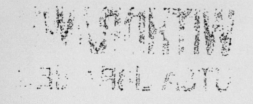

Material Properties and Manufacturing Processes

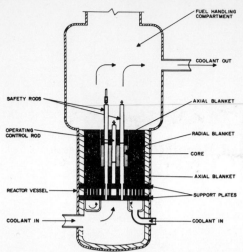

Scheme of a Reactor

From Concept to Reality...

The Engineer's Role

In order to build a reactor, much engineering effort in the subjects of material properties and manufacturing processes is necessary for the translation of the scientific concept of a reactor into the practicality of engineering drawings. (*Drawings Courtesy of Power Reactor Development Co.*)

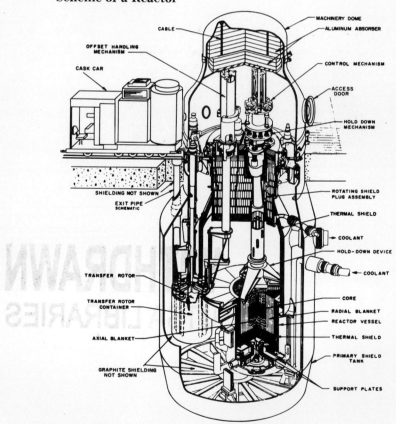

Engineering View of Reactor

Material Properties and Manufacturing Processes

JOSEPH DATSKO

Professor of Mechanical Engineering
University of Michigan

John Wiley & Sons, Inc.   New York · London · Sydney

To

Professor Orlan W. Boston

A pioneer in Metal Processing

Preface

The contents of this book were developed during my fifteen years of teaching materials and manufacturing processes. When I began teaching metal processing (the term then used for manufacuring processes by the leading engineering educational institutions and professional societies of the day), the emphasis was on the machining and casting processes; the objectives of the courses taught at the "better" engineering schools were not to teach the students how to operate the machines (although this was actually done), but rather to acquaint the student with the latest "state of the art" technology as practiced in industry.

During the last fifteen years many changes have taken place in the study of manufacturing processes because engineering knowledge has increased tremendously and the kind of work the graduate engineer is expected to perform has been radically altered. A few schools, either requiring more hours to teach science, or else being unable to alter their processing courses and not wanting these in their traditional scope, have abandoned the subject of manufacturing processes. The majority of the engineering schools realize that a proper knowledge of the manufacturing processes is essential to an engineer, and that it is one of the differences between the education of an engineer and a scientist. Therefore they have retained the subject area, but altered the content to meet present-day needs.

This book is the result of the latter approach to the manufacturing processes. It is the accumulation of new concepts, and principles that have resulted from my eight years of teaching the processing courses, with the following objectives: (1) to teach the engineering fundamentals of *all* the processes, not just one or two of them; (2) to emphasize the competitiveness of all the processes; (3) to show how the physical properties of a material limit or control its fabrication by processing; and (4) to demonstrate how the processing of a material into a specific part alters its mechanical properties.

This approach to processing, which is a combination of engineering fundamentals of materials with those of the mechanisms of the processes as opposed to the "state of the art" approach, will enable the student or engineer who is faced with a processing situation to solve it on the basis of "this is how it could or should be done" rather than on the basis "this is how it would have been done." The latter method or approach attempts to enable the student to solve processing problems by giving him a small part of the experience of a machine operator; the former method attempts to enable the student to take a creative, fundamental approach to solve processing problems.

I have found through experience that the best way to teach engineering principles to a sufficient depth so that the students can apply their knowledge, is by working a large number of problems. Consequently, a problem-solving approach to the processes is emphasized in this text. By having the student solve two or three problems, similar to those appended to every chapter, for each class period, his knowledge of the engineering aspects of the manufacturing processes will be greatly enhanced. In fact, the student will then be several years ahead of "the state of the art" in industrial processing.

This book goes very deeply into the subject of mechanical properties because one of the most important problem areas requiring engineering effort in the manufacturing industries, particularly in the space-travel field, is the interdependency of the mechanical properties and the manufacturing processes. Thus, the design engineer must be familiar with a great number of concepts in regard to the properties of materials; and he must know how to use a large variety of handbook data in such areas as creep, fatigue, impact, high temperature, and stress corrosion. However, in order to make a feasible or "engineering" design, he must also know the ordinary mechanical properties thoroughly in order to determine if and how a given part can be made.

All of the subject matter of processing cannot be presented in one book. The individual instructor can supplement this book by penetrating deeper into those areas in which he has personal experience. This has the additional benefit of stimulating the student's interest, which is a vital ingredient of the learning process. A course on the subject of the manufacturing processes can be taught from this textbook without active student participation in a laboratory or shop, but it must be supplemented with demonstrations on real manufacturing equipment.

In the four chapters that discuss individually each of the four manufacturing processes, the subjects are presented in the following order: (1) definition and brief general discussion of the process; (2) brief description of the most commonly used equipment and techniques associated with each of the processes; and (3) presentation and discussion of pertinent engineering concepts necessary to solve engineering problems associated with the process. The amount of descriptive material included is only that which is necessary to make the reader who has had no "shop" experience familiar with each of the manufacturing processes.

This textbook is written for use in a one-semester three- or four-credit hour course in which the material should be covered in the presented sequence. However, it could very well be used in a sequence of two quarter-term courses. In this event, the first course should cover Chapters 2, 3, and 4, and the second course Chapters 1, 5, and 6.

I wish to acknowledge with thanks the encouragement and assistance I have received from friends and colleagues, both in industry and at the University.

I am particularly grateful to Professor-Emeritus O. W. Boston and Dr. W. W. Gilbert for their inspiration which led me into this field. I owe special thanks to Dean G. J. Van Wylen, who encouraged the development of this new approach to the teaching of the Manufacturing Processes, and to Professors M. G. Wille and W. J. Mitchell, who assisted in the development of some of the new relationships presented in this book. I am very grateful to my fellow instructors who used the notes for this textbook in teaching their classes and offered their own helpful suggestions. I would like to give thanks to the students, both graduate and undergraduate, who have encouraged me with their favorable responses to this new approach to the subject matter; also the mechanics who made the specimens and collected some of the data that developed into the supporting structure of this book.

Finally, my public thanks to my family for their patience and understanding during the busy years this book was being created.

JOSEPH DATSKO

March 1966

Contents

List of Symbols Used in This Book

Chapter 1

A	Area
A_o	Original area
A_x, A_i	Instantaneous area
A_r	Per cent reduction of area (at fracture of tensile bar)
D	Diameter of spherical indenter
d	Diameter of indentation; or any diameter
E	Modulus of elasticity
e	Base of natural logarithms
G	Shear modulus
H_B	Brinell hardness number
H_M	Meyer hardness number
I	Impact strength
L	Load
l	Length
l_f, l_o	Final length and original length
l_l, l_s	Large length and small length
m	Strain-hardening exponent of σ–ϵ curve
n	Nominal (engineering) strain
n_f, n_u, n_y	Nominal strain at fracture, ultimate load, yielding
n	Strain-hardening exponent of L–d curve
R	Area ratio (A_o/A_x)
R_f	Area ratio at fracture of tensile specimen
R_B, R_C, R_E	Rockwell hardness, B, C, E, etc., scale
S	Nominal (engineering) stress
S_u, S_y	Ultimate tensile strength, yield strength
W	Cold work (per cent reduction of area)
W_f	Fraction coldworked $(W/100)$
$\epsilon_f, \epsilon_u, \epsilon_y$	Natural strain at fracture, ultimate and yield load

σ Natural stress
σ_o Natural stress of original material strained to $\epsilon = 1$
σ_u, σ_y Natural stress at ultimate and yield loads
ϵ Natural (true) strain
μ Poisson's ratio

Chapter 2

$\mathring{A}$ Angstrom (10^{-8} cm)
a, b, c Unit cell lengths
B Bainite
CT Continuous cooling transformation
E Eutectic, eutectoid
F force
H_B Brinell hardness
H_K Knoop hardness
IT Isothermal transformation
M Martensite
M_p, M_s, M_t Martensite: primary, secondary, tempered
M_sM_f Martensite start; martensite finish
P Pearlite
P_c, P_f, P_m, P_s Coarse, fine, medium spheroidized pearlite
R_c Rockwell C hardness
TTT Time, temperature, transformation diagram
α, β, γ Unit cell angles
$\alpha, \beta, \gamma, \delta$ Single-phase solid solutions
α Ferrite (alpha iron)
γ Austenite (gamma iron)
δ Delta iron
$\theta, \theta_1, \theta_2$ Intermetallic compounds

Chapter 3

A Area
C_p Heat capacity
F Force
g Acceleration due to gravity
h Head (height); surface heat transfer coefficient
Q Flow rate
q Heat loss
T Temperature
t Time

v Velocity
ρ Density

Chapter 4

A Area
b Arc potential as arc length approaches 0
E Voltage
E_i Intercept of generator curve
E_o Open circuit voltage
E_p Preferred voltage
HAZ Heat-affected zone
h Length (thickness)
I Current
I_p Preferred current
I_s Short circuit current
IGSA Inert gas shielded arc
JE Joint efficiency
K Ratio of E_i to E_o
k Thermal conductivity
l Arc length
m Slope of electrode characteristic curve
n Slope of generator curve
p Penetration
q Heat
R Electrical resistance
t Time
v Welding velocity
W Watts
ρ Electrical resistivity
σ Stress

Chapter 5

A Area
D Diameter
F, H Forces
H_K Knoop hardness
l Length
N Neutral or no-slip point
P Power
R Radius

R_H Rockwell H hardness
t Time, thickness
V Volume
v Velocity
W Work
α Entering angle
β No-slip point angle
ϵ Strain
θ Friction angle
μ Coefficient of friction, Poisson's ratio

Chapter 6

A Area, tool shape, tool life constant
B Work material constant
BUE   Built-up edge
C Proportionality constant in Taylor tool-life equation
C_p Heat capacity
C_v Volume specific heat $= \rho C_p$
d, w Depth of cut, width
F Feed (ipm), force (lb)
F_c Cutting force
F_F Feeding force
f, h Feed (ipr, ips, ipt), thickness
hp Horsepower
hp_c Horsepower at the cutter
hp_u Unit horsepower (hp/in³/min)
hss High-speed steel
J Mechanical equivalent of heat
K Proportionality constant
k Thermal conductivity
N rpm
n Slope of Taylor tool-life curve
P Power
Q Volume removed/min
q Size of cut constant
R Resultant force
S_p Stress for plastic flow
T Temperature
t Time
v Velocity or cutting speed
v_x Cutting speed for x minutes tool life

α Rake angle, thermal diffusivity
β Friction angle
η Mechanical efficiency
μ Microinch (10^{-6} in.), coefficient of friction
ϕ Shear angle
ρ Density

1

Mechanical Properties of Materials

This chapter was prepared with the understanding that the student has previously been introduced to the principles and traditional concepts of stress and strain in physics, materials and mechanics courses. Consequently, the common definitions and terms encountered in the area of mechanical properties are simply stated. However, since there are no universally accepted standards for the symbols that designate the various mechanical properties and terms employed in solving problems in this area, a complete list of the symbols used in this text is included at the front of the book. Although most of the symbols, and the concepts they represent, are identical to those found in handbooks and other texts on mechanical properties, a few are not. Some of the concepts and symbols used in this text are original and were created (through years of teaching this subject) to fulfill the need of systematizing and coordinating some of the mechanical properties so the student would have a more thorough understanding of the subject. Whenever possible, the most commonly accepted symbols were adopted; with new symbols, continuity has been obtained through using special symbols with meaningful subscripts in each of the areas studied, such as mechanical properties, welding, or machining.

One of the stimuli that created some of the new stress-strain concepts presented in the following sections of this chapter was the plea from the engineering students, "But how do we know which data to believe?" when they were confronted with conflicting data. For example, one widely used authoritative handbook on the properties of steel lists on one page the tensile strength and per cent reduction of area as 118,000 psi and 22%, respectively, for annealed AISI 1080 steel. But on the very next page the tabular data include a tensile strength of 89,250 psi and a reduction of area of 45% for annealed AISI 1080 steel. The same discrepancies exist for the yield strengths, hardnesses, and impact strengths. And this is true not only of the 1080

1

steel, but also for most of the materials tabulated in the handbook.

In another case of comparing stainless steel, one manufacturer's data sheets lists the annealed tensile strength of type 304 as 85,000 psi and type 305 as 78,000 psi while trying to prove that types 304 and 305 strain harden greatly during coldworking as opposed to the type they are promoting which strain-hardens only a little. After 50% cold-work, the tensile strengths of these two types are listed as 205,000 psi and 170,000 psi, respectively. The manufacturer's own low strain-hardening brand has an annealed tensile strength of 78,000 psi and a 50% coldworked strength of 152,000 psi. Of course, this proves their point. However, another stainless steel manufacturer's handbook of mechanical properties lists the annealed tensile strengths of types 304 and 305 as 86,300 psi and 85,260 psi, respectively. And after 50% coldwork these values are raised to 158,000 psi and 154,400 psi. If this is true, then the strain hardenability of both types of stainless steel are the same. Which set of data is correct?

The handbook referred to in the first example lists a tensile strength of 130,000 psi and a Brinell hardness of 514 for AISI 1040 steel which is water quenched and tempered at 400°F. However, experimental data obtained by students in laboratory experiments on standard $\frac{1}{2}$ in. diameter specimens of 1040 steel, water quenched and tempered at 400°F, always show the tensile strength to be about 280,000 psi and a Brinell hardness of 560. When confronted with a situation of this type, a student is hesitant to believe even his own data.

One of the principal advantages of the relationships given in this, and the following chapter, is that the graduate or student engineer can now for the first time determine whether a given set of published mechanical properties of a material are valid, or whether undetected and misleading discrepancies are present. To illustrate how these relationships enable one to discriminate between valid and unreliable data, consider the above three examples. In the first case, annealing a 1080 steel can result in either coarse lamellar pearlite having a tensile strength of 120,000 psi or a spheroidized pearlite having a strength of 90,000 psi, so the difference obviously is one of microstructures. On the other hand, the variations in the reduction of areas, may be the result of the microstructures present or they may simply be the random variations expected in commercial metals. Indeed, for some properties, such as the reduction of area, a variation of nearly 100% is a normal random variation. In fact, the yield strength of different samples of the same material may have a variation almost as great as this. Type 304 stainless, for example, has a published range of yield strength of 30,000 to 50,000 psi, or 67% variation.

In the second illustration, if one is aware of the fact that the tensile strength of a coldworked material $(S_u)_w$ is equal to the annealed tensile strength S_u, divided by one minus the fraction coldwork, then it is obvious which set of data is valid. Thus for 50% coldwork, as shown in the following sections of this chapter, $(S_u)_w = 2S_u$ and, if S_u is 80,000 psi, then the tensile strength of the 50% coldworked material should be 160,000 psi. On this basis it would appear that the manufacturer of the so-called low-work hardening stainless steel has presented biased data to encourage the sale of his product.

In regard to the third example, knowing that for stress-relieved steels the ratio of tensile strength to Brinell hardness = 500 is a valid relation, then it should be obvious that something is wrong when a steel has a Brinell hardness of 514 and a tensile strength of only 130,000 psi.

A second major advantage of the relationships given in the following sections is that they enable the substitution of only three "fundamental" tensile properties in place of many pages of traditionally tabulated data. This is discussed in detail later and is mentioned here simply to alert the reader.

The need for going as thoroughly into the subject of mechanical properties as is done in this first chapter of a text on the manufacturing processes is the recent realization that the biggest and most important problem area requiring engineering effort in the manufacturing industries, particularly in the space-travel field, is the interdependency of the mechanical properties and the manufacturing processes. For example, in order for the design engineer to ascertain whether a specific component part, such as the high pressure oxygen or helium tank to be used in a space capsule, can be fabricated to a required shape, and by which process, he must be first aware of the properties of the materials as well as how they are altered during manufacturing. Of course, if someone is simply going to redraw last year's model that has been "selling" satisfactorily, his knowledge of the properties of materials can be nil and he can still perform his function. But is this engineering? The design engineer must constantly also be aware of the fact that the mechanical properties of a part fabricated from a material such as an aluminum extrusion, a precipitation treated stainless steel, or annealed tungsten are not the same as the mechanical properties listed in the handbooks or the manufacturers' data sheets for the original material. The manner in which the properties of the material are influenced by the processing of a part from the original material can be understood only after one has a thorough knowledge of the fundamentals of material properties.

DEFINITIONS OF TENSILE PROPERTIES

The Nominal (Engineering) Stress and Strain

Stress has been defined for many years as the intensity of force or the unit force, that is, the load divided by the area. Thus $S = L/A$. All of the early tensile data collected on the strength properties of materials consisted of stress values obtained by dividing the load by the original area of the specimen (Figure 1-1). This was done for simplicity and convenience and it served the needs of early engineering design. However, at the turn of the century another concept of stress and strain evolved in which the stress was considered as the load divided by the instantaneous area, and the strain was an integrated strain (Figure 1-2) rather than the average one associated with the earlier concept. To distinguish between the two types of stress and strain, it became customary to refer to the former as the "engineering" stress and strain, and the latter as the "true" stress and strain. Because the present-day engineer uses both of these stress concepts in his calculations, and also because the implication is that whatever is contrasted to "true" is false, it is now becoming customary to refer to the older (engineering) stress concept as the "conventional" or the "nom-

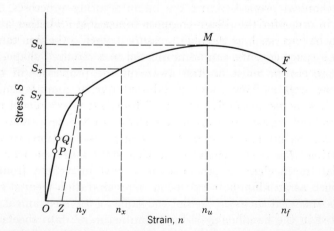

Figure 1-1. Nominal (engineering) stress-strain curve. Plotted on cartesian coordinates.

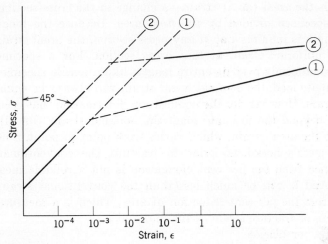

Figure 1-2. Natural (true) stress-strain curves. Plotted on log-log coordinates.

inal" stress. Since the word *nominal* is more descriptive than either engineering or conventional, it will be favored in this text. Therefore we define the *nominal stress as the unit force obtained when the load is divided by the original area,* or

$$S = \frac{L}{A_o} \tag{1-1}$$

Similarly, we define the *nominal strain as the unit elongation obtained when the uniform change in length is divided by the length over which this change occurred.* Care should be utilized when using this concept of strain, for when the unit elongation is not uniform along the entire length of the bar, as when necking is present, misleading results may be obtained. It is for this reason that the author feels that the per cent elongation is a poor and inappropriate tensile property and should hurriedly be made extinct, especially since the areal strain, as explained below, is easier to obtain and is much more meaningful.

While discussing necking, it is well to point out that although the strain does vary along the length of the specimen, in some cases it may be fairly constant in that portion outside the neck, and is fairly close to the strain at the ultimate load. However, in most cases the portions of the gage length on either side of the neck are conical all the way to the shoulder.

Another very worthwhile concept of strain, particularly so in this course, is the areal (area) strain—a change in the cross-sectional area of the specimen divided by the *final* area. Because the longitudinal gage length is infinitesimal at any cross section, the areal strain is the actual "uniform" strain at that cross section. For a specimen that deforms uniformly over its entire length, like a tensile specimen up to the ultimate load, the nominal lineal strain will always be equal to the areal strain. However, for the nonuniform deformation that occurs with loading beyond the ultimate load, the nominal strain (lineal) is not equal to the areal strain, which varies from point to point. Since most ductile metals neckdown prior to fracture, the conventional strain determined from the per cent elongation is not a reliable measure of strain. And it will be much less than the conventional strain determined from the per cent reduction of area, which is a measure of the maximum or fracture strain of the material.

Thus, for tension

$$n = \frac{\Delta l}{l} = \frac{l_f - l_o}{l_o} \qquad \text{or} \qquad n = \frac{\Delta A}{A_f} = \frac{A_o - A_f}{A_f} \qquad (1\text{-}2)$$

For compression, two ratios may be used in addition to the preceding area relationship:

$$n_1 = \frac{\Delta l}{l_o} = \frac{l_f - l_o}{l_o} \qquad \text{or} \qquad n_2 = \frac{\Delta l}{l_f} = \frac{l_o - l_f}{l_f} \qquad (1\text{-}3)$$

There is no absolute standard that dictates which strain is exclusively correct. Most engineering mechanics texts suggest the use of the first ratio where the "length over which this change occurred" is the original length. In this case, when the true strains in tension and compression are equal, the nominal strains in tension and compression are not equal. When the second definition of compressive strain is used, then for tensile and compressive deformations that give equal true strains, the tensile and compressive nominal strains are equal. Thus for extension from $l_o = \frac{1}{2}$ in. to $l_f = 1$ in.

$$n = \frac{l_f - l_o}{l_o} = \frac{1 - \frac{1}{2}}{\frac{1}{2}} = 1$$

and

$$\epsilon = \ln (1 + n) = \ln 2 = 0.695$$

Where "ln" denotes the logarithm to the base e. For the same process in reverse, or compression then

$$n_1 = \frac{l_f - l_o}{l_o} = \frac{\frac{1}{2} - 1}{1} = -\frac{1}{2} \quad \text{and} \quad n_2 = \frac{l_o - l_f}{l_f} = \frac{1 - \frac{1}{2}}{\frac{1}{2}} = 1$$

and

$$\epsilon_1 = \ln(1 + n_1) = \ln \frac{1}{2} = -0.695$$

and

$$\epsilon_2 = -\ln(1 + n_2) = -\ln 2 = -0.695$$

Although either n_1 or n_2 may be used in solving problems in the forming process, with identical results from both, they should not be used interchangeably in any problem.

The tensile test is used to determine any of the following mechanical properties of a material: proportional limit and elastic limit; yield, tensile, and breaking strength; per cent elongation; per cent reduction of area; modulus of elasticity. These are defined next since they will be used throughout the text.

The *proportional limit* is the greatest stress which a material is capable of developing without any deviation from a linear proportionality of stress to strain. It is determined by drawing a straight line through the points that lie in the elastic region of an experimentally obtained stress-strain curve, and locating the position where this straight line departs from the stress-strain curve, as point P in Figure 1-1. The values of the proportional limit so determined vary greatly with the sensitivity and accuracy of the testing equipment, eccentricity of loading, and the scale of the stress-strain diagram. Consequently, the proportional limit is very seldom used in engineering specifications.

The *elastic limit* is the greatest stress which a material is capable of developing without any permanent deformation (strain) remaining after complete removal of the load. The elastic limit may be above the proportional limit, but not below it. Because of the complexity of the testing procedure, which requires many successive loadings and unloadings, the elastic limit is very seldom used in engineering calculations. Point Q, Figure 1-1, defines the elastic limit.

The *modulus of elasticity* is the ratio of stress to the corresponding strain, below the proportional limit. It is expressed as $E = s/n$, which is commonly known as Hooke's law. The value of E is determined by measuring the slope of the straight line drawn through the points of the stress-strain curve below the proportional limit. The units of E are psi divided by in./in., or in other words, simply psi. The engineering significance of the modulus of elasticity is very great since the modulus undergo. The greater the value of E, the smaller will be the corresponding strain for a given load. Consider, for example, the two commonly used engineering materials magnesium and steel, which have moduli of elasticity of 6.25 and 30 ksi, respectively. From these values it is apparent that a structural member, if made of magnesium, would undergo nearly five times as great an elastic distortion for a given load as an identical part made of steel.

The *yield strength* is the stress at which a material undergoes a specified strain slightly greater than the strain associated with the elastic limit. In other words, a structural part stressed to its yield strength by an axial tensile load will be slightly longer after the load is removed. The yield strength may be determined by several methods such as the two most common methods, the divider and the offset.

The divider method, although somewhat crude, is very simple and rapid and gives results which are quite satisfactory for most engineering work. This method consists of adjusting the legs of a pair of dividers so that their ends fall into both of the punch marks which define the gage length of the specimen. While the load is being applied to the specimen, the divider ends are periodically placed or "felt" into the punched holes. At the time when the divider ends will not fit into the punch holes due to the elongation of the specimen, the load on the specimen is recorded. This load divided by the original cross-sectional area of the specimen gives the yield strength of the material.

The offset method, on the other hand, requires that the stress-strain diagram be first drawn either by an automatic recorder or by obtaining stress and corresponding strain data and then manually drawing it. After the stress-strain diagram is drawn, as in Figure 1-1, a point Z is placed on the strain axis at a specified distance from the origin. This distance, OZ, is known as the offset and is expressed as per cent. For example, when the offset is specified as 0.2%, then point Z in Figure 1-1 would correspond to a strain of 0.002 in./in. as shown. Although a 0.2% offset is the most commonly specified one, in some cases offsets of 0.01, 0.1, and 0.5% are specified. In reporting values of yield strength obtained by this method, the value of offset used should be stated.

The *yield point* is the first stress, below the maximum load, at which there occurs an increase in strain without an increase in stress, that is, a horizontal portion on a stress-strain curve near the yield strength. Unhardened, low-carbon steel is the only commonly used structural material that exhibits this unique phenomenon of yielding. When soft steel is tested in a mechanically loaded testing machine, the yield point is dramatically revealed by a lowering of the counter-balance beam. Consequently, the determination of the yield point by observing the load at which the indicating needle suddenly reverses itself is referred to as the "drop-of-the-beam" method. The highest stress achieved before the load decreases is referred to as the "upper-yield point." The lowest value it drops to before rising again to the maximum load is called the lower-yield point. Technically, the phrase yield point should be used only when referring to this unique yielding characteristic and should not be used interchangeably with yield strength.

The *tensile strength* is the value of stress obtained when the maximum load that the tensile specimen sustained is divided by the original cross-sectional area of the specimen. This corresponds to point M in Figure 1-1. The value of stress obtained by this procedure is sometimes called the *ultimate strength* or the *maximum strength*. The tensile strength is commonly used in engineering calculations, although there is probably more justification for the use of the yield strength since any structural member will have undergone sufficient deformation to make the part useless by the time the tensile strength is reached. It must also be kept in mind that the value of stress designated as the tensile strength is a fictitious stress because the actual cross-sectional area of the specimen at the time it is supporting the maximum load is much less than the original cross-sectional area.

The *breaking strength* or the *rupture strength* is the value of stress obtained by dividing the load carried by the specimen at the time of fracture by the original cross-sectional area. This is designated as point F in Figure 1-1. The breaking strength has very little engineering significance outside of studies of fracture.

The *per-cent reduction of area* is defined as the maximum change in area times one hundred, divided by the original area. It can be used only when tensile deformation occurs. Thus

$$A_r = \frac{A_o - A_f}{A_o} \times 100 \qquad (1\text{-}4)$$

In compression, the area increases or expands. Thus

$$A_e = \frac{A_f - A_o}{A_o} \times 100 \qquad (1\text{-}5)$$

In general, the concern about whether a positive or negative sign should be used when determining the magnitude of the strain during plastic deformation can be avoided by defining the strain always as the larger length or area over the smaller one as

$$\frac{A_l}{A_s} = \frac{100}{100 - A_r} \tag{1-6}$$

In reality, it appears to the author after several years' experience working with and teaching mechanical properties, that engineering calculations and problem solving would be simplified if the per cent reduction of area concept were abandoned, and deformation or ductility was simply expressed as the ratio of original to final area and designated as R. Thus the ductility of a material would be $R = A_o/A_f$. For example, if during the testing of a material it is found that $A_o = 0.2$ sq in. and $A_f = 0.15$ sq in., then R is simply A_o/A_f or 1.33. To obtain A_r requires slightly more effort and space.

$$A_r = \frac{A_o - A_f}{A_o} \times 100 = \frac{0.2 - 0.15}{0.2} \times 100 = \frac{5}{0.2} = 25\%$$

Thus an R of 1.33 and an A_r of 25% both express equally well the material's ductility. However, if one desired to now obtain the equivalent true strain at fracture (ϵ_f) as defined in the following section, one may proceed immediately with R thus: $\epsilon_f = \ln R = \ln 1.33 = 0.29$. On the other hand, to make use of A_r one must use the expression

$$\epsilon_f = \ln R = \ln \frac{100}{100 - A_r} = \ln \frac{100}{100 - 25} = \ln \frac{100}{75} = \ln 1.33 = 0.29$$

Although the results are the same, it is obvious that there is a certain amount of "busy work" that one does when using the per cent reduction of area concept. Similarly, since it is impossible to determine a meaningful true strain from the per cent elongation, it is thus obvious that it is even a poorer measure of a material's ductility than is the per cent reduction of area.

It is appropriate at this time to make the reader aware of the fact that although nearly all handbooks, textbooks, and the material manufacturer's data sheets list the per cent elongation with the material's mechanical properties, only about half of them list the per cent reduction of area; and none of them lists the more convenient area ratio. Consequently if an engineer wants to know the significant plastic stress-strain characteristics of a common material he frequently must, conduct his own tensile tests.

Shear stress is the unit shear load, that is, the load acting along the cross-sectional area (rather than normal to the cross-sectional area) divided by the cross-sectional area as illustrated in Figure 1-3.

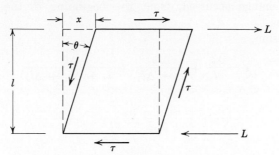

Figure 1-3. Element subjected to shearing stresses.

Thus

$$\tau = \frac{L}{A} \tag{1-7}$$

Shear strain is the angular distortion of an element acted upon by shear or torsional loads as shown in Figure 1-3. Thus

$$\gamma = \frac{x}{l} = \tan \theta \tag{1-8}$$

In some cases the shear deformations are small (this is especially true for elastic deformations) ; and for small angles the tangent of the angle is about equal to the numerical value of the angle. Therefore, in these cases $\gamma = \theta$. However, this simplification cannot be used for plastic deformations because the shear angle can be extremely large for severe deformations.

The *elastic shear modulus* G is the ratio of shear stress to shear strain, that is, $G = \tau/\gamma$. The elastic shear modulus is related to the modulus of elasticity and Poisson's ratio as follows:

$$G = \frac{E}{2(1 + \mu)} \tag{1-9}$$

The Natural (True) Stress and Strain

The *natural stress* or, as it is frequently called, the *true stress* is the unit force obtained when the load is divided by the instantaneous area. Thus

$$\sigma = \frac{L}{A_i} \tag{1-10}$$

The *natural strain,* or *true strain,* is the value of strain obtained by summing up all the ratios of infinitesimal changes in length over which the change occurred, from the beginning to the end of the deformations.

For tension,

$$\epsilon = \frac{\Delta l_1}{l_o} + \frac{\Delta l_2}{l_o + \Delta l_1} + \frac{\Delta l_3}{l_o + \Delta l_1 + \Delta l_2}$$

or

$$\epsilon = \sum_{l_o}^{l_f} \frac{\Delta l}{l}$$

And by integration

$$\epsilon = \int_{l_o}^{l_f} \frac{dl}{l} = \ln \frac{l_f}{l_o} \tag{1-11}$$

For compression, since compressive strains are defined as being negative,

$$-\epsilon = \ln \frac{l_f}{l_o} \quad \text{or} \quad \epsilon = \ln \frac{l_o}{l_f}$$

For the general case, where the sign may be disregarded as explained previously

$$\epsilon = \ln \frac{l_l}{l_s} \tag{1-12}$$

Also in plastic deformation, the volume remains constant so

$$V_0 = A_o l_o = A_f l_f \quad \text{or} \quad \frac{l_f}{l_o} = \frac{A_o}{A_f}$$

Thus

$$\epsilon = \ln \frac{l_f}{l_o} = \ln \frac{A_o}{A_f} \tag{1-13}$$

or in the general case where the sign may be ignored

$$\epsilon = \ln \frac{A_l}{A_s} \tag{1-14}$$

THE STRAIN-HARDENING EQUATION

The early investigators of the tensile properties of materials about a century ago first noticed that during the first stages of deformation that the stress was directly and lineally proportional to the strain, and it has become customary to refer to the proportionality constant as the elastic modulus E, as shown in Figure 1-1. About fifty years ago the scholars discovered that if the natural stress-strain data during plastic extension were plotted on log-log coordinates, the data fell reasonably well along straight lines, as in Figure 1-2, of the form

$$y = bx^m$$

where y and x are the natural stress and natural strain, respectively. The fact that this relationship is a straight line on logarithmic coordinates can be seen when it is expressed in logarithmic form

$$\log y = m \log x + \log b$$

which is identical to the expression $y = mx + b$ plotted on cartesian coordinates.

Up to the present time there have been no universally accepted symbols for the constants b and m although σ and ϵ are fairly well standardized for true stress and true strain, respectively. After several years of teaching these relationships to engineering students by way of working many problems, it became obvious that the use of meaningful symbols, rather than the already overly burdened constants K, A, and C, is a decided advantage when the goal is a thorough knowledge of the subject in a minimum time. From this effort, the symbols in the plastic stress-strain relationship decided upon are

$$\sigma = \sigma_o \epsilon^m \qquad (1\text{-}15)$$

The selection of σ_o for the proportionality constant was made on the basis of two important considerations. First, since ϵ is dimensionless the units associated with the proportionality constant are psi (the units of stress) and therefore it was found desirable to use σ, the symbol that denotes true stress, for this constant. Second, after solving many numerical problems concerning strain hardening, it gradually becomes apparent that this constant is actually a characteristic property of the annealed material; that is, it is a "fundamental" property of the original material and consequently a meaningful subscript is o. Thus σ_o is not just a proportionality constant, it is also an important property of the original material and has the units of stress. In a later paragraph, a physical meaning of σ_o is also given.

For a given material, the values of σ_o and m are the same for tensile and compressive deformation. In addition, experimental work, such as that shown in Figure 1-4 for 70-30 brass, indicates that the strain hardening due to rolling is identical to that obtained from the tensile test. In the experiment where we obtained the data plotted in Figure 1-4, a $\frac{1}{2}$ in. $\times$ $\frac{3}{4}$ in. cross-sectional area bar 4 in. long was cold rolled to a final cross section of $\frac{1}{4}$ in. $\times$ $\frac{13}{16}$ in. (a 46% reduction), and

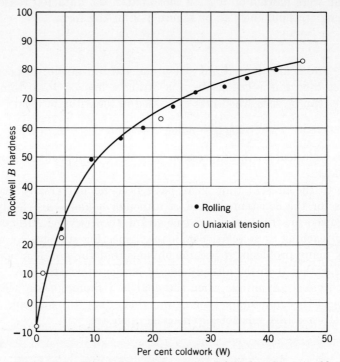

Figure 1-4. Comparison of the strain hardening due to cold-work by rolling and by uniaxial tension. The material is 70Cu-30Zn brass orginally annealed at 1300°F for 1 hr.

the final hardness was $83R_B$. When a similar piece, having a gage length cross section of $\frac{1}{4}$ in. $\times \frac{3}{4}$ in. was loaded on a tensile testing machine until the cross-sectional area was reduced 46% (with a slight neck occurring), the final hardness was also $83R_B$; for all deformations between 1% and 46%, a similar agreement was obtained.

In another experiment involving the same brass and the same size specimens mentioned in the previous paragraph, the yield strength was evaluated after both rolling and tensile deformations. The annealed yield strength of this material was 12,000 psi. First, a flat tensile specimen was loaded nearly to the maximum load and then unloaded. The reduction in area (or coldwork W) was 30%. Upon reloading this same specimen it was established that the new yield load was the same as the greatest previous load, and on the basis of the new coldworked area, the yield strength was found to be 54,000 psi, and the tensile strength was 54,500 psi. A second piece of this same annealed material was cold rolled to a 30% reduction. A flat tensile specimen was machined from the rolled bar and it was found to have a yield strength and tensile strength of 55,000 and 55,400 psi, respectively. The agreement here again is well within the range that is normally expected for different samples of the same material.

One common question that arises in regard to the strain hardening equation is, "Should the natural strain that is plotted be the total elastic plus plastic strain ϵ_t, or should it be simply the plastic strain ϵ_p?" Actually, both types of curves may be experimentally determined, and both are; but seldom is it clearly stated on a particular curve which natural strain was used. Although at first this may appear to be a careless practice, in reality the difference between the same data points plotted for both of the natural strains mentioned above is less than the difference between two curves obtained while using the same natural strain concept from different samples of the same material. Before we examine the quantitative differences between the plastic only and the elastic plus plastic strain curves, consider how the two types of curves may be obtained.

First, in conducting a uniaxial tension test it is most convenient to measure and record both the length (or diameter) of the specimen as well as the load at the instant a particular load is reached. The strains in this case are the total elastic plus plastic strains. (If at any time the loads were removed, the specimen would undergo a unit contraction equal to the stress divided by the elastic modulus.) If the load and diameter were measured in this manner from the beginning of extension until fracture occurred, a continuous stress-strain curve would be obtained that would be similar to either type A or B illustrated in Figure 1-8. For this type of curve, ϵ in the $\sigma = \sigma_o \epsilon^m$ relationship is the total strain ϵ_t.

However, consider the data obtained by cold rolling or cold drawing a material, followed by tensile tests on materials having varying amounts of coldwork to determine the coldworked materials' yield strength. In this case, the natural strain would be determined by the areas prior to and after rolling. There are no loads on the specimen during the measuring operation. Thus, for an initial cross-sectional area of 1 sq in. and a final cross-sectional area of 0.9 sq in., the natural strain would be 0.105. A tensile specimen machined from this coldworked material would then be tested and the yield strength determined. This combination of stress and strain gives one point on a natural stress-strain curve. A series of such points for a material having varying amounts of coldwork results in a strain-hardening curve expressed as $\sigma = \sigma_o \epsilon^m$ where ϵ is now the natural plastic strain only.

In Figure 1-5 the total elastic plus plastic natural strain as a function of natural stress (as determined from uniaxial tensile tests) are plotted as solid lines for two different classes of steel and one type of brass. The portions of the curves where the solid lines are replaced with dashes are the regions where experimental data were not sufficiently accurate to determine the true position of the lines. The entire stress-strain curve in this case may be considered as being made up of two straight lines: the elastic portion represented as

$$\sigma = E\epsilon_e \tag{1-16}$$

and the plastic portion represented as

$$\sigma = \sigma_o \epsilon_t{}^m \quad \text{or} \quad \sigma = \sigma_o (\epsilon_e + \epsilon_p)^m \tag{1-17}$$

Actually, the stress-strain relationship on the basis of total strain can be understood more easily by considering the strain as the dependent variable and the stress as the independent variable. Although it apparently is a universal habit to consider the strain as the independent variable (it is always plotted as the abscissa), it can just as easily and validly be considered as the dependent variable. If, as is customary in most tensile tests, specific loads are applied to a specimen and the resulting strain is recorded, then is not the strain really the dependent variable? In the same way it is apparent that for a given stress, the total strain is made up of an elastic strain plus a plastic strain. Thus

$$\epsilon_t = \epsilon_e + \epsilon_p$$

and if the given stress is low, $\epsilon_p = 0$ and only elastic deformation occurs. Thus in the elastic portion: $\epsilon_t = \epsilon_e = \sigma/E$. Similarly in the plastic portion

$$\epsilon_t = \epsilon_e + \epsilon_p = \left(\frac{\sigma}{\sigma_o}\right)^{1/m} \tag{1-18}$$

These stresses, σ, and total strains, ϵ_t, are the ones that are plotted as the solid strain-hardening lines in Figure 1-5.

To obtain the strain-hardening lines that include only the plastic deformation, it is simply necessary, for any given stress σ, to subtract the elastic strain from the total strain as follows:

$$\epsilon_p = \left(\frac{\sigma}{\sigma_o}\right)^{1/m} - \frac{\sigma}{E} \tag{1-19}$$

This has been done in Figure 1-5 and the resulting curves are represented by the broken lines.

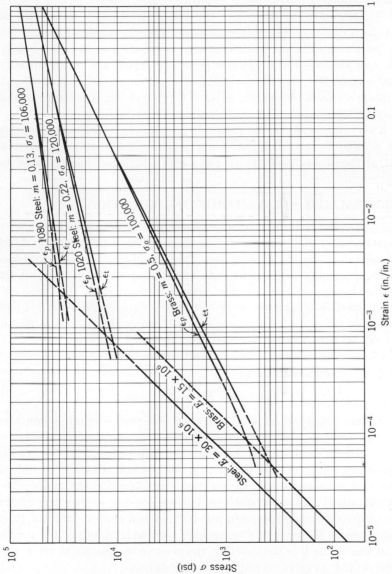

Figure 1-5. Comparison of strain-hardening curves on the basis of both the plastic strain ϵ_p only and the total (elastic plus plastic) strain ϵ_t.

From these several examples plotted in Figure 1-5 it is apparent
that the strain-hardening curves on the basis of the total strain and
on the plastic strain only are, for all practical purposes, identical since
their equations are (for 1020 steel) $\sigma = 120{,}000\epsilon^{0.22}$ and $\sigma = 121{,}$-
$000\epsilon^{0.21}$, respectively. Although the two extrapolated lines tend to
separate as the strain becomes very small, the magnitude of the stresses
and the stress differences also become smaller. For hot-rolled 1020
steel, the stresses for $\epsilon_t = 0.002$ and $\epsilon_p = 0.002$ are approximately
30,000 and 32,000 psi, respectively, or a difference of only 2000 psi.
Therefore $\sigma = \sigma_o(\epsilon_t)^m$ and $\sigma = \sigma_o(\epsilon_p)^m$ are about the same and we may
simply write $\sigma = \sigma_o\epsilon^m$.

A very important consideration to remember, regardless of whether
the ϵ_t or ϵ_p curve is used, is that a plastic strain less than the numerical
value of the elastic yield strain for a given material should never be
used since the results are meaningless in this range.

A GENERALIZED STRAIN-HARDENING EQUATION

After it was realized that σ_o was really a "fundamental" property
of a given material, it was inevitable to learn that a generalized strain-
hardening equation could be created that would replace the many specialized approximate equations that are now currently used in all the
texts and handbooks that include strain-hardening data. The past and
current practice is to present the strain-hardening data for a given
material in the annealed state as $\sigma = K\epsilon^n$, where the constants K and
n would be numerically specified. If this same material were coldworked to some amount x and its true stress-strain relationship were
obtained, it would be listed as

$$\sigma = K_x\epsilon^{n_x} \quad \text{where} \quad K_x > K \quad \text{and} \quad n_x < n$$

and for increasing amounts of coldwork, the proportionality constant
K_x would become greater and the exponent n_x would become smaller.
In other words, compared to the original annealed material, the plastic
stress-strain curve of the previously coldworked material would be
higher and of lower slope. In addition, the data for the coldworked
material would plot as a straight line on log-log coordinates if the
previously coldworked specimen was treated as a new one and the prior
strain ignored. However, by examining and understanding the definition of true strain it is obvious that the above concepts are in error, and
at best would serve as an approximation only.

To see the true effect of prior coldwork on the stress-strain relationship of a material, consider the simple case of extending a cylinder
from length l_o to some length l_x. The total true strain then, by defini-

tion, is

$$\epsilon_t = \int_{l_o}^{l_x} \frac{dl}{l}$$

If we consider this extension as first proceeding from l_o to l_1 and then to l_x, we may express it as

$$\epsilon_t = \int_{l_o}^{l_1} \frac{dl}{l} + \int_{l_1}^{l_x} \frac{dl}{l}$$

or

$$\epsilon_t = \epsilon_w + \epsilon_x$$

where ϵ_w is the strain of the prior coldwork, during the deformation from l_o to l_1, and ϵ_x is the strain of the additional coldwork in going from l_1 to l_x. Thus, from the straight-line plastic stress-strain relationship of the annealed material $\sigma = \sigma_o \epsilon_t{}^m$ we get by substitution

$$\sigma = \sigma_o \, (\epsilon_w + \epsilon_x)^m \qquad (1\text{-}20)$$

which is the generalized strain-hardening equation. Thus, for a given material, σ_o and m are fixed and do not vary with prior coldwork. The prior coldwork simply goes into the bracketed total strain as ϵ_w. For illustrative purposes, consider a 70-30 brass annealed at 1300°F for one hour.

Experimental data on the annealed material gave σ_o as 100,000 psi and m as 0.5. Since in the annealed condition $\epsilon_w = 0$, then the strain-hardening equation is $(\sigma)_{\text{ann}} = 10^5 \epsilon^{0.5}$. For 10% prior coldwork ($\epsilon_{10} = \ln 1.111 = 0.105$), $\sigma_{10} = 10^5 (0.105 + \epsilon_x)^{0.5}$. This latter equation, which has the form $y = b(a + x)^m$, is also a straight line on logarithmic coordinates having 0.105 as its minimum value of strain. This can readily be seen when the expression is put in logarithmic form

$$\log y = \log b + m \log (a + x) \qquad \text{or} \qquad y = b + m(a + x)$$

However, if the stress values obtained by solving the generalized equation are plotted for strains of ϵ_x rather than $(\epsilon_x + \epsilon_w)$, then the resulting curve will not be a straight line. Consequently, if a tensile specimen made of a previously coldworked material is tested and the original coldwork is not included in the calculations, then the resulting natural stress-strain curve will not be a straight line.

From the above generalized strain-hardening equation it is apparent that coldworked strains are additive. This is true for increasing strains of the same sign only, that is for compression following compression or tension following tension. Experimental work done by the author on cubes and cylinders has shown that alternating tensile and compressive strains of the same magnitude on a specimen does not appreciably increase the hardness of the metal beyond the hardness achieved with the first deformation. Thus, a material that is first stretched 10% is strain hardened by an amount indicated by the strain-hardening equation (hardness versus strain) of the material for an ϵ of 0.105. Compressing the same part to its original length does not strengthen the material by the amount obtained for $\epsilon = 0.2$, but rather the hardness remains approximately the same as it was after the first tensile deformation. Further deformations of 10% in either compression or tension do not strain harden the material additionally. To bring forth further strengthening, deformations greater than 10% must be utilized.

The Real Meaning of σ_o

The proportionality constant, σ_o, in the plastic true stress-true strain relationship (often referred to as the strain-hardening or strain-hardenability equation) is expressed in this text as

$$\sigma = \sigma_o \epsilon^m$$

It is apparent from this expression that σ_o *is the value of true stress (or the yield strength) when the material is plastically deformed to a true strain of 1.* That is, $\sigma_o = \sigma$ when $\epsilon = 1$. Some experimentally determined values of σ_o are listed in Table 1-1.

One question that the beginner always asks is, "Is σ_o really an attainable stress (or strength) for any of our common materials?" Or in other words, "Is it possible to deform a material to a true strain of 1?" The driving force behind this question is usually the realization that the elongation associated with an ϵ of 1 is very large. As a matter of fact, it is not a 100% uniform elongation, but rather a 271.8% uniform elongation. Of course, the answer is definitely yes; but a more quantitative answer can be obtained by considering the strain in terms of the traditionally more familiar per cent reduction of area, A_r. Although, as mentioned above, a 271.8% uniform elongation is required to give a true strain of 1, the equivalent A_r is 63.2%. This may be confirmed as follows:

$$\epsilon = \ln \frac{100}{100 - A_r} = \ln \frac{100}{36.8} = \ln 2.718 = 1$$

Thus a material may be subjected to a true strain of 1 if it has a per cent reduction of area greater than 63%. By referring to a hand-

TABLE 1-1. Some Typical Values of σ_o, m and ϵ_f

(All Values Are for Longitudinal Specimens Except as Noted)[1]

Material	Treatment	σ_o (psi)	m	ϵ_f
1100 aluminum	900°F 1 hr ann	26,000	0.20	2.30
2024 aluminum	T-4	100,000	0.15	0.13
Copper	1000°F 1 hr ann	78,000	0.55	1.19
Copper	1250°F 1 hr ann	72,000	0.50	1.21
Copper	1500°F 1 hr ann	68,000	0.48	1.26
70-30 leaded brass	1250°F 1 hr ann	105,000	0.50	1.10
70-30 brass	1000°F 1 hr ann	110,000	0.56	1.50
70-30 brass	1200°F 1 hr ann	105,000	0.52	1.55
1002 steel	Annealed	80,000	0.32	1.20
1018 steel	Annealed	90,000	0.25	1.05
1020 steel	Hot rolled	115,000	0.22	0.90
1212 steel	Hot rolled	110,000	0.24	0.85
1045 steel	Hot rolled	140,000	0.14	0.58
1144 steel	Annealed	144,000	0.14	0.49
1144 steel[2]	Annealed	144,000	0.14	0.05
4340 steel	Hot rolled	210,000	0.09	0.45
52100 steel	Spher. ann	165,000	0.18	0.58
52100 steel	1500°F ann	210,000	0.07	0.40
18-8 stainless	1600°F 1 hr ann	210,000	0.51	1.08
18-8 stainless	1800°F 1 hr ann	230,000	0.53	1.38
304 stainless	Annealed	185,000	0.45	1.67
303 stainless	Annealed	205,000	0.51	1.16
202 stainless	1900°F 1 hr ann	195,000	0.30	1.0
17-4 PH stainless	1100°F age	260,000	0.01	0.65
17-4 PH stainless	Annealed	173,000	0.05	1.20
Molybdenum	Ext. ann	105,000	0.13	0.38
Cobalt base alloy[3]	Solution H.T.	300,000	0.50	0.51
Cobalt base alloy[2,3]	Solution H.T.	300,000	0.50	0.40
Vanadium	Annealed	112,000	0.35	0.90

[1] These are values obtained from only one or two different heats. The values will vary from heat to heat because of differences in composition and annealing temperature. ϵ_f may vary by 100%.

[2] Tensile specimen machined from 4 in. diameter bar transverse to rolling direction.

[3] 20 Cr, 15 W, 10 Ni, 3 Fe, 0.1C, Balance Cobalt.

book on mechanical properties it may be seen that, for example, annealed 1020 steel has an A_r 60–70% and pure aluminum and copper have an A_r of 65 to 90%.

Another Meaning of E, The Modulus of Elasticity

The traditional concept of the modulus of elasticity E (Young's Modulus) is that it is the slope of the elastic portion of the conventional stress-strain curve. However, another meaning of the elastic modulus can be obtained by plotting the elastic stress-strain relationship as true stress-true strain on logarithmic coordinates. The curve depicting the elastic relationship is a straight line having a slope of 45°, and fits the equation $\sigma = E\epsilon^m$. Since the slope of a 45° line is 1, the equation simply becomes $\sigma = E\epsilon$ (Figure 1-2). (As pointed out below, for small strains $\sigma = S$ and $\epsilon = n$ and therefore we have the conventional form $S = En$). From the relation $\sigma = E\epsilon$ it is apparent that E *is the value of true stress for an extrapolated elastic true strain of 1*, or $E = \sigma$ when $\epsilon = 1$.

When looked at from this vantage point, we can see that the elastic curves of all materials are parallel lines having a slope of 45° and that their vertical position on the graph is determined by the magnitude of their elastic moduli, namely, the true stress for an extrapolated elastic true strain of 1. Thus, steel, magnesium and tungsten have elastic curves that intersect the $\epsilon = 1$ coordinate at stresses of 30×10^6 psi, 6.5×10^6 psi, and 50×10^6 psi, respectively.

The close similarity between E and σ_o is apparent when considered in the preceding manner.

SOME USEFUL STRESS-STRAIN RELATIONSHIPS

1. Relationship between Natural Strain and Nominal Strain

The expression $n = (l_f - l_o)/l_o$, which is a definition of strain, can be rewritten as $l_f/l_o = 1 + n$.

(This concept of nominal strain is valid for uniform extension only, and is not valid for the entire gage length after necking occurs.)

Therefore, by substitution, $\epsilon = \ln (l_f/l_o)$ can be expressed as

$$\epsilon = \ln (1 + n) \tag{1-21}$$

or as

$$e^\epsilon = 1 + n \tag{1-22}$$

Also, for small values of n (that is, in the order of 10^{-2} in./in. or less $\ln (1 + n) = n$ and, therefore, $\epsilon = n$.

Thus, for a uniform extension of 20%, $n = 0.2$, and $\epsilon = 0.182$. And for an extension of 0.2%, $n = 0.002$ and $\epsilon = 0.002$.

2. The Relationship between True Stress and Engineering Stress-Strain

The mathematical definition of true stress is $\sigma = L/A_i$
Now, since $A_i l_i = A_o l_o$ (volume remains constant during plastic deformation)

$$A_i = A_o \frac{l_o}{l_i}$$

Therefore

$$\sigma = \frac{L}{A_o} \cdot \frac{l_i}{l_o}$$

But $L/A_o = S$ and $l_i/l_o = 1 + n$. Therefore

$$\sigma = S(1 + n) \tag{1-23a}$$

At the maximum load, the equation may be rewritten as

$$\sigma_u = S_u(1 + n_u) = S_u e^m \tag{1-23b}$$

As an example, annealed 1020 steel has a tensile strength (S_u) of 60,000 psi and a strain at ultimate load (n_u) of 0.25; therefore it has a true stress at ultimate load (σ_u) of 60,000 $\times$ 1.25 or 75,000 psi.

3. Relationship between Lineal Strain and Areal Strain

Frequently it is desirable to convert directly from lineal strain to areal (area) strain, or vice versa. Although mathematically this conversion can be made easily, it must be remembered, as was pointed out in the initial discussion on this topic, that unless the deformation is uniform along the entire length of the part, the lineal strain is an average strain and consequently is more or less meaningless. Thus, converting the per cent elongation of a ductile tensile specimen, which is an average lineal strain times a hundred, to an equivalent areal strain, will not give the same areal strain that is obtained from the per cent reduction of area or area ratio of the same specimen. Although it is improper to convert from per cent elongation to areal strain, it is sometimes expedient to convert from the area ratio or reduction of area to an equivalent uniform lineal strain *provided one does not confuse this equivalent lineal strain with the per cent elongation of the specimen.*

The relation between the lineal strain n and the area ratio R may be obtained as follows.

From the definition

$$n = \frac{l_x - l_o}{l_o}$$

we get

$$\frac{l_x}{l_o} = (1 + n)$$

Since the volume of metal remains constant during plastic deformation

$$A_o l_o = A_x l_x \quad \text{or} \quad \frac{l_x}{l_o} = \frac{A_o}{A_x} = R$$

Therefore

$$\frac{A_o}{A_x} = 1 + n \quad \text{or} \quad n = R - 1 \tag{1-24}$$

and at complete fracture of a tensile specimen

$$\frac{A_o}{A_f} = 1 + n_f \quad \text{or} \quad n_f = R_f - 1. \tag{1-25}$$

A similar relation may be obtained between the lineal strain and the per cent coldwork W or the per cent reduction of area, A_r. Since by definition,

$$W = \frac{A_o - A_x}{A_o} \times 100 \quad \text{or} \quad \frac{A_o}{A_x} = \frac{100}{100 - W}$$

Since

$$\frac{A_o}{A_x} = 1 + n$$

then

$$n = \frac{100}{100 - W} - 1 \quad \text{or} \quad n = \frac{1}{1 - W_f} - 1 \tag{1-26}$$

or

$$W = 100 - \frac{100}{n + 1} \tag{1-27}$$

And for the fracture strain

$$n_f = \frac{100}{100 - A_r} - 1 \tag{1-28}$$

and

$$A_r = 100 - \frac{100}{n_f + 1} \tag{1-29}$$

Some insight may be gained regarding the quantitative values of the equivalent reduction in area W, the uniform elongation Ul, the area ratio R, and the strains n and ϵ from the values tabulated in Table 1-2.

TABLE 1-2.   Conversions of Per Cent Reduction of Area (A_r), Per Cent
Coldwork (W), Uniform Elongation (Ul),[1] Area Ratio (R),
Nominal Strain (n), Natural Strain (ϵ)

W or A_r, %	Ul,[1] %	R	n, in./in.	ϵ, in./in.
0	0	1	0	0
5	5.2	1.052	0.052	0.051
10	11.1	1.111	0.111	0.105
20	25	1.250	0.250	0.223
25	33.3	1.333	0.333	0.288
30	42.8	1.428	0.428	0.355
33.3	50	1.500	0.500	0.405
40	66.7	1.667	0.667	0.511
50	100	2.000	1.000	0.693
60	150	2.50	1.500	0.916
63.2	172	2.718	1.718	1.000
70	233	3.333	2.333	1.203
75	300	4.000	3.000	1.386
80	400	5.000	4.000	1.609
90	900	10.000	9.000	2.303
95	1,900	20.000	19.000	3.000
98.1	5,300	54.000	53.000	4.000
99.75	40,243	403.430	402.430	6.000
99.97	298,000	2,981.000	2,980.000	8.000
99.995	2,202,500	22,026.000	22,025.000	10.000

[1] Ul is the equivalent uniform elongation, not the total elongation of a
fractured tensile specimen, El.

4. Yield Strength versus Per Cent Coldwork (W)

Since $S = \sigma$ for small strains, and yield strains are very small
(about 10^{-3} in./in.), we may rewrite $\sigma = \sigma_o\epsilon^m$ as

$$S_y = \sigma_o(\epsilon_y)^m = \sigma_o(\ln R)^m = \sigma_o\left(\ln \frac{100}{100 - W}\right)^m \qquad (1\text{-}30)$$

This means that the σ versus ϵ curve is really the same as the S_y versus
ϵ curve or, in other words, that the σ *versus ϵ curve is the locus of yield
strengths for coldworked materials.* This concept is a very important
one in the subject of mechanical properties.

Another way to arrive at this same conclusion is to consider several
cycles of loading and unloading in tension. If a specimen is loaded to
any point X, as in Figure 1-1, having a strain n_x greater than n_y but less

than n_u, the stress S_x will be L_x/A_o. The load at this time is $L_x = S_x A_o$. Because the volume of metal during plastic deformation remains constant and ignoring the elastic volume change, the actual A_x under load will be

$$A_x = A_o \frac{l_o}{l_x} = \frac{A_o}{n_x + 1}$$

Since the elastic springback on unloading is small, this is also the new area of the unloaded specimen. On reloading this "new" specimen, yielding will now occur at load L_x and not the original yield load. The new yield strength of this coldworked material is also the same as its proportional limit and its elastic limit, and numerically it is

$$(S_y)_x = \frac{L_x}{A_x} = \frac{S_x A_o (n_x + 1)}{A_o} = S_x(n_x + 1) \qquad (1\text{-}31)$$

But for small strains $S = \sigma$ and therefore

$$(\sigma_y)_x = \frac{L_x}{A_x} \qquad \text{where} \qquad (\sigma_y)_x$$

is the yield strength for the metal that has been coldworked to a strain n_x. By repeating this loading and unloading process for all points between n_y and n_f, it is then apparent that the true stress-true strain curve is the locus of yield strengths for coldworked materials.

It was assumed in the above explanation that if a specimen were strained to some load above the yield load and then unloaded, that upon reloading the material would deform elastically and linearly proportionally until the previous maximum load was reached. However, this is not exactly true for most materials. Most materials, upon reloading, will cease to be linearly proportional at some load that is one-half to nine-tenths of the previous maximum load. Some materials will be linearly proportional all the way to the previous maximum load. And some materials are linearly proportional to loads that are actually slightly greater than the previous maximum load. The reasons for these variations are the tendencies for some materials to strain age or to strain relax. These phenomena are also influenced by temperature and the time that elapses between the unload and reload cycle.

Another observation that can be made here is the fact that the engineering or nominal stress-strain diagram up to the ultimate load may be determined for a material from the strain hardenability relationship $\sigma = \sigma_o \epsilon^m$ for the same material. In the previous discussion it was shown that for any strain n_x that $(\sigma_y)_x = L_x/A_x$ and therefore

$$\sigma_x = S_x(1 + n_x)$$

Since

$$\sigma_x = \sigma_o(\epsilon_x)^m$$

Then

$$S_x = \frac{\sigma_o \epsilon_x^{m}}{1 + n_x} \qquad\qquad (1\text{-}32a)$$

or

$$S_x = \sigma_o(\epsilon_x)^m (e)^{-\epsilon_x} \qquad\qquad (1\text{-}32b)$$

5. Tensile Strength versus Per Cent Coldwork

Up to the present time the only relationships considered between tensile strength and coldwork are the experimentally determined tables and graphs. Furthermore, it is believed that the curves are different for all materials. However, by looking more closely at the definition of tensile strength, it is apparent that there is one simple analytical relationship between tensile strength and coldwork that is *valid for all materials with deformations equal to or less than the strain at ultimate load*. And for strains beyond the ultimate load strain, the tensile strength is equal to the yield strength, which may be determined from the strain-hardenability equation. That is, $S_u = S_y = \sigma_y = \sigma_o \epsilon^m$ for strains greater than n_u.

From the definition of tensile strength, which is the maximum or ultimate load divided by the original area, and by reference to Figure 1-6 the following analysis is made.

For bar (a) in Figure 1-6

$$S_u = \frac{L_u}{A_o} \qquad \text{or} \quad L_u = S_u A_o$$

where S_u is the tensile strength of the annealed material. For bar (b) with deformations less than n_u the tensile strength by definition is

$$(S_u)_w = \frac{L_u}{A_x} = \frac{S_u A_o}{A_x} \qquad\qquad (1\text{-}33a)$$

Since

$$A_x = \frac{A_o}{n_x + 1}$$

Equation 1-33a can be rewritten as

$$(S_u)_w = \frac{S_u A_o}{A_o}(n_x + 1) = S_u(n_x + 1) \qquad\qquad (1\text{-}33b)$$

To put the above relationship in terms of the per cent coldwork rather than strain, it is more convenient to define the fraction coldwork

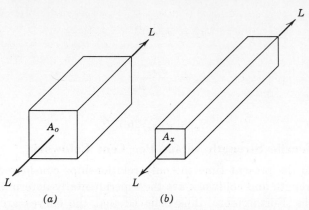

Figure 1-6. (*a*) Sketch of an annealed bar and the same bar (shown in *b*) after being coldworked under tensile loads. (*a*) Annealed $L_u = A_o S_u$. (b) Bar (*a*) after being coldworked to area A_x. If the coldworked strain n_x is less than n_u, the bar will still carry the same maximum load L_u that the annealed bar would carry.

(W_f) as the per cent coldworked (W) divided by 100. Thus,

$$W_f = \frac{A_o - A_r}{A_o} \quad \text{or} \quad \frac{A_o}{A_x} = \left(\frac{1}{1 - W_f}\right)$$

By substituting this latter expression into Equation 1-33a, the tensile strength of the coldworked material is found to be related to the annealed tensile strength and the amount of coldwork as given in Equation 1-33c.

$$(S_u)_w = S_u \frac{1}{1 - W_f} \qquad (1\text{-}33c)$$

For example, any material that is coldworked 10% will have a tensile strength after coldworking that is equal to its annealed tensile strength times the ratio of one over 0.9. Thus any material having an annealed tensile strength of 60,000 psi will have a tensile strength after it is coldworked 10% of:

$$(S_u)_{10} = 60,000 \frac{1}{0.9} = 60,000 \times 1.111 = 66,600 \text{ psi}$$

Similarly, an annealed material having a tensile strength of 30,000 psi will have a tensile strength of 30,000 × 1.111 or 33,300 psi after 10% coldwork. It must be remembered that this is true only if the material in this example has a strain at ultimate load n_u greater than 0.10.

If the 1020 steel were coldworked beyond the strain at maximum load, its tensile would be equal to its yield strength which could be calculated from the strain-hardening equation. Thus a 1020 annealed steel having a strain-hardening equation $\sigma = 100,000\epsilon^{0.23}$ would have a tensile strength after being coldworked 50% of

$$S_u = S_y = \sigma_y = 100,000 \ (\ln 2)^{0.23} = 100,000 \times 0.92 = 92,000 \text{ psi}$$

A comparison of experimentally determined tensile strengths with corresponding analytically calculated values for a coldworked material is given in Table 1-3. The second column of the table lists the tensile strengths that were actually obtained on samples of a 70Cu-30Zn alloy that were previously cold rolled to varying amounts up to a maximum of 60% reduction of area. The third column lists the expected values of tensile strength as calculated from Equation 1-33c for values of cold-work through 40% and from the strain-hardening equation for 50% and 60% coldwork. It can be observed that the analytically calculated values of tensile strength agree almost perfectly with the experimentally obtained values.

Strain aging or strain relaxation can affect the tensile strength of a coldworked material in a fashion similar to that discussed in the preceding section on yield strength where it was pointed out that the proportional limit could vary with the length of time between when the coldwork was done and when the material was then tested. Sim-

TABLE 1-3. Comparison of Experimental and Calculated Values of Tensile Strength after Plastic Deformation (70Cu-30Zn Brass)

Reduction by Cold Rolling, %	Tensile Strength, psi Experimental[1]	Calculated
0	43,000	43,000[2]
10	48,000	47,800[2]
20	53,000	53,700[2]
30	60,000	61,400[2]
40	70,900	71,600[2]
50	80,000	79,500[3]
60	90,000	90,700[3]

[1] R. M. Brick and A. Phillips, *Structure and Properties of Alloys*, McGraw-Hill Book Company, New York 1942.

[2] Calculated from $(S_u)_w = \dfrac{(S_u)_{\text{ann}}}{1 - W_f}$

[3] Calculated from $S_y = \sigma_y = 95,000\epsilon^{0.5}$

ilarly, the tensile strength may vary with time after coldworking. For example, the same 1020 steel mentioned above that had an annealed tensile strength of 60,000 psi, in round numbers, had a tensile strength of 67,000 psi when tested a couple of hours after it was cold rolled 10%. But the same material when tested a week after cold rolling has a tensile strength of 70,000 psi. This increase is due to strain aging. On the other hand, some materials such as 1100-0 aluminum do not appear to strain age in this fashion and have the same tensile strength several weeks after cold rolling as they have immediately after coldworking.

6. Relationship between m and ϵ_u

When the σ-ϵ curve is plotted on log-log coordinates, the slope of the plastic portion is constant and is designated as m, as illustrated in Figure 1-2. However, an interesting relationship may be obtained by considering a load (lb.)-strain curve as shown in Figure 1-7. The specimen stretches uniformly along the entire gage length, first elastically and then plastically, until the maximum load is reached. At this time, local straining occurs in a small length of the specimen and the phenomenon is referred to as "necking." When this phenomenon occurs, the load drops off from the maximum value continuously as the "necked down" area becomes smaller, until fracture occurs.

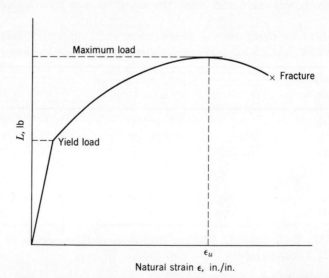

Figure 1-7. Load versus natural strain curve plotted on cartesian coordinates.

This analysis can start with the relation that the load on a tensile specimen is always equal to the product of the natural stress and the instantaneous area. That is

$$L = \sigma_i A_i \tag{1-34a}$$

Since

$$\sigma = \sigma_o \epsilon^m$$

we may rewrite (1-34a) as

$$L = \sigma_o \epsilon^m \times A_i \tag{1-34b}$$

Also

$$\epsilon = \ln \frac{A_o}{A_i} \quad \text{or} \quad e^\epsilon = \frac{A_o}{A_i}$$

so that

$$A_i = \frac{A_o}{e^\epsilon}$$

Thus,

$$L = \sigma_o A_o \epsilon^m e^{-\epsilon}$$

We then differentiate the load with respect to strain and equate it to zero since at the maximum load the slope of the load-strain curve is zero.

Thus,

$$\frac{dL}{d\epsilon} = -\sigma_o A_o (\epsilon^m)(e^{-\epsilon}) + \sigma_o A_o (e^{-\epsilon}) m(\epsilon^{m-1}) = 0$$

By canceling $\sigma_o A_o e^{-\epsilon}$ the equation reduces to $\epsilon^m = m(\epsilon)^{m-1}$. Since the strain at maximum load is designated as ϵ_u, we get

$$(\epsilon_u)^m = m(\epsilon_u)^{m-1}$$

or

$$1 = m(\epsilon_u)^{-1}$$

and finally

$$m = \epsilon_u \tag{1-34c}$$

Therefore the strain-hardening exponent m is numerically equal to the natural strain at the maximum load.

7. The Relationship of σ_o to the Elastic Properties of a Material

By writing the true stress-true strain equation as $\sigma_o = \sigma/\epsilon^m$, and using for σ and ϵ the specific values of stress and strain associated with the yield strength, the following is obtained:

$$\sigma_o = \frac{\sigma_y}{(\epsilon_y)^m} = \frac{\sigma_y}{(\sigma_y/E)^m} = \sigma_y{}^{1-m}E^m \qquad (1\text{-}35)$$

Thus it may be observed that σ_o is equal to the product of the yield strength to the $1 - m$ power and the modulus of elasticity to the m power. *But this is valid only when the yield strength actually lies on the $\sigma = \sigma_o\epsilon^m$ line.*

However it must be appreciated at this time that neither the elastic nor the plastic stress strain curves are straight lines, with the slopes E and m, respectively, in the vicinity where they intersect. This is implied in Figure 1-2 where the elastic line is a dashed line for all strains greater than a slightly lower strain than that of the hypothetical intersection strain. The same is true for all plastic strains slightly greater than the intersection strain.

In reality there are three types of stress-strain curves, with reference to the elastic-plastic region, as illustrated in Figure 1-8. Curve I represents the so-called ideal material where the plastic curve is straight all the way to the elastic curve. Curve A has a slope that gradually decreases from E to m, with the 0.2% offset yield strength falling below the plastic strain hardening line. Curve B, which appears to be the more common one, has a slope that rapidly changes from E

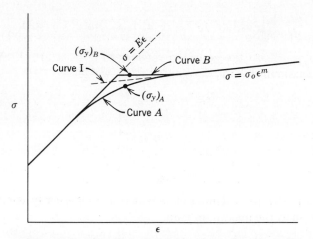

Figure 1-8. Schematic representation of two extreme types of actual stress-strain curves on log-log coordinates. Curve A is the less common type, whereas curve B is the type associated with a material that has or tends to have a "yield point" phenomenon.

to some value less than m. In some cases the slope actually drops off to zero, and for a few materials, such as annealed 1020 steel having a pronounced "yield point" phenomena, the slope becomes negative, and then gradually increases to m. For B-type materials, the 0.2% offset yield strength lies above the strain-hardening line. This is discussed in more detail under the next topic.

In general, the elastic region extends to strains of the order of magnitude of 10^{-3} in./in., the elastic-plastic region lies in the region of strains between 10^{-3} in./in. and 10^{-2} in./in. and the plastic or strain-hardening range is from 10^{-2} to 1 in./in.

Since not many of the real materials have stress-strain curves that are "ideal" and since Equation 1-35 was derived for an "ideal" material, *it should not be used to determine σ_o for a real material unless no other information is given other than S_y, E and m for the material.* On the other hand, if σ_o, S_y, m, and n_y are all known, then by calculating σ_y from $\sigma_y = \sigma_o(\epsilon_y)^m$ and comparing the calculated value to the experimentally determined value of S_y it is possible to determine how close to being "ideal" the material is.

8. Tensile Strength to Yield Strength Ratio (S_u/S_y)

For many years designers and engineers have known that the ratio of S_y to S_u is about $\frac{1}{2}$ to $\frac{5}{8}$ for soft steel, and for materials in general, the hard brittle materials have a ratio close to 1, whereas the soft ductile ones have a ratio near $\frac{1}{2}$. Considerable experimental data have been obtained for annealed and heat-treated carbon steels which, when plotted together on one set of coordinates, fit fairly well the line represented by the expression

$$S_y = 1.05S_u - 22,000 \qquad (1-36)$$

Another way of looking at this equation is that it is a straight line connecting the weakest and the strongest steels. The weakest steel is a very low-carbon steel having a microstructure of essentially 100% ferrite. It has a tensile strength of about 40,000 psi and a yield strength of approximately 20,000 psi. The strongest steel is a high-carbon martensitic, stress-relieved steel which has a tensile strength of about 400,000 psi. For a steel of this hardness having practically no ductility, the yield strength is nearly equal to the tensile strength.

The relationship expressed in Equation 1-36 is valid only for non-work hardened steels. It does not apply to other ferrous materials such as cast iron or stainless steels.

Much insight into the quantitative values of the S_u to S_y ratio for materials in general can be gained from studying the strain-hardenability equation. By solving this equation for the natural stress and then the nominal stress at both the ultimate strain and the yield strain, an interesting ratio is obtained.

From the strain-hardening equation $\sigma = \sigma_o \epsilon^m$ we get at the ultimate load

$$\sigma_u = \sigma_o m^m \tag{1-37a}$$

Also

$$\sigma_u = S_u \left(1 + n_u\right) = S_u e^m \tag{1-37b}$$

By combining the latter two equations

$$S_u = \sigma_o \left(\frac{m}{e}\right)^m \tag{1-37c}$$

By defining yield strengths as that value of natural stress that results when a material has been subjected to a 0.2% plastic deformation (that is, the elastic limit of a material after it has been cold-worked to a 0.2% plastic strain), we get

$$S_y = \sigma_o (0.002)^m \tag{1-38}$$

Therefore

$$\frac{S_u}{S_y} = \frac{\sigma_o \left(\dfrac{m}{e}\right)^m}{\sigma_o (0.002)^m} = \left(\frac{m}{0.002e}\right)^m$$

or

$$\frac{S_u}{S_y} = (184m)^m \tag{1-39}$$

and is valid for $m > 0.005$.

It must be pointed out at this time, however, that the 0.2% plastic deformation yield strength is not exactly the same as the 0.2% offset yield strength, although in many cases the numerical values of both are nearly the same. The advantage of using the 0.2% plastic deformation lies in the simplicity it affords in calculations employing the strain-hardening equations. To justify its use, we need only to recall that there is no one universal standard yield strength, or one method to determine the yield strength. For example, all of the following are acceptable ways to determine the yield strength, depending upon who does the specifying: (1) the dividers method; (2) the drop of the beam method; (3) the offset method, using either 0.5%, 0.2%, 0.1%, or 0.01% offset; (4) the 0.5% extension under load; (5) the proportional limit or the elastic limit. Obviously, when we look up the yield strength of a material in a handbook, we should also ascertain by which method the yield strength was determined.

Also, one may question the validity in the use of 0.2% plastic strain to calculate the yield strength of a material that may have a yield strain of 0.002 or slightly more. Again, by studying the stress-strain curves of annealed 1080 steel as plotted in Figure 1-5, it is obvious that the difference in the stresses for a strain of 0.002 and 0.004 are only in the order of magnitude of 5000 psi, which is less than the variation in published values of the 0.2% offset yield strength of different samples of annealed 1080 steel.

Thus we can see that the S_u to S_y ratio depends exponentially on the slope of the natural stress-strain curve. Table 1-4 lists some calculated values of the ratio for some discrete values of m covering the entire range of values normally encountered for metals deformed below their recrystallization temperature.

However, it must be recalled that in the derivation of Equation 1-39 and the compilation of Table 1-4, the yield strength was defined as the value of true stress for a true strain of 0.002. In other words, it is the value of σ that is obtained by solving the strain-hardening equation $\sigma = \sigma_0 \epsilon^m$ for a strain of 0.002. Thus Equation 1-39 is valid for a material having "ideal" mechanical properties, that is, a material having a plastic stress-strain relationship such as I in Figure 1-8. This relationship is a straight line (on logarithmic coordinates) all the way to its intersection of the linear elastic stress-strain curve.

TABLE 1-4. Calculated Values of S_u to S_y Ratio for a Range of m

m	0.005	0.05	0.1	0.15	0.20	0.25	0.30	0.40	0.50	0.60
S_u/S_y	1.000	1.12	1.34	1.64	2.05	2.60	3.33	5.55	9.60	16.8

But most real materials have curves that are similar to type B in Figure 1-8, and a few have curves that resemble type A. For these latter two types of materials, the S_u to S_y ratio calculated from the strain hardening exponent m will be different from the experimentally determined ratio. In fact, it can be determined how close to "ideal" a certain material is by comparing its "ideal" yield strength as calculated from Equation 1-39 with its experimentally determined value. Thus, if the calculated value is considerably lower than the experimentally determined value, then the material is of the B type.

The following examples of experimentally obtained properties of some common metals should serve as a guide in interpreting Equation 1-39 and Table 1-4. An annealed copper sample tested had a tensile strength of 34,000 psi, a yield strength of 5000 psi and a strain-hardening exponent of 0.5. Its experimental S_u to S_y ratio is 6.8. From Table 1-3, an "ideal" metal with an m value of 0.5 would have a S_u to S_y ratio of 9.6. Thus the copper sample is a B type material. However, a 70-30 leaded brass annealed at 1250°F has a tensile strength of 45,000 psi, a yield strength of 12,000 psi, and a strain-hardening exponent of 0.5. Its S_u to S_y ratio is only 3.75. This is much lower than the "ideal" ratio of 9.6. Thus this brass is very far from having an "ideal" type of strain-hardening curve.

Annealed aluminum has a tensile strength of 13,000 psi, a yield strength of 5000 psi, and a strain-hardening exponent of 0.2. The S_u to S_y ratio is 2.6. Since the "ideal" ratio is 2.05, pure aluminum is slightly nonideal and of the B type of material.

Hot-rolled 4340 steel has a tensile strength of 153,000 psi, a yield strength of 135,000, and a strain-hardening exponent of 0.088. Thus it has an actual S_u to S_y ratio of 1.13 where as the "ideal" material would have a ratio of about 1.27. Hardened steel has a low m (about 0.05) and an experimental S_u to S_y ratio close to one, again agreeing quite closely to the calculated value. On the other hand, 304 stainless steel has a tensile strength of 83,000 psi, a yield strength of 40,000 psi, and an m of 0.45. Its actual S_u to S_y ratio of 2.07 is considerably different from the "ideal" materials value of 7.3.

9. Tensile Strength versus Brinell Hardness

One of the advantages of the Brinell hardness test which assisted in its widespread acceptance, while the dozens of other hardness tests that were developed during the same period were dropped by the wayside, is its expediency. As an example, in steel when the Brinell hardness is multiplied by 500, the resulting number agrees closely with its tensile strength. Although it is generally known that the relationship $S_u = KH_B$ seems to apply for all materials, with the constant K being different for each material, it is also known that it varies greatly even in the same family of materials. For example, there is not one constant for all the aluminum alloys, but rather there is a different K for nearly all of the aluminum types.

As we have been shown previously in many other relationships concerning the mechanical properties, some new insight can be gained by referring to the true stress-true strain properties of the material. This is also true of the tensile strength and Brinell hardness. It was pointed out in a previous section that the tensile strength is a value of stress associated with a specific amount of strain—the strain at the maximum load. This strain is also numerically equal to the strain-hardening exponent of the material. Thus the tensile strength for a given material corresponds to a fixed amount of plastic deformation.

The Brinell hardness number, which has the units of kg/mm^2, is also a value of stress associated with a certain amount of plastic strain. However, in this case the stress is compressive, and the plastic strain is neither a fixed amount nor is it constant over the section that is deformed. The amount of plastic strain induced during the Brinell test depends upon the load that is applied to the indenting ball. Whereas there is only one load associated with the tensile strength of a specimen of given size and material, loads of different magnitude can be applied during the hardness test with resulting differences in the numerical value of the hardness number.

For example, ETP (electrolytic tough pitch) copper annealed at 1200°F will have a tensile strength of about 31,000 psi and a strain at the tensile load of about 0.5. But this same copper will have a Brinell hardness of 36 when a 200 kg load is applied to the standard indentor and a hardness of 48 when a 1500 kg load is used. The indentation with the lighter load is smaller and the amount of plastic deformation is less. The amount of plastic deformation that occurs during the Brinell test can be expressed as a d/D ratio, the ratio of diameter of the indentation to the diameter of the indentor. For this particular copper the d/D ratio is 0.25 for a 200 kg load and 0.60 for a 1500 kg load. Thus we can see that as the d/D ratio for copper varies from 0.25 to 0.60, the Brinell hardness number increases by 33%.

Since both the tensile strength of a material and its Brinell hardness number depend upon the strain-hardening characteristics of the material, it is to be expected that they are both related to each other by means of the strain-hardening exponent m. Although no analytical solution has been made for this relationship, Figure 1-9 illustrates empirically how the S_u/H_B ratio for all of the materials are related to the strain-hardening exponent. Two curves are drawn in this figure, one for a d/D of 0.5 and another for a d/D ratio of 0.3. Most Brinell tests are conducted with loads that result in a d/D ratio of approximately 0.5.

We can also see in Figure 1-9 that a material having a strain-hardening exponent of 0.5 to 0.6, such as annealed brass containing 30% zinc, will have a S_u/H_B ratio of 900 to 1000. Typical experimental values for the tensile strength and Brinell hardness are 47,000 psi and 50 kg/mm^2, respectively. This gives a S_u/H_B ratio of 940.

At the opposite end of the strain-hardening scale is the solution treated, or annealed, 17-4 PH stainless steel. It has a strain-hardening

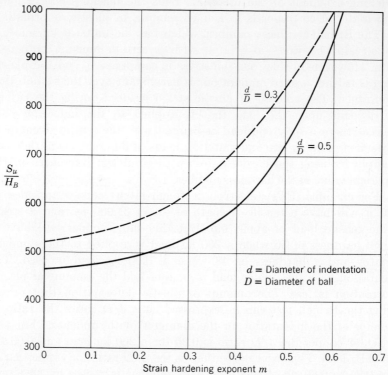

Figure 1-9.   Relationship between S_u/H_B ratio and the strain-hardening exponent.

exponent of about 0.05, a tensile strength of about 144,000 psi, and a Brinell hardness of 300 kg/mm². This results in a S_u/H_B ratio of 480, or about one-half that of the brass. As another example, annealed 18-8 stainless steel has a strain-hardening exponent of 0.44 to 0.52, a tensile strength of 85,000 to 95,000 psi, and a Brinell hardness of 140 to 150 kg/mm². This results in a S_u/H_B ratio in the range of 600 to 650.

10. Obtaining S_y, m, and σ_o from S_u, n_u, and n_f

It is becoming increasingly more important each year to have a more complete understanding of the mechanical properties of materials, since this knowledge is required for the many conditions under which each material is used. For example, 1020 steel may be annealed, normalized, heat treated by any one of many means and/or coldworked to various degrees. If all of the combinations of above treatments were tabulated, the data would be so bulky that it would be practically impossible to locate some desired information even if it were tabulated. One way to avoid compounding data in the above fashion is to tabulate only certain "fundamental" properties from which, by means of simple analytical and empirical relationships, the mechanical properties after any treatment can be easily determined. In regard to the tensile properties, it seems that S_u, n_u and ϵ_f (tensile strength, strain at ultimate load and strain at fracture, respectively,) are such "fundamental" properties, so that from them all of the presently required tensile properties can be calculated.

First, to determine the strain-hardenability exponent, it is simply necessary to convert the conventional ultimate-load strain to the true strain at the ultimate load, as follows:

$$m = \epsilon_u = \ln (1 + n_u) \tag{1-41}$$

The numerical value of σ_o, after m is known, can be determined by substituting the ultimate stress and strain into the strain-hardenability equation. Thus

$$\sigma_o = \frac{\sigma_u}{(\epsilon_u)^m} = \frac{\sigma_u}{m^m} = \frac{S_u(1 + n_u)}{m^m} \tag{1-42a}$$

or

$$\sigma_o = S_u \left(\frac{e}{m}\right)^m \tag{1-42b}$$

The "ideal" yield strength, on the basis of 0.2% plastic deformation can easily be determined by substituting 0.002 for ϵ in the strain hardening equation

$$S_y = \sigma_y = \sigma_o(0.002)^m \tag{1-43}$$

But, as discussed in Sections 7 and 8, the actual yield strength of a metal may be considerably different from this calculated value. Therefore it is necessary to determine experimentally the yield strength if the value must be known accurately.

From the relationships under Sections 4 and 5, the yield strength and tensile strength for any amount of coldwork can be determined.

Of course, ϵ_f determines the maximum tensile strain that a material can be subjected to without fracturing. This concept is discussed more thoroughly in Chapter 5.

The following illustration will demonstrate the use of the above mentioned three relationships with some familiar materials.

Ferrite (α) has an S_u of 40,000 psi and a n_u of 0.32. Pearlite (P_c) has an S_u of 120,000 psi and a n_u of nearly 0.12. Therefore

$$m = \ln (1.32) = 0.28 \qquad \text{for } \alpha$$

$$m = \ln (1.12) = 0.11 \qquad \text{for } P_c$$

$$\sigma_o = \frac{40,000 \times 1.32}{0.28^{0.28}} = \frac{53,800}{0.70} = 77,000 \text{ psi} \qquad \text{for } \alpha$$

$$\sigma_o = \frac{120,000 \times 1.12}{0.11^{0.11}} = \frac{138,000}{0.785} = 172,000 \text{ psi} \qquad \text{for } P_c$$

$$S_y = 77,000 \times 0.002^{0.28} = 77,000 \times 0.175 = 13,500 \text{ psi} \qquad \text{for } \alpha$$

$$S_y = 172,000 \times 0.002^{0.11} = 172,000 \times 0.505 = 87,000 \text{ psi} \qquad \text{for } P_c$$

REFERENCES

1. *1961 Book of ASTM Standards,* Part 3. Am. Soc. for Testing and Mater., pp. 1 to 226.
2. ASM, *Metals Handbook,* 1948 edition.
3. Everhart, J. L., W. E. Lindlief, J. Kanegis, P. G. Weissler, and F. Siegel, "Mechanical Properties of Metals and Alloys," *Nat. Bur. Standards,* C447 (1943).
4. *ASME Handbook,* "Metals Properties," McGraw Hill, New York, 1958.

STUDY PROBLEMS

1–1   A tensile test on a standard 0.505 in. diameter by 2 in. gage length specimen of a new material gave the following results: yield load 11,200 lb, maximum load = 62,000 lb, gage length at maximum load = 2.984 in., per cent reduction of area at fracture = 33%.
Determine the following:
a. Yield strength
b. Natural stress at the yield load
c. Tensile strength
d. Natural stress at the maximum load
e. Natural strain at the yield load
f. Natural strain at the maximum load
g. Natural strain at the fracture load
h. Nominal stress at fracture
i. Natural stress at fracture
j. Slope m of the natural stress-strain curve
k. The constant σ_o in the natural stress-strain curve

1–2   What amount of coldwork is required to produce a natural strain of 6? Of 10?

1–3   What initial length bar is required to have (after compression) a length of 1 in. with a natural strain of 10.

1-4 Nearly all common materials have a per cent elongation less than their per cent reduction of area. Is it possible for any material to have a per cent elongation greater than its per cent reduction of area? Explain.

1-5 A new material is developed, but because of the small amount available a subsize tensile specimen having a 0.505 in. diameter and 1 in. gage length is used to determine its mechanical properties. The resulting elongation is 30% and area reduction is 30%. Estimate these two values if a 0.505 in. diameter and 2 in. gage length specimen were used.

1-6 The strain hardenability of a 95-5 alloy in an annealed condition can be expressed as $\sigma = 100,000\epsilon^{0.25}$.
a. Estimate the yield and tensile strengths of the annealed material.
b. Estimate the yield and tensile strengths of this material after it has been coldworked 50%.

1-7 A particular metal in the annealed condition possesses the following characteristics:

$$E = 10 \times 10^6 \text{ psi} \qquad \mu = 0.25$$
$$S_u = 30,000 \text{ psi} \qquad \sigma = 60,000\epsilon^{0.33}$$
$$A_r = 40\%$$

a. When subjected to a strain-hardening treatment designated as X, the resultant yield strength is 30,000 psi. Determine the amount of coldwork imparted by the X treatment.
b. If a tensile specimen were machined from a bar of this material that was subjected to treatment X, and was tested on a tensile machine, what would the true tensile strain at fracture most likely be?
c. What will be the probable value of the per cent reduction of area of the specimen in part b?
d. What will be the probable value of the true fracture strength of the specimen in part b?

1-8 A steel supplier's stock handbook lists the yield and tensile strengths of cold drawn AISI 1045 steel as 90,000 psi and 103,000 psi respectively. This steel in the annealed condition has a yield strength of 58,000 psi and a per cent reduction of area of 50%. The generalized strain-hardening equation for this material is $\sigma = 137,000 \ (\epsilon + \epsilon_w)^{0.14}$ where ϵ_w is the true strain of any prior coldwork.
a. How much coldwork is given to this 1045 steel during the cold drawing operation?
b. What is the maximum tensile strength that AISI 1045 steel can be coldworked to?
c. What is the maximum tensile strength that AISI 1045 steel can be heat treated to?

1-9 It was determined experimentally that the strain hardening relationship for 1100-O aluminum is $\sigma = 27,000\epsilon^{0.18}$. An aluminum manufacturer's handbook lists the yield and tensile strengths of 1100-O as 5000 and 13,000 psi respectively. The respective values for 1100-H18 are given as 22,000 and 24,000 psi. What is the per cent coldwork that has been given to 1100-H18? How does this compare to the strain at maximum load?

1–10   A certain as-rolled AISI 1020 steel has the following properties: $\sigma =$ 115,000$\epsilon^{0.22}$; $A_r = 63\%$; $S_u = 66,000$ psi.
   a. Plot yield strength and tensile strength vs. per cent coldwork (on cartesian coordinates).
   b. Plot yield strength and tensile strength vs. true strain (of coldwork) on log-log paper.

1–11   The following mechanical properties are given for material X.

Annealed

$S_u = 40,000$ psi	$El = 35\%$	$H_B = 120$ kg/mm^2
$S_y = 23,000$ psi	$A_r = 30\%$	$E = 20 \times 10^6$ psi

% Coldworked

	5	10	20	30
$S_u =$	84,200	89,000	100,000	110,000
$S_y =$	64,000	79,000	97,000	109,000

Are all of the properties listed above valid? If not, which are not valid? Show all calculations.

1–12   A 0.505 in. dia. $\times$ 2 in. gage length standard threaded tensile specimen of annealed 1018 steel was loaded and strained until the minimum diameter was 0.340 in. During this loading it was established that this material has a yield point of 35,000 psi and a strain-hardening equation of $\sigma = 105,000\epsilon^{0.25}$. The specimen was unloaded before it fractured. (The handbooks list the A_r of annealed 1018 steel as 60 to 65%.)
   a. If this same piece were reloaded, what would the new maximum load be?
   b. If, instead of reloading immediately, the piece were machined to a uniform diameter of 0.300 in. over the entire length of the original gage length before retesting, what would be the new maximum load?
   c. 70–30 annealed brass has a strain-hardening equation $\sigma = 105,000\epsilon^{0.5}$. What would you expect its yield strength to be in comparison to the annealed 1018 steel above?

1–13   AISI 1040 cold-drawn steel has: $S_u = 90,800$; $S_y = 88,000$; $A_r = 52.5\%$; $n_y = 0.003$; $n_u = 0.087$; $E = 30 \times 10^6$ psi. In making this steel, a $1\frac{1}{16}$ in. dia. annealed bar is drawn to a 1 in. dia. (drawing through a die may be considered a tensile operation.)
   a. Derive the strain hardening equation for annealed 1040 steel.
   b. What is the value of A_r for the annealed steel?
   c. Does this annealed steel have a yield point phenomenon?

1–14   AISI C1141 annealed steel has $S_u = 85,000$, $S_y = 60,000$, $\%El = 25$, $A_r = 50\%$, $H_B = 170$. A bar of this material X in. diameter is cold drawn to 1 in. diameter and then has the following properties; $S_u = 94,500$, $S_y = 91,000$, $\%El = 14$, $A_r = 44.4\%$, $H_B = 189$. This cold drawn bar is now further cold drawn to a 0.950 in. diameter. It now has a $S_y = 104,500$ psi.
   a. What was the diameter X of the annealed bar?
   b. What is the strain-hardening equation of this annealed steel?

    c. What is the strain-hardening equation of the 1 in. diameter cold drawn steel?

1-15 A certain annealed nonferrous material has the following properties: $S_u = 90,000$; $S_y = 40,000$ psi; $A_r = 80\%$. If this material is coldworked 60%, what will be the A_r of a tensile specimen machined from the coldworked bar?

1-16 The standard Brinell test employs a 10 mm diameter ball and loads of either 500, 1000, 1500, 2000, 2500, or 3000 kg. For steels a 3000 kg load is generally used. If, on the same piece of annealed low carbon steel but at different locations, Brinell tests were conducted, first with a 3000 kg load and then with a 500 kg load, would the Brinell hardness number of the two tests be the same? Explain.

2

The Metallurgical Control of
Mechanical Properties

Chapter 1 defined the mechanical properties and demonstrated how some of them are interdependent. The mechanical properties of a material in a specified condition were listed, and we studied the manner in which they changed as the material was plastically deformed. No consideration was given as to what determined the original properties of the material, or how they could be altered.

The purpose of this chapter is to give the reader a thorough appreciation of the control of the mechanical properties of materials. Thus he may take a more creative approach, as opposed to the traditional handbook approach, to the problem of selecting and specifying materials for the "hardware" he designs. As in the other chapters, the problem solving method is emphasized here. This chapter is an *application* of the principles of the structure of solids with which it is assumed the reader is familiar from an earlier course in materials science. If there has been a considerable lapse in time since the reader has had such a course, we recommend his reviewing the subject while studying this chapter.

The mechanical properties are dependent not only on the atomic or molecular structure of the material, but also on the microstructural or phase arrangement of the material. To an engineer concerned with the design of structures, it is the dependency of the mechanical properties on the microstructures, or phases, that is most important. The range of mechanical properties that exist for any material, regardless of whether it be a common material such as iron or aluminum, or an exotic material such as an alloy of one of the refractory metals, can best be explained and understood on a microstructural basis.

In the following discussions, the emphasis will be on the strength (yield, tensile, and hardness) of the material. The ductility, either in

44

terms of impact strength or fracture strain, will be discussed briefly
wherever appropriate. Otherwise it will be sufficient to remember that,
in general, the ductility decreases for any given material as its strength
is increased.

DEFINITION OF STRENGTH

In this chapter, unless otherwise stated, the term strength will
always refer to the yield strength of the material. In view of this,
*strength is defined as a measure of a material's ability to resist the
mass sliding movement of one body of atoms, with respect to the remaining body of atoms, along crystallographic planes.* This motion is
referred to as slip, and the planes along which the motion occurs are
called slip planes. It is sufficient for an understanding of the control
of the mechanical properties to define slip as an avalanche of disloca-

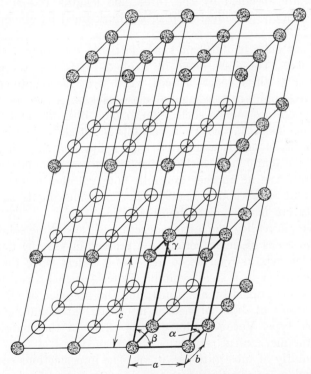

Figure 2-1. Schematic diagram of a space lattice and
its unit cell (atoms on the three visible faces and on
the unit cell are shown as dark circles).

tions which terminates at grain boundaries or inclusions, rather than to consider the movement of individual dislocations.

In order to become reacquainted with some of the terms used in discussing the structure of crystalline solids, we shall briefly review them. The atoms of a crystalline solid are arrayed in a three-dimensional network of straight lines known as a *space lattice*. This is schematically illustrated in Figure 2-1 where the center of the atoms are represented by small circles: solid circles on the three visible faces and hollow circles on the interior planes or faces. There are two important characteristics of a space lattice. First, the space lattice network divides space into equal-sized prisms whose faces contact each other in such a manner that no void spaces are present. Second, every lattice point of a space lattice has identical surroundings.

The individual prisms that make up a space lattice are referred to as *unit cells*. In a given space lattice, all of the unit cells are identical in regard to shape, size, and orientation. The size and shape of a unit cell are specified by the three side lengths (a,b,c) and the three angles (α,β,γ), as illustrated in the dark-lined parallelopiped of Figure 2-1.

There are only 14 different space lattices, with only 7 different systems of axes. These are listed in Table 2-1. Most of the common metals belong to three space lattices, which are: face-centered cubic, body-centered cubic, and hexagonal close-packed. A few of the low melting temperature metals such as antimony, bismuth, and mercury have a rhombohedral lattice. However, this is not an indication that a certain type of lattice is associated with a low-melting temperature material, since many high melting temperature compounds are also rhombohedral. And as another example, both gallium, a metal which melts at about 85°F, and cementite (Fe_3C), which melts at a very high temperature, have an orthorhombic lattice.

However, in reality, the lattice structure of crystalline solids is not perfect. Two types of imperfections are present in varying degrees in all solids. One type is referred to as a point defect since the imperfection is localized to a small volume. Defects such as vacancies (a lattice point unoccupied by an atom), and the presence of either substitutional atoms of different size or interstitial atoms are imperfections of this type. Vacancies have little effect in the metallurgical control of the mechanical properties; but they do affect the diffusion rate, particularly of substitutional atoms. The imperfections caused by substitutional or interstitial atoms do have a large effect upon the mechanical properties, and this influence is discussed in a following section on single-phase alloying.

TABLE 2-1   Crystal Systems and Space Lattices

Crystal System	Space Lattice	Number Of Axes	Side Lengths	Interaxial Angles
Cubic	Simple Body centered Face centered	3	$a = b = c$	$\alpha = \beta = \gamma = 90°$
Tetragonal	Simple Body centered	3	$a = b \neq c$	$\alpha = \beta = \gamma = 90°$
Orthorhombic	Simple Body centered Base centered Face centered	3	$a \neq b \neq c$	$\alpha = \beta = \gamma = 90°$
Rhombohedral	Simple	3	$a = b = c$	$\alpha = \beta = \gamma \neq 90°$
Monoclinic	Simple Base centered	3	$a \neq b \neq c$	$\alpha = \beta = 90° \neq \gamma$
Triclinic	Simple	3	$a \neq b \neq c$	$\alpha \neq \beta \neq \gamma \neq 90°$
Hexagonal	Simple	4	$a_1 = a_2 = a_3 \neq c$ or $a_1 = b \neq c$	$\alpha = \beta = 90°,$ $\gamma = 120°$

The second type of imperfection is a line defect and is referred to as a dislocation. Although there are several special types of dislocations, the two most commonly discussed line defects are the edge and the screw dislocation. An edge dislocation is a lattice defect in which the imperfections lie on a straight line extending from one end of the crystal to the other. When looking at a crystalline plane that is perpendicular to the dislocation line, the imperfection consists of an extra row (actually a plane) of atoms on one side of a crystalline plane that is not present on the other side. This is sketched in Figure 2-2, where the small circles represent the centers of the atoms. An edge dislocation is symbolically represented by the symbol $\perp$ where the vertical leg represents the extra plane of atoms. When the vertical leg is above the horizontal leg, as in Figure 2-2a, the dislocation is considered to be positive. When the extra plane of atoms is in the bottom portion of a crystal, the vertical leg is placed below the horizontal leg and the dislocation is then considered to be negative.

A screw dislocation is a lattice defect in which the lattice points lie on a spiral or helical surface that revolves around a center line which is called the dislocation line. The emergence of a screw dislocation at a crystal surface is illustrated in Figure 2-2b.

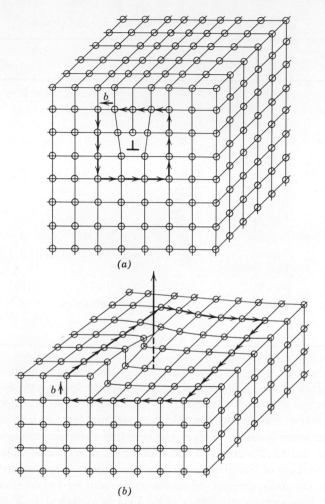

(a)

(b)

Figure 2-2. Line type surface imperfections in a lattice structure: (*a*) Edge dislocation. (*b*) Screw dislocation.

Dislocations are defined quantitatively by means of a Burgers vector. A Burgers vector is the distance, in multiples of the lattice parameter, that is needed to close a straight-sided loop around a dislocation when going the same number of lattice distances in all four directions. It is generally represented by a vector labeled **b**. Figure 2-2 illustrates a Burgers vector of unity in both an edge and a screw dislocation. A characteristic of an edge dislocation is that it lies perpendicular to its Burgers vector. Similarly a screw dislocation lies parallel to its Burgers vector.

The above introduction to dislocation theory serves as a background for understanding the theories behind each of the strengthening mechanisms, and for applying them to the control of the mechanical properties of real materials. To go further into dislocation theory is necessary only if one is to do research in that field. It is more meaningful to discuss the control of mechanical properties on the basis of slip, which is the sliding movement of enormously large numbers of atoms along a crystalline plane.

The first movements of dislocations in a nonplastically deformed metal are reversible and occur in the elastic range of loading. This phenomenon is submicroscopic or atomic in scale, but that of slip is microscopic in scale.

The evidence of slip is seen in metallographically prepared specimens on a metallurgical microscope as slip lines, which are the intersection of the crystallographic planes along which slip occurred and the etched surface of the specimen. Slip results in a narrow band on each side of the slip plane in which the lattice structure of the metal is severely distorted. These slip lines (bands) do not appear on the face of a specimen that is polished after the specimen is plastically deformed below the recrystallization temperature. It is only after chemical etching with a reagent which dissolves the particular metal being examined that the slip lines appear. The slip lines become visible since the internal energy within the distorted band is considerably higher than that within the rest of the crystal because of the great distortional mechanical strain in this region. The metal at the higher energy level reacts and goes into solution in the reagent much more rapidly than the rest of the crystal, thus leaving a narrow groove where the severely distorted band intersects the surface. This is the same reason that grain boundaries are visible under a metallurgical microscope.

On the other hand, slip lines do appear on a previously polished face of an annealed specimen when it is subsequently plastically deformed below its recrystallization temperature.

Slip terminates at the grain boundaries or free surface of the grains in the form of substantial steps or jogs. This is illustrated schematically in Figure 2-3. Experimental studies on the spacing of the slip planes and the size of the jog have been made on some of the common metals. The spacing of the slip planes varies randomly, but the average distance between them is about 2000 atom diameters. The displacement of one mass with respect to that on the other side of the

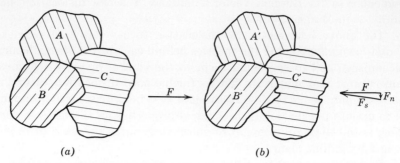

Figure 2-3. Schematic illustration of a distortion produced by slip. (a) Before slip. (b) After slip, which resulted from component F_s of the force F.

slip plane, or the size of the step at the surface of the grain, is of the order of magnitude of 200 to 700 atom diameters or 500 to 2000Å. (An angstrom equals 10^{-8} cm).

The atomic movement associated with slip, unlike that of the initial movement of dislocations, is irreversible in that the "slip" or change in shape is permanent. That is, it is plastic deformation. Thus slip and yielding, as defined in Chapter 1, are two terms that express the concept of plastic deformation from two different points of view: a microscopic and a macroscopic, respectively.

PRINCIPLES OF MECHANICAL STRENGTH

The mechanical behavior of a material can be best understood on the basis of three principles or precepts which in a coordinating fashion encompass all of the strengthening mechanisms used in the control of mechanical properties. These three rules will be enumerated first, and then applied to all the heat-treating techniques, as well as to problems concerned with the use of materials on the basis of mechanical strength.

The first principle of mechanical strength is: *a material is strengthened when slip is made more difficult to initiate.* This rule is self-evident from the definition of strength presented. Thus any treatment given to a material that retards the avalanche of dislocations or "pegs" the slip planes, or, in other words, anything that makes slip occur at a higher stress level, makes the material stronger. The magnitude of this effect is great: the yield strength of pure aluminum can be raised from 5000 psi in the annealed condition to 25,000 psi in the coldworked condition; the yield strength of iron can be raised from 20,000 psi in the "commercially pure" condition to about 400,000 psi when less than 1% carbon is dissolved in it.

The second principle of mechanical strength is: *slip is retarded by inducing mechanical strains, or distortions, in the lattice structure of the material.* These mechanical strains are residual elastic strains which are present when the atoms of the parent material are not at their equilibrium distances from each other, which is also their lowest energy position. Thus it is apparent that the internal energy of the material is proportional to the magnitude of the mechanical strains present. On this basis the second principle may be restated as: *the stress level at which slip occurs in a material is proportional to its internal mechanical energy caused by the lattice distortion.* It is necessary to restrict this energy to the mechanical portion since some forms of energy have negligible effects on strength, and thermal energy has an inverse effect on strength.

The third principle of mechanical strength is: *there are three methods to induce mechanical strains or increase the internal mechanical energy, namely: subrecrystallization plastic deformation, increase of the grain boundary surface area, and alloying.* These three methods are discussed in detail in the following sections since a thorough understanding of them is a prerequisite to a knowledge of the metallurgical control of the mechanical properties.

Subrecrystallization Plastic Deformation

The quantitative aspects of strain hardening due to plastic deformation were presented in detail in Chapter 1 by means of the strain-hardening Equations 1-15 and 1-20; so only a summary will be given here.

The amount of strain strengthening that may be acquired by a material is determined by the value of its σ_o, m, and ϵ_f. The strength coefficient is σ_o, m is the rate of strengthening due to plastic deformation, and ϵ_f determines the amount of deformation the material can be subjected to before it fractures. This last characteristic is discussed in considerable detail in Chapter 5 on Forming. For a review and interpretation of the material given in Chapter 1, let us look at the following examples.

Material A strain hardens according to the equation $\sigma = 100,000\ \epsilon^{0.5}$ up to $\epsilon_f = 0.7$, and material B according to $\sigma = 100,000\ \epsilon^{0.2}$ up to $\epsilon_f = 0.6$. Both these materials have the same strength coefficient, that is, a stress value of 100,000 psi for $\epsilon = 1$. However, A has a higher strengthening rate (0.5 versus 0.2) than B, and thus it must have a lower yield strength. Before continuing, the reader should convince himself that material A does in fact have a lower yield strength than B.

Neither of these two materials can be coldworked in tension to acquire a yield strength of 100,000 psi. After a deformation ϵ of 0.7, material A will have a yield strength of 83,600 psi. After a deformation of 0.6 material B will have a yield strength of 90,300 psi. This is higher than the yield strength of A because of its higher initial yield strength.

Material C strain hardens according to the equation $\sigma = 75,000$ $\epsilon^{0.5}$ up to $\epsilon_f = 1.5$. Although its strength coefficient is lower than that of material A or B, it may be strengthened to a higher value (92,000 psi) because of its greater ductility.

This review, in addition to the material in Chapter 1, should serve as a background for an understanding of the quantitative aspect of the subrecrystallization plastic deformation portion of the third principle of mechanical strength. An interpretation of strain hardening in terms of the first and second principles is also necessary, and is given below.

When a material is plastically deformed, there is an avalanche of dislocations that terminate at the grain boundaries. This may be considered as a mass flow of atoms along a crystalline plane of one portion of the grain with respect to the remaining portion. In a polycrystalline material, this flow creates a distortion of both the grain boundaries and the crystalline planes in the "flowed" grain as well as in the adjacent grains. This is illustrated in Figure 2-3 where slip is depicted as having occurred along two planes in crystal C due to the action of component F_s of the applied force F.

The crystallographic planes in grains A' and B' as well as those in the "slipped" grain C' are deformed, especially in the vicinity of the grain boundary where the slip terminated. These planes are "mechanically" distorted because of the change in shape which results from the mass movement of atoms called slip. And consequently the atoms are not in their lowest energy position. This displacement of the atoms from their equilibrium positions is referred to as mechanical strain.

Thus it can be seen that the second principle of mechanical strength which states that "slip is retarded by inducing mechanical strains in the lattice structure of the material" is fulfilled in the strain-hardening type of plastic deformation. And the first principle states that whenever slip is made more difficult to initiate, a material is strengthened.

This micromechanical interpretation of the mechanism of the phenomenon of strain hardening is also very helpful to gain an overall appreciation of the control of mechanical properties.

Grain-Boundary Surface Area

During the solidification process when a polycrystalline material is being formed, the grains grow outward from their center into the melt. As solidification nears completion, the liquid separating the grains decreases until finally the last few remaining atoms attach themselves to the surface of the contacting grains at what is referred to as the grain boundaries. Because the grains are not exact-fitting polyhedrons, perfectly aligned with their crystallographic planes identically oriented, a considerable mismatch occurs at the grain boundaries. This results in the atoms that are at the grain boundaries, as well as neighboring atoms, to be forced out of their lowest energy positions.

This local distortion of the lattice structure in the vicinity of the grain boundaries results in substantial mechanical strains in these regions. This lattice distortion impedes slip, and consequently the material adjacent to the grain boundaries is stronger than the material within the grains of most metals at room temperature.

The surface area to volume ratio of a sphere is proportional to the reciprocal of the diameter. Thus as the diameter of a sphere decreases, its ratio of surface area to volume increases. Similarly, as the size of other more irregularly shaped solids decrease, their area to volume ratio also increases. For a given weight, or total volume, of a polycrystalline metal, the grain-boundary surface area varies inversely with the grain size. Since the grain-boundary material is stronger than the remainder of the interior material, the strength of a given material varies inversely with the grain size. For simplicity and convenience, this strengthening phenomenon is referred to as a grain-size effect rather than grain-boundary surface area effect when discussing the control of mechanical properties.

Figure 2-4 illustrates the exponential nature of the relationship between some of the mechanical properties and the grain size of annealed 70Cu-30Zn brass. The shape of this curve is typical of the strength versus grain-size relationship for all single-phase metals. However, not all of the single-phase metals have such a pronounced grain-size effect as this particular composition of brass.

Although the hardness of a material is a measure of its tensile strength, the hardness scale used for such a comparison must be an "absolute" scale such as the Brinell or Knoop. Relative hardness scales

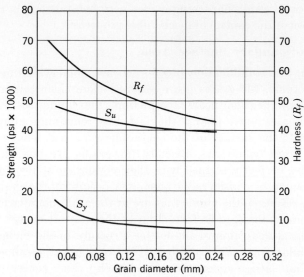

Figure 2-4. Relationship between grain size and strength for annealed brass (30% zinc).

such as the Rockwell cannot be used for such comparisons, or the results are misleading. For example, the Rockwell F hardness increases from 43 to 70, a 65% increase, as the grain size is reduced from 0.24 to 0.02 mm in diameter. (This is a 12 to 1 ratio of grain size.) The tensile strength increases from 38,000 to 52,000 psi, or a 37% increase. The equivalent Brinell hardnesses are 44 and 62, which is a 41% increase. The yield strength increases much more than the tensile strength; from 7000 psi to 15,000 psi, or a 114% increase. From these figures it can be seen that the tensile strength is closely related to Brinell hardness, but not the Rockwell hardness.

Another aspect of the severe lattice distortion at the grain boundaries is the associated higher internal energy of the strained material. Consequently when thermal energy is added to a polycrystalline material by raising its temperature, the total energy of the grain boundaries is always greater than that of the central portion of the grains. As the temperature of a polycrystalline metal is raised gradually, a point is reached where the strength of the grain-boundary material is reduced more than the rest of the grain so that both the grain boundary and interior material have the same strength. This temperature is referred to as the *equicohesive temperature*, and it is very important in the casting and welding processes which we will discuss further in Chapters 3 and 4.

As a metal is heated above its equicohesive temperature, the grain boundaries become weaker than the interior portion of the grains. Because of this characteristic of crystalline solids, metals that are subjected to loads at high temperatures where creep occurs are specified to be coarse-grained rather than fine-grained in order to keep the amount of grain-boundary material to a minimum.

Alloying

The third, and by far the most widely used, method of controlling the strength of a metal is by alloying, which is the addition of a second element (or several elements) to a pure metal. As mentioned at the beginning of this chapter, the strength of a crystalline solid is increased when slip is made more difficult to initiate: when dislocations are "pinned" or otherwise have their movement impeded. From a lattice structure viewpoint, this can be associated with the distortion of a perfect lattice and the induced mechanical strains. Alloying, unlike coldwork and grain boundaries, strains and distorts the lattice structure more uniformly throughout the entire mass. Consequently greater increases in strength can be achieved by alloying a pure metal than can be achieved by reducing the grain size or by coldworking it. But to achieve this high strength, select alloying elements must be used since not all alloys have high strength. The following examples will illustrate this point.

The average values for yield strength and tensile strength of commercially pure aluminum in the annealed conditions are 5000 psi and 13,000 psi, respectively. These values vary only slightly as a function of the grain size of the annealed aluminum, but not nearly as much as the brass which we discussed previously. Both the yield strength and the tensile strength can be raised to the range of 25,000 to 30,000 psi by coldwork. But the greatest improvement in strength occurs when the aluminum is alloyed with about 8% total of zinc, copper, and magnesium and properly heat treated. The yield and tensile strengths for this alloy are approximately 78,000 psi and 85,000 psi respectively. This is nearly a sixteenfold increase in yield strength.

The typical values for the yield and tensile strengths of commercially pure ferrite are 20,000 psi and 40,000 psi respectively. Like the aluminum just described, the strength varies only modestly with grain size. By means of coldwork alone, the ferrite can be strengthened to have both yield and tensile strengths of the order of magnitude of 100,000 psi. And also like aluminum, its greatest strength is achieved

by alloying and heat treating (with 1% or less carbon). In this way
it is possible to raise the yield and tensile strengths to approximately
400,000 psi.

As a final illustration, let us examine copper. The typical values
for the yield and tensile strengths of annealed copper are 5000 psi and
32,000 psi, respectively. By coldworking alone, the yield and tensile
strengths can be raised to about 60,000 psi each. Alloying the copper

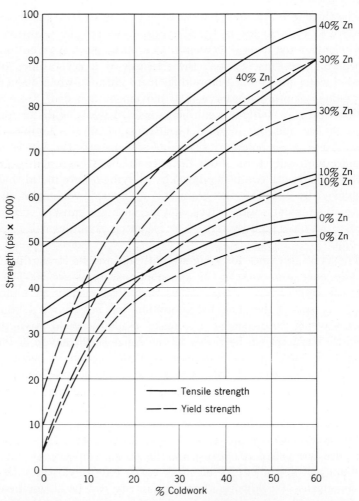

Figure 2-5. The effect of coldwork and zinc content on the strength
of brass (grain size: brass, 0.080 mm; copper, 0.030 mm).

with up to 40% zinc raises the yield strength to about 18,000 psi, and the tensile strength to 55,000 psi. Unlike the aluminum and ferrite, copper is not strengthened as much by being alloyed with zinc as it is by being coldworked. On the basis of mechanical strength, zinc is not a good alloying element for copper. This is because the atoms of copper and zinc are very similar to each other in terms of their atomic diameters and number of valency electrons. Thus substituting zinc atoms for copper atoms does not distort the lattice severely. Figure 2-5 shows the effect of both alloying and coldwork on the strength of copper-zinc alloys.

However, if the copper is alloyed with a more favorable element in terms of its strengthening effect, strengths much greater can be achieved than those possible by coldwork alone. For example, if 1.9% beryllium and 0.2% nickel are added to copper, and the alloy is heat treated properly, yield and tensile strengths of 150,000 psi and 190,-000 psi, respectively, can be achieved.

Although each alloy has characteristics and properties peculiar to itself, and even though there are literally thousands of different alloys, it is still possible to classify them into two main groups with five subgroups. And of course, they may also occur in various combinations. This classification is listed in Table 2-2.

TABLE 2-2. Outline of Alloy Types

I. *Single phase or solid solution*
   (May be undersaturated, saturated, or supersaturated.)
   A. Substitutional
   B. Interstitial

II. *Multiple phase*
   (Size, shape, distribution, and amount)
   A. Simple addition
   B. Precipitation
   C. Dispersion

Single-phase or *solid-solution alloying* is the inclusion of one or more types of solute atoms within the lattice structure of a parent or solvent element to the extent that only one solid phase is present after being given a proper heat treatment. When the solute atoms replace the parent atoms at the lattice points, the alloying is referred to as a *substitutional* type. This is the most common type of solid solution alloying. Or the solute atoms, if they are very small in diameter, may go into the void spaces (interstices) between the solvent atoms, and then the alloying is referred to as an *interstitial* type. The elements boron, carbon, hydrogen, and nitrogen have small enough diameters so that they form interstitial alloys with the transition metals, particularly iron.

Both types of single-phase alloying induce mechanical strains in the parent lattice structure. These strains are caused by the presence of the foreign atoms which force the solvent atoms out of their equilibrium or lowest energy positions. Figure 2-6 illustrates how the presence of an alloying atom distorts the crystallographic planes of a solid. Figure 2-6a is a portion of one plane, such as a face plane of a cubic structure, in which the atom centers are aligned in straight rows. Each row of atoms shown is also the intersection of a normal plane with the face shown. The distortion of the crystalline planes caused by the addition of a substitutional atom is illustrated in Figure 2-6b, where one larger atom is included. The addition of a smaller atom would have a similar effect. The addition of copper to nickel in any amounts or of zinc, up to 38%, to copper typifies substitutional alloying.

Figure 2-6c illustrates the distortion of the crystalline planes resulting from the presence of an interstitial atom. The interstitial atom is not in the same plane as the solvent atoms. The addition of small amounts of carbon (up to 0.01% at room temperature and 2.0% at 2000°F) to iron typifies interstitial alloying. In this case the diameter of the solute atom is greater than the interstices between the solvent atoms which are consequently forced out of their normal equilibrium sites.

The amount of mechanical strain, or strain energy, that is added to the parent material by solid solution alloying depends both on the

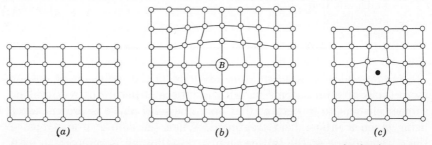

Figure 2-6. Distortion of crystalline planes due to the presence of a foreign atom. (a) Pure metal *A*. (b) One substitutional atom in metal *A*. (c) One interstitial atom in metal *A*.

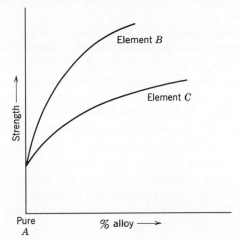

Figure 2-7. The effect of alloying elements
on the strength of a solid solution (atomic
diameter ratio *B/A* is further from unity
than is the ratio *C/A*).

amount of the solute added and the ratio of the solute to solvent atom
diameters. As illustrated in Figure 2-7, this relationship is an exponential one, in which initially a small addtion of a foreign element
increases the strength markedly, with further additions having a lesser
effect.

The magnitude of the strength increase due to single-phase alloying alone is as great as that achieved by any other strengthening
mechanism. For copper when slightly less than 40% zinc is substitu-
tionally added, the yield and tensile strengths are raised from 5000
psi and 32,000 psi to 20,000 psi and 57,000 psi, respectively.

A much more dramatic and common example is the interstitial
addition of carbon to iron. Although with slow cooling rates it is
possible to dissolve not more than 0.01% carbon in iron at room
temperature, it is possible, by means of fast cooling from the austenite
region where as much as 2% carbon can be in solution, to have a
supersaturated solid solution of 1% or more of carbon in iron at room
temperature. This supersaturated solution is known as primary martensite if the iron is in a body-centered tetragonal lattice structure, or
secondary (tempered) martensite if the lattice structure is body-
centered cubic. The yield strength of iron can be increased from 20,000
psi when it is pure to nearly 400,000 psi when 0.8% carbon is dissolved

interstitially in it. This is discussed in more detail in a following section on ferrous metals.

Multiple-phase alloying is the addition of one or more types of solute elements to a solvent element to the extent that more than one phase is present. It is the size, shape, distribution, and amount of the additional phases that determine the magnitude of the mechanical properties of this type of alloying. There are three ways of creating a multiple-phase alloy, and they are listed as the subtypes in Table 2-2. The first method, referred to here as the *simple addition* type, consists of adding enough of the alloying elements at an elevated temperature so that on slow cooling to room temperature more than one phase will be present. Annealed aluminum alloys as well as annealed and normalized steels fall in this type of multiple-phase alloying.

The second method of obtaining a multiple-phase alloy consists of adding enough of the alloying elements at an elevated temperature so that on fast cooling to room temperature a supersaturated solid solution is retained from which, either at room temperature or a slightly elevated temperature, the second phase precipitates uniformly throughout the solvent crystals. This method is known as the *precipitation* type. The simple addition type described in the preceding paragraph is actually a poor precipitation type in which the second phase is not fine and well dispersed, but rather it consists of large particles around inclusions or as a network in the grain boundaries. The precipitation method requires that the solubility of the alloying element in the parent metal be larger at a high temperature than at room temperature. Also, in all the precipitation type of alloys that are commercially used because of their high strength, the alloying element forms an intermetallic or metallic compound with the solvent element rather than just another solid solution. Some ferrous and many nonferrous alloys are included in this type.

The third method of obtaining a multiple-phase alloy consists of adding a compound, which is actually the second phase, directly to the parent material instead of adding the alloy as an element. Alloys made in this fashion are known as the *dispersion type*. This method is used when the desired second phase has a very limited solubility, if any, with the parent phase; or when there is no decrease of solubility with a decrease in temperature. The dispersion type of multiple-phase alloys is generally made by the sintered-powder process in which fine particles of the compound are mixed with fine particles of the parent phase, compacted to shape in dies under heavy pressure, and then heated in an oven until grain-boundary fusion (sintering) occurs. Two alloys of this type are in limited commercial use. One is a dispersion of aluminum oxide particles in aluminum, and the other is a dispersion of thorium oxide in nickel. Although materials such as sintered carbides, ceramics, and powder-metal parts are made by the same mixing-compacting-sintering process, they are not dispersion-type alloys in that they do not consist of a fine dispersion of particles in a host phase.

Multiple-phase alloying induces mechanical strains in the parent lattice structure because of the presence of inclusions or particles which may be submicroscopic in size, or as large as the host grains. These particles distort the crystallographic planes of the parent material in their vicinity in much the same fashion as the planes are distorted near grain boundaries. In fact, the second phases in reality are simply additional grains, with an increase in the grain boundary areas. And as the size of the second-phase particles decreases, the grain-boundary surface area increases, thus increasing the strength. In addition, if the second phase consists of small but very strong particles of an intermetallic compound finely dispersed throughout the parent grains, they prevent the avalanche of dislocations known as slip from going completely across the grain along the crystallographic planes. In this sense they act as "pegs" to prevent slip from occurring.

Figure 2-8 illustrates the effect of the presence of the additional phases on the strength of a material. It is shown that the strength increases exponentially with the amount of the second phase. Also, the rate of increase is greater as the particle size decreases.

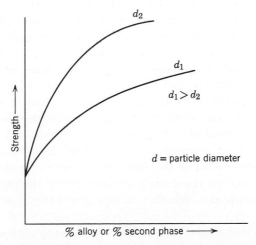

Figure 2-8. The effect of the amount and particle size of a second phase on the strength of a material.

The strength is also influenced by the distribution of the particles as well as their shape. A uniform distribution is the most beneficial because a low concentration of particles in one region would result in that portion having a lower strength. In regard to the shape of the particles, the strengthening effect increases directly with the surface area to volume ratio of the particle, being a minimum for particles having a spherical shape.

APPLICATION OF THE CONCEPTS OF ALLOYING TO HEAT TREATMENT

Rather than discuss the heat treatment of the ferrous metals in one section, and the heat treatment of the various families of non-ferrous metals in other sections, and the control of properties of non-metals through alloying in still another section, this chapter will apply the previously mentioned concepts to enough of the common materials so that the reader will thoroughly understand them. When the heat treatment of each material is discussed separately, the differences between them are emphasized even though it may be unintentional. The approach taken here is intended to emphasize the similarities between the various treatments given to the different materials. Single-phase alloying will be discussed first, followed by multiple-phase alloying.

Heat Treatment of Single-Phase (Solid Solution) Alloys

As illustrated in Figure 2-7 which we discussed previously, when a second element is dissolved in another, the strength increases exponentially. Although it is not possible to predict on the basis of solid-state physics what this relationship is for any given pair of elements, two generalizations may be used as a guide in solution strengthening. First, as we previously mentioned, the strengthening rate increases as the ratios of the atomic diameters of the two elements depart from unity, and also as the ratio of their valencies departs from unity.

Second, the mutual solubility of the two elements is best ascertained from their equilibrium phase diagrams. But it must be appreciated that the phase diagrams indicate only the solubility of the materials, and then only for equilibrium cooling; they do not relate any specific information concerning the strength of the materials. The strength relationships are determined experimentally, just as are the phase diagrams.

It is quite frequently stated that the strength of materials is directly related to their melting temperatures. That is, the high melting temperature materials also have a higher strength. Although there is a slight positive correlation to the above statement in considering the metals, large discrepancies can occur when comparing any two metallic elements. For example, a steep negative slope is obtained if the tensile strength versus melting temperature curve is drawn for the four common metals listed in Table 2-3.

TABLE 2-3. Tensile Strength and Melting Temperature
For Four Metals

Metal	Melting Temperature, °F	Tensile Strength, psi
Manganese	2273	72,000
Nickel	2651	46,000
Iron	2802	40,000
Platinum	3224	18,000

The control of the mechanical properties of metals is best discussed on the basis of their microstructures or microconstituents. Although the term microstructure refers to the metallurgical structure of the metal as seen through a microscope, the best means to determine what the microstructures of a metal are after a given heat treatment is to study the equilibrium phase diagram and nonequilibrium transformation diagrams for the metal. An actual microscopic examination can be used to verify the conclusions drawn from this study.

When studying microstructures, and especially when communicating with others about them, it is convenient to use as a symbolic language, encircled sketches of microstructures. It is customary to label or identify with Greek letters the various phases that exist as microconstituents. In this text the first letters of the Greek alphabet, α, β, γ, δ, are used to represent solid solution phases. Intermetallic compounds are identified by the letter θ, with numerical subscripts if more than one compound is being discussed at the same time.

To discuss microstructures on the basis of an equilibrium phase diagram, the phase diagram is altered to a microconstituent diagram. This alteration is very simple; it simply necessitates the drawing of vertical lines from eutectic or eutectoid points, and relabeling the diagram to include these two mechanical mixtures of phases. This is illustrated in Figure 2-9. In most instances, this alteration of the phase diagram need be done only mentally.

The inverse lever rule is applied to the microconstituent diagram for determining the amount and composition of the microconstituents exactly as it is applied to the equilibrium phase diagram in determining the amount and composition of the phases.

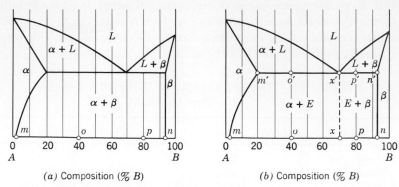

(a) Composition (% B)   (b) Composition (% B)

Figure 2-9. Alteration of an equilibrium phase diagram (*a*) to a micro-constituent diagram (*b*), *L* is a liquid; *α* and *β* are solid solutions; *E* is a eutectic of composition *x*.

The following examples will demonstrate these techniques.

Consider an alloy of *AB* consisting of 40% *B* at room temperature, such as point *o* in Figure 2-9*a*. By means of the inverse lever rule, the amounts and composition of the phases are:

$$\alpha = \frac{no}{nm} \times 100 = \frac{54}{92} \times 100 = 58.7\%$$

and consists of 2% *B* and 98% *A*.

$$\beta = \frac{om}{nm} \times 100 = \frac{38}{92} \times 100 = 41.3\%$$

and consists of 94% *B* and 6% *A*.

Similarly an alloy of 80% *B*, point *p* in Figure 2-9*a*, would consist of 15.2% *α* and 84.8% *β*. The composition of the *α* and *β* is the same as for the previous alloy.

The phase diagram gives no information concerning the mechanical properties of either the elements *A* and *B* or any of the alloys of the two. Also, if the mechanical properties of the phases *α* and *β* are experimentally determined, it is impossible to determine analytically on the basis of materials science what the mechanical properties of any of the other alloys are. On the other hand, the microconstituent diagram does make it possible to calculate with reasonable reliability the mechanical properties of any alloy on the basis of those properties of the individual microconstituents. The rule is: *the mechanical properties of any alloy are a weighted average of those of the individual microstructures that are present.* This is why the "modified" phase diagram is important in understanding the control of mechanical properties.

Now consider the previous alloy of 80% B on the basis of the microconstituent diagram of Figure 2-9b. At room temperature the microstructure consists of

$$\text{Eutectic } E = \frac{np}{nx} \times 100 = \frac{14}{24} \times 100 = 58.3\%$$

and

$$\beta = \frac{px}{nx} \times 100 = \frac{10}{24} \times 100 = 41.7\%$$

The eutectic itself consists of 26.1% α and 73.9% β.

If the mechanical properties of E and β are known, then the mechanical properties of alloy p can be determined from them in accordance with the preceding rule. Thus if the hardness and tensile strength of β is 150 Brinell and 90,000 psi, and the same properties of the eutectic are 200 Brinell and 120,000 psi, respectively, then the hardness of alloy p is $150 \times 0.42 + 200 \times 0.58$, or 179 Brinell. The tensile strength of alloy p is $90,000 \times 0.42 + 120,000 \times 0.58$, or 107,000 psi.

The microstructure for composition o in Figure 2-9b is somewhat more complicated because of the decrease in solubility of B in A as the temperature decreases from the eutectic temperature to room temperature. To understand what the microstructure of this composition actually appears like under the microscope, it is necessary to study both the solidification and the subsequent cooling of the alloy.

As an alloy of 40% B cools slowly from the all liquid region to a temperature just above the eutectic temperature, the material will consist of 40% liquid having a composition of 70% B and the 60% α solid solution will have a composition of 20% B. The balance of the composition of both the liquid and the solid solution is A. The α solid solution that forms above the eutectic temperature is referred to as proeutectic α to distinguish it from the α solid solution in the eutectic; or from any α that may precipitate on further cooling below the eutectic temperature due to a decrease in solubility with temperature of A in B. When the material cools to the eutectic temperature, the remaining 40% liquid transforms to 40% eutectic, which is a mechanical mixture, usually but not necessarily lamellar, of α and β. The material would have the microscopic appearance of Figure 2-10m at the eutectic temperature after complete solidification.

On cooling to room temperature, β will precipitate out of all the α solid solution since the solubility of B in A decreases from 20 to

2%. The space or volume occupied by the eutectic will remain practically the same at room temperature as it was at the eutectic temperature. The precipitated B will be present at the grain boundaries of the α microconstituent, at the α-β interfaces within the eutectic, and at other regions of high internal lattice stress. To understand what this microstructure might look like, it is necessary to study in detail the changes that occur during the cooling to room temperature.

As an example, consider 1 lb of alloy o which contains 0.6 lb of A and 0.4 of B at a temperature above the liquidus. As it slowly cools to a temperature just below the eutectic temperature, the microstructure will consist of 40% or 0.4 lb eutectic and 60% or 0.6 lb proeutectic α, as discussed above. Assume that this material now consists of two grains, one of α and one of eutectic as sketched in Figure 2-10m.

As the eutectic grain cools to room temperature, its average composition remains at 70% B, but the composition of the α phase in the eutectic decreases from 20% B to 2% B, and thus some post-eutectic β is precipitated within the eutectic. Thus the 0.4 lb of eutectic that was present at the high temperature is also present at room temperature. Within the eutectic grain there is 0.4 lb $\times$ 70% or 0.28 lb of B and 0.4 lb $\times$ 30% or 0.12 lb of A.

Now consider what happens to the one proeutectic α grain. At the eutectic temperature it weighs 0.6 lb and contains 20% or 0.12 lb of B and 80% or 0.48 lb of A, all uniformly dispersed in one phase. As the grain slowly cools to room temperature, β precipitates out in the grain boundaries and at inclusions within the grain. So instead of one homogenous grain of α solid solution containing 20% B, there is one smaller grain of α_2 solid solution containing 2% B plus some particles (small grains) of β containing 94% B. The subscript 2 on the room temperature solid solution signifies that it is not of the same composition as the higher temperature α solid solution. The amount of precipitated β is determined by means of the inverse lever rule as follows:

$$\beta = \frac{18}{92} \times 0.6 \text{ lb} = 0.188 \text{ lb}$$

And the amount of

$$\alpha_2 = \frac{74}{92} \times 0.6 = 0.482 \text{ lb}$$

On this basis the microstructure would consist of 40% eutectic, 48% α_2, and 12% precipitated β. The microstructure would appear something like the schematic sketch in Figure 2-10n. The total of 0.4

lb of B that is present in 1 lb of this alloy is distributed in each of the three microconstituents as follows:

In the eutectic

$$40\% \times 70\% \times 1 \text{ lb} = 0.28 \text{ lb} B$$

In the α_2

$$48\% \times 2\% \times 1 \text{ lb} = 0.01 \text{ lb} B$$

In the precipitated β

$$12\% \times 94\% \times 1 \text{ lb} = 0.11 \text{ lb} B$$

The microstructures are symbolically represented as sketched in Figure 2-10. The actual microstructure of a single-phase metal appears as sketched in a, b, and c. The first of these is representative of most of the face-centered cubic metals in that the grains tend to be angular, that is, have straight lines as grain boundaries. Another distinguishing

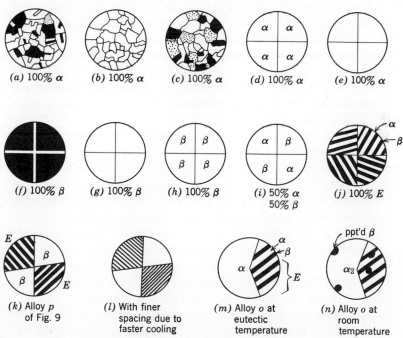

Figure 2-10. Representative sketches of microstructures.

feature is the presence of annealing twins, or twin bands, in many of the grains. If the specimen is lightly etched after polishing, the grains will be entirely light, or bright, in color, with the grain boundaries showing up as dark lines; and the twins will appear as long rectangles within some of the grains as sketched in Figure 2-10a. However, if the specimen is deeply etched after polishing, then some of the grains appear black, some gray, and others white. In this case the twins appear as white bands in dark grains and dark bands in white grains. Figure 3-23a is a photomicrograph of a brass specimen that very clearly demonstrates these latter characteristics.

All the body-centered cubic metals and a few of the face-centered cubic have microstructures that resemble the sketch in b. The distinguishing characteristics of these grains are that they are quite rounded and contain no twins. With deeper etching, some grains become dark, whereas others remain light as in c. Although the appearance of the various grains in a single-phase microstructure are different, their chemical composition is all the same.

Figures 2-10a, b, and c were made by tracing the outlines of the grain boundaries from actual photomicrographs. Even so, some of the fine details of the actual microstructure are missing from the reproduction, because it is rather time consuming to make such elaborate sketches as illustrated in a, b, and c. Furthermore, no two regions of even the same specimen look exactly alike. For these two reasons, the microstructures are sketched as in Figure 2-10 d and e; since in this way they can be made more efficiently, and communicate just as much information. Either one of these sketches can represent the α solid solution of Figure 2-9.

But what about a different solid solution, such as β in Figure 2-9? It can be represented as f in Figure 2-10. However, this also requires considerable time to draw, so it is sketched as g or h. Except for the identifying symbol, these latter two sketches are identical to d and e for the α solid solution. If the two phases α and β are present as microstructures in the same sample, they could be sketched as in i.

An eutectic or eutectoid, which is a mechanical mixture of two phases, is drawn as in j. The two phases in an eutectic are usually drawn as parallel lines to imply that the phases in many eutectics are lamellar, or in the form of platelets. Also, it is a very convenient way to make a sketch that indicates that two phases are present.

The microstructure of an alloy such as p in Figure 2-9 is represented as in sketch k of Figure 2-10. The portion of the circle representing the eutectic was purposefully made larger than that representing the β microconstituents. This was done because the amount of eutectic present as determined by applying the inverse lever rule to Figure 2-9b is 55%. Drawing the lamellae of the eutectic thick and relatively few in number signifies that the material solidified rather slowly. Only a few nuclei formed because each had sufficient time for considerable growth. (If the microstructure were an eutectoid rather than an eutectic, it would signify a slow cooling rate at the transformation temperature. This would be the equivalent of coarse pearlite if the material were a steel). Sketch l illustrates what the microstructure would be like if the cooling rate were greater. In this case the number of nuclei is great and the amount of growth is small. Consequently, there are many thin lamellae.

The microstructure of an alloy such as Figure 2-9o that has a decreasing solubility with a decrease in temperature is represented in sketches m and n of Figure 2-10. A description of how this microstructure is formed was given in a preceding section when the slow cooling of this alloy from the liquid region to room temperature was studied.

Some representative phase diagrams of the more commonly used alloys are included in Appendix C. *The Metals Handbook*, 1948 Edition, is the best source of equilibrium-phase diagrams for metals. In the following pages a few examples of the combined use of phase diagrams, microstructures, and mechanical properties of some common metals are given.

Undersaturated Alloying

Copper and nickel are completely soluble in each other in all proportions in the solid state, as evidenced by their phase diagram. Thus any alloy of the two is unsaturated. The tensile strength of copper is 32,000 psi and the tensile strength of nickel is 46,000 psi. The strength of either one is raised when a little of the other is alloyed with it. As seen in Figure 2-11, the maximum strength occurs with an alloy containing 35% Cu and 65% Ni.

As can be seen in the copper-zinc phase diagram, alloys containing less than 38% zinc consist of a single-phase unsaturated solid solution. The variation of the strength with composition and microstructure of copper-zinc alloys is illustrated in Figure 2-12. All of the alloys included here consists of a single micro constituent, the composition of which is different for each of the alloys.

In the aluminum-copper system, alloys containing less than about 0.1% copper are single phase and single microconstituent alloys. Alloys with less than about 0.008% carbon in the iron-carbon system are single-phase alloys. And up to 9% tin is soluble in iron. All these values pertain to solubility at room temperature.

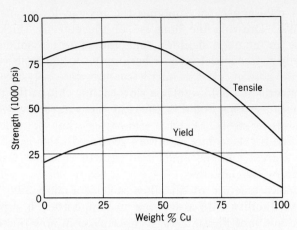

Figure 2-11. Strength of Cu-Ni alloys.

Saturated Alloying

Saturated alloying, as the term implies, refers to the condition in which the amount of a second element in solid solution in the first corresponds to the maximum room temperature solubility of the two. This situation prevails whenever two phases are present under near equilibrium conditions.

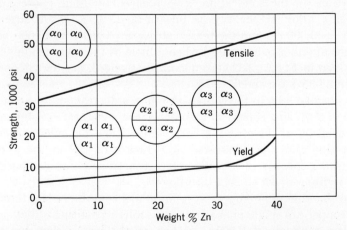

Figure 2-12. Strength and microstructures of Cu-Zn alloys up to 40% Zn (α_0 is pure Cu; α_1 is 10% Zn-90% Cu; α_2 is 20% Zn-80% Cu; α_3 is 30% Zn-70% Cu).

Supersaturated Alloying and Multiple Phase Alloying

Much higher strengths can be obtained by achieving a super-saturated solid solution, that is, an alloy consisting of a single phase but containing in solution more than the saturation amount of the solute element. This fact can be expected from the shape of the curve of the strength versus the per cent of alloy drawn schematically in Figure 2-7.

Nonequilibrium cooling during heat treatment must be resorted to in order to acquire an alloy in this condition. And since it is a non-equilibrium microstructure it may be considered as being unstable. That is, it can in time decompose into a multiple-phase system. For some materials, such as copper-alloyed aluminum, this decomposition may occur at room temperature in hours. But for some materials, such as iron-carbon alloys (steel), it may not occur for hundreds of years.

Figure 2-13 outlines the various heat treatments applied to aluminum-copper alloys along with the associated microstructures and hardness. From this figure we can see that the Brinell hardness of commercially pure aluminum is raised from 23 to 48 when it is alloyed with 5% copper and heat treated (annealed) in such a way that the second phase ($CuAl_2$ compound) is slowly precipitated out in the grain boundaries. The hardness is increased to 64 Brinell when the alloy is heat treated by cooling rapidly from the one phase region so that all of the 5% of copper is retained in solution at room temperature. Since the room temperature solubility of copper in aluminum is only 0.1%, the alloy with 5% of copper in solution is supersaturated.

The maximum hardness for this alloy is obtained when it is "aged," that is, when the second phase is allowed to precipitate slowly from the supersaturated solid solution in very fine submicroscopic particles uniformly dispersed throughout the material.

This precipitation can occur in several weeks at room temperature or in several hours at 200°F. In this precipitated condition the hardness is about 95 to 100 Brinell. However, if the alloy is overaged, that is, heated to a temperature of about 600°F for the precipitation process to occur, the precipitated particles coalesce into a smaller number of relatively large particles. The hardness of such an overaged alloy drops to about 55 Brinell. All of the above Brinell hardness numbers are for a 500 kg load.

Figure 2-14 outlines the various heat treatments applied to an eutectoid steel, and illustrates the microstructures that result. The close similarity between the heat treatment and microstructures of hardened steel and those of the previously described aluminum alloy should be

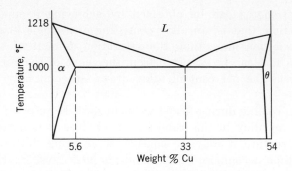

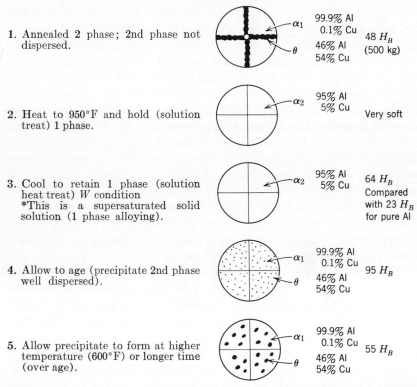

1. Annealed 2 phase; 2nd phase not dispersed.

    α_1 99.9% Al   0.1% Cu   48 H_B
    θ 46% Al   54% Cu   (500 kg)

2. Heat to 950°F and hold (solution treat) 1 phase.

    α_2 95% Al   5% Cu   Very soft

3. Cool to retain 1 phase (solution heat treat) *W* condition
*This is a supersaturated solid solution (1 phase alloying).

    α_2 95% Al   5% Cu   64 H_B Compared with 23 H_B for pure Al

4. Allow to age (precipitate 2nd phase well dispersed).

    α_1 99.9% Al   0.1% Cu   95 H_B
    θ 46% Al   54% Cu

5. Allow precipitate to form at higher temperature (600°F) or longer time (over age).

    α_1 99.9% Al   0.1% Cu   55 H_B
    θ 46% Al   54% Cu

Figure 2-13. The heat treatment, microstructures, and hardness of a 95% Al-5% Cu alloy.

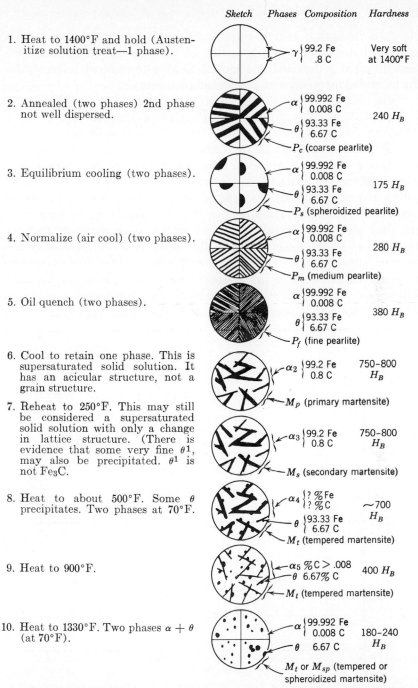

| Sketch | Phases | Composition | Hardness |

1. Heat to 1400°F and hold (Austenitize solution treat—1 phase). — γ { 99.2 Fe / .8 C } Very soft at 1400°F

2. Annealed (two phases) 2nd phase not well dispersed. — α { 99.992 Fe / 0.008 C }, θ { 93.33 Fe / 6.67 C }, P_c (coarse pearlite) — 240 H_B

3. Equilibrium cooling (two phases). — α { 99.992 Fe / 0.008 C }, θ { 93.33 Fe / 6.67 C }, P_s (spheroidized pearlite) — 175 H_B

4. Normalize (air cool) (two phases). — α { 99.992 Fe / 0.008 C }, θ { 93.33 Fe / 6.67 C }, P_m (medium pearlite) — 280 H_B

5. Oil quench (two phases). — α { 99.992 Fe / 0.008 C }, θ { 93.33 Fe / 6.67 C }, P_f (fine pearlite) — 380 H_B

6. Cool to retain one phase. This is supersaturated solid solution. It has an acicular structure, not a grain structure. — α_2 { 99.2 Fe / 0.8 C }, M_p (primary martensite) — 750–800 H_B

7. Reheat to 250°F. This may still be considered a supersaturated solid solution with only a change in lattice structure. (There is evidence that some very fine θ^1, may also be precipitated. θ^1 is not Fe$_3$C. — α_3 { 99.2 Fe / 0.8 C }, M_s (secondary martensite) — 750–800 H_B

8. Heat to about 500°F. Some θ precipitates. Two phases at 70°F. — α_4 { ? % Fe / ? % C }, θ { 93.33 Fe / 6.67 C }, M_t (tempered martensite) — ~700 H_B

9. Heat to 900°F. — α_5 %C > .008, θ 6.67% C, M_t (tempered martensite) — 400 H_B

10. Heat to 1330°F. Two phases $\alpha + \theta$ (at 70°F). — α { 99.992 Fe / 0.008 C }, θ 6.67 C, M_t or M_{sp} (tempered or spheroidized martensite) — 180–240 H_B

Figure 2-14. The heat treatment, microstructures, and hardness of a 99.2% Fe-0.8% C.

observed through a critical comparison of Figures 2-13 and 2-14. A simplified sketch, or working model, of the iron-carbon microconstituent diagram is included in Figure 2-15 as a convenient reference for the following discussions on ferrous microstructures.

For this discussion we will assume that the alloy contains 99.2% Fe and 0.8% C so that the iron-carbon phase diagram can be used. Although this alloy is called "steel," in reality it is not a commercially available steel since all steels contain a small amount of impurity elements. For example, the steel nearest to this alloy in composition is AISI 1080 which contains the following: 0.75 to 0.88% C; 0.60 to 0.90% Mn; 0.10 to 0.30% Si; 0.04% max P; 0.05% max S. The small amount of impurities present in the plain carbon steels, as opposed to the alloy steels, has a negligible effect on the phase diagram. In some cases however, the grain size and the manganese may influence the hardenability of a plain carbon steel to the extent that microstructures normally expected for a faster cooling rate than the one being used will result. That is, for a coarse-grained, high manganese and silicon content 1080 steel it is possible to obtain martensite in a thin section

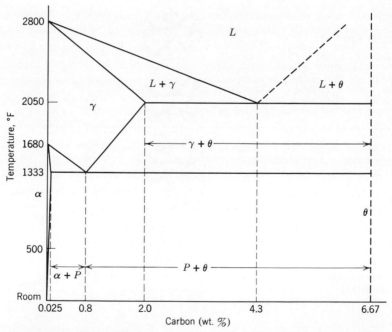

Figure 2-15. A simplified (working model), iron-carbon microconstituent diagram.

upon oil quenching. The microstructure normally expected for an oil quenched 1080 steel is fine pearlite.

The first step in the heat treating process of a ferrous metal is to austenitize it. That is, to heat the steel into the austenitic region of the microconstituent diagram. For a plain carbon eutectoid steel this means it is heated above 1333°F. The industrial practice is to heat hypoeutectoid steels to 75 to 100°F above the upper critical temperature, and to heat hypereutectoid steels to 75 to 100°F above the lower critical temperature. They are held at this austenitizing temperature for approximately one hour per inch of thickness of the steel before being cooled to room temperature. Thus this eutectoid steel would actually be heated to (austenitized at) 1400 to 1425°F.

The austenitizing treatment of steel is a special case of solution treating, that is, heating a metal to an elevated temperature to homogenize it. At this high temperature the eutectoid steel consists of a single phase, austenite, containing 99.2% Fe and 0.8% C. It is also a single microstructure at this temperature, as illustrated in sketch 1 of Figure 2-14. The austenite is very soft at this high temperature. In the following discussions it is assumed that small pieces, $\frac{1}{2}$ in. diameter or less, are treated.

If the austenitized specimen is allowed to cool very slowly, say at a cooling rate of approximately 0.01°F/sec at 1300°F as would occur if it were left to cool in the furnace after the heating energy was turned off, the resulting microstructure would be coarse lamellar pearlite as illustrated in sketch 2. The pearlite is a mechanical mixture of the two phases α (ferrite) and θ (cementite). Although two phases are present, there is only one microconstituent or microstructure, namely pearlite. The hardness of coarse lamellar pearlite is 240 H_B.

Although the above cooling rate is slow, it is still much faster than equilibrium cooling. A closer approximation to equilibrium cooling would be obtained if instead of the heating energy being completely turned off it would be slowly diminished in amount. If the cooling were so slow that it required several weeks to cool from 1350° to 1300°F, then the resulting microstructure would be spheroidized pearlite rather than lamellar pearlite. It would have the appearance of Figure 2-14 (3) and a hardness of approximately 175 H_B.

Most high-carbon steels have a tendency to spheroidize during the annealing process. This trait is probably related to the impurities that are present in steel, but the manner of this dependency is unknown. As a result of the variability of a given type of material's composition and microstructural traits, it is possible to have one heat of 1080 steel with an annealed hardness of 180 Brinell while another heat has a hardness of 240 Brinell. For the same reason it is possible for an annealed 1080 steel to have a 220 Brinell hardness, whereas an annealed 10100 steel may have an annealed hardness of only 190 Brinell.

If the austenitized specimen is taken out of the furnace and is allowed to air cool in the open, where the cooling rate at 1300°F is about 1°F/sec, the microstructure will consist of platelets of ferrite and cementite of intermediate thickness, as sketched in Figure 2-14 (4). This microstructure is referred to as medium pearlite, and it has a hardness of about 280 Brinell.

With a slightly faster cooling rate, such as 30°F/sec at 1300°F which occurs when small pieces are being oil quenched, the ferrite and cementite lamallae are very thin. This microstructure, which is sketched in Figure 2-14 as 5, is called fine pearlite and has a hardness of 380 Brinell.

The strengths and the hardnesses of the preceding four microstructures vary from 175 Brinell to 380 Brinell (88,000 psi to 190,000 psi tensile strength) even though they all consist of the identical amounts of the same two phases, ferrite and cementite. These four microstructures are all different, and yet they are all the same. That is, they are all *pearlite,* but they are all different types of pearlite. The differences in the strengths of these four specimens can be explained on the basis of the strengthening mechanisms discussed at the beginning of this chapter.

The fact that all four specimens are harder than 80 Brinell, the hardness of ferrite, is due to the presence of the second phase, cementite. The strengthening mechanism in all of these specimens is multiple-phase alloying. The differences in the mechanical properties of the four microstructures are due to the differences in the size, shape, and distribution of the second phase. As can be seen from the curves in Figure 2-8 and the related discussion, the least beneficial shape for a second phase on the basis of its effect on strength is a sphere. Thus the spheroidized pearlite is somewhat weaker than the coarse lamellar pearlite. And for a given shape, the smaller the particle size, the greater is the strengthening effect. This may be considered as being caused by the shorter distance that dislocations must move to reach the grain boundaries in the microstructure containing the finer laminations. The higher strength of the fine lamellar pearlite as compared to the coarse lamellar pearlite can also be considered as the result of grain-boundary or grain-size strengthening since, in reality, each individual platelet of ferrite and of cementite is an individual grain. The fine lamellar pearlite has a much larger amount of phase boundary, or grain boundary, surface area than does the coarse lamellar pearlite, and consequently a much higher strength.

The iron-carbon alloys known as steel do not get their maximum hardness by multiple-phase formation but rather upon the formation of a supersaturated solid solution. This supersaturated single phase is obtained by quenching the austenitized specimen from a high temperature, where a single phase exists under equilibrium conditions, with a cooling rate fast enough to prevent the precipitation of the second phase. This results in an unstable supersaturated solution at room temperature. You may recall from the discussion on the heat treatment of aluminum, and from a comparison of Figure 2-14(6) to Figure 2-13 (3), that the heat treating procedure of getting the steel specimen in the as-quenched single-phase condition is identical to that used in getting the aluminum alloy in the W condition.

Although there is no difference in the heat treating procedure, there is a metallurgical difference between the two. With the aluminum alloy, the same phase is present at both the high temperature and at room temperature. With the steel, the same phase is not present at room temperature that exists at the high temperature.

The steel at the austenitizing temperature consists entirely of the phase, or microconstituent, austenite which is a solid solution of carbon dissolved interstitially in face-centered cubic (gamma, γ) iron. When the specimen is rapidly cooled to room temperature, as in water quenching a small piece where the cooling rate is about 300°F/sec at 1300°F, the plain carbon austenite transforms to primary martensite in the temperature range of 750 to 250°F. Martensite is a supersaturated solid solution of carbon dissolved interstitially in either body-centered tetragonal iron or body-centered cubic iron. The former is known as primary martensite and the latter as secondary martensite.

Primary martensite is a single phase and a single microstructure although it appears as two phases when observed under the microscope because of its acicular structure. It is illustrated in Figure 2-14(6). The hardness of martensite, as would be expected of a solid solution, varies with the amount of carbon dissolved in it. The hardness of primary martensite having 0.8% carbon is $67R_c$, which is equivalent to 750 to 800 Brinell.

Many textbooks on mechanical metallurgy, and most metallurgical engineers, consider the martensitic reaction as one of the strengthening mechanisms, and refer to it as phase-transformation hardening or direct hardening. However, the phase transformation is only the means by which the strengthening mechanism is achieved and it is not in itself the strengthening mechanism. The phase transformation is a process type mechanism and not a slip inhibiting or strengthening mechanism. In other words, the phase transformation is a means to an end, but is not an end in itself. The actual strengthening mechanism in primary martensite is the supersaturated solid solution alloying of carbon in iron. Consequently, phase-transformation hardening, or direct hardening, is not included in the list of strengthening mechanisms in Table 2-2. Instead, the strengthening mechanism of primary martensite is the alloying type listed as I.B in the table, namely interstitial solid solution alloying.

The hardness achieved in plain carbon eutectoid steel by this strengthening mechanism, 800 Brinell, is as high as can be obtained in any steel of modest size by any treatment other than chemical conversions such as nitriding, cyaniding, or plating.

A second phase will precipitate out of the supersaturated solid solution if it is heated sufficiently above room temperature, as was true in the case of the aluminum alloy previously discussed. But unlike the aluminum alloy, the steel also undergoes another phase transformation upon reheating to a temperature of about 250°F. As illustrated in Figure 2-14(7) the primary martensite which is body-centered tetragonal transforms to body-centered cubic secondary martensite. The primary martensite in sketch 6 is identified as α_2 and the secondary martensite of sketch 7 is identified as α_3. The different subscripts are used to indicate that these two phases are different from the α ferrite which contains the saturation amount of carbon.

The only observable difference between primary and secondary martensite when etched specimens are studied under the microscope is the white appearance of primary martensite and the faint yellow tint of the secondary martensite. For this reason they are frequently called white and yellow martensite. Although there is evidence that some of the carbon may precipitate out of the solution in the form of complex carbides (not Fe_3C though), the α_3 solid solution is still very supersaturated. Experimental evidence as to the exact nature of this first stage of tempering is inconclusive. The hardness does not decrease measurably during this transformation, but remains in the range of 750 to 800 Brinell.

As the tempering temperature is raised from 250°F to about 400°F, some carbon definitely precipitates out of the solution in the form of transition carbides. The decrease in hardness is very slight. As the tempering is raised to about 500 to 600°F, more carbon precipitates from the solution and the transition carbides transform to cementite, Fe_3C. Two phases, θ and α_4, are now present as two microconstituents and are illustrated in Figure 2-14(8). The α_4 phase still has more than

0.008% carbon in solution, so it is not α ferrite. Upon etching for the same length of time normally used when etching primary martensite, this low-temperature tempered martensite appears dark or black when viewed through a microscope, and is so called. As the tempering temperature is raised above 400°F, the hardness decreases nearly linearly with temperature so that when the tempering temperature is just below the lower critical temperature, the hardness of the steel is very close to that of the annealed steel. *Thus a linear interpolation can be made for the approximate hardness of a steel tempered at any intermediate temperature between 400 and 1300°F.* The hardness for this steel is about 700 Brinell when tempered at 500°F.

When tempered at 900°F, nearly all of the carbon is precipitated as cementite; the cementite particles begin to grow in size at this and higher temperatures. The microstructure now consists of α_5 solid solution and θ, and has the appearance of Figure 2-14(9). The Brinell hardness is about 400.

Upon tempering at 1330°F for a sufficiently long time, the microstructure approaches that of the equilibrium cooling. The microconstituents are α ferrite and θ cementite. The cementite is present as small particles, randomly distributed throughout the ferrite matrix. Because the size of the particles is influenced by the impurities in the steel, the hardness may vary from 180 to 240 Brinell.

FERROUS MICROSTRUCTURES AND THEIR PREDICTIONS

The preceding section of this chapter dealt with the subject of microstructures in general and how they are represented. This following section discusses in detail all the microstructures associated with ferrous metals. The mechanical properties of the microstructures are included and examples of using empirical data and charts for predicting microstructures that should result from any thermal treatment of a ferrous alloy.

The microstructures that can be present in steel are listed in Table 2-4 along with the approximate cooling rate needed to produce each microstructure. The first column of microstructures contains those that would normally be present throughout a piece of eutectoid plain carbon steel (AISI 1080) that is less than $\frac{3}{8}$ in. diameter if it were quenched under either of the four more or less standard cooling conditions specified in the table. If the steel were hypoeutectoid plain carbon, then pro-eutectoid ferrite would be present as a second microconstituent. Similarly a hypereutectoid steel would contain proeutectoid cementite as a second microconstituent. However, if the cooling rate is fast enough, then the pro-eutectoid phases, α and θ, may not be present even for the noneutectoid steels. This does not mean that α and θ are not present. It simply means that no α and θ form above 1330°F. Or to be more specific, it means that no α and θ form before the eutectoid reaction starts.

If the steel is a low-alloy structural steel, that is, contains less than about 4% alloy, it is generally referred to as oil hardening. The microstructures that are obtained with these steels are, to a first approximation, those that are obtained with a plain carbon steel quenched at the next fastest cooling rate listed in Table 2-4. That is,

TABLE 2-4.   Austenite Transformation Products

(For plain carbon steel, less than $\frac{5}{8}$ in. diameter, quenched with severe agitation from above the upper critical temperature.)

Quenching Medium	Cooling Rate, °F/sec at 1300°F	Microstructures[1]		
		Eutectoid	Hypoeutectoid	Hypereutectoid
Water	300	M	M	M
Oil	30	P_f	$P_f + \alpha$	$P_f + \theta$
Air (normalize)	1	P_m	$P_m + \alpha$	$P_m + \theta$
Furnace (anneal)	0.01	P_c	$P_c + \alpha$	$P_c + \theta$

[1] M—martensite; P_f—fine pearlite; P_m—medium pearlite; P_c—coarse pearlite; α—ferrite; θ—cementite, B—bainite does not occur in plain carbon steels on continuous cooling.

γ_r—retained austenite can occur along with martensite in steels that are severely quenched.

Alloy steel (oil-hardening type): For a given quench, the resulting microstructures are moved down one line in the table.

Alloy steel (air-hardening type): For a given quench, the resulting microstructures are moved down two lines in the table.

a small piece of low-alloy steel will transform to martensite upon oil quenching. And it will transform to fine pearlite, plus a second microconstituent if it is not of eutectoid composition, upon air cooling.

Increasing the alloy content to approximately 4 to 10% makes the steel air-hardening, providing the alloys added increase the hardenability of the steel. These steels transform to martensite when the austenitized material is taken out of the furnace and allowed to air cool.

An alloy steel need not have 0.8% carbon to be of eutectoid composition. AISI 4150 and AISI 4340 steel are both of approximately eutectoid composition even though their carbon contents are 0.5% and

0.4%, respectively. If these two steels are cooled slowly from the austenitizing temperature, they will transform to a 100% pearlitic microstructure having a hardness that is approximately equal to that of an annealed AISI 1080 (plain carbon eutectoid) steel, which is approximately 240 Brinell.

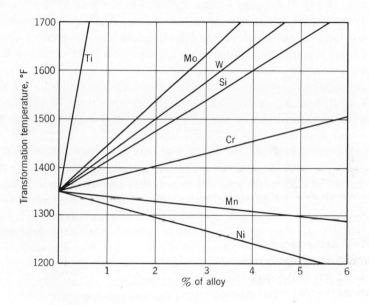

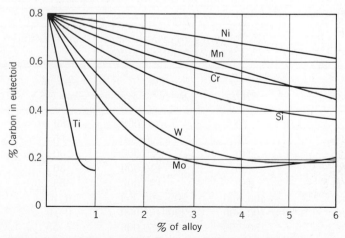

Figure 2-16. Effect of alloys on the transformation temperature and carbon content of pearlite.

Figure 2-16 illustrates the effect of some alloys on the carbon content of the eutectoid and temperature of the eutectoid reaction. Thus it can be seen that if a steel contains 1% chromium, the carbon content of the eutectoid is 0.7%. Or if the steel contains 1% molybdenum, the eutectoid will contain 0.53% carbon. If more than one alloy is present, the effect of each one is added to get the total effect. That is, if 1% chromium lowers the carbon content by 0.1% carbon and if 1% molybdenum lowers the carbon by 0.27%, then a steel containing both of these alloys has its eutectoid carbon content lowered by 0.37%. Its eutectoid composition is, therefore, 0.80 − 0.37 or 0.43% carbon.

Appendix E-1 contains the AISI and SAE designations for structural steel, and Appendix E-2 gives the compositions of some of the common structural steels. For example, a 4150 steel contains about 1% chromium and $\frac{1}{4}$% molybdenum. These two alloys lower the eutectoid carbon content by 0.1% and 0.12% carbon, respectively. In addition, the 1% Mn and the $\frac{1}{4}$% Si lower the carbon another 0.1%. The resulting eutectoid composition is 0.48% carbon, which is approximately equal to the carbon content of the 4150 steel. In similar fashion it can be demonstrated that a 4340 is also of approximately eutectoid composition. In view of this, *pearlite is defined as a mechanical mixture of ferrite and cementite, usually but not necessarily lamellar, and of eutectoid composition.*

Table 2-5 lists the mechanical properties of the ferrous microstructures. These are valid for plain carbon and alloy structural steels alike. However, they do not pertain to stainless steel. Thus coarse

TABLE 2-5.   Relationship of Mechanical Properties and
Ferrous Microstructure

Microstructure	BHN	T.S. BHN × 500	Red of Area (%)	Impact Izod
α	70	40,000	80	100
P_s	180	90,000	55	10
P_c	240	120,000	30	5
P_m	280	140,000	30	5
P_f	380	190,000	35	10
M^1	400–800	200–400,000	0–10	1–5
B^1	400–800	200–400,000	0–10	1–5
M_t	180–700	90–350,000	5–55	1–80

[1] Depends on carbon content—stress relieved.

pearlite has a hardness of approximately 220 to 240 Brinell. And a slowly cooled eutectoid steel will have this hardness regardless of its actual carbon content. Likewise if a 1040 plain carbon steel and a 4340 alloy steel are both quenched to form martensite, they will both have a hardness of about 57 R_c or 580 Brinell. The only difference in these two steels is the severity of quench needed to obtain martensite.

Table 2-6 lists several practical relationships between the carbon content and the mechanical properties of steel. The first of these relationships states that the tensile strength of a plain carbon annealed steel is equal to 40,000 plus 1000 times the points (per cent $\times$ 100) of

TABLE 2-6.   Relationship between Carbon Content and
Mechanical Properties of Steel

$S_u = 40,000 + 100,000$ C for annealed plain carbon steel where C = % carbon

$H_B = 80 + 200$ C—for annealed plain carbon steel

$H_B = 80 + 160$ P_c (P_c is fraction of pearlite present) for annealed carbon and alloy steel.

$H_B = 900$ $C^{0.45}$—for primary martensite up to 0.65% C—which has maximum hardness.

$S_u = 500$ H_B for all stress relieved steels, but not coldworked.

$S_y = 1.05$ S_u—22,000 for non-coldworked steel.

$S_y = 1.05$ S_u—30,000 for annealed alloy steel.

$I_{max} = 120$–120C (maximum possible impact strength for a given carbon content).

---

carbon. Thus the tensile strength of a 1030 annealed steel is 70,000 psi and that of a 1090 steel is 130,000 psi. The second relationship is simply the first one divided by 500, which is the proportionality constant that equates the tensile strength of steel to the Brinell hardness.

The third relationship equates the Brinell hardness number to the amount of coarse pearlite present in the microstructure, and consequently it applies only to annealed steel. Since pearlite was defined above as being of eutectoid composition, this relationship applies equally well to alloy steels, whereas the two previous relationships are valid only for plain carbon steel. It is derived from the facts that the hardness of ferrite is 80 Brinell, the hardness of coarse pearlite is 240 Brinell, and the hardness of any combination of the two is a weighted average of the hardness of these two microconstituents.

The fourth relationship provides a convenient means to determine the hardness of primary or untempered martensite. It is valid for both alloy and plain carbon steels having carbon contents between 0.2%

and 0.65%. The hardness of martensite containing more than 0.65% carbon is the same as that of martensite containing 0.65% carbon since the hardness reaches an asymptote of 67 R_c (about 800 Brinell) at this carbon content. The hardness of tempered martensite is discussed in a following section.

The fifth relationship in Table 2-6 states that the ratio of the tensile strength over the Brinell hardness is 500. This relationship is usually accurate to within 3% for all stress-relieved steels. It does not apply to coldworked steel.

The sixth relationship is only a rough approximation that can be used to estimate the yield strength of annealed or heat-treated steel if only the tensile strength and nothing else is known about the steel. It cannot be used for coldworked steel. For coldworked steels, the relationships developed in Chapter 1 can be used. It is derived from the observation that the yield strength of ferrite (about 20,000 psi) is half of the tensile strength (40,000 psi) of ferrite; and that the yield strength is nearly equal to the tensile strength when the steel has its maximum tensile strength of about 400,000 psi. The seventh relationship is slightly more valid if used for annealed low-alloy steel.

The last relationship is included in Table 2-6 to illustrate the detrimental effect of carbon on the impact strength of steel. The maximum impact strength that can be achieved with a very low-carbon steel is about 100 to 120 ft-lb. But as the carbon content approaches 1%, the impact strength approaches zero. In reality, the maximum impact strength that a 1095 steel can have, regardless of the heat treatment, is about 5 ft-lb.

All the microstructures that austenite can transform into are listed in Table 2-4. The type of quench needed to produce each of the microstructures in small pieces of steel is also included. However, some type of empirical hardenability data is needed in order to predict what microconstituents are most likely to be present in various sizes of bars subjected to common quenching operations. *Hardenability* is that characteristic of a structural steel that is a measure of the slowness of cooling rate that can be employed in quenching the steel from its proper austenitizing temperature and still obtain all martensite.

There are at present two types of hardenability data that are both convenient to use and that give fairly reliable results. These are the isothermal transformation diagrams and the end-quench hardenability data or, as the latter are frequently referred to, Jominy curves. A brief discussion of how each type is used follows.

Figure 2-17 contains an isothermal transformation diagram for an AISI 1080 steel austenitized at 1500°F. Since the diagram correlates

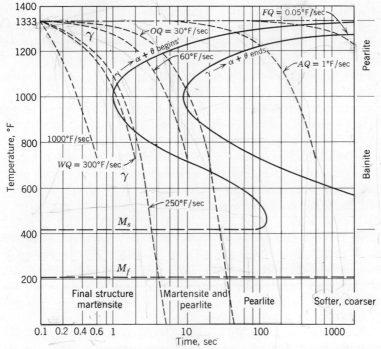

Figure 2-17. Isothermal transformation diagram for AISI 1080 steel with continuous cooling rate curves superimposed.

time, temperature, and transformation products, it is frequently referred to as a *TTT* diagram. The diagram is also occasionally called the *S* curves because of the shape of the lines. The first, or left-most line, indicates the time necessary for austenite to begin to transform to $\alpha + \theta$ when it is instantaneously cooled from the austenitizing temperature to some temperature between the critical temperatures but above the M_s temperature, and held at that temperature. The second curve, or the one on the right, indicates the time necessary for the completion of the transformation of austenite to $\alpha + \theta$ while the temperature is maintained constant at the value it is instantaneously quenched to.

The portion of the transformation curve where it reaches its extreme left position, exclusive of the martensite region, is referred to as the nose, or the knee, of the curve. A better appreciation of the effect of a specific cooling rate on the microstructures that may result in any steel during heat treatment can be realized if one remembers two features of the *IT* diagram of AISI 1080 steel. First, the edge of the nose of the curve occurs at a temperature of approximately 1000°F. Second, the times for the beginning and end of the isothermal transformation at 1000°F are 1 and 10 sec respectively. The curves are displaced to the right for steels having a greater hardenability. That is, longer times are necessary for the completion of the transformation of austenite to ferrite plus cementite.

Superimposed on the isothermal transformation diagram in Figure 2-17 is a series of continuous cooling rate curves. They vary from the low-cooling rate of an anneal or furnace cool to one that is faster than a water quench. The cooling rate curves plotted here are not just the cooling rate at 1300°F, but the specified cooling rate exists over the entire range of temperature for each curve. They should not be interpreted as being continuous cooling curves, which have a decreasing cooling rate with a decrease in temperature at which the rate is measured. Thus the 60°F/sec curve has the temperature drop from 1333 to 1273°F in the first second and to 1213°F by the end of 2 sec, and so on. Since the cooling rate for a given type of quench does not vary appreciably in the temperature range that is important (1300 to 1000° F), the use of cooling rate curves which are easier to construct than cooling curves is justifiable.

The *critical cooling rate* is a term frequently employed when discussing hardenability—it is a quantitative means of defining a steel's hardenability. The critical cooling rate of a steel is the slowest cooling rate that can be given to the steel and have it transform to all martensite. The critical cooling rate is also defined as the cooling rate that is tangent to the nose of the *TTT* curve for a particular steel.

Not all isothermal transformation diagrams have the same appearance as that of the AISI 1080 steel, which is of eutectoid composition. There are two typical variations or modifications of this basic diagram. The first modification is illustrated in Figure 2-18. This diagram indicates that when austenite of noneutectoid composition transforms at a temperature above 1000°F, a pro-eutectoid phase, either α or θ, will precipitate or transform before the simultaneous transformation to α and θ occurs. This should be anticipated from the iron-carbon phase diagram. When a noneutectoid steel is cooled from the single phase austenite region through the two phase region between the upper and the lower critical temperatures, a pro-eutectoid reaction occurs in which some austenite transforms to either ferrite for a hypoeutectoid steel or to cementite for a hypereutectoid steel.

Although the equilibrium phase diagram indicates that austenite will transform to another phase upon being cooled below the critical

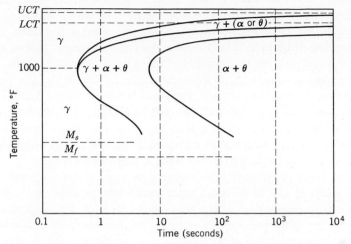

Figure 2-18. Schematic isothermal transformation diagram for a noneutectoid steel.

temperatures, it does not indicate how much time is necessary for the transformation to occur. The isothermal transformation diagram, on the other hand, does indicate how much time is required for austenite to transform to another phase when it is cooled below the critical temperatures. By referring to Figure 2-17, it can be seen that an austenite of eutectoid composition will not begin to transform to ferrite and cementite until after many hours have elapsed if it is cooled to just a few degrees below the lower critical temperature. But if the austenite were cooled rapidly to 1200°F and maintained at that temperature, it would begin to transform in about 5 secs and would be completely transformed in about 1 min. Thus it is apparent that austenite can exist at temperatures below the critical one; but only for a limited period of time which depends upon the temperature it is held at.

If a hypoeutectoid steel, such as AISI 1040, were instantaneously cooled to some temperature such as 1250°F and held at that temperature, it would require several seconds before any austenite would begin to transform. When the austenite does begin to transform at this temperature, as can be seen in Figure 2-18, the first transformation product to form is ferrite. As much as 50% of the austenite can transform to ferrite before any simultaneous transformation of ferrite and cementite occur with a 1040 steel. And this proeutectoid ferrite does not transform at the upper critical temperature, but instead it forms at a temperature of 1250°F only after several seconds have elapsed.

The second modification of the simple eutectoid transformation diagram is the type that contains a bainite nose in addition to the pearlite nose (Figure 2-19). It does not exist with plain carbon steels, but in varying degrees it is typical of the alloy structural steels. Three features are characteristic of most diagrams of this type: the pearlite nose occurs in the temperature range of about 1100 to 1200°F; the bainite nose occurs in the range of 800 to 900°F; the pearlite nose is positioned to the right of the bainite nose. For these reasons it is possible to obtain bainite with continuous cooling of an alloy steel of this type, whereas it is impossible with a plain carbon steel.

Very little production heat treating of steel is done by this inter-rupted quench, the isothermal transformation process. It is not as convenient or economical as the continuous quench. Although the *TTT* diagrams are obtained experimentally by isothermally transforming steel, they are intended to be used to predict the microstructures that will result upon continuous cooling. As would be expected, the trans-formation of austenite to ferrite and cementile during continuous cool-ing does not begin to occur at the time and temperature that corre-sponds to the intersection of the cooling curve and the first isothermal transformation line. The transformation actually begins at a lower temperature and at a longer time. But after the transformation begins

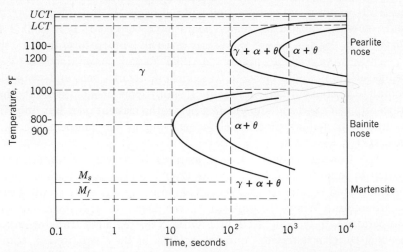

Figure 2-19. Schematic isothermal transformation diagram containing a bainite nose.

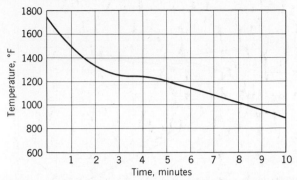

Figure 2-20. Cooling curve for a ¾ diameter AISI 1080 steel during air cooling.

during a continuous cool, the transformation may occur at constant temperatures if the cooling rate is not too high since the transformation is an exothermic reaction. The heat evolved during the transformation of an eutectoid steel is sufficient to prevent the temperature from dropping until the transformation is nearly complete. This is analogous to the "hold," or constant temperature portion, of a cooling curve of a pure element during solidification when the heat of fusion is evolved.

Figure 2-20 is a cooling curve obtained experimentally on the surface of a ¾ in. diameter bar of AISI 1080 steel during air cooling.

It is apparent that the austenite began to transform to medium pearlite at a temperature of about 1245°F approximately 50 sec after its temperature dropped below 1333°F. The temperature remained above 1240° for about an additional 75 sec. This cooling curve is superimposed on a *TTT* diagram for 1080 steel in Figure 2-21. From this figure it can be seen that for all practical purposes the transformation of the austenite to pearlite was isothermal at a temperature nearly 100°F below the lower critical temperature.

To use the isothermal transformation diagram of any steel to predict what microstructures will most likely result with a given thermal cycle, or to estimate what cooling rate will be necessary to obtain a desired microstructure, it is necessary to modify the *IT* diagram to a continuous transformation or *CT* diagram. This alteration is usually done mentally similarly to that described previously where a phase diagram was modified into a microconstituent diagram. Figure 2-21 points out the manner in which the *IT* diagram must be altered

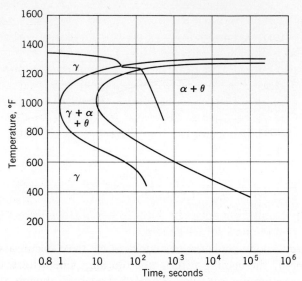

Figure 2-21. Cooling curve of Figure 2-20 superimposed on a TTT diagram for 1080 steel.

to predict when austenite will transform on continuous cooling as well as what the transformed products will be.

Figure 2-22 is an *IT* diagram for a 1080 steel that is modified to a *CT* diagram. The original *IT* diagram is shown by means of the narrow lines. The *CT* diagram is the pair of heavy lines. The austenite-transformation-begins line (the left line) of the *CT* diagram lies approximately one-third to one-half of the shortest distance between the beginning and the ending line of the *IT* diagram. It usually is about one-third of the distance near the nose of the *IT* diagram and one-half of the distance at the far right end of the *IT* diagram. The autenite-transformation-ends line (the right line) of the *CT* diagram lies an equal amount to the right of the equivalent curve of the *IT* diagram.

Three cooling curves are superimposed on the transformation diagrams of Figure 2-22. Curve *A* represents the critical cooling rate as described previously. However, from the preceding discussion it is apparent that curve *B* is really the slowest cooling rate that will give 100% martensite. Consequently, curve *B* is in reality the critical cooling rate. Curve *C* passes through both the transformation of austenite-to-pearlite begins- (left) and-ends (right) curves of the *IT* diagram. However, since curve *C* is a continuous cooling curve, and also since it does not cross the transformation-ends curve of the CT diagram, some austenite is still present at a temperature designated as point X on curve C. This austenite will transform to martensite rather than to pearlite, but at a much lower temperature.

Several isothermal transformation diagrams are included in Appendix F. When used in the previously described way, reasonable predictions can be made of the microstructures that will result with conventional heat treatments. However, it must be realized that a given isothermal transformation diagram for a specific steel is valid only for the one sample tested. Another sample of the same type of steel from another heat, or a sample austenitized at a different temperature, will yield a significantly different isothermal transformation diagram because of differences in the grain size or in the chemical composition. This limitation must be borne in mind whenever a steel is being studied on the basis of hardenability.

The most convenient manner of presenting the experimental hardenability data for steel is by means of Jominy end-quench hardness data. Hardenability data in the form of Jominy end-quench curves are easier to interpret than are the data in the form of TTT curves. And when the end-quench hardenability data are presented in tabular form, as in Appendix G, they are much more compact than in any other form.

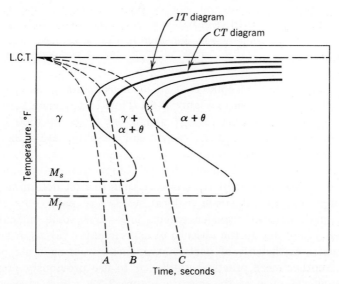

Figure 2-22. Alteration of an isothermal transformation diagram to a continuous transformation diagram.

The data that are included on two pages in Appendix G would require several dozen pages if presented in the form of curves. An additional advantage of hardenability presented in the form of end-quench hardness data is that they are very simple to use in conjunction with cooling rate data as a function of bar size and shape. It should be noted that end-quench hardenability curves are included beneath the isothermal transformation curves in Appendix F.

There are two characteristics of the so-called structural steels, the plain carbon and the low alloy steels of low and medium carbon content, that make it possible for the end-quench hardenability data to be so practical. The first characteristic is: *the cooling rate for a given steel determines the resulting microstructure*. This means that regardless of how a specific cooling rate for a given steel is achieved, the microstructure that results is the same. For example, the center of a large bar quenched in brine with severe agitation can have the same cooling rate as a small bar quenched in oil with no agitation. The microstructures at the center of both bars will be identical, and so will the mechanical properties. However, the microstructures and properties of the steel at the surface of both bars probably will be different.

The second characteristic is: *the thermal conductivities of all the structural steels are sufficiently close to being identical so that they all have nearly the same cooling rate when cooled under the same conditions*. This means that for purposes of hardenability calculations the center of a 4 in. diameter bar of AISI 8640 steel and a 4 in. diameter bar of AISI 1040 steel will both have the same cooling rate if they are identically quenched in the same media. This also means that all structural steels have the same cooling rate at a specified Jominy distance.

The cooling rates at 1300°F at $\frac{1}{16}$ in. increments along a Jominy end-quench bar are given in Figure 2-23. Thus end-quench specimens of all steels have a cooling rate of about 490°F/sec at 1300°F at a distance of $\frac{1}{16}$ in. from the quenched end and a cooling rate of 32°F/sec at a distance of $\frac{1}{2}$ in. from the quenched end.

In order to use end-quench hardenability data to predict the microstructures in a given part, it is necessary to first determine what the cooling rates are at strategic locations in the part. This can be done by making heat transfer calculations—but some difficulty is encountered here due to the absence of experimental values of surface heat transfer coefficients of parts having heat treating scale on the surface. Another more practical method is to use previously prepared tables or charts, such as the ones in Figure 2-23, which give cooling rates under a variety of quenching conditions for simple geometrical

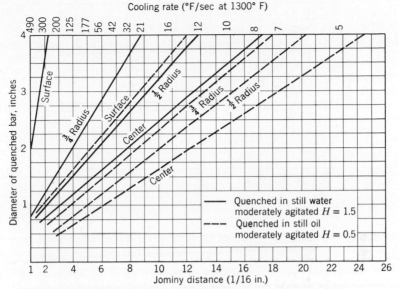

Figure 2-23. Equivalent Jominy distances of round-quenched bars.

shapes such as cylinders, spheres, and plates. Several different types of tables and charts of time-temperature relationships are available in handbooks.

The equivalent cooling rates in Figure 2-23 are for round bars that have a length to diameter ratio greater than 3. The values are valid for positions along the length of bar that are not less than a distance equal to one diameter from the ends of the bar. These values are only approximate inasmuch as the cooling rate at 1300°F is affected by the austenitizing temperature from which the piece is quenched. The cooling rate is also influenced by the austenitizing time and furnace atmosphere since these two variables determine the amount of scale that is formed on the surface of the bar.

Jominy end-quench curves for several low, medium, and high-carbon steels are drawn in Figure 2-24. However, a single curve for one class of steel such as 4140 is only representative of one sample. End-quench specimens from different heats of the same class of steel will give a considerable range of hardness distributions. If steels are selected and the design of structural parts is made on the basis of hardenability calculations, then steels manufactured to have guaranteed limits to the end-quench curves should be specified. These steels are designated as H steels since the letter H follows the AISI number.

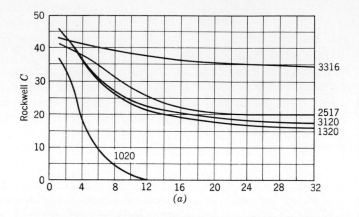

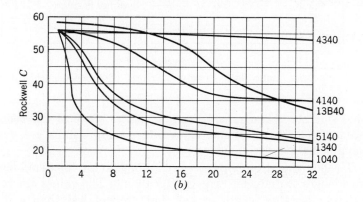

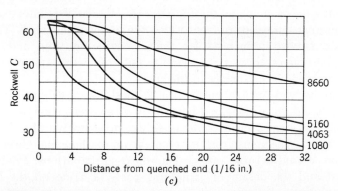

Figure 2-24. Jominy-end quench curves for some low, medium, and high-carbon steels. (*a*) Low-carbon. (*b*) Medium-carbon. (*c*) High-carbon.

Thus a 4140 steel has a guaranteed chemical composition, but no restrictions on its hardenability. A 4140 H steel guarantees both the chemistry and the hardenability. The guaranteed limits of the H steel are referred to as hardenability bands.

The hardenability bands of two steels are drawn in Figure 2-25. The hardenability limits for most of the structural H steels are given in Appendix G in compact tabular form. Although the H steels are sold with guaranteed hardenability limits it should be noticed that the difference between the maximum and minimum hardness at a given distance from the end of the specimen may be as much as 20 R_c, or a variation of 100,000 psi in the tensile strength.

Structural parts made of heat-treated steel should always have a tempering process included as part of the heat treatment. The tempering may be done in the low temperature range of 300 to 450°F, where it is referred to as stress relieving. It may be done in a temperature

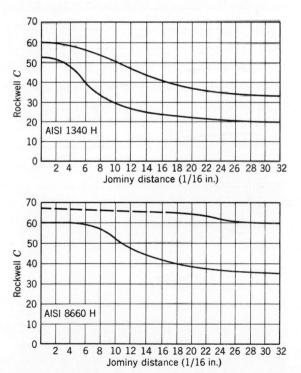

Figure 2-25. Jominy-end quench bands for AISI 1340 H and 8660 H steels.

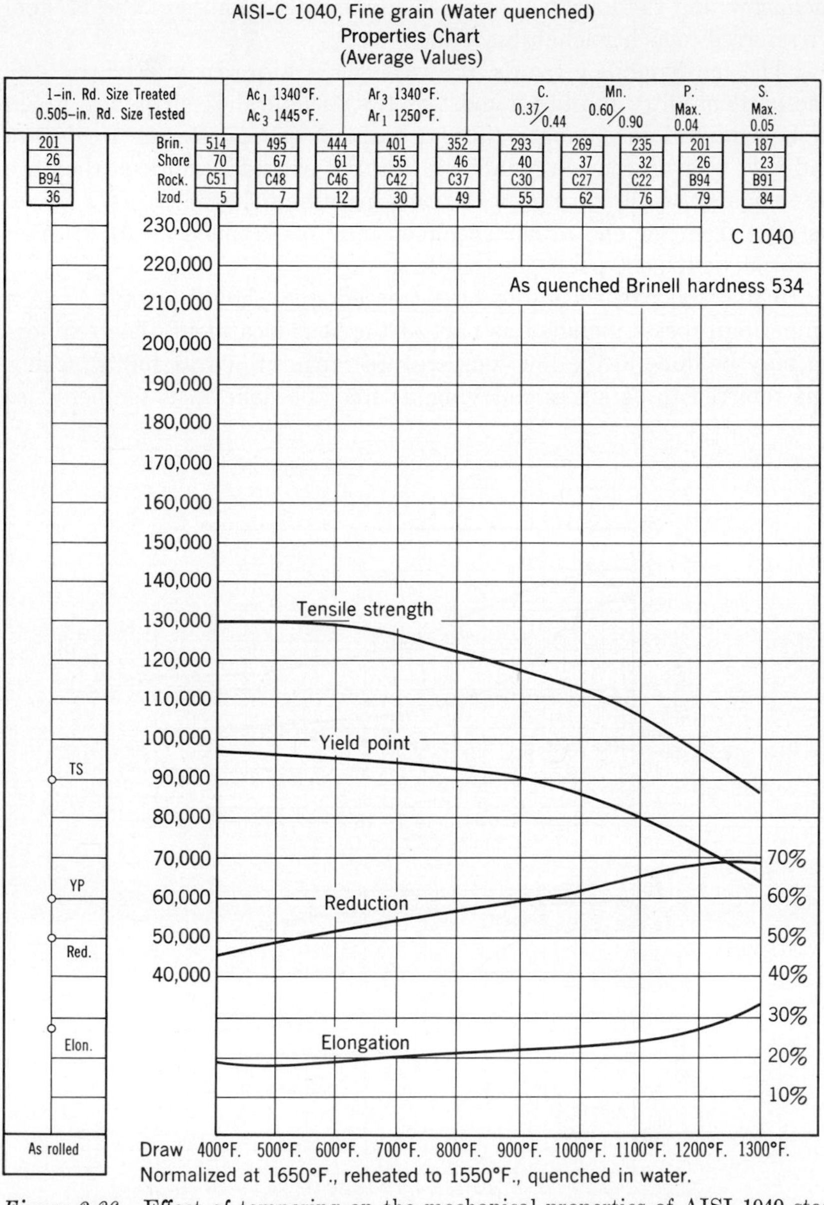
AISI-C 1040, Fine grain (Water quenched)
Properties Chart
(Average Values)
1-in. Rd. Size Treated
0.505-in. Rd. Size Tested
Ac1 1340°F.
Ac3 1445°F.
Ar3 1340°F.
Ar1 1250°F.
C. 0.37/0.44
Mn. 0.60/0.90
P. Max. 0.04
S. Max. 0.05
Brin. Shore Rock. Izod.
201 26 B94 36
514 70 C51 5
495 67 C48 7
444 61 C46 12
401 55 C42 30
352 46 C37 49
293 40 C30 55
269 37 C27 62
235 32 C22 76
201 26 B94 79
187 23 B91 84
C 1040
As quenched Brinell hardness 534
230,000
220,000
210,000
200,000
190,000
180,000
170,000
160,000
150,000
140,000
130,000
120,000
110,000
100,000
90,000
80,000
70,000
60,000
50,000
40,000
Tensile strength
Yield point
Reduction
Elongation
70%
60%
50%
40%
30%
20%
10%
TS
YP
Red.
Elon.
As rolled
Draw 400°F. 500°F. 600°F. 700°F. 800°F. 900°F. 1000°F. 1100°F. 1200°F. 1300°F.
Normalized at 1650°F., reheated to 1550°F., quenched in water.

Figure 2-26. Effect of tempering on the mechanical properties of AISI 1040 steel (Courtesy of Bethlehem Steel Corp.).

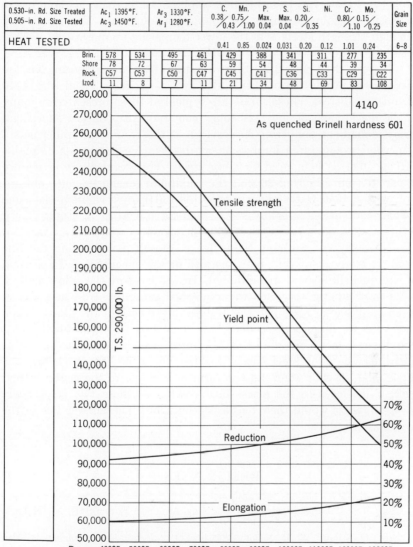

AISI-4140 (Oil quenched)
Properties Chart
(Single Heat Results)

0.530-in. Rd. Size Treated 0.505-in. Rd. Size Tested	Ac₁ 1395°F. Ac₃ 1450°F.	Ar₃ 1330°F. Ar₁ 1280°F.	C. 0.38/ /0.43	Mn. 0.75/ /1.00	P. Max. 0.04	S. Max. 0.04	Si. 0.20/ /0.35	Ni.	Cr. 0.80/ /1.10	Mo. 0.15/ /0.25	Grain Size
HEAT TESTED			0.41	0.85	0.024	0.031	0.20	0.12	1.01	0.24	6–8

Brin.	578	534	495	461	429	388	341	311	277	235
Shore	78	72	67	63	59	54	48	44	39	34
Rock.	C57	C53	C50	C47	C45	C41	C36	C33	C29	C22
Izod.	11	8	7	11	21	34	48	69	83	108

4140

As quenched Brinell hardness 601

Tensile strength

Yield point

T.S. 290,000 lb.

Reduction

Elongation

Draw 400°F. 500°F. 600°F. 700°F. 800°F. 900°F. 1000°F. 1100°F. 1200°F. 1300°F.
Normalized at 1600°F., reheated to 1550°F., quenched in agitated oil.

Figure 2-27. Effect of tempering on the mechanical properties of AISI 4140 steel (Courtesy of Bethlehem Steel Corp.).

range of 500 to 600°F to retain a high hardness with a slight increase in toughness. Much design of mechanical components specify a tempering range of 900°F to 1050°F. This is done on the philosophy that steel tempered in this range has the "optimum" combination of mechanical properties. However, this optimum combination is really a compromise between maximum strength and maximum toughness. The trend with the high-strength steels is to the lower tempering temperatures and the resulting higher strengths.

Figures 2-26 and 2-27 illustrate the effect of tempering on the mechanical properties of AISI 1040 water-quenched steel and 4140 oil-quenched steel. These curves are typical of those presented in many of the mechanical design textbooks. Too frequently only a superficial study is made of tempering curves such as these, and the reader gets a somewhat exaggerated impression of the relative properties of plain-carbon steel as compared to alloy steels. For example, it is readily apparent from Figure 2-26 that the maximum tensile strength obtainable with a 1040 water-quenched steel is 130,000 psi whereas the same carbon content in an alloy steel, such as the 4140 in Figure 2-27, achieves a maximum strength of 290,000 psi.

However, by studying these figures closely and reading the fine print, it is apparent that both the size of the specimen and agitation of the quenching fluid are different. In the case of the alloy steel, a 0.530 in. diameter specimen was quenched in agitated oil and then a 0.505 in. diameter specimen was tested. In the case of the plain carbon steel, a 1 in. diameter specimen was quenched in nonagitated water and then a 0.505 in. diameter specimen was tested. For the sizes quenched, the alloy steel formed martensite to the center whereas the larger plain-carbon steel did not form martensite to the center. However, if the sizes of the pieces heat-treated of these two steels were reversed, what would their tensile strength be? The answer lies in the hardenability data.

REFERENCES

1. ASM, *Metals Handbook*, 1948 edition.
2. ASM, *Strengthening Mechanisms in Solids*, Am. Soc. For Metals, Metal Park, Ohio, 1960.
3. Clark, D. S., and W. R. Varney, *Physical Metallurgy for Engineers*, D. Van Nostrand Co., New York, 1962.
4. Grossman, M. A., *Principles of Heat Treatment*, Am. Soc. For Metals, Metals Park, Ohio, 1953.
5. Holloman, J. H., and L. D. Jaffe, *Ferrous Metallurgical Design*, John Wiley and Sons, New York, 1947.

6. Samans, C. H., *Metallic Materials In Engineering,* Macmillan Co., New York, 1963.
7. Smith, M. C., *Alloy Series in Physical Metallurgy,* Harper and Brothers, New York, 1956.

STUDY PROBLEMS

2-1   A bronze of 85 Cu–15 Sn is a good bearing material, whereas a brass of 85 Cu–15 Zn is not. On the basis of the equilibrium diagrams, explain why.

2-2   List all of the practical ways the following materials may be strengthened without changing the composition: (a) 70 Cu–30 Zn brass, (b) 5 Cu–95 Al alloy, (c) 1 C–99 Fe alloy, and (d) pure magnesium.

2-3   A commonly used silver solder for low welding temperatures has the following weight composition: 50% Ag; 16% Cu; 16% Zn; 18% Cd. The material welded is steel.
    a. If silver solder produces a metallurgical bond, what are the "active" metals?
    b. What is the function of the other metals?

2-4   By means of the data below, illustrate (including sketches of microstructures):
    a. The magnitude of the effect of coldwork alone on pure aluminum.
    b. The magnitude of the effect of solution hardening alone on aluminum.
    c. The magnitude of the effect of precipitation hardening alone on aluminum.

Material	S_y	S_u	H_B
1100-O	5,000	13,000	23
1100-F	14,000	16,000	28
1100-H18	22,000	24,000	44
2011-O	15,000	30,000	48
2011-W	18,000	36,000	63
2011-T3	48,000	55,000	95
2011-T4	45,000	50,000	90

2-5   If 1020 annealed steel has an A_r of 66 and 1040 steel has an A_r of 58, what is the per cent reduction of area of ferrite and of coarse pearlite?

2-6   Calculate the properties of the following materials on the basis of their microstructure.
    a. Brinell hardness number (Bhn) of 1060 steel—annealed.
    b. Tensile strength of 1030 steel—small piece, oil-quenched.
    c. Yield strength of 1010 steel cold-drawn 12%.

2-7   Two shafts of $\frac{1}{2}$ in. diameter were made of AISI 1040 steel and heat treated as outlined below. What are the percentages of each microstructure present and what are the probable tensile and yield strengths?
    a. γ'd at 1400°F; water-quenched and tempered at 450°F.
    b. γ'd at 1550°F; water-quenched and tempered at 450°F.

2-8   A cylindrical bar 24 in. long is needed that will support a load of 50,000 lb with a factor of safety of 2 based on the yield strength. If 9262 steel costs $0.16/lb and 4140 steel costs $0.14/lb, which would be the more economical to use?

2–9   Why are hypoeutectoid steels heated above the upper critical temperature while hypereutectoid steels are heated to slightly above the lower critical temperature in the hardening operation?

2–10   Aluminum can be treated to change its mechanical properties by cold-work, grain size, and alloying (single and multiple phase). Discuss quantitatively the effect of each of these techniques.

2–11   Express the data of Figure 1-4 in the form $R_B = Kd^n$, where d is the deformation.

2–12   What is the critical cooling rate for a 4130 steel? For a 9262 steel?

2–13   What is the critical cooling rate for an E4340H steel?

2–14   What axial load would cause yielding in a 2 in. diameter bar of 1340H steel oil-quenched and tempered at 400°F?

2–15   a. What composition of A and B could not be coldworked? Why?
       b. What composition would probably be best to achieve precipitation hardening? Why?
       c. Specify compositions and heat treatments of two materials that will illustrate "solution hardening" and nothing else. Include a sketch of the microstructures.

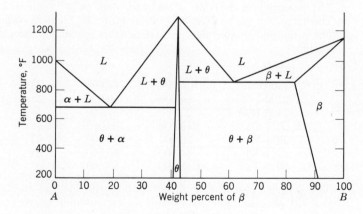

2–16   A 4 in. diameter by 18 in. long solid cylinder of 4140 steel is quenched in still water with moderate agitation.
       a. Sketch and label the microstructure at the surface.
       b. Sketch and label the microstructure at the center.
       c. What is the hardness at the center? Tensile strength? Yield strength?
       d. What diameter bar, when oil quenched, would have the same hardness at the center? Explain how you obtained your answer.
       e. Estimate the hardness at 64 Jominy distances on a Jominy end-quench bar of 1030 steel? Explain how you obtained your answer.
       f. What is the function of carbon as an alloy in steel?

2–17   Four small pieces of 1040 steel are heated to 1350°F and cooled as indicated below. Sketch and label the microstructures and give the hardness of each: (a) furnace cool, (b) air cool, (c) oil quench, and (d) water quench.

2–18 One-half inch diameter pieces of the following are heated to 1550°F and water quenched. Sketch and label the microstructures and give the hardnesses: (a) 1100 F aluminum, (b) copper 20% C.W., (c) 4 C–96 Fe, (d) 1040 steel, (e) 4140 steel, (f) 2 C–98 Fe, and (g) 70 Cu–30 Zn brass.

2–19 Four small pieces of 1050 steel are heated to 1340°F and cooled as indicated below. Sketch and label the microstructures and give the hardnesses: (a) furnace cool, (b) air cool, (c) oil quench, and (d) water quench.

2–20 A typical strain-hardening relationship for 1100-O aluminum is $\sigma = 23{,}000\epsilon^{0.2}$. The maximum A_r of a tensile specimen is about 85%. The strongest aluminum alloy is 7078T6 which has a tensile strength of 85,000 psi, a yield strength of 74,000 psi, and an 8% reduction of area after heat treating (solution heat-treated and artificially aged). Can aluminum be strengthened as much by coldwork as by alloying and heat treating?

2–21 Can iron be strengthened as much by coldwork as by alloying and heat treating?

2–22 What would you estimate the hardness and yield strength of an annealed 5140 steel to be? Include calculations.

2–23 In what condition is the lead present in a leaded (free machining) steel?

3

The Casting Process

Casting is probably the oldest process used to manufacture metallic articles. Archaeological studies have unearthed artifacts and utensils of cast metal dating back to 4000 B.C. These first castings were made of metals that were easy to extract from the earth and had relatively low melting temperatures. Casting was the first process employed to make hollow articles such as vases and pots. The barrels for the early cannons were also made by this process out of copper-tin (bronze) alloys.

Very little in the way of equipment is needed to make simple castings (parts made by the casting process) in small quantities. The minimum requirements are a wooden pattern, a sand-clay mixture to make a mold, and a furnace to melt the material being cast. However, considerable equipment is required for the mass production of high-strength sound castings. Equipment is needed for materials handling, for molding and melting, and for process and metallurgical control.

The casting process has the advantage of making a part almost to the finished shape before any machining is done. This advantage plus the cheapness of ferrous metals as compared to the price of all other metals is the basis of the statement "cast iron is cheap" by mechanical design engineers. But this is really not true, since the minimum price for which cast iron can be purchased is about 11 cents per pound, whereas wrought steel can be purchased for approximately half that price. The correct way to express the advantages of casting is to note that cast iron as such is not cheap in comparison to wrought steel but that parts made of cast iron are relatively cheap only if the casting process enables the elimination of a substantial amount of machining that would ordinarily be required.

DEFINITION

Casting is the manufacturing process whereby the desired material is heated to the liquid state, then poured into a previously prepared mold cavity of proper design, and allowed to solidify in the mold before being extracted, trimmed and cleaned.

From this definition it is apparent that a study of the casting process must include the following areas: patterns and molding; melting and pouring (flow); solidification and cooling; cleaning and inspection. In considering the castability of a specific material, the properties and relationships to be taken into account are: (1) the relative melting temperatures of the material in question and suitable mold materials; (2) the solubility or chemical reactivity of the part material and the mold material; (3) the solubility in the material of its atmosphere at low and high temperatures; (4) the thermal expansion and thermal conduction of both the part and mold materials; and (5) the cost and availability of both the part and mold materials.

There are many casting processes, which are generally classified by the type of mold used to make the casting. The more common of the processes as listed in order of decreasing application are: green sand, die, permanent mold, shell, investment, baked sand, plaster. These processes will be discussed in more detail later.

The manufacturing plant in which castings are made is called a *foundry*. In the past, the process of casting was called *founding*, and it is occasionally called that today. Individual foundries are specialized according to the molding processes they use and the materials they cast. Thus, some foundries make only gray iron castings in sand molds, others make only permanent cast iron, whereas others restrict themselves to die casting zinc or aluminum base alloys. Some die casting plants make only castings of plastics, which are frequently called injection moldings.

PATTERNS

A pattern is a replica of the part to be cast and is used to make the mold cavity into which the liquid material is poured.

The type of pattern used is determined by the number of castings required as well as the casting process itself. When only a few castings are to be made, a pattern is made by gluing together sections of soft wood which are then finished to the shape of the desired part. If a larger number of casting is to be made, the pattern may be made of hard wood. When the number of castings to be made is very large, in the thousands, the pattern is made of aluminum or some other metal and generally is mounted on a match plate or on a molding machine. Patterns are divided into five types which are described next.

A *loose pattern* is simply a replica, usually made of wood, of the desired casting. It is slightly larger than the casting, and it may have several projections or bosses called core prints that the resulting casting does not have. The reasons for these differences between the pattern and the casting is discussed on p. 106. Loose patterns obtained their name because they are not attached or mounted on a plate or frame.

Loose patterns are used when the number of castings to be made is very small—roughly, up to 100. If an existing part is available, it may be used as a loose pattern if the slight difference in size of the resulting casting is not significant, or if a thin layer of "padding" can be attached to the part before the molding begins.

Loose patterns may be one solid piece, exactly like the desired casting, or they may be split along a plane or irregular surface to facilitate the extraction of the pattern out of the mold before the pouring operation.

A *gated pattern* is simply one or more loose patterns having attached gates and runners, which are the channels through which the liquid flows from the pouring sprue to the cavity. Since the molder does not have to form these channels by hand, gated patterns reduce the molding time somewhat. Because of a higher cost than loose patterns the gated patterns are used when the size of the castings is small, and the amount required is about a thousand.

Gated patterns are frequently set on a follow board which is shaped to the parting surface of the mold. This serves as an interface where the mold separates, which enables the pattern to be removed after the mold is constructed as we will see in the discussion on the construction of molds.

A *match plate pattern* is a split pattern having the cope and drag portions mounted on opposite sides of a wood or metal plate, called the match plate, that conforms to the contour of the parting surface. The match plate is accurately located between the cope and drag halves of the flask by means of locating pins. (The flask is a four-sided frame in which a sand mold is made.) When the match plate is withdrawn after the sand is molded around the pattern, and the mold is closed by bringing the two halves together again, the cope portion of the mold cavity thus "matches" with the drag portion.

This type of pattern is used for a large number of castings. Several patterns can be mounted on one match plate if the size of the castings is small. In this case the patterns need not all be for the same casting.

When match plate patterns are used, the molding is generally done on a molding machine on which the sand is forced around the pattern by either jolting or squeezing rather than by hand ramming.

The gates and runners are also mounted on the match plate so that very little hand work is required.

A *cope and drag pattern* is a split pattern having the cope and the drag portions each mounted on separate match plates. The patterns are accurately located on the plates, so that when the two separately made mold halves are brought together the mold cavity is properly formed. For a higher rate of production each half of the pattern is mounted on a separate molding machine. (For production work of this type less skilled molders are needed than is required for hand molding with loose patterns.)

Pneumatic vibrators are usually attached to cope and drag patterns as well as to match plate patterns to facilitate the withdrawal of the pattern from the mold without crumbling the mold walls.

Shell molds are made with patterns that can be classified as cope and drag type, with two primary differences from those used for green sand molds: First, the pattern is equipped with ejector pins, similar to those on a die-casting mold or a press drawing-die, to enable the shell mold to be stripped from the pattern. Second, the pattern is heated to temperatures between 350 and 550°F to form the mold.

Sweeps and skeleton patterns are wooden cross-sections of very large castings that are used by the molder as a guide to hand form the molds for casting. A complete pattern is not necessary and would be quite expensive for a very large casting where the tolerances are large.

A sweep is a section or board of proper contour that is rotated about one edge to shape mold cavities having circular shapes. This is frequently referred to as the loam molding process since a special molding mixture, loam, with a large amount of plasticity must be used. The loam consists of a mixture of silica sand, sawdust, fire clay and enough water to give it a consistency of paste. A framework of brick or wood supports the loam.

For large castings having simple geometrical shapes, skeleton patterns are used. These patterns are simple wooden frames that outline the shape of the part to be cast and are also used as guides by the molder in the hand shaping of the mold.

Since sweeps and skeleton patterns are used in the making of very large castings, the molds are made either in a pit or on the foundry floor. Thus this type of molding is referred to as pit and floor molding in contrast to the bench and machine molding used with the previously described patterns.

It was stated that a pattern is slightly larger than the finished part of which it is a replica. There are two reasons for this—the contraction that occurs from the cooling of the cast material, and the need to provide excess material for removal when a machined surface is required. This oversize is referred to as *pattern allowance;* the former is the shrinkage allowance and the latter is the machining allowance.

The shrinkage allowance represents the increase that is added to the length of any dimension of a cast part to obtain the corresponding length of the pattern. It is expressed as inches per foot. The shrinkage allowance for cast iron is $\frac{1}{8}$ in./ft., which means that the pattern length for a 6 in. casting will be $6\frac{1}{16}$ in.

The total shrinkage that occurs in a casting during cooling is composed of three separate contractions: (1) the contraction of the liquid on cooling from the pouring temperature to the freezing temperature; (2) the contraction associated with the change from the liquid state to the solid state; and (3) the contraction of the solid during cooling from the freezing temperature to room temperature. These are illustrated in Figure 3-1 where the contraction is evidenced by a reduction in the specific volume.

The contraction associated with the solidification of a pure metal, a compound, or an eutectic occurs at a fixed temperature as demonstrated in Figure 3-1a. Figure 3-1b shows the contraction resulting from the solidification of a liquid solution into a solid solution which occurs over a temperature range that is equal to the difference between the liquidus and the solidus temperatures.

Figure 3-1c illustrates the specific volume versus temperature for an AISI 1080 (eutectoid) steel during very slow cooling, and also during sufficiently fast cooling to form martensite. In addition to the contraction discussed, there is an expansion during the allotropic transformation that occurs in the solid state. On slow cooling, the transformation of austenite to pearlite at the lower critical temperature results in a volume expansion of about 0.3%. On fast cooling, austenite transforms to martensite, with about the same 0.3% volume increase, while cooling through the temperature range of 450 to 250°F.

The liquid shrinkage is the smallest of the three contractions, being about 0.5% for the common metals poured with the normal amount of superheat. The liquid shrinkage, as well as the solidification shrinkage, does not affect the pattern allowance because risers (reservoirs of liquid metal) are provided in the mold to feed liquid metal into the casting cavity during cooling and solidification. Thus, in a well-designed mold the solid metal while at the freezing temperature completely fills the mold cavity. The size of the riser needed is influenced by both the liquid and solidification shrinkages and by the area and volume of the casting.

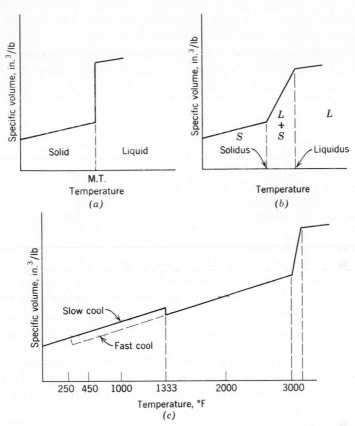

Figure 3-1. Specific volume temperature. (*a*) Pure materials, compounds, and eutectics. (*b*) Solid solutions. (*c*) AISI—1080 steel.

Table 3-1 lists the solidification and solid contraction and typical pattern shrinkage allowances for some common casting materials. The freezing shrinkage is greatest for the aluminum copper alloy, being 8.7%, and thus requires a large riser. The freezing shrinkage of cast iron is only 1.8%, and may be as low as 0% if the graphitic carbon content is greater than 3%. Since the riser feeds liquid metal into the mold cavity during the solidification of the casting, this contraction does not influence the pattern allowance.

The solid contraction of a material is obtained by multiplying the difference between its melting temperature and room temperature by its average coefficient of thermal expansion over the same temperature

TABLE 3-1.   Shrinkage and Pattern Shrinkage Allowance for
Some Common Metals

(Shrinkage is the percent of room temperature volume. Shrinkage allowance
is in./ft to the nearest $\frac{1}{32}$. Liquid shrinkage is about 0.5% with normal
superheat.)

Material	Solidification Shrinkage	Solid Shrinkage	Pattern Shrinkage Allowance
Aluminum	7.0	5.6	$\frac{3}{16}$
Aluminum, 8% Cu alloy	8.7	5.0	$\frac{5}{32}$
Aluminum, 10% Mg alloy	7.5	4.4	$\frac{5}{32}$
Aluminum, 12% Si alloy	3.5	4.0	$\frac{5}{32}$
Cast iron, gray	1.8	3.0	$\frac{1}{8}$
Cast iron (>3% graphite C)	0	3.0	$\frac{1}{8}$
Cast iron, malleable	5.0	6.0	$\frac{1}{4}$
Cast steel, low carbon	3.0	7.2	$\frac{1}{4}$
Copper	4.5	7.5	$\frac{3}{16}$
Copper tin (bronze)	5.5	6.0	$\frac{1}{4}$
Copper zinc (brass)	5.2	8.0	$\frac{3}{16}$

range. This is a linear contraction. To obtain the volume contraction
from small linear contractions, it is sufficiently accurate to simply
multiply by three. The solid shrinkage values listed in Table 3-1 were
obtained in this fashion.

The pattern shrinkage allowance is obtained by multiplying the
total solid contraction by 12 to get the contraction on an inch per foot
basis. This latter number is then converted to a fraction equal to the
nearest $\frac{1}{32}$. Thus for gray cast iron having an average coefficient of thermal expansion of 5×10^{-6} in./in./°F and an eutectic temperature of
about 2070°F, the linear contraction is 0.010in./in. or 0.12 in./ft. The
nearest fraction to 0.12 is $\frac{1}{8}$ and so the pattern shrinkage allowance for
cast iron is expressed as $\frac{1}{8}$ in./ft.

Typical values for pattern machining allowances for sand castings
are given in Table 3-2. These allowances indicate how much larger the
rough casting should be over the finished casting to allow sufficient
metal to insure that machining will "clean-up" the surfaces. This
machining allowance is added to all surfaces that are to be machined.
Thus a 10 in. external diameter on a finished gray iron casting would
require a $10\frac{3}{16}$ in. as cast diameter. Likewise a bore that is 10 in.
diameter when machined should be $9\frac{3}{4}$ in. diameter as cast.

TABLE 3-2. Typical Pattern Machining Allowances for Sand Casting

(The allowances are in inches per side. For internal surfaces such as bores, the allowance is about $\frac{1}{32}$ in. greater and is negative.)

	Overall Length of External Surfaces			
Material Cast	0 to 12 in.	12 in. to 24 in.	24 in. to 42 in.	42 in. to 60 in.
Aluminum alloys	$\frac{1}{16}$	$\frac{1}{8}$	$\frac{5}{32}$	$\frac{3}{16}$
Brass, bronze	$\frac{1}{16}$	$\frac{1}{8}$	$\frac{5}{32}$	$\frac{3}{16}$
Cast iron	$\frac{3}{32}$	$\frac{1}{8}$	$\frac{3}{16}$	$\frac{1}{4}$
Cast steel	$\frac{1}{8}$	$\frac{3}{16}$	$\frac{5}{16}$	$\frac{3}{8}$

Pattern draft is the taper that is intentionally placed on the pattern surfaces that are parallel to the direction in which the pattern is withdrawn to prevent the crumbling of the mold surfaces during the drawing operation. Figure 3-2 illustrates what happens when a pattern with and without draft is withdrawn from a sand mold. When no draft is present, the sand in contact with the pattern face is sheared and torn loose from the mold face, and the top edges crumble away. Some of the loose sand drops into the bottom of mold cavity and will result in a "dirty" casting being made.

The draft on average patterns varies between $\frac{1}{4}$ and 2 degrees, depending upon the method of molding, the sand mixture used as well as the design, and economic restrictions imposed on the casting. For a

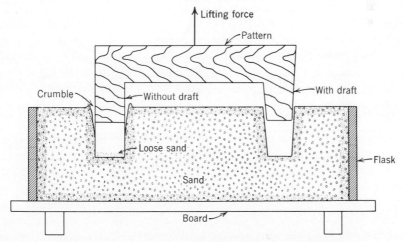

Figure 3-2. A pattern and mold with and without draft.

¼ degree draft, the pattern sides should be very smooth and the drawing should be done in a straight line with no side movement. A taper of
1 degree is quite sufficient for most patterns.

Core prints are the projections on a pattern and the corresponding
portion of the mold cavity that serve to firmly locate the core in the
mold during the pouring process. As stated before, one of the differences between a pattern and the resulting casting is that the former
may have core prints. A core print is not present on the casting because
a portion of the core fits into the core print cavity in the mold and
prevents the liquid metal from flowing into that portion of the original
mold cavity.

Figure 3-3 illustrates the differences between a casting and a
split loose-piece pattern that is used to make the casting. In the following section on molding, this same pattern is employed to demonstrate the steps in the making of a mold. All of the previously
mentioned characteristics of a pattern are summarized in this figure
and in the following discussion.

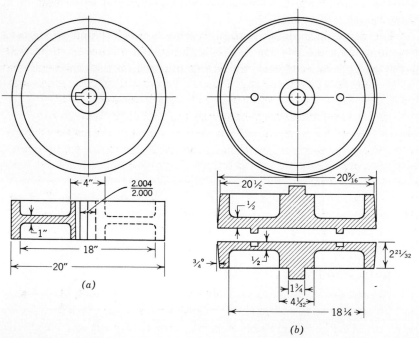

Figure 3-3. A casting and its loose-piece pattern. (*a*) Cast iron casting. (*b*) Wood
pattern.

The pattern is split about its midplane to facilitate molding. cope half has two dowel pins that mate with two guide holes in drag half of the pattern. Since the machined diameter of the casting 20 in., the outside diameter at the edge of the pattern is $20\frac{1}{2}$ in. This increase of $\frac{1}{2}$ in. is made up of $\frac{1}{4}$ in. shrinkage allowance and $\frac{1}{4}$ in. machining ($\frac{1}{8}$ in. on the radius) allowance. The maximum diameter of the pattern is $20\frac{9}{16}$ in.; the additional $\frac{1}{16}$ in. is due to the draft. Since the face is to be machined, the half thickness of the pattern rim is $2\frac{21}{32}$ in. The core print diameter, which is equal to the diameter of the core to be used, is $1\frac{3}{4}$ in., which allows $\frac{1}{8}$ in. per side for machining stock.

MOLDS

A mold is an assembly of two or more blocks of metal, or bonded refractory particles, with a primary cavity which is a negative of the desired part. It contains secondary cavities for pouring and channeling the liquid material into the primary cavity. If necessary, it has a large cylindrical cavity for storing the liquid material for "feeding" into the primary cavity during solidification when the specific volume of the material at the melting temperature is greater for the liquid than it is for the solid.

Metal molds are permanent in the sense that thousands of castings can be made from one mold. But molds made of bonded refractory particles, such as sand, can be used only once; therefore a new mold must be made for each casting. This is true not only for the green-sand mold, but also for the baked sand, shell, and investment molds.

Molds are identified by the following means: material used in their construction, such as green sand or plaster; the way the liquid is forced into the cavity, such as die casting or permanent mold; the way a mold is made, such as shell or investment. A description of each of the mold types follows, with a detailed procedure for making a green-sand mold given in order to focus separately on each of the components of a mold. An understanding of the functions of each of these components is necessary to understanding the characteristics of a cast material as well as the origin of defects in a cast part.

Green-Sand Molds

A green-sand mold is composed of a mixture of sand, clay, water, and an organic material such as wood flour. In regard to color, "green sand" is actually either black if it has been used previously or brown if it is a new mixture. It gets its descriptive name because the bonding agent that holds the sand and clay particles together is water. The

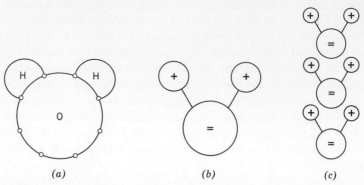

Figure 3-4. Polarization in a water molecule. (*a*) Structure illustrating two hydrogen atoms, each sharing two electrons with an oxygen atom. (*b*) Centers of charge. (*c*) Attraction between the O= pole of one molecule and the H+ of another molecule.

name "green sand" originated in the days when the word "green" was associated with the condition of wetness or freshness, as in the expression "green" lumber which referred to freshly cut boards before they were dried.

The manner in which the water bonds the sand and clay together can be explained on the basis of the crystalline structure of sand and clay. Quartz sand, SiO_2, and silicate rocks, $K_2O \cdot Al_2O_3 \cdot 6SiO_2$, have as a primary structural unit the SiO_4 tetrahedron in which the silicon atom lies interstitially within four closely packed oxygen atoms. These tetrahedra line up in a three-dimensional chainlike structure. Since the oxygen atoms are on the outside surface, an electrical unbalance or polarization is present at the surface. Water molecules have electrical dipoles because the centers of the positive charge and the negative charge do not coincide, as illustrated in Figure 3-4*b*. Because of this polarization, water molecules are adsorbed on the sand surface. And because of the attraction of opposite magnetic poles of water molecules as illustrated in Figure 3-4*c*, the grains of sand are "bonded" together by the mutual attractive forces between the water molecules adsorbed on one grain to those on another grain. This is actually a type of welding and is described as such in Chapter 4.

The crystalline structure of kaolinite clay $(Al_2O_3 \cdot 2SiO_2 \cdot 2H_2O)$ is an alternately stacked or layered structure of two individual sheet-type tetrahedron units. One of the sheets consists of tetrahedra composed of the OH radical, aluminum atoms, and oxygen atoms. The

alternate sheet consists of tetrahedra composed of oxygen atoms, the
OH radical, and silicon atoms.

Each double layer of tetrahedra sheets consists of five parallel
planes, each plane containing one type of atoms, except the center
plane which contains both oxygen atoms and the OH radical. Figure
3-5a illustrates this layered structure where one surface consists of a
layer of OH radicals which has a negative charge of unity and the
opposite surface is a layer of oxygen atoms which has a negative
charge of four.

Water molecules can adsorb on both surfces of the clay particles
because of their magnetic dipoles and thus "bond" the clay particles
together as illustrated in Figure 3-5b.

The clay particles are colloidal in size, that is, they cannot be
seen with the ordinary optical microscope. The thickness of a clay
particle is about 1.5×10^{-6} mm. The clay particles are platelike in

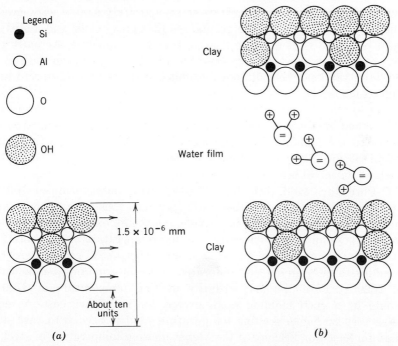

Figure 3-5. Layered structure of kaolite clay. (*a*) Five planes within each
sheet. (*b*) Bonding of two clay particles with a water film.

shape, having a width and breadth approximately 10 to 100 times the thickness. For such small-sized particles the surface area to mass ratio is extremely large, and consequently the "bond" strength of clay is greater than that of the much larger sand grains.

Clay moistened with water exhibits a high degree of plasticity because the individual platelets of clay can slide with respect to each other over the intervening film of moisture. If forces act on the two clay platelets in Figure 3-5b such that shear stresses are induced in the water film, the platelets can readily slide with respect to each other.

Green Sand Preparation. Green molding sand is a mixture of the following ingredients, on a weight basis: 68 to 86% sand; 10 to 20% clay; 3 to 6% water, 1 to 6% additives such as wood flour, dextrin, sea coal, and silica flour. These percentages are for gray iron molding sand and may vary slightly for steel and nonferrous castings. Each of these ingredients is briefly described, and their function in the mixture is explained as follows:

Sand. The two types of sand used for making molds are natural and synthetic. A *natural* sand is one having a mixture of sand grains and clay, as mined from the ground, so that only water and additives need be added to it to make it satisfactory for molding. Actually the clay content of most natural sands is slightly higher than desired so that new sand can be continuously added to the used sand to replenish that which is lost.

A *synthetic* sand is one having a specified type of sand grain and a specified type of clay as well as the water and other additives all mixed in the foundry. Synthetic sands have the advantage that sand grains of specified composition and properties can be selected on the basis of the metal being cast.

Pure silica sand, SiO_2, has a high melting temperature of 3140°F and consequently is a desirable sand. However, most silicate rocks also contain in a combined form iron oxide, potassium oxide, and aluminum oxide. These impurities lower the melting temperature of the sand. For example, it is evident in Figure 3-6 that when 5.5% alumina, Al_2O_3, is added to SiO_2 an eutectic is formed that has a melting temperature of 2820°F. Pure alumina, with its melting temperature of 3720°F would be a good molding sand, except for its higher cost. A more refractory or higher melting temperature sand is needed to cast steel than for cast iron because of the higher melting temperature of steel.

Sand is used as a molding material because it is plentiful (or cheap), and has good refractory characteristics as well as good molding properties. The molding properties of a sand are influenced by the

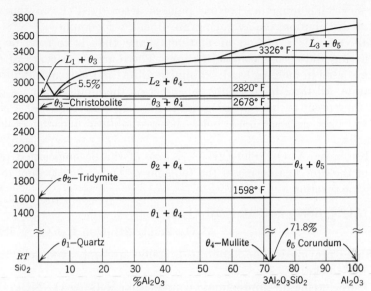

Figure 3-6. Al$_2$O$_3$-SiO$_2$ equilibrium phase diagram. θ_1—quartz, SiO$_2$. θ_2—tridymite, SiO$_2$. θ_3—christobolite, SiO$_2$. θ_4—mullite, 3Al$_2$O$_3$·2SiO$_2$. θ_5—corundum, Al$_2$O$_3$. (After Bowen and Grieg, *J. Am. Soc.* **7**, 243, 1924.)

shape of the sand particles, which vary from smooth round grains to sharp angular ones. These properties are discussed below in more detail.

The grain size of the particles, and especially the distribution of grain size in a particular sand mix, influences the mold properties. If all the sand particles in a mix are the same size, then the bulk density is low and the permeability (the ability of gas to flow through the mixture) is high because of the voids between the sand particles. Angular grains that are randomly oriented will have a lower bulk density than spherical grains. A sand mixture containing grains of all sizes from the largest that can be used to grains that are only microns in diameter will have a bulk density that approaches the true density of the sand. In this case the permeability of the mixture will be very low.

The size and distribution of the particles in a molding sand are determined by a standard screening test specified as the AFS (American Foundrymen's Society) sieve analysis. In this test 50 grams of the dried sand are placed on the top of a stack of 11 sieves in which the top one has 4 openings per linear inch and the bottom one has 270. The stack is shaken for 15 min and then the weight of sand retained on each sieve, including the bottom pan, is determined. From this frequency distribution, the average grain fineness is computed.

Clay. Clay is a colloid of platelet shape that is formed by the weathering and decomposition of rocks. There are three types of clay that are used in molding sand: kaolinite, illite, and montmorillonite or bentonite. All three have a different effect on the mold properties. And since they occur in different geographic locations, the clay that a given foundry uses depends upon both the availability and the molding properties.

Kaolinite, $Al_2O_3 \cdot 2SiO_2 \cdot 2H_2O$, is one of the decomposition products of the slow weathering of the feldspar orthoclase, according to the following reaction.

$$K_2O \cdot Al_2O_3 \cdot 6SiO_2 + CO_2 + 2H_2O \rightarrow$$
$$Al_2O_3 \cdot 2SiO_2 \cdot 2H_2O + K_2CO_3 + 4SiO_2.$$

As stated previously, the kaolinite platelets are approximately 1.5×10^{-6} mm thick.

Illite, having the approximate composition $K_2O \cdot Al_2O_3 \cdot SiO_2 \cdot H_2O$, is formed from the weathering of mica rocks which are complex silicates of Al_2O_3, K_2O, MgO, FeO, and Li_2O. The particle size of illite clay is about the same as kaolinite clay, and has similar molding properties.

Montmorillonite, or bentonite as it is more frequently called in the foundry industry, is also formed from the weathering of volcanic or igneous rocks. Its general composition is $MgO \cdot Al_2O_3 \cdot SiO_2 \cdot H_2O$. There are two types of montmorillonite: western bentonite, typical of that found in South Dakota, which contains some sodium; Southern bentonite, typical of that found in Mississippi, which contains some calcium.

One of the significant differences between the bentonite clay and the kaolinite clay is in their crystalline structure. The bentonite clay has some $Mg(OH)_2$ tetrahedra replacing $Al(OH)_3$ on the surface layer of the kaolinite illustrated in Figure 3-5, plus the calcium or sodium. The thickness of the platelets of the bentonite clay is about 1×10^{-6} mm. Because of this finer particle size with its greater surface area to mass ratio, the amount of bentonite clay needed in a molding sand is only about 4%, whereas 12% kaolinite is needed for the same strength. A smaller amount of water is required to obtain a given degree of plasticity when bentonite clay is used. That is a desirable feature since less steam is formed when the molten metal is poured into the mold, permitting a lower permeability in the molding sand.

The refractoriness of the clay is influenced by both the size of the particles and their composition. Since melting occurs first at the surface, and at grain boundaries of polycrystalline materials, the coarser particles will have a smaller amount of liquid present when the clay is heated for a short time to the minimum temperature at which a liquid phase is present.

The effect that the composition has on the refractoriness of clay is evident in the equilibrium phase diagram of Al_2O_3-SiO_2 presented in Figure 3-6. Although all the clays contain combined water, as does portland cement, the clay dissociates between 700 and 1000°F and all the water of hydration is evolved. For kaolinite clay, this dehydrated mineral consists of only Al_2O_3 and SiO_2 and so the phase diagram of Figure 3-6 is applicable in this case.

The dehydrated mineral consists of 46% Al_2O_3 and 54% SiO_2. Below 1598°F two phases exist, namely quartz (SiO_2) and mullite which has the composition $3Al_2O_3 \cdot 2SiO_2$. Above 1598°F the quartz changes to a different crystalline structure, that of tridymite. This transformation occurs with a considerable increase in specific volume which tends to cause cracks in the material and is the reason pure quartz is not widely used commercially. At 2820°F an eutectic consisting of $5\frac{1}{2}$% Al_2O_3 is formed, so if kaolinite is heated above this temperature, some liquid will be present. This limits the temperature to which a sand mold may be heated during the casting process.

Clay, in combination with the temper water defined in the next paragraph, is the bonding agent in a green sand. Although moist sand particles do adhere to each other slightly, by coating them with moist clay the strength (tensile and shear) of the sand mix is increased about threefold.

Temper Water. Temper water is the water added to molding sand to give it the needed strength and plasticity. The way in which water bonds together the particles of sand and clay was described in the previous section under green sand molds.

Dry clay is powdery and has no tensile strength or plasticity. If a little (1 to 3%) water is added to the clay, the particles will adhere to each other and if the clay is "worked" into shape it will have a tensile strength of a few psi. Although it can be plastically worked by squeezing, it does not flow easily and relatively large pressure has to be exerted on it. When 4 to 10% of water is added to clay it reaches its maximum strength. It can then be plastically worked more easily and still will not stick to the surfaces squeezing it. When still more water is added to the clay it becomes "sticky" and behaves as a viscous fluid. In this condition it is referred to as a "slip." Such a mixture is used for coating the pattern in the "investment" casting process.

When a green molding sand has the proper amount of water added to it to give a high strength with sufficient plasticity, the sand is said to be "at temper" or "tempered."

Additives. Although sand, clay, and water are the basic ingredients required to make a green-sand mold, other materials must frequently be added to the mixture to make a satisfactory casting. These additives may be necessary to give a good surface finish on the casting or to eliminate casting defects that arise from either the expansion of the molding sand as it is heated or the contraction of the casting as it cools in the mold. Descriptions of the more common of these additives follow.

Cereal. Foundry cereal is finely ground corn flour or corn starch. Corn starch has a strength that is greater than that of the clay in a molding sand; so a small amount of it is added to increase the strength of the sand. Since the cereal is organic, it is "burned out" when hot iron comes in contact with it and the resulting void spaces permit the heated sand particles to expand into them without buckling the mold surface. Because of the low density of the cereal, about 1% is generally sufficient.

Wood Flour. Wood flour is ground wood particles or other cellulose materials such as grain hulls. It serves the same purpose as cereal except that it does not increase the green strength as much. When it is required, about 1% is added.

Silica Flour. Unlike the cereal and wood flour, silica is not an organic material, but as the name implies it is very fine silica. It is generally mixed with about twice as much conventional molding sand to make a "facing" sand that is used to surround the pattern. Because of its higher cost it is not used to make the backsides of the mold. Because of its purity the silica flour increases the hot strength of the mold face. And because of the fine particle size it improves the surface finish of the resulting casting.

Sea Coal. Sea coal is finely ground soft coal. It is added to molding sands used to make ferrous castings. The sea coal reduces the adherence of sand particles to the casting, thus making the cleaning of the casting easier. It also improves the surface finish of the casting. And because of the small particle size, it also increases the strength of the molding sand. It is added in amounts up to 8%. Other carbon rich materials such as finely ground coke, asphalt, or pitch are sometimes substituted for sea coal.

Molding Sand Properties. The success of the casting process depends in great part on the making of a satisfactory mold. To make satisfactory green-sand molds on a production basis requires that the molding properties of the sand be controlled. The important molding properties are strength, permeability, deformation, flowability, and refractoriness. These are briefly discussed.

Two standard specimens are used to determine all of these molding sand properties. A 2 in. diameter $\times$ 2 in. high cylindrical specimen is used for determining the room temperature properties, and a $1\frac{1}{8}$ in. diameter $\times$ 2 in. high cylinder is used for the elevated temperature testing to determine the "hot" properties. The latter size was selected because its cross-sectional area is 1 sq in.

These specimens are prepared by ramming the sand under standard conditions. These conditions consist of placing a weighted sample of sand in a hardened steel cylinder of the proper diameter and placing a piston or cap at both ends. Then a weight of specified size is dropped from a specified height onto the piston. This is repeated twice for a total of three blows.

Strength. Although the strength of the bond is discussed in terms of tensile and shear strength, the strength of molding sand is determined by means of a compression test. The strength of the molding sand is the value of compressive stress that causes the test cylinder to break when loaded axially, and is generally less than 100 psi. The testing is done in a special apparatus that gradually increases the load and simultaneously indicates the change in length or deformation of the specimen.

To determine the *green strength* of the sand, the specimen is tested immediately after ramming before any of the water dries out. The *dry compressive strength* of the sand is determined by loading the specimen at room temperature after it has been thoroughly dried at 225°F. The *hot strength* of the sand is determined by applying the load on the specimen in an oven after the specimen is heated to the specified test temperature.

Deformation. The deformation of molding sand is the reduction in length of the standard specimen at the time it fractures during the compression test, and is expressed in thousandths of an inch. The *green deformation* is that deformation associated with the green strength, and the *hot deformation* is the deformation of the hot specimen at failure.

Permeability. The permeability of molding sand is the measure of its ability to permit air to flow through it. In a sense it is an indication of the porosity of the molding sand. The permeability number is the quantity of air in cubic centimeters per minute that will pass through a specimen 1 cm high and 1 sq cm cross-sectional area under a pressure of 1 gm/sq cm. The permeability test is conducted on a 2 in. $\times$ 2 in.

standard specimen previously mentioned while it is still in the ramming cylinder immediately after ramming. The permeability is also determined in the "shop" by measuring the rate of air flow through the sand under a specified pressure and through a standard orifice.

Flowability. The flowability of a molding sand is a measure of its ability to flow around and over a pattern during ramming. Flowability is determined in the same apparatus that the 2 in. $\times$ 2 in. specimen is made. Instead of taking the specimen out of the cylinder after the third drop of the weight, the weight is dropped two more times on the sample. The height of the cylinder is measured after the fourth drop and after the fifth drop. The flowability is reported on an arbitrary scale in which the flowability is 100% if the difference in heights is zero and the flowability is 0% if the difference is 0.1 in. It means simply that if a molding sand has 100% flowability, then only four blows by the weight are needed to compact it to its apparent maximum density.

Refractoriness. Refractoriness of a molding sand is a measure of its ability to remain solid as a function of both the temperature it is subjected to and the liquid metal it is in contact with. Refractoriness is greatly dependent upon the purity of the sand particles.

Figure 3-7 summarizes the effect of the water content upon the molding properties of green sand. For this particular sand-clay ratio, $7\frac{1}{2}$ to 8% water should be used since both a high permeability and a high flowability are desirable.

It is interesting to note how low the permeability is for a dry water-clay mixture. This is because the dry clay particles, being much smaller than the sand particles, nearly fill completely what would be the void spaces between the sand particles. Therefore the flow of air through the mix is very low. (If no clay were present, the air flow through the sand would be very high.) However, when the proper amount of water ($7\frac{1}{2}$% in this case) is added, it is adsorbed on both the clay and sand particles. This results in the clay now forming a coating over the surface of the sand particles. In this condition, the sand particles are slightly further apart than when the mix was dry and also the clay no longer fills the voids between the particles. Thus the permeability is high. However, upon the addition of more water, the water begins to fill the voids and the permeability decreases.

Mold Preparation. The sequence of operations performed in the making of a green sand mold is outlined below. These details are given here because the reader will then be able to understand more clearly exactly what a mold is regardless of whether it be of the permanent type or expendable type. The reasons for selecting the green-sand

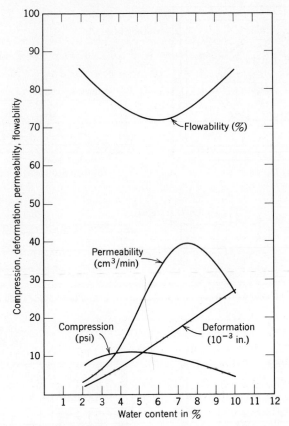

Figure 3-7. The effect of moisture on molding sand
properties.

mold as the subject to illustrate the mold details are twofold. First,
green-sand molds are made in tremendously greater numbers than are
any of the others, partly because they can be used only once. Second,
the "molding" of sand into a mold is much simpler and more easily
demonstrated than is the "machining" of a metallic permanent mold.

Figure 3-8 illustrates the sequence of operations performed in
making the mold to cast the gray iron wheel of Figure 3-3. A loose
piece split pattern is used for this example on the basis that only a
few castings are to be made.

The first steps in making of the mold are shown in Figure 3-8a.
The drag half of the pattern (the half with dowel holes rather than
the dowel pins) is placed with the split face down on a flat bottom

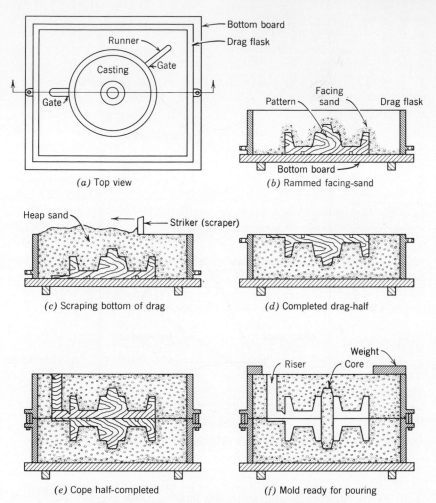

Figure 3-8. The construction of a green-sand mold.

board or mold plate, and the drag half of a flask is also placed on the plate with the lugs containing the locating holes near the plate. Both the bottom board and the flask should be larger than the pattern so that several inches of sand surround the pattern on all sides. In addition, they must be large enough so that if the gating and risering is on the side rather than on the top of the mold cavity, which is normally the case, sufficient space is provided for them on one or more sides.

In Figure 3-8a, patterns to form the gates and runners are in position with the casting pattern. As an alternative, the gate and runner patterns could be placed in the cope half rather than the drag half of the mold; or else the gates and runners could be "cut" by hand after separating the two halves if they were molded without these auxiliary patterns.

The second step as shown in (b) consists of dusting a parting compound such as nonwetting talc over the pattern and bottom board to facilitate both the removal of the pattern and the separation of the two mold halves. Following this a layer of facing sand (used sand to which additional clay has been added) is riddled into the flask to cover the pattern. The facing sand is "peened" or packed into the corners of the pattern and the mold board to insure that the mold cavity will be well defined after the pattern is withdrawn.

The third step, shown in (c), consists of the following operations: filling the drag half of the flask with sand; compacting the sand by ramming to obtain the proper strength and permeability (if the molding is done on a machine, the compacting is done by jolting, vibrating or squeezing); scraping (frequently called striking) the excess sand off the top (actually the bottom of the drag) to level it to the same height as the flask. If the permeability of the sand mold is considered to be too low so that the gases cannot flow through it rapidly enough, vent holes are made in the mold by forcing a $\frac{1}{8}$ in. diameter wire into the mold from the back side, but not all the way through to the pattern, for the gases to flow through.

The operations performed in the fourth step are: placing a second bottom board or plate on the molded drag half, and clamping it if the mold is too heavy to be turned over conveniently by hand; turning the mold over 180° and removing the original bottom board. The mold now appears as in Figure 3-8d.

In the fifth step, the cope flask is mounted onto the drag half; the cope half of the pattern is properly positioned over the drag half; the riser and pouring sprue patterns are placed over the gates.

The second and third steps are repeated on the cope half of the pattern.

In the sixth step, a pouring basin is formed adjacent to the sprue, and then the riser and sprue patterns are withdrawn. The sprue pattern is tapered not so much as to obtain draft but rather to have a decreasing cross-sectional area corresponding to the increase in velocity of the liquid as it flows down the sprue hole. This is done to prevent turbulent flow which would draw in bubbles of air along with the liquid.

The cope is temporarily separated from the drag while the patterns are removed. If cores are to be used, as is true in this case, they are properly located in the core prints of the drag, and then the cope is gently positioned over the drag. If the lifting force on the cope due to the hydrostatic pressure of the liquid in the mold cavity is greater than the weight of the cope, the cope must either be clamped to the drag or else weights must be placed on top of the cope.

The vertical force tending to lift the cope is the sum of all the projected areas of liquid in contact with the cope times the hydrostatic pressure acting on each of these areas. This relationship can be expressed as

$$\mathbf{F}_v = A_c h_c \rho_m + A_r h_r \rho_m$$

where ρ_m is the density of the liquid metal, A_c and h_c are the projected area and effective head of one part of the mold cavity (the casting cavity for example), and $A_r h_r$ are the corresponding features of another part of the mold cavity (the runners and gates for example).

The effective head is the vertical distance in inches between the top of the cope and the surface of the cope in contact with and above the liquid metal. The lifting force so calculated is the static lifting force. Since the liquid metal during pouring has momentum, the general foundry practice is to double the static lifting force to obtain the dynamic lifting force.

This vertical lifting force is opposed by the weight of the cope, which is approximately equal to the volume of sand in the cope times its density which is 0.06 lb/in.[3] The weight that must be added on top of the cope to prevent it from floating on the liquid metal is the differ-

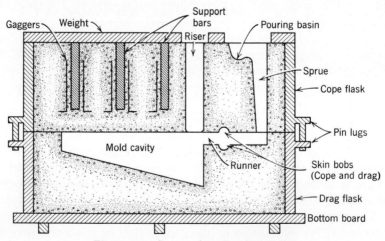

Figure 3-9. Support bars in a large cope.

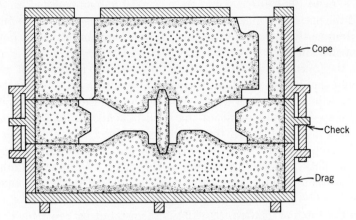

Figure 3-10.   A three-part sand mold.

ence between the dynamic lifting force and the weight of the cope. The sketch in Figure 3-8*f* shows the mold completely assembled and weighted and ready for pouring.

When large sand molds are made, the sand would drop out of the cope half when it is raised to remove the pattern unless some support is provided within the cope flask. Figure 3-9 illustrates two types of such support, namely support bars and gaggers. The support bars are attached to both ends of the cope flask but do not extend to the bottom in the event that part of the casting is to be in the cope. If the bars have a thicker section at the bottom they give more support to the sand. Gaggers are L-shaped wires of $\frac{1}{4}$ in. to $\frac{1}{2}$ in. diameter that are placed in the cope to help support the sand as illustrated in the sketch. The gaggers are generally dipped in a clay slurry to improve the bonding of the mold sand to the gagger.

Sometimes a casting has reentrant surfaces which make it more convenient to use a three or more part mold rather than a two part mold. The sections of the mold between the cope and drag are referred to as *cheeks*. Figure 3-10 illustrates how a cheek is utilized to cast a wheel having a groove in the rim.

Molding Machines. The hand-molding process just described is suitable when the number of molds to be made is small. But when a large quantity of molds are required, the molding is done on a machine. Molding machines are quite simple in construction in comparison to the machine tools used in forming and machining, and consequently are fairly inexpensive. However, they greatly reduce the time required to make a mold. The three common methods of compacting the sand around the pattern to make a mold are: jolting, squeezing, and slinging. Quite frequently jolting and squeezing mechanisms are incorporated into one machine.

In the jolting method the pattern and flask are mounted on a mold plate and the flask is filled with sand. The entire assembly is raised a small amount by means of an air cylinder and is then dropped against a fixed stop. The compacting of the sand is achieved by the deceleration forces acting on it. In the squeezing method, a pressure plate is placed on top of the sand in the flask in such a manner that it does not touch the flask. A force, by means of an air or hydraulic cylinder, is applied to the pressure plate which causes the sand to flow around the pattern.

In the slinging method the sand is thrown out by centrifugal force from a rapidly rotating single bladed impeller and directed over the pattern in the flask. This type of compacting results in a mold having a more uniform density throughout than does the jolting or squeezing method. The molding machines employing this method of compacting are called sandslingers. Sandslingers are generally used only in the making of large molds.

The simplest of the molding machines is the jolt machine. It consists of a flat table attached to the end of the piston rod of a short stroke pneumatic cylinder. During jolting, the table is raised about 2 in. and then dropped with no cushioning at the bottom of the stroke. About 25 to 50 drops are needed to compact the sand, and the average machine operates at about 200 strokes per minute. During molding, the flask and pattern are not clamped to the table.

The jolt squeeze machine is the next simplest. It is similar in appearance to the jolt machine, but in addition it has a vertical column rising above and behind the table to which is fastened a rigid support that overhangs the table. In addition, the base contains two concentric air cylinders: the smaller one to provide the jolting and the larger one to squeeze the mold against the overhead support. On this type of machine the pattern can be attached to a match plate, and both the cope and drag halves of the mold can be made either on one machine or on two separate machines.

The jolt squeeze strip or jolt squeeze vibrate molding-machine is similar to the jolt squeeze machine except that it has an air hose attached to the match plate so that the pattern can be vibrated while it is being withdrawn from the mold. Figure 3-11 is a photograph of this type of molding machine. As illustrated here the operator has completed the drag half of the mold and is about to squeeze the cope half.

Figure 3-11. Jolt-squeeze vibrate-molding machine. (Courtesy International Molding Machine Co.)

The match plate, with its attached air hose, is assembled between the cope and drag. On this size and type of machine the operator raises and turns over the mold halves by hand.

The jolt squeeze rollover draw-type of molding machine is required when the size of the mold is too large to be turned over by hand. They are generally not used for making the smaller molds since the manual operation is faster. Figure 3-12 shows this type of machine. Only a half of the mold is made at one time on this type of machine. The mold is compacted by jolting on the table in the foreground to which it is clamped. The table is raised and the mold is rolled over the center column onto the roller table in back of the column. The pattern is stripped from the mold and returned to the jolting table while the

Figure 3-12. Jolt-clamp rollover draw-molding machine. (Courtesy SPO, Inc.)

completed mold is rolled onto a conveyor that transports it to the assembly and pouring area.

In all these molding machines, the sand can either be shoveled into the flask by hand or deposited into the mold by pneumatic or mechanical conveyors.

Other Types of Expendable Molds

The other types of expendable molds will be described briefly since their design features are similar to those of the green-sand mold which were already discussed in considerable detail.

Dry Sand Molds

Dry sand molds are basically green-sand molds that are baked in an oven at 225 to 500°F for several hours. Consequently, the operations performed in making a dry sand mold are identical to those described above. The sand mixture that is used for dry molds contains 1 or 2% cereal flour and or 1 to 2% pitch, whereas a green molding sand may not contain these additives. These additives increase the hot strength due to the evaporation of the water as well as by the oxidation and polymerization of the pitch. The dry sand molds reduce the incidence of the casting defects such as gas holes, blows, or porosity which occur because of the presence of steam generated in the mold.

Cores and Core Sand Molds

A stronger mold can be obtained by the addition of an oil, such as linseed or soybean oil, or a thermosetting plastic to a green-sand mixture so that during the baking or curing, the resin or oil oxidizes and polymerizes around the sand particles, thus bonding them together. The strength of the polymerized resin is greater than that of the pitch used in the dry sand molds; consequently this type of molding sand is used to make cores. Cores require a higher strength because they generally are subjected to bending forces produced by the hydrostatic pressure of the liquid trying to lift the core. The baking times and temperatures are similar to those used with dry sand.

Shell Molds

A fairly skilled molder is required to make all of the previously described molds. Thus the combination of a high labor rate and a long molding time results in a high mold cost. A process developed in Germany in the 1940's and introduced into United States industries in the early 1950's makes it possible to mass produce sand molds having a smoother surface with a shorter molding time and with an unskilled laborer as an operator. In fact, the process can be completely automated, eliminating the operator. This process is called shell molding since the finished mold consists of a "shell" of bonded sand about $\frac{1}{4}$ in. thick around the mold cavity.

The molding sand for a shell mold consists of only dry silica sand and approximately 6% by weight of a thermal setting plastic. The sand and resin may be a simple mechanical mixture of the two ingredients, or the resin may be present as a thin coating around each sand particle. To obtain the sand in this latter condition, the resin is dissolved in an alcohol and then mixed with the sand. When the alcohol evaporates, it leaves the sand particles coated with the dry resin. New sand is used to make each mold since it is cheaper to purchase the sand than it is to "reclaim" the bonded sand.

The pattern for a shell mold resembles the match plate pattern described above for green-sand molding. However, the pattern is always made of metal such as aluminum because it is heated to 400 to 600°F during molding, and the match plate itself is considerably more complicated and expensive because it must contain stripper-pins to separate the bonded shell from the pattern. In reality, a match plate pattern for a shell mold resembles a die casting die having a protruding "cavity" rather than a recessed one.

The sequence of operations in making a shell mold, after the pattern is made, is as follows. An open-topped box which is mounted so that it can easily be inverted is partially filled with a dry sand-resin mixture. The pattern and its mounting plate, which is kept at a temperature of 400 to 550°F, is clamped onto the dump box. The dump box is inverted and the dry sand mixture falls onto the plate and pattern. The resin softens and begins to polymerize when it is in contact with the hot metal. It takes about 15 seconds for the heat to flow sufficiently into the sand mixture to cause polymerization to begin at a distance of $\frac{1}{4}$ in. from the surface. The dump box is now righted and all of the sand except for the $\frac{1}{4}$ in. heated layer falls back into the box. The match plate is unclamped from the dump box and placed in a heating chamber maintained at a temperature of about 550°F for another half minute. This heating results in a complete polymerization of the resin as well as reheating the pattern. The shell of bonded sand is stripped from the match plate and pattern by the ejector pins as soon as the assembly is withdrawn from the oven, and the shell is conveyed to the pouring area.

This shell constitutes only one-half of the mold. When two such halves are placed together, they make a complete mold including all the gates, runners and risers. For small castings, the molds are simply held together with mechanical or spring clamps during the pouring operation. But for large castings the shells are placed in flasks and dry, loose sand or shot is packed around the shells to prevent them from breaking because of the hydrostatic pressure. Figure 3-13 is a photograph of a three-cavity shell mold in both the open position before assembly and after pouring.

Investment Molds

An investment mold is one made from a slurry of very fine silica (silica flour), ethyl silicate and either water or alcohol. The advantage of this type of mold is that castings can be produced that contain very fine detail, good surface finish, and close tolerances out of high melting temperature metals. For this reason the process is sometimes referred to as "precision casting." Die castings have equivalent, if not better, surface finishes and accuracies but are restricted to low melting temperature metals. Because the labor cost in making an investment casting is high, the process is competitive only for those metals that are difficult to machine or form by plastic deformation.

Figure 3-13. Photograph of a shell mold. At left, two halves open to show mold cavities, riser and locating surface. At right, mold assembled and poured. (*a*) Sprue. (*b*) Riser.

The investment casting process is also unique in that not only is the mold used only once, but a new pattern must be made for each mold. The patterns are generally made of wax, but in some cases a thermoplastic plastic is used. The patterns themselves are cast in metal molds or dies. But since the pattern material has such a low melting temperature, the dies to mold them can be made of easy-to-fabricate metals such as aluminum or zinc base alloys.

The sequence of operations in making an investment casting is briefly outlined.

The wax pattern is attached to runners and a sprue. If the pattern is small, several of them can be attached to a common sprue to form a "tree." This pattern assembly is then dipped into the investment slurry, withdrawn, and dried. This leaves a very thin layer of fine-grained silica over the pattern. This operation may be repeated several times to increase the thickness of the coating. The coated pattern is then placed into an empty container that is just slightly larger than the pattern assembly and a thicker, coarser slurry is poured into the flask to completely surround the pattern assembly. The mold is then allowed to dry and harden for several hours.

The next step is to remove the pattern from the mold. This is very simply done by warming the mold until the pattern melts. If the mold is not inverted so that the wax flows out through the pouring sprue, the molten wax will seep through the walls of the mold. The investment process is sometimes called "the lost wax" process because of this characteristic.

After the pattern has been removed, the mold is slowly heated to a higher temperature to drive off all of the moisture and volatile matter. In some cases, the mold is heated to a temperature approaching the freezing temperature of the metal being cast. This is done to permit the casting of thinner sections or to reduce the thermal stresses in the mold and casting.

High quality, precision castings are made by melting the metal and pouring it into the mold all within a vacuum chamber. This eliminates the possibility of gas porosity within the casting, but it does not eliminate shrinkage porosity.

Plaster Molds

Plaster molds are made by pouring a slurry of plaster of paris (the half-hydrate of gypsum, $CaSO_4 \cdot \frac{1}{2}H_2O$) over either a wax or a permanent pattern. The half-hydrate combines with $1\frac{1}{2}$ molecular weights of water to form the crystalline hydrated gypsum $CaSO_4 \cdot 2H_2O$ in a matter of minutes. The pattern is then separated from the mold, and the mold is thoroughly dried, and usually preheated, before pouring. Since the plaster is not as refractory as silica sand, these molds are not used for high melting temperature metals. But since fine details can be reproduced by this process, it is frequently used in making jewelry.

Nonexpendable Molds

There are two common casting processes that employ nonexpendable molds, permanent mold and die casting. The *permanent mold* process is the casting process in which the liquid is poured into a metal mold under the force of gravity. The *die casting* process is the casting process in which the liquid is forced under high pressure into a metal mold where it solidifies. There are many similarities and many differences between these two processes, which are now discussed.

The permanent mold process is used to make cast iron, and occasionally nonferrous castings. Permanent mold castings are competitive price-wise to sand castings and generally have a better surface finish and tolerance. The molds are usually made of a heat resistant cast iron, and are air-cooled by the use of fins. The mold cavity is sprayed with an oil-carbon silica mixture before each injection of the molten metal. The casting is withdrawn from the mold as soon as it has solidified to prevent hot tears.

The die casting process is used to make castings of low melting temperature metals, particularly aluminum and zinc base alloys. Iron is not cast by this process. When plastics are cast by this process, it is referred to as injection molding. The surface finish and tolerances obtained by this process are the best of all the casting processes. The molds, more frequently called dies, are made of medium carbon, low-alloy tool steel, and are water-cooled during use to prolong their life as well as to shorten the solidification and casting time. Since the liquid is forced into the die cavity under high pressure, much thinner sections can be cast by this process than by the permanent mold or green sand processes.

Figure 3-14 is a photograph of a hot chamber type of die casting machine. The square box on the right end of the machine houses a gas-heated melting pot in which is a gooseneck type of piston pump that forces the liquid into the die cavity. On the extreme left end are

Figure 3-14. A hot chamber die casting machine. The gas-heated melting pot is on the right, and the hydraulic pump and accumulators are on the left. (Courtesy Kux Machine Co.)

the hydraulic pump and accumulators that actuate the movable platten and the injection piston.

Die casting machines are classified as either hot chamber or cold chamber, depending upon the method of transporting the liquid from the melting pot to the sprue of the die. These two methods are illustrated in Figure 3-15. The advantage of the cold chamber process is that the liquid metal is in contact with the injecting cylinder walls for

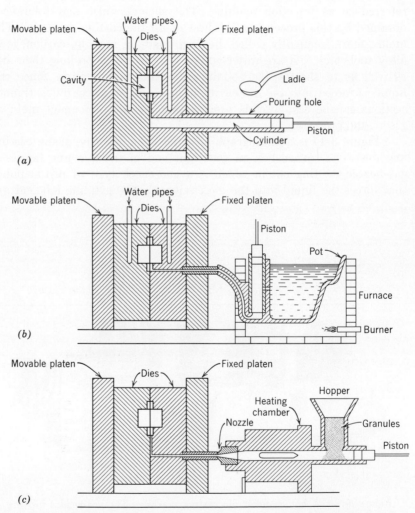

Figure 3-15. Sketches of die casting processes. (*a*) Cold chamber. (*b*) Hot chamber. (*c*) Injection molding.

only a short time. This prolongs the life of the cylinder when high melting temperature metals that also alloy with iron, such as aluminum or zinc, are used. The advantage of the hot chamber process is that it is more completely or more simply automated.

The operating cycle of the cold chamber type of machine is as follows: the dies are closed and locked together under high pressure; enough liquid for one casting and its runners is ladled into the heated injection cylinder; the injection piston forces the liquid into the die cavity; the liquid solidifies, the die is opened, and the cast part is ejected. The cycle time is approximately one minute. The operating cycle of the hot chamber machine is similar to that of the cold chamber machine described except that the liquid is not "ladled" into the injection cylinder but is automatically fed in by means of a submerged piston-pump.

Miscellaneous Casting Processes

There are many specialized casting processes that are used in industry to achieve certain geometrical features or economical advantages. Some of these are now discussed.

Centrifugal Castings. Centrifugal castings are made in sand or permanent molds that are rotated during the time the casting solidifies either to make a hollow casting or a casting in which the less dense nonmetallic inclusions are segregated near the center of rotation. To make a hollow part, the axis of rotation is at the center of the casting. However, solid parts can be made by having all the casting on one side of the axis of rotation. In fact, several castings can be made simultaneously in one mold having several cavities. The advantages of this process are twofold: by making the part hollow, the material cost is less and no core is required; a more dense casting can be produced.

Slush Casting. Slush castings are made by pouring the liquid into open-top permanent molds and inverting the mold after a thin layer of liquid has solidified on the mold surfaces to allow the remaining liquid in the center portion of the cavity to flow out. This results in a shell-like casting which is widely used for ornamental objects such as lamp bases, sculpture figures, and toys. Low melting temperature materials such as tin, lead, and zinc are used.

Frozen Mercury. The frozen mercury process is a process in which the pattern is frozen mercury. The pattern is made by pouring mercury into permanent molds that are cooled below the freezing point of mercury. In other respects, the process is similar to other investment processes.

TABLE 3-3. Summary of the Casting Processes

Characteristic	Sand Green and Baked	Shell	Permanent	Die Casting	Investment
			Type of Mold		
Pattern Material	Wood or metal	Metal	Cast iron or steel	Steel	Wax or plastic
Materials cast	All common metals	All common metals	Melting temp., < 2500°F	Melting temp., < 1500°F	High melting temp.
Labor cost	Medium	Low	Low	Low	High
Equipment cost	Low	Medium	Medium	High	Medium
Economical tolerance[1] (across parting)	±$\frac{1}{16}$ in. ferrous ±$\frac{3}{32}$ in. Al, Mg	±0.030	±$\frac{3}{32}$ in. ferrous ±0.020 nf.	±0.010	±0.010
Minimum tolerance[2] (in one part of mold)	±0.005 in./in.	±0.005	±0.010	±0.002	±0.004 ferrous ±0.002 spec.
Minimum section thickness[3]	$\frac{1}{8}$ in.	$\frac{1}{16}$ in.	$\frac{1}{8}$ in.	0.050 in. Al 0.030 in. Zn	$\frac{3}{32}$ in.
Surface finish[4]	250–2000	125–250	125–250	32–125	64–125

[1] For lengths up to 12 in.
[2] These tolerances are for small castings or dimensions of only a few inches. Also, they are the minimum value for dimensions less than 1 in.
[3] Average values for common metals. Thinner sections can be cast if the length is very short.
[4] RMS. These values are not directly comparable to machine surface finish since the surface topography of the two are different.

CO₂ Process. The Co_2 process is a sand molding process in which sodium silicate $(Na_2O \cdot SiO_2)$ is used as a bond rather than clay. Water is added to the molding sand to give it sufficient plasticity. After the mold is made, CO_2 gas is caused to flow through the mold to cause it to harden. This reaction is quite rapid, requiring only about 1 min. This is considerably less than the several hours required to produce baked or core-sand molds. Since, the strength of the CO_2 hardened molds is not as high as the others and the cost is apparently about the same, the process is little used.

Table 3-3 summarizes the characteristics of the common casting processes.

MELTING EQUIPMENT

Several different types of heating units or furnaces are available for melting the material that is to be poured into the mold to make a casting. These range from the small gas fired crucible furnaces used for low melting temperature metals to large direct arc furnaces used to melt steel and high melting temperature metals. The characteristics and applications of each are presented next.

Crucible Furnace

The simplest and oldest of the melting equipment is the crucible furnace. It consists of a firebrick-lined steel shell with a movable lid and some means of heating an enclosed crucible (Figure 3-16a). The crucibles are made either of a clay-graphite mixture or a clay-silicon carbide mixture. They vary in size from about 2 in. outside diameter for a number 1 crucible to approximately 20 in. outside diameter for a number 400 crucible. The crucible number is the weight of aluminum, in pounds, that the crucible can safely hold during handling without spilling over the top. If some other metal is to be melted, the weight of this other metal that a given crucible can hold is the product of the crucible number and the ratio of densities of the other metal over aluminum. Thus a number 400 crucible can hold $400 \times 540/180$, or 1200 lb of brass that has a density of 540 lb/ft³.

The earliest fuels for crucible furnaces were wood, coal, and coke. The most common fuels today are natural gas and fuel oil blown into the combustion zone with compressed air. In some cases, particularly where small quantities are required at infrequent intervals, the metal in the crucible is melted by setting the crucible inside a high frequency electrical coil.

The crucible may be lifted out of the furnace for pouring, or the entire furnace may tilt or roll to pour out the melt. Crucible furnaces

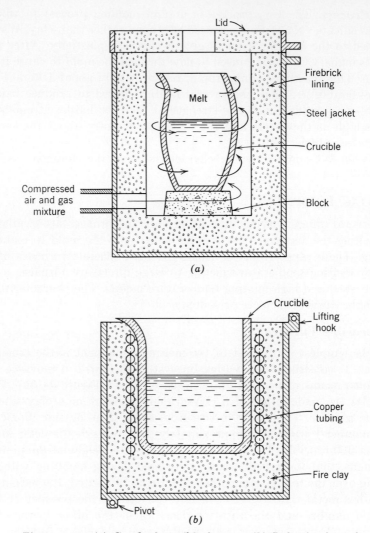

Figure 3-16. (*a*) Gas-fired crucible furnace. (*b*) Induction-heated crucible-type melting furnace.

are sometimes referred to as pot furnaces. They are generally used for melting the low melting temperature metals. Except for the induction-heated type, they are not used to melt the ferrous metals. The equipment and operating costs are very low for the gas and oil-fired crucible furnaces.

Induction Furnace

In an induction furnace the material is heated by means of either a high frequency or a low frequency electromagnetic field. In melting furnaces, as illustrated in Figure 3-16b, the crucible has a coil of copper tubing wrapped around it. The crucible and coils are imbedded in a fire clay lining. The coils conduct a high frequency (1000 to 30,000 cps) alternating current at a high power level. This creates an alternating magnetic field, which in turn induces a high alternating current in the surface of the metal inside the coil. The heat so generated in the surface of the metal is conducted into the center, thus the entire mass is melted quite rapidly. The copper coils have water circulating through them to keep them from getting too hot.

The cost of the furnace itself is quite low, but the high frequency power source is fairly expensive. The operating cost is fairly high for this equipment, so it is not used when a lot of molten metal is required. All metals can be melted in an induction furnace, and the time to melt a heat is quite short, normally a matter of minutes for a small heat. The same power source, when operated at the higher frequencies, can be used for surface hardening and brazing processes.

The low frequency furnace generally operates on standard 60 cycle current. The heating unit resembles the primary windings of a transformer and is imbedded near the bottom of the furnace. This type of furnace cannot melt directly from the solid, but some liquid metal must first be poured into the furnace to cover the insulated primary coils. This liquid then serves as the secondary winding and has a current induced in it which causes it to heat. Solid metal is then added to the furnace. This type of furnace is more economical than the high frequency one, but its starting characteristics retard its use.

Cupola Furnace

The cupola, Figure 3-17, is the principal melting furnace in the cast iron foundry because it is the most economical. The cupola is a vertical shaft-type furnace in which the heat to melt the iron results from the combustion of coke. The size of cupolas vary from a minimum of about 2 ft to a maximum of about 9 ft inside diameter. The height is approximately five times the diameter. The smaller size can produce about 1 ton of cast iron per hour and the largest can produce as much as 40 tons per hour.

A cupola is not operated continuously as is a blast furnace, which normally operates 24 hr a day for several years without being shut

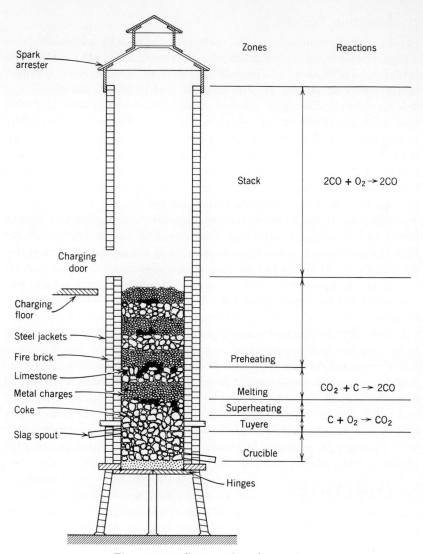

Figure 3-17. Cross section of a cupola.

down for repairs. In smaller foundries the cupola may operate only 4 hrs a day and in larger foundries it may operate 10 to 16 hrs a day. At the end of each day's run the bottom doors are opened and the remaining melted and solid material is dropped onto a sand layer on the foundry floor. Minor repairs are frequently and periodically made to the cupola lining. If molten metal is required 24 hrs a day, three or more cupolas are used so that at least one is in operation at all times. A brief description of the operation of a cupola follows.

After the lining is inspected and repaired, the bottom doors are closed and held shut by means of a vertical prop. A layer of sand about 6 in. thick is placed over the doors and sloped towards the tap hole. A fire of kindling wood and coarse coke is started on the sand bottom. When the coke in this preliminary fire ignites, a layer of coke is dropped onto the fire to a height of several feet above the tuyeres, depending on the air pressure being used, to form a coke bed. As soon as the coke bed is well ignited, the metal, flux, and fuel are added in weighted portions called a "charge."

The size of a charge is determined on the basis of the weight of coke that will form a uniform layer about 6 ins. deep in the cupola. The limestone ($CaCO_3$) is added on top of the coke and is placed near the center of the cupola to keep it away from the silica lining of the cupola. Since the limestone is basic and the silica is acidic, the life of the lining is extended by this means. The purpose of the limestone is to reduce the viscosity of the slag that normally forms in the operation of a cupola. The amount of limestone needed depends upon the impurities in the metal and the coke, but is generally about 20% of the amount of coke used.

The metal for the charge is added next. The total weight of the metal in each charge varies between 6 and 12 times the weight of the coke. The metal to coke ratio influences the temperature of the liquid in the crucible zone, usually referred to as the tapping temperature. The higher metal to coke ratio results in a lower tapping temperature. The tapping temperature, as well as the composition of the original pig iron, determines the silicon and manganese content of the cast iron. A lower tapping temperature results in a lower silicon and manganese content. The lump size of the coke as well as the porosity of the coke influences the metal to coke ratio and the burning rate of the coke. These factors, and more, must be controlled by the foundryman to achieve the desired properties in the cast iron and to manufacture it at a competitive rate.

The metal is added so that the melting will be uniform throughout the entire charge. The metal of each charge consists of pig iron, cast iron scrap (rejected parts plus gates and risers), and steel scrap in the proper proportions to give the desired chemical composition. The steel scrap which has a carbon content of 0.2% is added to lower the carbon content of the cast iron since the pig iron has a carbon content that may be as high as $4\frac{1}{2}\%$. These ingredients are preferentially placed within the cupola to achieve uniform melting in the following fashion. The steel scrap with its higher melting temperature is placed near the center of the cupola where the temperature is higher. The pig iron is placed in a ring around the steel scrap, and the smaller sections of cast iron scrap are placed over the top to level off the metal charge. Subsequent charges are added until the cupola is filled to the charging door.

The molten iron and slag accumulate in the crucible part of the cupola. When the crucible becomes full, the slag is first drained off through the slag spout. The "bot," clay plug in the tap hole, is punctured with a long bar and the cast iron flows out the tap spout into a holding ladle. When the crucible is emptied of cast iron, another bot is rammed into the tap hole to accumulate another melt. The cast iron from the holding ladle is transferred to pouring ladles and poured into the previously prepared molds.

The amount of air that must be blown in through the tuyeres is determined on the basis of the amount of oxygen needed to combine with the carbon of the coke. The carbon content of the coke is about 90%. From experience it has been found that with good operating conditions the composition of the stack gases at the bottom of the charging door is about 13% CO_2, 13% CO and 76% N_2. Since 12 lb of carbon combine with 32 lb of oxygen to form CO_2 and with 16 lb of oxygen to form CO, each pound of coke requires $(\frac{32}{12} \times \frac{1}{2} + \frac{16}{12} \times \frac{1}{2})$ $\times$ 0.9 or 1.8 lb of oxygen to form equal amounts of CO and CO_2.

Near the end of each melting period (4 to 16 hr) additional charges are not added to the cupola and the height of the materials in the cupola decreases gradually. Thus at the end of the melting period only a small amount of material is in the cupola. At this time the prop is knocked out and the bottom doors open and drop the remaining hot charge onto a sand layer on the foundry floor. Water is sprayed over this hot pile to cool it more rapidly. The dropped materials are separated and reused. After cooling, the cupola lining is inspected, and then the cupola is prepared for another run.

Blast Furnace

Blast furnaces are not generally used for melting purposes in ferrous foundries because their output is so high that even a large foundry cannot use all of the liquid metal that one furnace produces. However, since the output of the blast furnace is the pig iron that is used in the foundry, a brief description of it is given here.

A blast furnace is a very large shaft-type furnace that converts iron ore (iron oxide) to pig iron (iron saturated with carbon). It is very similar in construction and operation to the cupola furnace discussed above. The blast furnace is much larger than the cupola. A typical blast furnace is about 25 ft in diameter and 90 ft high and produces about 600 tons of pig iron per day. The lining of the blast furnace is water-cooled in the regions where the temperature is highest which permits the furnace to be operated continuously for years. In fact, it is a major undertaking to "stop" a blast furnace and to start it up again at a later date.

Iron ore, coke, and limestone are charged into the top of a blast furnace in much the same fashion but in larger quantities than in the cupola. Preheated air is blown in through water-cooled tuyeres at the bottom of the furnace. Slag and pig iron are periodically withdrawn from the bottom.

Whereas the melting reactions in the cupola are simply the combustion of the coke to generate enough heat to melt the ferrous materials in the charge, the reactions in the blast furnace are more involved. Near the bottom of the furnace the hot air combines with the coke to form CO at temperatures of 2500 to 2800°F. As the CO rises it combines with the iron ore (principally Fe_2O_3) to form iron plus CO_2 and the liberation of additional heat. The liquid iron, in contact with the hot coke, is saturated with carbon. The purpose of the limestone is again to form a low melting temperature, fluid slag.

The liquid pig iron that is tapped from the blast furnace that is to be sold to foundries is cast into simple open-topped molds about 5 in. wide, 3 in. high, and 18 in. long. Pig iron is the cheapest of all the metals, selling for about $0.03 per pound.

Air and Open Hearth Furnaces

The air furnace and open hearth furnace consist of a large dish-shaped refractory hearth onto which a charge of solid or liquid iron is placed for refining while a stream of hot combustion gases flow over it to keep it hot (Figure 3-18). Although these furnaces can melt iron or steel, they usually are used in conjunction with a cupola or a blast furnace to refine the already melted metal.

The air furnace is principally used in the malleable iron foundry, and sometimes in the gray iron foundry when a lower carbon content iron is desired. Because the liquid metal is not in contact with coke, the carbon content of the iron can be reduced. If cast iron from a cupola is transferred to an air furnace, the carbon content is lowered by adding either iron ore or scrap steel to the melt.

The open hearth furnace is used to convert pig iron to steel, either in a steel mill making wrought steel or in a steel foundry making

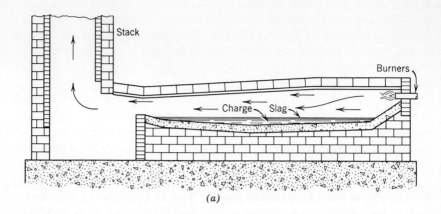

(a)

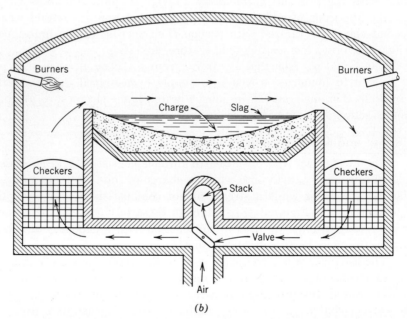

(b)

Figure 3-18. Cross section of: (a) an air furnace, (b) an open-hearth furnace.

steel castings. In the open hearth furnace, pig iron and iron ore are combined to give the low carbon ferrous material known as steel. Since the melting temperature of steel is higher than the melting temperature of cast iron, the open hearth must operate at higher temperatures than the air furnace. To achieve these higher temperatures, the incoming air is preheated before it is burned by passing it through a refractory heat exchanger called a "checker." The hot gases, after passing over the hearth, flow through one checker to heat it before exhausting to the atmosphere while the incoming air goes through a second checker. Periodically, the checker valve is reversed so that the incoming air passes through the previously heated checker while the hot gases reheat the cooled checker. When the checker valve is reversed, the burners which are located on opposite ends of the hearth are also reversed. That is, one is extinguished while the opposite one is ignited. This reverses the direction of flow of the combustion gases (Figure 3-18b).

In both of these furnaces, slag plays a very important role in determining the content of the impurities such as sulfur, phosphorus, silicon, manganese, and oxygen. The composition of the slag, and also the melt, is influenced by the composition of the hearth. A furnace is referred to as being acid or basic, depending upon whether the hearth lining is made of a silica base refractory which is acidic or a basic refractory containing magnesite ($MgCO_3$) or dolomite ($CaCO_3 \cdot MgCO_3$).

The acid furnace requires the use of ore and scrap containing low sulfur and phosphorus contents since these two ingredients cannot be removed with an acid slag. The sulfur and phosphorus contents can be lowered with a basic slag.

Converter

The converter is an open-top pot-type refining furnace that converts molten pig iron or cupola iron into low carbon steel by blowing air either through the melt or over the melt (Fig. 3-19). The bottom blow converter, developed in 1855 and now known as the Bessemer converter after its inventor, was the first practical process to make steel out of pig iron commercially.

One of the advantages of the converter is the short time needed to oxidize the carbon. The carbon content of the melt is lowered from 3 to 4.5% carbon to about 0.1% carbon in 15 to 20 min. The silicon and manganese oxidize more rapidly than the carbon does, and so at the end of the blow these two elements are also present only to the extent of about 0.1%.

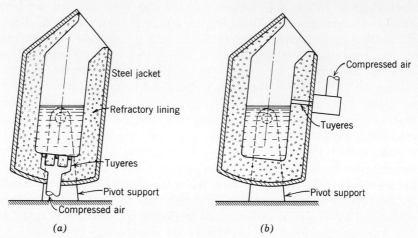

Figure 3-19. Cross section of a converter: (*a*) Bottom blow (Bessemer). (*b*) Side blow.

The principal disadvantage to this process is that about 12% of the iron is also oxidized. In addition, the "blow" creates a large amount of dark smoke that creates a nuisance to the entire neighborhood. The converters generally are smaller in size than the open hearth furnace, and thus result in a higher operating cost.

Electric Arc Furnaces

As the name implies, electric arc furnaces are melting furnaces in which the heat is generated from an electric arc maintained within the furnace. These furnaces are classified as either direct or indirect arc furnaces depending upon whether the arc is maintained between one electrode and the metal being melted, as in the former, or between two electrodes, as in the latter type. Figure 3-20 illustrates these two types of furnaces. The direct arc furnace generally has three electrodes, each one connected to one of the leads of a three-phase power source. They range in capacity from 1 to 100 tons.

In melting ferrous metals, the electrodes generally are made of carbon. The furnace can be used as a melting furnace where solid metal is charged into it or it can be used as a refining furnace in conjunction with a cupola. In the manufacture of some high melting temperature metals, such as molybdenum, the electrodes are made of the same material that is being melted. This is done when carbon and

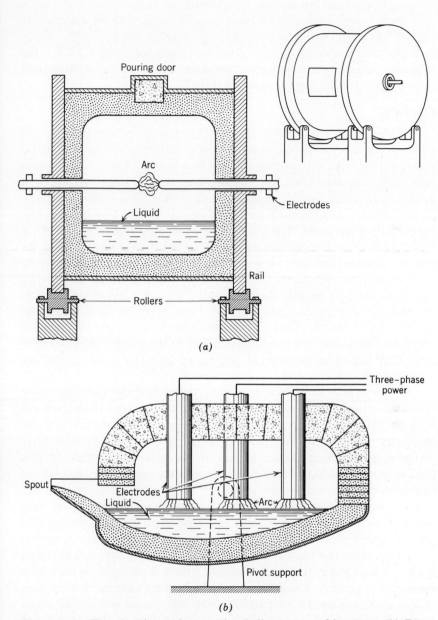

Figure 3-20. The electric arc furnace. (*a*) Indirect arc, rocking type. (*b*) Direct arc, tilting type.

other impurities are to be kept to a minimum. The arc furnaces are not used to melt the low melting temperature alloys.

Arc furnaces have either a basic or acid lining, with an appropriate slag, to give the required chemical composition in the melt. These furnaces are capable of operating at higher temperatures than are the chemical fuel-fired furnaces. Arc furnaces are used for making tool steels as well as high quality structural steel.

POURING

After the melting process, the metal is poured or injected into the mold cavity. Except for die castings and injection moldings, the metal is transferred from the melting furnace to a pouring ladle. The pouring ladle varies in size from the smaller one that a man carries on a handle to a larger mechanically handled one. The metal must be rapidly poured into the mold cavity or else it will solidify before completely filling the mold. The alternative of using a higher superheat is undesirable since the amount of gas dissolved in the liquid metal increases with an increase in superheat. Not only must the mold be filled rapidly but the metal must flow with a minimum of turbulence; must not impinge against the mold with enough energy to erode it, particularly in a green sand mold; must not carry impurities into the mold cavity. These restrictions are necessary to avoid casting defects, which are discussed in a later section. Some of the characteristics of a mold that influence the flow of the liquid into the mold cavity are presented next.

If the liquid is poured from the ladle directly into the mold cavity, as illustrated in Figure 3-21a, liquid strikes the bottom of the mold cavity with a velocity $v = \sqrt{2gh}$, where g is the acceleration due to gravity and h is the vertical distance of free fall. Since the kinetic energy is proportional to the square of the velocity, pouring in this fashion is undesirable in that it can cause considerable erosion of the bottom of the mold cavity.

The simplest type of pouring and gating arrangement used in sand molds is sketched in Figure 3-21b. It is referred to as a parting line gate. As illustrated here, the metal from the ladle is poured into a basin formed in the top of the cope adjacent to the sprue. The sprue is the vertical channel, usually tapered about 2 degrees, down which the metal is poured. A *gate* is a short horizontal channel terminating at the mold cavity by means of which the liquid enters the mold cavity. If several gates are needed, or if the bottom of the sprue is far from the mold cavity, then long horizontal channels called *runners* connect the gates to the sprue.

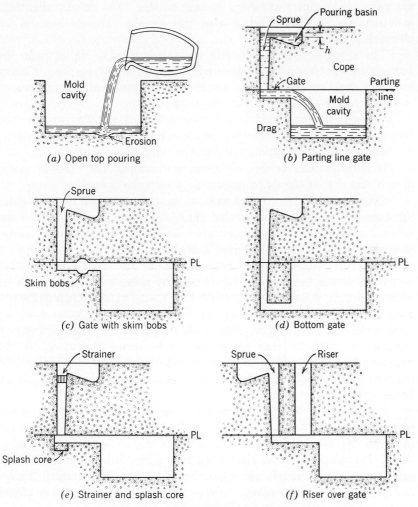

Figure 3-21. Illustrations of pouring sprues.

The time to fill the mold cavity is determined by the cross-sectional areas and lengths of the sprue, gates and runners. When the pouring basin is full, the maximum flow rate is determined by the cross-sectional area of the bottom of the sprue and the "head" of the liquid above this plane. The head determines the velocity of the liquid into the sprue by the relationship $v = \sqrt{2gh_s}$. Thus the rate of flow into the sprue is $Q = A \times v = A \sqrt{2gh_s}$ in.³/min. The minimum time to fill a mold having a volume of V in.³ is then V/Q. This assumes that the gates and runners are large enough so that they do not offer constrictions to the flow, and it also ignores the friction loss in the channels.

The sprue is tapered so that the faster flowing liquid near the bottom does not aspirate air through the mold and drag the air along into the mold cavity. If the sprue were cylindrical, the increased velocity due to the greater head near the bottom of the sprue would result in a lower pressure and thus the inflow of air. To prevent this, the sprue is tapered so that the product of the area and velocity at the bottom equals the product of the area and velocity at the top.

If several gates branch off from one runner, the cross-sectional area of the runner should be decreased after each branching gate.

Skim bobs, which are recesses to trap either heavier or lighter impurities such as dross or eroded sand, are sometimes placed on the gates. This prevents these impurities from going into the mold cavity. Skim bobs are illustrated in Figure 3-21c.

The erosion of the bottom of the mold and the turbulence of metal flow into the mold cavity can be reduced by using a bottom gate. This type of gate is sketched in Figure 3-21d. Gates of this type generally are more difficult to make than are parting line gates.

Another means of preventing dross from entering the mold cavity is to use a ceramic strainer at the top of the sprue, and to reduce the amount of eroded sand, a ceramic or baked sand splash core can be inserted in the mold directly beneath the sprue. Both these features are sketched in Figure 3-21e.

A side riser is quite often placed over a gate rather than either placing it on top of the casting or else putting it on the opposite side of the cavity from the sprue. This arrangement is sketched in Figure 3-21f. The purpose of the riser is to feed metal into the mold cavity after the pouring into the sprue has ceased and solidification shrinkage has begun in the mold cavity. Risers are discussed in more detail in the following section covering solidification.

The lengths of gates and runners are kept to a minimum to reduce the amount of heat loss from the liquid before it enters into a wide cavity; streams of liquid coming together from different directions in the cavity may freeze before they merge and result in a defect known as a cold shut.

COOLING AND SOLIDIFICATION

Because most metals contract during solidification, special consideration must be given to the construction of the mold for the resulting casting to be sound. Except for the few castings made in a vacuum, the decrease in solubility of gases in the metal as the temperature drops is another source of casting defects. Although the shrinkage and the gas solubility are separate and unrelated phenomena, they do have the same influence on some aspects of proper casting design.

Coring

In Chapter 2 it was assumed that the only variation in composition and microstructure in a given part was due to the part being heated to a two-phase region in an equilibrium phase diagram and cooled either slowly or rapidly to produce the room temperature phases. Thus the microstructure of a medium carbon steel shaft could be different at the surface than at the center. However, the heat treatment of a 70 Cu-30Zn brass shaft would always result in the same composition and the same phase at both the center and the surface. But a cast shaft having a nominal composition of 70% Cu and 30% Zn could have a different composition at the surface and at the center. To see how this occurs, reference to Figure 3-22 is made for the following discussion.

If this material is heated in a crucible to 2000°F, it will be liquid with about 300°F of superheat. If this metal is now poured into a room temperature mold, a thin layer immediately solidifies adjacent to the mold wall at a temperature of about 1740°F. The composition of this material is not the nominal composition of the original melt. Instead it will contain about 76% Cu and 24% Zn as indicated by point 1 in Figure 3-22. The liquid within this shell will contain slightly more than 30% Zn.

This surface layer cools to nearly room temperature very rapidly, particularly if it is cast in a permanent mold. As heat flows out from the interior of the shaft, the temperature at the center drops until at point 2, 1690°F, it is completely solid. The composition of the last liquid that freezes is approximately 65% Cu and 35% Zn. If the casting were kept at a temperature just below 1690°F for several hours, diffusion of the copper and zinc atoms would result in a uniform composition throughout the shaft of 70% Cu and 30% Zn. However, the shaft in reality cools too fast for equilibrium conditions to prevail so this variable composition of a copper rich surface and a zinc rich center persists in the cast shaft. This variable composition that results in a casting due to nonequilibrium cooling is referred to as *coring*. A casting having a cored structure can be homogenized by reheating and holding for several hours in a furnace at a temperature near the solidus temperature.

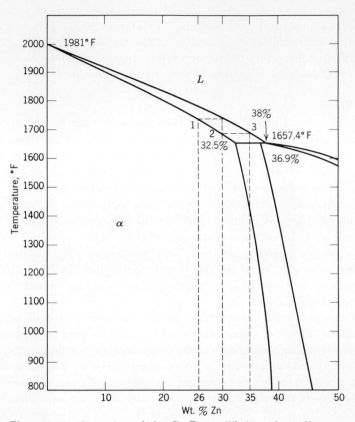

Figure 3-22. A portion of the Cu-Zn equilibrium-phase diagram.

The compositions stated in the above discussion are only approximately correct. In reality, with rapid cooling the phenomenon known as undercooling would be present and the temperatures at points 1 and 2 would be suppressed with a resulting lower copper content in the initial solid.

The microstructure of a cast alloy usually is different from that of the same alloy in the wrought or homogenized condition. Figure 3-23 contains photomicrographs of a 70 Cu-30 Zn brass alloy in the wrought and cast condition. The wrought microstructure contains the typical light and dark grains, the angular grain boundaries, and a large number of twin bands. The as-cast microstructure has large columnar grains and no twin bands. Coring is not readily evident in this particular casting.

Figure 3-23. Photomicrographs of **70 Cu-30Zn** brass (50×). (*a*) Wrought. (*b*) Cast.

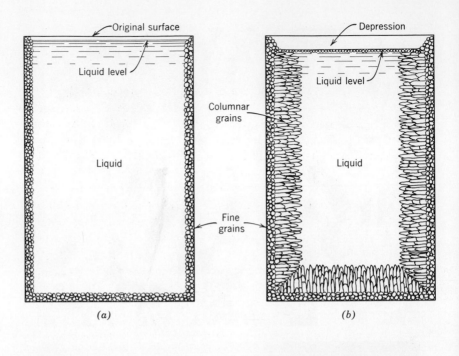

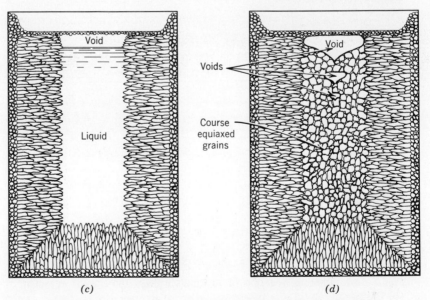

Figure 3-24.   Cast structure and shrinkage cavities of an ingot.

In addition to these microstructural characteristics of a casting, another characteristic is illustrated in Figure 3-24. This is the shape of the grains within a casting, as well as the line of demarcation between the dendritic grains growing toward each other from two different directions.

The chilled layer at the surface of the ingot consists of fine equiaxed grains. As the heat flows outward through this layer, solidification proceeds inward. The grains that form during this time cannot grow sideways because of their neighbors, so all of the growth is inward. The result is long needlelike dendritic grains. Near the bottom of the ingot the grains growing horizontally meet the vertically growing grains and form a line of demarcation at a 45-degree angle.

The top surface of the liquid for an open-top ingot is lowered during this early solidification. Generally a thin shell will freeze over the top of the ingot before all of the center metal solidifies. This layer consists of equiaxed grains.

The cooling rate of the metal near the center of the ingot is considerably lower than that near the surface, and the heat is flowing outward in all directions from this central mass. Consequently, equiaxed grains form here and, because sufficient time is available, these grains grow to a much larger size than do the surface grains.

Gas Solubility

The presence of gases in the liquid metal may cause defects in the resulting casting known as gas holes, pin holes, or porosity. This comes about because of the decrease in solubility of the common gases in the common metals with a temperature decrease as schematically shown in Figure 3-25 by three lines.

The solubility of the common gases such as hydrogen, nitrogen, moisture, and carbon monoxide in liquid metal increases with a temperature rise. The desirability of keeping the amount of superheat to a minimum when melting a metal is readily apparent. Although the gas liberated as the liquid metal cools to the liquidus temperature can escape from an open-top casting, it requires a considerable permeability in a mold that completely surrounds the casting. Also, when a casting is made in a completely enclosed mold, a thin shell of solid forms around the hot liquid metal. As this encased liquid cools to the freezing temperature, the liberated gas collects into large bubbles that result in large gas holes within the casting.

For most metals a more serious aspect is the large decrease in solubility of gas as the metal transforms from the liquid to the solid state. This is demonstrated in Figure 3-25 by having a long vertical

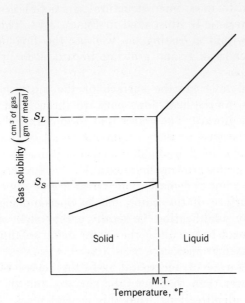

Figure 3-25. The solubility of a gas in a
metal as a function of the temperature.

line at the melting temperature of the metal. An appreciation of the
magnitude of this decrease in solubility can be obtained from the data
in Table 3-4.

TABLE 3-4. Solubility of Hydrogen in Some Metals
At Their Melting Temperature
(At a pressure of 1 atm.)

Metal	Melting Temp., °F	Liquid Solubility, cm^3/gm	Solid Solubility, cm^3/gm	Gas Liberated	
				cm^3/gm	cm^3/cm^3
Ni	2640	0.38	0.18	0.200	0.022
Fe	2780	0.27	0.07	0.200	0.025
Mg	1202	0.26	0.18	0.080	0.045
Cu	1981	0.055	0.02	0.035	0.004
Al	1218	0.007	<0.001	0.006	0.002

From Table 3-4 we see that the solubility of hydrogen decreases
from 0.27 cm^3 to 0.07 cm^3 when 1 gm of iron transforms from liquid
to solid at 2780°F. Thus 0.2 cm^3/gm of hydrogen are liberated. Since

iron has a density of about 7.8 gm/cm³ at this temperature, the amount of gas liberated is 0.025 cm³/cm³ or 2.5% on a volume basis. With aluminum, the amount of hydrogen liberated is less than 0.5%.

Much of the gas that is liberated during solidification becomes trapped within the growing dendrites. In this case the gas is well dispersed in very small (microscopic) bubbles throughout the solid, and is referred to as microporosity.

Several techniques are used in foundries to reduce or eliminate gas from liquid metal. Vacuum melting or vacuum degassing are the most thorough of the degassing techniques. In vacuum melting, the actual melting of the material as well as the pouring is done in a vacuum chamber. By employing sufficiently low pressures, such as 10^{-3} mm Hg, just about all of the gas is removed from the liquid. In the vacuum degassing technique, the metal is melted in a conventional furnace and then is transferred to a chamber in which the pressure is then reduced. After a few minutes in this low pressure chamber, the gas content of the melt is reduced considerably. The crucible of liquid metal is then taken out of the degassing chamber and the pouring is done in the normal atmosphere.

Probably the most common degassing technique in the brass and aluminum foundries to remove the hydrogen from the liquid is to bubble a gas that has a low solubility and no harmful effects, such as chlorine, nitrogen, or argon, through the liquid. This process is very simple since a carbon or ceramic tube through which the gas flows slowly is moved around throughout the melt. As the bubbles of the scavaging gas leave the tube, the partial pressure of hydrogen within each bubble is zero. As the bubbles flow upward, the dissolved hydrogen within the liquid diffuses to these hydrogen depleted regions and mixes with the scavenging gas to form a uniform hydrogen content throughout. As the bubbles float to the surface, the hydrogen as well as the scavaging gas diffuse out to the atmosphere. If this bubbling is continued for a few minutes, most of the dissolved hydrogen is removed.

Another technique is to stir the melt with a solid material that decomposes at the temperature of the melt to liberate a gas such as chlorine which will bubble up through the liquid.

Risers

Probably the major problem that a foundry must solve to satisfactorily make a new casting is the design and location of the riser or risers. If the riser is too small, shrinkage cavities will result in the casting proper. If the riser is too large, too much metal is melted for each casting and thus the cost of the casting is increased. The function of a riser was briefly discussed in the preceding section on pattern allowance, and will be discussed in more detail now. Since a riser is intended to supply liquid to the mold cavity during the cooling and solidification of the casting, a discussion on riser requirements or characteristics must include the size (volume) of the riser as well as its shape (surface area to volume ratio).

To obtain a quantitative appreciation of riser requirements, consider the cooling and solidification of a simple casting as illustrated in Figure 3-26. For this discussion assume that the mold cavity is a unit cube (1 in. on a side) and that aluminum at a temperature of 1450°F is poured into the cavity through the parting line gate. Assume also that a barrier is placed across the gate at the cavity face as soon as the cavity is filled and no additional metal can flow into the cavity. Fine details such as the expansion of a thin layer of the mold material around the mold cavity and evolution of gas will also be ignored.

If the heat were extracted slowly from the mold, as would be true if the mold were preheated to the freezing temperature of the metal being poured, the liquid aluminum would cool from 1450 to 1218°F with no solid being present. Since the liquid contraction is about 0.5%, the liquid would now occupy a volume of 0.995 in.^{3} (Figure 3-26b). The casting now would have the dimensions 1.000 in. $\times$ 1.000 in. $\times$ 0.995 in. high. Thus there would be a 0.005 in. space between the top of the liquid and the top of the mold cavity.

As the heat slowly flows out through the mold walls, the casting will solidify at a constant temperature of 1218°F. At first a thin shell freezes around the mold cavity. Because of the space above the casting, the top face will solidify more slowly than the sides so that the layer of solid on top is thinner than that at the sides and bottom. Also, since the solidified metal occupies a volume that is 93% of the liquid volume, the top face of the liquid is now lower. Since the layer of solid metal on the top is so thin and has such a low strength, it settles or drops down with the receding liquid surface (Figure 3-26c).

In Figure 3-26d it is assumed that sufficient time has elapsed so that a $\frac{1}{8}$ in. thick layer has solidified on all four sides and on the bottom. The solidified layer on the top is somewhat thinner. At this time the total volume of solid is about $\frac{1}{2}$ in.^{3} and the volume of the liquid is about $\frac{1}{2}$ in.^{3} Actually, $\frac{1}{2}$ in.^{3} of liquid will solidify to 0.5 $\times$ 0.93 (7% contraction from Table 3-1) or 0.465 in.^{3} This contraction is illustrated as the 0.05 in. depression on the top face of the casting.

As solidification continues to completion as illustrated in e, the top layer does not drop any further because it now supports itself. As the remaining liquid within the casting solidfies, the contraction results

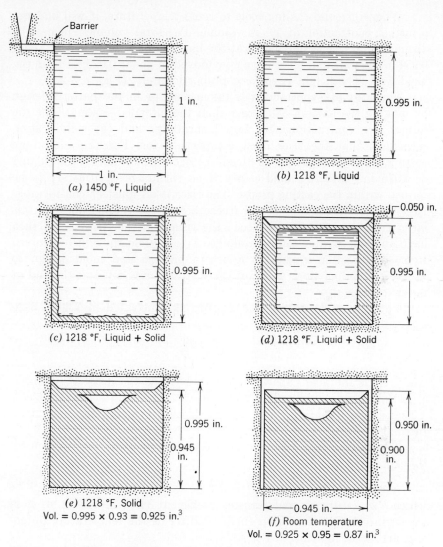

Figure 3-26. The contraction of an aluminum cube during slow cooling.

in the creation of a void near the top center of the casting. At this point the entire casting is solid and has a temperature of 1218°F. The bottom base is still 1 in. × 1 in. but the height varies from approximately 0.995 in. at the edges to 0.945 in. near the center. These latter two dimensions are only approximate inasmuch as the top face in reality is not flat but rather it is dished. The total volume of solid metal at 1218°F is about 0.925 in.³, not including the internal void.

When the solid casting cools to room temperature, it will undergo a further contraction of 5% in volume. The total volume will now be about 0.87 in.[3]. The side length at the base of the casting is now about 0.954 in. and all four sides have now moved in about 0.023 in. from the mold wall. The height is reduced proportionately (Figure 3-26*f*).

This last 5% contraction is taken care of in the pattern design by making the pattern 5% larger than the intended casting. It is the former two contractions, the liquid shrinkage and the solidification shrinkage, that the riser must compensate for. For this aluminum casting, the riser will have to "feed" $7\frac{1}{2}\%$ of the volume of the casting or 0.075 in.[3] into the mold cavity if no shrinkage cavities are to be formed within the casting proper. The riser itself must be considerably larger than 0.075 in.[3] or it will freeze before the casting does. In this latter case the casting will "feed" the riser and the casting will then have an even greater total shrinkage. A few guide rules have evolved from solidification studies to assist in pattern and mold design to insure a sound casting. A few of these studies are listed at the end of the chapter.

The rate of heat loss of a casting as illustrated in Figure 3-26 is given by the expression

$$q = \rho C_p V \frac{dT}{dt} \tag{3-1}$$

where C_p is the heat capacity (Btu/lb°F), ρ is the density (lb/in.[3]), V is the volume (in.[3]), T is temperature (°F), and t is time (sec). This assumes a material with a high thermal conductivity so that no thermal gradients exist in the casting.

The rate of heat flow across an interface or a surface is given by the expression

$$q = hA \, \Delta T \tag{3-2}$$

where h is a surface heat transfer coefficient (Btu/min°F in.[2]), A is the surface or interface area (in.[2]), and ΔT is the temperature difference across the interface (°F).

For a casting completely surrounded by a mold, all of the heat will flow through the casting surface into the mold. By equating equations 3-1 and 3-2, the rate of cooling of the casting is given by

$$\frac{dT}{dt} = \frac{h \, \Delta T}{\rho C_p} \frac{A}{V} \tag{3-3}$$

Although these relationships do not include the heat of fusion that is evolved as the metal solidifies, nor does the interface temperature remain constant, they do serve to illustrate the importance of the area to volume ratio. Thus if a casting has a high area to volume ratio, it will have a high cooling rate. Similarly, since it is desired to have the riser freeze more slowly than the casting it is feeding, the riser should have a low area to volume ratio.

Probably the first study that yielded quantitative values for the design of risers is the one by Chvorinov[4] in which he showed that the solidification time for a simple casting is related to its shape as follows:

$$t_f = K \left(\frac{V}{A}\right)^2 \tag{3-4}$$

where t_f is the time required for the casting to freeze, K is a constant that includes the thermal properties of both the mold and the melt, V is the volume, and A is the area of the casting. The numerical value of K is 5.5 sec per sq in. for steel casting in green-sand mold.

Since the guiding rule of riser design is that the riser be the last to solidify, the riser itself can be considered as another casting. Then if

$$(t_f)_R > (t_f)_c$$

it follows that the ratio

$$\left(\frac{V_R}{A_R}\right) \quad \text{must be greater than} \quad \left(\frac{V_c}{A_c}\right)$$

The subscripts R and c refer to riser and casting. This relationship is only approximate since some of the original volume of the riser metal flows into the casting during the early stages of solidification. However, it is accurate enough for a good engineering first approximation in designing riser sizes. Some of the references at the end of the chapter go into the subject in more detail than space permits in this text. A quantitative appreciation of the significance of the volume to area ratio can be achieved by considering the casting in Figure 3-26.

The volume to area ratio for a 1 in. cube is $\frac{1}{6}$. If a cylindrical riser 4 in. high is to be used to feed this casting it would require a diameter of $\frac{8}{11}$ in. This size is determined as follows:

$$V_R = \frac{\pi D^2}{4} \times 4 \quad \text{and} \quad A_R = 4\pi D + \frac{2\pi D^2}{4}$$

By setting $V_R/A_R = \frac{1}{6}$ and solving for D, D is found to be equal to $\frac{8}{11}$ in. The volume of this riser is 1.66 in.³ compared to 1 in.³ for the casting.

If a riser having a diameter equal to its height is used, then

$$V_R = \frac{\pi D^3}{4} \quad \text{and} \quad A_R = \pi D^2 + \frac{\pi D^2}{2}$$

For $V_R/A_R = \frac{1}{6}$, $D = 1$ in. Thus a riser 1 in. diameter by 1 in. high could be used. Since its volume is only 0.785 in.^{3}, from an economics point of view it would be more efficient than the previous riser.

From these two examples it is apparent that the height and the diameter of a riser determine, for a given V/A ratio, the total volume of metal in the riser. At this time it is appropriate to consider what the optimum dimensions for a riser are. This will be referred to as the *optimum riser*. For a cylindrical riser, the optimum dimensions can be calculated as follows.

The volume of a cylinder is given by expression:

$$V = \frac{1}{4}\pi D^2 h \tag{3-5}$$

By differentiating Equation 3-5 with respect to h and equating it to zero, the relationship between diameter and height is obtained.

$$\frac{dV}{dh} = 0 = \tfrac{1}{4}\pi D^2 + \tfrac{1}{2}\pi Dh \frac{dD}{dh}$$

or

$$\tfrac{1}{2}D + h \frac{dD}{dh} = 0$$

and

$$\frac{dD}{dh} = -\frac{D}{2h} \tag{3-6}$$

Similarly, the surface area of a cylinder is

$$A = \pi Dh + \tfrac{1}{2}\pi D^2 \tag{3-7}$$

To obtain the minimum area for a given volume, Equation 3-7 is differentiated with respect to h and equated to zero.

$$\frac{dA}{dh} = 0 = \pi D + \pi h \frac{dD}{dh} + \pi D \frac{dD}{dh}$$

or

$$\frac{dD}{dh} = -\frac{D}{h + D} \tag{3-8}$$

By equating Equations 3-6 and 3-8, the relationship between the height and the diameter for the optimum riser is obtained:

$$\frac{D}{2h} = \frac{D}{h + D}$$

so

$$h = D \tag{3-9}$$

Thus the optimum V/A ratio in terms of the diameter is:

$$\frac{V}{A} = \frac{\frac{1}{4}\pi D^3}{\pi D^2 + \frac{1}{2}\pi D^2} = \frac{D}{6} \qquad (3\text{-}10)$$

In the previous example where the diameter was arbitrarily made equal to the height and the V/A ratio was specified as $\frac{1}{6}$, the diameter was calculated to be 1 in. From Equations 3-9 and 3-10 we see that in reality this is the optimum cylindrical riser for the specified casting.

However, if the 1 in.^{3} casting discussed above had the dimensions $\frac{1}{4}$ in. $\times$ 2 in. $\times$ 2 in. it would have a V_c/A_c ratio of $\frac{1}{10}$. A cylindrical riser of equal height and diameter would now be 0.6 in. diameter and 0.6 in. high. It would have a volume of only 0.17 in.^{3}.

Although the freezing times for a casting $\frac{1}{4}$ in. $\times$ 2 in. $\times$ 2 in. and a cylindrical riser 0.6 in. diameter $\times$ 0.6 in. high are equal, the total volume of the riser is less than 20% of the volume of the casting. Consequently, the riser probably will not be able to supply all of the liquid metal that the casting requires, so a partial shrinkage cavity will be present in the casting adjacent to where the riser is attached if the metal has such a large solidification shrinkage as some aluminum alloys. However, if the metal being cast is a high-carbon gray iron with a very low solidification shrinkage, then a riser this small would be satisfactory.

In order for the riser to supply liquid metal into the mold cavity during the solidification of the casting, the gate between the riser and the casting must not freeze over before the casting does. A gate as small as possible is desired not only because a smaller volume of metal has to be poured into the mold, but also because it is then easier to separate the riser from the casting. This latter operation is done by either breaking or by sawing the riser off with a conventional or an abrasive saw. Usually, the gate is kept open simply because the liquid metal flows through it either on its way to the mold cavity or to the riser. Thus the first metal flowing into either the mold cavity or the riser is cooled as it flows through the gate, and at the same time the mold material surrounding the gate is heated. By the time the mold cavity or riser is filled, the mold around the gate is quite hot and as a consequence the heat flow from the metal in the gate to the surrounding mold is low.

Another aspect of the feeding problem is referred to as *feeding distance*. It is closely related to the gating problem discussed previously. It occurs in long thin sections, where the feeding is through the end of a bar or plate; but most of the heat flow is through the sides with the result that freezing may occur too soon at a point between the riser and some portion of the casting. To prevent this from happening, the concept of *directional solidification* is used. That is, in a properly designed casting, solidification occurs first at points farthest removed from the riser and gradually progresses toward the riser.

Figure 3-27 illustrates several different types of solidification patterns found in plates when influenced by the feeding distance. As illustrated in *a*, a sound casting will result in plates ($w/t > 5$) if the distance between the edge of the riser and the end of the plate is less than $4\frac{1}{2} t$ in. The location of the solid-liquid interface at successively longer times is indicated by lines S_1, S_2, etc., to S_6. The shrinkage cavity is entirely contained within the riser. At no time did all of the metal in a vertical plane of the casting freeze while liquid was between that plane and the edge of the casting. The reason for the metal in the plate adjacent to the riser freezing at a slightly later time than that in a plane near the far end of the casting is that both the heat from the riser and warmer liquid which feeds into the casting tend to produce a slightly lower cooling rate near the riser.

If the feeding distance in the plate is greater than $4\frac{1}{2} t$, as illustrated in *b*, voids will occur in the midthickness of the plate in a region between the riser and the far end of the plate. This defect is referred to as center-line shrinkage. The far end of the plate is sound because of the directional solidification resulting from the heat flow out the end of the casting. The plate adjacent to the riser is also free of voids because after the metal at the plane *x* is completely solidified, liquid metal was able to flow toward plane *x* from the riser as the solidus line moved to the left. However, when plane *x* became completely solid, there was still some liquid metal at the midthickness to the right of plane *x*. As this liquid froze, no feeding occurred, with the result that the shrinkage cavities formed.

The effective feeding distance can be increased by the insertion of a chill, or chill block as it is sometimes called, at the far surface of the mold as illustrated in *c*. This chill block is a solid piece of metal, usually steel, which, because of its high thermal conductivity and heat capacity in comparison to a sand mold, causes the far end of the plate to cool very rapidly, and thus promotes directional solidification toward the riser.

Rather than a chill block, a second riser could be placed at the opposite end of the plate to cast a longer section. And for a very long casting, top risers could also be added at frequent intervals.

Another very common technique to enable the use of longer feeding distances without the formation of voids is to taper the casting so that the cross section becomes greater in the direction toward the riser,

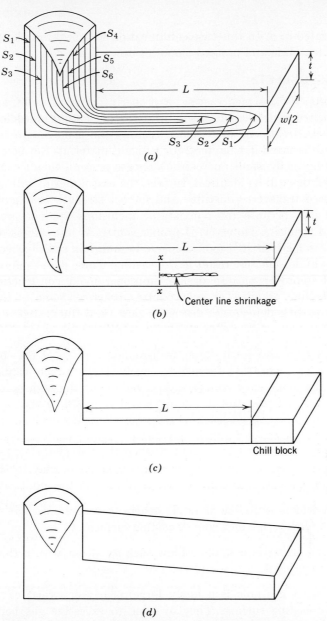

Figure 3-27. Solidification pattern in plates as influenced by the feeding distance. (a) For a sound casting: $L < 4\frac{1}{2}t$ for plates $w/t > 5$; $L < 6t^{0.5}$ for bars $w/t < 3$. (b) Unsound casting: $L >$ restrictions listed in (a). (c) For a sound casting: $L < 4\frac{1}{2}t + 2$ in. for plate, $L < 5\frac{1}{2}t$ for bars. (d) Tapered section. Sound casting if riser is large enough.

as illustrated in *d*. In this case solidification will begin at the farthest point in the plate and proceed smoothly toward the riser.

CASTING DEFECTS

A properly designed casting, a properly prepared mold, and correctly melted metal should result in a casting having no defects. By proper heat treatment of a sound casting, the same microstructures that were discussed in Chapter 2 for wrought materials can be obtained in a casting; if the same microstructures are present, then the mechanical properties will be identical. In fact, the cast material will not have the reduced transverse ductility and impact strength that a wrought material has, because the nonmetallic inclusions are not present as elongated stringers. However, if proper control is not exercised in the foundry—sometimes it is too expensive to maintain sufficient control— a variety of defects may result in the casting. These defects may be the result of improper pattern design, improper mold construction, improper melting practice, or poor pouring practice. Some of the more common casting defects are described next, and illustrated in Figure 3-28.

Blows. A blow is a fairly large, well-rounded cavity at the cope surface of a casting. It is formed by evolved gas which cannot flow through the mold, so it collects into a bubble at the high points in a mold cavity and prevents the liquid metal from filling that space. It may be due to excess gas such as steam or CO being evolved from the mold surface because of a high moisture or organic content of the sand mold. The steam and CO is formed when the hot metal contacts the green sand. Another cause is an excessive amount of clay in the sand mixture, or excessive ramming of the sand around the mold cavity.

Scars. A scar is a shallow blow. It generally occurs on a flat surface, whereas a blow occurs on a convex casting surface.

Blisters. A blister is a shallow blow such as a scar with a thin layer of metal covering it.

Gas Holes. A gas hole is a fairly large, nearly spherical cavity beneath the casting surface. They are due to excessive gas being dissolved in the liquid metal or else to mold-reaction gases that get trapped within the casting.

Pin Holes. Pin holes are small gas holes either at the surface or just slightly below the surface. What may appear as a pin hole from a surface examination of a casting may actually be a surface opening of a gas hole. When pin holes are present, they occur in large numbers and are fairly uniformly dispersed over the surface.

Porosity. Porosity refers to very small holes uniformly dispersed through the entire casting. These are present within the dendritic network of the cast microstructure.

Drops. A drop is an irregularly shaped projection on the cope surface of a casting. It results from a cavity that forms in the surface of the cope above the mold cavity when a lump of sand breaks loose from the cope and drops down into the mold cavity. The lump of sand drops out because of a combination of a low green strength in the molding sand and a jarring or jolting of the cope as it is placed over the drag in the closing of the mold. The loose sand that falls into the cavity will also cause a dirty casting surface, either on the top or bottom surface of the casting, depending upon the relative densities of the sand and the liquid.

Inclusions and Dirt. Inclusions are nonmetallic particles, either oxides or intermetallic compounds, in the metal matrix. The inclusions are objectionable only if they are present in large quantity, or if they are segregated. If loose sand is present in the mold cavity, as when a drop is formed, the loose sand becomes embedded in the cope surface of the casting.

This condition is referred to as *dirt*. Actually, when such a dirty casting is cleaned, the sand particles are for the most part removed from the casting surface, leaving small angular holes in the casting surface.

Wash. A wash is a low projection on the drag face of a casting that commences near one side of the casting and extends along the surface toward the opposite end of the casting, decreasing in height as it progresses. This type of defect is also called a *cut*. It occurs with bottom-gated castings in which the molding sand has insufficient hot strength, and when too much metal is caused to flow through one gate. It is caused by erosion as the liquid stream flows from the gate into the mold cavity (the eroded sand also causes the dirt defect described before).

Buckle. A buckle is a long, fairly shallow, broad, vee depression that occurs in the surface of flat castings. It extends in a fairly straight line across the entire flat surface. A buckle results when the molding sand has insufficient hot deformation.

To illustrate how a buckle originates, consider a simple mold cavity that is 1 in. deep with a 12 in. width and length made in a

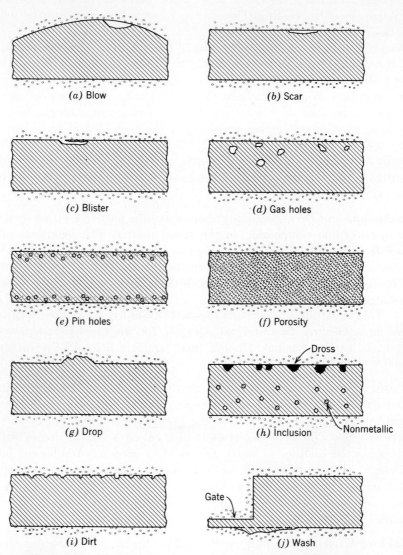

Figure 3-28. Illustrations of common casting defects. The array of small circular particles surrounding each casting represents the mold.

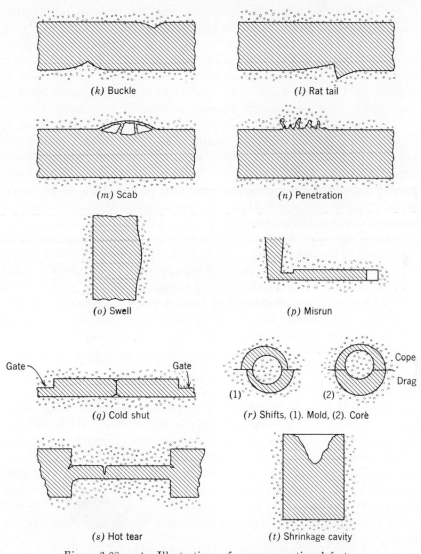

Figure 3-28 cont. Illustrations of common casting defects.

molding sand containing only sand, clay, and water. The mold is originally at room temperature and is filled with a liquid metal, such as cast iron at a temperature in excess of 2000°F. A layer of the molding sand in contact with the hot liquid is heated very rapidly. Because of the low thermal conductivity of the sand, the layer of hot sand is thin and the temperature rise is considerable. As the sand and clay particles experience this rise in temperature, they also undergo an increase in volume. Since the solid particles are in physical contact with each other at room temperature, the expansion of the sand is resisted by the mold flask, with the result that the heated sand is subjected to large compressive stresses parallel to the casting face.

This thin layer of sand becomes hot before a noticeable layer of liquid freezes against it. This combination of conditions causes the sand in the heated layer to buckle or bulge outwards into the mold cavity in a broad vee shape. When the casting solidifies within the mold cavity, the surface of the casting conforms to the shape of the mold surface and thus the upheaved vee projection of the mold causes a mating depression in the casting surface.

Buckling is avoided by adding organic particles, such as cereal or wood flour to the molding sand, so that these organic particles separate the refractory particles. When the hot metal is poured into a mold containing these additives and the adjacent layer of sand gets hot, the organic particles are oxidized and pass through the mold as a gas. Thus, they leave small void spaces for the expanding refractory particles to move into without inducing severe compressive stresses.

Rattail. A rattail is a long, shallow, angular depression in the surface of a flat casting and resembles a buckle except that it is not shaped like a broad vee. The cross section of a buckle has the two sides of the vee sloping in opposite directions. The cross section of a rattail either has the two sides of the angle sloping in the same direction, but one side steeper than the other, or else one of the sides is nearly perpendicular to the casting surface. A rattail is generally found on thinner castings than is a buckle. It is formed by the same conditions that cause a buckle except that instead of the expanding sand upheaving, the compressed layer fails by one mass flowing up over the other in a shear type failure. The difference between a buckle and a rattail can be seen in Figure 3-28k and l.

Scab. A scab is a rough, thin layer of metal protruding above the casting surface on top of a thin layer of sand, and held onto the casting by stringers of metal through the sand. A scab is created generally when the sand is upheaving to form a buckle and the upheaved sand separates from the mold and liquid metal flows into the space between the mold and the displaced sand.

Penetration. Penetration is a rough, porous projection on top of a casting surface which consists of a mixture of molding sand and metal. It results when the mold surface is too soft and porous. When the liquid metal is poured into the mold cavity, at those places where the sand is too loosely packed, some metal will flow between the sand particles for a distance into the mold wall. After this metal solidifies and the casting is removed from the mold, the lump of metal that seeped into the mold remains attached to the casting. Although it can be removed by chipping or grinding, this additional operation adds to the cost of the casting.

Swell. A swell is a slight, smooth projection or bulge usually found on vertical faces of castings that is caused by a local outward movement of the cavity face due to the hydrostatic pressure of the liquid metal. It occurs when the green deformation of the molding sand is high because of too high a water content, or when the mold is not rammed to a sufficient hardness.

Misrun. A misrun is a casting that is incomplete in its outermost sections because either the length to thickness ratio is too large or because the metal was poured with insufficient superheat. When liquid metal is flowing from one side in a thin section, it may lose sufficient heat so that the leading edge of the stream may freeze before it reaches the far end of the cavity. When this happens, the extremities of thin sections are missing. It is this defect that determines the minimum thickness that can be cast for a given metal, superheat, and type of mold.

Coldshut. A coldshut is an interface within a casting that lacks complete fusion, and is formed when two streams of liquid from two different directions come together after the leading surfaces have solidified. It is caused by the same conditions that create a misrun.

Shifts. A mold shift is a step at the parting line of a casting caused by the cope half of the cavity being displaced sideways with respect to the drag half. A core shift is a variation in wall thickness or section size between the cope and drag halves of a casting produced by a vertical displacement of the core during casting.

Hot Tears. A hot tear is an intergranular failure (along the grain boundaries) that occurs while the casting is at a high temperature within a mold. A hot tear may form in a larger section of a casting that is at a temperature just above the solidus temperature and is sub-jected to tensile strains induced by the solid contraction of an adjacent thinner section. While the mass is just above the solidus temperature, it consists of grains of metal that are surrounded by a thin film of liquid that cannot support a tensile load. Actually, since most cast metals contain nonmetallic inclusions, many of which have lower melt-ing temperatures than the metal being cast, this type of hot tear can also occur at temperatures just slightly below the solidus.

A second type of hot tear occurs at temperatures above the equi-cohesive temperature, but below the solidus in sections of a casting whose ends are constrained. For example, consider an I cross-sectional casting that solidifies uniformly in all parts of the casting. As the casting cools from the solidus to temperatures somewhat above the equicohesive temperature, the restraint caused by the ends of the cast-ing induce mechanical strains in the central part of the casting that are equal to the thermal contraction. Since the metal within the grain boundaries at this temperature has a lower strength than the grains themselves, and since this strength is very low at the high temperature, the metal fails (tears) through the grain boundaries.

To avoid hot tears, a mold having a low hot strength and large hot deformation should be used. When this is impossible, as is true with die and permanent mold casting, then the casting should be ex-tracted from the mold immediately after solidifying before it has a chance to cool significantly.

Shrinkage Cavities. A shrinkage cavity is a depression or an internal void in a casting that results from the volume contraction that occurs during solidification. The way in which shrinkage cavities originate in a casting were described in the previous section on solidification. A few examples are given next to demonstrate how a part design can be modified to eliminate or reduce shrinkage cavities.

There are two principles of casting design that must be adhered to if shrinkage cavities are to be avoided. Although they were stated in the previous section, on risers, they are repeated here for illustra-tion. The first principle is that a riser must be thicker than any part of the casting so that the riser solidifies last. The second is that in order for the riser to feed all parts of a casting, there must not be any decrease in section thickness in the direction toward the riser. This was illustrated in the examples of Figure 3-27. However, intersecting parts of a casting such as L's, T's, vees, etc., usually have a larger section thickness than do the adjoining legs, with the result that the center of these larger masses are "hot spots" and freeze last with a shrinkage

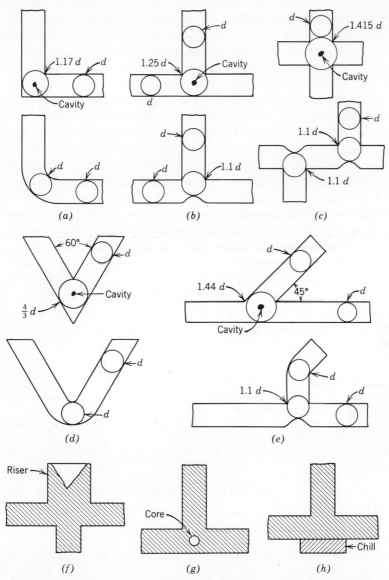

Figure 3-29. Illustrations of methods for eliminating shrinkage cavities at intersecting surfaces.

cavity being formed. A rule of thumb relationship to apply in casting design for avoiding shrinkage cavities is this: position the surfaces of the casting so that in any cross section the same diameter circle can be inscribed within the surfaces at any point in the casting.

Several methods of eliminating shrinkage cavities at intersecting surfaces are illustrated in Figure 3-29. With an angle section such as a, the outside surface should have a radius, R, at the corner that is equal to $r + d$, where r is the inside radius and d is the plate thickness. A tee section as at b simply requires a depression in the flat surface. For a cross such as at c, two legs may be displaced laterally and the opposite faces depressed. In the vee and Y sections shown in d and e, in addition to having a shrinkage cavity in the metal, there is also a hot spot in the mold at the sharp point because of a restricted heat flow. This condition can be improved by not only rounding the corner of the vee, but also by further separating the legs and making it a combination of a vee and a U section.

Several alternate methods of eliminating the cavity in a T are shown in f, g, and h, where either a riser, a core, or a chill is used.

REFERENCES

1. Adams, C. M., Jr., and H. F. Taylor, "Fundamentals of Riser Behavior," *Trans. A.F.S.*, **61**, p. 686, 1953.
2. Briggs, C. W., *The Metallurgy of Steel Castings,* McGraw-Hill Book Co., New York, 1946.
3. Caine, J. B., *A Theoretical Approach to the Problem of Dimensioning Risers,* *Trans. A.F.S.*, **56**, p. 492, 1948.
4. Chvorinov, N., "Control of the Solidification of Castings by Calculation," *Foundry Trade Journal,* Aug. 10, 1939.
5. Heine, R. W., and P. C. Rosenthal, *Principles of Metal Casting,* McGraw Hill Book Co., New York, 1955.
6. Ruddle, R. W., *The Solidification of Castings,* Inst. of Metals, London, 1957.

STUDY PROBLEMS

3–1   Discuss briefly the reasons for adding each of the following ingredients to a green sand mix: (a) sand, (b) water, (c) silica flour, (d) cereal, and (e) clay.

3–2   An aluminum hand wheel, as sketched, is cast in a permanent mold and is taken out of the mold when it cools to 100°F. Assume the strength-temperature relationship shown is correct and the temperature-gradients across any section are negligible.

$$\alpha = 13 \times 10^{-6} \text{ in./in./}°F$$

$$E = 10 \times 10^6 \text{ psi}$$

Are there any stresses in the radial spokes? If no, describe why. If yes, how large are they and how did they originate?

3-3   In casting a part such as is illustrated, what is the most likely type of defect that may occur from poor sand control? What would be another way, other than sand control, to prevent this defect?

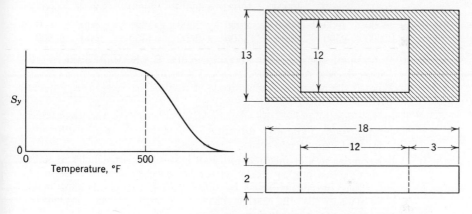

3-4   Distinguish between "porosity" and "voids" when these terms are used to describe casting defects. This should briefly describe their origin.

3-5   Estimate the cost of the pulley casting in Figure 3-3 if it were sand cast of gray iron in quantities of 50. Assume it is cleaned (with risers and gates removed) but not machined. Show all calculations (see Appendix H).

3-6   Estimate the lowest unit cost that a flat plate 1 in. x 6 in. x 9 in. could be purchased from a foundry in lots of 1000 pieces (see Appendix H).

3-7   If a pulley of Problem 3-5 above were made by pouring the liquid metal into a mold that was rammed too hard, what defects would probably be present and how serious would they be to the functioning of the part?

3-8   An "I" section die casting of "pure" aluminum is made in a mold that is maintained at a temperature of 100°F. The part is taken out of the mold when it is at a temperature of 300°F and is allowed to cool to room temperature (70°F) (ignore temperature gradients across any section). For aluminum:

$$\alpha = 13 \times 10^{-6} \text{ in./in./}°\text{F}$$
$$E = 10 \times 10^6 \text{ psi}$$

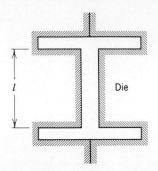

	70°F	300°F	400°F	500°F	600°F	700°F	800°F	900°F
Y.S.	5000	4000	3000	2000	1500	1000	500	0
T.S.	13,000	8500	6000	3500	2500	1500	1000	500

    a. If the length l of the die is 1.0000 in. at 100°F, what will be the length l of the die cast part at 70°F?

    b. What is the nature and magnitude of residual stresses, if any, of the part in (a) above?

3–9   State two advantages of the shell molding process over the green-sand molding process. (The two advantages must be reasonably different, that is, don't express one reason two ways.)

3–10   A link, similar to a connecting rod with bosses and cored holes at both ends, may be cast of gray iron in either green sand molds or permanent molds. What precaution must be taken during the permanent mold process to insure that the casting comes out in one piece that may not be a precaution necessary during the green-sand process?

3–11   If ferrite has a tensile strength (T.S.) of 40,000 psi and coarse pearlite has a T.S. of 120,000 psi, estimate the T.S. of gray cast iron. Explain your answer.

3–12   A plain carbon steel casting containing 1% carbon is specified for a certain wear-resistance application. Outline a heat treatment, after the original casting has cooled to room temperature and has the gates and risers removed, that will provide a microstructure that has the best wear resistance. Give temperatures, times, and cooling rates.

3–13   List and briefly describe five ways in which a pattern differs from the resulting casting made.

3–14   What are the advantages and limitations of the shell molding process?

3–15   What is the approximate cost of a 3 in. diameter x 10 ft long bar of the following material purchased from a warehouse (see Appendix H): 2024T4 aluminum, 70–30 brass, and 1020 steel.

3–16   List three reasons why a surface on a green sand casting would have to be machined.

3–17   Outline a procedure by means of which an aluminum alloy casting containing 95% Al, 5% Cu could be precipitation hardened without reheating the casting after the metal was poured into the mold.

3–18   Explain the metallurgical or microstructural changes that occur during the "holding period" in the malleableizing cycle of making malleable cast iron.

3–19   What is the major metallurgical difference between the steels and the cast irons?

3–20   Other than color, what is the primary difference between gray cast iron and white cast iron? To what difference in composition is this due?

3–21   Estimate the cost of a 2 in. diameter x 10 ft bar of the following (see Appendix H): (a) AISI 1018 H.R. steel, (b) 1100-F alloy, (c) 70 Cu–30 Zn brass, (d) 18-8 type stainless steel, and (e) gray cast iron.

3–22   Estimate the cost of a 4 in. diameter x 1 ft long bar of the following (see Appendix H): (a) AISI 1045 C.D. steel, (b) aluminum alloy, (c) copper, (d) stainless steel, (e) cast iron, and (f) teflon.

3–23   a. Sketch and label the microstructures of the following cast irons: (1) white, (2) gray, (3) pearlitic malleable, and (4) permanent mold ferritic gray.
       b. List two significant problems that are associated with permanent mold casting of gray iron that are less severe with the green-sand process.
       c. What casting defects (at least 2) most likely would result in the casting of a "H" section if good foundry practice were not followed?

3–24   It is desired to cast a cube that is 1 in. on a side of pure aluminum. Assume that the normal amount of superheat will be used.
       a. What will be the size of the mold cavity?
       b. What will be the volume of metal at the pouring temperature needed to make the cube. (This does not include the gates, runners or risers.)
       c. Why *must* a permanent mold casting of an "I" section of gray iron be removed from the mold immediately after solidification, whereas the same part made of aluminum need not be removed so soon?

3–25   A 1 in. diameter by 10 ft long cylinder of pure aluminum is made by casting in a sand mold. A second cylinder is made by casting in a permanent mold (made of steel). Discuss briefly why or why not residual stresses are present in either bar.

4

The Welding Process

Before the student considers the details of the various welding processes and the equipment associated with them, he will find that it is educationally profitable to first become aware of the overall scope and the fundamental problem of the welding process. Having gained this insight, he will be able to appreciate its development and its present status, as well as its capabilities and limitations. The close dependency of an engineering knowledge of welding upon a knowledge of materials and their properties will then become distinct to the student, and he will see that the mere cataloging or listing of the names and descriptions of the current processes and equipment is wholly unsatisfactory.

DEFINITION OF WELDING

There are many definitions of welding in the technical literature, with some of them explanations rather than definitions. The definitions vary from the all-inclusive "joining together of two or more members" to the all-exclusive "joining together of two or more pieces of metal by melting or fusing their contacting surfaces." The first definition is completely unsatisfactory to a student of the manufacturing processes because it does not exclude the joining operations of riveting, bolting, press fits, tying together with wire, or, if the author is permitted an extreme liberty, the bonding of a bride and groom by a marriage ceremony. The second definition is equally unsatisfactory since it does not include cold-pressure welding, recrystallization welding, welding with adhesives, and includes only part of the heterogeneous welding processes.

A suitable definition of welding for an engineer might be: *Welding is the manufacturing process of joining two or more pieces of material together by utilizing only the fundamental attracting forces that hold the atoms of a solid into their fixed positions.* Since the memorizing of a definition is but the first short step toward understanding a

178

subject (the application or use being the major step), the following discussion should clarify what welding is and is not.

Since all physics, chemistry, and materials textbooks describe sufficiently well the four fundamental bonding forces, it is assumed that the reader is already familiar with them and can now begin to apply this knowledge. These forces are therefore simply listed here in order of decreasing bonding strengths: (1) covalent, (2) ionic, (3) metallic, and (4) molecular. Thus the joining of two pieces of plastic or the joining of two pieces of metal or ceramic by means of an "adhesive" is truly welding if the forces holding the pieces together are van der Waal's molecular attractive forces. Plastic materials which are used as adhesives are usually noncrystalline, so it is not appropriate to refer to grain boundaries when discussing them. In describing their growth from small individual units or particles into larger masses, we refer to the crosslinking and interlocking of chainlike molecules (Figure 4-1a) as well as the mutual attraction of dipole molecules.

On the other hand, all the materials that are held together by the three remaining types of bonding forces are crystalline in structure and form polycrystalline solids. Single crystals are crystals in which all the crystalline planes of one type, such as the (001), are parallel and, in addition, the crystal surfaces (grain boundaries) are free or exposed surfaces. When two or more crystals form in such a way that some of the crystal surfaces, in particular the surfaces between the contacting crystals, are not free surfaces, the solid is said to be poly-crystalline (Figure 4-1b and 1c). In this condition nothing but grain boundaries separates the individual grains from each other—the atoms at the contacting surface of one grain are separated from the atoms of the adjacent grain by a distance that is approximately equal to the lattice parameter for that material. In this context, the terms grains

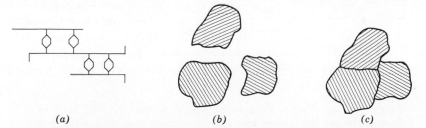

(a)   *(b)*   *(c)*

Figure 4-1. Schematic sketch of solids: (a) benzene base hydrocarbon chain, (b) single crystals of solid, and (c) polycrystalline solid. Cross section refers to same family of crystalline planes.

and crystals are used interchangeably. This condition, in reality, is welding as it applies to crystalline solids. The fundamental mechanism of welding crystalline materials is obvious in its simplicity—the bringing together of two or more pieces so that nothing but grain boundaries separate them. As sketched in Figure 4-1, the similar crystalline planes of adjacent crystals need not be, and usually are not, of the same orientation. This concept, then, guides us naturally to the basic welding problem.

THE FUNDAMENTAL WELDING PROBLEM

The fundamental welding problem (to us on earth) is simply the *removal of the adsorbed gas and oxide layers from large areas of the intended contacting surfaces* of the mating parts so that only grain boundaries separate them. It must be understood that this welding problem is only one of atmosphere or environment, and in the past we never had to seriously consider joining or unjoining materials in any other environment than that on the surface of the earth. However, in the vacuum of outer space, on the moon, or on other planets, welding may not be a problem—but unwelding may. Let us consider for a moment some of these situations.

Two pieces of clean metal brought into contact in a vacuum will have nothing but grain boundaries separating them at the contact surfaces. The area of the contacting surfaces will be dependent upon

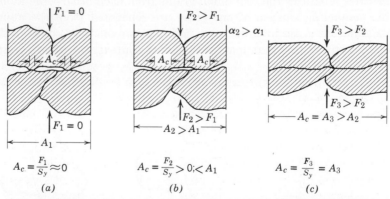

$$A_c = \frac{F_1}{S_y} \approx 0 \qquad\qquad A_c = \frac{F_2}{S_y} > 0; < A_1 \qquad\qquad A_c = \frac{F_3}{S_y} = A_3$$

$$(a) \qquad\qquad\qquad (b) \qquad\qquad\qquad (c)$$

Figure 4-2. Sketches of clean surfaces under several different loads in a vacuum. In (a) the force is zero and the contact area A_c is zero. In (b) the force is modest and the contact area A_c is a small fraction of A_1. In (c) the force is large enough to deform all the asperities and the contact area equals the projected area.

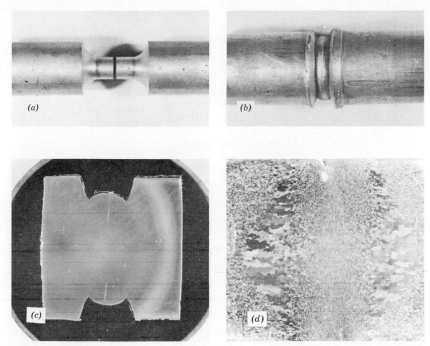

Figure 4-3. Photomicrograph of a cold pressure weld of two pieces of aluminum as depicted in Figure 3c. (Note dispersion of oxide and compare with spot weld of Figure 4-46.) (*a*) Two pieces before welding. (*b*) After welding. (*c*) Section at weld joint after polishing. Only center half is welded. (*d*) After annealing, coarse grains in critically strained region.

the forces pressing the two parts together, and, if the force is large enough, the asperities on the surfaces will be plastically deformed until the entire cross-sectional areas of the parts are in intimate contact (Figure 4-2). When this occurs, the parts are completely and perfectly welded together. If tensile forces are then applied to separate the parts, failure will occur outside the "weld area" because the metal in the weld area has been strengthened by strain hardening, as is demonstrated in Figure 4-3 which is a photomicrograph of a cold weld of two pieces of aluminum. What problems will be involved in separating a passenger vehicle and a freighter vehicle after they have been in contact in space if their surfaces are made of crystalline solids? How can tools such as pliers or wrenches be used in a vacuum and not have their sliding parts weld together? Will a metal screw rotate in a metal nut on the surface of the moon? The need to prevent welding in situa-

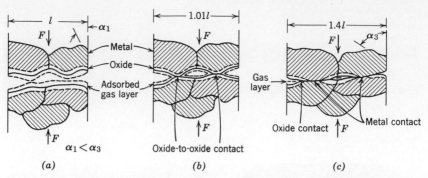

Figure 4-4. Sketches of actual smooth surfaces, highly magnified, under several different loads in air. In (*a*) the force is nearly zero and there is no oxide-to-oxide contact. In (*b*) the force is modest and there may be some oxide-to-oxide contact at the asperities where lateral elastic force may have separated the moisture film. In (*c*) the subsurface metal grains have sufficiently flowed laterally to fracture the oxide layer and leave nearly 50% of the surface exposed as new metal surfaces with some metal-to-metal contact.

tions similar to those described above is stimulating research and bringing forth data that are equally useful in teaching the subject of welding from a fundamental rather than a "this is how it is done" manner.

Smooth surfaces such as those prepared by finish grinding or lapping are really not perfectly plane surfaces but rather, when looked at microscopically, consist of a continuous array of asperities. Furthermore, in our normal atmosphere, this metallic surface is coated with two thin films (about 100 to 200Å thick); one an oxide layer and the outer one an adsorbed gas layer as sketched in Figure 4-4*a*. Until a few years ago the traditional way in which these two films were removed from a weld interface was by heating the parts until the interface material was melted and thus flowed out of the interface. The more recent technique of exposing clean metal at the weld interface by means of severe plastic deformation is illustrated in Figure 4-4*c* where the mechanism is also briefly described.

Welds can be made between two pieces of metal without removing the adsorbed gas or the oxide layer, but the strength of such a weld is very low, and was not considered as a "weld" in the days when weld was synonymous with fusion. Such a low-strength weld occurs when two gage blocks (hardened and precision lapped pieces of steel used as reference or standards of length in industry) are "wrung" together (Figure 4-5*a*). The actual process of wringing gage blocks together consists of wiping the mating surfaces, which are about $\frac{1}{4}$ in. $\times$ 1 in. in cross section, on the inside of one's wrists and then sliding the two blocks together. It has been demonstrated that two properly joined blocks can support a load as high as 100 lb if it is applied normally to the contacting surfaces, whereas the gage blocks can be separated by sliding with a force only a fraction of 1 lb applied parallel to the contacting surfaces. Thus the tensile strength of this weld is of the

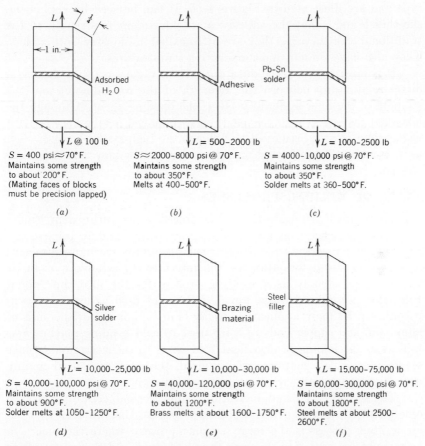

Figure 4-5. Approximate relative strength of various types of welded joints. The welded pieces are $\frac{1}{4}$ in. $\times$ 1 in. cross-sectional steel blocks in all cases.

order of 400 psi—much less than the strength of steel, but also much greater than atmospheric pressure. What holds the blocks together? Actually, it is the adsorbed moisture layer that is attached to both surfaces that holds the blocks together; the molecular attractive forces of the dipole water molecules and the surface tension of the moisture. This has been substantiated by tests conducted in dry atmospheres where it was found that the blocks would not "weld."

The strength of the weld can be raised somewhat by placing a molecularly bonded film with a higher Van der Waal's attractive force between the two pieces of steel to be joined together. The common adhesives, epoxies, and plastic cements on the market today are of this type and are illustrated in Figure 4-5b. It can be seen by comparing sketches b and c that the adhesives are equivalent in strength to the traditional lead-tin or, as they are often called in industry, soft solders. They also have similar upper operating temperatures.

It is apparent from the data outlined in Figure 4-5 that there is a direct relationship between the strength of the welded joint and the strength of the filler material used as the bonding agent. Although the adsorbed gas and oxide layer need not be removed for the low-strength welds, they must be removed to achieve the high-strength welds such as d, e, and f. The following paragraphs will show how this is accomplished.

TYPES OF WELDING PROCESSES

There are five types of welding processes, as outlined in Figure 4-6, when considered on the basis of the energy used to remove the gas and oxide layers. The first type listed uses only mechanical means, or severe plastic deformation at the interface, to achieve a weld. It was used industrially as a welding process for the first time about 1950. Because of its relative newness it is not used as extensively as it could be. Its main application today is in the joining of the ends of aluminum and copper coils of wire used in cold heading machines as well as in the joining of electrical lead wires to their terminals. Since severe plastic deformations are required, the process is used mainly with ductile materials such as aluminum and copper.

The second type listed, mechanical plus thermal, contains both the oldest and the newest of the welding processes. Undoubtedly the oldest welding process is the forge welding process, where the pieces to be joined were heated in an open fire or "forge," and then the ends to be joined were placed, one on top of the other, on an anvil and hammered (or forged) together. Considerable skill was shown many centuries ago by the practitioners of this trade in the joining of bars

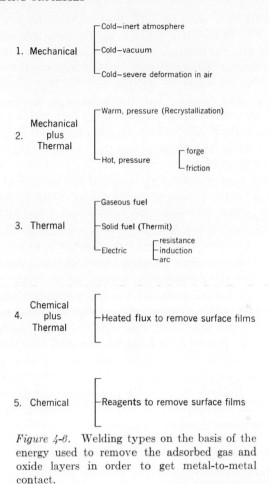

Figure 4-6. Welding types on the basis of the energy used to remove the adsorbed gas and oxide layers in order to get metal-to-metal contact.

or plates of iron. Because of the limitations in the size of castings and forgings that could be produced, whenever large parts were required, it was necessary to employ the forge welding process. The welding artisan of those days achieved surprisingly good welds by first crowning or beveling the mating surfaces to facilitate squeezing out the oxides. Also by throwing silica sand onto the areas to be welded, they converted the iron oxide to a more fluid slag which aided its expulsion from the interface. Forge welding is used quite extensively today to join large diameter pipe and shafts end to end. The heat is supplied by oxyacetylene flame heads or by induction heating coils, and the pressure is supplied by hydraulic cylinders.

Recrystallization welding and friction welding are very recent innovations. The former has limited applications because it lies between the cold and the hot processes and does not have the advantages of either. Because of its simplicity, friction welding is becoming more widely applied as an industrial welding process. The equipment will be described in a later section, but the process is briefly described as follows: one part is clamped and then its end rotated while lightly contacting the mating part (which is also clamped) and, after a short time, the two parts are pressed together with a large force as the relative motion is stopped.

During the past half-century most of the industrial welding was done by means of the processes listed under Type 3, thermal, in the outline of Figure 4-6. The most common gaseous fuel is the combination of compressed oxygen and acetylene. Originally the d-c electric arc was by far the most common of the electric heat sources, but now the a-c arc and the resistance processes are also being very widely used.

In some cases the melting temperature of the oxide is higher than that of either the parent metal or the filler material and then a flux must be used that will combine chemically with the oxide layer to form a low-melting-temperature slag that can be displaced easily from the weld interface. This is Type 4, or the chemical plus thermal process. In the past this would be associated with the brazing and soldering processes.

Type 5 was included in order to distinguish the processes that use a reagent at room temperature for removing the oxide layer from those processes that require a heated flux.

Welding Classes According to Composition

It is helpful to distinguish the welding processes on the basis of composition changes that may occur in addition to the previous cataloging on the basis of the energy used to remove the surface films. On the basis of composition changes in the weld zone, all of the welding processes can be grouped under three classes: (1) autogenous, (2) homogeneous, and (3) heterogeneous.

Autogenous welding is a class of welding processes in which no filler material is added to the joint interface. This includes nearly all of the cold and hot pressure welding processes and the electric resistance processes.

Homogeneous welding is that class in which the filler material is of the same type as the parent metal. Thus the welding of 1100 aluminum with an 1100 aluminum rod, the welding of 70-30 brass with a 70-30 brass rod, and the welding of plain low carbon steel with a low carbon rod are all homogeneous processes.

Heterogeneous welding is a class of welding processes whereby the filler material is of a different type from the parent metal. This class includes the brazing and soldering processes as well as those that use adhesives or other plastics as a filler material. There are literally thousands of different compositions of alloys, many of which are so-called low melting temperature, on the market today for the heterogeneous welding process. Nearly all of them are identified by the manufacturer's trade name or number rather than by the actual composition, which accounts for their large number.

All of these three classes of welding may be used with any of the types of energy sources outlined in Figure 4-6. For example, two plates of AISI 1020 steel can be joined by autogenous welding using every one of the welding processes in this figure.

Autogenous welding is the fastest and least expensive of the three classes. However, when using those welding types that employ no pressure, the cross-sectional area of the fused metal at the interface will be less than that of the parent metal during autogenous welding because of the lack of perfect "fit-up" at the interface. Thus it is apparent that homogeneous welding is used when it is desired to compensate for this lack of sufficient metal at the interface by adding filler metal.

Sometimes it is desired to weld two pieces together, such as precision investment castings, without melting either of them. This can be accomplished by a heterogeneous process using a filler material of lower melting temperature than the castings, which is also soluble in them. Sometimes it is necessary to weld two pieces together without a phase transformation occurring. An example of this is the rapid welding of a high-hardenability cast iron rotor onto a steel shaft without forming martensite in the rotor because of the fast cooling after welding. This also can be done by a heterogeneous process using a soluble filler material with a melting temperature about 200°F below the lower critical temperature of the cast iron.

Another problem encountered occasionally is the welding of two materials that are not soluble in each other. An example of this is the welding of a silver plug onto a steel bar, for according to the equilibrium phase diagrams in the Appendix, iron and silver are insoluble in each other in both the liquid and solid states. This problem can also be readily solved by using a filler material such as tin or copper that is soluble in both silver and iron.

Nearly all welding problems in which the difficulty lies in joining the parts together can be solved by approaches similar to the above. To determine whether materials can be bonded together, we must determine to what extent they are soluble in each other. This can be done by referring to the equilibrium phase diagrams of the materials in question, the best source of which is the 1948 edition of the ASM *Metals Handbook.*

This broad overlook of the fundamentals of welding should assist the reader in approaching a welding situation where he is expected to make an optimum design or solution better equipped than if he were indoctrinated with the traditional, and current, lists of do's and don'ts.

SURVEY OF WELDING EQUIPMENT

The common equipment, or hardware, as it is now called in many engineering circles, in current use in the various welding processes is briefly described next. In some cases, a summary of some of the techniques required in the process is also included.

Gaseous Fuel Processes

Gas welding as we know it today is a comparatively young process, the present-day welding torch having been developed about 1900. Although the early Egyptians, Greeks, and Romans used a liquid fuel to produce a flame, the resulting flame temperature was too low to melt copper or iron alloys. However, those early weldors were able to make satisfactory weldments by using the flame to simply heat the metal to make it soft and ductile so that by means of hand hammering, joining was accomplished by the forge welding process. The present industrial success of gas welding is due to the development of fuels capable of producing flame temperatures in excess of 5000°F. But even our current gaseous fuels are not satisfactory to weld many of the refractory materials by the autogenous or homogeneous processes.

Several combinations of gases may be used as welding fuels, some of which are: hydrogen and oxygen, propane and oxygen, propane and air, and natural gas and air. However, because it has the highest flame temperature, as illustrated in Table 4-1, the most widely used combination is acetylene (C_2H_2) and oxygen, frequently referred to as oxyacetylene welding.

Acetylene was first produced in 1836 by Edmund Davy, but it was a French chemist, Marcellin Berthelot, who identified it and named it acetylene in 1862. Also in 1862 Wöhler discovered the material calcium carbide, from which all present-day acetylene is generated by dropping calcium carbide particles into water in a closed container.

TABLE 4-1. Some Properties of Gases Suitable As Welding Fuels

Gas	Formula	Specific Gravity (60°F)	Specific Volume (ft³/lb) (60°F)	Heat of Combustion H_c Btu/ft³ (1 atm, 60°F)		Theoretical Flame Temperature (°F)	
				Gross	Net	With Air	With Oxygen
Acetylene	C_2H_2	0.9056	14.45	1483	1433	4770	6300
Hydrogen	H_2	0.0696	188.70	325	275	4010	5400
Butane	C_4H_{10}	2.0100	6.51	3261	3010	3870	5300
Propane	C_3H_8	1.5223	8.61	2509	2309	3840	5300
Ethane	C_2H_6	1.0494	12.48	1762	1612	3820	5100
Methane	CH_4	0.5545	23.64	1012	912	3750	5000
Natural gas	$CH_4 + C_2H_6$	0.68	19.20	1100	1000	3740	4600

The products of the reaction are acetylene and calcium hydroxide or slaked lime as shown by the equation:

$$CaC_2 + H_2O \rightarrow C_2H_2 + Ca(OH)_2 + 166\,Btu/ft^3\,C_2H_2$$

But calcium carbide was an expensive material used only in the laboratory at this time. An economical way of manufacturing calcium carbide was accidentally developed in 1892 when Wilson in the United States was trying to produce metallic calcium by heating a mixture of coke and limestone in an electric furnace.

Two important developments in the history of oxyacetylene welding occurred in 1895: (1) Le Chatelier discovered that when equal volumes of oxygen and acetylene were burned, the flame temperature was 6000°F, and (2) Linde developed the liquid air machine that made it possible to produce oxygen economically.

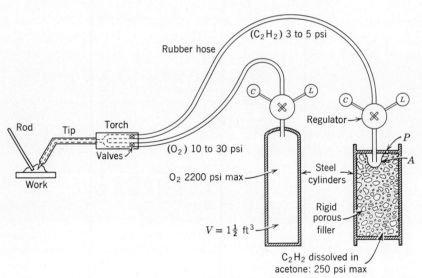

Figure 4-7. Sketch of a typical gas welding setup. The oxygen cylinder is charged with 220 ft³ of atmospheric oxygen when pressurized to 2200 psi. The acetylene cylinder has a unique construction. The steel tank is originally filled with a mixture of diatomaceous (spongelike) earth, charcoal, and cement. After hardening, this porous material is filled with acetone, and then the acetylene is dissolved in the acetone.

C = cylinder pressure gage, L = line pressure gage, P = temperature sensitive plugs, and A = asbestos wick.

Before oxyacetylene welding could be used extensively, a means of transporting acetylene was necessary for the smaller users of the gas since the manufacture of acetylene was not feasible for them. Acetylene could not simply be stored by compressing it into steel cylinders, as is done now with the other gases such as oxygen, hydrogen, helium, etc., which are stored and transported at pressures of 2200 psi, because acetylene is an endothermic compound and decomposes into carbon and hydrogen readily. If in a confined space, this decomposition results in an increase in pressure and, above 25 psi pressure, it is violently explosive even in the absence of oxygen when subjected to sparks or shock. This storage and transporting problem was solved in 1897 when Claude and Hess noted the very high solubility of acetylene in acetone. Twenty volumes of acetylene will dissolve in one volume of acetone at 15 psi and increases somewhat proportionally with pressure, being 300 volumes at 175 psi. Acetylene is usually stored in these cylinders at a maximum pressure of 250 psi.

The oxyacetylene torch and the oxyacetylene process as we know them today came into the industrial scene between 1900 and 1903. A typical gas welding setup is sketched in Figure 4-7. The brief description given in that figure as well as the operating data given in Tables 4-2, 4-3, and 4-4 are sufficient for a general understanding of the gas welding process. A description of the details of welding techniques is too time consuming for both the author and the reader. However, a 15 min demonstration, either live or with movies, is far superior to a written text and the author recommends this practice.

TABLE 4-2. Tip Size and Gas Consumption in Welding Steel
(Data from *Welding Directory*, 1958–1959)

Metal Thickness (in.)	Average Flame Length	Orifice Diameter (in.)	Approx Gas Consumption ft^3/hr		Welding Time, min/ft
			Oxygen	Acetylene	
$\frac{1}{16}$	$\frac{3}{16}$	0.037	5.0	5.0	4–6
$\frac{1}{16}-\frac{1}{8}$	$\frac{1}{4}$	0.042	6.0	6.0	3–10
$\frac{1}{8}-\frac{3}{16}$	$\frac{5}{16}$	0.055	9.0	9.0	5–20
$\frac{3}{16}-\frac{1}{4}$	$\frac{3}{8}$	0.0635	12.0	12.0	6–17
$\frac{1}{4}-\frac{3}{8}$	$\frac{7}{16}$	0.076	21.0	21.0	7–8
$\frac{3}{8}-\frac{1}{2}$	$\frac{15}{32}$	0.086	23.0	23.0	14–25
$\frac{1}{2}-\frac{5}{8}$	$\frac{1}{2}$	0.098	36.0	36.0	20–30
$\frac{5}{8}-1$	$\frac{9}{16}$	0.1065	50.0	50.0	28–35

TABLE 4-3. Material Consumption Data For Manual
(Oxyacetylene Welding[1])

Thickness (in.)	Joint Preparation (Degree Spacing)	Rod Diameter	Oxygen ft³/hr	Acetylene ft³/hr	Rod, lb/hr	Time, min/ft
$\frac{1}{64}$	Square groove	—	0.7	0.7	—	2.0–2.3
$\frac{1}{32}$	Square groove	—	1.0	1.0	—	2.4–2.7
$\frac{1}{16}$	Square groove	$\frac{1}{16}$	2.4	2.3	0.23–0.27	2.8–3.2
$\frac{1}{8}$	Square groove	$\frac{1}{8}$	8.8	8.5	0.58–0.69	4.6–5.5
$\frac{1}{4}$	90° single Vee	$\frac{3}{16}$	27.0	26.0	1.59–1.86	8.5–10.0
$\frac{3}{8}$	90° single Vee	$\frac{1}{4}$	45.7	44.0	2.39–2.98	12.0–15.0
$\frac{1}{2}$	60° single Vee	$\frac{1}{4}$	58.2	56.0	2.90–3.48	10.0–12.0
$\frac{3}{4}$	60° single Vee	$\frac{5}{16}$	91.5	88.0	3.27–4.57	17.0–24.0

[1] Compiled from data in Welding Handbook, 5th Edition.

TABLE 4-4. Average Data For Machine Cutting Low Carbon Steel[1]

Thickness Plate (in.)	Diameter of Cutting Orifice (in.)	Oxygen Pressure (psi)	Cutting Time, min/ft	Gas Consumption ft³/hr Oxygen	Acetylene
$\frac{1}{8}$	0.0200–0.0400	15–30	0.38–0.55	17–55	5–9
$\frac{1}{4}$	0.0310–0.0595	11–35	0.43–0.60	36–95	6–11
$\frac{1}{2}$	0.0310–0.0595	20–55	0.50–0.70	63–125	8–13
1	0.0465–0.0595	28–55	0.63–0.86	130–174	13–16
2	0.0670–0.0810	22–60	0.86–1.2	185–260	16–20
4	0.0810–0.0860	40–60	1.3–1.8	293–384	21–26
8	0.0980–0.0995	60–90	2.5–3.2	505–625	31–39
12	0.1100–0.1200	69–105	3.5–5	780–880	42–52

[1] Data from *Welding Directory*, 1958–1959.

The three types of flames obtained with an oxyacetylene welding torch are illustrated in Figure 4-8. In most welding situations it is theoretically desirable to use a neutral flame, but, in practice, because there is no way to discern whether the flame is neutral or oxidizing, either a slightly reducing or a slightly oxidizing flame is used. The former is used for those materials that oxidize rapidly like steel or aluminum. The latter flame is used when welding materials such as copper or gold which are not oxidized readily and which have a high solubility of hydrogen in the molten state and low solubility in the solid state.

The complete combustion of acetylene requires $2\frac{1}{2}$ mols (or volumes) of oxygen for each mol of acetylene as evidenced from the reaction:

$$C_2H_2 + 2\frac{1}{2}O_2 \rightarrow 2CO_2 + H_2O \tag{4-1}$$

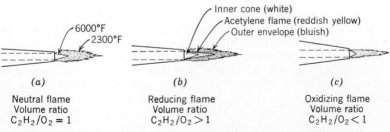

Figure 4-8. Three types of flames obtained with a gas welding torch.

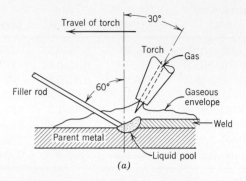

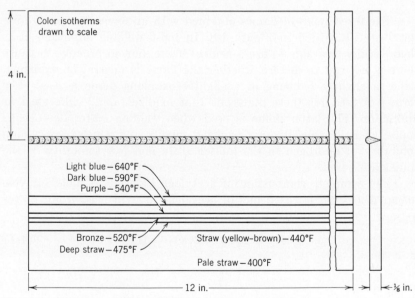

Figure 4-9. Sketch of oxyacetylene gas welded cold-finished steel plates showing: (a) The position of torch, rod and work during forehand welding. For backhand welding, the position of the torch and rod are reversed.

(b) Position of the color isotherms after welding drawn to scale.

Average welding rate: 4.5 min/ft. Rod diameter: $\frac{1}{16}$ in. Gas consumption: acetylene—0.15 ft^3/min, oxygen—0.15 ft.^{3}/min, and $H_c = 543{,}000$ Btu/lb mol.

The reaction at the inner cone for the neutral flame where equal volumes of cylinder oxygen and acetylene are used is

$$C_2H_2 + O_2 \rightarrow 2CO + H_2 \qquad (4\text{-}2)$$

Thus it is apparent that the environment within the outer envelope consists of hydrogen and carbon monoxide and is relatively inert to materials that oxidize readily. During actual welding, the outer envelope spreads out over the surface of the work material and serves as a protective shield from the ordinary atmosphere.

The reactions at the outer envelope are

$$2CO + O_2 + N_2 \rightarrow 2CO_2 + N_2 \qquad (4\text{-}3)$$

$$H_2 + \tfrac{1}{2}O + N_2 \rightarrow H_2O + N_2 \qquad (4\text{-}4)$$

Since bottled oxygen is expensive compared to atmospheric oxygen, it is used only for the inner cone reaction, Equation 4-2, and atmospheric oxygen is used for the combustion at the outer envelope which accounts for the nitrogen being included in Equations 4-3 and 4-4.

Figure 4-9a illustrates the position of the torch, rod, and work material during the actual welding operation. Illustrated in b to scale is the position of the color isotherms of two pieces of $\tfrac{1}{8}$ in. thick steel welded under typical conditions. By comparing this to Figure 4-33 which illustrates the same plates arc-welded, it is obvious that much of the heat of the flame is wasted in heating up a large volume of adjacent metal.

Some data on material consumption during gas welding are given in Tables 4-2 and 4-3. Some cost data on the economics of welding are given in Tables 4-14 and 4-15.

Flame Cutting. The manufacturing process of flame cutting has been traditionally included with the list of welding processes although on a rational basis there is more justification to list flame cutting as a machining process and thus change the name to flame machining. Certainly it cannot be denied that flame cutting is an unjoining rather than a joining process. It would then fall in a category that would include such processes as: electroarc machining, electron-beam machining, shearing, electro-chemical machining etc. Figure 4-10 illustrates a typical flame cutting operation.

The torch for flame cutting is the same as the welding torch, with two exceptions. First, as illustrated in Figure 4-11, the welding tip contains only one hole in the center of the tip through which the mixed C_2H_2 and O_2 gases flow, whereas the cutting tip contains a center hole through which pure oxygen, which does the actual "cutting,"

Figure 4-10. Photograph of a flame cutting setup. (Courtesy Linde Co.)

flows. There are also several concentric holes that provide the required preheat by supplying a mixture of C_2H_2 and O_2. Second, the cutting torch has an additional, or third, valve for controlling the flow of pure oxygen.

Flame cutting is done both manually and with motor-driven heads. The latter, sometimes called a cutting machine, may be of the simple type that cuts only along straight lines with one cutting head; or they may be very elaborate cam-controlled devices that trace directly from

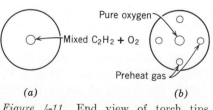

Figure 4-11. End view of torch tips. (*a*) Welding. (*b*) Cutting.

blueprints by means of photoelectric tubes and employ many cutting torches in a line. The surface finish of manual cut pieces is not very good, about 1000 or more RMS, but the surface finish of machine-cut surfaces may be as good as 100–150 RMS which is comparable to some machined surfaces and better than most sawed surfaces.

Nearly all flame cutting is done on steel. Cast iron cannot be flame cut satisfactorily because the graphite oxidizes more readily than the ferrous matrix and it simply melts the matrix. Aluminum cannot be cut because of its high thermal conductivity; and stainless steel because of its oxidation resistance.

Some data for gas consumption during the flame cutting of steel are given in Table 4-4.

Arc Welding Processes

The first description of the electric arc is probably the one made by Sir Humphry Davy in 1809 after he accidentally created arcs while experimenting on the decomposition of some of the alkaline metals. However, it was not until 1885 that arc welding became an industrial process. In that year two Russians received a patent on a joining process in which fusion was obtained by maintaining an arc between a carbon electrode and the work to be joined. A few years later the process was modified to have the arc between two carbon electrodes held in one holder, but since the heat for welding the work pieces is radiated from the arc, the thermal efficiency of the process is poor, thus it is very rarely used today. The atomic hydrogen process that is used in a few special applications today is a descendant of the double-arc process.

The number of rapid improvements that were made in the arc welding process attests to the fact that the manufacturing industries had a great need for such a process. In 1892 a German conceived the idea of using a consumable metallic electrode in place of the "non-consumable" carbon electrode. Since he used an ordinary metal wire, both the arc and the weld pool were unprotected from the oxygen, nitrogen, and moisture in the atmosphere, and so the welds were, by today's standards, very inferior due to the presence of gas and oxide inclusions in the weld zone. A Swedish engineer in 1907 got the first patent on a coated electrode, but the coating was basically only a protective gas former and arc stabilizer and did not protect the hot weld metal after the arc moved by. The first gas plus slag-forming electrode coatings were developed in both England and the United States about 1910, and with these heavy-coated electrodes it was possible for the first time to obtain weldments free of oxide inclusions.

198 THE WELDING PROCESS

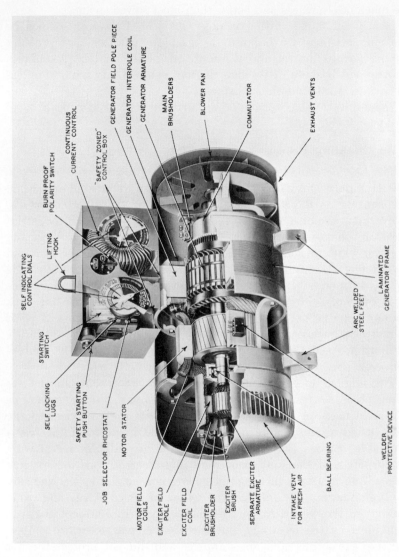

Figure 4-12. Photograph of a cutaway section of a motor-driven d-c welding generator. (Courtesy Lincoln Electric Co.)

In those early days, the control of coatings and arc-welding techniques were poor and consequently some welds were good, whereas others were not. Therefore, when critical parts were arc welded it was necessary to also inspect every inch of weld metal by x-ray photographs to make sure no inclusions or gas holes were present. Because of improved controls, today this practice of x-ray inspection has reduced simply to spot checks or sample inspection.

Direct-Current Generators. The most common type of arc-welding unit is the electric motor or gasoline engine driven d-c generator, one model of which is shown in Figure 4-12. Basically, the welding generator is a differentially compound-wound self-excited d-c generator with two sets of magnetic poles—the main field and the cross field (Figure 4-13).

The main field poles are designed to be magnetically saturated, so their magnetic flux is constant for all values of armature current. Since these poles are saturated, they generate a constant potential across the armature which is designed to be approximately 50 volts for welding purposes.

The cross pole pieces have two windings, one in series with the armature and the other in series with the shunt field of the main pole, and are designed to be nonsaturated. Therefore the magnetic flux of the cross poles is affected by the armature current in such a way that when the current increases, the armature potential due to the cross field decreases. The output potential of the generator is the algebraic

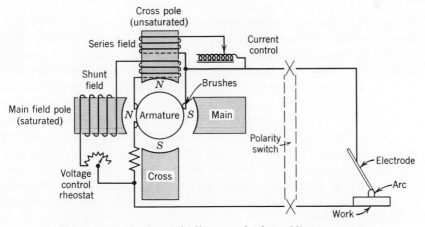

Figure 4-13. A schematic diagram of a d-c welding generator.

sum of the potentials generated in the armature due to both the main-field flux and the cross-field flux.

When the external arc circuit is open, no current flows through the series field of the cross pole, and the magnetic flux of the cross pole is due entirely to the second cross pole winding. The output potential of the armature in this case is referred to as the open circuit voltage. When the voltage control rheostat is set at its maximum value, the output potential is maximum. The maximum value is about 100 volts for most machines, with 50 volts being generated by the main field pole, and 50 volts generated by the second cross pole field. When the voltage control switch is set to its minimum value, the potential produced by the main field pole is 50 volts and by the cross pole is zero, so the resulting output potential is equal to the minimum value of 50 volts.

When the electrode is shorted to the work, the armature current is maximum for any particular setting of the current control switch, and is referred to as the short circuit current. The series field creates a flux in the cross pole that is equal and opposite to that created by the main field pole, and as a result the output potential is nearly zero, being large enough to overcome the resistance of the short circuit.

During an actual welding operation, the conditions lie between these two extremes. The arc current is constantly fluctuating as a result of changes in the arc length, changes which are due to the passage of molten globules of metal through the arc column. The response of the welding generator to these variations in welding conditions is referred to as the generator characteristics and they are illustrated in Figure 4-24 and discussed in detail in a following section.

One advantage of the d-c generator over the a-c welding trans-former that offsets its higher cost is that the ratio of the arc energy going into the work surface or the electrode end can be varied. With a d-c arc, about five-eighths of the arc energy goes to the anode surface and about three-eighths is liberated at the cathode surface. Thus for straight polarity where the work is positive, about 62% of the arc energy is liberated at the work surface, which is desirable for welding thick sections. On the other hand, in welding thin sections such as automobile bodies, it is advantageous to use reverse polarity to prevent the melting or "burning" of holes in the metal, since only 38% of the arc energy is liberated at the work surface in this case. In a-c welding, since the polarity is changing at the rate of 60 cycles per second, half of the arc energy is liberated at the work surface and half at the electrode.

Direct-Current Rectifier. A more recent addition to the d-c welding equipment is the dry plate rectifier shown in Figure 4-14. The a-c supply current is transformed to between 60 and 70 volts, depending on the current flow, and rectified with no "moving" parts. Consequently, the maintenance cost is lower than for the generator type. An additional benefit is that three-phase current can be used, thus making it possible to achieve a close balance in using the three phases of the power supply. In most other respects this type of a welding machine is also similar to various aspects of d-c generators and a-c transformers.

Alternating Current Transformer Welders. Alternating-current welding machines were not used industrially until quite recently because of the need of good "arc stabilization," which is the ability of

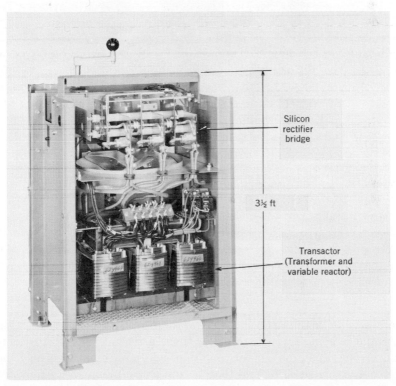

Silicon rectifier bridge

3½ ft

Transactor (Transformer and variable reactor)

Figure 4-14. Photograph of a cutaway section of a rectifier-type d-c welding machine. (Courtesy Westinghouse Electric Co.)

Figure 4-15. Photograph of a cutaway model of an a-c welding transformer. (Courtesy Miller Electric Mfg. Co.)

the arc to be maintained during the short periods of time when the potential is going through zero 120 times a second. The first attempt to overcome this problem was made by adding a high frequency unit to the basic transformer so that a low current high frequency was superimposed on the 60-cycle welding current. However, this increased the cost of the welding machine and made it less competitive. More recently, the development of low-ionization-potential electrode coatings has made it possible for a simple transformer to be used successfully as a welding machine with the advantage of both a low initial and low maintenance cost. A typical unit is shown in Figure 4-15.

How the current is varied, by leakage reactance, is shown in Figure 4-16. The amount of the leakage reactance is determined by the distance between the primary and the secondary coils. This distance can be changed very easily for different welding conditions by means of a screw which moves the primary coil with respect to the secondary coil. When the distance between the two coils is great, there is a large leakage and the welding current is low (Figure 4-16). Most of the a-c welding transformers provide only one open circuit voltage, as shown in Figure 4-25, and the output characteristics (volts versus amperes) are approximately elliptical in shape.

An advantage of the a-c welder, in addition to its lower maintenance and operating cost, is that there is little "magnetic arc blow" associated with it. The phenomenon known as "arc blow" is the erratic or wandering arc that occurs during the welding of magnetic materials such as steel with d-c current when the cross section of the metal being welded is not symmetrical about the electrode. The unbalanced magnetic forces in this situation cause the d-c arc column to wander from what should be its normal position.

Submerged-Arc Welding. The submerged-arc welding process is different from the previously discussed consumable electrode arc welding process in two respects: first, the filler material is a long bare wire (sometimes a mile in length) in the form of a coil rather than a 14 in.

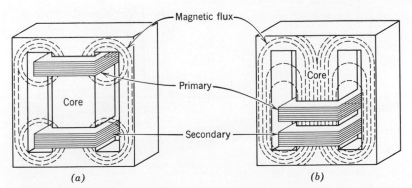

Figure 4-16. Control of current in a-c welding transformer by means of leakage reactance. (*a*) Low current. (*b*) High current.

long "stick"; second, the shielding material, instead of being a coating on the electrode wire, is a dry granular flux that is continuously fed by gravity through a pipe directly in front of the arc so that the arc and all the adjacent hot metal are covered and protected from the oxygen in the air. It is for this reason that the process gets its name, submerged arc. Figure 4-17 illustrates the process.

In most instances of submerged-arc welding, the process can be classified as homogeneous welding since the filler wire has the same composition as the parts being joined. Steels are the most common metals joined by this process, but nonferrous metals can also be joined.

Although the same flux may be used for many different compositions of steel, a different flux must be used for each of the different families of nonferrous metals. A thin layer of the flux that is in contact with the molten metal melts and reacts chemically to form a brittle, glassy coating over the hot metal which will, after cooling to near room temperature, peel off freely, exposing a clean metal surface. This is caused by the difference in coefficients of thermal expansion of the flux and the metal being welded. This surface may then be painted without resorting to handchipping to remove the slag. The fused flux is discarded, but the unfused flux is collected, screened, and reused.

Considerably higher currents are used in this process than are possible with stick electrodes because the electrical contact to the filler wire is made a short distance from the welding end of the wire which is rapidly moving away from the contact. Consequently, it is possible to tolerate much higher values of I^2R heating. For example,

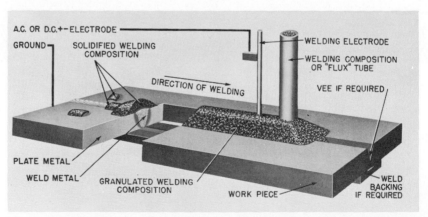

Figure 4-17. Schematic illustration of submerged-arc welding. (Courtesy Linde Co.)

$\frac{1}{8}$ in. diameter wire can use as much as 600 amperes and a $\frac{3}{16}$ in. diameter may employ 1000 amperes. These values are three to six times as large as the currents used in the manual stick welding processes. The arc voltage is about the same as those used with stick electrodes, and either a-c or d-c can be used.

Because of these large currents, great penetration is possible with this process; $1\frac{1}{2}$ in. thick steel plates can be welded in a single pass if a vee joint is used. In a following section it is shown that the penetration varies directly with the current to the $1\frac{1}{3}$ power, whereas it varies only as the square root of the voltage. Also, because of this high rate of heat input, high welding speeds are possible. Velocities as large as 100 ipm are possible, although 20 to 50 ipm are probably more common. This compares to speeds of 6 to 30 ipm with stick electrodes.

This process is widely used for making straight welds in the flat position with the welding head moving on a track. However, when special work positioners are provided that incorporate the welding motion in the positioner itself, irregular welds may be very efficiently made. A simple example of this is the circumferential welding of a cylinder by rotating the cylinder under the welding head.

Arc-Welding Electrodes. As mentioned in the historical outline at the beginning of this chapter, the first electrodes used for arc welding were "nonconsumable" carbon rods. Then followed the bare electrodes and coated consumable electrodes and, in 1930, tungsten was developed as a nonconsumable electrode material. The present status of the use of electrode types is this: coated stick electrodes are used almost exclusively for job-shop (nonproduction and repair) work, and also in many high production operations; however, bare wires are seldom used as electrodes but are used as filler rods for the nonconsumable electrode processes; bare wire in the form of a coil having the same composition as the material to be welded is used for much of the production welding and sometimes for job-shop work; the nonconsumable electrode process is not used nearly as extensively as the consumable electrode processes, and tungsten is the most common nonconsumable electrode material.

There is no standard designation used to classify the bare wire electrodes. They are purchased on the basis of the metal to be welded. Although the composition of the electrode is basically the same as the parent metal, small amounts of special additives such as deoxidizers are included by many manufacturers to improve the weld quality.

A classification (code designation) for coated stick electrodes was formulated in 1937 by the American Welding Society and the American

Society for Testing Materials that consisted of the letter E followed by four or five numbers. The prefix E indicates that the electrode is part of an electric circuit. The first two numbers (three, if the strength is 100,000 psi or over) represent the minimum as welded tensile strength in 1000-lb units. Thus the most common type of electrode, the E60 – –, has minimum tensile strength of the weld metal of 60,000 psi. The third number indicates the welding positions that the electrode can be used in, as follows: 1—all positions; 2—horizontal and flat positions; 3— flat position only. The last number indicates the type of current and polarity that must be used. Table 4-5 summarizes the electrode types.

TABLE 4-5. Classification of Steel Electrodes[1]

Type	Current	Position	Coating	Penetration	Slag
Exx10	d-c-R[2]	All[3]	High cellulose + sodium	Deep	Thin
Exx11	a-c, d-c-R	All	High cellulose + potassium	Deep	Thin
Exx12	a-c, d-c-S[2]	All	High titania + sodium	Medium	Heavy
Exx13	a-c, d-c-S	All	High titania + potassium	Shallow	Medium
Exx14	a-c, d-c-S	All	High titania + iron oxide	Medium	Medium
Exx15	d-c-R	All	Low hydrogen + sodium	Medium	Medium
Exx16	a-c, d-c-R	All	Low hydrogen + potassium	Medium	Medium
Exx20	a-c, d-c	H, F	High iron oxide	Medium	Heavy
Exx30	a-c, d-c	F	High iron oxide	Shallow	Heavy

[1] Courtesy American Welding Society or after *Welding Handbook*, 4th ed., Section 5.
[2] R—Reverse polarity, electrode positive.
   S—Straight polarity, electrode negative.
[3] All positions: V = vertical, OH = overhead, H = horizontal, F = flat.

The first coating was developed by Kjellberg in Sweden and was simply an asbestos-coated steel wire. It stabilized the arc somewhat and provided only meager protection to the melt. When a combination of cotton cloth and asbestos was used for a coating, the weld quality was greatly improved; the asbestos stabilized the arc and the cotton, which is nearly pure cellulose, decomposed to form a protective atmos-

TABLE 4-6. The Functions of Compounds in the Electrode Coatings

---

1. Provide a protective gaseous atmosphere.
2. Stabilize the arc (low ionization potential or long "ion" life).
3. Lower the melting point of other oxides.
4. Provide a protective slag over hot metal.
5. Act as a flux—remove impurities.
6. Provide strength to the coating.
7. Act as bonding agent to hold ingredients together.
8. Reduce weld metal spatter—when coating burns off slower than core.
9. To add alloying elements.[1]
10. Control arc characteristics (volts versus arc length).
11. Act as a deoxidizer.
12. To make a refining slag, as in E6020.

---

[1] See Table 4-7.

phere according to the reaction

$$C_6H_{10}O_5 + \tfrac{1}{2}O_2 \rightarrow 6CO + 5H_2 \qquad (4\text{-}5)$$

You may recall that this is the same atmosphere that is provided by the oxyacetylene process.

The more common reasons for adding various ingredients to an electrode coating are listed in Table 4-6, and are self-explanatory.

Table 4-7 lists the per cent of the alloying element that had been added to an electrode coating that ends up in the weld metal. Since the

TABLE 4-7. Recovery of Elements From Electrode Coatings[1]

Alloying Element	Form of Material in Electrode Coating	Recovery of Element, %
Carbon	Graphite	75
Manganese	Ferromanganese	75
Phosphorus	Ferrophosphorus	100
Silicon	Ferrosilicon	45
Chromium	Ferrochromium	95
Nickel	Electrolytic nickel	100
Copper	Copper Metal	100
Columbium	Ferrocolumbium	70
Titanium	Ferrotitanium	5
Molybdenum	Ferromolybdenum	97
Vanadium	Ferrovanadium	80
Beryllium	Copper-beryllium	0

[1] From Henry and Claussen, *Welding Metallurgy*, 2nd ed.

recovery of the elements is about the same regardless of whether it is initially present in the core wire or in the coating, it is often times advantageous to use a plain carbon wire and add the alloys to the coating rather than use a more expensive alloy wire.

The compositions of the coating of the most common types of electrodes is given in Table 4-8. Again, since the table is quite self-explanatory, no additional discussion is given.

TABLE 4-8. Compositions of Some Electrode Coatings

(E6011 and E6013, a-c electrodes, are made by substituting potassium silicate for the sodium silicate in the E6010 and E6012 electrodes)

Compound	Source	Function[1]	E6010	E6012	E6016	E6020
SiO_2	Clay + Na_2SiO_3	3,4	39	26	16	31
$TiO_2 + ZrO_2$	Rutile	2,3,4	14	45	6	16
FeO	Iron Oxide	5,12	2	7	—	31
MgO	Asbestos	6	3	2	1	3
Na_2O	Clay + Na_2SiO_3	2,7	5	2	2	4
Al_2O_3	Clay[2]	1,2,3,4	—	—	37	—
CaF_2	Flurospar	3	—	—	27	—
Na_3AlF_6	Cryolite	3	—	—	6	—
Mn	Ferromanganese	11	7	7	2	14
Volatiles	Cellulose	1	30	5	—	—
Atmosphere formed			CO,H_2	CO,CO_2	CO,CO_2	Slag

[1] The number refers to the list of functions in Table 4-6.

[2] Clay has variable compositions such as $Al_2O_3 \cdot 2SiO_2 \cdot 2H_2O$ (kaolinate) and $K_2O \cdot Al_2O_3 \cdot 6SiO_2$ (orthoclase).

The first of the modern electrode coatings was similar to the present E6010 type. From Table 4-8 it is apparent that the E6010 rod protects the weld metal from the air to a large extent by providing a gaseous envelope through the combustion of the cellulose. Since the amount of the slag producing ingredients is small, the slag which forms on top of the weldment is very thin, thus making this a good rod for out-of-position welding; that is, overhead and vertical. This rod, as may be seen in Table 4-11, requires a larger arc potential for a given arc length than the other d-c rods and therefore it will give deeper penetration, as explained in a latter section.

The coating on the E6011 electrode, which is the a-c counterpart of the E6010 d-c rod, has basically the same composition as those listed in Table 4-8 for the E6010 coating, except that potassium silicate is substituted for the sodium silicate. The ionization potential of potassium is 4.3 electron volts, sufficiently lower than the 5.1 electron volts of sodium to give it ample arc stability for a 60 cycle current. The ionization potential for some other gases is listed in Table 4-9.

For many welding operations a "cooler" rod, that is, one that gives less penetration and a slower burn-off rate, is desired. This is accomplished with the E6012 type of coating which requires a lower arc potential than the E6010 rod. Electron emission can be made to occur more freely with lower cathode temperatures by adding certain metal oxides; thoriated tungsten oxide is a very common one in the electronics industry. Apparently the increased emissivity and the lower arc potential of the E6012 coating are produced by the much larger amount of titanium dioxide present. This larger amount of rutile also results in a thicker slag being formed over the weldment.

The E6013 rod is modified from the E6012 exactly as the E6011 described above is a modified E6010 coating.

The cooling rate after arc welding is quite high, and is sufficient when high strength steels are welded to result in the formation of some

TABLE 4-9. Ionization Potentials for Some Elements and Compounds Encountered in Arc Welding[1]

Element		Ionization Potential (electron volts)	Compound or Molecule		Ionization Potential (electron volts)
Symbol	Name		Symbol	Name	
Al	Aluminum	5.96	CH_4	Methane	14.5
A	Argon	15.68	CO	Carbon monoxide	14.1
C	Carbon	11.22	CO_2	Carbon dioxide	14.4
Ca	Calcium	6.09	Cl_2	Chlorine	13.2
Cl	Chlorine	12.95	H_2	Hydrogen	15.6
Cs	Cesium	3.87	H_2O	Water	12.56
Cu	Copper	7.67	N_2	Nitrogen	15.51
Fe	Iron	7.83	O_2	Oxygen	12.5
H	Hydrogen	13.53			
He	Helium	24.46			
K	Potassium	4.32			
Mg	Magnesium	7.61			
N	Nitrogen	14.48			
Na	Sodium	5.12			
O	Oxygen	13.55			
Si	Silicon	8.12			
W	Tungsten	8.1			

[1] From *Handbook of Chemistry and Physics,* 38th ed.

martensite in the weld zone. Normally, this martensite would not be considered detrimental, but if hydrogen is present in the metal, then a failure called "underbead cracking" occurs. This descriptive name is used since the cracks form in the parent metal just beneath the fusion zone. The generally accepted theory for the formation of underbead cracks is: the atomic hydrogen dissolved in the metal diffuses and comes out in the regions of misalignment at the edges of the martensite needles (sometimes called microcracks or transient cracks). The atomic hydrogen then combines into molecular hydrogen, creating such large pressures that the "underbead cracks" form.

The low hydrogen electrodes, the Exx15 and Exx16, were developed to eliminate the problem of underbead cracking. This was accomplished by eliminating all ingredients such as cellulose and hydrated oxides like $Al_2O_3 \cdot H_2O$ from the coating that would form hydrogen or water vapor in the arc region. This is evident in Table 4-6 where the composition of the E6016 coating is given. The cellulose is completely eliminated, the amount of the acidic silica is reduced, and calcium fluoride and calcium oxide are added in substantial amounts. In some similar coatings, iron oxide and calcium carbonate are the principal ingredients. For this reason many of the low hydrogen electrodes are referred to as "lime-ferrite" rods in the United States and as "basic electrodes" in England.

The E6020 rod is typical of the so-called heavy-coated electrodes in which the coating may account for half the total weight of the electrode. These rods are the more recently developed ones, and they illustrate the results of engineering effort on the problem of welding. These rods were developed to obtain deep penetration with high welding speeds, fast deposition rates, and oxide-free weldments. To get deep penetration, the metal oxides such as TiO_2 that promoted emissivity were either eliminated or reduced so that the arc potential would be higher. Under similar conditions, the arc voltage of the E6020 electrode is 20% greater than the E6010 and 40% greater than the E6012. To obtain a high deposition rate without entrapped oxides, about 30% iron oxide and one-half as much manganese were used in the coating. The manganese, being a good oxidizing agent, reduces the iron oxide to metallic iron, evolving heat in the process and increasing the amount of iron added to the weldment. These electrodes are referred to as "iron powder" rods and as "hot" rods.

Another of the more recently developed electrodes is the E6014 type or "drag" rod as it is called by many welders. Its name is derived from the fact that very good weldments are made when the end of the electrode coating continuously touches the work piece during the entire welding operation. This is possible because the coating has a much lower burn-off rate than the iron core, and being a nonconductor of electricity, it permits the arc column to be maintained within its confines between the end of the recessed core and the work piece. This characteristic is a decided advantage since it permits good weldments to be made with welders of less skill and experience than is needed when using electrodes which require good control of arc length in order to realize uniform penetration.

The core wire of all the E60xx electrodes is basically the same, being made of AISI 1010 rimmed steel. The preference of rimmed steel over killed steel for an electrode material is because the former has entrapped small pockets of carbon monoxide gas, whereas the killed steel is completely deoxidized with aluminum. These gas pockets play a vital part in the mechanism of transfer of metal from the electrode to the work. Although any type of material would be suitable for welding in the flat position where the force of gravity can transfer the molten electrode to the work material below, only rimmed steel is satisfactory for welding in the overhead position. Here the globules of electrode material must be projected vertically against the force of gravity. This is also obvious by observing the random directions in which the steel globules leave the electrode end.

Gas-Shielded Arc Welding. The gas-shielded arc processes are relatively recent innovations to the family of welding processes. Hydrogen and helium have been used commercially as shielding gases for about thirty years and carbon dioxide which was commercially developed about thirty years ago and was applied industrially as a shielding gas only about ten years ago is now rapidly becoming the most popular gas because of its low cost. Other inexpensive gases will certainly be developed during the next decade.

Unfortunately, from an educational point of view, all of the welding equipment manufacturers who have developed equipment of this type have selected different trademark names for basically similar equipment. Thus we have numerous gas-shielded processes that have such titles as: MIG; TIG; SIGMA; Heliarc; Fillerarc; Thermal Arc; Closarc; etc. All of the gas-shielded arc processes can be classified into two types, those using inert gas and those not using inert gas. A brief description of both follows.

Noninert Gas-Shielded Arc Process. Since the shielding gas in this process is not inert, it will react chemically with its environment. The most common example of this process is the atomic hydrogen welding process (Figure 4-18). As can be seen from the detailed sketch of the

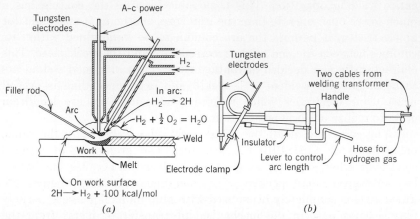

Figure 4-18. Sketch of atomic hydrogen welding process. (*a*) Details of the welding head. (*b*) General arrangement of welding head.

welding head, the molecular hydrogen, which comes from a storage cylinder similar to that used for oxygen, flows by the tungsten electrodes in the holder, keeping them cooler and lengthening the electrode life. In the vicinity of the arc, which extends in a fan shape (a result of the magnetic fields of the inclined electrodes) between the two electrodes, the molecular hydrogen dissociates into atomic hydrogen with the absorption of about 100,000 cal/mol of heat. This atomic hydrogen recombines to form molecular hydrogen outside the arc, particularly on the relatively cold surfaces of the work that is being welded, with the evolution of this previously gained heat. At the outer surfaces of this gaseous shield, the hydrogen combines with the oxygen of the air to form water vapor, making a bright orange flame.

In performance, the atomic hydrogen process is slightly superior to the oxyacetylene process in that it has a higher intensity heat source, but its higher cost of operation restricts its widespread application. It is used to a limited extent in the welding of very thin sheets or small diameter wire, particularly those made of the noble metals and the refractory metals. It is restricted in its application to thin materials because of its much lower thermal efficiency as compared to the direct arc processes, since the arc heat is radiated to the work material. As is true of all the processes that utilize two electrodes, non-conducting materials such as ceramics may be arc welded. Alternating current is used usually so that both electrodes burn off at the same rate.

Inert Gas-Shielded Arc (IGSA) Processes. In both job-shop and mass production work the various IGSA processes are gradually being applied to operations that in the past would be done solely by coated stick electrodes. This trend is due to the fact that much greater penetration and higher welding speeds are possible because of the higher currents that can be used. In our discussion of the submerged-arc process we explained why a much higher current can be used in these processes than is possible with stick electrodes. The power sources for the shielded arc processes are identical to those described previously under arc-welding equipment, except that frequently higher current capacity is available.

The mechanism of the IGSA process is obvious in Figure 4-19. The welding head consists of a lightweight handle, or gun as it is usually called, with provisions for holding either a stationary tungsten electrode in the nonconsumable electrode process or a continuous wire of the same composition as the material to be welded in the consumable electrode version. In this latter type, the wire is automatically fed from the reel by a variable speed motor at a preset rate that is determined by the arc voltage; that is, the wire feed increases with an increase in arc voltage caused by an increase in the arc length. In all welding heads the shielding gas flows by or along the electrode through a nozzle at the end of the gun into the arc region. This is done to keep the electrode cooler and permits higher currents to be used. Most guns are also water cooled.

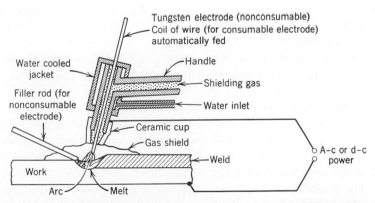

Figure 4-19. Inert gas-shielded, arc-welding process (IGSA). The separate filler rod is not used when the wire-feed, consumable-electrode process is used.

The external manually fed filler rod (see Figure 4-19) is never used with the consumable electrode process and is sometimes not used with the nonconsumable electrode process. In this latter case the welding would then be an autogenous type.

The IGSA process was developed in the early 1940's in an attempt to find a means to weld magnesium, which burns or oxidizes almost explosively when oxygen comes in contact with it while it is hot. It is interesting to note that the casting of magnesium posed an identical problem, and it was partially solved in the foundries by using a covering gas of sulfur dioxide over the molten metal and during pouring of the casting. In the welding processes, helium and argon were the first industrially used shielding gases.

The process was then applied to the welding of aluminum and stainless steels. The incentive for this change from coated electrodes was mainly because with the gas-shielded process there is no slag to clean off after welding. The higher welding speeds also partially offset the higher cost of the process. But the majority of welding is done on ordinary steels and the use of argon and helium is prohibited by their high cost. However, with the introduction of carbon dioxide as a shielding gas about ten years ago, the IGSA process is now beginning to replace the coated electrode process in many steel welding operations, particularly in the automotive industries and appliance industries.

The operating conditions for the IGSA processes are very similar to those of the submerged-arc. Electrode diameters of $\frac{1}{32}$ in. to $\frac{3}{16}$ in. are commonly used with welding speeds ranging from about 20 ipm to over 120 ipm. With the larger electrodes, the current may be as high as 1200 amperes, resulting in a very deep penetration as explained in a later section.

The ionization potential of some gases are listed in Table 4-9. Helium has the highest ionization potential of all the gases listed.

Potential Drops and Power Dispersal in Arc Welding. The total voltage drop in an arc welding circuit consists of the following individual drops: (1) voltage drop in the cables or lead wires connecting the electrode and work to the welder; (2) voltage drop in the electrode and in the work piece, and (3) voltage drop in the arc.

The potential drop in the first two regions listed is quite small, normally being only 1 to 2 volts as determined when the electrode is shorted to the work piece. This voltage drop is simply determined by the product of the current and the resistance of the circuit. Thus, most of the total voltage drop occurs in the arc. The potential drop in the arc is composed of the cathode drop, the column drop and the anode drop.

Morris and Gore[3] made a calorimetric study of the heat loss at the three zones of an arc as influenced by the arc length which is worthwhile to consider along with the potential drops. For this study a water-cooled copper anode, a water-cooled tungsten cathode, and a controlled flow of argon gas by the arc were used. The incoming and outgoing temperatures were measured along with the flow rates. The values were recorded for various arc lengths after a steady-state condition was achieved.

Figure 4-20 illustrates the results obtained under one set of conditions. With an arc length of 0.5 mm, the cathode region extends nearly to anode surface and there is no arc column or plasma as can be seen in sketch a. The total arc potential was 9.5 volts with a current of 60 amperes, resulting in a total of 570 watts. Of this power, 98 watts was dissipated through the cathode, 92 watts was radiated from the cathode region and the balance, and 380 watts or 67% was dissipated through the anode.

With an arc length of 1 mm as sketched in b, the arc potential increased to 9.9 volts; the 0.4 volt increase being the potential drop in the arc column. The total arc power was 594 watts, with the same loss through the electrode and cathode region. Of the additional 24 watts generated in the arc column, 4 watts were lost by radiation to the atmosphere and an additional 20 watts, for a total of 400 watts, were dissipated at the anode. This amounts to $67\frac{1}{2}$% of the heat going out at the anode.

As the arc length is increased to 3 mm, as sketched in d, the total potential drop increased to 11.3 volts, 1.8 volts being the column drop. As in the previous cases, the power loss through the electrode and cathode region remains at 98 and 92 watts respectively. Of the additional 108 watts generated in the arc column, 54 watts go into the anode. The total anode power loss was 434 watts or 64%.

In all of these conditions the arc efficiency, which is the per cent of arc power going into the workpiece, is about 65%. It would have been very enlightening if longer arc lengths, say up to about 20 mm, would have also been studied, for it is probable that the arc efficiency begins to decrease rapidly for arc lengths greater than $\frac{1}{4}$ in.

Temperature Distribution in the Arc Column. By experimentally studying the particle density in arcs in various gases and determining the effect of temperature on particle density by means of Saha's equation, Olsen[6] calculated the temperature distribution in welding

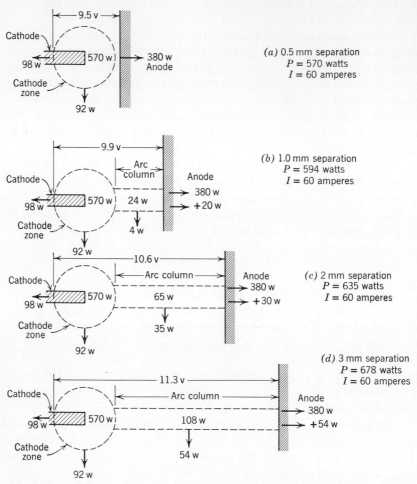

Figure 4-20. Power dissipation in an electric arc. (0.04 in. tungsten cathode, copper anode, argon gas.) (From Morris and Gore.[3])

arcs. Figure 4-21 is a plot of some of his results using a tungsten arc in an argon atmosphere for several arc lengths. The temperature at the outer surface of the arc column is the familiar 10,000°C that is reported in most welding texts as the temperature of the arc, which is also the lowest temperature present in an arc. However, with short arc length or with large values of arc power the temperature in the arc adjacent to the cathode spot is more than twice the above minimum value.

Arc Welding Characteristic Curves

The Arc Characteristics. Most of the early studies on arc characteristics (voltage versus current) were made with relatively low currents,
usually less than seven amperes[4,5] in order to prevent the rapid "burn
off" of the electrode. Nottingham[5] showed that for these low current
arcs, the arc potential was related to the current as follows:

$$E = A + BI^{-a} \qquad (4\text{-}6)$$

where A, B and a are constants. Since the exponent a is negative, the
potential decreases as I increases from zero as shown for the low
currents (less than 10 amperes) in Figure 4-22. Nottingham's experimental data also demonstrated that the numerical value of A was a
function of the absolute boiling temperature of the anodic electrode
and varied between 0.4 and 0.8 for most metals. For carbon electrodes,
a is nearly 1. However, nearly all industrial arc welding is done with
currents of 50 to 350 amperes for stick electrodes and up to 1000
amperes for continuous wire electrodes, which are 10 to 100 times the
maximum values studied by Nottingham.

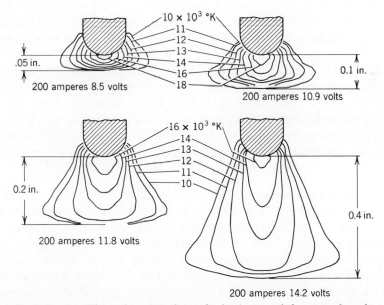

Figure 4-21. Effect of arc length on the isotherms of the normal-mode
argon arc at 1 atm. (From Olsen.[6])

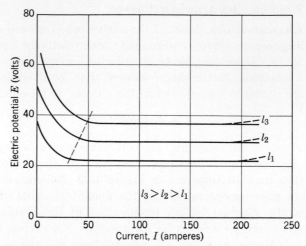

Figure 4-22. Metal-arc characteristics in air. (Values shown are typical for iron.)

Easton[1] studied the characteristics of arcs between iron electrodes in air with typical welding currents and found that the voltage remained constant as the current increased above 30 amperes for short arc lengths and above 50 amperes for long arc lengths, as illustrated by the solid lines in Figure 4-22. Actually, more recent experimental data obtained by the author using coated stick electrodes and others using arcs in inert gases indicate that the arc potential increases slightly over the minimum value as the current increases beyond 200 amperes (see dashed lines in Figure 4-22). However, since this is nearly the maximum current used with stick electrodes, and since the increase appears to be slight, it is assumed in the following discussions that the potential drop across a welding arc· is constant for a given arc length and for the range of currents used in welding.

Electrode Characteristics. The electrode characteristics are arc characteristics considered on a different basis, that is, the potential drop as a function of the arc length rather than the arc current, as shown in Figure 4-23. Again, most of the electrode characteristic studies have been made with bare electrodes and, except for the SIGA processes (shielded inert gas arc), low currents. All of these studies indicate that for the arc lengths associated with welding, the arc potential is directly and lineally proportional to the arc length or, as shown in Figure 4-23, plotted as straight lines with a positive slope. To appreciate and understand the significance of the electrode characteristics, an objective that can be achieved through solving engineering problems that require their application, it is desirable to express them in a mathematical form such as

$$E = ml + b \qquad (4\text{-}7)$$

The constant b may be considered as the arc potential when the arc length approaches zero; it is not the voltage drop at the contact point when the electrode contacts the work. The slope m determines the rate at which the arc potential changes with arc length.

Although experimental data is available in the published literature that includes values of b and m for arcs between such bare metals as aluminum, titanium, tungsten and steel in atmospheres of argon and helium (see Table 4-10), there is no such data available for coated-stick electrodes. Several years ago the author conducted a series of tests for several of the common types of stick electrodes and obtained the electrode characteristics that are listed in Table 4-11. These results indicate that b can vary between 15 and 25 volts and that m can vary between 20 and 40 volts/in. All of the electrode types listed in this table, some of which are plotted in Figure 4-23, have the same com-

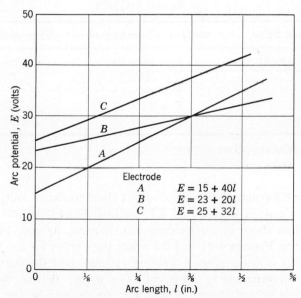

Figure 4-23. Electrode characteristics (bare and coated). They approximate straight lines of the form $E = b + ml$.

TABLE 4-10. Typical Characteristics of Some Shielding Gases
Used in the SIGA Processes

Shielding Gas	Anode Material	Cathode Material	Current Ampere	Characteristics
Helium	Titanium	Tungsten	300	$E = 26l + 14$
Argon	Titanium	Tungsten	300	$E = 20l + 8$
Neon	Titanium	Tungsten	300	$E = 15l + 10$
Krypton	Titanium	Tungsten	300	$E = 20l + 7$
Argon	Aluminum	Aluminum	100	$E = 15l + 14$
Argon	Aluminum	Aluminum	200	$E = 28l + 17$
Helium	Aluminum	Aluminum	150	$E = 20l + 23$

position of iron wire or core and differ only in coating ingredients. Thus, it is apparent that one of the unpublicized functions of electrode coatings is to control the electrode characteristics.

TABLE 4-11. Experimentally Determined Characteristics of Some
Common Types of Electrodes

(Only one series of tests was run, and then only on electrodes made by one manufacturer, so these relationships should be used as a guide only until they are further verified.)

Electrode Type	Electrode Characteristic	Type of Current
Bare (steel)	$E = 40l + 15$	d-c, S^1, R^2
6010	$E = 32l + 25$	d-c, R
6012	$E = 26l + 18$	d-c, S
6014	$E = 20l + 23$	a-c, d-c, R, S
6020	$E = 24l + 23$	a-c, d-c, R, S

[1] S = Straight polarity.
[2] R = Reverse polarity.

Generator Characteristics. The output characteristics, output of voltage versus output current, of d-c welding generators are markedly different than those of a-c welding transformers, as may be observed by comparing Figures 4-24 to 4-25 where the curves for the former are straight lines in the region of welding voltages and the curves for the latter are approximately elliptical. The motor driven d-c welding generator has output characteristics that are defined by the expression

$$E = nI + E_i \quad \text{or} \quad E = nI + kE_o \quad\quad (4\text{-}8)$$

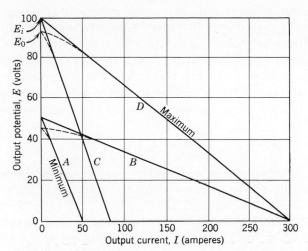

Figure 4-24. Motor driven d-c generator characteristic curves. They approximate straight lines of the form $E = E_i - nI$.

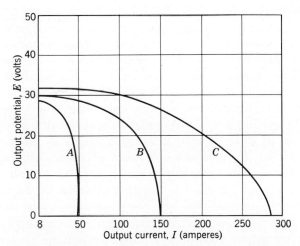

Figure 4-25. Alternate-current transformer characteristic curves. They approximate ellipses of the form $aE^2 + I^2 = c^2$.

throughout the entire range of useful welding voltages. It is only at
the very high potentials, near the open circuit voltages, that the actual
generator output curve falls below the extrapolated straight line, as
shown by the dashed lines in Figure 4-24. In the above equations, E_i
is the intercept of the straight line with the E axis; E_o is the open
circuit voltage set on the generator; n is the slope of the line, is negative and is equal to E_i/I_s; k is a constant. For the generator that was
tested to obtain the curves plotted in Figure 4-24, k was found to be
equal to 1.15 for all of the curves and so the characteristics can be
expressed as

$$E = nI + 1.15E_o. \tag{4-9}$$

It is difficult to measure accurately the voltage and current output
of a generator or transformer during arc welding even when the arc
length is maintained constant since they vary erratically because of the
presence of molten globules of metal moving in the arc column from
the electrode to the work material. To overcome this difficulty, the
output energy of the welding unit is dissipated between movable steel
plates in a brine tank so the current and voltage remain constant for
a given setting. Inasmuch as it is the generator characteristics that
are being determined, there is no reason why the output energy must
be dissipated in an arc. The data in Figures 4-24 and 4-25 were obtained this way.

From a series of tests made on one d-c rectifier type welding unit
it appears that the output of this type of welding equipment may also
be approximated by a straight line in the range of voltages used for
welding. However, unlike the motor generator, the constant k does not
have the same numerical value for all output curves of the given unit;
but instead k varies with the slope n, increasing as n decreases.

All d-c welding units are designed to operate with an open circuit,
E_o, potential of 70 to 90 volts although voltages as low as 45 and as
high as 110 can be obtained on many of them. Although the arc
potential during welding is in the range of 15 to 35 volts, the much
higher open circuit potential is required to assist in the initiation of
the arc. For in "striking" the arc, the electrode may be inadvertently
withdrawn to an excessive arc length with a resulting high arc voltage.
Also, a larger output voltage is required for striking an arc on scaled
or contaminated surfaces, or for welding with unusually long leads
from the welding unit to the workpiece where the potential drop may
be considerable. As we can see from Figure 4-24, there are two operator controls on this type of d-c welding generator. One control varies
the output current for a given open circuit voltage as shown by curves

C and D or A and B. The second control varies the open circuit voltage, but not without its affecting the short circuit current I_s. This may be seen in Figure 4-24 where curves A and C were obtained by simply changing the open circuit voltage control and leaving the current control rheostat fixed. On the other hand, a change in the short circuit current made by the current control rheostat has no noticeable effect on the open circuit voltage.

Most of the a-c welding units have only one control, a current control that is accomplished by changing the distance between the secondary and primary coils of the transformer. As may be seen in Figure 4-25 which is a plot of experimental data obtained from an a-c welding unit, there is a slight increase in the open circuit voltage E_o when the short circuit current I_s is increased. The data shown as curves A and B in Figure 4-25 are quite accurately defined by the ellipses $2.7E^2 + I^2 = 2100$ and $13.4E^2 + I^2 = 12,000$ respectively. Curve B represents a typical setting of the a-c welding unit when welding with $\frac{1}{8}$ in. diameter electrodes. It is also apparent that the open circuit voltage of the a-c welding transformer is much lower than that of the d-c units. For this reason the initiation and maintenance of the arc are much more difficult, and this explains why the much cheaper a-c transformers followed so far behind the d-c welding units in being developed and used industrially. Actually it was not until the industry began to add alkaline earths having low ionization potentials and materials having a low thermionic work function to the electrode coatings that the welding arc became stable enough to be used with 60 cycle a-c current.

However, it is important to appreciate that once the welding machine controls are set, the welder has a fixed operating characteristic curve. That is, it will have only one value of output current for each operating voltage.

Combined Arc Welding Characteristics. The combined arc welding characteristics are a plot of the arc power expressed in watts as a function of the arc length (Figure 4-26). They are a combination of the electrode characteristics and the generator characteristics.

For a given arc length, the electrode characteristics determine the arc potential. This specific arc potential then becomes the output voltage of the welding generator whose characteristics in turn then determine the arc current. The product of this arc voltage and current is the arc power for the given arc length.

In reality, when the electrode contacts the work (is shorted) there is no arc and the voltage drop across the contact region is not equal to the value b but rather is very nearly zero. Consequently, for a short-circuited arc the power or watts will approach zero. But as soon as a short arc is established the power will jump to some finite value as illustrated in Figure 4-26. Then, depending upon the electrode and generator characteristics selected, as the arc length is increased three different types of arc power curves can result. First, as illustrated by curve A, the arc power will immediately start to drop off. The second type of power curve, as depicted by curve B, is one that rises gradually for short arc length but reaches a maximum value in the useful welding arc length region. The third type, curve C, reaches its maximum power at arc lengths greater than the useful arc lengths. Curve D is a theoretical constant-power output curve that may be obtained with a hyperbolic generator characteristic as explained in a following section.

The arc power may be converted to arc heat by means of the conversion: 1 watt = 0.0568 Btu/min or 1 watt hr = 3.4 Btu. Thus, a 3000 watt arc operating for one minute liberates 170 Btu's, which is enough to heat a $\frac{1}{4}$ in. $\times$ $\frac{1}{2}$ in. $\times$ 12 in. bar of steel to its melting temperature if all this heat went into the bar. Of course, this is not so. Although very little data concerning arc efficiency (the per cent of

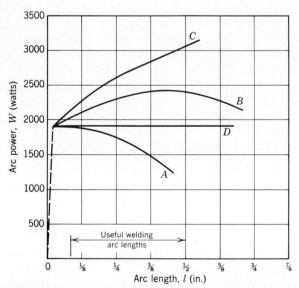

Figure 4-26. Combined arc-welding characteristic curves. Obtained by combining the electrode and the generator characteristics. The arc length where power is at a maximum varies for the three curves shown.

the arc heat that actually goes into the weldment) are available, the author has found reasonably good agreement between calculated and experimental temperature distributions about an arc weld when using an arc efficiency of 80% for an arc length of $\frac{1}{8}$ in. and 65% for an arc length of $\frac{1}{4}$ in. These values will apply only to coated consumable electrodes where most of the heat going to the electrode eventually ends up on the weldment. The arc efficiency for arc lengths greater than $\frac{1}{2}$ in. is very low. In fact, it is practically impossible to form a weld bead with a $\frac{3}{4}$ in. arc length using a $\frac{1}{8}$ in. diameter electrode.

Table 4-12 lists average and maximum values of current and voltage for various sizes of steel electrodes.

TABLE 4-12.   Average Values of Arc Voltage, Current and Power
for Various Steel Electrode Sizes

(The maximum current is about twice the average current)

Electrode Diameter (in.)	Voltage	Current	Power, kw
$\frac{3}{32}$	24	60	1.44
$\frac{1}{8}$	25	100	2.50
$\frac{5}{32}$	26	140	3.64
$\frac{3}{16}$	28	180	5.04
$\frac{3}{8}$	33	460	15.2

The restriction on the maximum current that a given diameter electrode can carry is because the entire electrode will become red hot and droop from the I^2R heating if greater currents are used.

Table 4-13 gives some deposition data that are useful when considering some aspects of the economics of welding. Some additional data concerning the economics of welding, particularly the costs of labor and materials, are included in Tables 4-14 and 4-15.

The Constant-Power (Hyperbolic) Generator Characteristic Curve. The concept of the constant-power (hyperbolic) generator characteristic was created by the author as an analytical tool to help in the solving of many of the welding problems concerning the proper selection of electrodes and generator settings for a specific welding operation, as will be illustrated in the following section of this chapter. No welding generators have characteristics of this type, however. It is often desirable to have a constant arc power over most of the range of useful arc lengths, as when attempting to get uniform heat penetration while using less skilled arc welders. What electrode type and

TABLE 4-13. Deposition Data Concerning The Economics of Arc Welding[1]

(E6010 Electrode. Flat position unless otherwise noted.)

Item No.	Item		Electrode Diameter			
			$\frac{3}{32}$	$\frac{1}{8}$	$\frac{3}{16}$	$\frac{3}{8}$
1	Pound of metal in 12 in. electrode		0.023	0.042	0.094	0.375
2	Feet of electrode per pound weld metal		42.50	23.97	10.65	2.663
3	Total length of electrode, in.		12.0	14.0	14.0	18.0
4	Total coating, % of total weight		15.0	12.0	8.0	14.0
5	Weight of one complete electrode, lb		0.028	0.055	0.119	0.655
6	Electrodes per pound full length, coating included		36.0	18.0	8.4	1.5
7	Arc volts		24.0	25.0	28.0	33.0
8	Current, amp		60.0	100.0	180.0	460.0
9	Arc seconds to melt 12 in. of electrode		60.0	60.0	70.0	100.0
10	Pound metal melted per arc hr		1.4	2.50	4.83	13.5
11	Spatter/metal melted, %		12.0	14.0	18.0	25.0
12	Arc time, %		58.0	60.0	60.0	65.0
13	Pound metal deposited per hr		0.72	1.30	2.37	6.63
14	Output at the arc, kwhr per arc hr		1.44	2.50	5.04	15.20
15	Heat input into joint, Btu per hr		2860.0	5150.0	10,300	34,000
			Arc time			
16	Approximate pounds of	Flat	as above			
	metal deposited		0.7	1.3	2.4	6.6
17	per hr	Horiz x 0.9	0.6	1.2	2.2	6.0
18		Vert x 0.8	0.5	1.1	1.9	—
19		O.H. x 0.6	0.4	0.8	1.5	—

[1] Compiled from data in *Welding Handbook*, 3rd Ed.

TABLE 4-14. Some Cost Factors Concerning the Economics
of Gas Welding (1963)

Cost of Welding Regulators and Torch	$300.00
Cost of Gas	
Oxygen	$0.01/ft³
Acetylene	0.025/ft³
Cost of Labor	
Welding	3.00/hr
Overhead	5.00/hr
Cost of Welding Rods ($\frac{1}{8}$ in. dia)	$/lb
Aluminum	1.10
Steel	0.22
Cast iron	0.80
Stainless steel	2.88

generator settings will give a constant power curve such as D in
Figure 4-26? Actually, none of the generator characteristics discussed
previously will give such a constant arc power curve that is horizontal
throughout the entire range of useful arc lengths. The welding generators discussed previously will give curves similar to A, B, or C,
some of which may be made tangent to curve D at a desirable arc
length.

In order to get a constant arc power curve, say W equal to
approximately 2000 watts as curve D, it is obvious after some reflection to realize that all that is required is for the product of E and I
to be constant—in this case, 2000 watts. Thus $EI = W = 2000$ watts,
or $E = W/I$. This is not the equation of a straight line, but rather a

TABLE 4-15. Some Cost Factors Concerning the Economics
of Arc Welding (1963)

Cost of Electricity	$0.03/kwhr
Cost of 300 Amp Arc Welder	$500.00
Cost of Electrodes ($\frac{1}{8}$ in. dia)	$/lb
Aluminum (bare)	1.10
Aluminum (coated)	1.25
Steel (coated)	0.22
Stainless steel (coated)	2.88
Cast iron (bare)	0.80
Cost of Labor	
Welding	$3.00/hr
Overhead	6.00/hr

hyperbola. Thus we obtain a hypothetical generator that has the output characteristics as sketched in Figure 4-27. To obtain curve D in Figure 4-26, we use the lower or 2000 watt hyperbola. Then, regardless of what electrode type is used, if the arc length is such that the potential is 20 volts, the current will be 100 amperes. Similarly, if the arc length is increased to some value that results in a potential drop of 30 volts, the current will decrease to 66.7 amperes so that the product EI remains constant at 2000 watts.

Application of Characteristic Curves to Welding Problems. Several types of problems may be solved by means of the characteristic curves and will be illustrated by a typical problem of each type. For the reader to appreciate more fully the significance of these problems, a comparison of welding to another manufacturing process will be enlightening.

About two hundred years old, machining, as we know it today, is the use of power-driven machine tools as opposed to its original method of whittling or chipping. On the other hand, arc welding was first used as a manufacturing process less than a century ago. Up until about 1940, the machinist was considered an "artist"; he selected the tools, the speeds, and feeds, as well as the sequence of machining operations on his own. But now, by and large, the machinist has been replaced by an operator who simply provides the manual work needed during the machining. The selection of tools, speeds, feeds, and se-

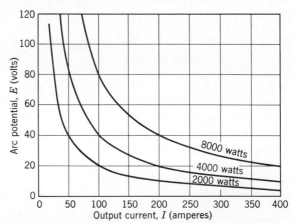

Figure 4-27. Constant-power (hyperbolic) characteristics of an idealized welding generator.

quency of operations is now being done by manufacturing engineers or technicians who work under engineering supervision. The manufacturing industries today are too competitive, the costs of labor are at a premium, and the complexity of the materials used are too great to permit anyone without an engineering background to have responsible control of manufacturing and design.

Welding has just recently entered the era where an engineer, rather than the welder or the operator, will determine the welding conditions to be used. The engineer will specify the electrode type, the volt-ampere settings on the welding unit, the preheat temperature, the arc length, and welding speed. The operator will then manipulate the electrode to maintain the proper welding speed and arc length. Obviously it would be best to have even the latter two variables under the control of the welding equipment rather than the operator, and in many automatic welding operations it is done. But there is still a very large amount of nonproduction welding that can most economically be done with consumable stick electrodes where the welder (operator) manipulates the electrode to maintain a specified arc length and welding speed; the other conditions being controlled by someone with a more technical background. The following problems will illustrate this same approach to the arc welding process.

Flat-Position Welding. The flat position, where the work lies in a horizontal plane and the electrode is in a nearly vertical line above the work to be welded, is the easiest position for welding. As large a weld pool as is either necessary or else possible without "burning" through the plate can easily be run along the top of the work material. For uniform heat penetration, the welder has to maintain both a uniform speed and a constant arc length. However, with the proper choice of generator settings and electrode type it is possible to have a nearly constant arc heat for the practical range of arc length variations so the operator needs to concentrate only on maintaining a uniform welding velocity. The texts that discuss this aspect of arc welding say that a steep (high E_o and low I_s) generator characteristic should be used for flat-position welding because the weld pool size is insensitive to arc length. The argument for this concept says that for a given voltage change, a steep characteristic curve will have a smaller change in current than a flat curve and thus, less heat variation. As will be seen in the following problem, when the arc power is considered on the basis of the constant-power hyperbola, the fallacy in the above concept is apparent; namely, that the constant power portion occurs at arc lengths greater than those useful for welding.

Problem: What electrode type and what generator (d-c motor driven) settings should be used to weld $\frac{3}{16}$ in. steel plates in a square butt joint using $\frac{1}{8}$ in. diameter-coated stick electrodes. Assume that on an economic basis, the best combination of heat input and welding speed is 4000 watts and 15 in./min. *Note:* A reasonable range of arc lengths for a fair welder is $\frac{1}{16}$ in. to $\frac{1}{4}$ in.

Solution: To avoid the embarrassment of ending the calculations with a solution that has the flat portion of the power curve occurring at a 1 in. or greater arc length, it is logical to begin by selecting a preferred arc length. Since the arc length can vary from $\frac{1}{16}$ in. to $\frac{1}{4}$ in., the most direct solution is to consider the preferred arc length as approximately the average, or $\frac{3}{16}$ in. Next, the electrode type should be selected inasmuch as it determines the arc potential. An electrode having a low slope m in Equation 4-7, $E = ml + b$ should be used, because this will result in the least variation in voltage for a given change in arc length. If two or more electrodes have the same slope, then the electrode having the largest constant b should be used if the arc heat desired is very large; and the electrode having a low value of b should be used if a low arc heat is desired. A very good electrode type for this problem would be one having the characteristic $E = 20l + 22$, although an E6014 or an E6020 electrode (see Table 4-11) would be satisfactory. In this case E_p (the preferred voltage) is $E_{3/16}$ and is equal to 25.75 volts. Also $E_{1/16}$ and $E_{1/4}$ are 23.25 and 27 volts.

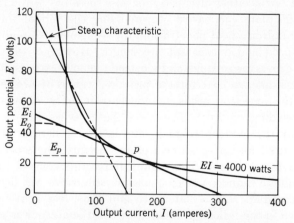

Figure 4-28. Use of constant-power hyperbola to obtain the best generator characteristic for flat welding.

To illustrate this solution graphically, Figure 4-28 will be constructed simultaneously with this analysis. The constant-power hyperbola $EI = 4000$ has been plotted, and E_p is then located on this curve. The current for a potential of 25.75 volts is 4000/25.75 or 155.5 amperes. If the generator actually had a characteristic curve like the hyperbola shown, the arc heat would be constant as the potential changed (because of arc length variation) from 23.25 to 27 volts. But since the generator has real characteristics that are represented as straight lines of the type $E = nI + E_i$ (see Equation 4-8), it is obvious that the best characteristic is the straight line tangent to the hyperbola at E_p. This also assumes that the power is not to exceed 4000 watts for any arc length. Thus n, the slope of the generator characteristic, is the tangent to the ideal characteristic at E_p, and may be determined as follows:

$$n = \frac{dE}{dI} \quad \text{and since} \quad E = \frac{W}{I}$$

$$\frac{dE}{dI} = -\frac{W}{I_2} = -\frac{EI}{I_2} = -\frac{E}{I} \tag{4-10}$$

Therefore, the slope n at any point on the hyperbola is equal to the ratio $-E/I$ for that point. For our particular problem the slope n is $-25.75 \div 155.5$ or -0.165. This line may now be drawn on Figure 4-28.

The next step is to determine E_o and I_s. This may be done graphically by drawing the above tangent line, or it may be done analytically as below. It will be assumed that for this generator that $E_i = 1.15E_o$ as discussed previously in the section on generator characteristics. From Equation 4-8,

$$E_i = E - nI \quad \text{and} \quad \text{at point } p$$

$$E_i = E_p - nI_p = E_p - \frac{-E_p}{I_p} I_p = 2E_p \tag{4-11}$$

Thus it is apparent that E_i will always be twice E_p, or for our example $E_i = 2 \times 25.75 = 51.5$ volts. The open circuit generator setting, E_o, will then be $51.5 \div 1.15$ or 45 volts. It should be pointed out that an open circuit voltage of 45 is the lowest obtainable on d-c generators and that some machines will actually not go that low. In that case, either an electrode having a larger b value should be used or else a steeper generator characteristic will have to be used even though it does not give the least variation in arc power.

The short circuit setting, I_s, may be determined as follows:

From Equation 4-8, $E = nI + E_i$ for $E = 0$, $I = I_s$
then

$$I_s = \frac{-E_i}{n} = -\frac{2E_p}{n}$$

but

$$n = -\frac{E_p}{I_p}$$

so

$$I_s = \frac{2E_p}{E_p} I_p = 2I_p \qquad (4\text{-}12)$$

Just as E_i is twice E_p, so also is I_s twice I_p. Realizing these relationships makes the solving of this type of problem extremely simple. For the values used in the above problem, $I_s = 2 \times 155.5 = 311$ amperes.

Thus, the solution to this problem is to use an electrode having a low slope m and then set the generator for a very flat characteristic, that is, $E_o = 45$ volts and $I_s = 311$ amperes. Under these conditions the arc heat will be about 3995, 4000, and 3999 watts for arc lengths of $\frac{1}{16}$ in., $\frac{3}{16}$ in., and $\frac{1}{4}$ in. respectively. Actually a more refined solution can be made by considering the heat input into the plate instead of the arc heat as was done in this example. This refinement would consist of applying a correlation coefficient to account for the decrease in arc efficiency with an increase in arc length. Because these correlation coefficients are unavailable at present and the arc length varies only between $\frac{1}{16}$ in. and $\frac{1}{4}$ in., in normal welding the simpler approach is sufficiently reliable.

Consider what the results would be if a steep generator characteristic was used, such as $E_i = 100$ volts and $I_s = 150$ amperes, as shown by the broken line in Figure 4-28. Then for the same electrode used in the previous analysis, the arc heat will be 950, 2860, and 2960 watts for arc lengths of $\frac{1}{16}$ in., $\frac{3}{16}$ in., and $\frac{1}{4}$ in. These values are much lower than the desired 4000 watts. However, the steep characteristic when used with an arc potential of 50 volts will give an arc heat of 3750 watts—but the arc length will have to be 1.4 in., an imaginary arc because arc lengths greater than $\frac{3}{4}$ in. cannot be maintained during normal welding.

By comparing the above two solutions to this welding problem the advantage of the constant-power hyperbolic concept is affirmed.

Overhead Welding. Overhead welding, or out-of-position welding as
it is descriptively called, poses some unique problems simply because
the work piece being welded is above the electrode and the weld pool
has a tendency to fall down as droplets due to the force of gravity.
In this situation, an approach exactly opposite to that used in the
analysis for flat-position welding is required. In out-of-position welding
it is generally desirable to have the generator controls set so that the
operator can change the heat input by changing the arc length while still
continuing his welding. Inasmuch as the arc length normally is about $\frac{1}{8}$
in. to $\frac{3}{16}$ in. and the minimum arc length possible without short cir-
cuiting across the molten droplets is $\frac{1}{16}$ in., if an appreciable change of
arc heat is to be effected then the arc length must be increased rather
than decreased. Furthermore, since the arc efficiency decreases with an
increase in arc length, the best control of the weld pool size will be
achieved by having the generator settings arranged to have a decrease
in arc heat as the arc length increases beyond the preferred arc length.
Curve A in Figure 4-26 illustrates such a condition.

The above analysis is shown in Figure **4-29**, again making use of the
ideal constant-power hyperbola, while considering the following problem: "What electrode type and what generator settings should be used
for welding in the overhead position?" To keep the weld pool man-
ageable, an arc power of **2000** watts is to be used. A typical solution
follows.

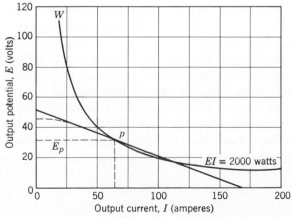

Figure 4-29. Use of constant-power hyperbola to obtain
the best generator settings for overhead welding.

After constructing the hyperbola $W = EI = 2000$ watts in Figure 4-29, it can readily be deduced from the previous discussion that the best straight-line generator characteristic will be that line having the lowest obtainable value of E_o and intersecting the hyperbola at the preferred arc voltage E_p. Any point that lies to the left of the hyperbola will have a product of voltage and current, or wattage, less than the value of the constant-power hyperbola. Since it is desired during overhead welding to have a substantial decrease in arc heat as the arc length increases beyond the normal value, it is then necessary for the generator characteristic to lie to the left of the hyperbola for those voltages greater than E_p. Furthermore, to obtain as large an angle as possible between the tangent to the ideal characteristic curve at the preferred voltage and the straight-line characteristic, it is necessary to select as low an open circuit voltage E_o as is possible on the welding machine. To obtain a large angle between these two lines it is also necessary to select an electrode that gives as high an E_p as possible. So, again, the electrode type must be selected first.

Upon first glance at the electrode characteristics, one concludes that the best electrode is the one having large values for both the constant b and the slope m. This is true, but with two precautions: first, that the electrode coating be a thin or light one since the falling molten slag from a heavily coated electrode will prove to be more than an annoyance to the operator standing below; second, that the electrode be suitable for d-c reverse polarity since five-eighths of the arc energy is expended at the anode, which is the electrode during reverse polarity welding. From Table 4-11 it appears that the electrode type E6010 is best suited for overhead welding, having the characteristic $E = 32l + 25$. For a $\frac{3}{16}$ in. arc length, E_p is 31 volts and I_p will be 64.5 amperes for a desired arc heat of 2000 watts. If the lowest open circuit voltage E_o on the welding generator is 45, then the E_i intercept is 1.15×45 or 51.5 volts. This gives the straight-line generator characteristic of $E = 51.5 - 0.315\,I$, and a short circuit I_s of 164 amperes.

The proper welding conditions for the previously stated overhead welding problem are: electrode type, E6010; $E_o = 45$ volts, $I_s = 164$ amperes. For these conditions, the arc heat will be 2000 and 1700 watts for arc lengths of $\frac{3}{16}$ in. and $\frac{3}{8}$ in. respectively.

Arc Length for Maximum Arc Power. Sometimes it is desirable to select and use the arc length that yields the maximum power. However, this calculated arc length also must fall in the range of arc lengths useful for welding. This arc length can be calculated by combining the electrode and generator characteristics.

From Equation 4-8 we get $I = (E - E_i)/n$ and from Equation 4-7 $E = ml + b$. By combining these two we get the arc power

$$W = EI = (ml + b)\left(\frac{E - E_i}{n}\right)$$

$$W = (ml + b)\left[\frac{(ml + b) - E_i}{n}\right] \qquad (4\text{-}13)$$

By differentiating Equation 4-13 with respect to the arc length and equating to zero, we get the arc length for maximum power.

$$\frac{dW}{dl} = (ml + b)\frac{ml^{-1}}{n} + ml^{-1}\left[\frac{(ml + b) - E_i}{n}\right] = 0$$

and by collecting terms we get

$$l = \frac{E_i - 2b}{2m} = \frac{kE_o - 2b}{2m} \qquad (4\text{-}14)$$

Thus it is apparent that the arc length for maximum arc power depends upon the open circuit voltage setting of the generator as well as the electrode constants b and m.

For a given arc length, say $\frac{1}{8}$ in., it is possible to solve Equation 4-14 for E_i in terms of the electrode constants and get

$$E_i = \frac{m}{4} + 2b \qquad (4\text{-}15)$$

Now we see how this applies for the electrode in the previous problem that had the characteristic $E = 20l + 22$. We then get

$$E_i = \tfrac{1}{4} \times 20 + 44 = 49 \text{ volts}$$

For an E6010 electrode having the approximate characteristic $E = 32l + 25$, the maximum arc power for a $\frac{1}{8}$ in. arc length will occur with the generator set for $E_i = \tfrac{1}{4} \times 32 + 50 = 58$ volts.

Output-Voltage Yielding Maximum Arc Power for a Given Generator Setting. Once a given generator setting has been made, that is E_i and I_s are fixed, it is interesting to note that the maximum arc power will occur when the operating or output potential is one-half the intercept voltage E_i. This can be demonstrated as follows:

$$W = EI = E\left(\frac{E - E_i}{n}\right)$$

To obtain the solution we differentiate W with respect to E and equate to zero.

$$\frac{dW}{dE} = \frac{2E}{n} - \frac{E_i}{n} = 0$$

or

$$E = \frac{E_i}{2} \qquad\qquad (4\text{-}16)$$

Weld Penetration

In the preceding sections we saw how it is possible to use the electrode and generator characteristics to control the changes in arc heat produced by random variations in arc length. A more significant effect of the arc conditions is the weld penetration, where penetration is defined as the depth of the fusion zone (melt) beneath the original plate surface. It is not the distance to the edge of the heat-affected zone. In the following sections we will see how it is possible to control the actual penetration by appropriately selecting the operating variables: voltage, current, and welding velocity.

It is obvious that the penetration will increase with an increase in the arc heat that is dissipated at the work surface. Thus the penetration increases with a rise in the arc current since this induces a greater amount of heat at the work surface.

The effect of the arc voltage on the penetration is somewhat more complicated since the effect is also a function of the type of arc welding process being used. This is true because the arc voltage is increased, not by manipulating the power source as is done for the current, but by increasing the arc length. And as the arc length is extended, the heat loss from the arc column by radiation increases greatly. (In fact, the work piece is not melted when the arc length is greater than about $\frac{5}{8}$ in. when welding with $\frac{1}{8}$ in. diameter coated-stick electrodes.) Thus, depending upon the type and thickness of coating on a stick electrode, the penetration will first increase with arc length for short arc columns which are recessed within the coating. But as the arc length increases further so that most of the arc column is exposed and loses heat to the surroundings by radiation, the penetration reaches a maximum and then starts to decrease as the arc length is further increased. For the gas shielded arc processes, the penetration probably varies inversely with arc length for all practical arc lengths since there is no thermal shielding present. On the other hand, the submerged arc process is completely blanketed by a layer of insulating flux and so the radiation is very low.

For this latter process it would be expected that the penetration varies in the same direction as the arc length for all practical arc lengths.

Also, it is intuitive that the penetration will vary inversely with the welding velocity when the voltage and current are maintained constant.

Some insight into the magnitude of the influence of each of these three operating variables can be obtained from Figures 4-30, 31, and 32, which are plots made from published experimental data obtained on steel with the submerged arc process.[2] Although complete data is not yet available for all types of arc welding and all materials, it does appear that the effect of the operating variables on penetration is predictable when welding with coated electrodes, submerged arc, or the SIGA process if only a little amount of experimental data is obtained.

Figure 4-30 illustrates the effect of the arc potential on weld penetration when the current is maintained constant at 500 amperes with a welding speed of 30 in./min. The experimental data points fall very accurately along a line that can be expressed as:

$$p = 0.025 \, E^{0.56} \tag{4-17}$$

where p is the penetration in inches and E is the arc potential in volts.

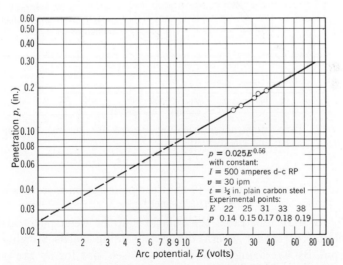

Figure 4-30. Penetration versus arc potential with constant welding velocity and current. (Data from Jackson and Goodwin.[2])

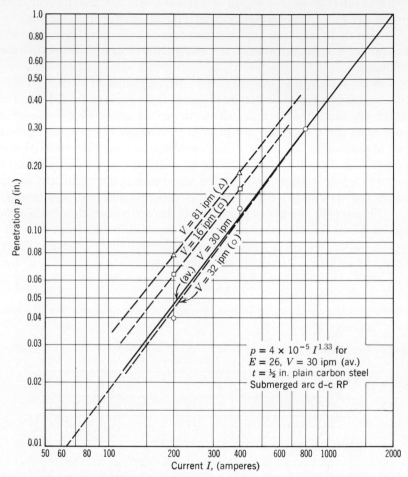

Figure 4-31. Penetration versus welding current for several welding speeds. (Data from Jackson and Goodwin.[2])

Thus we see from Equation 4-17 that the penetration increases approximately as the square root of the arc voltage.

Figure 4-31 illustrates the relationship between penetration and the welding current for several different welding speeds, varying from 8 to 32 ipm. By averaging these curves, we see that for an arc potential of 26 volts and a welding velocity of 30 in./min., the penetration is related to the current density as follows:

$$p = 4 \times 10^{-5} I^{1.33} \tag{4-18}$$

From this it is apparent that the welding current influences the penetration more than the arc potential does even though the voltage and current both affect the total heat input equally. A few examples will demonstrate the manner in which the empirical relationship designated as Equation 4-18 facilitates the understanding of some of the advantages of the SIGA processes over the stick welding process.

From Figure 4-31 we can see that the penetration is 0.155 in. when welding with 500 amperes, 26 volts, 30 ipm, and a $\frac{3}{16}$ in. diameter electrode in the submerged-arc process. When welding with a $\frac{3}{16}$ in. diameter coated-stick electrode, the operating conditions would be about 26 volts and 200 amperes (see Table 4-12). The lower current is required because the I^2R heating would cause the entire electrode to overheat if higher currents were used. Under these conditions, if the welding speed

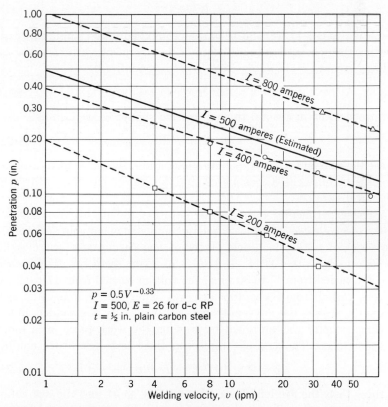

Figure 4-32. Penetration versus welding velocity for several values of current. (Data from Jackson and Goodwin.[2])

240   THE WELDING PROCESS

were 30 ipm, the penetration would be only 0.046 in. However, a welding speed of about 12 ipm would be more reasonable, and this would result in an increase of the penetration to about 0.063 in.

Considerably higher current densities are possible with the SIGA processes; since typical values are about 400 amperes with a $\frac{1}{8}$ in. diameter wire (similar to those for the submerged arc) with a welding velocity of 30 ipm, these conditions would result in a penetration of about 0.125 in.

Figure 4-32 shows the way penetration depends upon the welding velocity for several combinations of current and arc potential. For all of the data shown in Figure 4-32, the penetration varies inversely to the one-third power of the welding velocity. With the operating conditions used in the previous examples, namely, a current of 500 amperes and potential of 26 volts with a $\frac{3}{16}$ in. diameter electrode, the penetration versus velocity relationship is defined by Equation 4-19

$$p = 0.5V^{-0.33} \tag{4-19}$$

Equations 4-17, 18, and 19 can be combined into a single expression relating the penetration to all three of the operating variables. For arc-welding steel with the submerged arc, this equation is

$$p = 2 \times 10^{-5}E^{0.56}I^{1.33}V^{-0.33} \tag{4-20}$$

For arc welding in general this expression should be written as

$$p = kE^a I^b V^c \tag{4-21a}$$

where the constant k and exponents a, b, and c, will be slightly different for arcs in different atmospheres and for work materials other than structural steel.

The experimental data for penetration during arc welding with coated-stick electrodes are very meager and somewhat contradictory. In one series of tests $\frac{1}{2}$-in. thick plates of low carbon steel were welded semimanually with E6014 electrodes of $\frac{1}{8}$ in. diameter. The welding velocity varied from $4\frac{1}{2}$ to 30 ipm; the voltage varied from 17 to 37; the current varied from 85 to 195 amperes. The welding was done semimanually, that is the arc length was controlled by the welder, but the welding velocity was obtained by moving the work piece on a motor-driven carriage. The data obtained from these tests best fit the equation

$$p = 2 \times 10^{-5}E^{0.56}I^{1.40}v^{-0.29} \tag{4-21b}$$

In these tests the arc length was kept fairly short and the arc column was recessed within the coating, which probably accounts for the positive exponent on the voltage.

In a later series of tests $\frac{1}{2}$-in. thick plates of steel were welded by down-feeding the electrode by means of a motor-driven screw to maintain a constant arc length. The welding velocity was also obtained by attaching the work piece to a power driven carriage. In these tests $\frac{1}{8}$-in. diameter E6014 electrodes were used. The welding speed was varied from 5 to 30 ipm; the voltage ranged from 27 to 35 (indicating fairly long arc lengths); and the current varied from 70 to 165 amperes. Under these conditions the penetration best fit the expression

$$p = 4.5 \times 10^{-5}E^{-0.7}I^2v^{-0.33} \qquad (4\text{-}21c)$$

The exponent for the voltage in this second series of tests is negative, whereas it is positive for the first series. As stated earlier, this difference is probably due to the fact that shorter arc lengths (potential drops as low as 17 volts) were used in the first tests. Until sufficient data of this type are available to show the effect on the penetration of such variables as the moisture content in the coating and the angle that the electrode makes with the work piece, precise predictions of the penetration cannot be made. On the other hand, these relationships are significant because they illustrate what the important variables are in regard to weld penetration as well as the effect that each of the variables has on penetration. And they do give a *reliable estimate* of the depth of penetration.

All of these relationships for weld penetration are valid only for plain carbon and low alloy steels (less than 4% alloy) and cannot be used for stainless steel or nonferrous materials because their thermal conductivity and diffusivity are markedly different. In general, the penetration will vary inversely with the thermal conductivity and thermal diffusivity. However, the depth of the heat-affected zone will vary directly with these two thermal properties.

Heat Utilization Efficiency (per cent of total heat that is used to melt the nugget). Jackson and Goodwin[2] have demonstrated with their studies that, for a given total heat input per unit length of weld, the penetration and the heat utilization efficiency are both greater when high currents with high welding speeds are employed. This is verified by the data compiled in Table 4-16. The total energy input per inch is approximately 43 Btu's for all five of the operating conditions listed. The first set of conditions consists of both low current and low velocity; namely, 125 amperes, 4 ipm, and 24 volts. The last set of conditions was 800 amperes, 27.4 ipm, and 26 volts. The penetration is 0.05 in. with the low current and speed but is 0.26 or five times as deep for the high current and speed. The width of the nugget increases

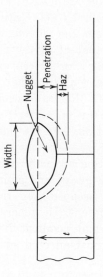

TABLE 4-16. Efficiency of Heat Utilization in Welding[1]

Current, Amperes	Potential, Volts	Velocity, ipm	Total Energy Input Watt sec/in.	Total Energy Input Btu²/in.	Penetration, in.	Nugget Width, in.	Area, sq.in.	HAZ Depth, in.	Energy to Melt nugget[3], Btu/in.	Efficiency[4], %
125	24	4.0	45,000	42.7	0.05	0.45	0.042	0.109	7.03	16.4
170	27	6.0	45,700	43.3	0.10	0.59	0.067	0.101	11.0	25.4
300	32	12.6	46,500	44.1	0.15	0.59	0.094	0.078	15.65	35.5
410	26	14.0	45,700	43.3	0.16	0.62	0.101	0.066	16.85	39.0
800	26	27.4	45,500	43.2	0.26	0.56	0.140	0.054	23.0	53.0

[1] Data compiled from Reference 2 at end of chapter.
[2] Btu = 1052 watt sec; 1 watt = 1 joule/sec.
[3] Approximately 167 Btu/in.³ to melt steel.
[4] Btu/in. to melt nugget divided by total Btu/in. × 100.

only about 25%, from 0.45 to 0.56 in., for these same conditions, so that the increase in nugget area is almost entirely because of the penetration increase. Also, a very noteworthy fact is that the depth of the heat-affected zone for the low current setting is twice that of the high current. In fact, for the low current, the depth of the HAZ is two times the penetration, whereas with the high current the depth of the HAZ is only 20% as large as the penetration. All of these effects imply that the efficiency of heat utilization increases with an increase in the welding current and the calculations bear this out, the efficiency being only 16% for the low current and 53% for the high current.

Figure 4-33 shows the distribution of the maximum temperature about an arc-welded butt joint in a thin plate.

Electric Resistance Welding

The electric resistance welding processes rely on the heat generated by the contact resistance at the weld interface to melt the oxide layer, and a simultaneous application of a light-pressure across the weld interface for squeezing out some of the molten oxide as well as for insuring intimate contact of the mating surfaces.

The first weldment made by the electric resistance process is probably that by the English physicist, James Joule, who in 1856

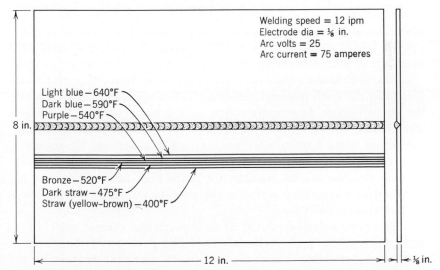

Figure 4-33. Sketch of arc welded, cold-finished steel plates showing positions of color isotherms drawn to scale.

heated wires by the passage of electric current through them, and then pressure-welded them together. In 1880 resistance-welding machines utilizing light pressures to insure contact of the joining faces were put on the industrial market under the name incandescent welding.

The most common types of electric resistance-welding processes (spot, butt, and seam) will be described individually after briefly discussing the general principles applying to all of them.

The total heat for all of the electric resistance welding processes is generated in the weld zone in accordance with the relationship

$$q = I^2Rt \qquad\qquad (4\text{-}22)$$

However, the heat remaining in the weld zone that is directly used to achieve the weld is given by the expression

$$q = KI^2Rt \qquad\qquad (4\text{-}23)$$

where q is in Btu's, I is the current in amperes, R is the resistance in ohms, t is the time in minutes, and K is a proportionality constant (less than 1) that compensates for the heat losses by radiation to the surroundings and conduction to the work holders or electrodes as well as the colder work material outside the electric circuit.

To experimentally determine the value of q it is best to simply measure the current and the voltage drop for a given period of time. Equation 4-23 can be rewritten as

$$q = K\,(\dot{E}I\cos\phi)\,t \qquad\qquad (4\text{-}24)$$

where $\cos\phi$ is the power factor or lag between the voltage and the current and is equal to 1 for dc. The potential drop is about 1 to 5 volts for all processes except the flash upset which uses 10 to 15 volts.

The heat is not generated uniformly either across the joint interface or in the work material between the two electrical contacts where the current flows. In our discussion of the basic welding problem it was pointed out that when two smooth surfaces are pressed together, the actual contact takes place only at a few asperities. By means of Figure 4-34 it can be seen how this limited "contact" makes the resistance welding process possible, for if the high temperature was not localized at the contact surfaces, the process would be too inefficient for industrial application.

The same value of current flows through the contact interface as flows through the cross-sectional A_o of the part, or of the electrode end in spot welding. Since the real metal-to-metal contact at the interface is small, in the order of 10^{-3} times A_o, the current density through these "bridges" is high. Another way to look at it is that the

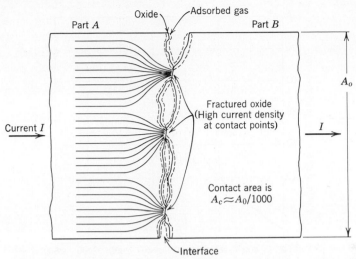

Figure 4-34. Schematic drawing of the interface of an electric-resistance welding operation showing current flow lines.

electrical resistance per unit length is the reciprocal of the resistivity times the area. Since the contact area is so small, the electrical resistance at the interface is in the order of 10^3 times that of the bulk metal. The same current that heats the metal interface to the melting temperature in about one second will heat the bulk metal only slightly above room temperature. This has been demonstrated experimentally by butt welding two $\frac{1}{2}$ in. diameter by 4 in. long pieces of steel together. The time for welding was about one-tenth of a minute; the interface had been melted and about $\frac{1}{4}$ in. on each of the interface was red hot. Following this, one piece of steel $\frac{1}{2}$ in. diameter by 8 in. long was clamped in the electrodes and the same current was caused to flow through it for one minute. The piece of steel was heated so slightly that after it was withdrawn from the machine it could be held in one's bare hand.

During the early stages of the resistance-welding cycle, as the above-mentioned contact areas became hot, their strength also decreases and the metal flows plastically, thereby increasing the contact area. Also, some of the oxide is removed which increases the contact area further. And, the contact area of the interface soon increases to nearly the bulk A_o. Why doesn't the temperature now drop at the interface? Because the electrical resistance depends not only on the area but on the resistivity which in itself is a function of temperature.

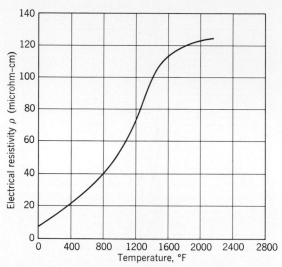

Figure 4-35. Effect of temperature on the electrical resistivity of iron.

Figure 4-35 illustrates how the electrical resistance of steel varies with temperature. The resistance increases by a factor of 10 as the temperature changes from room temperature to 1800°F. Consequently, the hot metal will become even hotter. If the current flow is maintained for a sufficiently long period, the position of the high temperature will move from the interface all the way back to the electrode contacts on the part.

The entire contact area at the weld interface may not always be free of oxides after resistance welding, as can be seen from Figure 4-36, which is a photomicrograph of a spot weld in low carbon steel. The black oval-shaped globules consist of part of the oxide layer that was present on the surfaces of the mating parts prior to welding. The fact that martensite can easily be formed with carbon contents as low as 0.15% with the fast cooling rates associated with electric resistance welding is demonstrated by the high hardness ($45R_c$) in the heat-affected zone in this same figure.

A brief discussion of the equipment and techniques associated with the common electric resistance welding processes is given next.

Electric Resistance Butt Welding. There are two types of electric resistance butt welding processes, the *upset* and the *flash*. The equipment for the latter type is a little more sophisticated than the former,

Figure 4-36. Photomicrograph of an electric-resistance spot weld of low carbon steel.

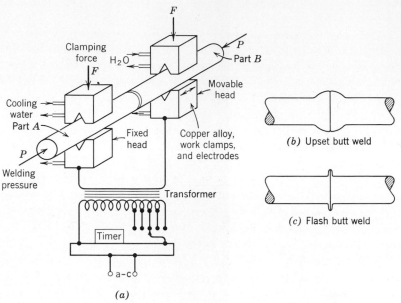

Figure 4-37. Schematic drawing of electric-resistance butt welding. (*a*) Line drawing of typical equipment for both upset and flash butting welding. (*b*) and (*c*) Typical cross sections resulting in the completed weldments.

but both can be described by the schematic drawing in Figure 4-37. When special electrodes or work clamps are used, irregularly shaped parts can be easily welded.

The sequence of operations in the upset butt process is as follows. The two pieces to be welded together are clamped in position in the electrodes. The movable head is moved toward the fixed head until the mating surfaces of the work pieces are in light contact. Then the proper current is made to flow across the interface for a preset time, while the slight pressure between the two parts is maintained. When the current stops, the interface is at the proper welding temperature and the pressure forcing the two parts together is increased to form an "upset" (Figure 4-37*b*). In a matter of a few seconds the heat from the interface flows into the adjacent cold metal and the welded parts are withdrawn. Of the oxide layer that was originally present at the interface, some is eliminated by the decomposition of the FeO into Fe + O, with some of the released oxygen dissolving in the steel if it is not already saturated. Also, some of the oxide is squeezed out when the interface is molten, and some remains as small isolated particles at the interface.

The equipment for the flash butt welding process is slightly different from the upset butt process. The movable head on the flash butt equipment is fed toward the fixed head at a slow controlled rate, with no pressure between the mating parts until after the current ceases. The exact sequence of operations is similar to the upset butt process. After the parts are properly positioned and the correct current, head speed, and time, are selected, a cycle start button is actuated. This causes the movable head to approach the fixed head. As the highest asperities at the interface contact each other, the large current flows through these small areas and instantly melts and boils away these small projections. As the next highest asperities come in contact, they too are boiled off, with the molten particles ejected from the interface with considerable force and "sparking," thus giving the process its name "flash" butt. As this process continues for a few seconds, a very thin layer at the interface is melted, and then the current is shut off and the two parts are rapidly pressed together causing a small upset as illustrated in Figure 4-37c.

Electric Resistance Spot Welding. The spot welding process is very similar to the previously described upset butt process as may be seen by comparing Figures 4-37 and 4-38. In reality, the only difference is in the shape of the electrodes and the parts being welded: spot welding

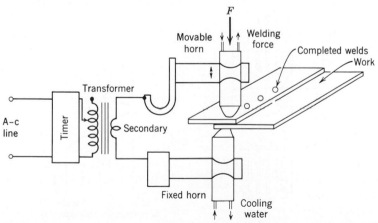

Figure 4-38. Schematic drawing of the electric-resistance spot-welding process.

is generally done on sheets, whereas the butt processes are generally used on bars. As is true of all the electric resistance welding processes except the flash butt, the parts are held together by light pressure, usually about one-tenth of the yield strength of the material being welded, during the time the current is flowing through the interface. The oxide layer is partially eliminated in the same manner as was described previously under the topic of butt welding.

The temperature distribution in spot welding at the instant the current is interrupted is illustrated in Figure 4-39. This temperature distribution is also typical of all the electric resistance welding processes. The maximum temperature occurs at the interface of the two parts being welded for the same reasons given for electric-resistance welding. As soon as the temperature at this region exceeds the melting temperature, the weld is complete.

To achieve successful spot welding, it is necessary to prevent the temperature at the electrode-work interfaces from rising to the melting temperature. This is accomplished by using copper alloy electrodes which deform more than steel at the contact points, thus giving a larger contact area. The electrical resistance is lower and the thermal conduction is higher for copper than steel, which also tends to keep the temperature lower. And, finally, the electrodes are usually water cooled to maintain a lower ambient temperature. By these means the temperature at the electrode work interface is kept below that of the

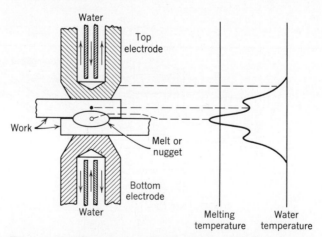

Figure 4-39. Temperature distribution in electric-resistance spot welding at the time the current is stopped.

SURVEY OF WELDING EQUIPMENT

251

weld interface, but is higher than the temperature near the mid-thickness of the sheets being welded (Figure 4-39).

In the spot welding process it is desirable to keep the weld nugget (melt) symmetrical about the joint interface. If the two sheets are of the same thickness and material, then a symmetrical nugget can be achieved simply by keeping the two electrodes the same diameter. However, if the sheets are of a different thickness or composition, then the electrodes must be of different diameter or, in some cases, of different composition.

To determine what the relative sizes of the electrodes should be, it is necessary to consider what is required to obtain a symmetrical nugget. A symmetrical nugget will result with a proper balance of the heat being generated in each piece and the heat flowing away from the hot interface. Obviously in the electric resistance processes the heat generated depends upon the electrical resistivity ρ and the heat flow depends on the thermal conductivity k.

The electrical resistance for a sheet of thickness t where the current flows through an area A (electrode contact area) is defined by the expression

$$R = \frac{\rho t}{A} \tag{4-25}$$

Similarly the thermal conductance is

$$K = \frac{kA}{t} \tag{4-26}$$

When spot welding two sheets of the same material but of different thicknesses, it is desirable to keep the thermal conductance through both sheets equal or

$$\frac{kA_1}{t_1} = \frac{kA_2}{t_2} \quad \text{so that} \quad \frac{A_2}{A_1} = \frac{t_2}{t_1} \tag{4-27}$$

Thus to get equal penetration into each sheet the electrode contact area should be directly proportional to the thickness of the sheet it is in contact with.

When spot welding two sheets of the same thickness but different material, the electrical resistance of both sheets should be equal. Thus

$$\frac{t\rho_1}{A_1} = \frac{t\rho_2}{A_2} \quad \text{so that} \quad \frac{A_2}{A_1} = \frac{\rho_2}{\rho_1} \tag{4-28}$$

That is, the electrode contact area should be directly proportional to the electrical resistivity of the material it is in contact with. In spot welding copper to steel, a larger contact area should be provided for the electrode that is in contact with the steel. For most metals, the electrical and thermal conductivities are about equal, and so the reciprocal of the thermal conductivity can also be used in the above ratio in place of the electrical resistivity.

Electric Resistance Seam Welding. Figure 4-40 illustrates the electric-resistance seam-welding process. In reality, seam welding consists of a continuous overlapping series of spot welds. It is more convenient to use two rotating electrodes, with the work being welded moving continuously by the electrodes, than to have an interrupted work movement which would be required if spot welding electrodes were used. The current does not flow continuously during seam welding, but rather it flows for a few cycles and is off for a few cycles to give an overlap of spot welds.

   In seam welding, or in spot welding where more than one spot weld is made on a part, the current must be increased to compensate for the fact that some of the electricity will flow through the previously completed welds. In most cases of seam welding, a stream of water is directed over the disc electrodes and the area of the work pieces being welded to keep everything cool except the joint interface.

Electric Resistance Projection Welding. The projection welding process is depicted in Figure 4-41. The projections on sheet metal may

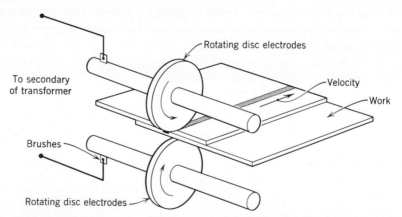

Figure 4-40. Schematic drawing of electric-resistance seam welding process.

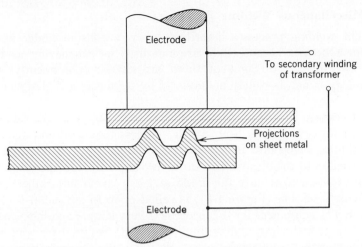

Figure 4-41. Schematic drawing of electric-resistance projection-welding process.

be produced by embossing, coining or bending or they may be machined or upset on the ends of bars or shafts. The operation of forming the projection can be combined with other forming operations if the parts have to be previously formed by means of dies and tools in punch presses or lathes. Projection welding is a modification of either the spot or the butt process, depending on the shape of the parts being welded, to the extent that it enables close control of the location of the current flow and contacting pressure. Simpler shaped electrodes can be used and flat-faced cylinders are usually sufficient. Because larger diameter electrodes can be used with a greater heat capacity, the need for water cooling is often eliminated. Also, many "spot" welds can be made simultaneously on one piece, resulting in a lower cost of operation.

To develop uniform heating in the two pieces being welded by the projection process, the projections should be formed on the thicker of the two pieces for autogeneous welding. If the welding is of the heterogeneous type, then the projections should be formed on the material having the higher conductivity.

There are many applications for projection welding, but there are no governing principles for their use. The use of this welding process depends primarily upon the designer's creativity and consequently nothing further need be said here concerning its application.

Miscellaneous Welding Processes

The welding processes described below are listed under miscellaneous processes because they are not used as extensively as those previously described. Some of them are newer; consequently, their technology is not as widely understood by engineers and designers.

Cold Pressure Welding. Although lead was cold-pressure welded as early as the seventeenth century, the process that we know today as cold welding came into industrial usage about 1950. This process is quite similar to the electric resistance process with the exception that no heat is used to remove the oxide and gas layers but rather severe plastic deformation (Figure 4-3), is relied upon to get metal-to-metal contact. The equipment for this process is very simple and inexpensive: light presses with simple "dimpling" dies being required for cold welding thick sections and special pliers similar to bolt cutters being sufficient for thin sections.

By studying Figure 4-42 and considering the mechanism by which the weld is achieved in the cold welding process, it is evident that a thorough understanding of the process requires a knowledge of the forming process and associated strain-hardening as well. The sketches labeled (a) illustrate the mechanism of butt welding wires or bars. The two wires are clamped in specially shaped dies in such a way that when the two wires are contacting at their interface, the die faces are separated by a distance l which is determined by the amount of deformation needed to have the volume lA_o equal to the volume V_d of the die cavity. The cavity V_d is made elliptical for two reasons: first, the displaced metal will fill the die cavity more readily; and second, the displaced metal is attached to the wire by only a small area and this "flash" can easily be trimmed off.

To acquire satisfactory bonding, deformations resulting in natural strains of nearly 1 are required for aluminum, and strains greater than 1, and sometimes nearly as large as 2, required to join copper, iron, and other metals. When it is recalled that an area ratio of 2.7, that is, the final area is 2.7 times the initial area, is equivalent to a strain of 1, the magnitude of the deformations required is more apparent.

Joint efficiencies, on the basis of the yield strength, greater than 100% can be obtained easily when welding annealed materials. Consider, for example, the joining of $\frac{1}{4}$ in. diameter 1100-0 aluminum wire having a yield strength of 5000 psi and a strain hardenability that can be expressed as $\sigma = 26{,}000\epsilon^{0.18}$. If the interface is deformed to a

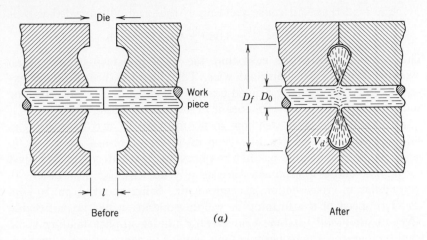

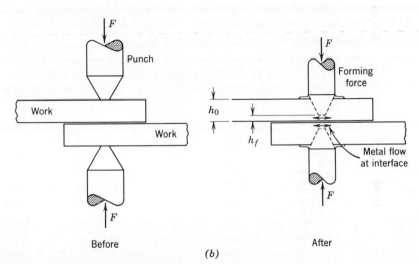

Figure 4-42. Schematic drawing of typical cold-welding operations. (*a*) Butt weld of bars. (*b*) Lap-spot weld of sheets.

natural strain of 1, that is, to a $D_f = 0.412$ in., the interface material will then have a yield strength of 26,000 psi. After the flash is removed, and assuming that only one-half of the interface is a real metal-to-metal weld, the interface weld area is then 0.025 in.^{2} The load to cause yielding at the interface is then

$$L_y = S_y \times A_c = 26{,}000 \times 0.025 = 625 \text{ lb}$$

The load that will cause yielding of the original annealed wire is

$$L_y = S_y \times A = 5{,}000 \times 0.05 = 250 \,\text{lb}$$

Thus we can see in this case that the weld interface is more than twice as strong as the original wire. This fact has been verified experimentally where many welded bars were loaded in a tensile machine and the resulting failure would occur in the parent metal.

Figure 4-42*b* illustrates how sheets are cold welded together. The deformations required for this type of joint, expressed as the h_o/h_f ratio, is about the same as that required for the butt joint described above. The end of the punches are usually not circular but rather are rectangular in cross section, a common size being about $\frac{1}{16}$ in. $\times \frac{1}{4}$ in.

The speed of the forming or welding operation has no noticeable effect on the weld quality. Conceivably, under impact loading some local temperatures may become high enough to cause recrystallization, but the area affected and the time at temperature would be so small that its influence would be negligible. The recrystallization temperatures of some metals are listed in Table 4-17.

TABLE 4-17. Recrystallization Temperatures, for Some Metals

Metal	Per Cent Cold Work	$R_x °F$	Metal	Per cent Cold Work	$R_x °F$
Aluminum	10	685	Nickel	10	1157
(2S)	20	602		30	1060
	30	530		50	969
	60	510		70	878
	80	505		80	780
Copper	10	510	Platinum	20	1265
	25	365		40	1130
	50	280		60	968
	70	260		80	842
	90	190		90	680
Iron	5	968	Silver	10	482
	10	950		30	383
	50	847		60	266
	75	770		90	230
Magnesium	30	525	70-30	10	800
	50	440	Brass	25	752
	60	400		50	700
	75	345		75	662

An experimental test was also conducted to verify that the interface temperature rise was slight, much lower than the recrystallization temperature, as calculations seemed to imply. For these tests, very small diameter Chromel-constantan thermocouples were embedded at the weld interface and the temperature was recorded during the welding operation. For modest rates of loading, the maximum temperature rise during the butt welding of aluminum bars was only 10°F.

The best surface preparation prior to welding appears to be either a filing or wire-brushing of the intended contacting surface. Other than performing the operation in a vacuum, preliminary experimental work seems to indicate that the process is no more efficient when carried out in an inert atmosphere such as helium or argon than when performed in air. This seems to imply that the adsorbed gas layer is more of a handicap than the oxide layer when making room temperature welds.

Friction Welding. The friction welding process came into limited industrial use in the late 1950's after having been widely proclaimed in Russia for several years. Although the cold pressure welding process is most readily performed on small cross sections, the friction process lends itself more to the joining of large sections, particularly large diameter shafts or tubes. In this latter case the friction welding process closely resembles the cold welding operation of Figure 4-42*a*, the electric resistance butt welding operation of Figure 4-37*a*, and the hot pressure welding process.

The techniques of this process can be described by referring to Figure 4-42*a*. Instead of the work being held in specially shaped dies, the work is clamped in three or four jaw chucks or in collets. One chuck is stationary and the other rotates at a fairly high speed. At the beginning of the weld cycle, the two bars are brought into light end-to-end contact and one bar is rotated, generating frictional heat at the interface. After a few seconds the rotating spindle is stopped quickly and the pressure between the two bars increased to cause an upset at the interface. The welds obtained by this process are comparable to those of the other competitive processes described above.

The equipment used for this process resembles very closely a heavy-duty engine lathe consisting of a base or bed upon which are mounted a rotating spindle and a stationary chuck with provisions for moving the two heads together under high pressure. The welding times and contact pressures must be accurately controlled to insure good welds, but this is not a disadvantage since all industrial manufacturing processes require control of the operating conditions for satisfactory results. However, at the present time there is no way to calculate the amount of frictional heat that will be generated at the interface, so experience is necessary in this field. The amount of welding done by this process is very small, as is true of all the miscellaneous welding processes listed.

Electron Beam Welding. The electron beam welding process is an autogenous arc-welding process done in a vacuum, usually in the order of 10^{-5} mm of mercury. It is different from the ordinary shielded and unshielded arc-welding processes in that the voltage and currents are reversed in order of magnitude. For the arc processes described previously, typical potentials and currents are 25 volts and 250 amperes. Typical values for the electron beam process are 25,000 volts and 250 milliamperes.

The arc column, or electron beam as it is called by the manufacturers of the equipment to distinguish it from the other arc processes, is much smaller in diameter than in the other arc processes. The diameter of the arc column is slightly greater than that of the electrode used in the others, but in the electron beam process the diameter of the arc column is in the order of 10^{-2} in., resulting in a more localized heating.

Deep penetrations with a very narrow heat affected zone is quoted for this process. Penetration of $1\frac{3}{4}$ in. in aluminum and $1\frac{1}{4}$ in. in stainless steel with a total width (melt plus HAZ) of only one-tenth of the penetration is reported by the manufacturers of the equipment. Shallow welds are made equally well.

Welding done by this process is quite a bit more expensive than with common arc processes for two reasons: first, the initial equipment cost is ten to twenty times as great; and second, the welding times are longer since there is a five minute or more delay after the parts are placed in the vacuum chamber until the gases are evacuated before welding. However, welds made by this process are superior to those made by the other arc processes. Since no gas is dissolved in the melt, there is no porosity or pin holes present. Where clean, sound welds such as these are required, the election beam process is very feasible.

Stud Welding. Stud welding is a special type of autogenous arc welding in which the electrode, usually a headless bolt called a stud or a similarly shaped piece, is allowed to remain in the melt that was created by maintaining an arc for a short time between the stud (electrode) and the part with which is is joined.

The end of the studs have a cap that encases a dry flux, and a ceramic ferrule that is used to maintain a gap between the end of the stud and the work, making the process an electric arc rather than an electric resistance one.

The sequence of operations during stud welding is as follows: the stud, or other projection to be welded to the work part, is loaded into the end of the special "gun," which very often is a portable hand tool. The stud is then properly positioned on the work piece and the trigger of the gun is pressed. This causes an arc to form between the stud and the work which is maintained for about a second. The stud is then pushed by means of a spring into the weld pool and the current is stopped to allow the end of the stud to freeze in place.

This process is widely used to attach bolts and other projections onto work pieces without the need for drilling and tapping holes and is therefore very economical.

Thermit Welding. The thermit welding process is a special process used mainly to repair steel or cast iron parts of large cross sections by constructing a mold around the broken area and pouring into the cavity the ferrous metal that was melted by igniting a "thermit" mixture of aluminum powder and iron oxide. Actually this process is as much a casting process as it is a welding process. But with the development of the automatic and shielded arc processes, the use of the thermit process has decreased.

The technique of this process consists of the following steps. The broken parts have a large bevel, flame cut or machined, at the fractured interface so that they meet in a vee joint. The vee is then filled with wax and a sand mold constructed around it, leaving a pouring sprue as well as a riser, if the parts are extremely large. The mold is then heated to melt the wax, causing it to flow into the sand mold and leaving a void space in the vee joint. The thermit mixture, which had previously been prepared in a bottom-pour ladle, is ignited with a torch, or by other means, that can heat it to the temperature of 2000°F required for the oxidation of the aluminum according to the reaction.

$$8Al + 3Fe_3O_4 \rightarrow 9Fe + 4Al_2O_3 + \text{heat} \qquad (4\text{-}29)$$

The reaction is nonexplosive and requires about a half-minute to go to completion. The stopper is knocked out of the bottom of the ladle and the liquid is poured into the mold cavity. Since the molten metal is at a temperature of about 4500°F as it goes into the mold cavity, it melts the faces of the vee joint and when solidification occurs the two broken parts are welded together.

Ultrasonic Welding. Ultrasonic welding is another of the welding processes developed in the 1950's. There are two types of ultrasonic welding equipment in very limited use today, mostly for the joining of aluminum. The first type uses no external heating. The equipment quite closely resembles electric resistance spot and seam welding equipment, where the electrodes, rather than carrying a current, simply vibrate or impact the two mating surfaces together. The second type is a "gun"-type soldering iron having a vibrating tip. This latter type is used for the soft soldering of aluminum, which is difficult to do with ordinary acid core or rosin core solders because of the inability of these two fluxes to remove the aluminum oxide layer. The success of the ultrasonic soldering gun is its effect in breaking up the oxide layer which then permits the soft solder to alloy with the parent metal. However, it should be pointed out at this time that there are now chemical fluxes that dissolve the aluminum oxide layer and permit the soft solders to function in the traditional manner.

In regard to the ultrasonic welding process, there are some conflicting theories concerning the means by which the metallic bond is obtained. Some shroud it in mystery and claim the oxide simply "disintegrates" and metal contact results. Obviously, matter cannot be destroyed without the evolution of a tremendous amount of heat, which is lacking in this process. And the oxide cannot be dissociated to metallic aluminum so easily, as evidenced by the manufacturing process required to obtain pure aluminum from the ore.

The most logical explanation seems to be a combination of the fracturing of the brittle oxide layer and a softening or melting of the asperities due to the localized high velocity rubbing of the two contacting surfaces. The oxide layer, if fractured and dispersed in a noncontinuous volume at the interface, will not prevent bonding but may actually increase the strength of the metal. In reality, this is the mechanism of both precipitation and dispersion hardening. Any photomicrograph of polished and etched 1100—0 aluminum will show many particles of aluminum oxide dispersed through the matrix. An increase in the number of these particles, if they are small and well dispersed, will strengthen the aluminum.

THE STRENGTH OF WELDMENTS

The subject of the strength of weldments can be divided into two areas: the interrelationship between the strength and the microstructure (metallurgical), the effect of the geometry of the joint design on the stresses (stress raisers). The latter area is traditionally included in textbooks and courses on machine design and is discussed only briefly here.

Geometrical Considerations of Welded Joints

The data summarized in Table 4-18 illustrates the influence of both the welding technique and the geometry of the joint on the strength and the cost of the weldment. It must be kept in mind that in some cases the relative strengths listed in this table depend more upon the quality of the welding than upon the type of the joint. Consequently, the cleaning and welding techniques must be carefully studied in conjunction with the joint design when appraising the efficiency of a weldment. The four joints in Table 4-18 can serve as a basis to illustrate some of the considerations that must be given to the design of butt joints.

Since the entire cross section of joint A has been fused, the tensile strength of the welded joint is equal to that of the parent plate, assuming that the same microstructure is present in all cases. In order to achieve complete fusion throughout the entire depth of the weld it is necessary to chip out thoroughly all of the slag before making each welding pass. When both the bottom and the top of the plate are to be welded, it is especially important, after the first side is welded and the plate turned over, to clean the root of the joint before starting to weld from the second side. This was done in the case of joint A but not for joint B, with resulting relative tensile strengths of 100% and 85% respectively. This latter value of 85% is only a rough guide to demonstrate what may happen under reasonable conditions if the joint design is proper but the welding is done carelessly. If the depth of the U in joint A or the double V in joint B is insufficient and if in addition the welding conditions are such that shallow penetration is achieved, then the relative strength of both these joints may approach that of joint D, namely 60%.

The relative cost of joint A is given as 100%, with all the other joints being considerably cheaper. The reasons for the high cost of this first joint are threefold. First, the U or J joint is the most expensive shape to machine; a V or bevel is easier to machine, and, of course, the square-end simple butt requires no machining other than cutting the pieces to the proper length. The second reason for the cost being high is that all the slag was chipped and the welding was carefully done. The third reason is that a single U or V joint for full penetration requires more filler metal to be deposited than for a double U or V. In fact, for welding the same thickness of plate, with the same bevel angle, the single V requires exactly twice as much filler metal as the double V. The reader can verify this for a 60° or 90° V in a 1 in. thick plate on the basis of geometric considerations only.

If the same careful welding was done on joint B as was done on joint A, then a 100% relative strength with a cost of 50 to 80% would

TABLE 4-18.   Relative Values of Joint Characteristics[1]

	A.	B.	C.	D.
Sketch of Joint				
Description of Joints	Single "U"	Double "V"	Single "U"	Simple butt
Cleaning and Welding Techniques	"U" completely welded first. All slag chipped from bottom before welding underneath side.	Top V welded first. bottom of V not chipped before welding second V.	"U" groove filled. Not chipped or welded from underneath. Penetration not complete.	Top and bottom welded with no chipping. Penetration not complete.
Tensile Strength[2]	100%	85%	70%	60%
Relative Cost	100%	30–50%	40–50%	15–35%

[1] (Abstracted from *Steel Plates and Their Fabrication*, by Lukens Steel Company).
[2] Relative to strength of parent metal, assuming the same microstructures are present in all cases.

be possible because of the cheaper edge preparation and the smaller amount of filler metal required.

For plates less than $\frac{1}{2}$ in. thick, it is possible in many arc welding processes to achieve penetration equal to one-half the plate thickness. In this situation, relative strengths of 100% can be achieved with the D type of joint, with a very low relative cost. Whenever possible, this latter approach should be used.

Another consideration is the stress concentration that occurs in the welded plate adjacent to the weld bead. This stress concentration is due simply to the change in cross section, and is more severe when the bead is excessively high.

Analyses similar to the above can be made for other types of joints and for fillet welds.

In many weldments, such as the welding of heads onto the ends of cylinders or the welding of forgings and castings, stress raisers resulting from changes of cross section or bending moments because of eccentric loading may be present. If the design cannot be modified to eliminate features of this kind, then the weldment must be reinforced in the high stress regions. Figure 4-43 illustrates one way in which the eccentric loading of a lap joint can be eliminated by forming a jog on the end of both plates making the lap. Many similar illustrations can be found in design and welding handbooks.

There is one beneficial aspect in regard to the geometry of a weld joint that should be mentioned at this time; namely the circumstance of triaxial stresses that exist in the joint of a butt weld made with a filler material that has a lower strength than the parent metal, even though the external loading is uniaxial. This condition of triaxial stresses has the effect of raising the uniaxial load-carrying capacity of the welded part, as shown by the curve in Figure 4-44 where the tensile strength of the joint is much greater than that of the filler material when the proper joint thickness is used. In fact, experimental data have shown that when butt-welded bars of stainless steel have been welded with silver solder having a tensile strength of approximately 40,000 psi, the tensile

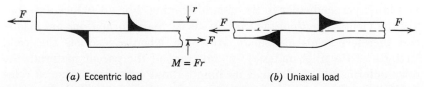

(a) Eccentric load   (b) Uniaxial load

$M = Fr$

Figure 4-43. Sketches of lap joints showing how eccentric loading can be eliminated. (a) Eccentric load. (b) Uniaxial load.

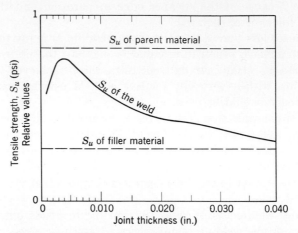

Figure 4-44. The influence of joint thickness on the tensile strength of a heterogeneous-welded butt joint where the strength of the filler material is considerably lower than that of the parent metal.

strength of the weld can be in excess of 120,000 psi for a joint thickness of 0.002 in., which is a threefold increase.

When a specimen is subjected to either pure hydrostatic (equal in all three directions) tension or compression, the resolved shear stress is zero and the specimen should not fail during compression, and in tension only when the stresses become numerically equal to the solid atomic bonding forces of the material. Bridgeman's experiments with hydrostatic compression and Joffe's with hydrostatic tension demonstrated that under hydrostatic loading, stresses considerably higher than uniaxially tensile strength of a material can be endured by the material. Also, a notched specimen has a higher tensile strength than a plain one.

Figure 4-45 illustrates how hydrostatic or triaxial stresses originate in a uniaxially loaded heterogeneous butt weld in which the filler metal has a lower strength than the parent metal. When a uniaxial load is applied, such as F in Figure 4-45a, a uniaxial stress σ_z is present across all planes perpendicular to the axis of loading. For all values of σ_z below the yield strength of the filler material the deformations are elastic and therefore relatively small. However, when σ_z exceeds the yield strength of the filler material but not that of the parent material, the filler deforms plastically and its longitudinal extension becomes relatively large. To maintain a constant volume of filler material, the cross-sectional area decreases proportionately to the increase in length. This condition of a large reduction of area in the filler material and a small reduction of area in the parent metal creates shear stresses at the filler-parent material interface, thus inducing compressive stresses within the planes normal to the longitudinal axis of the parent material and tensile stresses in the equivalent planes of the filler materials (Figure 4-45a).

The effect of these triaxial stresses can be appreciated more by isolating elements B and C of Figure 4-45a and looking at the applied stresses acting on them. Figure 4-45b shows that only uniaxial stresses equal to $(\sigma_z)_u$ act on element B which is located in the parent metal far enough removed from the interface to be unaffected by the induced stresses. On the other hand, element C sketched in Figure 4-45c has the triaxial stresses $(\sigma_x)_t$, $(\sigma_y)_t$, and $(\sigma_z)_t$, which in themselves would not cause plastic deformation or failure. In addition, a stress $(\sigma_z)_e$ that is equal to $(\sigma_z)_u - (\sigma_z)_t$ acts in the direction of the uniaxial applied load and is the tensile stress responsible for failure to occur in the filler material. Element C is drawn in Figure 4-45d without the triaxial stresses, showing only the effective uniaxial tensile stress $(\sigma_z)_e$ acting along the loading axis. Thus it is apparent that for a load resulting in an average stress $(\sigma_z)_u$ which is greater than the yield strength of the filler material, the effective uniaxial stress $(\sigma_z)_e$ which acts across an element of the filler material near the interface is less than $(\sigma_z)_u$ by the amount of the induced triaxial tensile stresses.

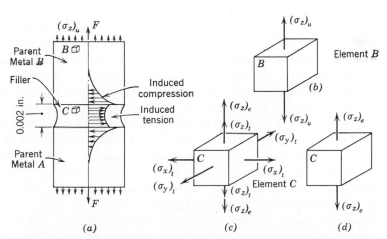

Figure 4-45. Sketch of heterogeneous butt weld illustrating how triaxial stresses increase the load carrying capacity of the joint. (a) Sketch of the joint showing the type of induced stresses. (b) Stresses acting on element B. (c) and (d) Stresses acting on element C.

As sketched in Figure 4-45a, the induced stresses normal to the loading axis are maximum at the parent-filler interface and decrease toward the center of the joint thickness. If the joint thickness is too large, the beneficial aspect of the triaxial stresses is lost. Also, if the joint thickness is too small, the filler material will not fill the entire joint, resulting in a lower load-carrying capacity. The optimum clearance appears to be in the range of 0.002 to 0.005 in. for the common nonferrous filler materials.

Microstructural Considerations of Welded Joints

Except for the few geometrical considerations described previously, the entire subject of the strength of a weldment is best discussed on the basis of the microstructures that are present. The answer to the important question "where will a welded joint fail?" can be determined by knowing what microstructures are present across the weldment and the relationship of the mechanical properties to the microstructures.

The dependency of the mechanical properties of a material upon its microstructure is thoroughly discussed in Chapter 2. The microstructures that are present in a weldment depend entirely upon the following:

1. The composition of the parent materials.
2. The composition of the filler rod, if any is used.
3. The temperature to which the material is heated.
4. The time the material is at temperature.
5. The cooling rate after welding.
6. The amount of deformation for cold pressure welding.

For a fusion weld, all of the first five items of this list must be known before the strength of a welded joint can be appraised. In the case of cold-pressure welding, the temperature and cooling rates are generally unimportant, but the amount of plastic deformation is very important. Determining the strength of a welded joint requires the application of all the principles of mechanical metallurgy. Since this book is written on the premise that the reader has already had one or two courses in the principles of the solid state of materials or mechanical metallurgy, we will start immediately in the application of the already learned principles. But first, two concepts must be defined; joint efficiency (JE) and heat-affected zone (HAZ).

The term *joint efficiency* is used to designate either of two per cent ratios: the strength of the weakest microstructure in the weld zone to the strength of the weakest parent metal: or the lowest load that the weld zone will support to the lowest load the parent plate will carry. Either the tensile strength, the yield strength, or the hardness may be used for this comparison. For example, consider a bar of cold-drawn AISI 1020 steel that is electric-resistance butt welded to a bar of annealed AISI 1020 steel, with the average cooling rate of the heat-affected zone being about 30°F sec at 1300°F. This cooling rate for a 1020 steel results in a microstructure consisting of three-quarters ferrite and one-quarter fine pearlite with a resulting average hardness of 155 Brinell. The hardness of the annealed 1020 steel is 120 Brinell and the cold-drawn steel has a hardness of 137. Thus, the JE is 155/120 × 100, or 129%, assuming the thickness of the weld zone is equal to the thickness of the plate. These hardnesses should be verified.

A cross section of the above-described weld is sketched in Figure 4-46 to illustrate the *heat-affected zone*, which is defined as the region of the weld zone extending from the material heated to melting temperature to the lowest temperature where the microstructure of the parent material is changed. Thus, for the 1020 cold-drawn steel the HAZ includes all the metal that was heated in the range of 800 to 2700°F and for the 1020 annealed steel the HAZ extends from the edge of the melt to the lower critical temperature of 1333°F. The lower HAZ temperature of some coldworked metals may be determined from Table 4-15 which lists the recrystallization temperature as a function of the prior deformation.

As another example of the strength of a weldment, consider the microstructures present along the weld made by joining 1040 annealed

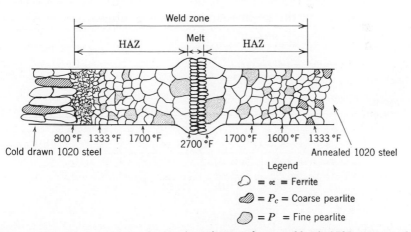

Figure 4-46. Cross section of electric-resistance butt weld of AISI 1020 steel illustrating the microstructures found in the weld zone. (1700°F is the grain-coarsening temperature for an inherently fine grained steel.) Temperatures shown are the maximum values at each location during welding.

steel to 4140 annealed steel with a single V joint using 0.1% carbon steel filler metal. The results are summarized in Figure 4-47 where the microstructures are identified by symbols rather than by grain structures. It is assumed in this example that all the metal that was heated above the lower critical temperature cooled after welding at an average rate of 30°F/sec at 1300°F. It makes no difference, from a microstructure point of view, what the cooling rate is of steel that is heated to temperatures below the lower critical temperature since no phase transformations will occur.

The annealed AISI 1040 steel in the parent metal will have a microstructure, determined by applying the "inverse lever rule" to the iron-carbon equilibrium diagram, of 50% ferrite and 50% coarse pearlite. The bulk hardness of this steel is $160H_B$, being a weighted average of the hardness of the ferrite and the coarse pearlite which are $80H_B$ and $240H_B$ respectively.

The heat-affected zone begins at the lower critical temperature, so the metal heated to just above 1333°F will have a microstructure of 50% ferrite and 50% fine pearlite. Since the hardness of fine pearlite is $380H_B$, the bulk hardness of this material is about $230H_B$.

There is no further change in the microstructure of the 1040 steel heated to temperatures slightly in excess of 1700°F, the grain coarsening temperature for inherently fine grained steels. The microstructure of the metal that was heated to the temperature range between the grain coarsening temperature and the melting temperature in most cases will be identical to that of the metal heated to the range between the upper critical and the grain coarsening temperatures. Because of the

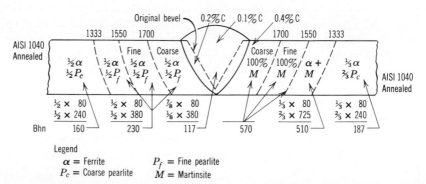

Figure 4-47. Cross section of a V weld between AISI 1040 and 4140 steel with 0.1% C filler rod. Assumed average cooling rate of 30°F/sec at 1300°F in the HAZ. (Temperatures shown are the maximum values at each position during welding.)

fact that hardenability is proportional to the grain size, if a plain carbon steel has traces of some alloys present as impurities it is possible to have martensite form with a cooling rate of 30°F/sec at 1300°F under this combination of conditions.

At the center of the melt the carbon content is only 0.10% and therefore the microstructure consists of seven-eighths ferrite and one-eighth fine pearlite with a bulk hardness of $177H_B$.

Consider now the opposite end of the weldment. The microstructure present in the annealed 4140 steel is approximately 33% ferrite and 67% coarse pearlite with a bulk hardness of about $187H_B$. The reason that 4140 steel has about 33% ferrite compared to the 50% ferrite for a 1040 steel is that the alloys in the former steel lower the carbon content of the eutectoid to nearly 0.6%.

The metal heated to just above the lower critical temperature will consist of one-third ferrite and two-thirds austenite. However, the alloyed austenite will transform to martensite of eutectoid composition. Thus, the bulk hardness of the metal heated just above the lower critical temperature will be about $510H_B$.

As the temperature is raised from the lower critical to the upper critical, the ferrite will be transformed proportionately to austenite so that at the upper critical temperature and above the metal will be 100% austenite. The hardness of martensite having a 0.4% carbon is about $570H_B$. The metal that was heated to temperatures between 1700°F and the melting temperature will have a microstructure of coarse martensite, but the hardness will remain at $570H_B$.

The joint efficiency in the above problem is $117/150 \times 100$ or 78%. Although hardness values were used in the above analysis, the tensile strengths of all the microstructures are in the same proportion to each other as the hardness values. The tensile strength of all the steels can be obtained by multiplying the Brinell hardness number by 500. In Chapters 1 and 2 several methods of determining the yield strength are given. Therefore the joint efficiency would also be 78% on the basis of the tensile strength and somewhat near this same value on the basis of yield strengths.

All of the preceding discussions of weld strength were on the basis of slowly applied loads. Before considering the strengths of other welded joints, let us look briefly at the impact strength. Without going into the tabulation of experimental data for each specific material, generally the most that can be said is that the impact strength varies inversely with the tensile strength.

Figure 4-48 illustrates a very common type of weld joint; namely, the brazing of cast iron to steel. In this particular case the cast iron is

70 Cu-30 Zn
Brazing metal
S_u = 45,000
Hot rolled
1020 steel
S_u = 65,000
Class 20
Cast iron
S_u = 20,000
1333° F
1600° F
1900° F

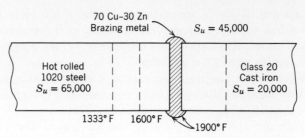

Figure 4-48. Cross section of a butt-brazed joint between steel and cast iron. (Temperatures shown are the maximum values at each location during welding.)

by far the weakest of the three metals present and the joint efficiency is 225%. However, if two pieces of hot-rolled 1020 steel were brazed together, the joint efficiency would appear to be 45,000/65,000 or 70%. But if the joint clearance was small, say 0.002 to 0.004 in. then because of the hydrostatic tensile components induced in the filler material, the joint efficiency would approach 100%.

Joint Design

Figure 4-49 illustrates the symbols that are recommended by the American Welding Society for use on blueprints to specify the type of

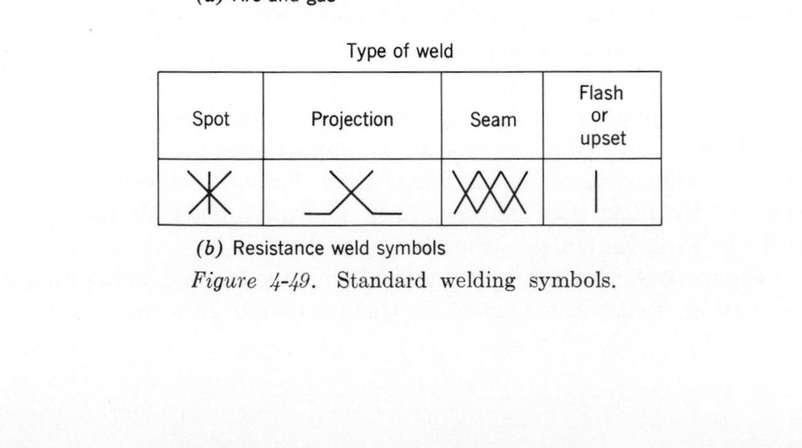

Type of weld
Bead
Fillet
Plug or slot
Edge preparation (groove)
Square
V
Bevel
U
J
(a) Arc and gas
Type of weld
Spot
Projection
Seam
Flash or upset
(b) Resistance weld symbols

Figure 4-49. Standard welding symbols.

welding that is to be done on a part. A *bead* weld is one in which the filler material is deposited at a joint where the two surfaces adjoining the joint are in the same plane as in the butt joint of Figure 4-50. A fillet weld is one in which the filler material is deposited at the corner of two intersecting surfaces, such as a T. A *plug* or *slot* weld is one in which a hole is formed through one of the pieces to be welded and the filler material is then deposited into this hole and fused with the mating part.

The edge preparation symbols and the terminology used to describe the five basic types of chamfers and grooves put on the mating edges of parts prior to welding are also illustrated in Figure 4-49. The square edge is the simplest and most economical, since it is the type of edge normally obtained on sheets or bars that are sheared, sawed, etc. In the bevel or J joint, only one of the parts is beveled. The V joint has a bevel on both parts, and the U joint has a J on both parts.

If only one side of a plate or bar has a prepared edge, it is referred to as a single bevel or a single J, etc. However, if both sides of a plate have a prepared edge, it is referred to as a double bevel or a double J.

Figure 4-50 illustrates the five basic types of weld joints and Figure 4-51 illustrates how these symbols are used on engineering blueprints to specify a desired weld.

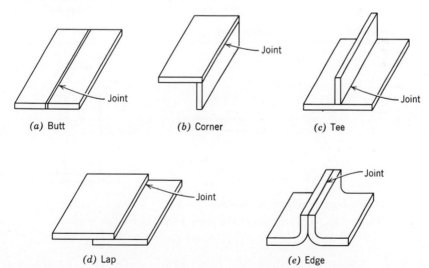

(a) Butt   (b) Corner   (c) Tee

(d) Lap   (e) Edge

Figure 4-50. Basic types of weld joints (after the American Welding Society).

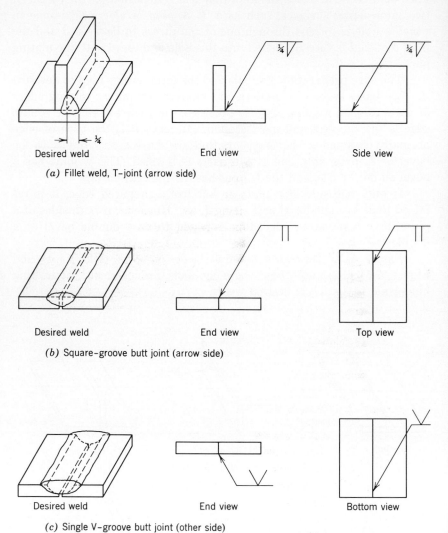

(a) Fillet weld, T–joint (arrow side)

(b) Square-groove butt joint (arrow side)

(c) Single V–groove butt joint (other side)

Figure 4-51. Illustrations of the use of standard welding symbols.

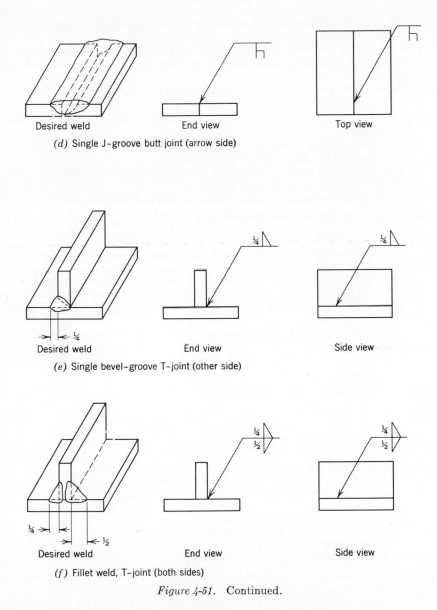

Desired weld   End view   Top view

(d) Single J-groove butt joint (arrow side)

Desired weld   End view   Side view

(e) Single bevel-groove T-joint (other side)

Desired weld   End view   Side view

(f) Fillet weld, T-joint (both sides)

Figure 4-51. Continued.

REFERENCES

1. Easton, E. C., "Discussion of Arc Stability," *Trans. AIEE,* **52,** p. 993, December 1933.
2. Jackson, C. E., and W. J. Goodwin, "Effect of Variations in Welding Technique on the Transition Behavior of Welded Specimens," *Welding Journal,* **27,** p. 2536, 1948.
3. Morris, A. D., and W. C. Gore, "Analysis of the Direct Current Arc," *Welding Journal,* p. 153 s, March 1956.
4. Myer, J. L., "New Studies of the Arc Discharge," *Trans. AIEE,* **52,** p. 250, March 1933.
5. Nottingham, W. B., "New Equation for Static Characteristics of the Normal Arc," *Trans. AIEE,* **42,** p. 302, February 1923.
6. Olsen, H. N., "Temperature Measurements in High Current Arc Plasmas," *Am. Phy. Soc. Bulletin,* p. 81, January 29, 1958.
7. *The Welding Directory,* Industrial Publishing Corp., Cleveland, 1957.
8. *Welding Handbook,* Am. Welding Soc., New York, 1962.

STUDY PROBLEMS

4–1   a. What happens when a piece of aluminum having a flat, smooth face is placed against a similar mating piece of copper such that the normal pressure is one-tenth the yield stress? This is done under room temperature.

   b. What happens to the piece at 900°F?

   c. What happens to the two pieces at room temperature when the normal pressure is increased to the point where the stresses at the interface approach the fracture stress?

4–2   How would you weld the following?

(a)

(b)

4–3   List the principal advantages of:
   a. Arc welding over gas welding.
   b. Gas welding over arc welding.
   c. D-c arc welding over a-c arc welding.

4–4   Two pieces of 2SO aluminum were pressed together as sketched below. What is the "actual weld area" if the welded assembly failed with a tensile load of 2400 lb? The following data are valid for 2SO aluminum.

% Red (C.W.)	0	20	40	60	80
Y.S.	5,500	15,000	18,000	20,000	23,000
T.S.	13,000	17,500	21,000	23,500	25,000

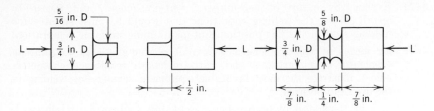

Before pressing   After welding

4-5' Refer to Problem 4-4. Is this really cold welding, or is there enough heat during squeezing to raise the metal to its recrystallization temperature? Assume all the heat remains in the metal, and the maximum temperature at the interface is twice the bulk temperature after welding. The force displacement curve below is valid during this welding sequence. C_p for aluminum = 0.22 Btu/lb°F.

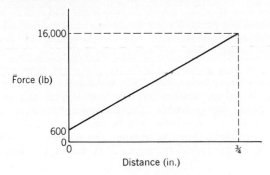

Distance (in.)

4-6 Refer to Figure 4-9. Assume that 50% of the heat of the flame goes into the steel plates, and there is no loss of heat from the plates. (a) What will be the average, uniform temperature of the plates? (b) How does this compare with color isotherms on the plates? Explain the differences. (c) What is the thermal efficiency of this welding operation? Assume that ideally only a $\frac{1}{32}$ in. thick layer of material on each face would have to be heated to the melting temperature.

4-7 Refer to Figure 4-33. Assume that 70% of the heat of the arc goes into the steel plates and there is no loss of heat from the plates.
  a. What will be the average, uniform temperature of the plates?
  b. How does this compare with the color isotherms on the plates? Explain any differences.
  c. What is the thermal efficiency of this welding operation? Assume that ideally only a $\frac{1}{32}$ in. thick layer of material on each face would have to be heated to the melting temperature.

4-8 Explain how the metal is transferred from the welding rod to the weldment when using low carbon steel "stick" electrodes.

4-9 Plot arc power vs arc length (watts vs inches) for a bare electrode and an E6014 electrode for the following two generator settings.
  a. $E_o = 100$ volts, $I_s = 100$ amperes.
  b. $E_o = 50$ volts, $I_s = 300$ amperes.

4–10   Explain, by means of *volt-ampere, volt-arc length,* and *power-arc length curves,* the welding conditions that would be most suitable for welding steel in the flat position and maintaining uniform penetration.

4–11   By means of volt-arc length (electrode characteristics), volt-ampere (generator characteristics) and watt-arc length (combined characteristics), illustrate the most favorable equipment settings for welding in the overhead position.

4–12   a. $\frac{1}{2}$ in. thick steel plates are being welded in a square butt joint with $\frac{1}{8}$ in. diameter coated stick electrodes using the average or recommended values listed in Table 4-13. The welding velocity is 10 ipm. What is the cross-sectional area of the bead?
       b. If the welding of part *a* were done on a submerged arc welding machine with 600 amperes, what welding speed would be necessary to maintain the same size bead?
       c. What would be the approximate depth of penetration in part *b*.

4–13   If an E6012 electrode having voltage-arc length characteristic represented by $E = 18 + 26l$, where E is in volts and l is in inches, is used on a d-c welding generator set on open circuit voltage of 90 and short circuit current of 300 amperes, what is the change in "heat output" of the arc as the arc length varies from $\frac{1}{8}$ to $\frac{1}{4}$ in.?

4–14   Many pieces of $\frac{1}{4}$ in. thick AISI steel plates are to be arc welded with $\frac{3}{16}$ in. diameter stick electrodes. The welding is to be in the flat position, and in order to use welders having as little skill as possible, it is desired to preset the generator controls (open circuit voltage and short circuit current) so that there will be the least variation of heat input as arc length varies from $\frac{1}{16}$ to $\frac{3}{8}$ in. The desired arc length is $\frac{1}{8}$ in. If 6,000 watts is the maximum power a $\frac{3}{16}$ in. stick electrode can carry, specify:
       a. Electrode type.
       b. E_o.
       c. I_s.

4–15   Calculate the total cost ($/ft) to make a $\frac{1}{4}$ in. fillet weld. Assume a $\frac{3}{16}$ in. electrode is used, and do not include the setup or positioning time.

4–16   Calculate the approximate cost to fabricate the angle shown by arc welding pieces of AISI 1018 steel with $\frac{3}{16}$ in. diam E6010 electrodes. Assume a one-minute positioning time, and a $3.00/hr labor rate. The cost to shear the steel prior to welding is $0.01/lb.

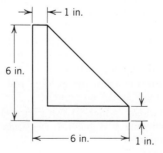
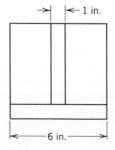

4-17   The welding time (min/ft) to gas fusion weld $\frac{1}{8}$ in. thick pieces of AISI 1020 steel is about 5 minutes and for 1100-O aluminum it is about 3 minutes. Estimate the welding time, using an oxyacetylene torch, to fusion weld tantalum plates of the same thickness.

4-18   Estimate the time to weld a 1 ft length of the following: (butt joint)
        a. $\frac{1}{8}$ in. thick 1020 steel plates with oxyacetylene torch.
        b. $\frac{1}{8}$ in. thick 1020 steel plates—arc welded.
        c. $\frac{1}{8}$ in. thick 1100-O aluminum—oxyacetylene.
        d. $\frac{1}{8}$ in. thick 18-8 stainless steel—arc welded.
        e. $\frac{1}{8}$ in. thick molybdenum—oxyacetylene.

4-19   Define weldability as it pertains to ferrous materials.

4-20   One of the main difficulties encountered with the welding of cast iron arises from the fact that it has a low yield strength and practically a 0% elongation. Explain what this difficulty is by means of an illustration.

4-21   What is the purpose of preheating a part to be welded, and how would you select a preheat temperature?

4-22   4640 steel plates are to be arc welded. What is the "critical cooling rate" for this steel?

4-23   Two pieces of extruded 7075 T6 aluminum are to be welded together to make an axially loaded structural part. The parts have an I cross section with an area of 1 in.^{2} and length of 2 ft. Discuss the load carrying capacity of this weldment if welded (a) by gas, (b) by arc.

4-24   A $\frac{1}{4}$ in. thick plate of 15% coldworked AISI 1320 is welded to a $\frac{1}{4}$ in. thick plate of annealed 4640 steel with a 0.2% carbon (no alloy) electrode.

        Make a complete sketch of the cross section of the plates, indicating the microstructures and hardness that will most likely be present. Assume a cooling rate equal to an oil quench (30°F/sec at 1300).

4-25   Two pieces of AISI-1010 hot rolled steel $\frac{1}{16} \times 1$ in. $\times 8$ in. are brazed together with a butt joint to make one piece 16 in. long. The filler material used as $\frac{3}{32}$ in. diam 50% coldworked brass containing 70% Cu and 30% Zn. What tensile load, if applied parallel to the long axis, will cause fracture to occur? Show all calculations.

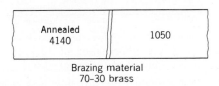

Brazing material
70-30 brass

4-26   For the welded joint sketched:
        a. Draw curves of hardness vs distance.
        b. List microstructures.
        c. Calculate joint efficiency.
        (Calculations should refer to the room temperature properties after the joint is made. All joints heated above 1300°F cooled at a rate equal to that at 8 Jominy distances.)

4-27. a. What is the joint efficiency (ignore stress raisers) when $\frac{1}{8}$ in. thick plates of AISI 1020 steel cold rolled 20% are welded to $\frac{1}{4}$ in. thick plates of AISI 5140 annealed steel with 0.2% C electrodes, under such conditions that the cooling rate is observed to be 30°F/sec at 1300°F?

      b. Where will the welded plates fail?

4-28 A $\frac{1}{4}$ in. $\times$ $1\frac{1}{2}$ in. $\times$ 4 in. piece of annealed AISI 1020 steel is heated on one of the $\frac{1}{4}$ in. $\times$ 4 in. faces by moving an electric arc of 2000 watts at a speed of 6 in./min. After the piece has cooled to room temperature the face opposite the welded one is now circular rather than plane, the radius of curvature being 400 in. Assume that the neutral axis is at the half thickness and all the stresses are due to bending. Calculate the magnitude of the residual stress on the face opposite the welded one.

4-29 If one edge of a $\frac{1}{4}$ in. $\times$ 1 in. $\times$ 20 in. bar of aluminum is heated so that one of the $\frac{1}{4}$ in. $\times$ 20 in. faces is momentarily and instantaneously heated to 400°F to a depth of 0.100 in., on "position vs. stress" coordinates similar to those in the sketch, draw the probable residual stress pattern after the top face has cooled.

$$\alpha = 12 \times 10^{-6} \text{ in./in.°F}$$

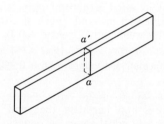

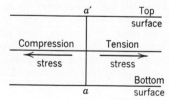

4-30 A square butt weld of $\frac{1}{2}$ in. thick steel plates is made using a $\frac{3}{16}$ in. diam. electrode and a welding speed of 12 imp at 30 volts and 150 amperes. What is the amount of the penetration?

4-31 a. Determine the minimum time (arc minutes) to weld a 1 ft. length of square groove butt joint in $\frac{1}{2}$ in. thick 1020 steel using $\frac{3}{16}$ in. diameter E 6010 electrodes if the area of the bead is not to exceed 0.03 in.² (along with maximum penetration).

      b. What will be the penetration in a?

4-32 a. Determine the minimum time (arc minutes) to weld a 1 ft. length of square groove butt joint in $\frac{1}{2}$ in. thick 1020 steel using a $\frac{1}{16}$ in. diameter wire-feed welding machine with CO_2 shielding. Assume the electrode characteristic is $E = 32l + 16$ for this process, and that the burn off rate, for a given current, is the same as for stick electrodes. The area of the bead must not exceed 0.03 in.[2] The currents used for welding with $\frac{1}{16}$ in. diameter wire and the gas shielded wire feed process are in the range of 50 to 350 amperes. (Extrapolate data in Table 4-13)

    b. What will be the penetration in a if the penetration equation for stick electrodes is valid in this case?

4-33 A square butt joint of $\frac{1}{4}$ in. thick AISI 1020 steel is welded with $\frac{1}{8}$ in. diameter E 6010 electrodes in the flat position. Using the data in Table 4-13, and other data as needed, calculate the following.

    a. Assuming that the deposited bead is triangular in cross section having a base that is six times the height, what is the height of the bead if the welding velocity is 10 ipm?

    b. What is the amount of penetration?

    c. If the cooling rate of the metal in the HAZ and the melt is assumed to be 30°F/sec at 1300°F and the core wire has 0.10% carbon, what load (per unit length) applied across the joint will cause failure? Assume it is welded on two sides, and that there are no stress raisers (stress concentration) in the weld.

    d. What E_o and I_s should the generator be set for, if a d-c motor generator is used?

5

The Forming Process

Forming is on its way to becoming the most important of the manufacturing processes. It is the fastest way to change the shape of a part. Generally speaking, if the shape of a part is such that it can be made by one of the forming operations, then forming is the most economical process to use. Furthermore, on a weight and strength basis, wrought steel is the cheapest of the structural materials available. Therefore, forming parts of steel is the trend in the manufacturing industries today. And if a given part is too complex in shape to be formed as one piece, it is frequently possible to form it as two or more parts and then either mechanically or metallurgically join the pieces together.

There are two other important reasons why *cold forming* is a favorable manufacturing process. The surface finish and tolerance obtainable with smooth forming tools are competitive with those obtained by grinding. The second reason is the increase in strength due to strain hardening that results from coldworking the material. When the design engineer takes advantage of these characteristics of cold forming, he can in some cases replace a part that is made by a machining-heat treating-grinding sequence with a part made by simply cold forming.

DEFINITION:

Forming is the manufacturing process by which the size or shape of a part is changed by the application of forces that produce stresses in the part which are greater than the yield strength and less than the fracture strength of the material. The applied forces may be tensile, compressive, bending, shearing, or a combination of all.

According to our definitions of forming and machining presented in this text, the manufacturing operations called shearing, blanking, and punching are not forming operations but rather they are machining operations. (The metal deformation during shearing and machining is very similar, as you can see by comparing Figure 5-1a and b.) The

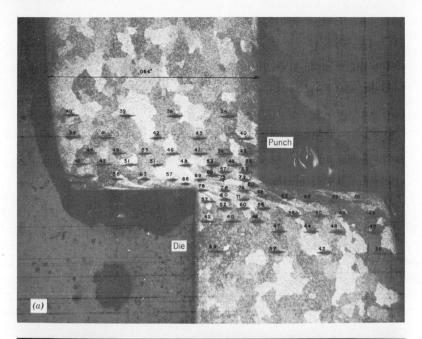

Figure 5-1. Photomicrographs of material being cut. (*a*) Sheared. (*b*) Machined. The numbers are Knoop hardnesses. The material is 1100-0 aluminum.

machine tools on which these operations are performed are generally the same as, or similar to, those used for the forming operations and not at all like the "conventional" metal cutting machine tools. Thus they are discussed in this chapter on forming, the place where they are traditionally discussed.

The number of different plastic working operations is very large and frequently they are associated with "trade" names. Many of the more common processes will be described in the following section under the title "equipment." All of the forming operations may be done either hot, cold, or warm; the distinction being made on the basis of the temperature at which the material is worked.

A forming operation is *hot-working* if the temperature of the material during working is above the recrystallization temperature of the material being worked, and it is *cold-working* if the temperature of the material is below its recrystallization temperature. A forming operation is referred to as *warm-working* if the temperature of the material is significantly above room temperature, but below the material's recrystallization temperature.

The recrystallization temperatures of lead, zinc, and tin are below 80°F. Consequently these three materials are hot worked when they are formed at room temperature. The recrystallization temperature for a variety of materials as a function of the amount of prior coldwork is given in Table 4-15. From an examination of this table, it is evident that copper is hot worked if it is deformed to the extent of 90% reduction of area at a temperature of 200°F, and it is cold (or warm) worked if it is deformed 10% at a temperature of 500°F.

Since a material is heated while in the process of being formed due to the work being expended on it, a bar of copper that is being rolled with heavy passes to a reduction of 90% need not be heated above room temperature prior to rolling and it will still be hot working because the bar will come out of the rolls at a temperature above 200°F.

The strength of metals vary inversely with temperature, but the ductility may vary directly or inversely with temperature. The relationships are not linear, as can be seen in Figures 5-2 to 5-4. The principal reason for heating a metal prior to forming is to lower its strength so that reasonable sized presses can be used to form parts having large cross-sectional areas. It is also desirable to have the ductility increase, as is true with aluminum. As is quite often the case, though, one advantage is gained at the expense of another. This is illustrated in Figure 5-3 where the ductility of the cobalt-base alloy, which is difficult to form at room temperature because of its high strength and high strain-

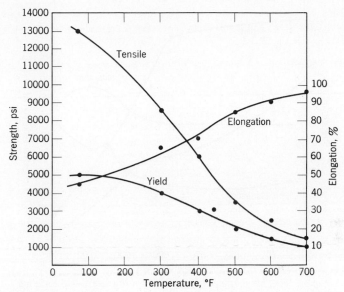

Figure 5-2. Mechanical properties of 1100-0 aluminum as a function of temperature.

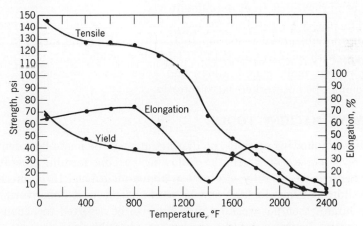

Figure 5-3. Mechanical properties of a cobalt base alloy as a function of temperature. (Composition: Co-balance; Ni—9.00 to 11.00; Cr—19.00 to 21.00; W—14.00 to 16.00; Fe—3.00 max; C—0.05 to 0.15; Si—1.00 max; and Mn—1.00 to 2.00.)

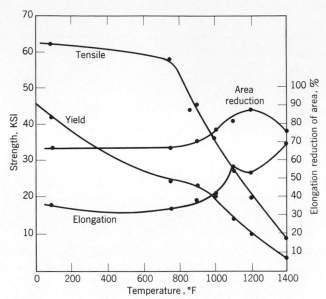

Figure 5-4. Mechanical properties of a low plain-carbon steel (0.15 C).

hardening exponent, decreases at the high temperature thus making hot-working without fracture difficult.

The proper temperature for hot working is one that is high enough to cause a substantial reduction in the strength of the metal in combination with sufficient ductility and a low oxidation rate. For this latter reason, molybdenum alloys and a few other "refractory" materials cannot be hot worked satisfactorily.

FORMING MACHINE TOOLS

In the following sections, no distinctions will be made between hot, cold, or warm working. All the following specific forming operations described can be done by any of the above-mentioned three methods. The following generalization can be made. If the part being formed is "very large," then hot working may have to be resorted to because of the capacity limitation of the equipment available.

The machine tools upon which all of the forming operations are performed can be divided into four basic types, which are illustrated schematically in Figure 5-5. They are: presses, hammers, rolls, and drawbenches. These basic machine tools will be described briefly in conjunction with the common forming operations that are performed on them.

Presses and Hammers

The following two types will be discussed together since they are so closely related.

A *press* is a machine tool having two plattens or heads, one fixed and the other movable, upon which tools or dies are mounted to plastically deform materials to a required configuration.

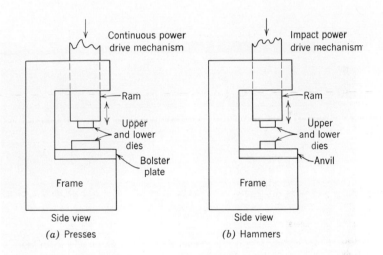

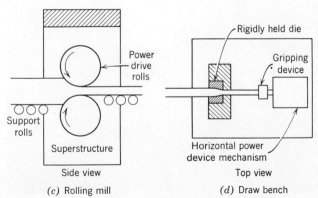

Figure 5-5. Schematic drawings of the four basic types of forming machine tools.

A *hammer* is a special type of press that either has a very heavy movable head that is "dropped" with the force of gravity onto the workpiece on the bottom anvil; or it has the head accelerate toward the workpiece by means of a steam or pneumatic cylinder. The deformation of the work piece is a result of its absorbing the kinetic energy ($\frac{1}{2} mv^2$) of the moving head. Hammers are simpler in construction and less expensive than presses.

Figure 5-6 is a photograph of a press. This is not a "typical press"—there are so many different presses in use that it is impossible to pick out one as being typical. But it is a "typical" inclinable single-action, crank-type mechanical punch press of 110-ton capacity. In the

Figure 5-6. Photograph of a mechanical press. (Courtesy E. W. Bliss Co.)

photograph shown, the operator loads the parts by hand into the dies. The ropes attached to the operator's hands are a safety mechanism to withdraw his hands from between the dies when the latter are closed.

Figure 5-7 illustrates the six common types of mechanisms that transmit power to the ram of presses and hammers. The mechanisms depicted in a and f are used on hammers. Hammers are built in sizes of from 50 to 25,000 lb capacity. The stated size is the weight of the movable head and die. Although the board-drop hammer sketched in a relies only on the force of gravity, the hammer illustrated in f utilizes a pneumatic or steam cylinder to accelerate the movable head in addition to the gravity force. Hammers having the mechanism sketched in a are called board-drop hammers because the vertical member, shown in sketch a, to which the head is attached and which is raised by the rotating rollers is a series of 2 in. $\times$ 12 in. boards several feet long.

The mechanisms illustrated in sketches b and c are the common ones used on small mechanical presses of. 5 to 200-ton capacity. The size rating, or capacity, of punch presses or mechanical presses is the maximum "equivalent" force that the press is capable of exerting. It is determined by multiplying the maximum area that can be sheared of a given material by its tensile strength. The tensile strength is used rather than the shear strength to account for the friction losses in the dies and machine tool.

For example, a 200-ton capacity press could punch a slug out of 1 in. thick AISI 1018 hot-rolled steel (S_u = 60,000 psi) having a periphery of 6.67 in. —200 $\times$ 2000/1 $\times$ 60,000—or about 2 in. diameter.

From the above, it is apparent that the press capacity is not equal to the force necessary to shear, which is the product of the area being sheared and the shear strength of the material.

The knuckle-joint mechanism illustrated in d is used on large capacity (up to 5000 ton) mechanical presses, especially for those operations such as coining that require a high pressure at the bottom of the ram stroke. As the crank in d rotates counterclockwise, it first straightens the knuckle to lower the ram and then bends it again to raise the ram. This mechanism has the greatest mechanical advantage when the rotating crank is in the left, horizontal position at which time the ram is at the bottom of the stroke.

The toggle-joint mechanism illustrated in e is used on punch presses designed for punching and drawing operations. Since either two or three slides (rams) may move during forming, these presses are frequently referred to as double-action or triple-action. The toggles are so designed that there are at least two dead-center positions which create a dwell or zero relative velocity between the two slides at

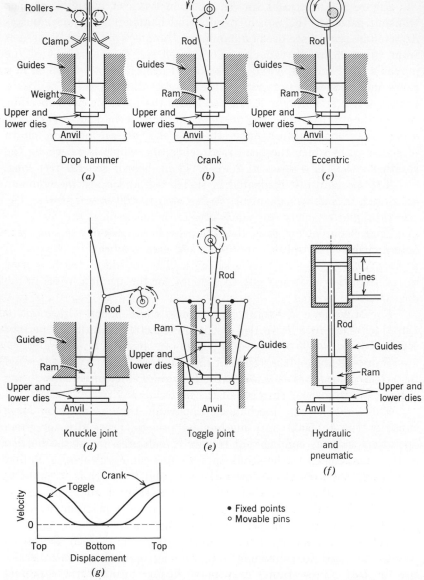

Figure 5-7. Sketches of mechanisms used to power the ram of presses and hammers.

the bottom of the stroke, as illustrated by Figure 5-7g. The main slide, which delivers the large forming force, is attached to the upper die or punch. The second slide, which delivers a much smaller force, is attached to the blank (work piece) holder and prevents the flanges from wrinkling during the drawing operation. Presses of this type are used to form large parts such as automotive bodies, and have capacities up to about 5000 ton.

The hydraulic mechanism of f is used on all sizes of presses from the small 5 to 20-ton capacity up to the largest capacity built. The largest presses in the United States are of 50,000-ton capacity. Only two of these presses are in existence, and they were built in the 1950's under Air Force sponsorship to form large precision forgings for aircraft structures. This approach to forging was originated by the Germans during World War II.

Double-acting hydraulic presses delivering high pressure to the main ram and lower pressure to the holddown platten are also used for drawing operations, as are the toggle presses.

When the power mechanism of f is pneumatically or steam-actuated, the machine tool is referred to as a hammer.

Rolls or Rolling Mills

A *roll* or *rolling mill* is a forming machine tool having two or more circular or contoured rotating cylinders which, by means of the friction force between the cylinders and the work piece, draw the work piece through the opening between the cylinders, thus reducing the thickness and cross-sectioned area of the part. Figure 5-8 is a photograph of two commercial rolling mills. The first shows a "typical" two high, single-stand, one-way, narrow-strip mill. It shows a strip being cold rolled and coiled. The second photograph illustrates a 56-in. semicontinuous hot strip mill for rolling stainless and alloy steel. It consists of five stands of four high rolls.

A rolling mill may be two high, three high, four high, or six high depending upon the number of rolls stacked above each other, as illustrated in Figure 5-9. The two high rolls are the most common for both hot and cold rolling since they are the least expensive.

The reduction in thickness of the bar or plate is normally about 1 to 10% per pass. The maximum reduction per pass is limited by either the ductility of the material, in which case fracture occurs, or by the surface condition and diameter of the rolls which determine whether the material will be "drawn" through the rolls. If too large a reduction per pass is attempted, the bar will simply not be pulled into the rolls. For high production work a series of rolls are lined up

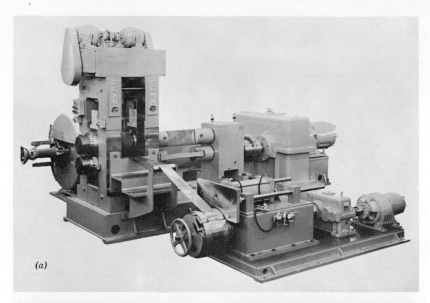

Figure 5-8. Photograph of rolling mills. (*a*) Single-stand, two high cold strip mill. (Courtesy Fenn Co.) (*b*) Five-stand, four high semicontinuous hot strip mill. (Courtesy Blaw-Know Co.)

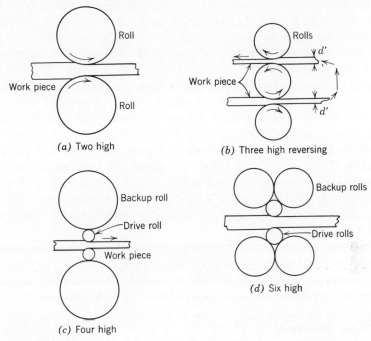

Figure 5-9. Sketches of arrangements of rolls in a rolling mill.

so that each succeeding pair is spaced slightly closer together and rotate correspondingly faster. This enables the bar or plate to move continuously through the plant until the final thickness is achieved.

The alternate procedure is to use a single pair of rolls and reverse their direction of rotation after each pass. The rolls are brought closer together after each pass and the bar or plate reciprocates many times between the rolls before the final thickness is achieved. Much power is consumed and heavy forces are induced in the roll-drive mechanism when they are reversed. To avoid this disadvantage, the three high rolling mill was developed. In this mill a third roll is employed and the bar or plate is raised and lowered after each pass as illustrated in Figure 5-9*b*.

The two high reversing mill and the three high mill are used to roll bars and plates that are up to 40 ft. long. The continuous mills are used to roll strip, coils, or sheets that may be many thousands of feet in length.

The four high and six high type of mill is needed to cold roll either wide sheets, thin sheets, or severely strain-hardened sheets. The reason for this need is the fact that the rolls bend during the rolling operation which results in a sheet that is thicker at the center than at the edges. This tendency is minimized through the proper selection of work-roll and back-up roll diameters on the basis of the following considerations.

For a given width of sheet and reduction per pass, the bending of the cylindrical roll will be less as the diameter of the roll is increased. Therefore large diameter rolls should be used to prevent crowning. However, to accomplish this by simply increasing the roll diameter is not the best solution. The roll separating force, which is the force that causes the bending, for a given reduction increases as the roll diameter increases. This is due to the longer arc of contact between the roll and plate. Therefore by combining a small diameter work-roll to obtain a small area of contact with a larger diameter back-up roll, the roll separating forces are reduced and a smaller total cross-sectional area of rolls is required.

In some operations, such as forge rolling, the rolls are not circular in cross-section, and in some operations, such as power spinning and tube piercing, the rolls do not have parallel axes of rotation. These processes are illustrated and described in a following section.

Draw Benches

A *draw bench* is a very simple forming machine tool that consists of a die and a power driven mechanism to either pull a wire or bar through a conical orifice of the die, or stretch a bar or sheet over a convex die. Figure 5-5d is a schematic diagram of a draw bench.

The entering angle of the die, which is half of the included angle, is generally about 6°. This value is used since it is an average value of the friction angle (the angle whose tangent is equal to the coefficient of friction) for hard steel rubbing against other metals under high pressure. A high pressure lubricant is essential for successful wire drawing, as is true for all the forming operations, to prevent the material being severely deformed from seizing onto the forming tools.

FORMING OPERATIONS

The common forming operations are presented in Tables 5-1, 5-2, and 5-3 by means of a diagramatic sketch and a definition. By placing the definition parallel to the sketch and all the operations listed in condensed tabular form, the reader is able to perceive an overall view of the entire field of forming. Word descriptions of how an operation is performed are given only for those operations in which the sketch and definition are not sufficient.

TABLE 5-1. Forming Operations Performed on Presses and Hammers

Operation	Definition or Description	Sketch	Uses or Applications
Open die forging	Forming by uniaxial compression between flat parallel plates (dies)		Discs or blanks used as preforms. Very large shafts or forgings of simple shape
Closed die forging	Forming by a uniaxial compressive force using dies with cavities which control lateral flow		Shaped parts small to medium size such as connecting rods, handles, levers, gear blanks
Upsetting	A special type of closed die forging operation on bars in which a longitudinal force causes a local flow		Heads on bolts, valves. Flanges and shoulders on shafts
Forward extrusion	Forming by axial flow of a billet through a die orifice in the direction of an applied compressive force		Regular or irregular structural shapes such as window moldings, angle sections, circular, or irregular tubing
Back extrusion	Forming by axial flow of a billet through a die orifice opposite to the direction of an applied compressive force		Regular or irregular structural shapes, tubes for grease and cosmetics
Coining	Special type of closed die forging operation in which the lateral surfaces are restrained resulting in a variable thickness and a well-defined imprint of the die faces		Shallow configurations on flat objects, such as ornamental designs or structural ribs and bosses

293

TABLE 5-1. (*Continued*)

Operation	Definition or Description	Sketch	Uses or Applications
Hobbing (Hubbing)	Forming a very smooth, accurately shaped die cavity by pressing a hardened punch into a softer metal die block		Making many duplicate cavities, e.g. plastic molds for molding typewriter keys, plastic wall tile
Embossing	Forming a design on thin materials by raising or lowering portions of the material by localized bending		Forming ribs to increase rigidity. Making ornamental or communicative designs
Drawing (Deep, Cup)	Forming by pushing a formed punch against a flat sheet and forcing it over a shaped die-edge into the die cavity to take the shape of a recessed vessel.		Cups, shells short tubes, automotive bodies, gas tanks, appliance covers
Ironing	Forming by reducing the wall thickness of deep drawn parts by forcing them through a die with a punch wherein the clearance is less than the original wall thickness		For thinning and sizing walls of predrawn parts
Sizing	Finish forming operation, usually done on a preformed part, in closed dies to obtain very accurate dimensions		Accurate control of height or area of a formed part such as bosses

TABLE 5-1. (*Continued*)

Operation	Definition or Description	Sketch	Uses or Applications
Braking (Bending)	Forming of structural shapes such as angles and channels by bending sheets or plates in a long press called a brake		Structural shapes such as automobile and truck chassis. Angle and channel sections having large moment of inertia to weight ratio
Hydroform (Guerin Process) (Rubber Punch)	Bending or drawing operation in which either the punch or the die is a piece of constrained rubber		Low quantity of parts that could be made by drawing
Swagging	Forming operation in which the diameter of bars or tubes is changed by repeated blows of radially actuated shaped hammers		Flaring ends of tubes, reduction of tube or shaft diameter
Staking	Forcing a shaped punch into the top of a projection to complete a riveting operation		As a substitute to drilling and riveting
Shearing	A material separation operation using two knife blades or a punch and die wherein the material deformation is localized and due to shear forces		Rapid method of cutting bar stock or plates to length

295

TABLE 5-1. (*Continued*)

Operation	Definition or Description	Sketch	Uses or Applications
Blanking	A material separation process using a punch and die to shear a useful blank from a thin piece of material		Making discs, washers or flat blanks which may be drawn afterwards
Piercing	A material separation operation using a punch and die to shear a hole in a thin piece		Rapid method of making holes or slots in a part

TABLE 5-2. Forming Operations Performed on Rolls

Operation	Definition or Description	Sketch	Uses or Applications
Rolling	Forming operation on cylindrical rolls wherein the cross sectional area of a bar or plate is reduced with a corresponding increase in length		Rapid method of producing bars of uniform cross section
Roll forming	A continuous bending operation generally performed on originally coiled strip material and resulting in long shaped sections such as angles, channels and tubes		Rapid method of forming long lengths of tubes or structural shapes
Forge rolling	A closed die forging operation in which the die cavities are machined in the periphery of cylinders		Similar to closed die forging except longer parts can be forged

296

TABLE 5-2. (*Continued*)

Operation	Definition or Description	Sketch	Uses or Applications
Power spinning	Forming of a conical part from a disc in which the diameter does not change by progressively forcing the disc against a conical mandrel by means of a small roller moving from the center out		For low production forming since cost of tooling is low
Roll straightening	Straightening of a bar or plate by passing it through a series of rolls which are not all in the same plane, causing the material to be bent so that it is straight after the bending forces are removed		To straighten sheets that have been rolled
Tube piercing	Tube piercing is a rolling process in which a solid cylindrical bar is formed into a rough seamless tube by means of two conical rolls oppositely skewed a few degrees from the axis of the bar		To originate holes in seamless tubing
Thread rolling	A plastic deformation process in which threads are formed on a cylinder that has an original diameter equal to the final pitch diameter		To form threads by plastic flow rather than machining. Gear teeth and splines can be formed by a similar process

297

TABLE 5-3. Forming Operations Performed on Draw Benches

Operation	Definition or Description	Sketch	Uses or Applications
Wire or bar drawing	Reducing the diameter of a bar or wire by pulling it through a tapered orifice in a die		Forming small cross sectional parts of uniform cross section and close tolerance
Tube drawing	Reducing the wall thickness of a tube by pulling it simultaneously over a mandrel and through a die orifice		Forming close tolerance tubing
Stretch forming	Simultaneously stretching and bending, over a die, a bar or plate that would fail by compressive buckling if bending alone was attempted		Bending "I" or "L" sections to small radii
Stretcher levelling	Straightening a sheet or plate by performing slight tensile deformation		Straightening sheets or plates previously rolled

Of all the operations performed on presses, combinations of blanking and drawing are the most common ones. Many of the parts used on automobiles and home appliances are made of steel by a combination of these two operations. Closed-die forging and extruding are the next most commonly used processes.

Of all the operations performed on rolls, the rolling of bars, plates, strip, structural shapes, and so on, is by far the most common. Nearly all the wrought materials, except wires, are formed by this process.

Of all the operations performed on draw benches, wire drawing is the one used most frequently.

Forming Tools—Dies and Rolls

The tools used to deform the material in the forming operations are called *dies*. Dies are to the forming operations what molds are to the casting operations. There are four general classes of dies: (1) squeezing (forging, upsetting, extruding); (2) shearing; (3) stretching (drawing); and (4) bending.

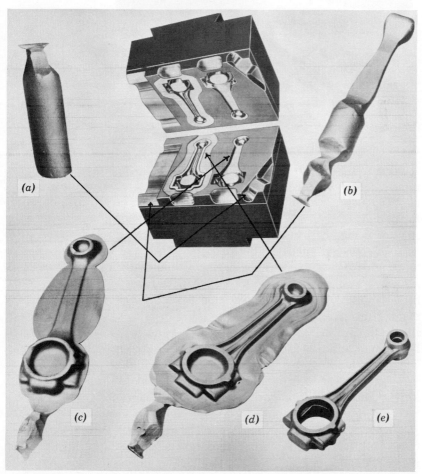

Figure 5-10. Photograph of forging dies. (*a*) Stock. (*b*) Fullering and edging. (*c*) Blocking. (*d*) Finished forging. (*e*) Trimmed. (Courtesy Drop Forging Association)

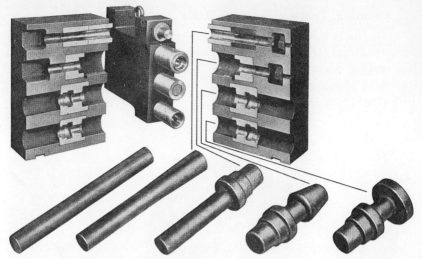

Figure 5-11. Photograph of upsetting dies. (Courtesy Drop Forging Association)

Figures 5-10 and 5-11 show two squeezing-type dies. The first is referred to as a closed-die forging die and the second is an upsetting die. These dies, as well as extrusion dies, are subjected to quite large forces and consequently they are made of either a medium-carbon alloy steel or a high-carbon steel heat treated to a hardness level of 45 to 60 R_c, depending upon the application.

Figure 5-12 illustrates a shearing or blanking die, and Figure 5-13 a deep drawing die. It is quite common to have both these types of dies combined into one combination blanking and drawing die. The manner in which these dies operate is fairly self-explanatory from the illustrations. One aspect of the deep drawing die that is not obvious is the importance of having the correct pressure on the pressure pads. This may be illustrated with the following example.

Consider the drawing of a 4 in. diameter blank into a flanged cup having an outside diameter of $3\frac{1}{2}$ in., as in Figure 5-14. If the proper hold-down pressure is applied, the flanged cup is formed satisfactorily. However, if the hold-down pressure is insufficient, the flange of the cup wrinkles (becomes corrugated) as the metal flows inward from a 4 in. diameter to a $3\frac{1}{2}$ in. diameter. This wrinkling or buckling is due to the compressive circumferential strains induced in the flange. On the other hand, if the hold-down pressure is too great, the flange will not slide inward between the faces of the die and hold-down pads with the result that the punch will shear out the bottom of the cup as in a blanking or piercing operation (Figure 5-14*d*).

Action of rolls. The rolling operations illustrated in Table 5-2 are fairly self-explanatory. However, it is interesting to observe the plastic deformation-recrystallization-grain growth cycle that occurs during hot rolling. This is illustrated schematically in Figure 5-15. The time necessary for recrystallization and grain growth is a function of the hot working temperature, the amount of deformation, and the material being deformed.

The forces acting between the rolls and the work material, as well as the velocities of the work piece and rolls, are illustrated in Figure

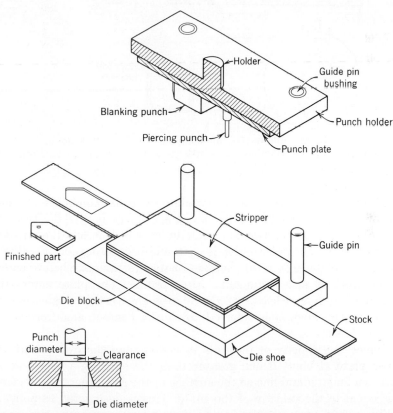

Figure 5-12. Illustration of the components of a blanking and piercing die. A two-stage or progressive die. The small hole is punched first, then the stock is moved to the left and the part is blanked out.

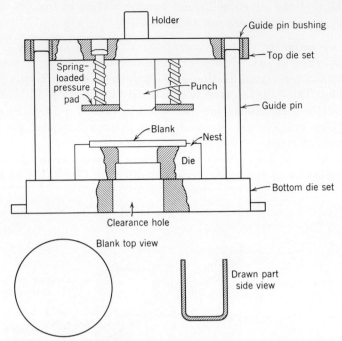

Holder

Guide pin bushing

Top die set

Spring-
loaded
pressure
pad

Punch

Guide pin

Blank

Nest

Die

Bottom die set

Clearance hole

Blank top view

Drawn part
side view

Figure 5-13. Illustration of components of a drawing die
(cup).

5-16. In this illustration a sheet or plate of initial thickness t_i enters
the rolls at a velocity v_i and leaves at a velocity v_f and thickness t_f.
The rolls rotate at a peripheral velocity v_r, which is less than v_f and
greater than v_i. The deformation is quite uniform throughout the thickness of the plate, that is, an element that is rectangular before entering the rolls is also rectangular after rolling. The plate enters the
rolls at point A and leaves at B which is the vertical center line of
the rolls. The angle α is referred to as the contact angle or as the
angle of bite.

    Since the velocity of the rolls v_r is less than the exit velocity v_f
of the plate at point B and greater than the entering velocity at A,
there is a longitudinal line on the surface of the rolls where the velocity
v_r is equal to the velocity of the plate. This is designated as point N
in Figure 5-16 and is referred to as the *neutral point* or *no-slip point*.
The angle between N and B, β, is the no-slip angle. The difference between the velocity v_f and v_r at point B is referred to as *forward slip*.

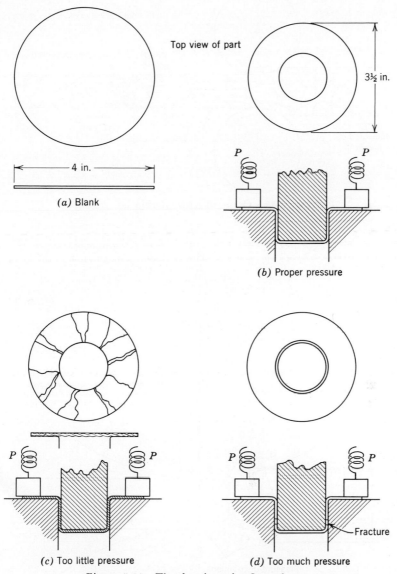

Figure 5-14. The drawing of a flanged cup.

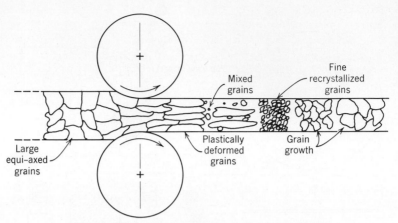

Figure 5-15. Grain structure during hot rolling.

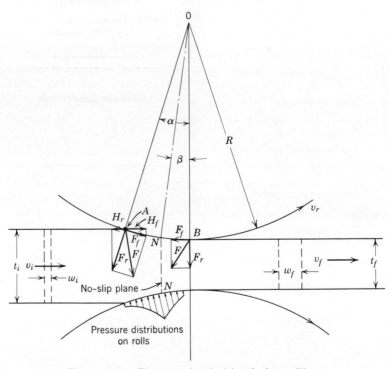

Figure 5-16. Forces and velocities during rolling.

The pressure distribution along the arc of contact varies, as illustrated schematically on the bottom roll in Figure 5-16. The radial pressure is maximum at the no-slip point. However, for many of the studies on the roll separating force or neutral point, the pressure distribution is assumed to be constant along the arc of contact.

The forces acting at any point along the arc of contact between the rolls and plate are a radial force F_r and a friction force F_f. These forces are illustrated for points A and B in Figure 5-16. The magnitude of the radial force varies along the arc of contact in accordance with the pressure distribution described above. The friction force F_f is equal to μ times the radial force, where μ is the coefficient of friction between the rolls and plate.

The radial force at all points along the arc of contact except B acts at an angle toward the incoming material and consequently has a horizontal component H_r which acts in a direction opposite to the rolling direction. At point A the horizontal component of the radial force F_r is H_r and $H_r = F_r \sin \alpha$.

The friction force F_f acts in the direction of the roll velocity at all points between the entering point A and the no-slip point N; the friction force acts opposite to the direction of the roll velocity at all points between the no-slip point N and the exit point B. In order for the plate to continue to pass through the rolls, the sum of all the H_f's along the arc of contact must be greater than the sum of the H_r's. Because of the uncertainties concerning the magnitude of the radial force and the coefficient of friction along the entire length of contact, it is extremely difficult to evaluate all the horizontal forces. However, it is possible to determine the maximum amount of reduction in thickness that may be given to a plate in one pass for a specific rolling condition in terms of whether the plate will be "drawn into" the rolls, that is, whether the rolls will "bite" the plate and pull it in or whether the rolls will simply slide by the edges of the plate.

By examining the forces acting at the entering point A in Figure 5-16, it can be seen that a plate of thickness t_i brought into contact with the rotating rolls at point A will be drawn "into" the rolls if the horizontal force H_f is equal to or slightly greater than H_r. Since $H_r = F_r \sin \alpha$ and $H_f = F_f \cos \alpha$, then the plate will be drawn in when

$$F_r \sin \alpha = F_f \cos \alpha$$

or when

$$\frac{F_f}{F_r} = \frac{\sin \alpha}{\cos \alpha} = \tan \alpha \qquad (5\text{-}1)$$

However, the ratio F_f/F_r is defined as the coefficient of friction μ and the angle θ whose tangent is equal to μ is the friction angle. That is,

$$\mu = \tan \theta = \frac{F_f}{F_r} \tag{5-2}$$

By equating 5-1 and 5-2, it is seen that for the plate to be drawn into the rolls the friction angle θ must be equal to or slightly greater than the entering angle α.

The friction angle θ is determined by the smoothness of the rolls and type, if any, of lubricant used. The entering angle is determined by the diameter of the rolls and the amount of reduction being made. Thus, to obtain large reductions with smooth rolls it is necessary to use rolls having large diameters.

To calculate the power needed for a rolling operation it is necessary to know the velocity of the work material through the rolls. Generally, the peripheral velocity of the rolls is known. Since the velocity of the work material is equal to the roll velocity at the no-slip line, the no-slip angle must be determined. This is extremely difficult to do for actual rolling conditions. However, by assuming a constant coefficient of friction μ and a uniform distribution of force along the arc of contact, the no-slip angle can be calculated by equating the sum of the horizontal components of force to the left of the no-slip joint to those on the right side. This manipulation results in the expression

$$\beta = \frac{\alpha}{2} - \frac{1}{\mu}\left(\frac{\alpha}{2}\right)^2 \tag{5-3}$$

where the angles are measured in radians.

The angle of contact α can be expressed in terms of the thickness of the plate and the roll diameter. By dropping the second-order terms, the equation reduces to

$$\beta = \left(\frac{t_i - t_f}{2D}\right)^{\frac{1}{2}} - \frac{t_i - t_f}{2D\mu} \tag{5-4}$$

where D is the roll diameter in inches.

A more detailed analysis of the forces and power required for both hot and cold rolling is given in References 5 and 7 at the end of the chapter.

Tube Piercing With Rolls. In the tube piercing operations illustrated in Table 5-2, a solid bar is transformed into seamless tubing. The operation is done hot. The surface finish is poor and the wall thickness is not constant, requiring a finish sizing operation which is generally done cold. During this operation, the length of the bar increases

greatly. For example, a 3 in. diameter bar 5 ft long will result in a
seamless tube 3 in. O.D. and about $16\frac{1}{2}$ ft long if the wall thickness
is $\frac{1}{4}$ in.

The hole in the seamless tubing is not created simply by forcing
the bar axially over the mandrel. Instead it is the transverse com-

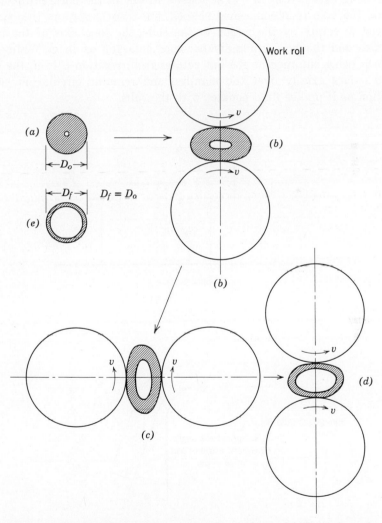

Figure 5-17. Creating the hole in seamless tubing. (*a*) End view of
bar with shallow drilled hole. (*b*) Bar flattened by action of rolls. (*c*)
Bar after rotating 90°. (*d*) Bar after rotating several turns. (*e*) Section
of finished tube.

pression with its associated normal tensile strains that create the hole which is then "sized" over the mandrel. The way in which this is done is illustrated in Figure 5-17.

A small center hole is drilled or punched in the end of the bar as in a. The bar is then fed into two rotating, skewed rolls having a clearance considerably less than the diameter of the bar. This results in the bar being flattened as in b. The tensile strains in the normal direction cause the hole to become oval shaped, but also larger. As the bar is forced to rotate by the action of the rolls, the long axis of the hole rotates and the hole gradually becomes enlarged as in d. While the hole is being enlarged as the bar rotates from position b to d, the bar also moves axially over the mandrel and remains circular in cross section as it makes final contact with the rolls.

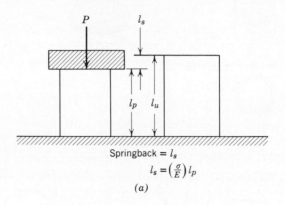

$$\text{Springback} = l_s$$

$$l_s = \left(\frac{\sigma}{E}\right) l_p$$

$$(a)$$

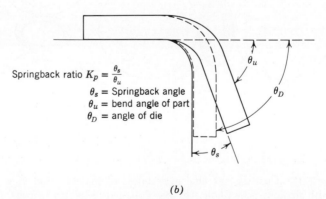

$$(b)$$

Figure 5-18. Illustration of springback after forming. (a) Uniaxial compression. (b) Bending.

Springback. One of the practical problems associated with the bending type of forming operations is *springback*, which is the elastic recovery that occurs when the pressure being exerted to form a part is removed. This is illustrated in Figure 5-18. This recovery is not uniform through the thickness of the plate after bending, and consequently residual stresses are present in parts that are formed by bending.

FORCES AND POWER FOR FORMING

Since forming is becoming an increasingly more popular process and more materials are being developed with which the "shops" have no experience, it is frequently necessary for the design engineer to be able to estimate whether a given part he is specifying can actually be formed on the existing equipment. The following sections will illustrate how the mechanical property relationships presented in Chapter 1 can be utilized to estimate the forces and power required for forming, as well as the maximum deformation possible for a given material.

In these analyses, the friction between the work piece and the dies is neglected. In well-lubricated operations and for very small deformations, the friction forces are truly negligible. But for poorly lubricated operations and very large deformations, the friction forces themselves are as large as the forces needed to deform the material when there is no friction.

Plastic flow will occur in a material when it is subjected to stresses equal to its yield strength. For uniaxial tensile and compressive forces, the stress distribution is assumed to be uniform across any transverse section. During bending and twisting the stresses vary from surface to center. When forces are applied in more than one direction, the effective stresses $\bar{\sigma}$ and effective strains $\bar{\epsilon}$ must be used. They are defined as follows:

$$\bar{\sigma} = \frac{\sqrt{2}}{2} \left[(\sigma_1 - \sigma_2)^2 + (\sigma_2 - \sigma_3)^2 + (\sigma_3 - \sigma_1)^2 \right]^{\frac{1}{2}} \qquad (5\text{-}5)$$

$$\bar{\epsilon} = \frac{\sqrt{2}}{3} \left[(\epsilon_1 - \epsilon_2)^2 + (\epsilon_2 - \epsilon_3)^2 + (\epsilon_3 - \epsilon_1)^2 \right]^{\frac{1}{2}} \qquad (5\text{-}6)$$

where $\sigma_1, \sigma_2, \sigma_3$ and $\epsilon_1, \epsilon_2, \epsilon_3$ are the three principal stresses and strains. σ_1 is always the largest and σ_3 is the lowest of the three stresses. For uniaxial loading, as in a tension specimen, $\sigma_2 = \sigma_3 = 0$, so $\bar{\sigma} = \sigma$ and $\bar{\epsilon} = \epsilon$.

In the following illustrations, only simple tension and compression are considered.

Force to Deform a Nonstrain-Hardening Material

Before examining the force-deformation relationships for a non-strain-hardening material it is appropriate to consider what the stress-strain relationships for such a material would be like and whether such materials actually exist.

Figure 5-19 illustrates what the stress-strain curves for a non-strain-hardening material would look like. Two important character-istics are: (1) the strain-hardening exponent m is zero; and (2) the tensile strength is equal to the yield strength. That is, the maximum load occurs at the onset of plastic deformation.

Lead is frequently used as a nonstrain-hardening material in ex-perimental studies of plastic deformation. This is done because lead is soft, ductile, inexpensive, and recrystallizes below room temperature. It is because of this last characteristic, the low recrystallization tem-perature, that many researchers consider lead as a nonstrain-hardening material. However, this is not a justifiable conclusion when lead is be-ing continuously deformed, that is, when the deforming force is un-interrupted.

Figure 5-20a is a typical nominal stress-strain curve for com-mercially pure lead tested at room temperature (80°F) and at the customary strain rate of about 10^{-2} to 10^{-3} in./in./min. The tensile strength of lead is 2600 psi and the yield strength is 1300 psi. This means that lead strain hardens under the plastic deformation condi-tions of a tensile test. Also, from Figure 5-20a, since the nominal strain at the maximum load is 0.42, the strain-hardening exponent m is 0.35

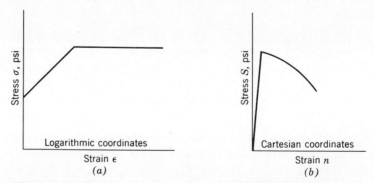

Figure 5-19. Stress-strain curves for a nonstrain-hardening material. (a) Natural stress-strain. (b) Nominal stress-strain.

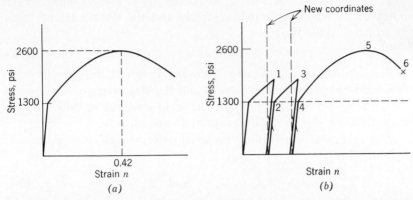

Figure 5-20. Stress-strain curves for lead. (*a*) Continuous loading. (*b*) Interrupted loading. A short time interval included between unloading and reloading.

$[\epsilon_u = \ln (1 + n_u)]$. Actually this is a strain-hardening rate 50% greater than that of either pure aluminum or low carbon steel,

Figure 5-20*b* illustrates what the stress-strain curve for lead looks like during a tensile test in which the load is interrupted. By comparing this to Figure 1-7, the difference in behavior between lead and a strain-hardening material is evident. When lead is loaded beyond its yield strength, the stress increases to some value such as point 1 in Figure 5-20*b*. Upon unloading, the specimen contracts elastically. When the specimen is reloaded again, its new yield strength is identical to the original yield strength, point 0. This does not mean that the new yield *load* is identical to the original load. On the contrary, since the new area is less than the original area the new yield load is actually lower than the original yield load.

If the test is continued the stress will rise beyond that of point 2. If the load is again withdrawn after stress 3 is reached, the specimen contracts elastically. Upon reloading, the stress-strain curve will go through points 4, 5, and 6, whereupon it fractures. From these curves it is apparent that lead does not recrystallize at room temperature while it is being deformed, but rather it recrystallizes after it is unloaded.

Very likely the main reason that lead is considered by many to be nonstrain-hardening is the fact that lead rolled at room temperature has the same yield strength as annealed lead. Why this condition exists is readily explainable on the basis of the stress-strain curves just discussed.

The force to deform a material plastically is always equal to the product of the yield stress (flow stress) and the cross-sectional area over which it acts. That is,

$$F = \sigma_y A_i \qquad (5\text{-}7)$$

For a nonstrain-hardening material deformed plastically, the strain-hardening exponent m is zero and the stress-strain relationship $\sigma = \sigma_o \epsilon^m$ is simply $\sigma = \sigma_o$. That is, the yield strength or flow stress is constant during plastic deformation and is equal to σ_o.

The volume of any "solid" material deformed plastically remains constant. Thus

$$A_i l_i = A_o l_o = V_o \qquad \text{and} \qquad A_i = \frac{V_o}{l_i} \qquad (5\text{-}8)$$

where V_o is the initial volume. Equation 5-7 can be written in terms of the instantaneous length and flow stress as

$$F = \sigma_o A_i = \sigma_o \frac{V_o}{l_i} \qquad (5\text{-}9)$$

Figure 5-21 illustrates quantitatively the manner in which the force varies when a nonstrain-hardening material is loaded in tension and in compression. For the tension specimen, the maximum force occurs when the yield strength is reached; and the force drops to one-half the maximum value when the length of the specimen is doubled, for then the cross-sectional area is $\frac{1}{2} A_o$. For the compression specimen, the force is twice the yield load when the length is reduced to one-half the original length. The force never reaches a maximum value, but continues to increase exponentially as the length is reduced.

To calculate the work done during a forming operation, the work expended during the elastic deformation can be ignored. Therefore, the work done is

$$W = \int_{l_o}^{l_i} F \, dl = \sigma_o V_o \int_{l_o}^{l_i} \frac{dl}{l_i} = \sigma_o V_o \ln\left(\frac{l_f}{l_o}\right) = \sigma_o V_o \epsilon \qquad (5\text{-}10)$$

For the tensile deformation in Figure 5-21, the work is

$$W_t = \sigma_o V_o \ln\left(\frac{2l_o}{l_o}\right) = 0.694 \sigma_o V_o$$

For the compressive deformation, the compressive stress is considered negative and the work done is

$$W_c = -\sigma_o V_o \ln\left(\frac{l_o}{2l_o}\right) = -\sigma_o V_o(-\ln 2) = 0.694 \sigma_o V_o$$

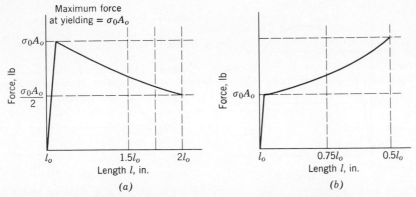

Figure 5-21. Force versus displacement for a nonstrain-hardening material under a uniaxial force. Initial size: A_o and l_o. (*a*) Tension. (*b*) Compression.

Thus it is apparent that for the same true strain, the tension work and compression work are identical.

Power is the time rate of doing work, or $P = W/t$. The English unit of power is the horsepower, which is equal to the rate of doing work equal to 33,000 ft-lb per min. To express power in the absolute system, the conversion factor is 1 hp = 746 watts.

Force to Deform a Strain-Hardening Material

As stated previously, the force necessary to deform a material plastically is equal to the product of its yield strength and cross-sectional area or $F = \sigma_y A_i$

The yield strength for a strain-hardening material is related to the amount of plastic deformation it is subjected to by the strain-hardening equation

$$(\sigma_y)_i = \sigma_o (\epsilon_i)^m$$

By substituting the latter expression into the former

$$F_i = \sigma_o (\epsilon_i)^m A_i$$

Since the volume remains constant during plastic deformation, $A_i = V_o/l_i$ so

$$F_i = \sigma_o \left(\frac{V_o}{l_i}\right) (\epsilon_i)^m \tag{5-11}$$

Figure 5-22 illustrates quantitatively how the force varies when a strain-hardening material is loaded in tension and in compression.

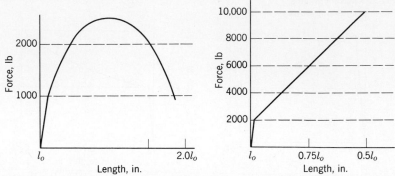

Figure 5-22. Force versus displacement for a strain-hardening material under a uniaxial force. Initial size: A_o and l_o. (*a*) Tension. (*b*) Compression.

Values obtained for aluminum having $\sigma = 25,000\ \epsilon^{0.22}$, $S_y = 5000$ psi, $E = 10 \times 10^6$ psi, $A_o = 0.2$ in.

The work done in plastically deforming a strain-hardening material is equal to the area under the force-displacement curve. The work done, per unit volume of material, in deforming a material is also equal to the area under the natural stress-strain curve. The work done in the plastic region is equal to the area between the yield strain and the final or instantaneous strain. Thus for an initial volume V_o the work for plastic deformation is

$$W = V_o \int_{\epsilon_y}^{\epsilon_i} \sigma\, d\epsilon$$

and since

$$\sigma = \sigma_o \epsilon^m$$

$$W = V_o \sigma_o \int_{\epsilon_y}^{\epsilon_i} (\epsilon_i)^m\, d\epsilon$$

or

$$W = V_o \sigma_o \frac{\epsilon_i^{m+1}}{m+1} \tag{5-12}$$

In calculating the work done in any forming operation, it must be remembered that σ_o and m are mechanical properties of the material, V_o is the total original volume, and that ϵ_i is the total or maximum strain the material is subjected to and is always equal to

$$\ln\left(\frac{l_l}{l_s}\right) \quad \text{or} \quad \ln\left(\frac{A_l}{A_s}\right)$$

THE MAXIMUM DEFORMATION POSSIBLE DURING FORMING

It is frequently necessary to know the maximum amount of deformation that a material can be subjected to during forming without interposing an annealing cycle. This need is experienced by both the engineer who designs the part and the engineer who is responsible for its satisfactory fabrication. There are several failure theories that are used to predict failure on the basis of initiation of yielding such as the maximum-stress theory, the maximum-strain theory, the maximum-shear theory, and the maximum-strain energy theory. However, there are no such theories for total failure or failure by fracture at the present time.

In the field of the forming operations, many "rule of thumb" relationships are used to predict forming failures. Also, some handbook data on the basis of shop tests are available, such as values of the R/t ratio for a variety of materials.

The author has developed a failure theory which predicts when to expect a material to fail during forming: a theory which he has found to be reliable in both the laboratory and in industry. This concept is the *maximum-deformation theory*, which states *"the maximum deformation that a material in a given condition can be subjected to in forming is that deformation that results in a natural tensile strain being induced in some direction in the part that is equal to the natural strain at fracture of a tensile specimen of that particular condition of the material."*

The strains can be easily calculated for the deformation of simple shapes, but not for the deformation of complex shapes. In this latter case it is necessary to resort to at least a partial experimental study to determine the magnitude and distribution of strains in the formed part. It is possible to greatly simplify this experimental aspect by making a micro-hardness study of the formed part and then determining the strains from the strain-hardening characteristics of the material. This technique will be discussed later.

Recognition must be made of the fact that the fracture strain of wrought or forged materials is lower in the transverse direction than it is in the direction of rolling, even though the yield strength and tensile strength are the same in both directions. The correct value of fracture strain must be used for the successful application of the maximum deformation theory.

A tensile specimen cut transversely from a bar or plate may have a fracture strain $(\epsilon_f)_t$ that is only 60% of the fracture strain $(\epsilon_f)_l$ of a tensile specimen cut longitudinally. If a flat-bend specimen were cut out transversely from the plate and bent, the transverse fracture strain $(\epsilon_f)_t$ would be the correct one to use. The longitudinal fracture strain $(\epsilon_f)_l$ would have to be used for a longitudinal bend specimen. Since the longitudinal fracture strain is greater than the transverse fracture strain, plates that are bent longitudinally can be bent to smaller radii than if they are bent transversely. It is common knowledge among "shop people" that materials can be deformed more "with the grain" than "against the grain."

A few examples of experimental studies that were made to verify the maximum deformation theory are presented next, according to the forming operation performed.

Bending

The first relationship derived and verified experimentally was the minimum radius that a sheet or plate can be bent to is related to the strain at fracture of a tensile specimen.[4] When applied to this operation, the theory states that "failure will occur as a transverse crack in the outer fiber of a material being bent when the natural tensile strain in the outer fiber is equal to the natural-strain at the instant of fracture of a tensile specimen of the same material."

The tensile strain in the outer fiber of a bent sheet, as sketched in Figure 5-23, is

$$\epsilon_{of} = \ln \left(\frac{l_{of}}{l_o} \right) = \ln \left[\frac{\phi(R + t)}{\phi(R + t/2)} \right]$$

The natural strain at fracture of a tensile specimen is

$$\epsilon_f = \ln \left(\frac{A_o}{A_f} \right) = \ln \left[\frac{100}{100 - A_r} \right]$$

By equating ϵ_{of} to ϵ_f, the result is

$$\left(\frac{100}{100 - A_r} \right) = \left(\frac{R + t}{R + t/2} \right)$$

By solving for R/t as a function of A_r,

$$\frac{R}{t} = \frac{50}{A_r} - 1 \tag{5-13}$$

The above analysis was made by assuming that the neutral axis remains at the midthickness of the bent sheet. This relationship has been verified by laboratory tests as well as by industrial shop tests for a broad range of materials that include brittle cast iron, high car-

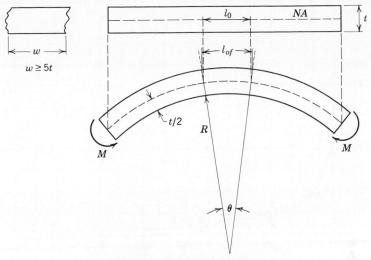

Figure 5-23. The bending of a plate.

bon steel, and precipitation-hardened aluminum as well as ductile materials such as brass, low carbon steel, and soft aluminum. For very ductile materials, with $A_r > 50$, the equation predicts negative radii, which are physically impossible. The correct interpretation of the use of this relationship for very ductile materials is this: If a material has an A_r of 50, it may be bent, for all practical purposes, to a 0 in. radius without fracture.

The above relationship can be modified to take into account the shift in the neutral axis as the material is bent to give the following:

$$\frac{R}{t} = \frac{(100 - A_r)^2}{200A_r - A_r^2} \qquad (5\text{-}14)$$

This latter relationship does not predict a negative radius with A_r approaching 100, and it is more useful than the former equation in some research studies. However, from a design and manufacturing point of view, the simpler equation with its correct interpretation is more convenient and just as reliable when one appreciates the fact that the A_r of a specific material may vary by as much as 50% from one sample to another.

Figure 5-24 illustrates the results of an experimental study to verify the analytical relationships derived above. The experimental data correlate very well with the analytical curves drawn. The only experimental point that is significantly off the theoretical curve, K, is

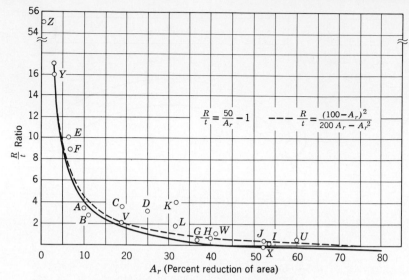

Experimental Data Superimposed on Analytical Curves of R/t versus Per Cent Reduction of Area.

A	¼ in. Mg Tooling Plate	K	³⁄₁₆ in. RC 130 B Ti
B	⅛ in. Mg Tooling Plate		(This specimen was strained
C	0.050 in. AZ 31 BH24 Mg Alloy		during machining.)
D	0.032 in. HK 31 XI H24 Mg Alloy	L	¼ in. RC 130 B Ti
E	¼ in. 2011 T 6 Al	U	⅛ in. B and S Tool Steel
F	⅛ in. 2011 T 6 Al	V	¼ in. 70–30 Brass (50% CW)
G	¼ in. 70–30 Brass (CR 10%)	W	¼ in. B and S Tool Steel
H	⅛ in. 70–30 Brass (CR 10%)	X	¼ in. 2 Sh Al
I	¼ in. 1018 Steel (25%)	Y	⅛ in. Polystyrene
J	⅛ in. 1018 Steel (CR 25%)	Z	⁹⁄₆₄ in. Cast Iron

Figure 5-24. Experimental and analytical values of R/t ratio versus A_r.

for a titanium specimen that was unintentionally strained during machining. Also, it is apparent from this figure that the difference between Equations 5-13 and 5-14 is insignificant. Figure 5-25a is a photograph of an aluminum alloy plate that failed by exceeding the bending limit.

Another practical consideration, in addition to the possible variation in the per cent reduction in area of the material, is the springback that occurs when the bending forces are removed after a sheet is bent. Both of the above equations give the minimum radius to which a sheet can be bent *while the load is applied.* When the bending moment is removed, the sheet elastically springs back as we discussed before.

Figure 5-25. Photograph of bending and upsetting failures. (*a*) Bending. (*b*) Upsetting.

Upsetting or Forging in Open Dies

The second relationship that was derived, but verified at the present only on a few materials, is that a material can be compressed without failure occurring until the circumferential or transverse tensile strain is equal to the natural strain at fracture of a tensile specimen of the same material.

When a cylinder is compressed along its axis, there are compressive stresses and strains across a plane normal to the axis, and there are tensile stresses and strains in the radial and circumferential directions. This is true during both the elastic and plastic deformations. Failure in upsetting and forging, as is true in bending, is defined as occurring when a crack or physical separation is created at the surface of the material. Figure 5-25b is a photograph of a cylinder that failed due to axial compression inducing circumferential tensile strains greater than ϵ_f.

The significance or the application, of this failure theory for upsetting can best be illustrated with the following examples that were verified in the laboratory.

For a brittle material, such as cast iron, that may be elastically deformed but whose plastic deformation is extremely small (A_r between 0 and 1), the failure may be predicted with sufficient accuracy by considering only the elastic deformation. If the cylinder in Figure 5-26 is cast iron and is loaded in compression as shown, then during the elastic deformation $n_{cf} = \mu n_l$ where μ is Poisson's ratio. Or $\epsilon_{cf} = \mu \epsilon_l$, since for very small strains $n = \epsilon$. For elastic deformations

$$\epsilon_l = \frac{F}{A_o E} = \frac{S}{E}$$

And since μ for cast iron may be assumed to be equal to 0.3, then

$$\epsilon_{cf} = 0.3\epsilon_l$$

Before determining the maximum compression deformation possible, the simpler tensile deformation will be reviewed.

In general, for a brittle material having only an elastic range

$$F = A_i S_i = A_i E \epsilon_i$$

Failure in tension occurs, for brittle materials, when $\epsilon_l = \epsilon_y$. Also, for small deformations up to ϵ_y, $A_i = A_o$. Therefore

$$F_t = A_o S_y = A_o E \epsilon_y \qquad (5\text{-}17a)$$

where F_t = tensile force or load at failure.

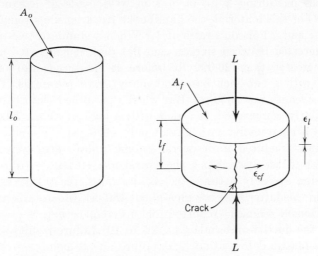

Figure 5-26. A cylinder with perfectly lubricated ends deformed by an axial compressive force.

Failure in compression, on the other hand, will occur when $\epsilon_{cf} = \epsilon_y$. Thus, from the general equation $F = A_o E \epsilon_l$, since $\epsilon_{cf} = \mu \epsilon_l$ at fracture

$$F_c = \frac{1}{\mu} A_o E \epsilon_{cf} = \frac{1}{\mu} A_o E \epsilon_y \qquad (5\text{-}17b)$$

where F_c is the compressive force or load at failure. Therefore, it is apparent that

$$F_c = \frac{1}{\mu} F_t \qquad (5\text{-}18)$$

or, in other words, the load that causes failure in compression for a brittle material is $1/\mu$ times the load that causes tensile failure.

For the cast iron with $\mu = 0.3$, F_c is $3\frac{1}{3}$ times as large in compression as it is in tension. Experimentally, F_t was found to be 4000 lb and F_c was between 12,000 and 15,000 lb on a 0.505 in. diameter specimen.

An interesting demonstration for the reader to have at this time is the compression testing of two cylinders or cubes of concrete, mortar, or chalk. One should be tested as is and the second one should be coated with a film of parafin on the two faces that contact the dies before testing. The relative load-carrying capacity of the lubricated (parafined) specimen to the plain specimen should be compared. In the absence of a live demonstration, the following typical experimental data can be analyzed.

Cubes measuring 2 in. on a side were made of a sand-cement mortar. (For this material, the handbooks list a tensile strength of 250 to 500 psi and a Poisson's ratio of $\frac{1}{4}$.) When a standard two-inch cube was compressed between smooth and flat dies, it supported a load of slightly greater than 20,000 lb before it fractured into one main pyramid with a two-inch base and many small pyramids. The compressive strength was 5000 psi. But when a parafined (lubricated) cube was similarly compressed, it failed with a load of about 7800 lb and thus had a compressive strength of only 1950 psi. This cube, on the other hand, fractured into several prisms whose faces were all perpendicular to the base. Since the transverse (tensile) strains during compression are only μ times the axial strains, the transverse tensile stresses in this latter cube are then about 480 psi, which falls within the range of tensile strengths reported for this composition.

For the ductile materials ($A_r > 5$ to 10) failure results after considerable plastic deformation, and failure due to compressive loading will occur as a longitudinal crack when the circumferential tensile strain ϵ_{cf} equals the strain at fracture of a tensile specimen ϵ_f.

The size and shape of a cylindrical specimen at the instant when such a failure occurs can be calculated as follows. The tensile fracture strain, in terms of the reduction of area of a tensile specimen, is

$$\epsilon_f = \ln\left(\frac{100}{100 - A_r}\right)$$

The circumferential tensile strain during compression is

$$\epsilon_{cf} = \ln\left(\frac{\pi D_f}{\pi D_o}\right) = \ln\left(\frac{D_f}{D_o}\right)$$

Since $\epsilon_f = \epsilon_{cf}$ is the criteria for failure during the compression of a cylinder

$$\frac{D_f}{D_o} = \left(\frac{100}{100 - A_r}\right) \quad \text{or} \quad D_f = \left(\frac{100 D_o}{100 - A_r}\right) \tag{5-19}$$

where D_f is now the diameter of a compressed cylinder at impinging failure, D_o is the original diameter of the compression cylinder, and A_r is per cent reduction of area of a tensile specimen of the same material. The above analysis is on the basis of perfect lubrication and no barrelling, or a constant diameter from top to bottom of the specimen.

The cross-sectional area of the compressed cylinder at fracture is then

$$A_f = \frac{\pi D_f{}^2}{4} = \frac{\pi}{4}\left(\frac{100 D_o}{100 - A_r}\right)^2 \tag{5-20}$$

The load at fracture may be determined by multiplying the fracture area of Equation 5-20 by the true stress at fracture, which may be determined from the expression

$$\sigma = \sigma_o \epsilon^m = \sigma_o \left(\ln \frac{A_f}{A_o} \right)^m$$

Therefore

$$F_c = \frac{\pi \sigma_o}{4} \left(\frac{100 D_o}{100 - A_r} \right)^2 \left(\ln \frac{A_f}{A_o} \right)^m \tag{5-21}$$

For a steel having the mechanical properties: $A_r = 60\%$; $\sigma = 120{,}000 \epsilon^{0.20}$; and a cylindrical shape with an original diameter $D_o = 0.25$ in. ($A_o = 0.05$ in.^{2}); the cross-sectional area and diameter at failure due to a compressive load are, theoretically

$$A_f = \frac{\pi}{4} \left(\frac{100 \times 0.25}{40} \right)^2 = \frac{\pi}{4} \left(\frac{2.5}{4} \right)^2 = 0.307 \text{ in.}^2$$

The theoretical maximum final force is

$$F_c = \frac{\pi \times 120{,}000}{4} \left(\frac{2.5}{4} \right)^2 \ln \left(\frac{0.307}{0.05} \right)^{0.20} = 52{,}000 \text{ lb}$$

In a laboratory experiment to verify these calculations, a $\frac{1}{4}$ in. diameter specimen was compressed to a final diameter of approximately $\frac{5}{8}$ in. with a final load of 50,000 lb, at which time circumferential cracks developed on the surface.

Instead of comparing the size and shape of a compressed cylinder on the basis of the tensile reduction of area, the comparison can be made on the basis of the strains induced in the part.

The maximum tensile strain of a tensile specimen at fracture is

$$\epsilon_f = \ln \left(\frac{A_o}{A_f} \right) = \ln \left(\frac{4\pi D_o{}^2}{4\pi D_f} \right) = 2 \ln \left(\frac{D_o}{D_f} \right) \tag{5-22}$$

The circumferential tensile strain during the compression of a cylinder is

$$\epsilon_{cf} = \ln \left(\frac{\pi D_f}{\pi D_o} \right) = \ln \left(\frac{D_f}{D_o} \right) \tag{5-23}$$

The axial (longitudinal) compressive strain during the compression of a cylinder is

$$(\epsilon_l)_c = -\ln \left(\frac{4\pi D_o{}^2}{4\pi D_f{}^2} \right) = 2 \ln \left(\frac{D_f}{D_o} \right) \tag{5-24}$$

Now for a material having a tensile fracture strain of ϵ_f, the limiting compressive deformation is when $\epsilon_{cf} = \epsilon_f$. Then

$$\epsilon_f = \epsilon_{cf} = \ln\left(\frac{D_f}{D_o}\right)$$

or

$$(e)^{\epsilon_f} = \frac{D_f}{D_o} \quad \text{and} \quad D_f = D_o(e)^{\epsilon_f} \tag{5-25}$$

But when a cylindrical specimen is compressed from D_o to D_f, the longitudinal or areal strain $(\epsilon_l)_c$ is given by Equation 5-24. By comparing Equations 5-23 and 5-24 it is apparent that for a given axial compression, the longitudinal compressive strain $(\epsilon_l)_c$ is numerically twice the circumferential tensile strain ϵ_{cf}.

That is

$$(\epsilon_l)_c = 2\epsilon_{cf} \tag{5-26}$$

This same relationship is also true for tensile deformation.

Another way of arriving at this same relationship is to make use of Poisson's ratio μ which equates the lateral or normal strain to the axial strain thus: $\epsilon_n = \mu\epsilon_l$. Since the normal (radial) strains are equal to the circumferential strains, then $\epsilon_{cf} = \mu\epsilon_l$.

For plastic deformation, where the volume remains constant, μ is equal to exactly $\frac{1}{2}$. Therefore $\epsilon_l = 2\epsilon_{cf}$. To designate a compressive strain, ϵ_l is written as $(\epsilon_l)_c$.

A very interesting observation can be made here, namely that a material can be strain hardened to the extent that it will have a *yield strength that is greater than its true fracture stress*. This conclusion appears to be, at first thought, both impossible and ridiculous. How can a material possibly have a strength greater than the true stress at fracture? The answer to this paradox lies in the above relationships.

From Equation 5-26 it is apparent that when a cylinder is axially compressed, the longitudinal compressive strain $(\epsilon_l)_c$ is two times the circumferential strain ϵ_{cf}. And the maximum circumferential strain that can be endured by a cylinder in compression is equal to the fracture strain of the material in tension, ϵ_f. Thus since

$$(\epsilon_l)_c = 2\epsilon_{cf}$$

and

$$\epsilon_{cf} = \epsilon_f$$

then

$$(\epsilon_l)_c = 2\epsilon_f \tag{5-27}$$

That is, a cylinder can be plastically deformed in compression to a longitudinal or areal strain that is numerically twice the tensile strain at fracture of a tensile specimen of the same material. And since tensile and compressive strain hardening are identical, as shown in Figures 5-29 and 5-31, then the true stress of the final compressed cylinder is greater than the true fracture stress of the tensile specimen.

Consider, as an example, an annealed 18-8 type of stainless steel having $\sigma_o = 200,000$ psi, $m = 0.5$ and $\epsilon_f = 1.2$ as determined from a tensile test. The true fracture stress, after correcting for the triaxial stresses at the neck is

$$\sigma_f = 200,000 \times 1.2^{0.5} = 219,000 \text{ psi}$$

A cylinder of this same material compressed to a longitudinal strain $(\epsilon_l)_c$ of 2.4 will have a true stress of $\sigma_c = 200,000 \times 2.4^{0.5} = 310,000$ psi.

This value of true stress is also the compressive yield strength of this deformed cylinder. The tensile yield strength is probably about 10 to 20% lower than this, as explained in a following section on the directional aspects of strain hardening.

The above example demonstrates the greater amount of strain hardening that can be achieved by compressively deforming a material than by means of tensile deformation.

Another limitation to the amount of upsetting that can be given to a bar is the ratio of the unsupported length to the diameter. This ratio is influenced by the type of tooling or clamps that are used in the upsetting operation. Four special cases follow.

(1). When compressing a cylinder between two flat dies, the length to diameter ratio should not exceed two. Some barrelling may result because of friction at the die faces under these conditions. However, if the length to diameter ratio exceeds 2 or $2\frac{1}{2}$ then buckling in the form of one face moving laterally with respect to the opposite face is likely to occur. The tendency for this type of buckling to occur is increased as the surface finish and lubricity at the contacting faces are improved. Figure 5-27a illustrates the compression of a cylinder between two flat dies.

(2). When upsetting a cylinder between one flat and one recessed die, the ratio of unsupported length to diameter of the bar should not exceed three. Buckling may result otherwise (Figure 5-27b).

(3). When upsetting a cylinder in a closed die, unsupported length greater than $3 D_o$ can be employed provided the final diameter

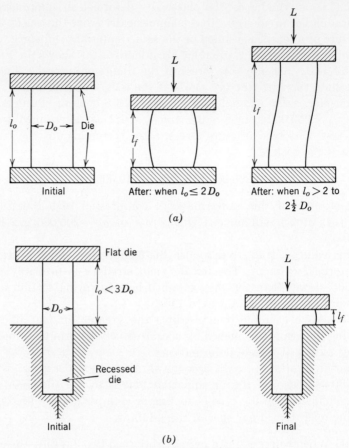

Figure 5-27. Length to diameter ratio limits for upsetting. (*a*) Pressing between two flat dies. (*b*) Pressing between one flat and one recessed die. (*c*) Pressing a cylinder in a closed die. (*d*) Upsetting a cylinder to a $D_f > 1\frac{1}{2} D_o$ by use of intermediate upsetting.

of the upset part is less than $1\frac{1}{2} D_o$. In this type of upsetting, the final diameter of the upset bar is equal to the inside diameter of recessed forging die (Figure 5-27*c*).

(4). When upsetting a cylinder that requires an unsupported length greater than $3 D_o$ and a final diameter of $1\frac{1}{2} D_o$ in a conical closed die, the length of unsupported bar between the faces of the die should not exceed $1 D_o$ (Figure 5-27*d*). Generally, the part formed in the conical recess is an intermediate part in the formation of a final

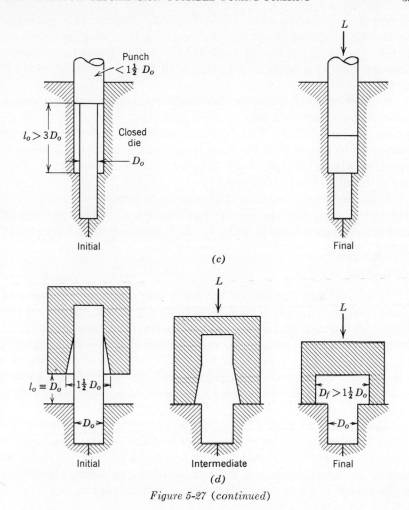

Figure 5-27 (continued)

part having a diameter greater than $1\frac{1}{2} D_o$ and an initial unsupported length greater than $3 D_o$.

Stretching or Stretch-Forming

In any stretching or combination of stretching-bending operation, failure will occur, just as in the simple tensile test, when the longitudinal tensile strain equals the natural strain at fracture. Again, failure in this case is determined when a crack or physical separation occurs. In simple stretching, however, failure of the forming operation may be considered as occurring when and if "necking" begins. This condition can also be predicted in advance by recalling that necking begins at the time the maximum load is applied to a part and that the strain at maximum load ϵ_u is equal to the slope m of the true stress-true strain curve.

Another mode of failure in the bending of a part having a cross-sectional shape such as a tube or an I section is by compressive buckling on the inside fibers. This buckling occurs at quite low levels of plastic strain. However, if the part being bent is also simultaneously loaded axially in tension, much smaller radii can be formed. This process is called stretch-forming.

Thus, for simple stretching, failure may be considered as occurring when $\epsilon_l = \epsilon_u = m$, whereas for the combination of stretching-bending operations failure will occur when $\epsilon_l = \epsilon_f$ if sufficient stretching load is applied.

Rolling

If an originally square bar having a side length of s inches and original length l_o is rolled to a thickness of $\frac{1}{2} s$, the width and the length will increase significantly but neither will be twice the original dimension. If a bar of rectangular cross section with a width w_o greater than six times the thickness t_o, or a plate, is rolled to a thickness of $\frac{1}{2} t_o$ then the width increase is negligible and the length is $2l_o$. In this latter case the per cent reduction in thickness is equal to the per cent reduction in area.

The criteria for failure in rolling, as is true in the previously described forming operations, is that amount of deformation that induces tensile strains in the material that are equal to the natural strain at fracture of a tensile specimen. The tensile strains in rolling are defined by the change in length of the part during rolling, that is,

$$\epsilon_r = \ln\left(\frac{l_f}{l_o}\right) \tag{5-28}$$

For plates or wide bars, as described above, the longitudinal strain ϵ_r is equal to the cross-sectional area strain ϵ_a, or the thickness strain ϵ_t, since the volume remains constant. The width strain ϵ_w is zero. Thus for a 50% reduction in the thickness of a plate:

the rolling strain

$$\epsilon_r = \ln\left(\frac{l_f}{l_o}\right) = \ln 2 = 0.694$$

the thickness strain

$$\epsilon_t = \ln\left(\frac{t_o}{t_f}\right) = \ln 2 = 0.694$$

the area strain

$$\epsilon_a = \ln\left(\frac{t_o w_o}{t_f w_o}\right) = \ln 2 = 0.694$$

the width strain

$$\epsilon_w = \ln\left(\frac{w_o}{w_o}\right) = \ln 1 = 0$$

Thus failure in rolling will occur when the maximum tensile strain due to rolling, ϵ_r, is equal to the natural strain at fracture of a tensile specimen ϵ_f. Figure 5-28 shows rolling failures in paraffin, magnesium, and brass.

It is interesting to note the type of failure that occurs during rolling. When a fractured tensile specimen of ductile materials is examined, we see that generally the fractured surfaces make an angle

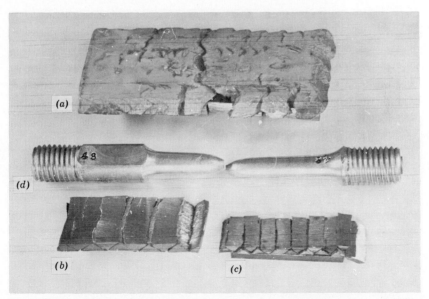

Figure 5-28. Photograph of rolling failures. (*a*) Wax. (*b*) Magnesium. (*c*) 70Cu–30Zn brass. (*d*) Aluminum tensile specimen.

of 45° with the axis of the specimen. This is the plane of maximum shear stress. The rolling failures in Figure 5-28 are a series of these 45° "ductile" tensile failures.

STRAIN DISTRIBUTION IN SOME FORMING OPERATIONS

As mentioned previously, the strain induced in some of the simple deformation operations can be calculated directly from the change in shape of the part. However, this cannot be done in some of the more complicated forming operations. The strain distribution determined experimentally for some forming operations by means of micro-hardness studies are presented below to serve as a guide as to how the strains in more complicated operations can be studied.

Figure 5-29 is a comparison of the natural stress-strain curves of annealed aluminum in both tension and compression. The compression curve is a plot of the instantaneous compressive load divided by the instantaneous area. The loading was frequently interrupted to measure the hardness of the specimen and to reapply a high pressure lubricant to the contacting faces. For strains greater than 0.8 the lubricant is

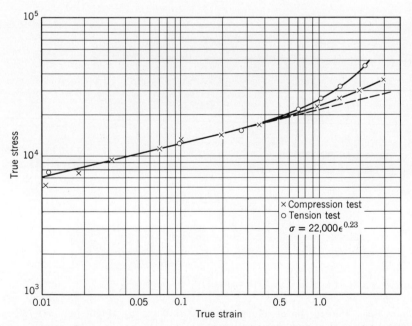

Figure 5-29. Stress-strain curve in tension and compression (material: 1100-0 aluminum).

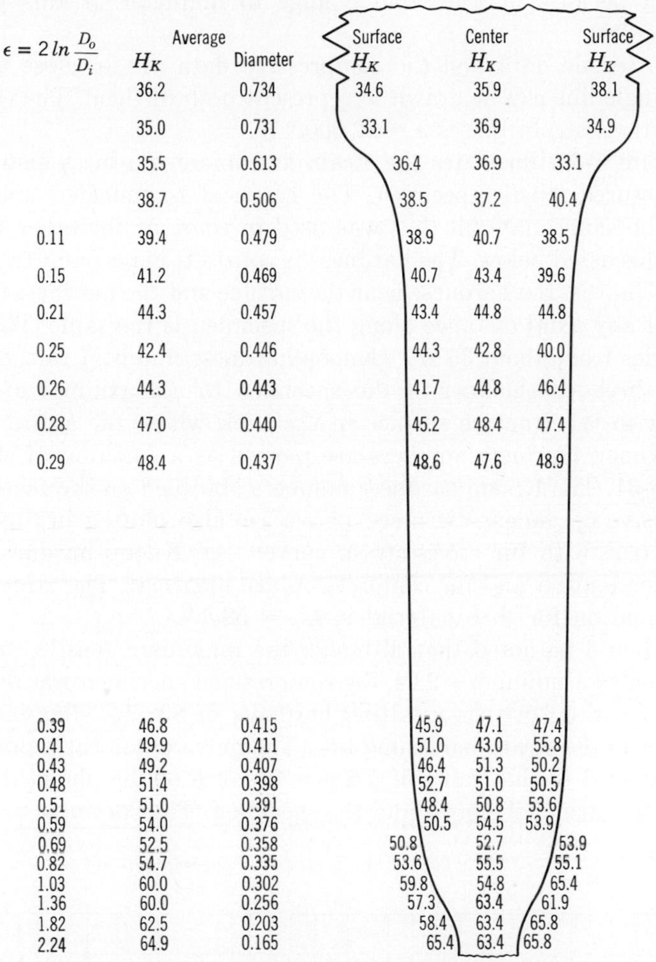

$\epsilon = 2\ln\dfrac{D_o}{D_i}$	Average H_K	Diameter	Surface H_K	Center H_K	Surface H_K
	36.2	0.734	34.6	35.9	38.1
	35.0	0.731	33.1	36.9	34.9
	35.5	0.613	36.4	36.9	33.1
	38.7	0.506	38.5	37.2	40.4
0.11	39.4	0.479	38.9	40.7	38.5
0.15	41.2	0.469	40.7	43.4	39.6
0.21	44.3	0.457	43.4	44.8	44.8
0.25	42.4	0.446	44.3	42.8	40.0
0.26	44.3	0.443	41.7	44.8	46.4
0.28	47.0	0.440	45.2	48.4	47.4
0.29	48.4	0.437	48.6	47.6	48.9
0.39	46.8	0.415	45.9	47.1	47.4
0.41	49.9	0.411	51.0	43.0	55.8
0.43	49.2	0.407	46.4	51.3	50.2
0.48	51.4	0.398	52.7	51.0	50.5
0.51	51.0	0.391	48.4	50.8	53.6
0.59	54.0	0.376	50.5	54.5	53.9
0.69	52.5	0.358	50.8	52.7	53.9
0.82	54.7	0.335	53.6	55.5	55.1
1.03	60.0	0.302	59.8	54.8	65.4
1.36	60.0	0.256	57.3	63.4	61.9
1.82	62.5	0.203	58.4	63.4	65.8
2.24	64.9	0.165	65.4	63.4	65.8

Figure 5-30. Strain and microhardness distribution in a fractured tensile specimen (material: 1100-0 aluminum).

only partially effective, as evidenced by the upswing of the compressive stress-strain line. The area of the compressive specimen was determined with the load removed from the specimen, whereas the area of the tensile specimen was determined with the load applied.

The tensile stress-strain curve swings upward appreciably for strains greater than 0.4. Since the strain at the maximum load is only 0.23 for this material, this rise in the stress-strain curve is due to the presence of triaxial stresses which are induced in the "neck" of the specimen because of the rapid change in diameter at this location (Figure 5-30).

The tensile data and the compressive data are so close together that a single line can be drawn to represent both of them. The equation of this stress-strain line is $\sigma = 22{,}000\epsilon^{0.23}$.

Figure 5-30 illustrates the strain and micro-hardness distribution in a fractured tensile specimen. The material is annealed aluminum, and is the same material that was used in some of the other forming studies discussed below. The hardness is constant across any transverse section. That is, the hardness near the surface and the hardness near the center at any axial distance along the specimen is the same. The hardness varies from about 35 H_K (Knoop hardness number) in the underformed threaded shoulder of the specimen to a maximum of 66 H_K adjacent to the fracture surface in the neck where the strain is 2.24. These Knoop hardness numbers are plotted as a function of strain in Figure 5-31. The Knoop hardness numbers obtained on the faces of the compressive specimens discussed above are also plotted in this figure. As was true with the stress-strain curves, the Knoop hardness-strain curves for tension and for compression are identical. The strain-hardening equation for this material is $H_K = 58\epsilon^{0.2}$.

It should be noted that although the maximum tensile strain for this annealed aluminum is 2.24, the compression specimen was deformed to a strain of 5.6 with a resulting hardness of 83 H_K. This last point also falls on the strain-hardening line. The only reason the deformation was restricted to this value of 5.6 was because of the physical limitations of the size of the press and the specimen. The specimen originally

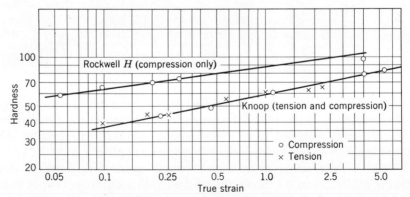

Figure 5-31. Microhardness versus strain for tensile and compressive deformation (material: 1100-0 aluminum).

was 2 in. high and was compressed to a final height of about 0.004 in.

Rockwell H hardness readings were also taken on the faces of the compression specimens to permit a comparison of Knoop hardness numbers with the more common Rockwell hardness number. The strain hardening in terms of Rockwell H is also exponential, and as can be seen from the data in Figure 5-31, very consistent. The strain-hardening equation on this scale is $R_H = 86\epsilon^{0.13}$.

If a solid cylinder is compressed axially without "perfect" lubrication at the faces, the phenomenon known as barrelling occurs and the diameter of the deformed cylinder is not constant. The diameter is smallest at the two faces and largest at the mid-height. This is due to the friction forces acting on the faces which prevent the material from flowing radially. When this condition is present, the strain hardening is not uniform throughout the cylinder.

"Perfect" lubrication is easy to achieve by interrupted loading and reapplication of lubricant with low strength materials such as aluminum; but is nearly impossible to achieve with a ductile high-strength material.

Figure 5-32 illustrates the variation in strain hardening within a solid cylinder compressed axially to a strain of 0.58. The material is a cobalt base alloy having a strength coefficient of 300,000 psi and a strain-hardening exponent of 0.5, which indicates that this alloy can be strengthened very significantly by coldwork. This is confirmed by the fact that this alloy in the solution-treated (single-phase) condition has a hardness of 20 R_c and, when coldworked to a strain of 0.58, it has a hardness of 51 R_c. It is interesting to note that this same alloy can be strengthened by precipitation hardening. In an experiment to determine the magnitude of this effect, it was found that precipitation hardening increased the hardness by 4 R_c numbers. This was true for the solution-treated material with no coldwork where the increase was from 20 to 24 R_c, as well as for the material with all degrees of coldwork up to $\epsilon = 0.58$ where the hardness was 55 R_c after aging.

As can be seen in Figure 5-32, the hardness varies considerably and consistently throughout the deformed cylinder. The maximum hardness on the deformed face of the cylinder is 45 R_c and at a distance $R - \frac{1}{4}$ in. from the edge the hardness drops to a minimum of 40 R_c. However, on a plane $\frac{1}{8}$ in. beneath the face, the maximum and minimum hardnesses are 51 and 45 R_c. And it should be noted that the maximum hardness on this plane occurs at a radial distance where the hardness was minimum on the deformed face. At the mid-height, the hardness is minimum near the outer surface of the cylinder and fairly uniform throughout the central portion.

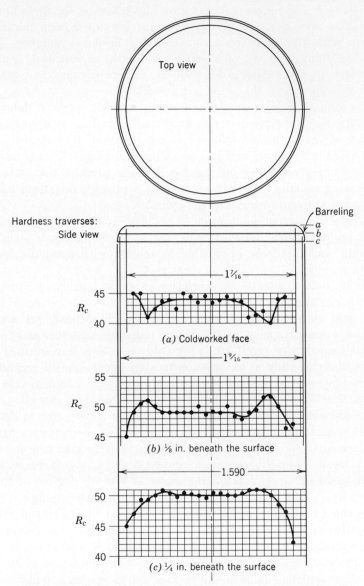

Figure 5-32. Variation in strain hardening in a cylinder compressed with poor lubrication. Cobalt alloy with an initial hardness
of 20 R_c. Diameter is 1 in. $\times$ 1 in. high-annealed solid cylinder compressed to $\frac{9}{16}$ in. (*a*) Coldworked face. (*b*) $\frac{1}{8}$ in. beneath the surface.
(*c*) $\frac{1}{4}$ in. beneath the surface.

Figure 5-33 is a cross-sectional sketch of a 1 in. diameter bar of annealed aluminum that was forward extruded for a portion of its length to a $\frac{1}{2}$ in. diameter. Micro-hardness readings obtained experimentally on the sectioned bar are included in the sketch. The aluminum used for this study was not from the same heat as that from which Figures 5-29 to 5-31 were obtained. The strain-hardening characteristics for the material used in this extrusion study are: $\sigma = 26,000\epsilon^{0.2}$ and $H_K = 62\epsilon^{0.19}$.

Several observations concerning the strain hardening of an extrusion can be made by examining the data in Figure 5-33. The material at the center of the forward surface of the extruded bar is not strain hardened, whereas, the corners are slightly strain hardened. The hardness increases rapidly along the length of the extrusion in the direction opposite to the extruding direction to certain maximum values. For this particular bar with a 75% reduction of area, the maximum uniform hardness at the center of the bar is about 62 H_K which corresponds to a tensile or compressive reduction of area of about 63%. On the other hand, the uniform maximum hardness for a thin layer at the surface of the extrusion is about 80 H_K which corresponds to about a tensile or compressive reduction of area of about 95%.

A tensile specimen was machined from the extruded bar to evaluate the yield strength and tensile strength of the extruded material. The objective of this particular test was to ascertain whether the strength-hardness relationship for the extruded bar was equal to the strength-hardness relationship for a uniaxially deformed tensile specimen.

To conduct this test the $\frac{1}{2}$ in. diameter extrusion was machined in the gage section to a 0.357 in. diameter (a 0.1 in.^{2} area). By examining Figure 5-33 it is apparent that the material in the 0.357 in. diameter portion of the extrusion has a hardness of about 60 to 65 H_K. From the previously obtained strain-hardening data on an annealed tensile specimen of this material, namely, $H_K = 62\epsilon^{0.19}$ and $\sigma = 26,000\epsilon^{0.2}$, the strain in the machined portion of the extrusion is about 1.0. Therefore, if the strain hardening during extrusion is the same as the strain hardening in uniaxial tension, then the tensile specimen of the extruded materal should have both a yield strength and a tensile strength of 26,000 psi. Upon testing the specimen of extruded aluminum, it was found to have a yield strength of 26,000 psi and a tensile strength of 26,200 psi!

In conclusion, we can then say that although it is necessary to determine experimentally the strain distribution in an extrusion, once the strain is determined the strength of the material can be calculated from the tensile strain-hardening relationship for the annealed material.

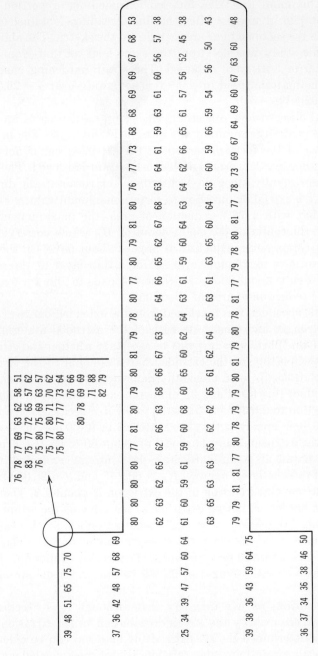

Figure 5-33. Strain-hardening distribution in a forward extruded bar (material: 1100-0 aluminum. Sizes: $D_o = 1$ in. $D_f = \frac{1}{2}$ in. Reduction: 75%).

It can also be observed from Figure 5-33 that the portion of the billet in the extrusion chamber adjacent to the piston is not strain hardened until it comes near the die orifice. It is also apparent that the "dead" metal in the corners of the extrusion chamber is very severely strained along a 45° line extending from the edge of the die opening.

Figure 5-1 illustrates the magnitude and distribution of strain hardening in a material being sheared in a die as well as being machined into a chip with a cutting tool. The material is again 1100-0 aluminum. By comparing the values of Knoop hardness obtained in the two pieces illustrated in Figure 5-1 with the typical strain-hardening data for annealed aluminum, it is apparent that strains considerably greater than 1.0 are present in the deformed material.

DIRECTIONALITY OF STRAIN HARDENING

In all the previous discussions on strain hardening incurred during a forming operation, it was assumed that the strength of the material given after deformation was the strength and direction in the same sense as the deforming force. But what about the properties in a direction perpendicular to the direction of the deforming force? And what are the properties in the direction of the deforming force, but in the opposite sense? That is, what is the compressive yield strength of a part previously deformed in tension; or what is the tensile yield strength of a cylinder previously deformed in compression? The Bauschinger effect is the concept that is frequently used to *qualitatively* answer the latter question.

The textbooks and handbooks state the Bauschinger effect as follows: when a material is plastically deformed in one direction, as in tension, than its yield strength in that same direction is raised but its yield strength in the opposite sense (compression) is lowered. The inference is also usually made that if a part is deformed in one direction, such as compression, then its tensile yield strength after cold-working is actually lower than the yield strength of the annealed material. If this effect is true, then designs using cold formed parts must certainly take it into consideration. Unfortunately, the handbooks do not give any quantitative data for the magnitude of the Bauschinger effect, especially after large plastic strains.

Several studies [3,6] have been made recently to obtain quantitative data on the directionality of strain hardening. These studies do not confirm all the above-mentioned aspects of strength versus prior deformation described as the Bauschinger effect. These studies reveal that for the amount of plastic deformation associated with the forming operations, the yield strength in both tension and compression, and for all directions in the deformed metal, is greater than the annealed yield strength. In fact, for severe deformations, the yield strength in both senses in all directions is four or more times the annealed yield strength. This will be discussed in more detail later.

The reason there appears to be some confusion regarding the Bauschinger effect is probably because many translators and interpreters take Bauschinger's "elastic limit" to mean "yield strength." In his original expression of the phenomenon he noted, Bauschinger concluded[2]: "By applying a tensile or compressive load beyond the elastic limit, the elastic limit for compression, or for tension respectively, is reduced considerably, and the more it is the more these loads exceed the elastic limit. Exceeding the elastic limit in one direction rather slightly may bring the elastic limit in the other direction down to zero."

The property that Bauschinger reported on was the elastic limit. At times in engineering discussions, the terms elastic limit and yield strength are considered to be synonymous since the end of elastic deformation is the beginning of plastic deformation. Consequently many people use the two terms interchangeably. In most of the introductory courses in mechanics and materials, the stress-strain curve for the common materials other than low carbon steel is presented as in Figure 5-34. The proportional limit and the elastic limit are about the same,

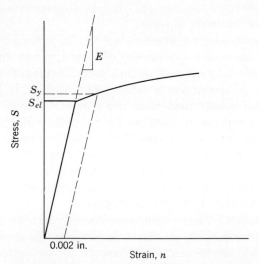

Figure 5-34. Idealized stress-strain curve for small strains.

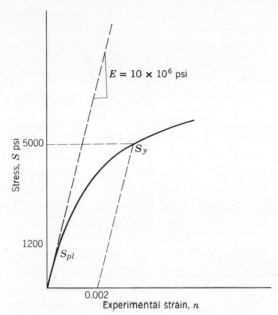

Figure 5-35. Stress-strain curve for 1100-0 aluminum.

and the yield strength is only slightly above them. The reader should review the definitions of these properties in Chapter 1 at this time.

Figure 5-35 is an actual stress-strain curve drawn from experimental data on annealed aluminum. This is the type of curve that is associated with cast iron. However, with cast iron there is no straight portion to the elastic curve. The modulus of elasticity in this case (for cast iron) is a "tangent" modulus. The aluminum specimen in Figure 5-35 does have a linear portion on the elastic curve with a slope of 10^7 psi. However, the proportional limit is only 1200 psi whereas the yield strength is 5000 psi. Although the elastic limit was not determined for this material, it probably is not much over 1200 psi.

Figure 5-36 illustrates the change in the proportional limit of annealed aluminum as a result of small prior plastic deformation. The results shown here for the proportional limit are in agreement with those reported by Bauschinger for the elastic limit. The following explanation is given to assist you in interpreting Figure 5-36.

The proportional limit in tension A and the proportional limit in compression B for the annealed material are equal. Consider a specimen that is deformed in tension to point C having a strain slightly greater

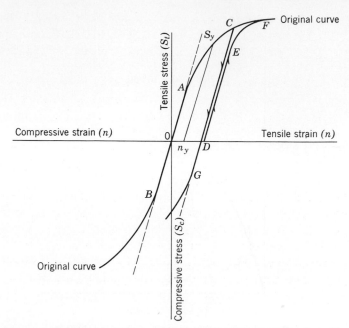

Figure 5-36. Change in the proportional limit as a result of small plastic deformation.

than the yield strain, and then unloaded. It springs back to point D. If this same specimen is now loaded in tension, its new proportional limit is at point E, which is above the original proportional limit A but below the prior maximum tensile stress C. If loaded further, the specimen will begin to follow what would have been the extension of its original stress-strain curve at point F.

However, if the specimen after unloading from C to D is stressed in compression rather than in tension, its new proportional limit is at G, which is lower than B and may actually be at 0 psi.

All of the above data are on the basis of the proportional and elastic limits for small strains. The results are completely different when the yield strengths are considered after significant plastic deformation has occured. Figure 5-37 illustrates this latter condition for annealed aluminum having a proportional limit of 1200 psi and a yield strength of 4800 psi.

Consider a specimen that is deformed in tension to point A and then unloaded to B. If it is now loaded in tension it has a proportional limit at C and a yield strength at D. However, if it were to be reloaded in compression its proportional limit would be E which is considerably lower than C but greater than the annealed *yield strength*. Its yield strength in compression is at F, which is about 10 to 20% lower in value than the yield strength in tension D. The same results are achieved when the original prior deformation is compressive.

Table 5-4 gives numerical values for yield strengths D and F as a function of the prior deformation B. With only 10% coldwork, the yield strength is raised by 113% in the direction opposite to that of the prior deformation. Rather than the yield strength in the opposite direction being lower than the annealed yield strength, it is more than doubled! And for 85% deformation, the yield strength in the opposite sense is more than four times the annealed yield strength.

The yield strengths in the opposite direction to the prior deformation for the aluminum listed in Table 5-4 are about 20% lower than the yield strengths in the same direction as the prior deformation. Also, tensile tests conducted on specimens cut out transversely from the deformed material gave results in good agreement with those cut out in the longitudinal direction. For example, a bar of annealed aluminum, after it was stretched in simple tension to a 10% reduc-

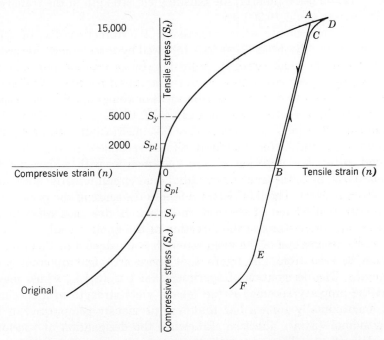

Figure 5-37. Change in the yield strength as a result of large plastic deformation.

TABLE 5-4. Tensile and Compressive Yield Strengths as a
Function of Prior Coldwork

Material 1100-0, aluminum $\sigma = 23,000\epsilon^{0.26}$ from a tension test
on annealed material

Prior Uniaxial Deformation	Yield Strength (0.2% offset) psi	
	In the Direction of Prior Strain	Opposite Direction of Prior Strain
0%	4,800	4,800
10	12,500	10,200
15	13,400	11,500
20	14,400	12,200
33	17,500	14,400
50	19,000	15,000
75	22,400	17,700
85	26,500	20,000

tion of area, had a compressive yield strength in the transverse direction of 12,500 psi. Similarly, the tensile yield strength in the transverse direction was about 10,200 psi.

It is convenient, when discussing the directionality of yield strength, to use the designation (S_y) followed by three letters. According to this code the yield strength would appear as $(S_y)_{123}$, but with the numbers replaced with letters as follows. The first letter is either a lower case t or c to designate tensile yield or compressive yield respectively. The second letter is either a capital L to designate a longitudinal specimen; a capital T for a transverse specimen; capital R for a radial specimen; capital C for a circumferential specimen. In regard to the second letter, the direction of the specimen is with respect to the original bar. Also, the transverse, radial, and circumferential specimens are all equivalent. The third letter refers to the sense of the prior strain in the axial direction of the test specimen. It does not refer to the sense of the prior strain in the direction of the applied load.

This designation of the yield strength is illustrated in Figure 5-38. It can be seen from this figure that there are eight different yield strengths. The designation of specimen No. 1 is $(S_y)_{tLc}$, which means that the property specified is the tensile yield strength of a specimen cut longitudinally from a bar that was previously compressed in the longitudinal (axial) direction. Likewise, the designation of specimen No. 4 is $(S_y)_{cTt}$. This means that the property specified is the compressive yield strength of a specimen cut transverse to the original

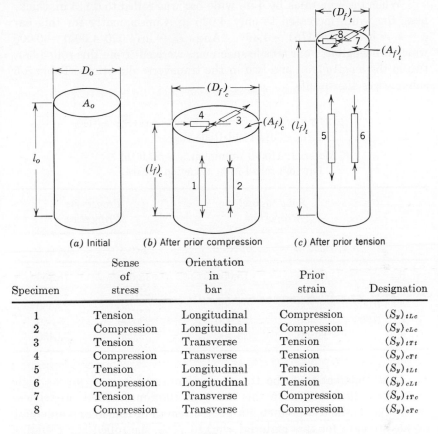

Specimen	Sense of stress	Orientation in bar	Prior strain	Designation
1	Tension	Longitudinal	Compression	$(S_y)_{tLc}$
2	Compression	Longitudinal	Compression	$(S_y)_{cLc}$
3	Tension	Transverse	Tension	$(S_y)_{tTt}$
4	Compression	Transverse	Tension	$(S_y)_{cTt}$
5	Tension	Longitudinal	Tension	$(S_y)_{tLt}$
6	Compression	Longitudinal	Tension	$(S_y)_{cLt}$
7	Tension	Transverse	Compression	$(S_y)_{tTc}$
8	Compression	Transverse	Compression	$(S_y)_{cTc}$

Figure 5-38. Designation of eight different yield strengths of a plastically deformed bar.

loading direction, and the strain during the original deformation was tensile in the transverse direction. The reader should study all eight specimens in Figure 5-38 to be sure that he can interpret all of them.

In another experiment to determine whether there is any significant variation in strength in a material deformed so that the strains in one direction are zero, $\frac{1}{2}$ in. thick by 4 in. wide bars of aluminum were rolled. This aluminum in the annealed condition had a stress-strain relationship of $\sigma = 22,000\epsilon^{0.2}$. This relationship would predict, if strain hardening by rolling is identical to strain hardening by uniaxial tension, a yield strength and tensile strength of 23,300 psi in a bar cold rolled to a 77% reduction of area. ($\epsilon = 1.467$).

When the $\frac{1}{2}$ in. thick by 4 in. wide bar was rolled to 0.115 in. thickness, the width increased to only 4.020 in. Consequently for this bar $\epsilon_r = \epsilon_t = \ln(0.500/0.115) = 1.467$.   And $\epsilon_w = \ln(4.020/4.000) = 0.005$ which is negligible. Four tensile specimens were cut from this rolled bar, two in the longitudinal and two in the transverse directions. Table 5-5 summarizes the results.

TABLE 5-5.   Longitudinal and Transverse Strengths
of a Cold-Rolled bar

Material: 1100-0 aluminum. $\sigma = 22,000\epsilon^{0.2}$.
Bar cold-rolled 77% reduction of area.

	Longitudinal Properties		Transverse Properties	
	Spec. A	Spec. B	Spec. C	Spec. D
S_{pl}	15,000	15,000	18,600	18,350
(S_y) 0.001	18,900	20,400	21,450	22,000
(S_y) 0.002	21,300	21,900	22,250	22,650
(S_y) 0.006	23,400	22,900	23,400	23,350
S_u	23,500	23,400	23,950	23,450

It is apparent that the transverse tensile properties are as high (actually a little higher in this case) as the longitudinal properties. Where the tensile test predicted a yield strength of 23,300 and an equal tensile strength for this material worked 77%, the rolled bar actually had a 0.2% offset yield strength of slightly greater than 22,000 psi and a tensile strength of about 23,500 psi. However, the 0.6% offset yield strength is about 23,400 psi. The reason for the 0.2% offset yield strength being slightly lower than the tensile strength even though the coldworking strain was greater than ϵ_u is the fact that the material after coldworking does not have an elastic line that is linearly proportional all the way up to the value of prior maximum stress. This can be seen by comparing points C and D in Figure 5-36.

REFERENCES

1. ASM, *Cold Working of Metals,* Am. Soc. for Metals, Metal Park, Ohio, 1949.
2. Bauschinger, J. *On The Change in Elastic Limit and Strength of Iron and Steel,* Mitt. Mech. Tech. Lab. Der K. Polytechnische Schule, Munchen, Germany, Vol. 2, No. 13, 1886.

3. Datsko, J. and graduate students, Unpublished research reports, Mechanical Engineering Dept., University of Michigan.
4. Datsko, J. and C. T. Yang, "Correlation of Bendability of Materials with Their Tensile Properties," *Trans. ASME, Series B,* **82,** No. 4, p. 309.
5. Ekelund, S., "The Analysis of Factors Influencing Rolling Pressure and Power Consumption in the Hot Rolling of Steel," *Steel,* **93,** August 21, 1933.
6. Khan, A., *An Investigation of the Anisotrophy of Tensile and Comprehensive Properties of Commerically Pure Aluminum Prestrained Under Simple Direct Stress,* Ph.D. Thesis, Mechanical Engineering Dept., University of Michigan.
7. Underwood, L. R., *The Rolling of Metals,* Vol. 1, John Wiley and Sons, New York, 1950.

STUDY PROBLEMS

5-1   A formed sheet metal part is found to be too flexible. List three ways of making the part more rigid.

5-2   In the cold rolling of brass sheets, reductions in thickness of more than 60% are seldom made without including an annealing step because the material may fracture during rolling. However, during cold extrusion a 2 in. diameter $\times \frac{1}{2}$ in. thick disc of this same brass may be formed into a tube (closed at one end) having a 0.030 in. wall thickness and a length of several inches. Explain briefly.

5-3   Polystyrene is a very common thermoplastic plastic. A standard tensile test showed that it had a 3% reduction area (A_r). In bending a $\frac{1}{8}$ in. thick specimen, fracture occurred when it was bent to a 2 in. radius and it was permanently bent.

CR 39 is a special plastic material used in photoelasticity studies. A standard tensile test showed it had nearly a 0% A_r. However, a $\frac{1}{8}$ in. thick piece of it was also bent to a 2 in. radius before it fractured. The bend specimen was straight after fracture. Explain briefly.

5-4   a. List (and briefly discuss) two reasons why rolled threads and splines are cheaper than machined ones.
       b. Discuss one reason why rolled threads and splines are better (other than cost) than machined ones.

5-5   The fork as illustrated is made of a one-piece ferritic malleable iron casting (T.S. = 30,000 psi, % elongation = 20%). A process engineer submits a report showing that the manufacturing cost can be reduced 20% by making the part from two pieces of AISI 1018 H.R. steel, cold-bending Det. A and welding Det. B to it. What minimum % A_r must be specified when purchasing the steel for Det. A?

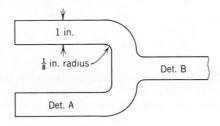

5-6   In forming the turbine wheel shown in (b), a disk (a) is cold pressed by
       means of an "open" die, one-half of which is sketched and distinguished
       by the shading.

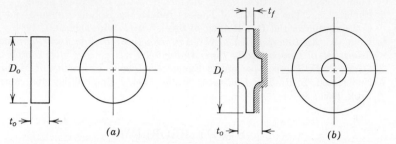

(a)   (b)

a. If D_o is 10 in., D_f is 15 in. and for this material $\sigma = 158,000\epsilon^{0.2}$ $E =$
   40×10^6, $\sigma_y = 37,500$ psi, what is the tensile yield strength of the
   material at the periphery of wheel in the circumferential direction?
b. The compressive yield strength?

5-7   Assume lead and aluminum have the following properties at room
       temperature:

Lead	Aluminum
$S = 2 \times 10^6 \, n$ (up to yield strength)	$S = 10,000,000 \, n$
$\sigma = 2,000 \, \epsilon^0$ (from yield to fracture)	$\sigma = 26,000 \, \epsilon^{0.18}$

a. If a $\frac{1}{2}$ in. diameter $\times$ 1 in. long specimen of lead is stretched to a 2 in.
   length (with uniform cross-sectional area), (1) what is the final load
   on the part? (2) how much work was done on it?
b. If a $\frac{1}{2}$ in. diameter $\times$ 1 in. long specimen of lead is compressed to $\frac{1}{2}$
   in. length (ignore friction between die and specimen), (1) what is the
   final load on the part? (2) how much work was done on it?
c. If a $\frac{1}{2}$ in. diameter $\times$ 1 in. long specimen of aluminum is compressed
   to $\frac{1}{2}$ in. length (ignore friction), (1) what is the final load on the part?
   (2) how much work was done on it?

5-8   In bending I section beams as sketched, "failure" always occurs in the
       nature of buckling on the inside flange.

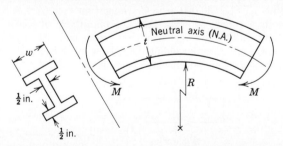

a. If buckling commences when the compressive longitudinal strain is
   five times the yield strain, to what minimum radius R can an aluminum beam be bent that has the following properties and shape?

$$\sigma = 28{,}000\epsilon^{0.20}, \qquad \sigma_y = 10{,}000 \text{ psi} \qquad A_r = 64\%$$

$$t = 6 \text{ in.}, \ w = 4 \text{ in.}, \qquad E = 10 \times 10^6 \text{ psi}$$

    b. If tensile forces were applied longitudinally to the beam while it was being bent, what minimum radius could it then be bent to?

5–9   The following information is available from a tensile specimen of material X.

        Initial size: 0.505 in. diameter; 2 in. G.L.

        Final size: 0.300 in. minimum diameter; 0.420 in. diameter of uniform section outside of necked down region; 2.60 in G.L.

        Loads: Yield = 1600 lb., Maximum = 20,000 lb.

        Bhn = 250 kg/mm^2. Strain at yielding = 0.000152 in./in.

        Assume strain-hardening slope = strain at maximum load.

    a. To what radius can a $\frac{1}{2}$ in. thick sheet be bent?

    b. What "theoretical horsepower" would be required to cold roll a $\frac{1}{2}$ in. thick by 4 ft wide sheet in one pass to the minimum thickness possible without annealing if the peripheral velocity of the rolls is 100 fpm? Assume the no-slip point is at the mid-reduction, and the diameter of rolls is large.

    c. What is the maximum diameter head that can be cold upset on the end of a 1 in. diameter shaft of this material?

    d. How much springback would occur on unloading a cylinder 0.505 in. diameter and 1.0000 in. long (initial unloaded size) after it was compressed to a loaded length of 0.8000 in.?

5–10 A stainless steel is being, considered to make a valve for an internal combustion engine. The following mechanical properties were obtained on an annealed specimen at room temperature: $A_r = 60\%$; the 2 in. gage length is 2.006 in. long when yielding occurs and 2.500 in. long when the maximum load is applied; $E = 28 \times 10^6$ psi.

How many annealing cycles would be required to cold form (upset) a 1 in. diameter head on the end of a $\frac{1}{4}$ in. diameter annealed bar? The piece need not be annealed after the last forming step. Show all of your calculations.

5–11 What is the yield strength of the material in the "head" of the valve in Problem 5–10 after the last forming step? (If you did not solve 5–10, assume the last step deformed the material from 0.8 in. diameter to 1.0 in. diameter.)

5–12 What is the *maximum* yield strength that stainless steel of Problem 5–10 can have?

5–13 In regard to forming equipment, what is the difference between a "hammer" and a "press"?

5–14 The turbine wheel shown below is to be rotated at a very high speed. Design "A" calls for the wheel to be made as a hot forging and machined all over. Design "B" specifies that the wheel be made by cold pressing a flat disc that is 3 in. thick and about 8 in. O.D. into the shape shown here. Which design would you prefer, and why? The material is an austenitic stainless steel.

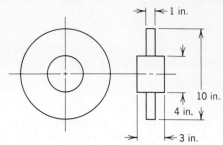

5-15 a. It is desired to cold roll a flat bar of a new experimental material to a smaller thickness. The initial size is $\frac{1}{2}$ in. $\times$ 6 in. $\times$ 72 in. This material has a Y.S. = 150,000 psi, T.S. = 200,000 psi, $E = 40 \times 10^6$ psi, $\sigma_f = 350,000$ psi, per cent reduction area = 10. What minimum thickness do you estimate this bar can be rolled to without annealing?

b. If the peripheral velocity of the rolls is 120 fpm in the problem above, and ignoring friction, what horsepower motor is required to drive the rolls?

5-16 A new high-strength alloy has been developed that is being considered for use in missile skins. Tensile tests have been conducted on this material, both at room temperature and and at elevated temperatures in as much as this is a high speed missile. One of the results of these tests is the following relationship: $\epsilon_f = 0.000645 \ T^{0.84}$ for temperatures above 50°F, where T = temperature in °F and ϵ_f is the true strain at fracture.

Can the manufacturing department form a $1\frac{1}{4}$ in. radius in a sheet that is $\frac{1}{16}$ in. thick? Explain.

5-17 The mechanical properties of steel and cast iron are listed below:

Steel	Cast Iron
Y.S. = 40,000 psi	Y.S. = 30,000 psi
T.S. = 60,000 psi	T.S. = 30,000 psi
$A_r = 60\%$	$A_r = 0\%$
$m = 0.25$	$m = $ is nonexistent
$\mu = 0.3$	$\mu = 0.3$
$\sigma = 120,000\epsilon^{0.25}$	

Cylinders as sketched of each metal are loaded axially:
(1) What tensile load will cause failure on the basis of Y.S.?
(2) What tensile load will cause fracture (or appearance of cracks)?
(3) What compressive load will cause failure on the basis of Y.S.?

(4) What compressive load will cause fracture (or cracks)?

(5) Is cast iron relatively strong in compression?

5-18 Define or describe the following: (1) wrinkling, (2) ironing, (3) hobing, (4) die, (5) drawing, (6) roll forging, and (7) stretch forming.

5-19 Define or describe the Bauschinger effect and explain how it applies to forming.

5-20 Define or describe: (1) swagging, (2) spinning, and (3) mandrel.

5-21 An annealed material has the following mechanical properties:

$$E = 15 \times 10^6 \text{ psi}; \ \sigma = 100,000 \ (\epsilon + 0.015)^{0.5}$$

a. Estimate its annealed yield strength and tensile strength.

b. Which of the two values calculated is more reliable?

5-22 A given 1020 steel has the following mechanical properties:

$$S_y = 40,000 \text{ psi}; S_u = 60,000 \text{ psi}; A_r = 60\%;$$

$$m = 0.25; \ \mu = 0.3; \ \sigma_o = 120,000 \text{ psi}.$$

If a $\frac{1}{2}$ in. diameter $\times 1$ in. long cylinder is compressed axially between flat frictionless dies, what compressive load will cause failure (cracks) to occur?

5-23 A material has a strain hardenability that can be expressed as $\sigma = 10^5 \epsilon^{0.25}$. Also $\epsilon_y = 0.002$ and $\epsilon_f = 0.91$. Plot the curves of yield strength versus per cent coldwork and tensile strength versus per cent coldwork for this material.

5-24 A 1 in. thick plate of hot rolled 1020 steel is bent to a 1 in. inside radius. Assume the neutral axis remains at $t/2$ and for this steel $\sigma = 120,000\epsilon^{0.2}$, $\epsilon_f = 1$, $E = 30 \times 10^6$, and $S_y = 30,000$ psi. On coordinates as illustrated, plot the stress versus radial position while the bar is subjected to the bending load.

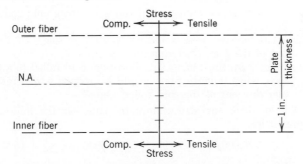

5-25 It is desired to have a ring of 1100 aluminum that is 2 in. O.D. $\times 1\frac{7}{8}$ in. I.D. $\times 2$ in. wide with a yield strength of 18,000 psi. For this aluminum $\sigma = 25,000\epsilon^{0.2}$ and $A_r = 85\%$. If the part is to be formed by "ring rolling" an annealed ring as illustrated in the sketch, what should be the size of the annealed ring? (*Note:* As the ring rotates, the outer roll feeds in slowly until the final wall thickness is obtained.)

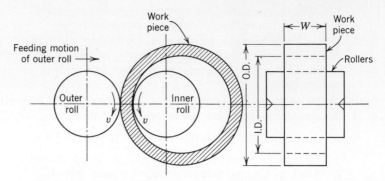

5–26   An annealed stainless steel has these tensile properties: $\sigma = 250,000$
$(\epsilon + 0.008)^{0.52}$, and $A_r = 70\%$.
a. What is the true fracture stress of a tensile specimen of this material?
b. To what final height could a cylinder 3 in. in diameter $\times$ 6 in. long
be compressed without annealing?
c. What would be the final load on the cylinder?
d. If a tensile specimen were machined in an axial or longitudinal direction from the coldworked cylinder, what would be its yield
strength?

5–27   Some aluminum bars tested gave the following data: $\sigma = 26,600\epsilon^{0.21}$,
$\epsilon_f = 2.2$, and $(S_y)_{ann} = 4800$ psi.
a. A $\frac{1}{2}$ in. thick $\times$ 24 in. wide plate of this annealed material is cold
rolled to a thickness of $\frac{1}{8}$ in. A $\frac{1}{8}$ in. thick $\times$ 1 in. wide $\times$ 2 in.
gage length "transverse" tensile specimen is machined from the
plate. What should be its tensile yield strength?
b. If the tensile specimen of (a) were a "longitudinal" one, what maximum load should it support?
c. To what inside radius could the $\frac{1}{8}$ in. thick cold rolled plate of (a)
be bent?
d. What tonnage press would be required to shear a 3 in. diameter disc
out of the $\frac{1}{2}$ in. thick annealed plate?
e. If the $\frac{1}{2}$ in. thick annealed plate were cold rolled to a 0.450 in. thickness, what tonnage press would be required to blank a 3 in. diam-
eter disc out of the cold rolled plate?

5–28. A 1 in. thick annealed aluminum plate has the following mechanical
properties:

$$\sigma = 26,000\epsilon^{0.2}, A_r = 90\%, S_y = 5000 \text{ psi}, S_{pl} = 1500 \text{ psi}$$

a. What is its tensile strength?
b. The above plate is cold rolled to a thickness of $\frac{1}{2}$ in. A longitudinal
tensile specimen is machined from the cold-rolled plate. What are the
yield and tensile strength of the specimen?
c. What should be the per cent reduction of area of the tensile specimen
of (b)?

6

The Machining Process

The technological advances in the field of machining during the past 100 years have made this manufacturing process a very important and essential one. It may be said that the machine tool is to our mechanized era what power was to the industrial revolution. In fact, without our machine tools the engines that provide our industrial and domestic power would be nonexistent. For example, although James Watt *designed* a steam engine with a separate condenser in 1775, it took 25 years to *make it*—even with the help of one of England's best machine builders. In his day, it was considered a major achievement when a cylinder was bored so that "when a piston was tightly fitted at one end, a clearance not greater than the thickness of a shilling was present at the other end." Today, cylinders can be bored to an accuracy of a thousandth of an inch (0.001 in.) without much difficulty and with care to a ten-thousandth of an inch (0.0001 in.).

During the past 150 years, our American manufacturing industries have been much superior to those of the rest of the world in terms of quantity and efficiency of production. This all stems from "mass-production," a manufacturing technique conceived in the United States in 1800 by Eli Whitney in the manufacture of muskets. Prior to that time, even in the government's armory at Springfield, Massachusetts, muskets were custom-made; soft parts were fitted together by the "trying and filing" technique, then hardened and set. Consequently, no two muskets were exactly alike, and their parts could not be interchanged. At that time, when France and England were at war and the United States was increasing its military facilities in case it became involved, there was a tremendously impressed board of government officials and army officers who saw the first demonstration of the results of "mass-production." Out of a box containing ten dismantled muskets, parts were selected at random and before the astonished eyes of the officials, ten complete muskets were rapidly and easily assembled. But even more amazing than this feat, the jigs and fixtures and machine tools of Whitney's factory could produce with ease thousands and thousands of muskets, all exactly alike. Out of this arose our American industrialization. Without machine tools and the machining process, this would not have been possible.

DEFINITION

Machining is the manufacturing process in which the size, shape, or surface properties of a part are changed by *removing* the excess material. This is in contrast to forming where the materials is simply *moved*. Machining may be accomplished by locally straining the material to fracture through the relative motion of a tool and the work piece, as is done in the conventional processes. However, the material-removal mechanism may be chemical, electrical or thermal as in the case of the unconventional processes such as chem-milling, electrolytic, or electro-arc machining, respectively. In this light, flame cutting is a chemical machining process.

Machining is a relatively expensive process that should be specified only when high accuracy and good surface finish are required, which, unfortunately, is necessary for almost all mating parts. Machining today is almost exclusively performed by means of *machine tools*, which are power-driven machines that have provisions to hold and move the work piece as well as to hold and move a *cutting tool*. These new terms will all be described briefly.

Cutting Conditions

The cutting conditions in machining usually refer to those variables that are easily changed at the machine tool by the operator and that affect the rate of metal removal. They are: the tool material and shape, the cutting speed, and the size of cut, which refers to the feed and depth. The tool materials and the effect of tool shape on the performance of the tool are discussed in following sections. In general, we can say that the keener or sharper the cutting edge, the better the performance of the tool.

The *cutting speed, v,* is defined as the largest of the relative velocities between the cutting tool and the work material, and is expressed with the units of feet per minute. In some machines it is the work that reciprocates or rotates to provide the cutting speed, whereas in other machine tools it is the cutter that moves to provide the cutting speed. The effect of the cutting speed on the tool life (the number of minutes that a cutting tool can cut before the cutting edge is worn away) is an exponential relationship that may be expressed as: $t = Kv^{-m}$, where t is the minutes of cutting time until the tool becomes dull, v is the cutting speed, and K and m are constants for a given cutting condition. The constant K is very large, of the order of 10^8, and the exponent m is of the order of 10. Thus, it is apparent that for a small decrease in the cutting speed, the tool life will be increased greatly.

In general, it is more convenient in referring to the cutting speed-tool life relationship to violate the principles of dependent and independent variables and to rewrite the expression as $vt^n = C$. In this form, C is a constant for each cutting condition with a range of values from 10 for very hard steel to 10^4 for very soft magnesium when the machining is done with a high speed steel tool. In general, for a given work material, the value of C for a carbide tool is three to five times as large as for a HSS tool; for a ceramic tool it is five to eight times as large. In reality, C is the cutting speed that results in a one-minute tool life. Thus a material having a C value of 150 will cause the tool to fail in one minute if it is machined at a cutting speed of 150 fpm.

The exponent n varies from 0.05 to 0.15 for most work materials when a high speed steel tool is used and whenever actual values are not known, the value of 0.1 may be used. The average value of n for carbide and ceramic tools is generally given as 0.2 and 0.4, respectively. This equation, known as the Taylor equation, is discussed in more detail in a following section entitled "Tool Life."

The *depth of cut d* is defined as the distance the cutting tool projects below the original surface of the work and is expressed in thousandths of an inch. The depth of cut determines one of the linear dimensions of the cross-sectional area of the size of cut. In general, an increase in the depth of cut will result in a nonlinear increase in temperature and a decrease in tool life.

The *feed f* is defined as the relative lateral movement between the tool and the work during a machining operation. On the lathe and drill press it is expressed with the units inches per revolution (ipr). On the shaper it is expressed as inches per stroke (ips). On the milling machine it is expressed in inches per tooth (ipt) although the machine controls are designed with the units inches per minute (ipm), which is the product of the basic feed times the number of teeth in the cutter times the revolutions per minute of the cutter. The feed is the second linear dimension that determines the cross-sectional area of the size of the cut. In determining the cutting time for a given operation the feed F (in./min.) is used. It is the product of the feed f and the rpm or spm (strokes per minute).

The product of the proper speed, feed, and depth of cut determines the rate of metal removal which is expressed as cubic inches per minute. On the lathe, in turning operations, the rate of metal removal is obtained from the expression 12 *vfd*. In drilling, for example, it would be the product of the feed (ipr) times the RPM of the drill times the cross-sectional area of the drilled hole. The effect of the size of cut on the efficiency of machining is discussed in detail in two following sections under the headings "Tool Life" and "Machinability."

CHIP-FORMING MACHINE TOOLS

There are six basic types of machine tools: lathe or turning machine; drilling or boring machine; shaper or planer; milling machine; grinder; and press. The first four, referred to as the basic machine tools, are similar in that they use cutting tools that are sharpened to a predetermined shape; whereas, the cutting edges on a grinding wheel are not controlled. In general, the accuracy and surface finish obtainable on these machine tools may be summarized as follows: (1) for the basic machine tools, a surface finish of 50 to 250 rms (microinches), and an accuracy of ±0.005 in. with ease; (2) for the grinding machines, a surface finish of 5 to 60 rms, and an accuracy of ±0.0001 in. with care and ±0.001 in. with ease.

Although presses are used for shearing, blanking, and piercing operations which are chip-forming processes and as such can be included with chip-forming machine tools, they are more commonly associated with the forming (chipless-machining) operations. Con-

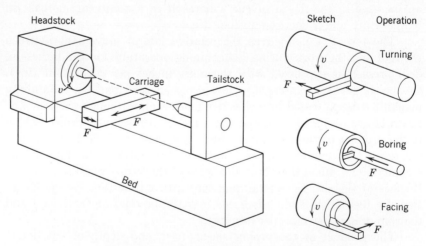

Figure 6-1. Schematic drawing of a lathe.

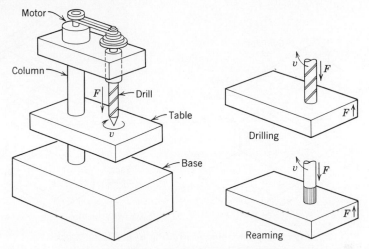

Figure 6-2. Schematic drawing of a drill press.

sequently, in this text, they are discussed as is traditionally done in Chapter 5 on Forming.

The basic motions possible with metal-cutting machine tools and the most commonly performed operations are illustrated in Figures 6-1 to 6-5. The surfaces that may be generated by machine tools fall into four general types: (1) plane, (2) external cylindrical, (3) internal cylindrical, and (4) irregular. In general, plane and irregular surfaces are machined on the shaper, milling machine, and lathe. External and internal cylindrical surfaces are created on lathes and

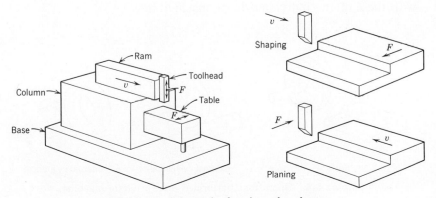

Figure 6-3. Schematic drawing of a shaper.

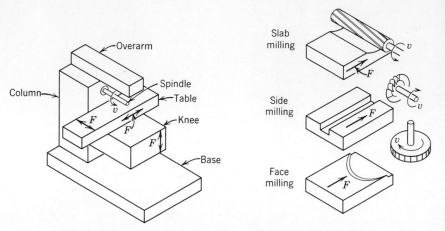

Figure 6-4. *Schematic drawing of a milling machine.*

drilling machines. Although drilling machines usually produce internal cylindrical surfaces, they are sometimes used to produce internal flat surfaces in operations such as spot-facing or counter boring. The grinding machines can produce any of the surfaces that the four basic machine tools can produce and with much better surface finishes and greater accuracy, but with correspondingly reduced rates of metal removal. Consequently, grinding is usually performed only as a final finishing operation.

In today's era of "mass-production" and "automation" many special-purpose machine tools are designed and built that combine operations of all four of the basic machines. Consequently they cannot be readily classified even though their basic motions are identical with those of the individual basic machine tool.

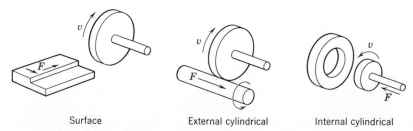

Surface   External cylindrical   Internal cylindrical

Figure 6-5. Operations performed on a grinding machine.

One design feature common to all machine tools is the materials they are made of. Except for parts such as gears and bearings, all of the machine tools in the past were made of cast iron, and the better ones had the ways (sliding surfaces) flame hardened. Several years ago, some of the more expensive machine tools replaced the integral flame-hardened cast iron ways with hardened and ground tool-steel inserts to give them longer life. But more recently several machine tool builders have designed and constructed all-steel-welded machines in both the light duty and heavy duty sizes.

The advantage of a welded steel structure over a cast iron one is that greater strength and rigidity are obtained for a given weight. Also in many cases, especially for heavy parts and those requiring only a little machining, a welded steel structure is less expensive than a cast iron one. As may be seen in Appendix H, the basic cost of cast iron is two or more times the cost of wrought steel.

One advantage of cast iron over steel is its greater vibration dampening capacity, which is one of the main reasons why cast iron was the exclusive material used for machine bases. But more recently it has been found that the vibration dampening capacity of cast iron decreases with an increase in the applied stress so that when the cast iron is under load this advantage is markedly reduced. Also, by incorporating a vibration analysis in the functional design of a machine, it is possible to control the vibrations in a machine so they are less objectionable.

The capabilities, characteristics, and design features of the individual types of machine tools are described in detail in the following sections.

Lathes and Turning Machines

Lathes and turning machines, as illustrated in Figure 6-1, are those machine tools that have provisions for: rotating a clamped work piece to obtain the cutting velocity and slowly moving a cutting tool that is attached to a carriage or tail stock to obtain the "feeding" motion. The cutting tool may be a single-point tool bit, a form tool, a drill, a reamer, and so forth.

The feeding motion is parallel to the axis of rotation of the work piece when "turning" an external cylindrical surface or "boring" an internal cylindrical surface. Plane surfaces are "faced" on a work piece by feeding the tool in a direction perpendicular to the axis of rotation. To form a tapered or conical surface, the line of the feeding motion is inclined to the axis of rotation of the work; that is, both parallel and perpendicular components are present. And finally, irregular contours are machined by using variable ratios of parallel and normal components of feeding directions. The surfaces formed by the four processes described are referred to as generated surfaces. Of course, all four generated surfaces can be obtained by using "form" tools, that is, tools that have the desired part contour ground onto their end. When making form cuts, the feeding motion is perpendicular to that used to generate the same surface.

The efficiency of a turning cut, as is true of all machining operations, depends upon the size of the cut, the tool shape, and the cutting speed. In a later section on machinability, relationships between the cutting speed for a given tool life and the size of cut are presented in detail. For now, it is sufficient to classify turning cuts into three arbitrary sizes—small, average, and large. Small, or light, cuts usually have a feed of less than 0.005 ipr and a depth cut of less than $\frac{1}{16}$ in. Average-sized cuts may be considered as those having a feed of 0.005 to 0.015 ipr and a range of depth from $\frac{1}{16}$ to $\frac{1}{4}$ in. Large, or heavy cuts are those having a feed of 0.015 to about 0.100 ipr and depths of cut varying between $\frac{1}{4}$ and 1 in. These three classes are quite arbitrary and are presented only as a guide to give the reader a quantitative appreciation of the capabilities of the industrial machining processes.

Figure 6-6 shows a lathe with its various components and attachments identified by name. This lathe is typical of the hundreds of models on the market today which all consist of the same five basic components: bed, headstock, tailstock, carriage, and feed box. The variations in the different models of lathes are in their size; type of motor drive; attachments, and the number of speeds, feeds, and carriages. The description of lathes and turning machines that follows is divided into two sections, basic components and attachments.

Basic Components of Turning Machines

Bed. The bed of a lathe or other type turning machine is the base of the machine tool: it is raised from the floor to the proper working height (approximately waist-high) by two or more legs and it serves as a support for the other four basic components. The top portion of the bed has two sets of longitudinal ways, usually a combination of vee or flat surfaces, that go the entire length of the bed. These ways serve two functions: (1) to provide accurate locating or aligning surfaces for the headstock, tailstock, carriage, and other attachments, and (2) provide sliding surfaces on which the carriage and tailstock can freely move.

Figure 6-6. Photograph of a toolroom-type engine lathe. This model has a step-less variable speed range. (Courtesy Monarch Machine Tool Co.)
(*a*) Headstock. (*b*) Tailstock. (*c*) Carriage. (*d*) Bed. (*e*) Feed box. (*f*) On-off.
(*g*) Forward -reverse switch. (*h*) Back gear lever. (*i*) Speed rheostat. (*j*) Tachometer. (*k*) Feed-thread selector. (*l*) Chart. (*m*) Coarse feed selector. (*o*) Fine feed selector. (*p*) Carriage feed. (*q*) Carriage feed clutch. (*r*) Feed reverse. (*s*) Cross slide. (*t*) Cross-slide clutch. (*u*) Compound screw. (*v*) Thread cut lever.

Headstock. The headstock is an enclosed power train accurately mounted on the ways, usually at the left end of the bed. The power is transmitted to the headstock from the motor that is usually mounted in a leg of the bed by means of multiple belt vee pulleys. On most modern lathes the power is transmitted inside the headstock to the spindle shaft with provisions for a range of speeds by means of gear trains. However, some low-priced lathes utilize belt-driven pulleys of varying diameters for a range of speeds.

The main shaft in the headstock is referred to as the spindle shaft, and is hollow so as to allow long bars of work material to extend through the headstock while being machined. The end of this shaft extends outside the headstock housing facing the tailstock and is called the spindle. The internal surface of the spindle is tapered to accommodate such work-holding devices as centers, sleeved chucks, and collets. The external surface of the spindle is either threaded or tapered so that work-holding devices such as chucks, face plates, and collets can be attached.

The speeds in rpm of the geared-head type of lathe usually vary in a geometric progression of the type

$$N = N_1 r^{n-1} \qquad (6\text{-}1)$$

where N is the speed in rpm, N_1 is the first or lowest speed, r is the geometric progression ratio, and n is the sequential number of the speed—first, second, third, and so forth. The ratio r for most machine tools varies from about 1.6 for an 8-speed head and 1.2 for a 20-speed head. A typical lathe may have eight speeds, the lowest being 20 rpm. Thus, the second speed would be

$$N_2 = 20 \times 1.6 = 32 \text{ rpm}$$

and the eighth speed would be

$$N_8 = 20 \times 1.6^7 = 540 \text{ rpm}$$

The reason for using a geometric progression of this type is to obtain well-balanced speed increments at both the low-speed range and the high-speed range.

A few lathes have an infinitely variable speed adjustment with a range of speeds extending from near zero rpm to several thousand rpm. Lathes of this type employ a dc motor, with the direct current being obtained either by using an ac motor-generator setup or else by rectifying the alternating current.

Tailstock. The tailstock is the component of the lathe that is mounted on the ways of the bed opposite the headstock and consists of two parts—the lower portion that contacts and is located by the ways, and the upper portion that contains the tailstock spindle. Unlike the headstock, the tailstock is not permanently fixed in one place on the bed, but it may be slid along the ways by hand and locked in place anywhere along the length of the bed. In addition, the top portion of the tailstock may be moved in a horizontal direction so that the tailstock spindle is parallel to, and offset a small amount from, the axis of the headstock. This adjustment is frequently made when it is desired to turn long tapers having small included angles.

The tailstock spindle is moved in and out of its housing by means of a hand wheel. The end of the tailstock spindle that faces the headstock is referred to as the quill, and contains an internal Morse taper. (A Morse taper is the standard taper used on taper-shank drills, reamers, and similar rotating tools and has a $\frac{5}{8}$ in. change in diameter per foot of length.) This tapered hole is provided to hold and locate centers to support long work pieces and such tools as drills, reamers, and so forth, to perform machining operations on the end of rotating work pieces.

Carriage. The carriage is an I-shaped component of the lathe which slides along the ways between the headstock and the tailstock. The carriage has two main functions—a combination support and carrier of the cutting tool, and a housing for the power-train which transmits the feeding motion to the tool.

The carriage is really an assembly of the following subcomponents: the carriage frame (which includes the cross-slide screw), the compound, and the apron. The operation of the carriage assembly will be briefly described since it is not very obvious to the beginner.

The *carriage frame* slides longitudinally on the outer ways of the bed with the top and bottom flange of the I-frame serving as the bearing surfaces. A set of dovetail slides and a cross-slide screw are incorporated in the center section of the I-frame, and they are perpendicular to the longitudinal axis of the bed. The *compound*, which has provisions for holding various types of cutting tools, has a mating set of dovetail slides along which it moves over the carriage frame. The power is transmitted by means of a nut that engages the cross-slide screw.

The *apron* is that part of the carriage that hangs in front of the bed, and includes the gears and clutches that translate the rotating motion of the feed rod and lead screw into the straight line motion of the carriage frame or the compound. The power for *feeding* is transmitted from the feed rod through friction clutches in the apron and consequently the motion is not considered positive. That is, if the resistance to motion of the carriage is large (a large feeding force), the clutch will slip and the carriage will not move.

On the other hand, for machining threads, the motion of the carriage should be accurate and positive. Consequently, the power for *threading* is transmitted from the threaded lead screw through a split nut in the apron.

Feed box. The feed box is a low speed-low power transmitting quick-change gear box that provides a range of rotational speeds to the feed rod and the lead screw. The power input to the feed box comes from a take-off gear on the headstock spindle. Thus, the rotation of both the feed rod and the lead screw, and consequently the translation of the carriage, is synchronized with the rotation of the spindle. Because of this, the basic feed (f) on a lathe or turning machine is expressed as "thousandths of an inch per revolution," that is, 0.001 ipr.

If a lathe is set up to provide a given feed such as 0.010 ipr with a particular rotational speed of the spindle, the feed will remain the same, 0.010 ipr in this case, if the spindle speed is doubled. However, the carriage will move twice as fast along the ways in terms of the bulk feed ($F = fN$) which has the units of ipm.

Specification of lathe size. The size of a lathe is specified by two linear dimensions—*swing* and *length*. The length is always given as the maximum distance between centers. That is, it is the length of the longest bar or cylinder that can be supported between the headstock and tailstock centers with the tailstock placed as far to the end of the bed as possible. There are two methods of determining and designating the swing. Therefore it is necessary to decide whenever a numerical value is given for the swing which method was used to measure it.

The more common of the two methods of specifying the swing is by giving twice the distance between the center line of the spindle and the highest point on the compound, exclusive of the tool-holder support. According to this method, if a lathe had the size specifications of 16 in. x 48 in. then it means that the longest bar which could be supported between centers is 48 in., and the largest diameter cylinder that could be turned between the centers is 16 in.

However, if a short cylinder is to be turned or faced by holding it in a chuck or on a face plate, then a much larger diameter cylinder than 16 in. can be machined on the same lathe mentioned above. In this case the swing is twice the distance between the spindle center line and the top of the flanges of the carriage frame. For a medium-duty lathe of the type mentioned above with an 8 in. distance from the spindle center to the compound, the distance from the spindle center to the flanges of the carriage frame would be approximately 12 in. Consequently, the swing as specified by the second method would be 24 in.

Lathe Attachments

The attachments or accessories that are frequently used on lathes or other turning machines are briefly described next. Since we are concentrating on only the fundamentals of the processes important to an engineer, and do it with a reasonable number of pages, a small number of photographs and sketches are used. (This same approach is taken in other portions of this textbook.) So, supplementary visual aids and live demonstrations are again recommended by the author for highlighting explanations of the uses and operations of all attachments and accessories. If the reader is not enrolled in a formal class, he should seek out as supplementary material any one of the dozens of texts that describe in detail the equipment associated with the manufacturing processes.

Work Holding Devices. The *three-jaw universal* (self-centering) chuck is probably the most frequently used of all the work holding devices on turning machines even though its use is restricted to work pieces having circular or hexagonal cross sections. The construction and the operation of this type of chuck is relatively simple.

To clamp a work piece, a square-ended chuck or tee wrench is inserted in the square-shaped recess in the end of the shaft of any one of three equally spaced pinion gears. These pinion gears are located beneath the chuck face with their longitudinal axes in a radical direction and the recessed ends of the shafts are flush with the circumferential surface of the chuck body. The pinion gears are enmeshed with the gear teeth which are on one side of a disc having its center on the axis of rotation of the spindle. The opposite face of this disc contains a scroll that is actually a spiral square thread. The three chuck jaws enmesh with the scroll so that they all simultaneously move inward or outward, depending upon the direction of rotation of the chuck wrench.

Three-jaw chucks that are new or in good condition will clamp circular work material to an accuracy of about 0.001 in; that is, the surface which is in contact with the jaws will be concentric to the axis of rotation to an accuracy of about 0.001 in. tir (total indicator reading). However, after considerable use the accuracy of a three jaw chuck will be closer to 0.01 in.

The main advantage of the three jaw chuck is that because it is selfcentering, the time required to clamp and locate a circular or hexagonal work piece is relatively short in comparison to the time required when a non-self-centering chuck is used.

The *four-jaw independent* chuck, as the name implies, is nonselfcentering but instead each jaw moves inward or outward independently of the others. This type of chuck is different in construction from the previously described chuck: the chuck wrench engages a shaft that has an acme thread machined on it and the inner face of the chuck jaw has a mating thread. In other words, it resembles a simple screw and nut arrangement.

When a skilled operator exercises care in clamping a work piece in an independent chuck, the clamped surface may be located to an accuracy of about 0.0001 in. However, this accurate clamping operation does require a considerable amount of time since each jaw is adjusted individually and the position of the work piece is checked continuously with a dial indicator type gage. But if accuracies in the order of 0.01 in. are satisfactory, the clamping time with an independent chuck is not much greater than with a universal chuck.

The four-jaw chuck is used to clamp work material having an irregular cross section as well as for accurate clamping of round parts.

Both the universal and the independent type of chucks are made in sizes ranging from a 6 in. diameter to a diameter of several feet.

Collets, or as they are some times called, *spring chucks*, are a special type of work or tool-holding device. The size of collets, which is really the diameter, or distance between flats, of the hole as well as the work material that it clamps, varies from as small as a fraction of an inch to as large as several inches.

Collets are hollow cylinders having a length equal to about four times its outside diameter and a $\frac{1}{8}$ to $\frac{1}{4}$ in. wall thickness. Although the outer surface has a circular cross section, the inner surface may have a circular, square, hexagonal, or irregular cross section. The end of the collet that fits into the headstock spindle is threaded so that it can be attached to the drawbar mechanism that provides the motion for clamping the collet over the work piece. See Figure 6-11*f*.

The opposite end of the collet has two distinct features. First, it has three equally spaced slots that go completely through the wall thickness and extend for a length slightly greater than one-half the length of the collet. These slots give the collet its "spring" effect; that is, it allows this end of the collet to be compressed to a smaller diameter and thus tightly clamp the work piece. The second feature on this end of the collet is the tapered, or conical, outer $\frac{1}{2}$ in. or so of the surface with the diameter increasing toward the end of the collet. This shape accounts for the contracting inner dimension of the collet as it is drawn into the mating taper of the headstock spindle sleeve by the drawbar mechanism.

The accuracy, in terms of concentricity, that can be obtained with collets is very good; as good as with an independent chuck. A second advantage of collets is that the clamping time is very short; it is usually less than that required with a universal chuck.

Centers which are inserted in the headstock and tailstock spindle are the type of work-holding device used to hold long shafts, that is, shafts having a length to diameter ratio greater than approximately 10. (If the slenderness ratio exceeds the value of about 50, then the midlength of the shaft must also be supported by either a *steady-rest* or a *follow-rest* during the time that cutting is taking place near the mid-length.) Also, short shafts that are to be heat treated and ground as well as those having several different and concentric diameters are supported by centers during machining.

Two types of centers are used. The older and most commonly used type is the *solid* center. The portion of the center that fits into the internal Morse-tapered headstock or tailstock spindle is a truncated cone having a maximum diameter that varies from about $\frac{1}{2}$ in. for the smallest size to about 2 in. for the largest size. The length of this section of the center is about five times the diameter. The opposite end of the center, which is the work supporting end, is a cone having a 60° angle. The solid centers are usually made of high speed steel, and a slightly more expensive variety has an inserted tip of a cast-nonferrous or sintered carbide alloy for that portion of the 60° cone that mates with the center drilled holes in the work piece.

The center that is inserted in the headstock spindle is sometimes referred to as the "live" center since it rotates with the work piece. Consequently, this center needs no lubrication. The tailstock center is referred to as the "dead" center, and since there is relative motion between it and the work piece, it must be well lubricated with a high pressure lubricant like white lead paste.

The second type of center is the *antifriction* bearing type. In this center the work-supporting cone is not integrally attached to the Morse taper shank as it is in the solid type. Instead, the two conical portions of the center are connected by means of an antifriction bearing so that the 60° cone can rotate with the work piece while the Morse taper shank is stationary in the tailstock spindle. This center is more expensive and less rigid than the solid type, but it can be used to support work pieces rotating at higher speeds.

Sometimes a shaft is clamped in a chuck at the headstock and supported with a center only at the tailstock end. The transmission of the power from the headstock spindle to the work piece is through the chuck. But when the work is supported between two centers, the chuck is replaced with a slotted disc called a *driving plate*. Also, a special clamp called a "lathe dog" is attached on the headstock end of the work piece in such a way that a projection (the "dog's tail") fits into one of the slots in the driving plate. The torque to rotate the work piece is thus transmitted through the driving plate and the dog.

In order for work pieces such as shafts to be supported between centers, it is necessary to first drill center holes in the ends of the shaft. Center holes are drilled with a combination drill and countersink that is frequently referred to as a *center drill*. See Figure 6-10a.

Mandrels are used to support hollow work pieces such as gear and pulley blanks which cannot have center holes drilled in them. In some cases, the mandrel is simply a shaft having a taper of about 0.005 in./ft. and with concentric center holes at the ends. The hollow, previously reamed or bored, work pieces are pressed onto the mandrel, machined and then pressed off the mandrel. Another type of mandrel, referred to as a stub-arbor, consists of a stepped or two-diameter shaft with a thread on the end of the small diameter shaft. With a mandrel of this type, the work piece or pieces are slipped onto the small diameter shaft. Then, by means of a washer and nut, the work piece is pressed tightly against the shoulder of the larger diameter.

Face plates, which are slotted discs somewhat larger in diameter than driving plates, are mounted on the headstock spindle and are frequently used to hold flat plates or irregularly shaped castings and forgings. Parts of this type are attached to the face plate by means of bolts and clamps. The proper location of the work piece on the face plate is usually made by means of dial indicators when only a few parts are to be machined. When there are many parts to be made, the special rapid locating fixtures are attached to the face plate.

Turret Lathes

A turret lathe is a lathe in which the tailstock is in the form of an indexing turret that is power fed by means of the same feed rod that powers the carriage. A typical one is illustrated in Figure 6-7. The hexagonal tailstock turret can hold a large variety of cutting tools, with as many as three or four tools mounted on each of the six turret faces. All tools are preset to the proper position to machine the work piece to the required dimensional tolerances. Each turret position has associated with it an adjustable stop that disengages the power feed and prevents any further advance of the turret, including manual feed. Consequently a turret lathe may be considered as a semi-automatic lathe since finished parts can be produced by an operator with little experience after an experienced "set-up man" had adjusted all the tools. The machine operator need only to continuously go through the following cycle of motions: advance the turret by rotating the large hand wheel counter-clockwise until the cutting tool nearly touches the work piece; raise the lever that engages the power feed; then while waiting for the cutting operation to terminate, he may file burrs or inspect the previous piece, depending on how cost conscious the management is; and retract the turret by rotating the hand wheel clockwise after the power feed is automatically disengaged (the turret automaticallly indexes in a clockwise direction to the next station during this retracting operation). This

Figure 6-7. Photograph of a ram type turret lathe. This model has a maximum capacity of 2 in. diameter bar stock. (Courtesy Warner & Swasey Co.)

sequence continues through six indexes, at which time the part is complete and, if bar stock is being used, this part is cut off by means of a special parting tool mounted on the carriage.

In addition to these described differences in the tailstock, the carriage of a turret lathe differs from that of an engine lathe in that it normally has two tool holders, a front one and a rear one. The front tool holder is usually an indexable square turret that holds single point cutting tools in each of its four corners. Like the tailstock turret, the carriage turret is equipped with preset stops that automatically disengage the power feed when the proper linear dimension on the part is reached. The rear tool holder normally contains either a form tool or a cutoff tool clamped in an inverted position.

The same type of facing, turning, boring, drilling, reaming, etc., tools that are used on lathes are also used on turret lathes. Threading with a single-point tool is not done on a turret lathe. Instead, collapsible taps and expanding dieheads that more or less automatically thread a shaft are used. They are described in more detail in the section on thread cutting.

Automatic Turning Machines

Although the automatic turret lathes and screw machines are usually special-purpose machine tools, and come in a large variety of shapes and sizes, they all may be generally called turret lathes which are fully operated by means of cams, hydraulic cylinders, or electric relays. Chucking-type automatic turret lathes that machine castings or forgings may have a completely automatic work loading attachment so that there is no interruption in the machining operation. Screw machines, which are automatic turret lathes that use 10 to 20 ft long bars of work material held in collets, have automatic work feeding and collet locking devices on them so that the spindle does not need to be stopped to advance the work material for the succeeding part. Figure 6-8 shows a typical automatic turning machine.

Automatic turning machines are divided into two classes: single spindle and multiple spindle. In the single spindle machines one piece is worked on at a time. However, in the multiple spindle machine as

Figure 6-8. Photograph of an automatic turning machine with covers removed to show the cams. (Courtesy Brown & Sharpe Co.)

many as four to eight pieces may be worked on simultaneously, each clamped in a separate spindle which indexes at the completion of each operation.

In summary, we can state as a general guide that lathes are used to make parts when the number required varies from one to several thousand; turret lathes are used when the number of parts required varies from several dozen to a hundred thousand; automatic turning machines are used when the number of parts required varies from several thousand to several million.

Taper Cutting

There are four common ways to machine a taper on a lathe. A taper attachment is very frequently used when the length of the taper being cut is in the range of several inches to several feet. The taper attachment consists of an auxiliary set of short ways, or dovetails, that are attached to the opposite side of the lathe from the apron. It is locked in place along the length of the lathe during the taper cutting operation. These auxiliary ways may be pivoted about an axis at their mid-length so that they may be set at an angle to the lathe bed equal to one-half of the included angle of the desired taper. A mating block that slides on the auxiliary ways is attached to the cross-slide of the carriage. The nut that is attached to the cross-slide and translates the rotational motion of the cross-slide screw to straight line motion of the cross-slide must be disengaged during machining with a taper attachment. This enables the cross-slide to move freely in a direction perpendicular to the bed ways as the sliding block moves along the auxiliary ways. The combination of the two feeding directions, the longitudinal travel of the carriage, and the perpendicular motion of the cross-slide, produces a conical or tapered section.

When it is necessary to cut a long, small-angle taper on a lathe that is not equipped with a taper attachment, or when it is necessary to machine a taper that is longer than the taper attachment, then the *tailstock offset* method is used. As the name implies, this technique of cutting a taper simply requires that the tailstock center be displaced in a horizontal plane so that its center is offset from the axis of rotation of the work piece. In this case the tool moves parallel to the bed ways. For small-angled tapers this method is competitive with the taper attachment method when used by a skilled machinist who employs a dial-indicator gage to determine the amount of offset.

When very short tapers are to be cut, two techniques may be used. Generally, if the number of parts to be made is small, then the taper is cut by setting the axis of the *compound* slide to the preferred angle and feeding the tool by means of the compound screw. If the number of parts is large, then a special *form tool* is ground to the desired angle and the taper is machined by plunge cutting the tool into the work piece.

Thread Cutting

Threads may be machined on a lathe in several ways. When only a small number of specific parts are to be threaded in a job-shop, a lathe having a *threading attachment* is used. This attachment consists of a split nut (half nuts) that is engaged with the lead screw by a lever, and a dial that indicates the proper time to engage the split nut. The threading dial enables the operator to engage the power feed to the carriage in such a manner that a single-point threading tool, which is moved radially a few thousandths of an inch after each cutting traverse (pass), will always follow the identical helical path of the preceding cuts.

When cutting a small quantity of standard size threads, many machinists use a *hand threading die* to machine external threads or a *tap* to cut internal threads. The tap or die handle is supported on the lathe bed and the torque is provided by rotating the headstock spindle at a low speed.

For threading large quantities of parts, special *collapsible taps* and *expandable die heads* are used. When the proper length of thread is cut, the cutting tools automatically spring in radially to clear the root diameter for the former and spring out radially to clear the outside diameter of the part for the latter. Only one pass or traverse is needed to complete a thread when using this type of tap or die head.

Recommended cutting speeds and feeds for thread cutting operations are given in the following section on drilling and hole producing processes.

DRILL PRESSES AND RELATED MACHINE TOOLS

Drill presses (Figure 6-2) are those machine tools that have provisions for: supporting a clamped, usually stationary, work piece; rotating a multiple-point cutting tool about its longitudinal axis to obtain the cutting velocity; advancing the cutting tool at a slow speed in a line coinciding with the axis of rotation to obtain the feeding motion. Unlike the other basic machine tools, all of which have provisions for feeding the cutting tool in two or three directions, the drill press has only this one feeding direction. The cutting tool may be a drill, reamer, tap, end mill, counterbore, and so forth, or in some special cases, it can be a tool with a single cutting edge. All of these are shown in Figure 6-10.

Although drilling operations are frequently performed on lathes and mills, these two machine tools are classified separately.

Components of Drill Presses

Figure 6-9 shows a typical drill press which consists of the following basic components: base, column, table, head, and spindle assembly.

The *base,* as the name implies, serves as a support for the other components. The base may be firmly attached to either the shop floor

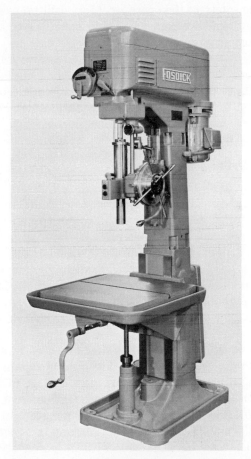

Figure 6-9. Photograph of an upright drill press. (Courtesy Fosdick Machine Tool Co.)

or to a waist-high bench or table. The former type is usually referred to as an "upright" drill press and the latter as a "bench" type.

The *column* is cantilevered from the base and supports the head, spindle assembly, and table. Its cross section may be circular, square, or an irregular built-up shape.

The *table* is provided to support the work and work-holding devices such as vises or drill-jigs during drilling and allied operations. The table may be raised or lowered along the face of the column to accomodate work pieces of varying height.

The *head*, which is mounted at the top of the column, includes the motor and either a gear or belt-driven power train which transmit the power to rotate the spindle. The power train is enclosed with a cover or guard for the safety of the operator. Most drill presses are designed to provide about nine different rotational spindle speeds, usually arranged in a geometric progression.

The *spindle assembly* transmits the torque and thrust to the cutting tool. It includes both the spindle and the feeding mechanisms, which may be manual or power driven. The tool holding end of the spindle, which is referred to as the quill, contains an internal Morse taper to hold either taper-shank cutting tools or a Jacobs type chuck to hold straight-shank tools.

Types of Drilling Machines

The simplest of all the drilling machines is the *portable hand drill*, or as it is frequently called, the *electric drill*. In addition to being a common home workship and garage tool, it is used industrially to drill rivet and bolt holes during the assembly of large structures, such as aircraft frames. To accurately locate the position of the holes, templets or drill jigs are used. The time required to drill a hole in steel with this type of drill is relatively long since the thrust force a person can exert without employing some type of a mechanical help is low, usually about 50 to 100 lbs. As the name implies, this tool is held and operated by hand.

By far, the most common drilling machine used in manufacturing plants is the *upright drilling machine*. A typical upright model is shown in Figure 6-9. Drill presses of this type have a range of 6 to 10 power feeds in addition to having a range of speeds. The feeds usually vary from about 0.001 to 0.015 ipr for small drill presses that are designed for use with drills up to 1 in. in diameter, and up to about 0.050 ipr for the largest drill presses. Drill presses with no power feed mechanism are called *sensitive* drill presses.

When more than one spindle is mounted on the column, or on adjacent columns, the machine is then referred to as a *gang drill press*. This is a very common arrangement for "production" work, that is when a large number of parts requires more than one drilling operation. For example, a housing may require six threaded holes and two reamed dowel pin holes. The sequence of operations may be as follows: for the first spindle, drill six holes with "tap size" drills (minor diameter of thread); second spindle, chamfer or countersink six holes; third spindle, tap six holes; fourth spindle, drill two dowel holes with a $\frac{1}{64}$ in. undersize drill; fifth spindle, ream two dowel holes.

When it is necessary to drill more than one hole in a production part, a *multiple-spindle drill head* may be attached to the drill press spindle and by this means all of the holes may be drilled simultaneously. Thus, in the above example, three six-spindle drill heads and two two-spindle drill heads could be used so that at each station the drill press spindle would have to be fed down only once to complete all of the holes.

A multiple-spindle drill head is not a machine tool but an attachment that can be mounted and dismounted in a matter of minutes on any drilling machine, provided it is of proper size.

A *radial drill press* is a drilling machine that has its spindle attached onto the head by means of ways so that the spindle may be moved radially with respect to the column. The column is usually circular in cross section so that the head and spindle assembly may rotate about the center of the column in addition to the radial motion of the spindle. Of course, clamps are provided to lock the spindle in place when it is properly positioned for a drilling operation. Since a radial drill press costs several times as much as an upright drill press of equivalent capacity, it is not used as much.

Special machine tools, usually referred to as *deep-hole* or *gun drilling* machines, are used to drill holes that have a depth of hole to diameter ratio greater than about eight. The drilling of rifle bores is a common example of deep-hole drilling. In most deep-hole drilling operations it is the work piece that is rotated to obtain the cutting speed rather than the drill as is done during conventional drilling.

Two types of drills are used for deep-hole drilling. One type is identical to an extra long, conventional, two-flute twist drill except that a hole extends along the length of the drill from the shank to the drill point. The purpose of this hole is to convey a coolant under high pressure to the bottom of the hole as it is being drilled so that the chips may more readily be expelled from the hole. The second type of deep-hole drill is a single flute, straight flute drill that has only one cutting edge at its point. It also has a coolant hole along the length of its body. This type is referred to as a gun drill.

The generation of accurate (precision) holes, in terms of either diameter or location, is done on either of two types of precision drilling machines, the *jig-borer* or the *boring mill*. The former is a vertical spindle drilling machine, is usually smaller, and finishes smaller holes than the latter which has a horizontal spindle. The accuracy of these two machine tools is primarily due to their precision spindles as well as precision lead screws and ways that move the table on the bed. Tolerances in the order of magnitude of $\pm 1 \times 10^{-4}$ in. are possible on these types of machine tools. Because of the high initial cost of precision boring machines and the relatively high cost of drilling a hole with them, they are not generally used as "production" machine tools but rather as tool-room machines.

Drilling Machine Size. The size of the upright type drill press is specified as twice the distance between the center line of the spindle and the nearest side of the column. This specification is frequently stated as the diameter of the largest disc in whose center a hole may be drilled. Thus, a 24 in. drill press would have the center of the spindle 12 in. from the surface of the column.

The size of the radial type drill press is specified by two dimensions: the diameter of the column expressed in inches and the maximum distance from the center of the spindle to the nearest surface of the column. Thus, a 10 in. $\times$ 4 ft radial drill press has a 10 in. diameter column and a distance of 4 ft between the spindle center and the nearest surface of the column.

The size of the portable hand drill is determined by the maximum diameter of a drill that can be clamped in its chuck.

Types of Drilling Operations and Tools

The holes or surfaces produced by the drilling operations as well as the tools for each of them are shown in Figure 6-10. Most drilling tools are made of high-speed tool steel. For the larger size drills, especially the taper shank ones, the shank is usually a piece of plain carbon steel that is butt welded to a high-speed steel body. The body of the boring bar illustrated in Figure 6-10h is plain carbon steel and the tool bit, or insert, is high-speed steel. Carbon tool steel is sometimes used for hand taps and inexpensive drills that are not used on production operations. Sintered carbide, in the form of inserts, brazed to the end

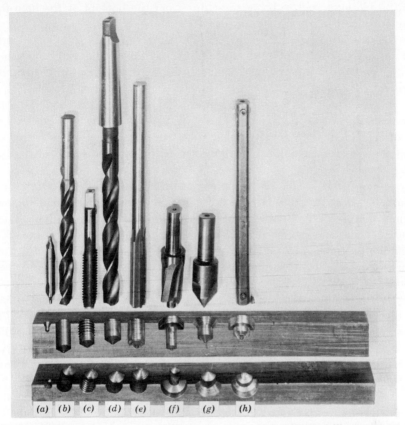

Figure 6-10. Photograph of drilling type tools. (*a*) Center drill. (*b*) Straight shank drill. (*c*) Tap. (*d*) Taper shank drill. (*e*) Machine reamer. (*f*) Counterbore. (*g*) Countersink. (*h*) Boring bar.

of the cutting tool to serve as cutting edges, are frequently used for high production operations. A brief description and a definition of each are given next.

Drilling is a hole originating or enlarging operation that utilizes an end-cutting tool having one or more cutting edges, where the cutting is done by rotating either the tool or the work piece about the center line of the hole (Figure 6-10 *b* and *d*). The most common drill is the two-fluted type (two cutting edges) in which the flutes are at a 30° helix along the body of the drill. The flutes are semicircular channels running along the body from the point to the shank. They are necessary for providing a way to bring the chips from the bottom of the hole to the surface.

A drill consists of three parts: the point which is usually ground to an included angle of 118°; the body; and the shank which may be either straight or tapered (the former being more common for the small drills).

The surface finish of drilled holes is relatively poor, being in the range of 63 to 500 rms. The accuracy of drilled holes is also relatively poor. The diameter of small drilled holes, such as $\frac{1}{8}$ in. may vary from 0 to 0.002 in. oversize and a 1 in. diameter drill may produce a hole 0.010 in. oversize.

Reaming is a hole sizing or smoothening operation in which the diameter of an existing hole is increased by 0.003 in. to 0.030 in. by a multiple-tooth, end-cutting tool called a reamer (Figure 6-10e). The cutting edges of a reamer are the intersections of the flutes and the 45° chamfer on the end of the tool. As is true of the drill, they are not the edges along the body formed by the intersection of the flutes and the land.

The diameter of a reamed hole is more accurate than that of a drilled one. Reamed holes greater than 1 in. in diameter may vary in diameter ±0.001 in. and those less than 1 in. may vary about ±0.0005 in. On the other hand, reaming does not improve the accuracy of the location or angular alignment of drilled holes. The surface finish of reamed holes is usually in the range of 16 to 125 rms.

Center drilling is the operation of originating a relatively small diameter shallow hole that serves as a starting hole for a standard drill, as illustrated in Figure 6-10a. Center drilling is performed with a short (for rigidity) combination drill and countersink tool which is also called a center drill. The most common type is the double-ended one (Figure 6-10a).

Center drilling is done to originate a hole prior to drilling with a standard drill since the centerline of a standard drill wanders or drifts from the axis of rotation when the drill is brought in contact with a flat surface while relative rotational motion is present. When this happens, either the drill breaks or the hole is not drilled in the intended place or direction.

The feed for center drilling is determined on the basis of the diameter of the "drill" portion of the tool, and the cutting speed is determined by the largest diameter of the countersink formed.

Tapping is the operation of making internal threads in a previously formed hole and is usually done by means of a tool called a tap, as illustrated in Figure 6-10c. A tap resembles a screw that has either straight or helical flutes machined in it which provide the cutting edges for the tap. Internal threading may also be done with a single point tool by taking successive cuts along the same helical path.

When a small number of holes are to be tapped, the tapping may be done by hand with the part clamped either on the drilling machine or in a bench vise. However, when a large number of holes are to be tapped, the tap is clamped in a "tapping head" where the tapping is done automatically and with practically no chance of breaking the tap. The tapping head is designed to accomplish the following motions: when an upward force is exerted on the tap, it rotates in a clockwise direction and transmits a preset maximum torque; when the vertical force on the tap is zero, it does not rotate; when a downward force is exerted on the tap (due to the weight of the part), it rotates in a counter clockwise direction.

In many mass production tapping operations, particularly those requiring a very accurate thread, tapping machines having a lead screw to feed the tap at a positive uniform rate are used.

Counterboring is a recessing operation whereby a larger diameter hole having a 180° (flat) bottom is formed part way along the length of an existing hole by means of a multiple-tooth, end-cutting tool called a counterbore, as illustrated in Figure 6-10f. Counterboring is generally done so that a square-shouldered head of a fastener or a nut may be placed beneath the surface of the work piece whenever the presence of the projecting head might interfere with the functioning of the part.

A counterbore has a pilot (projecting cylinder) on the end that is supported during cutting by the walls of the previously formed pilot hole. A counterbore is different from an end mill in this respect since the latter does not have a pilot. The cutting edges on an end mill may extend radially to the center of the tool and thus it may be used to originate a hole, which is not possible with a counterbore. Counterboring is also similar to boring, which is described next.

Another operation similar to counterboring is spot-facing, which may be done with either a spot-facer, counterbore, or an end mill. The purpose of spot-facing generally is to provide a flat, smooth surface for a washer or bolt head to seat on, and is performed mostly on castings and forgings. The primary difference between spot-facing and counterboring is the depth to which the surface is machined, and in the former only enough material is removed to give a smooth seat.

Boring is a hole enlarging operation that uses a single or multiple-tooth, end-cutting tool to achieve small tolerances on either the diameter of a hole or the location of a hole. Figure 6-10*h* illustrates a boring bar made of structural steel having a clamped insert-type tool bit at each end. The tool bit itself is made of a tool material such as high-speed steel or sintered carbide.

The tolerance and surface finish obtained by boring depend upon the diameter and length of the boring bar. For light cuts as in precision boring operations, tolerances in the order of ±0.0005 in. are common and the surface finish is comparable to that obtained by reaming, namely 16 to 125 rms. For rough boring operations, the tolerances and surface finishes obtained are comparable to those obtained by turning operations on lathes.

Countersinking is a recessing operation whereby a conical hole is machined at the top of an existing cylindrical hole as illustrated in Figure 6-10*g*. The cutting tool for this operation is called a countersink. Countersinking is performed so that the head of screw having a tapered shoulder will be beneath the surface of the work piece. The point-angle on a countersink is generally 82°.

Tool Holders

The tool holders employed for hole machining operations are illustrated in Figure 6-11.

Straight shank tools such as drills and reamers are commonly held in a *Jacobs-type chuck*, which is shown in Figure 6-11*a*. By engaging

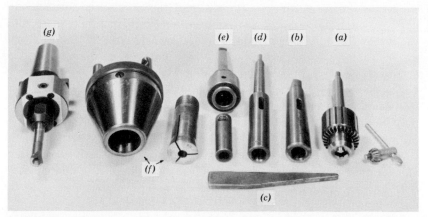

Figure 6-11. Photograph of tool holders used with drilling type tools. (*a*) Jacobs-type chuck and key. (*b*) Sleeve. (*c*) Drill drift. (*d*) Socket. (*e*) Magic chuck. (*f*) Collet. (*g*) Offset boring head.

the bevel-gear chuck key with the outer sleeve of the chuck body, and then rotating it, the three jaws of the chuck are forced downward and inward until they press tightly against the shank of the tool, thereby permitting the torque to be transmitted to the tool. Chucks of this type are most commonly used with drills up to a $\frac{1}{2}$ in. diameter and on occasion with drills up to 1 in. diameter. The shank of a Jacobs chuck consists of a Morse taper.

Taper shank tools are inserted directly into the quill of the spindle of drilling type machine tools. Since the taper is small ($\frac{5}{8}$ in./ft) it is self-holding. That is, when the taper shank is "rammed" into the quill, it is tightly locked in place by means of a press fit. In fact, the tool is so tightly held in place that a wedge, called a *drift* and shown as *c* in Figure 6-11, must be used to remove the tool. Although the taper fit does transmit some torque, its primary function is to properly locate the tool. The *tang* (flat section at the shank end) transmits the bulk of the torque.

A *sleeve*, which has a large external taper and a small internal taper as ilustrated in *b*, is placed on the shank of a tool having a smaller taper than that in the machine tool on which it is to be used.

A *socket*, as shown in d, has the external and internal tapers displaced from each other along the length of the holder. A socket is used on a tool that has a larger diameter taper than is present in the quill. Sometimes it is used when the distance between the quill and work piece is too large for the tool.

A *magic chuck* (see Figure 6-11e) is used whenever a sequence of operations such as drill, ream, and counterbore is to be performed on one hole for a low production item that does not warrant a gang-drill setup. By using this chuck the tools may be changed very rapidly without stopping the rotation of the spindle. To change tools in a magic chuck while the spindle is rotating, the operator simply raises the outer collars along the axis of the chuck. This motion releases the two balls which seat in the slots of the sleeve that holds the tool. When the balls are seated in the slots, the sleeve is held in the chuck and the torque is transmitted through the balls to the sleeve. When the balls are unseated, the sleeve may be withdrawn and another sleeve with a different tool may be attached.

Tools may also be clamped in *spring collets*, (see Figure 6-11f). Since these are discussed in the section on lathes, no further description is given here.

Boring bars are frequently clamped in adjustable boring heads in which the tool bit may be accurately moved radially to control the diameter of the hole being bored, as illustrated in Figure 6-11g.

Speeds and Feeds for Drilling Operations

The cutting speeds for most hole producing operations are lower than the cutting speeds used during turning,—these are discussed thoroughly in the section on *Machinability*. There are two reasons why a relatively low cutting speed is used during the drilling operations: (1) the body of the drill as well as the work material is in contact with the hot chips for a longer time and so for a given speed the cutting edges of a drill become hotter than the cutting edges of external cutting tools; and (2) the tool changing and grinding times are usually longer than for a turning tool so a longer tool life is required for a drill. The longer life is achieved by using a lower cutting speed.

The following list indicates typical values of cutting speeds that can be used for the various hole-producing operations when using high-speed steel tools (the values are given in per cent, with an "average" size turning cut being 100%): boring, 75%; drilling, 60%; reaming, 50%; and threading, 30%.

In regard to the magnitude of the feeds used for various hole-producing operations, the author has found the following relationships to be safe first choices for average conditions. The magnitude of the feed in ipr that can be used for drilling may be approximated by dividing the diameter of the drill by 100. Thus, feeds of 0.010 ipr and 0.001 ipr are typical for 1 in. and $\frac{1}{8}$ in. diameter drills, respectively.

The feeds for reaming generally are two to three times as large as the feeds used for drilling holes of equivalent diameter. No specific values of feeds can be given for boring because the maximum feed is determined by deflection of the boring bar, which in turn is determined by its diameter and length. And, of course, for threading, the feed is equal to the lead of the thread.

SHAPERS AND SHAPING-TYPE MACHINES

Shapers and shaping-type machines, as illustrated in Fig. 6-3, are those machine tools that have provisions for (1) relative reciprocating motion between the tool and the work piece to obtain the cutting velocity; and (2) movement of either the tool or work piece in small discrete steps, usually during the return stroke and perpendicular to the cutting direction, to obtain the "feeding" motion. The cutting tool may be a single-point tool bit, a form tool, or a sequence of cutting teeth mounted on one body as on a broach or saw.

Shapers and planers are very similar to each other in operation, and both are used for low production machining operations. In general, planers are much larger than shapers. The shaper's table and length of stroke seldom exceed 4 ft, whereas the planer's table and length of stroke are seldom less than 4 ft—with a bed greater than 6 ft in length. Another distinguishing feature between these two types of machine tools is the component that moves to obtain the cutting speed: on the shaper, the ram and tool reciprocate with respect to the work piece; on the planer, the table and work piece reciprocate past the tool.

On both planers and shapers the feeding motion is in a vertical or inclined direction when the feeding is accomplished with the tool head, as shown in Figure 6-3. The feeding motion is in a horizontal direction on a shaper when the feeding is done by traversing the table past the tool: on a planer, it is done by traversing the tool head along the rail.

Components of Shapers

A typical mechanical shaper is shown in Figure 6-12. All shaping type machine tools consist of the six basic components: base, column, ram, rail, table, and tool head.

Base. The base supports the column and the outside-end of the table. On some shapers it also supports the drive-motor and contains a reservoir for the lubricating oil for the power-drive mechanism, as well as a support for several of the basic components, as described below.

Column. The top of the column contains the Vee ways in which the ram reciprocates. It serves as a housing for the power-drive mechanism and a support for the basic components described below.

Ram. The ram reciprocates in the vee ways at the top of the column. This motion, the cutting speed, is produced on mechanical drive shapers by means of a link connecting the ram to the Whitworth linkage. On hydraulic shapers it is produced by a hydraulic cylinder. In addition to the possible changes in the stroke length of the ram, as described previously, the position of the ram stroke with respect to the table can be varied. The ram reciprocates horizontally on the standard shaper and vertically on the vertical shaper, or slotter.

Rail. The primary feature of the rail, or cross-rail, is its horizontal ways on which the table slides, thus providing the feeding motion. Attached to the square ways on the front of the column (and locked during machining), the rail may be raised or lowered along these ways by a hand-operated screw, depending on the size of the work piece being machined.

Table. The table is the boxlike block at the front of the shaper on which the work piece is clamped, usually in a large vise. The far end of the table is attached to the horizontal ways of the rail. The near end of the table is supported by a leg that rests on and slides

Figure 6-12. Photograph of a typical mechanical shaper. (Courtesy Norton Company)

along a machined way on the base of the shaper. On the planer type of shaping machine tools, the table reciprocates on two ways on the top of the planer bed.

Tool head. The tool head is attached to the front end of the ram. The tool head has provisions for clamping a cutting tool on it and feeding the tool, by hand on most machine tools, into the work piece. The tool head can be rotated about a horizontal axis so that this feeding motion may be vertical, horizontal, or diagonal. The tool head also contains a clapper-box, so called because at the end of each return stroke its movable portion strikes its fixed part with a resounding clap. This motion of the clapper-box is possible because it is hinged at the top, allowing the bottom to swing outward and upward. This motion is provided to prevent the tool flank from rubbing with high pressure against the machined shoulder during the return portion of the stroke. It should be recalled here that the feeding motion during shaping occurs during the return portion of the stroke, and it is for this reason that the rubbing would be severe.

Cutting Speed and Feed

The cutting speed during shaping varies along the length of the stroke (Figure 6-13). The velocity is not constant anywhere along the stroke of a mechanical drive shaper, but it is constant for about the middle three-quarters of the stroke for a hydraulic drive shaper. The return speed is higher than the forward or cutting speed on both types of shapers, as may be seen in Figure 6-13a. The ratio of the return speed to the cutting speed is not constant, and for the mechanical shaper it varies with the length of stroke, as described next. Typical values for the ratio of the time for the cutting half-stroke over the return half-stroke are 1.6 and 2.0 for mechanical and hydraulic shapers, respectively.

The shape of the velocity-displacement curve for the mechanical shaper is due to its power-drive mechanism, which is generally referred to as the Whitworth Link. This mechanism is illustrated in Figure 6-14 and it operates as follows. The pinion gear drives the large bull gear which has a channel running radially on one of its faces. A block which can be positioned at various radial distances along the face of the bull gear determines the length of stroke. When this block is set at the center of the bull gear the length of the stroke is zero; when the block is set at its maximum radius, the stroke length is maximum and equal to the specified size of the shaper.

A pin at the center of the sliding block is attached to the oscillating link, which is pinned at the bottom to the base of the machine and then attached at the top to a connecting link that reciprocates the ram. For the length of stroke shown in Figure 6-14, as the bull

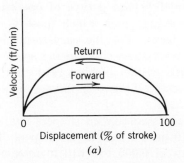

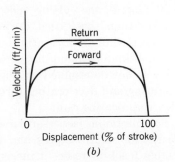

Figure 6-13. Velocity-displacement diagrams for shapers. (a) Mechanical model. (b) Hydraulic model.

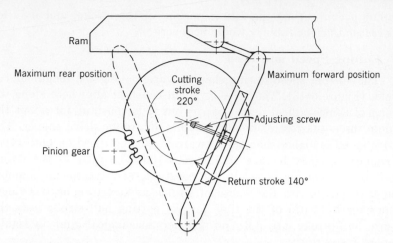

Figure 6-14. Sketch of Whitworth Link Drive mechanism for a mechanical shaper.

gear rotates through one revolution, the ram moves forward while the gear rotates through 220°, and returns during the remaining 140°. Thus the average return speed is 220/140 or 1.57 times the average cutting speed. As the length of stroke is decreased the ratio of the forward to return degrees of revolution approaches unity, and the ratio of the average return speed to the average cutting speed approaches one.

The power drive mechanisms for hydraulic shapers, planers, and the other miscellaneous shaper type machine tools are not described in this text, which merely surveys the equipment.

Unless otherwise specified, when the cutting speed for a shaping operation is given, it represents the average of the forward and return speed.

In general, the cutting speeds in the shaping type of operations are lower than those used during turning, upon which most of the tables of machinability ratings are based. For the easy-to-machine materials like aluminum, brass, and most steels, the cutting speed for shaping is not determined on the basis of tool life but rather on the accelerating and decelerating forces on the Whitworth linkage induced by the reciprocating ram.

The minimum power-operated feed available on shapers is about 0.005 ips for small shapers and 0.010 ips for the larger shapers. The available feeds increase in increments of 0.005 to 0.010 to maximum values of about 0.250 ips.

Other Shaping-Type Machine Tools

There are many special-purpose machine tools in industrial use that are referred to by means of their specific name. Some of the more common ones classified as shaping-type are described next.

Broaching Machines. A *broaching machine* is a machine tool that has provisions for pulling or pushing a special type of cutting tool, called a *broach* or *broaching tool*, over a face of the work piece or through a previously created hole in the work piece. A broach (cutting tool) is similar to a hacksaw blade or a file in that it consists of a series of cutting teeth placed in line with a regular pitch. One difference is that each succeeding tooth extends above the centerline of the broach about 0.001 to 0.005 in. beyond that of the preceding tooth. This rise-per-tooth, which is the "feed," depends upon the material being cut and the rigidity of the setup. On most broaches, the last three to six teeth are at the same height and are referred to as finishing teeth. The length of the broach (cutting tool) is determined by the amount of material that must be removed (depth of cut) and the feed and the pitch.

The pitch on a broach must be large enough to provide space for the chip to curl into during the cutting stroke. The pitch in general is much larger than that on a file or hacksaw blade because more metal is removed per stroke. A surface broach, like that used to machine the face of the heads of an automobile engine may have a pitch of approximtely 1 in. One limitation on the pitch of a broach is the requirement that at least two teeth must always contact the work piece during cutting. That is, the pitch must be less than the work piece width.

A broach for machining internal surfaces, such as a circular, square, or splined hole, consists of a series of rings of increasing diameter or dimension of similar cross section. A broach for machining external surfaces consists of a series of cutting teeth on one face with a flat smooth surface on the opposite face which contacts the ways of the machine base, thus obtaining the feeding force.

The cutting force and cutting speed on most broaching machines are obtained by means of a hydraulic pump and cylinder that moves the broach rather than the work piece.

Since a broach is a special-purpose machine tool, it is generally used for high production operations only. However, for machining square holes or straight keyways, broaching is used even for small quantities. Broaching generally gives a good surface finish and a tolerance of about ±0.005 to ±0.001 in.

Sawing Machines. There are three types of sawing machines: two shaping types and one milling type. The shaping types of sawing machines are the *band saw* and the *hack saw* (reciprocating blade saw). There are several different types of saws (cutting tools) used on band saws, depending upon the thickness and type of material being cut. The conventional saws are operated at cutting speeds approximately 80% of those used in turning operations. However, in the process called *friction sawing*, the cutting speed is in the range of 3000 to 15,000 fpm. Although conventional and friction saw blades are made of either tool steel or high-speed steel, the reason the high speeds used in friction sawing are possible is that each cutting tooth is not in contact with the work piece long enough for the cutting tooth to get hot. Consequently, friction sawing is feasible only on materials less than about $\frac{1}{4}$ in. thick. In some cases, as when "rocking" the work piece, pieces of steel as thick as an inch have been friction sawed. Band saws are used to cut materials in sheet and plate form, and bars when irregular edges are needed.

The power-driven hack saw is commonly used in low production operation to cut bars to proper length prior to machining them on the other machine tools. The bar stock is normally purchased from the mill or warehouse in 10 or 20 ft lengths of circular, square, rectangular, and so forth, cross sections.

The time to hack-saw a piece from a bar of large cross-sectional area such as a 4 in. or larger square, for example, is fairly long — 15 min or more. However, the saw-operator need not oversee the entire operation. After properly positioning the piece to be cut and starting the machines, the operator can then dispense tools from a crib or clean other parts since the hack saw will automatically stop when the part is cut off.

When the sawing time is more critical, a *circular saw* is used. Circular sawing is actually a milling type of operation and not a shaping one, but is listed here to keep all of the sawing processes together. A circular saw does not have the disadvantage of a reciprocating cutting motion like the hack saw, and it has greater rigidity than the band saw. Whereas band saws are normally about $\frac{1}{32}$ in. thick, circular saws are $\frac{1}{8}$ to $\frac{1}{4}$ in. thick. Consequently circular sawing is faster than band or hack sawing. Most circular saw blades are made of high-speed steel, although saws with carbide-tipped teeth are also used. The cutting speeds for sawing are equivalent to those for milling.

Abrasive sawing is circular sawing performed with a thin ($\frac{1}{32}$ to $\frac{1}{4}$ in. thick) grinding wheel bonded with a hard rubber or resin compound. The cutting speed during abrasive sawing is 5000 to 15,000 fpm. Very fast cutoff is achieved with this process. A typical value for cutting steel bars is 5 to 10 sec/in.² of cross section cut. This process is used for small as well as large cross sections.

MILLING MACHINES

Milling machines, as illustrated in Figure 6-4, are those machine tools that have provisions for: rotating a multiple-tooth cutting tool to obtain the cutting speed, and moving a work piece fastened to the table at a slow rate (feeding) in any one of three perpendicular directions. Cutting tools generally fall into two classes on the basis of how they are attached to the milling machine, namely shank-mount

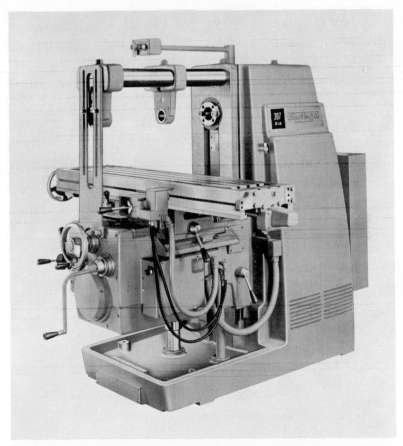

Figure 6-15. Photograph of a typical horizontal milling machine. (Courtesy Kearney & Trecker Corporation)

and arbor-mount. These are discussed in detail in a following section.

Milling machines are divided into horizontal and vertical ones, depending upon whether the spindle rotates about a horizontal or a vertical axis (Figures 6-15 and 6-16). Milling machines are also classified as either column and knee or production machines. The column and knee type is distinguished by the fact that the work piece may be moved (fed) with respect to the cutter in three perpendicular

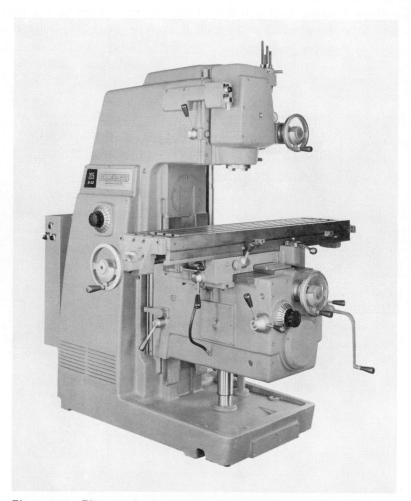

Figure 6-16. Photograph of a typical vertical milling machine. (Courtesy Kearney & Trecker Corporation)

directions: vertically, horizontally to the left or right, and horizontally in or out. The machines illustrated in Figures 6-15 and 6-16 are of this type.

The production type of milling machine, on the other hand, imparts a feeding motion to the work piece in only one direction. The table can be reciprocated over the bed, but generally not raised nor moved in and out. These latter two motions are usually obtained with the cutter and spindle during the machine setup prior to cutting.

Basic Components of Milling Machines

The six basic components of a milling machine illustrated in Figure 6-4 are briefly described next.

The *base* of a milling machine is a pan-shaped part about 2 to 3 ft wide, 4 to 5 ft long, and 6 in. high with a wall thickness of $\frac{1}{2}$ to 1 in. It lies flat on the floor and serves as a support for the column and the knee. It also serves as a tray or tank to hold the coolant.

The *column* is a vertical, cantilevered housing supported at the bottom by the base. The front face of the column contains vertical ways along which the knee is guided as it is raised and lowered, and to which it is locked during the cutting operation. At the top of the column are either ways or holes to which an overarm is attached. Also at the top of the column, just beneath the overarm, are the bearing supports for the spindle. In addition, the column serves as a housing for the power train and the electric motor.

The *knee* is a boxlike structure that is attached to the column by means of dove-tailed ways along which the knee can move in a vertical direction. The knee is raised and lowered by a vertical screw that protrudes downward from the center of the knee and rests on the base. This screw also serves as a support for the knee to give it additional rigidity.

The *table* is supported in dove-tailed ways on top of the knee which is perpendicular to the column face. The table can be moved (fed) along these ways during machining either toward or away from the column. The top of the table is attached to the bottom of the table by means of longitudinal ways that permit the top of the table to be fed in a direction parallel to the face of the column. The top face of the table contains three or four parallel equally spaced T slots in which the various work-holding devices are clamped onto the table.

The *spindle* is housed near the top of the column in the horizontal type of milling machine. It supports the portion of the gear train that provides the rotational motion for the cutting speed. It is supported at both ends of the column by bearings; it contains a tapered hole at the front end in which the various cutter-holding attachments, such as arbors and adaptors, are located.

The *overarm* is present only on the horizontal type of milling machine. It is cantilevered out from the top of the column; that is, parallel to, and above, the spindle. In some cases it may be supported on the front end by straps attached to the knee. The overarm has a bracket attached to its front end which contains a center or a bushing that is used to support the near-end of the arbor when arbor-mount type of cutters are being used. The overarm is provided to fulfill this latter function.

Size Specifications

The physical size of milling machines is generally designated by a number from 1 through 6. These numbers are assigned on the basis of the maximum longitudinal table travel of the machine as follows:

Maximum table travel in inches	22	28	34	42	50	60
Size number	1	2	3	4	5	6

In addition to the size number, most milling machines have a "size letter" such as M or H to designate whether the machine is a light, medium, or heavy-duty one. The motor horsepower generally varies from 3 for the small machines to 25 or more for the larger or heavy-duty machines.

Speeds and Feeds

The *cutting speed* of a milling operation is the maximum peripheral velocity of the rotating cutter, and is expressed as feet per minute (fpm). The speeds as specified on milling machines are expressed as revolutions per minute (rpm). In converting from spindle speeds, rpm, to cutting speeds, fpm, the diameter of the cutter which is normally specified in inches must be converted to feet.

Since the cost of milling cutters is considerably higher than the cost of turning (lathe) tools, and the tool changing time also is generally larger, the tool life for milling operations must be longer than for turning operations because of economic reasons. To obtain a longer tool life, the cutting speed must be reduced as explained in a following section under tool life. The proper cutting speed, as explained in a later section under the title of economics of turning, is that speed for which the sum of labor and tool costs are a minimum. Since more information is available for turning type of operations, it will suffice at this point to simply relate the speeds for milling to those for turning as follows: for a given size of cut (feed and depth) and tool geometry and material, the cutting speed for milling is generally about 80% of that for turning.

The *depth* of cut is the distance between the original and the final surfaces: it is the thickness of the layer of material that is machined away. The depth of cut may vary from a few thousandths of an inch to several inches.

Two feeds are used in describing milling operations. The *basic feed* is the relative speed between the work and cutter expressed as inches per tooth and designated generally as *f*. The *machine feed* is the relative speed between the work and cutter expressed as inches per minute and designated as F. $F = nNf$, where n is the number of teeth on the cutting tool and N is the rpm of the spindle.

Table 6-1 lists a range of feeds normally used for a variety of milling cutters. The lower feed is used, along with a higher cutting speed when a better surface finish is required. Also, if the arbor is out-of-round or if the setup lacks rigidity, the lower values of feed are used.

TABLE 6-1.   Basic Feeds for A Variety of High-Speed Steel Milling Cutters

Type of Cutter	Feed (ipt)
End mills	0.001–0.010
Face and shell end mills	0.005–0.025
Form cutters	0.002–0.008
Saws	0.001–0.005
Side mills	0.003–0.010
Slab mills	0.002–0.005

Milling Cutters

Figures 6-17 and 6-18 show a variety of shank-mount and arbor-mount types of milling cutters along with the surfaces they produce. The shank type of milling cutters, such as end mills or face mills, cut on the end of the tool when the feeding motion is along the longitudinal axis of the tool. However, they cut either on the corner or a short distance along the periphery of the cutter equal to the depth of cut when the feeding motion is perpendicular to the axis of the tool. Figure 6-17 illustrates how a "tee" slot is machined by first cutting a slot with an end mill, and then following through with a Woodruff keyway cutter.

Figure 6-17. Photograph of some shank-mount milling cutters. (*a*) Woodruff keyway cutter. (*b*) 4-flute double end mill. (*c*) Shell and mill.

Figure 6-18. Photograph of a variety of arbor-mount milling cutters. (*a*) Slitting saw. (*b*) Double angle cutter. (*c*) Gear cutter. (*d*) Form cutter. (*e*) Convex cutter. (*f*) Concave cutter. (*g*) Plain milling cutter. (*h*) Side milling cutter. (*i*) Slab mill.

The arbor-mount type of milling cutters, such as side mills and slab mills, cut on the periphery of the cutter. Side milling cutters and slab milling cutters are very similar, their primary difference being the ratio of the face width to the diameter of the cutter. For slab mills this ratio is generally greater than one, and for side mills it is less than one.

Milling cutters are divided into two classes, profile and form, on the basis of where they are ground during sharpening. The profile cutters, which are the more common of the two, are sharpened by grinding the cutting teeth on their periphery. This is not done by rotating the cutter during grinding, which would produce a convex cylindrical surface having the diameter of the cutter, but rather by keeping the cutter stationary while grinding the teeth one at a time. This produces either an inclined plane surface on the periphery of the tooth or a concave cylindrical surface having the diameter of the grinding wheel. The form cutters, on the other hand, are always ground on the face of the cutting teeth. The face of a tooth, on both the form and profile cutter, is a plane surface which provides the rake angles for the cutting tool, and it is approximately radial with respect to the cutter, depending upon whether the rake angles are zero or not.

Work-Holding Devices

A *vise* is the work-holding device that is most commonly used on milling machines. It is clamped onto the milling machine table by tee-bolts and straps. Screw-actuated vises are used for job-shop or general-purpose operations. For production-type operations, fast acting mechanical devices, such as cams or toggles, and air-hydraulic cylinders are used to open and close the movable vise jaw. Vise jaws having special grooves or contours are used to hold irregular work pieces.

Fixtures are special work-holding devices used to clamp and locate large or irregularly shaped work pieces that cannot be conveniently clamped in a vise. Since fixtures are fairly expensive, they are used only when the quantity of required parts justifies their expense. If only a small number of large or irregular parts is required, then they are clamped directly onto the milling machine table by tee-bolts and straps. The disadvantage of this method is the considerable amount of time is takes the machine operator to properly locate and clamp each piece before machining.

Mechanical chucks, clamped onto the table, are frequently used to hold parts of circular, square, or hexagonal cross section. *Vacuum chucks* are frequently used to hold thin sheet materials.

A *dividing head* or *index head* is used to hold work pieces on which any number of equally spaced holes, slots, or projections are to be machined. A dividing head is simply a worm-type gear box having a ratio that is generally 40 to 1. That is, each revolution of the handle rotates the work piece 1/40 of a revolution.

The amount that the index handle must be rotated for each equally spaced division is equal to 40 divided by the number of divisions. Frequently, the number of divisions required is such that the index handle is rotated a fraction of a revolution. To make the task easy for the machinist when using the plain indexing method, the dividing head is equipped with three standard, interchangeable index plates that are clamped concentrically under the indexing handle. Each of these index plates contains six rows of equally spaced, concentric holes, each row having a different number of holes. The standard index plates contain the following number of holes:

> *Plate No. 1.*   15, 16, 17, 18, 19, 20 holes
> *Plate No. 2.*   21, 23, 27, 29, 31, 33 holes
> *Plate No. 3.*   37, 39, 41, 43, 47, 49 holes

The index handle is adjustable radially so that a pin on its end may be positioned to fall into any one of six rows of concentric holes.

A simple illustration of the calculations required in plain indexing will make its use more clear. Consider the operation of machining a spur gear having 22 teeth. The number of revolutions of the index handle needed for each tooth is $\frac{40}{22}$ or 1 and $\frac{18}{22}$ (or 1 and $\frac{9}{11}$). Since there is not an index plate having 22 or 11 equally spaced holes, a circle having a multiple of 11 holes must be used. The outer circle of Plate No. 2 has 33 holes. Consequently, Plate No. 2 would be used and the indexing handle would be positioned so that its pin would fall into the outer row of holes. Then after each gear tooth is machined, the indexing handle is rotated one full turn plus 27 holes in the 33-hole circle.

GRINDING

Grinding is the precision machining process in which abrasive particles are used as the cutting tool. The abrasive particles are generally bonded together into a disc called a wheel, but sometimes they are used loose as in lapping. Each abrasive particle that comes into contact with the work piece acts as a miniature cutting tool with irregular inefficient cutting angles, producing extremely small, highly deformed chips. Because of the small size of cut, and the small chips, the surface finish is good (16 to 125 rms for grinding and 0 to 1 rms for lapping) and the tolerances are low ($\pm 10^{-3}$ to $\pm 10^{-4}$ in. for grinding and $\pm 10^{-6}$ in. for lapping). For the same reason, the cutting forces are low (1 to 10 lb) and the unit horsepower is high (5 to 20). In the normal grinding operations, the rate of metal removal is low (10^{-3} in.³/min). In recent years a process called *abrasive machining* has been developed in which heavier cuts on machine tools with higher horsepower ratings permit removal of metal at the rate of 1 in.³/min.

Grinding machines

Unlike the four basic types of chip-forming machine tools described, the grinding machines cannot be classified as a single type on the basis of the surface created or the motions used. Their use of abrasive particles as the cutting tool distinguishes them from other machine tools. Actually, grinding machines are special modifications of the four basic types of machine tools. This is implied in Figure 6-5 where the machine tool itself is not illustrated but only the work piece and cutting tool. Table 6-2 lists the common types of grinding machines along with the basic machine tools they resemble.

From this tabular listing it is apparent that the common (horizontal) surface grinder is a modified type of precision milling machine in which the milling cutter is replaced with a grinding wheel, and the spindle speeds increased by a factor of 10 to 100. And the cylindrical grinder is a turning type machine tool.

The graduations (least reading) on the dials provided to locate the work piece with respect to the cutter are in units of 10^{-4} in. in

TABLE 6-2. Grinding Machines and Their Basic Machine Counterparts

Grinding Machine Type	*Basic Machine Tool Counterpart*
1. Surface Grinder	
A. Horizontal	Horizontal milling machine
B. Vertical	Vertical milling machine
2. Cylindrical	
A. External	Lathe, turning
B. Internal	Lathe, boring; drilling machine
3. Centerless	Turning with steady rest
4. Lapping	Shaping, milling
5. Honing	Drilling machine, reaming
6. Special	
A. Thread	Lathe
B. Spline	Milling
C. Gear	Milling

contrast to units of 10^{-3} in. on the basic machine tools. This is one reason why the grinding machines are referred to as precision machine tools.

Abrasives

Three types of abrasive materials are used in the making of grinding wheels: aluminum oxide, Al_2O_3; silicon carbide, SiC; diamond, crystalline carbon. These materials are not intermixed in the making of grinding wheels; any given wheel consists of only one of these abrasive types.

Aluminum oxide is manufactured by heating bauxite (a clay containing Al_2O_3, SiO_2, FeO, TiO_2, combined H_2O) with coke and iron filings in an arc furnace. The products of the reaction are alumdum (99% Al_2O_3) and a slag. The large alumdum clinkers are fractured into abrasive particles and sorted as to size and composition.

Silicon carbide is manufactured by heating silica (SiO_2), coke, salt, and sawdust in an electric resistance furnace. The products are silicon carbide (SiC) clinkers, which are crushed and sorted, and a slag.

Industrial diamonds, usually referred to as bort, are different from "jewelry" diamonds in that they are black or off-color and consequently less expensive. Until the late 1950's all diamonds were natural, that is, they were mined. However, some industrial diamonds are now being manufactured commercially by subjecting graphitic carbon to high temperatures and pressure.

These three types of abrasives are also used loose, that is, un-

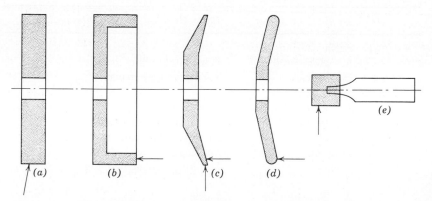

Figure 6-19. Shape designation of commonly used grinding wheels. (*a*) Straight. (*b*) Cup. (*c*) Dish. (*d*) Saucer. (*e*) Mounted. The arrows point to the cutting faces.

bonded and suspended in a liquid or paste, in the processes of lapping and polishing. Fine particles of iron oxide (rouge) and chrome oxide are also used as loose abrasives. More recently, compounds such as boron carbide and boron nitride have been developed which are harder than the other previously mentioned abrasives.

Wheel Designations

Two designations are employed to specify a grinding wheel. One is a shape designation and the other is a composition and structure designation. Figure 6-19 illustrates five of the common standard wheel shapes.

The composition and structure of grinding wheels are specified by a sequential listing of seven groups of letters and numbers. This code will be explained by means of the following example. Consider a grinding wheel with the designation

$$\underline{48} \quad \underline{A} \quad \underline{46} \quad \underline{K} \quad \underline{5} \quad \underline{V} \quad \underline{2}$$

The items in this code are: (1) manufacturer's prefix; (2) abrasive type; (3) grain size; (4) grade or strength; (5) structure or density; (6) bond type; and (7) manufacturer's mark. Each of these items will be described separately.

The first item in the code refers to the *quality* of the abrasive particles: their pureness, hardness, sharpness of fracture, etc. It is listed as a two-digit number such as 18, 32, 38, 48, 51, etc. These numbers have no systematic meaning and they are not always included in the specification.

The second item in the wheel marking indicates the *type of abrasive particles* that the wheel is made of. As stated above, grinding wheels are made of three abrasive materials: aluminum oxide, silicon carbide, and diamond. The code letter associated with these are A, C, and D respectively.

In general, wheels made of aluminum oxide abrasives are used to grind materials that are "tough"—that is, possess a high strength with some ductility. The grinding of all structural steels, tool steels, malleable iron, and bronze is done with aluminum oxide.

Wheels made of silicon carbide are used to grind materials that are either extremely brittle or else very soft and ductile. The former type of material includes: gray and white cast iron, sintered carbide, rocks and ceramic materials. The latter type of material includes: brass, aluminum, copper, rubber, and pressed paper.

Wheels made of diamond particles are used to grind sintered carbide and ceramic parts.

The *physical size* of the abrasive particles comprising the wheel is the third item. As mentioned previously, the manufactured "clinkers" of abrasive material are fractured and sorted on the basis of size. This sorting is accomplished by vibrating the particles over a series of sieves (Taylor sieves) made of very fine wire with an increasing number of.wires on each succeeding sieve. The coarsest sieve has eight openings per linear inch, and the very finest has 600 openings per inch.

In medium-sized abrasives the particle size ranges from 30 to 80. The abrasive size as listed is the smallest size openings in a standard screen through which the abrasive particles will pass. Thus a grain size of 46 means that those grains passed through a standard screen having 46 openings per linear inch but did not pass through the next smaller one having 50 openings per inch.

When a grinding wheel is manufactured to a specified grain-size rating, like 46, this does not mean that all the abrasive particles in it are of the same size as listed, 46 in this case. Some coarser and some finer particles are mixed with the stated size, depending upon the openness (denseness) desired and the manufacturer's experience as to what combination gives the best performance.

The fourth item in the code of wheel markings is the *grade*, which indicates the strength of the bond. It is a measure of the force necessary to pull the abrasive particles from the wheel. The grade is designated by one of the 26 letters of the alphabet with A being the softest and Z the hardest. The letters J to N indicate medium hardness.

The fifth item in the code refers to the *structure* of the grinding wheel and indicates the denseness or porosity of the wheel by numbers between 1 and 15. Number 1 indicates a very dense wheel and number 15 a very open or porous wheel.

The sixth group in the designation specifies the type of *bonding material* that welds the abrasive particles together. In the following description of the bonding material and process, a code letter for each of the six bonding materials is placed in parenthesis.

Vitrified wheels (V) are made by forming a mixture of the abrasive and clay (kaolinite, $Al_2O_3SiO_2H_2O$) by pressing in metal molds, drying, and then vitrifying. This latter process is accomplished by slowly heating the wheels to about 2275° F and holding at that temperature for 8 to 24 hr. At this temperature, the clay fuses and becomes a glasslike ceramic around the abrasive particles. The wheels are then slowly cooled, dressed, and trued.

Dressing is the removal of excess material from the wheel either to shape it or to remove dull, worn grains. This is done while the wheel is rotating by forcing a dressing tool across the face of the wheel and crushing or fracturing the particles and bond. Truing is a precise dressing operation where the periphery of the wheel is made concentric to the axis of rotation.

The majority of grinding wheels used in industry has a vitrified bond. They are harder and stronger than the wheels made with the other bond materials. Also, they resist attack by water, oil, and most acids.

Silicate wheels (S) are made in much the same fashion as the vitrified ones except that the bond material is sodium silicate or water glass ($NaSiO_3$). These wheels are cured at 500°F for several days. This bonding process is frequently used in the manufacture of very large wheels since the lower curing temperature presents less of a chance for the wheels to crack during cooling.

Resinoid wheels (B) are made by dissolving the bonding material, which is a thermosetting phenolic resin such as bakelite, in a solvent and mixing with the abrasive. After molding to shape, the wheels are cured at about 300°F for several hours. This bond has a "high" tensile strength in comparison to the vitrified and silicate bond because it is not as brittle. Consequently, this bond is used to make the thin grinding wheels needed for cutoff operations. These wheels can rotate at higher speeds because of their greater strength, as illustrated in a following section on "Speeds and Feeds."

Rubber wheels (R) are made from sheets consisting of a mixture of vulcanizable rubber and abrasive particles. The grinding wheels are punched out of these sheets by proper shaped dies and then vulcanized under pressure. Because of the hard rubber bond, these wheels are the least brittle. These wheels are used for "rough" operations such as snagging and cutoff where little rigidity is present. Very thin wheels can be made by this bonding process. Like the resinoid wheels, the rubber wheels also can rotate at higher speeds.

Shellac wheels (E) are made by baking at 300°F for several hours the performed mixture of abrasive particles and shellac. Because of the low strength of the bond and the ease of manufacturing these wheels, they are used for light finishing cuts where a bright smooth finish is required on the work piece.

Occasionally, *magnesium oxychloride* (O) is used as a cement to bond the abrasive particles together.

Speeds and Feeds

The vitrified, silicate, and shellac-bonded grinding wheels are rotated during grinding with a peripheral speed of 5000 to 6500 fpm.

The soft wheels are run at the lower speed, and the hard wheels at the higher speed. For ordinary grinding operations, the resinoid and rubber-bonded wheels are rotated with a peripherial velocity of 6000 to 9500 fpm. Cutoff wheels are used with speeds of 10,000 to 16,000 fpm.

In addition to the wheel speed, the work piece is also moved during cutting at a much lower speed, usually 10 to 50 fpm. On surface grinders this is done by reciprocating the work piece under the wheel. On cylindrical grinders it is accomplished by rotating the work piece.

The feed during grinding is larger than in turning, usually about $\frac{1}{8}$ to $\frac{1}{2}$ in. for each stroke or revolution of the work piece.

The depth of cut in grinding is very small. Depths of 0.002 to 0.010 in. are common in rough grinding and depths of 0.0001 to 0.001 in. are used for finishing cuts.

CUTTING TOOL MATERIALS

Although it is sometimes stated that the only essential requirement of a cutting tool material is that it be harder than the material being cut, for efficient performance this is not true. The dynamic conditions existing between the tool and the work are very severe: the chip slides along the tool face at a speed of about 10 to 1000 ft/min with a unit pressure in the order of magnitude of 10^5 to 10^6 psi and at a temperature of 300 to 1500°F. To withstand these conditions effectively, the tool material must have a high hardness with modest toughness at these high temperatures and also have a microstructure that is wear-resistant. In ferrous base materials, this is done by having a matrix of martensite with an excess of carbides of iron, tungsten, molybdenum, and chromium. In the sintered carbide materials, this microstructure is obtained by having a matrix of tungsten carbide (plus some titanium and tantelum carbide) bonded together with cobalt. Table 6-3 summarizes the most commonly used cutting tool materials, including their composition and relative performance.

Carbon Tool Steel

Plain carbon steels of about 1.2% carbon, with or without alloys, were the first effective cutting tool materials. This was the only tool material acceptable to the American industries up to World War I. When austenitized to just above the lower critical temperature, and then quenched to give a martensite plus cementite microstructure, these materials will possess a high hardness and a strength superior to any of the modern cutting tools. However, although its wear resistance is superior to any of the hypo or eutectoid steels, it is not as abrasive resistant as the newer steels that have an extremely large amount of tungsten carbide or chromium carbide present. Although these carbon tool steels have a sufficient hardness and wear-resistance at room temperature, the hardness decreases very rapidly when the cutting speed is increased so that the temperature between the tool-chip interface reaches values of 500°F or more (Figures 6-20 and 6-21). The carbon tool steels are the cheapest tool materials available today, ranging in price from $0.50 to $1.00 per pound. This tool material is used in industry for cutting tools only when the quantity of work to be done is very small or when maximum strength is required in the cutting tool, as in some small taps or drills.

High-Speed Steel

Although Taylor and White developed high-speed steel in 1903, it was not until the pressure of World War I put great demands on the American metal manufacturing industries that high-speed steel became accepted as a cutting tool material. The significant difference between the carbon tool steel and high-speed steel is that the high-speed steel maintains its high hardness to a temperature as high as 1000°F. One can see the reason by noting its heat treatment in

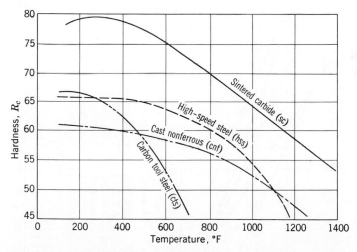

Figure 6-20. Relationship of hardness of several cutting tool materials to the testing temperature. R_c values for sintered carbide obtained by conversion from R_A.

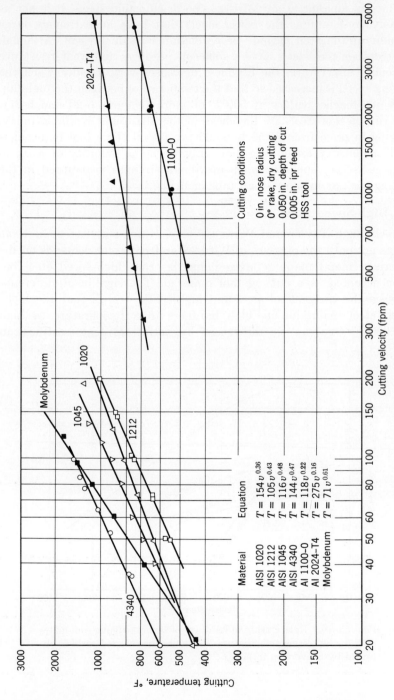

Figure 6-21. Relationship between cutting speed and tool-chip interface temperature for some metals.

Table 6-3. It consists of austenitizing at a temperature of approximately 2250°F and then either air cooling or oil quenching the material. Following this the material is tempered or drawn at a temperature between 1000 and 1100°F for a period of 2 to 6 hr. During this tempering process the hardness of the material increases from a value

TABLE 6-3. Cutting Tool Materials

Material	Composition	Relative Cutting Speed	Maximum Cutting Temp., °F	Manufacturing Process	Heat Treatment
Carbon tool steel (CTS)	1.2% C 0.2% alloy Balance Fe	50%	500	Machine, heat-treat, and grind	Austenitize at 1400°F W.Q. or O.Q. Temper at 450°F
High-speed steel (HSS)	18% W 4% Cr 1% Va 0.7% C Balance Fe	100	1000	Machine, heat-treat, and grind	Preheat to 1600°F austenitize at 2250°F, O.Q. or air cool, temper at 1050°F
Cast nonferrous (CNF)	48% Co 18% W 32% Cr 2% C	150	1500	Casting, grinding	None
Sintered carbide (SC)	95% WC (some TiC and TaC) 8% Co	300 to 500	2000	Sintering, grinding	None
Ceramics	Metal oxides + binder	500 (for light cuts only)	2000	Sintering, grinding	None
Diamond	Carbon	500 to 1000 for very light cuts	1500	Grinding	None

of about 63 to 65 Rockwell C in the as-quenched condition to a value
of 65 to 67 in the tempered condition. The improvement in the tem-
perability of this material is due to the extremely high alloy content
which includes approximately 18% tungsten and 4% chromium. It
is possible to substitute molybdenum for the tungsten, and when this
is done it requires only one-half as much molybdenum. The improved
wear-resistance of the high speed steel over the carbon tool steel is
due to the presence of an extremely large amount of tungsten carbides
which are considerably harder than iron carbide.

The cost of high-speed steel is about \$2.25 to \$3.00 per pound.
Although the cost of the high-speed steel materials is about five times
that of the carbon tool steel and the relative cutting speed is only
twice as high, it must be kept in mind that the cost of the tool material itself is only a small part of the total manufacturing cost; the
cost of labor is, by far, the most important. Any improvement that
will reduce the labor cost usually will produce a considerable savings
in the cost of a manufactured article.

Cast Nonferrous

When it was learned that the addition of tungsten, cobalt, chromium, etc., improved the performance of ferrous cutting tool materials so greatly, it took only a short time to develop tool materials
that contained no iron at all. These tool materials became known as
the cast nonferrous materials, and came on the market under many
tradenames, such as Stellite, Rexalloy, and Crobalt. However, they
did not become very popular because a much superior grade of tool
material, namely, the sintered carbides, were developed shortly after
these cast nonferrous alloys were introduced. Although the hardness
of the cast nonferrous tool is slightly less than the high-speed steel
at room temperature, it is at a temperature of about 1100 or 1400° F
that the cast nonferrous tool material becomes superior because its
hardness remains quite high, as may be seen from Figure 6-20. The
cost of the cast nonferrous tool materials is about \$6.00/lb. The dis-
advantage of these tool materials is that they are quite brittle, and
consequently, considerable care must be exercised in the grinding of
these tools; otherwise, the thermal-shock produced by the rapid cooling after grinding will cause cracks to form on the surface of the tool.

Sintered Carbides

These tools were developed in Germany and although they were
introduced into the research and development laboratories in the
United States in approximately 1930, it was not until World War II

in 1941 that these tools began to gain acceptance in American industry as a cutting tool material. Tools of this material must be made by the powder-metal process; namely mixing the powder of tungsten carbide and cobalt, compacting the mixture under considerable pressure, and then putting these compacts into a furnace and sintering them at temperatures of about 2500°F. After cooling to room temperature these tool materials are then ground and put into service. Their hardness is superior to that of the ferrous base materials; the hardness averages about 92 Rockwell A which would be approximately equivalent to 75 Rockwell C. As may be seen from Figure 6-20 these tool materials maintain their high hardness at temperatures up to 1500°F and greater. The cost of the sintered carbide tool materials is quite high, ranging from about $20.00 to $30.00 per pound. Consequently, only small tools are made of solid sintered carbide; larger tools are made by taking small inserts of sintered carbide and attaching them to a large body of less expensive steel by a brazing process. A new development is the use of small blanks (a common size being $\frac{1}{8}$ in. $\times$ $\frac{1}{2}$ in. $\times$ $\frac{1}{2}$ in.) that are mechanically held onto a large shank. Each corner on both the top and bottom face constitutes a cutting edge, making a total of eight for a square insert. The insert is indexed after each cutting edge gets dull or fails, and after all edges are used, the insert is thrown away rather than reground.

Because these tool materials are very brittle, and have a low tensile strength and high hardness, they must be very carefully handled. The grinding of these tools poses another problem; although the other tool materials may be ground with an aluminum oxide grinding wheel, it is necessary to use either a silicon carbide grinding wheel which wears down rapidly, or preferably a diamond grinding wheel. The latter consists of small particles of diamond powder impregnated on a bakelite wheel. Diamond grinding wheels are very expensive.

Ceramics

This is the newest tool material being developed at the present time. Although originally introduced in the late thirties, these tools did not achieve any acceptance by industry because they were too brittle. However, at the present time several companies are still continuing to develop these materials to cope with the problem of machining some of the very high strength, high temperature resistant materials that are being developed for our high-speed aircraft and missiles of today. The ceramic tools are finding application in machining at a very high speed with light cuts and relatively short tool life. Most of their applications are still in the research and development stages and only a few are used for production. The cost of these materials is approximately 50% greater than that of the sintered carbide tool materials.

TOOL CUTTING-EDGE TEMPERATURE

The temperature at the tool-chip interface depends primarily upon the cutting speed, the size of cut, the tool shape, the cutting fluid, as well as the thermal and mechanical properties of the work material. The relationship between the cutting-edge temperature and the cutting speed for a variety of metals is shown in Figure 6-21. Although the relationship indicated here is a straight line, it must be observed that the scales used on both axes are logarithmic, thus making the true relationship an exponential one rather than a linear one. Thus, in machining AISI 1020 HR steel, the cutting-edge temperature is related to the cutting speed by the expression $T = 154\,v^{0.36}$. (This equation is true only for a depth of cut of 0.050 in. and a feed of 0.05 in./revolution and a specific tool shape.) Inasmuch as the maximum cutting temperature that a high-speed steel tool can endure is 1000°F, it is evident that the maximum practical cutting speed in machining this steel is 160 ft/min. However, in machining 1100-0 aluminum with the same tool, a cutting speed of 8500 fpm must be achieved before the temperature reaches 1000°F. The use of cutting fluids reduces the cutting temperature slightly, with water-base emulsions being the most effective.

Figure 6-20 shows how the hardness of the common tool materials varies with temperature. Although carbon tool steel and high-speed steel have the same hardness at room temperature, the former material begins to soften very rapidly at temperatures above 500°F, whereas the latter retains considerable hardness up to 1000°F. The sintered carbide tool materials have higher hardnesses throughout the entire cutting temperature range. Although the hardness values of the sintered carbide are given on the R_c scale in Figure 6-20, no readings greater than 67 to 70 R_c are actually taken on the testing machine. For materials of such high hardness, the tests are conducted on the R_A scale and then converted to R_c values.

CHIP FORMING

To understand the basic mechanism of machining, a study should be made of what happens when a cutting tool extending below the surface of a piece of material is forced to move through this material. Figure 6-22 illustrates one concept of the mechanism of chip formation when a

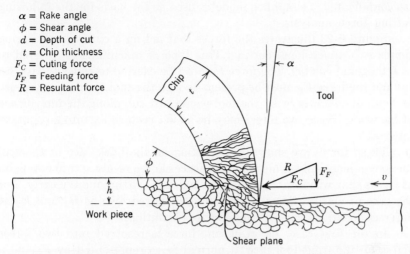

α = Rake angle
ϕ = Shear angle
d = Depth of cut
t = Chip thickness
F_C = Cuting force
F_F = Feeding force
R = Resultant force

Figure 6-22. Orthogonal or two-dimensional cutting.

tool, whose face is inclined from the vertical at an angle α and whose end projects a distance f beneath the work surface, is forced to move through the material with a velocity v due to the action of a resultant force R that is composed of a cutting force F_C and a feeding force F_F. By an analysis of this figure, it is apparent that the chip formation mechanism is one of plastic deformation beneath and in front of the tool, and shear progressing from the end of the tool to the work surface along a plane inclined at some angle θ to the surface. This plane is referred to as the *shear plane,* and the angle θ is called the *shear angle.* Two other characteristics are evident in this same figure: the extreme amount of deformation of the original metal when it is formed into the chip and the thin, superficial layer of strained metal beneath the machined surface.

Microscopic studies of metallurgically prepared samples during machining with a low cutting speed reveal that the above model is an over simplification of the actual chip formation mechanism. These studies reveal that severe plastic deformation occurs at a substantial distance in front of the so-called "shear plane" previously described, as well as beneath the new machined surface. A more correct model portrays the chip formation mechanism as a shearing of the metal in a line extending from the point of the tool in the direction of cutting and a plastic deformation by compression of this layer. Because the other is too complicated, a simplified model is used as the basis for the following cutting force analysis.

Figure 6-23 illustrates the forces that act on a cutting tool during simple two-dimensional cutting. This type of machining is referred to as orthogonal cutting. The force F_C must be exerted to cause the tool to cut and the force F_F must be present to feed the tool for the proper size or depth of cut; otherwise, the tool would just rub along the top surface of the work. These two forces may be added vectorially into a resultant force R.

These forces are shown to be acting on the back face of the tool for convenience only. This resultant force can be resolved into two pairs of forces that will illustrate the mechanics of cutting more clearly. For the sake of clarity, this resultant force R is redrawn as R_1 and R_2 at different locations when discussing its resolution.

In the first case, the resultant force is resolved into two forces acting on the front tool face; a normal force represented by F_n and a friction force represented by F_f. The normal force F_n causes a very high unit stress to exist between the chip and the tool and, along with the coefficient of friction, determine the value of the friction force F_f. As the chip slides up along the tool face with a velocity v, the friction force causes the chip to wear a crater on the tool face, particularly if the microstructure of the work material contains large abrasive particles. The ratio F_f to F_n is referred to as μ, the coefficient of friction in the machining process. And β, the arc tangent of μ, is referred to as the friction angle.

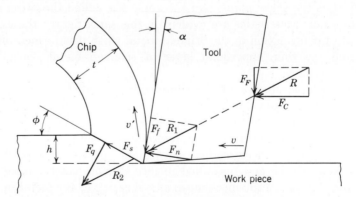

Figure 6-23. Forces acting between the cutting tool, the work material, and the chip.

Historical Background

Fundamental studies of the machining process have been made for over one hundred years, and they were especially profuse during the past thirty years because of the awareness that industrial and technological growth is spurred by engineering and scientific knowledge. These analytical and experimental studies may be divided into three chronological "periods": (1) mechanics or chip formation; (2) machinability; and (3) amplification and application. This does not include the study made by Count Rumford in 1798 since his main concern was not machining but the origin of the heat in the chips during the boring of cannons.

The first of these research periods, the mechanics or chip formation period, extended approximately from 1850 to 1900. The earliest studies made in this period were on the subject of cutting forces and power, and the first recorded study of this type was that of Cocquilhat in 1851. In 1858 Wiebe investigated the drilling process and concluded that the force necessary for drilling was related to the size of cut by the expression

$$F = Khw \qquad (6\text{-}2)$$

where K is a material constant, h is the thickness (usually the feed) of cut, and w is the width (usually the depth) of cut. The studies made during the latter half of this period were primarily concerned with the mechanism of the phenomenon of chip formation. Timme, in 1870, reported that the chip is formed during machining by fracture along successive shear planes which are inclined to the direction of cutting, a concept that is still favored by most machining researchers today. However, a few years later Tresca, who had contributed much in the field of plasticity, proposed a different concept of chip formation. He described the mechanism as a compression of the work material in front of the tool with subsequent shearing in a plane parallel to the cutting direction. Figure 6-24 shows a microscopic view of a piece of polished and etched AISI 1020 steel during orthogonal cutting. The depth of the cut, or feed in this case, is 0.012 in. This photograph clearly shows a crack about 0.010 in. long in front of the tool, as Tresca had proposed. The dark region in front of the tool is the region of severe plastic deformation.

Mallock made a microstructural study of polished and etched chips, and in 1881 he confirmed Timme's mechanism of chip formation and vividly described the process; his description is identical with the cur-

Figure 6-24. Photomicrograph of chip being formed illustrating crack formation.

rent "sliding deck of cards" analogy illustrated in Figure 6-25. According to this model, chip formation occurs in the following sequence. As the work moves to the right, the material in the lower right hand corner of area "4" is first elastically and then plastically deformed. As the work continues on to the right, more of the material in area "4" is

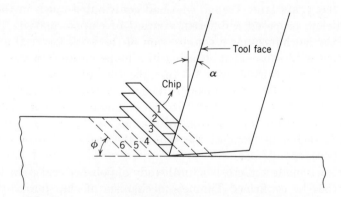

Figure 6-25. Schematic representation of the chip formation process. (After Mallock.)

deformed. In addition, the material directly beneath the tool point is deformed to a slight depth. As the work progresses to where the lower left corner of area "4" nears the tool point, the work material "slips" along the dashed line separating areas "4" and "5". Thus, after the work has moved a distance equal to the length of the base of a sketched area, area "4" occupies the position of "3" and is replaced by "5"; thus the process has completed one cycle and continues.

In 1893 Zvorikin published the results of an analysis he made of machining in which he derived, by minimizing the cutting force, the classic shear angle (Figures 6-22 and 6-23) relationship

$$\phi = 45 + \frac{\alpha}{2} - \frac{\beta}{2} - \frac{\beta'}{2} \qquad (6\text{-}3)$$

where ϕ is the shear angle, α is the tool rake, β is the friction angle at the tool-chip interface, and β' is the friction angle in the shear plane. A few years later in 1896 Hermann[7] derived a similar relationship by assuming that the shear plane is that plane in which the shear stresses are a maximum, namely

$$\phi = 45 + \frac{\alpha}{2} - \frac{\beta}{2} \qquad (6\text{-}4)$$

These relationships, with slight modifications, have remained unchanged to the present time.

The second of the research periods, the machinability period, extended roughly from about 1900 to 1930. Taylor[13] was probably the first person to study the speed-life relationships, including the tool shape and size of cut. His voluminous ASME paper presented in 1907 entitled, "On the Art of Cutting Metals," ushered in the empirical era of tool-life and tool-force testing.

The first use of the term "machinability" was in the middle 1920's in the papers and discussions of Herbert,[6] and Rosenhain and Sturney.[11] At that time machinability referred specifically to the speed-life relationship and not to criteria like surface finish, chip disposal, or dimensional stability as it occasionally is today. In that period machinability was considered to be a property of a material, which was in turn influenced by other properties such as hardness and toughness. The presence of the tool-chip interface temperature was also considered at this period. A relationship correlating the machinability of a material with its physical properties is given in a following section on theoretical machinability.

The third of the research periods, the Amplification and Application period, extends from the 1930's to the present. In this period the previously presented relationships of chip formation and machinability were studied in greater depth and with better instrumentation. Also, these relationships have been widely applied in industrial metal-working plants with very good success. In fact, the tremendous output of munitions required by the past two full-scale wars was made possible in part by the application of empirical machinability data to manufacturing problems. However, such a vast amount of test data is now being presented that the scientific and engineering literature is being diluted, and creative work is being stifled.

The number of researchers who have made contributions in the field of machining during this third period is too large to be included here. However, one study made during this period that is more of an innovation than an extension of the previous relationships is the work of the Bisacres and Chao[2]. These studies, made in the late 1940's, were the first to use the thermal properties of a material in the analysis of machining. They also introduced the dimensionless group vh/α, where v is the velocity, h is the thickness of the cut, and α is the thermal diffusivity.

Cutting Forces and Power

Before discussing in detail the second or machinability period, it is best to note more completely the subject of cutting force and power.

Since Wiebe's first study of cutting forces, and prior to 1930, many studies [3, 9, 10, 12] were made of forces and power from which several equations were presented of the type

$$F = K \times A \times f\,(\phi, \alpha, \beta). \qquad (6\text{-}5)$$

F is the cutting force, K is an experimentally determined material constant, A is the area (feed $\times$ depth) of cut, and $f\,(\phi, \alpha, \beta)$ represents some function of the shear, rake, and friction angles, respectively.

From the early 1930's to the present there were several modifications made on this force equation, but all of the newer equations still contained an experimentally determined material constant as well as experimentally measured shear and friction angles. Also, many experimental studies have been made of the influence of the size of cut, tool shape, cutting speed, etc., on the cutting force. Since there was no close agreement between the analytical solutions and the experimental data, the experimental data remained for the most part in tabular form.

It seems futile, from an educational point of view, to end a subject with a relationship of this type for the following reason: in order to obtain the equation by means of which we may calculate the cutting force for any specific cutting condition, we must first experimentally measure the cutting force. As well as being useful in orienting an engineering student, these relationships are very useful industrially in the testing and development programs on machinability. And for this latter reason, technical journals in mechanical engineering, during the past forty years, have been deluged with the empirical results of machining tests showing the effects on the cutting force of such variables as feed, depth, tool shape, coolants, and so forth. Table 6-4 illustrates this type of data. For the tool shape specified at the top of the table, the relationship

$$F_C = 133,000 \, f^{0.85} \, d^{0.98} \qquad (6\text{-}6)$$

is given for the cutting force for 1020 H.R. steel. For a 0.010 ipr feed and 0.100 in. depth of cut, the calculated cutting force is 281 lb. Although it is possible to calculate this value of cutting force from Equation 6-6 with a slide rule to an accuracy of about 1%, the validity of the equation itself is not nearly as accurate as the slide rule calculations. Consequently, a student of the subject must have a little experience and knowledge concerning the reliability of all these empirical cutting force equations.

Consider, as a specific example, AISI 1020 H.R. steel. Actually, it is not *one* steel, that is, it is not always exactly the same. The designation AISI 1020 H.R. indicates that it is a *type* or family of steels having

TABLE 6-4a

Experimentally determined relationships between the size of cut and the Cutting (F_C), Feeding (F_F), and Radial (F_R) forces for several materials and tool shapes.[1]

Tool Shape 8, 14, 6, 6, 6, 15, $\frac{3}{64}$	*Tool Shape* 8, 14, 6, 6, 6, 0, $\frac{3}{64}$	*Tool Shape* 8, 22, 6, 6, 6, 0, $\frac{3}{64}$
18-8 Stainless Steel: $F_C = 151,000 \, f^{0.85} \, d^{0.95}$ $F_F = 23,000 \, f^{0.48} \, d^{1.26}$ $F_R = 46,500 \, f \, d^{0.69}$	AISI 3135 Steel 207 BHN: $F_C = 259,000 \, f^{0.98} \, d$ $F_F = 950 \, d^{1.08}$ $F_R = 7,300 \, f^{0.74} \, d^{0.28}$	AISI 3135 Steel 207 BHN: $F_C = 174,000 \, f^{0.9} \, d$ $F_F = 950 \, d^{1.08}$ $F_R = 25,700 \, f^{0.84} \, d^{0.58}$
AISI 1020 H. R. Steel: $F_C = 133,000 \, f^{0.85} \, d^{0.98}$ $F_F = 113,000 \, f^{0.8} \, d^{1.46}$ $F_R = 3,565 \, f^{0.67} \, d^{0.47}$	AISI 1018 Steel 100 BHN: $F_C = 133,000 \, f^{0.83} \, d$ $F_F = 33,700 \, f^{0.48} \, d^{1.45}$ $F_R = 923 \, f^{0.56}$	AISI 1018 Steel 100 BHN: $F_C = 102,500 \, f^{0.8} \, d$ $F_F = 12,500 \, f^{0.42} \, d^{1.35}$ $F_R = 704 \, f^{0.46} \, d^{0.13}$
Yellow Brass: $F_C = 83,400 \, f^{0.81} \, d^{0.96}$ $F_F = 95,100 \, f^{0.91} \, d^{1.43}$ $F_R = 9,860 \, f^{0.97} \, d^{0.38}$		

[1] O. W. Boston, *Metal Processing*, 2nd Ed., John Wiley and Sons, 1951, p. 166.)[12]

TABLE 6-4b

Drilling torque and thrust formulas with constants for torque in (pound-feet) and thrust in pounds. (f = feed; d = drill diameter; w = web thickness.)[1]

SAE 33 Aluminum Alloy

Dry:
$$T = 646\, f^{0.83}\, d^{1.9}$$
$$B = 75{,}030\, f^{1.1}\, d^{1.2}$$

Soluble oil in water 1 to 10:
$$T = 553\, f^{0.83}\, d^{1.9}$$
$$B = 51{,}070\, f^{1.1}\, d^{1.2}$$

Cast Iron

Dry:
$$T = 370\, f^{0.6}\, d^{1.7}$$
$$B = 160{,}000\, f^{0.73}\left(\frac{d}{5}+\frac{w}{d}\right)^{1.9}$$

Soluble oil in water 1 to 10:
$$T = 344\, f^{0.6}\, d^{1.7}$$
$$B = 148{,}000\, f^{0.73}\left(\frac{d}{5}+\frac{w}{d}\right)^{1.9}$$

SAE 1020 Steel

Dry:
$$T = 2186\, f^{0.78}\, d^{1.8}$$
$$B = 906{,}000\, f^{0.87}\left(\frac{d}{5}+\frac{w}{d}\right)^{2.12}$$

Soluble oil in water
$$T = 1758\, f^{0.78}\, d^{1.8}$$
$$B = 785{,}000\, f^{0.87}\left(\frac{d}{5}+\frac{w}{d}\right)^{2.12}$$

Leaded Brass Screwstock

Dry:
$$T = 418\, f^{.73}\, d^{1.9}$$
$$B = 6938\, f^{.6}\, d^{1.0}$$

Soluble oil in water 1 to 10:
$$T = 418\, f^{.73}\, d^{1.9}$$
$$B = 6636\, f^{.6}\, d^{1.0}$$

SAE 3150 Steel

Dry:
$$T = 2215\, f^{0.78}\, d^{1.8}$$
$$B = 912{,}500\, f^{0.87}\left(\frac{d}{5}+\frac{w}{d}\right)^{2.12}$$

Soluble oil in water 1 to 10:
$$T = 2025\, f^{0.78}\, d^{1.8}$$
$$B = 773{,}000\, f^{0.87}\left(\frac{d}{5}+\frac{w}{d}\right)^{2.12}$$

a permissible range of chemical composition and cooling rate after being rolled to size. As a consequence, the tensile strength may vary from 55,000 to 70,000 psi, or nearly a 30% variation. The modulus of elasticity may vary from 27×10^6 to 31×10^6 psi,—a variation of 12%. In addition, the strain-hardening exponent may vary by a considerable amount. And it is well known that the tensile strength varies with temperature.

By summing up all these variations, is it any wonder that one investigator may get the expression

$$F_C = 90{,}000\, f^{1.0}\, d^{1.1} \tag{6-7}$$

and another investigator at a different time and place may summarize his findings as

$$F_C = 200{,}000\, f^{0.7}\, d^{0.8} \tag{6-8}$$

Each is greatly different from the published Equation 6-6, and yet all three were the results of machining AISI 1020 H.R. It must be kept in mind that sometimes empirical relationships show more reliably what *was* true rather than what *will be* true.

In the above brief historical review of the study of cutting forces it was shown that all of the published mathematical relationships for the cutting force include constants that must be determined from actual cutting tests. And in addition to this limitation of the cutting force equations, there are many new materials that are both expensive and scarce, making it impractical to run cutting tests even if one had the time. The author will now present the following analysis and Equations 6-14 and 6-15 as his solution to the educational problem of the cutting force.

When a piece of work material with its top surface above the end of a cutting tool is forced to move relative to the tool as indicated in Figure 6-26, it may be assumed that cutting will occur; that is, the tool will move through the work, when

$$F_C = F_f + F_p \qquad (6-9)$$

From this analysis we can assume that F_f includes, in addition to the friction force at the end of the tool, the horizontal component of the friction force along the tool face which will be very small when α is

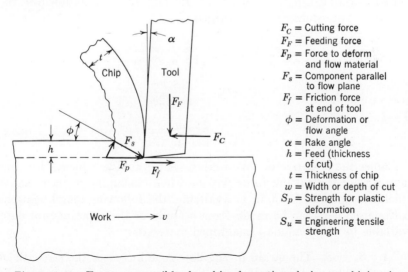

F_C = Cutting force
F_F = Feeding force
F_p = Force to deform and flow material
F_s = Component parallel to flow plane
F_f = Friction force at end of tool
ϕ = Deformation or flow angle
α = Rake angle
h = Feed (thickness of cut)
t = Thickness of chip
w = Width or depth of cut
S_p = Strength for plastic deformation
S_u = Engineering tensile strength

Figure 6-26. Forces responsible for chip formation during machining in simple cutting.

small and consequently, may be neglected. From the geometry of the chip-flow process depicted in Figure 6-26, it is apparent that

$$F_p = \frac{F_s}{\cos \phi} \qquad\qquad (6\text{-}10)$$

Also, the material will plastically flow in the inclined zone in front of the tool when the total force exerted along the flow (shear) direction is equal to the product of the "flow" strength of the material and its cross-sectional area. (For a strain-hardening material, the stress necessary for plastic deformation is dependent upon the strain that the material has undergone. This is usually expressed as $\sigma = \sigma_0 \epsilon^m$.) The stated relationship for the force in the flow direction can be written as

$$F_s = S_p A_s = S_p \frac{hw}{\sin \phi} \qquad\qquad (6\text{-}11)$$

(The symbols used here are defined in Figure 6-26.)

Experimentally it has been observed that

$$F_F = cF_C \qquad\qquad (6\text{-}12)$$

where the proportionality constant c varies between $\frac{1}{4}$ and 1 and is usually taken as $\frac{1}{2}$. By realizing that

$$F_f = \mu F_F \qquad\qquad (6\text{-}13)$$

and substituting Equations 6-10, 11, 12, and 13 in Equation 6-9, the following expressions can be obtained:

$$\begin{aligned}
F_C &= \mu F_F + \frac{S_p}{\cos \phi} \cdot \frac{hw}{\sin \phi} \\[2mm]
&= \mu c F_C + \frac{2S_p hw}{\sin (2\phi)} \\[2mm]
&= \frac{2S_p hw}{(1 - \mu c) \sin (2\phi)} \qquad\qquad (6\text{-}14)
\end{aligned}$$

Since the objective of this analysis is to provide a means for predicting what the cutting force will be when machining a material for which no experimental data is available, the following simplifications to Equation 6-14 can be made from a study of the experimental data available for the commonly machined materials:

1. $S_p = S_u$. The strain in the flow zone increases the strength of the material beyond the yield strength, and experimentally it appears to increase to a value equivalent to the engineering tensile strength, S_u.

2. $\mu = 0.3$ for dry metal to metal friction.

3. $c = \frac{1}{2}$ for sharp tools.

4. $\phi = 20°$ when $\alpha = 0°$. Although ϕ usually varies between $15°$ and $35°$, a typical value is $20°$. Also, as the rake angle α increases from $0°$, the flow angle ϕ increases.

By substituting these values in Equation 6-14, the simple expression

$$F_C = 3.5\,S_u hw \qquad\qquad (6\text{-}15)$$

is obtained. It must be realized that this equation should only be used when experimental cutting force data is not available. And, if the rake angle is greater than $0°$, the constant will be less than $3\frac{1}{2}$. Although Equation 6-15 is dimensionally correct with h and w having exponents equal to 1, it is observed experimentally that for very small values of h (from 0.5 to 5×10^{-3} in.) it has an exponent slightly smaller than 1. This discrepancy between the experimental and the theoretical value of the feed exponent probably exists because the theoretical analysis does not include the strain hardening of the surface cut. For most machining operations, h is numerically equal to the feed f and w is equal to the depth of cut d.

It can be noted that Equation 6-15 is identical to Wiebe's, and that his material constant K is equal to our $3\frac{1}{2}\,S_u$.

The work done in machining is the product of the cutting force and the distance cut. The power required for machining is the product of the cutting force and velocity and is expressed as ft-lb/min. Thus

$$P = Fv \qquad\qquad (6\text{-}16)$$

The equivalent horsepower is obtained by dividing by 33,000 ft-lb/min.:

$$\mathrm{hp}_c = \frac{Fv}{33{,}000} \qquad\qquad (6\text{-}17)$$

The subscript c is added to hp to designate this value as the horsepower that is required at the cutter; that is, the power at the tool point and not of the motor, which must be greater to overcome the friction in the driving mechanisms of the machine tool.

The horsepower needed at the motor is equal to the sum of the tare horsepower (power needed to "cut air") and the ratio of the cutting horsepower over the mechanical efficiency of the machine tool. Thus

$$\mathrm{hp}_m = \mathrm{hp}_t + \frac{(\mathrm{hp}_c)}{\eta} \qquad\qquad (6\text{-}18)$$

Another useful power concept is the unit horsepower, which is the ratio of the cutting horsepower over the volume (in.^{3}) of material removed in one minute, Q. Thus

$$\text{hp}_u = \frac{\text{hp}_c}{Q} \tag{6-19}$$

For turning cuts, Q may be approximated from $12\,vhw$ or $12\,vfd$ (the units of f in this latter expression is in. and not ipr). The cutting force depends upon the size of cut by either of the two following relationships:

$$F_C = Kh^a w^b \tag{6-20}$$

$$F_C = 3.5 S_u hw \tag{6-21}$$

Then the unit horsepower may be expressed in terms of the size of cut and material constants as follows:

$$\text{hp}_u = \frac{Kh^a w^b v}{33,000 \times 12 vhw} = K_1 h^{a-1} w^{b-1} \tag{6-22}$$

or

$$\text{hp}_u = \frac{3.5 S_u hwv}{33,000 \times 12 vhw} = 9 \times 10^{-4} S_u \tag{6-23}$$

The last relationship applies only for dry cutting with a zero rake tool and an average size of cut. As stated previously, h and w may be replaced with f and d respectively.

Table 6-5 lists representative values of hp_u for some common materials. Here it can be seen that hp_u for a given material varies with the size of cut.

The feeding force and radial force also depend on the size of the cut, as illustrated in Table 6-4. In general, these two forces are of

TABLE 6-5. Typical Values of Unit Horsepower

| Material | Size of Cut | | |
	Very Large	Average*	Very Small†
Plastic	0.1	0.2	5
Magnesium	0.1	0.3	8
Aluminum	0.2	0.4	10
Cast iron	0.3	0.6	15
Brass	0.2	0.5	12
Steel—120 H_B	0.5	0.8	20
Steel—400 H_B	0.5	1.2	20

*Average size cut is approximately $\frac{1}{8}$ by 0.010 in.
†Typical of grinding.

lower magnitude than the cutting force. Since the velocity in the feeding direction is very low, the power required for feeding is negligible. The velocity in the radial direction is zero and therefore no power is expended in that direction.

TOOL LIFE

The preferred method of describing the efficiency of machining is by stating the rate of removing metal,—cubic inches of metal removed per minute. However, since it is more convenient in the shop to evaluate cutting tools or work materials by means of their relative tool life under constant cutting conditions, the presently accepted way in industry of making this apraisal is by obtaining the values of n and C in the Taylor equation $vt^n = C$. These testing or data-collecting projects in machining are conducted most expediently when cutting speeds comparatively higher than those used commercially are employed. These higher speeds result in a shortened tool-life and a consequent saving in the expensive testing time. Figure 6-27 illustrates the results of a test conducted by the author several years ago to check the validity of extrapolating the tool-life curve from the short testing times to the longer commercial cutting times. Actually, the agreement between calculated and actual time in this particular instance is much better than would normally be expected. This is true because it is a common occurrence for three ex-

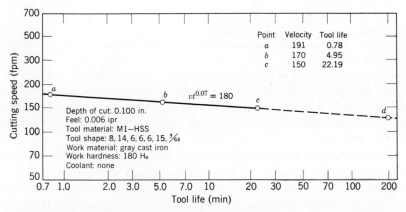

Figure 6-27. Validity of extrapolation of tool life curves. Points a, b, and c were obtained experimentally and were plotted on the chart. A straight line was drawn between them and extrapolated as indicated by the dashed line. From this line, it was predicted that to obtain a tool life of 200 min, the cutting speed should be 130 fpm. A fourth tool was tested at this speed with a resulting life of 195 min. This point, d, lies on the extrapolated line.

perimental points having tool lives between 1 and 20 min not to fall on a straight line because of minor variations in the material and the tool. Just as in specifying hardenability by a band rather than a line, so also should the machinability of a material be specified by a band. However, up to the present time, it is not.

A specific $vt^n = C$ equation is valid for solving problems only when all of the cutting conditions except speed and tool-life are kept constant. This restriction includes the tool material and shape, work material, and size of cut. In many engineering situations concerning machining, the appropriate equation is not available and an answer must be obtained by modifying some existing related data. For example, $vt^{0.1} = 90$ may be the only data available in the handbooks for machining a certain AISI steel. This relation may have been obtained with H.S.S. tools ground to proper shape with a $\frac{1}{8}$ in. depth of cut and 0.012 ipr feed. If carbide cutting tools are being contemplated for this operation, what can one do to obtain some knowledge of the cutting speed-tool-life relationship in this case without actually running a tool-life test? By referring to Table 6-6, it can be seen that the average value of n for a

TABLE 6-6.   Representative Value for n and C in $vt^n = C$

Tool Material	Range of n	Average	C
High-speed steel	0.06–0.12	0.1	X
Cast nonferrous	0.1 –0.15	0.12	1.25 to 1.5X
Sintered carbide	0.15–0.25	0.2	3 to 5X
Ceramic	0.30–0.60	0.4	5 to 8X

sintered carbide tool is 0.2 compared to the representative value of 0.1 for a high-speed steel tool; Also, the constant C for the carbide tool is about three to five times as large as the constant for a high speed steel tool. Thus, an approximate expression for the above problem would be $vt^{0.2} = 360$.

In considering the accuracy of such approximations it is necessary to appreciate the validity of any experimentally determined $vt^n = C$ relationship. Unfortunately, no quantitative studies have been made to indicate the absolute validity of a specific tool-life equation. However, experience has shown that variations in the cutting speed-tool-life relationship for a specific material when machining different batches of it will be at least as great or greater than the variations in the cutting force-size of cut relationship discussed previously. Or for ferrous materials, the variation in the machinability of a given type of steel is greater than the variation in the hardness between the upper and lower limit of the hardenability band.

In many instances, particularly in economical considerations, the effect of the size of cut on the speed-life relationship is very important. The cutting speed for a constant tool life, when only the depth of cut and feed are varied independently of each other, is related inversely to the feed and depth exponentially as follows:

$$v = k_1 f^{-a} \quad \text{and} \quad v = k_2 d^{-b} \tag{6-24}$$

By combining these two relations with the speed-life equation, the following useful expression is obtained:

$$v = K t^{-n} f^{-a} d^{-b} \tag{6-25}$$

The numerical values of a, as determined experimentally, seem to lie between 0.5 and 0.8 (0.65 av.) and the values of b are in the range of 0.3 to 0.6 (0.40 av.) for both high-speed steel and carbine tools. Representative values of n are given in Table 6-6 and were discussed previously. Obviously, use of the above relationships requires that n does not vary with the size of cut, when all other operating conditions are held constant. That is, for a given material and tool shape, n has the same numerical value for all values of f and d. This relationship is assumed to be true in the traditional method of applying the above speed-life equations. However, the more recent studies discussed in the following section entitled "Theoretical Machinability" indicate that n does vary with the size of cut.

In most industrial operations, the depth of cut is dictated by the initial and final size of the part and is not readily varied during manufacturing. On the other hand, the feed may be varied from small to large values depending on the surface finish requirements and rigidity of the setup. From an economics point of view, because the exponent of f is negative and less than one, it is desirable to machine with as large a feed as is possible since it is apparent from Equation 6-25 that for any specific increase in feed the cutting speed for a constant tool life is reduced by the ratio of the feed to the a power. That is,

$$v_1 f_1{}^a = k = v_2 f_2{}^a \quad \text{or} \quad v_2 = v_1 \left(\frac{f_1}{f_2}\right)^a \tag{6-26}$$

Similarly

$$v_2 = v_1 \left(\frac{d_1}{d_2}\right)^b \tag{6-27}$$

Since the numerical value of the exponent b is less than the value of a, it is actually more beneficial to use a large depth of cut rather than a large feed, if a choice is available.

It is worth while at this time to examine quantitatively the effect of changing only the feed and the depth of cut upon the rate of metal removal. This comparison is made on the basis of maintaining a constant tool life and assuming that n is constant. If the initial conditions are $v_1 f_1$ and d_1, then the rate of metal removal is

$$Q_1 = 12v_1f_1d_1 \quad \text{in.}^3/\text{min}$$

Upon doubling the feed $(f_2 = 2f_1)$ and without changing the original depth of cut, the new cutting speed for constant tool life is

$$v_2 = v_1 \left(\frac{f_1}{f_2}\right)^a = v_1 \left(\frac{f_1}{2f_1}\right)^{0.65} = 0.638v_1$$

The rate of metal removal with the increased feed is

$$Q_2 = 12v_2f_2d_1 = 15.3v_1f_1d_1 \quad \text{in.}^3/\text{min}$$

Thus it is apparent that by doubling the feed and correspondingly reducing the cutting speed to maintain a constant tool life, the rate of metal removal is increased by $\dfrac{15.3 - 12}{12} \times 100$, or 27.5%.

If the depth of cut were doubled $(d_2 = 2d_1)$ rather than the feed, the new cutting speed would be

$$v_3 = v_1 \left(\frac{d_1}{d_2}\right)^b = v_1 \left(\frac{d_1}{2d_1}\right)^{0.40} = 0.757v_1$$

The rate of metal removal with the increased depth of cut is

$$Q_3 = 12v_3f_1d_2 = 18.2\, v_1f_1d_1 \quad \text{in.}^3/\text{min}$$

The new rate of metal removal is 51.5% greater than the original rate and 19% greater than when the feed alone was doubled.

In using the above relationships in solving machining problems, when specific values for the constants K and exponents a and b are given, the angles at the tool point must not be varied from those used in obtaining the experimental data. The tool-point shape has a very marked effect on the performance or cutting efficiency of the tool. This effect is discussed in the following section.

Tool Shape and Cutting Efficiency

It is best when discussing single-point cutting tools to describe them by means of six angles and a nose radius as in Figure 6-28. These

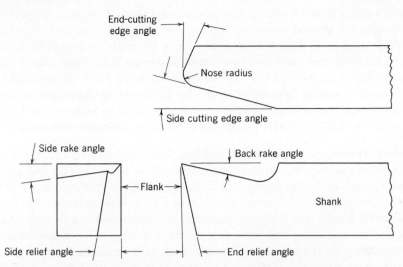

Figure 6-28. ASA nomenclature for a single-point cutting tool. The angles are specified in the following sequence: back-rake, side-rake, end-relief, side-relief, end-cutting-edge, side-cutting edge, nose radius.

have been adopted by the ASA* which specifies that they be listed in the following order: back-rake angle, side-rake angle, end-relief angle, side-relief angle, end-cutting-edge angle, side-cutting-edge angle, and nose radius. Each of these angles serves a definite purpose, and a knowledge of their effect upon the cutting speed for a given tool-life is essential for one to become proficient in the engineering applications in the machining processes. Each of these elements will be discussed separately, in order of increasing importance.

Back-rake Angle. The ordinary range of back-rake angles used on most cutting tools does not affect the cutting speed for a constant tool life. The back-rake is used on a tool primarily to control the direction of chip flow. With a zero back-rake angle, the chip would slide off parallel to the axis of the work in a turning operation; with no chip breaker, the metal would come off in long, straight chips which are extremely difficult to handle and salvage. A proper back-rake angle will cause the chip to flow at such an angle that it strikes the tool holder or the work material and curls or breaks into small segments.

In cutting steel and other ductile materials, a back-rake angle of approximately 8° works satisfactorily and will cause the chip to curl

* The American Standards Association, *Single-Point Tools and Tool Posts,* Bulletin No. 522, 1950, p. 3.

when cutting with all speeds except the very highest without a special chip breaker ground onto the top of the tool. For the more brittle materials, such as cast iron and bronze, a 0° angle is generally used since the material fractures into small irregular chips that break off the workpiece in front of the tool face regardless of which angle is used. The most desirable back-rake angle for any cutting operation is the smallest one that will give proper control of the chip because the time to grind the tool is directly proportional to the magnitude of the angles.

Relief Angles. As their name implies, both the end-relief and the side-relief angles are needed on a tool simply to keep the end and side flanks of the tool from rubbing against the work which would wear the cutting-edge away. The relief angles are also necessary to enable the tool to be forced into the work material to accomplish the feeding. An angle of 6° is usually sufficient, except where a large relief angle would be necessary on the leading side of the tool, as is encountered in thread cutting and similar operations. For hard materials, a slightly smaller relief angle may be used provided the feed is not large. When cutting with the crater-resistant type of sintered carbide tool, relief angles as large as 12° may be used with better performance than the traditional angle of 6°. Also, for very soft materials and materials with a low modulus of elasticity, slightly better results are obtained by increasing the relief angles up to 12°.

End-Cutting-Edge Angle. The end-cutting-edge angle is provided so that the end of the tool will not contact the work. If it did, the length of the cutting edge would become very large and would induce chatter. In a few operations such as planing cast iron, it is desirable to use a tool with a 0° end-cutting-edge angle to produce flat surfaces free of feed marks. For this type of work, the depth of cut must be very small, in the order of a few thousandths of an inch. However, for the majority of cutting operations, the end-cutting-edge angle should be kept as small as possible, the usual value being 6°. As is true of the relief angles, end-cutting-edge angles of this magnitude have no influence on the cutting speed for a constant tool-life.

Side-Rake Angle. For any machining operation there is an optimum side-rake angle which is determined by both the work and tool materials. Figure 6-29a illustrates the relationship between the side-rake angle and the cutting speed when machining annealed medium carbon, low alloy steel. By taking the cutting speed for a fixed tool-life obtained with a 0° rake angle and, for a basis of comparison arbitrarily setting it equal to a relative cutting speed of 100%, the relative cutting

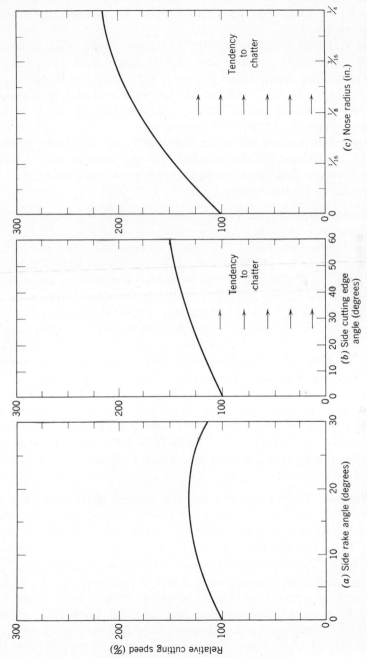

Figure 6-29. Effects of tool shape on cutting speed when machining annealed, low alloy medium carbon steel with HSS tool. Depth of cut = 0.100 in. and feed = 0.12 ipr.

speed increases to a maximum value of 130% with a side-rake angle of 25°. As the rake angle increases beyond 25°, the relative cutting speed decreases.

For materials which are softer and more ductile than annealed medium carbon steel, a rake angle slightly larger than 25° gives the maximum cutting speed, which is also a little greater than 130%. On the other hand, as the hardness of the work material increases, a larger force is placed on the cutting edge and in order to keep this edge from crumbling away, it is necessary to use a somewhat smaller rake angle with a resulting slight decrease in the maximum cutting speed. In machining alloy steels, especially those strengthened by cold-work or heat-treating, tools sharpened with a side-rake angle of 5° to 10° perform most satisfactorily.

Side-Cutting-Edge Angle. Figure 6-29b 'shows the influence that the side-cutting-edge angle has on the cutting speed for a given tool-life when machining a moderately soft steel. An increase in the side cutting edge (SCE) angle from 0° to 60° effects an increase of 50% in the relative cutting speed. Because of the tendency of chatter to occur when the length of the cutting edge is extended, it is seldom practical to use angles as large as 60°. However, in some instances when the depth of cut is very small, it is possible to employ a large angle in order to take advantage of the considerable increase in cutting speed that it makes possible. On most of the roughing work done in job shops, it is possible to use SCE angles of from 20° to 30°.

The high cutting speed resulting from a large SCE angle may be obtained without grinding a large angle on the tool, but simply by inclining the tool holder to the desired angle with the axis of rotation of the work (Figure 6-30). This practice is advantageous, since the SCE angle usually requires more grinding time than any of the other angles of the tool point.

Nose Radius. The nose radius has the greatest effect of all the elements of the tool point on the maximum cutting speed for any machining operation. Figure 6-29c shows that when turning a moderately soft steel, the cutting speed for a given tool-life increases exponentially. The speed for a constant tool life is increased by 120% as the nose radius is enlarged from 0 to $\frac{1}{4}$ in. Although a $\frac{1}{4}$ in. radius cannot be used very extensively on job-shop work, a $\frac{1}{8}$ in. radius can be used on much of the roughing and finishing work with cutting speeds 85% faster than when a sharp-pointed tool is used. In addition to its beneficial effect upon the velocity for a given tool life, the larger nose radius improves the surface finish of the machined work

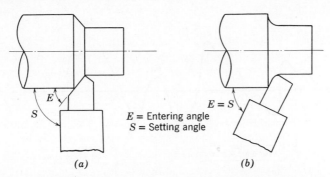

Figure 6-30. Tool bit and holder showing side-cutting edge angle and entering angle. With a 90° setting angle in (*a*), the entering angle is obtained by grinding a suitable side-cutting-edge. The same result can be obtained, as in (*b*), with much less grinding time simply by changing the setting angle.

material. Whenever a tool having a small radius is used in conjunction with a large feed, the resulting machined surface resembles a shallow thread.

SURFACE FINISH

In industrial practice there are many ways of specifying the surface finish that is desired on a part. Some companies use symbols such as "f" or "ff" or letters encased in a triangle like $\triangle{A}$ or $\triangle{B}$ to indicate the relative smoothness of the desired surface. These companies also have an intra-plant code that interprets the symbols into typical cutting conditions. For example, the symbol $\triangle{E}$ may specify that the referred surface be "machined with a light cut of $\frac{1}{16}$ to $\frac{1}{8}$ in. depth with a feed of 0.005 to 0.010 ipr and a tool having a small radius on the end."

However, today it has become increasingly common for industrial firms to specify the surface finish by means of either one of the two quantitative surface finish specifications that were developed during the past quarter century. The first of the quantitative measures of surface finish is the root mean square (rms) and the second is the arithmetic average (AA). The former is frequently specified by means of the symbol μ which designates microinches followed by the letters rms, whereas the latter is specified simply by the letter μ. Figure 6-31 illustrates these two surface finish designations in terms of the surface topography where h is the distance in millionths of an inch from an arbitrary reference plane to a specific point on the surface. The rms

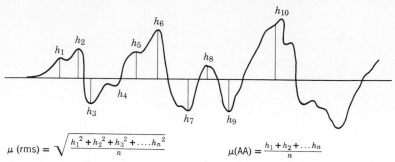

$$\mu \ (\text{rms}) = \sqrt{\frac{h_1{}^2 + h_2{}^2 + h_3{}^2 + \ldots h_n{}^2}{n}} \qquad\qquad \mu(\text{AA}) = \frac{h_1 + h_2 + \ldots h_n}{n}$$

Figure 6-31. Sketch of surface topography. Magnified in the Y-direction. The heights h are measured in microinches (10^{-6} in.) The numerical value of the surface finish is placed above the $\sqrt{}$ of the square root symbol, as: $\sqrt[32]{}$. Rms is the root mean square average; AA is the arithmetic average.

value in microinches, as shown in Figure 6-31, is the square root of the sum of the squared h values divided by the number of h values used. The AA value in microinches is, as the name implies, the simple numerical average of the h values. The numerical value of the surface finish is written above the v of the square root symbol as follows: $\sqrt[16]{}$ for a 16-microinch surface finish.

Figure 6-32 shows schematically the heads of instruments for determining the quantitative measure of surface finish for each of the two designations already described. The first type labeled *a* yields rms values. It consists of a coil that is attached to the stylus and positioned between the poles of a permanent magnet. In operation, the head is placed so that the two semispherical skids rest on the surface that is to be evaluated. Then, either by hand or by means of a motor-driven linkage, the head is reciprocated at a controlled speed over the surface. The tip of the stylus has a radius of 5×10^{-4} in.; consequently it rises and falls with the surface topography, whereas the large skids more or less ride on the peaks of the surface. An electric potential is generated in the coil as it moves up and down in the magnetic field. This potential is amplified and indicated on a meter as the rms value of the surface finish.

The instrument head illustrated in Figure 6-32*b* yields arithmetic average values of surface finish. This instrument is operated the same as the previously described one. The difference between the two is how the movement of the stylus creates an electric signal that is interpreted as a surface roughness measurement. In the latter type of instrument, the stylus is attached to a lever that protrudes into a vacuum tube. The enclosed end of the lever is designed to serve as the grid between the anode and the cathode of the vacuum tube. As the stylus moves up and down while tracing over the surface that is being evaluated, the distance between the grid and the anode changes. This produces a variation in the flow of electrons in the tube which registers on the meter as the arithmetic average of the surface roughness.

When a surface consists of random irregularities (normal roughness) superimposed on a wavy pattern, it is desirable to separate the two components. Most of the surface measuring instruments do not include in the numerical value of the surface finish the rise and fall of the stylus due to any waves having a pitch, p greater than $\frac{1}{32}$ in (Figure 6-33). Some instruments have the feature of recording both the waviness and the roughness.

Although surface finish designation and measurement is an important part of the manufacturing processes, the actual control of the surface finish is an even more important subject. There are two aspects to consider in the control of the surface finish of machined

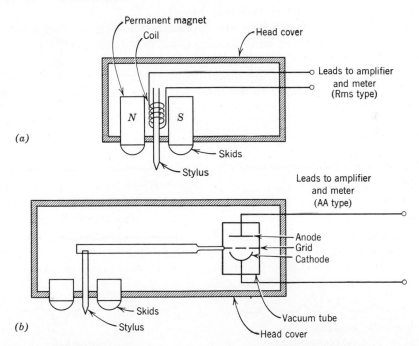

Figure 6-32. Schematic drawing of the heads of two types of surface finish measuring instruments.

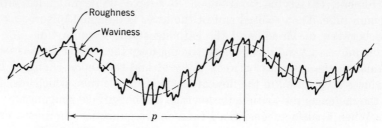

Figure 6-33. Roughness imposed on a regular wave pattern.

surfaces. One is geometrical, dealing with the feed and nose radius of the tool. The second is microstructural, dealing with the kind of chip formed and the presence of a built-up-edge.

Figure 6-34a shows us that the surface finish varies directly with the feed for a constant nose radius on the cutting tool. That is, the numerical value of the surface finish increases as the feed increases. Figure 6-34b shows how the opposite is true when the nose radius is varied with a constant feed. Thus the numerical value of the surface finish decreases as the nose radius increases.

Both of these illustrations are approximations because they ignore all other effects such as built-up edges, which will be described later, and abrasion. Also the preceding illustrations are only valid in describing the surface finish in the direction of feeding or across the feed marks. The surface finish in the direction of the feed marks or in the

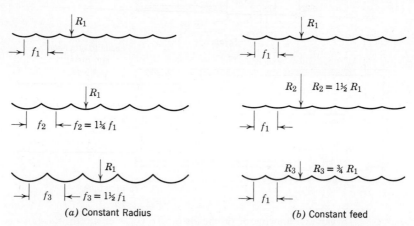

Figure 6-34. Effect of feed and nose radius on surface finish.

direction of the cutting velocity does not depend primarily on the feed
or nose radius, but rather it depends upon the amount of tearing or
abrasion that is associated with the chip forming process. In general,
the surface finish across the feed marks is rougher than the surface
finish along the feed marks.

The amount of tearing or galling that occurs during machining is
influenced primarily by two factors: the cutting velocity; and the
environment, that is, the cutting fluid. This is shown in Figure 6-35
where we see the general effect of velocity on the surface finish with
a light feed of about 0.005 in. and a modest radius of about $\frac{1}{16}$ in.
The abscissa is plotted as the relative cutting speed in terms of C_h
which is the velocity that results in a 1 min tool life when machining
with a high speed steel tool. Thus, if the Taylor equation for a given
set of cutting conditions with a hss tool is $vt^n = 180$, then C_h is 180
fpm.

When no cutting fluid is used, the band designated as A in Figure
6-35 represents reasonably well how the velocity affects the surface
finish. The finish is relatively poor until a velocity approximately
equal to C_h is reached, and for speeds slightly greater than this the
lowest values of surface finish are obtained. When machining with
some types of cutting fluids at very low velocities, it is possible to
achieve surface finishes that are comparable to those obtained at high

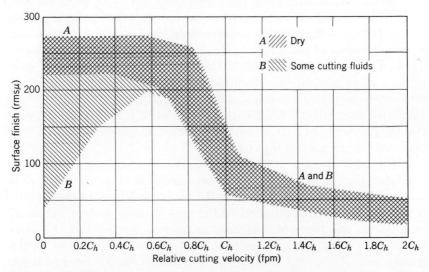

Figure 6-35. Effect of velocity on surface finish. C_h is the velocity that results in
a 1 min tool-life with an HSS tool and no coolant.

velocities when cutting dry. On the other hand, some cutting fluids have little or no effect on the surface finish. Very little engineering information is available regarding this phenomenon. However, some recent studies by the author seem to confirm the claim that a crack is formed in the work material ahead of the tool and in the direction of cutting—a claim made by several researchers about 1900. But this earlier concept was abandoned in the 1920's in favor of the sliding deck of cards model. On this basis, if a cutting fluid is to act as a lubricant, then either the fluid or its vapor must flow into the void space that is the crack and lubricate the bottom surface of the chip prior to when it slides up the tool face. Figure 6-24 is a photomicrograph made *during* the machining of a polished and etched specimen that clearly illustrates that above contention.

In nearly all industrial machining operations it is necessary, for purely economic reasons as discussed in a following section, to have tool lives in excess of 1 min by a factor of 10 or 100. Thus, it is obvious that usually surface finishes as good as 30 to 60 rms microinches cannot be obtained when using tools made of high-speed steel. Since the tool life constant for tungsten carbide tools, C_c, is three to five times the value of C_h for high-speed steel tools, it is readily possible to get good surface finishes when machining with carbide tools. The ceramic tools with a tool-life constant five to eight times that of the high-speed steel tools also gives good surface finishes.

The reason usually given for a rough surface being obtained with a low velocity and a smooth surface with a high velocity is the theory that a built-up-edge (BUE) is present on the cutting face of a tool when machining at low speeds but not when machining at high speeds. Thus in regard to Figure 6-35 it may be interpreted that a BUE is present when cutting at velocities less than C_h and that it is not present when cutting at velocities greater than C_h. There is a gradual transition from when a BUE is present to when it is not present, and this range where the BUE is unstable occurs at velocities slightly less than and slightly greater than C_h.

The built-up-edge is a small piece of the work material being machined that is separated from both the work and the chip; it is attached either mechanically or welded to the tool face, (Figure 6-36). A given BUE remains attached to the tool for only a short period of time. When one becomes detached, another is formed and this continues in an irregular cyclic pattern. Part of the BUE goes off on the bottom side of the chip and part of it remains on the finished work surface causing a very rough surface.

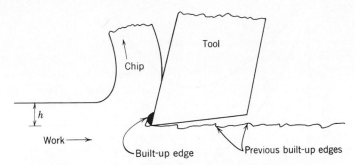

Figure 6-36. Sketch of a built-up-edge (BUE) and how it affects surface finish.

The height of the BUE varies with time, and many times it extends below the tool point. Thus the height of the machined surface, on a microscale, varies inversely with the height of the BUE.

When the BUE is present, it affects the machining operation in two additional ways. First, it protects the point of the tool from the sliding-rubbing action of the chip and causes the wear to occur further back along the tool face where the chip contacts the tool. Wear of this type is usually referred to as crater wear. The other aspect of the BUE is that it, in essence, acts as a second cutting tool with uncontrolled tool shape and usually with negative rake angles near its bottom. This has the effect of slightly increasing the forces and work needed for the machining operation.

COST ANALYSIS FOR A TURNING CUT

The total cost for any machining operation is comprised of four individual costs: loading and unloading cost, c_l; actual cutting cost, c_c; tool changing cost, c_{tc}; the tool cost (including grinding cost), c_g. The relationships between these costs, as well as the total cost, and the cutting speed are shown schematically in Figure 6-37. The nomenclature of the operating conditions included in this cost analysis is listed in Table 6-7. An analysis like the one presented next was first made by Taylor in 1907 in his classic book *On The Art of Cutting Metals*.[13]

The individual costs for a specific turning operation, such as turning the 5.925 in. diameter of Figure 6-38 to a 5.725 in. diameter, can be calculated in the following manner. Two expressions are derived for each of the three costs that are affected by the cutting speed (the

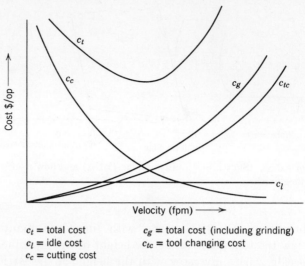

c_t = total cost c_g = total cost (including grinding)
c_l = idle cost c_{tc} = tool changing cost
c_c = cutting cost

Figure 6-37. Schematic relationship between cutting cost
cost and cutting speed.

loading cost is assumed to be unaffected by the cutting speed). The
first expression given is on the basis of using the cutting speed in terms
of rpm, and is the simpler of the two when the calculations are made
with a slide rule. The second expression uses the cutting speed in terms
of fpm and may be better for computer solutions. When the units for
the operating conditions are those listed in Table 6-7, the calculated
costs *have the units of dollars per operation.*

TABLE 6-7   Nomenclature of Operating Conditions Used
in Cost Analysis

K_1 = Labor rate: direct + overhead ($ per min)
K_2 = Tool cost ($ per cutting edge) (original cost + regrind cost)
t_i = Load, unload, and approach (idle) time per operation (min)
t_c = Cutting time (min/operation)
t_{tc} = Tool changing time (min)
L = Length of cut (in.)
D = Maximum diameter being cut (in.)
v = Cutting speed (fpm)
f = Feed (ipr)
n and C = Constants in tool-life equation
B_o = Tool failures per operation

The first cost is the loading cost per operation. This is sometimes referred to as the idle cost since the machine tool is idle during the time that the part is being loaded and unloaded. The loading cost is simply equal to the time in minutes required to load, unload, and advance the tool multiplied by the shop rate, K_1, in dollars per minute. That is,

$$c_l = K_1 t \qquad (6\text{-}28)$$

The second cost is the cutting cost per operation. It is equal to the product of shop rate, K_1, and the cutting time in minutes. That is,

$$c_c = K_1 t_c \qquad (6\text{-}29)$$

On the basis of the cutting speed expressed as rpm, since

$$t_c = \frac{L}{F} \frac{(\text{in.})}{(\text{ipm})} = \frac{L}{fN}$$

then

$$c_c = K_1 \frac{L}{fN} \qquad (6\text{-}30)$$

On the basis of the cutting speed expressed as fpm, since

$$N = \frac{12v}{\pi D}$$

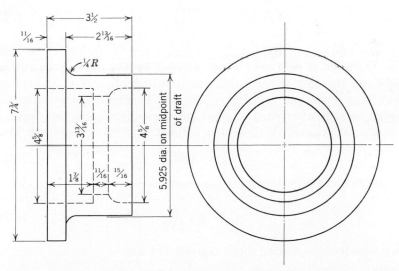

Figure 6-38. Drawing of a bearing housing. Material: permanent mold pearlite gray iron. Hardness: 187 Bhn.

then

$$c_c = \frac{L\pi D}{12fv} \qquad (6\text{-}31)$$

The third cost is the tool changing cost per operation. It is equal to the product of the shop rate K_1, the tool changing time t_{tc}, and the number of tool changes (or tool failures) per operation B_o. Thus

$$c_{tc} = K_1 t_{tc} B_o \qquad (6\text{-}32)$$

where B_o is the reciprocal of the number of pieces that can be machined for each tool sharpening. It is equal to the ratio of the cutting time per piece over the tool life at the particular speed being used. That is,

$$B_o = \frac{t_c}{t} \quad \text{where} \quad t = \left(\frac{C}{v}\right)^{1/n} \quad \text{in the Taylor equation}$$

and

$$t_c = \frac{L}{fN} \quad \text{or} \quad \frac{L\pi D}{12fv}$$

On the basis of the cutting speed expressed as rpm

$$c_{tc} = K_1 t_{tc} \frac{L}{fNt} \qquad (6\text{-}33)$$

On the basis of the cutting speed expressed as fpm

$$c_{tc} = K_1 t_{tc} \frac{L\pi D v^{(1/n)-1}}{12fC^{1/n}} \qquad (6\text{-}34)$$

The fourth cost item is the tool cost per operation. It includes both the original cost of the tool divided by the number of cutting edges and the cost of regrinding each cutting edge. With the throwaway type of carbide tool insert, the tool is intentionally made thin enough so that after each original cutting edge on the tool becomes dull, the tool (insert) is discarded without ever being reground. Thus

$$c_g = K_2 B_o \qquad (6\text{-}35)$$

On the basis of the cutting speed expressed as rpm

$$c_g = K_2 \frac{L}{fNt} \qquad (6\text{-}36)$$

On the basis of the cutting speed expressed as fpm

$$c_g = K_2 \frac{L\pi D v^{(1/n)-1}}{12fC^{1/n}} \qquad (6\text{-}37)$$

It is possible to determine the "theoretical minimum" cost for which a particular turning operation may be produced by calculating the cutting speed that results in the minimum cost per operation. This is accomplished by equating the total cost to the sum of the four individual costs, differentiating the cost with respect to the cutting speed and setting the result equal to zero, as follows:

$$c_t = c_l + c_c + c_{tc} + c_g \qquad (6\text{-}37)$$

By substituting Equations 6-28, 31, 34, and 37 into the above equation, and by letting $A = L\pi D/12f$ for simplification, then

$$c_t = K_1 t_l + K_1 A v^{-1} + K_1 t_{tc} A \frac{v^{(1/n)-1}}{C^{(1/n)}} + K_2 A \frac{v^{(1/n)-1}}{(C)^{1/n}}$$

$$\frac{dc}{dv} = 0 - K_1 A v^{-2} + K_1 t_{tc} A \left(\frac{1}{n} - 1\right) \frac{v^{(1/n)-2}}{C^{1/n}}$$

$$+ K_2 A \left(\frac{1}{n} - 1\right) \frac{v^{(1/n)-2}}{C^{1/n}} = 0$$

$$v^{(1/n)-2} \left\{ \frac{K_1 t_{tc}[(1/n) - 1]}{C^{1/n}} + \frac{K_2[(1/n) - 1]}{C^{1/n}} \right\} = K_1 v^{-2}$$

$$v^{1/n} \left\{ \frac{[(1/n) - 1](K_1 t_{tc} + K_2)}{C^{1/n}} \right\} = K_1$$

$$v_m = C \left\{ \frac{K_1}{[(1/n) - 1](K_1 t_{tc} + K_2)} \right\}^n \qquad (6\text{-}38)$$

The subscript m is used to denote the cutting speed for minimum cost.
For further simplification, let

$$R = \frac{K_1 t_{tc} + K_2}{K_1} = t_{tc} + \frac{K_2}{K_1} \qquad (6\text{-}39)$$

and

$$v_m = C \left\{ \frac{1}{[(1/n) - 1]R} \right\}^n \qquad (6\text{-}40)$$

The tool life for minimum cost is an even simpler relationship that is more convenient to use in industrial manufacturing situations in which cutting speed tool-life data are represented graphically. To obtain the equation for tool life for minimum cost, Equation 6-40 is solved simultaneously with the Taylor equation

$$v_m = C \left(\frac{1}{t}\right)^n$$

to obtain

$$t_m = \left(\frac{1}{n} - 1\right) R \qquad (6\text{-}41)$$

In some manufacturing situations it may be considered worthwhile to perform a certain operation at a cutting speed greater than the speed that results in the minimum cost. Such a situation might be where a plant is already producing or working during the maximum number of hours possible and increased orders require an increase in production. This increase in production can be achieved by either purchasing new equipment or by increasing the cutting speed beyond the speed for minimum cost. In many instances, the latter choice is desirable. In this situation, it is very important to know what the *maximum* production rate for a specific operation is. This can be determined from the relationships previously worked out for the minimum cost by assuming that the tool cost is unimportant, that is, setting $K_2 = 0$.

Then

$$R = \frac{K_1 t_{tc} + K_2}{K_1} = t_{tc} \qquad (6\text{-}42)$$

Therefore the cutting speed for maximum production is

$$v_p = \frac{C}{\{[(1/n) - 1]t_{tc}\}^n} = \frac{C}{(t_p)^n} \qquad (6\text{-}43)$$

where the tool life for maximum production, t_p, is

$$t_p = \left(\frac{1}{n} - 1\right) t_{tc} \qquad (6\text{-}44)$$

The cutting speed and the tool life for maximum production as defined above are the speed and resulting tool life that enable the greatest number of parts to be made in a given time. That is, for any speed higher or lower than the maximum production speed, the number of pieces produced in a given time will be less. It is interesting to observe that when machining with a hss tool ($n = 0.1$) requiring a tool changing time of 1 min that $t_p = 9$ min. And when machining with a carbide throwaway insert ($n = 0.2$) having a tool changing time of $\frac{1}{2}$ min, then $t_p = 2$ min. That is, the tool should last for only 2 min of actual cutting.

The use of these concepts of the economics of machining is demonstrated in the following illustrative sample problem.

A Problem and Solution On Economics of Turning

Problem. Machinability tests on the castings illustrated in Figure 6-38 were conducted with a depth of cut of 0.100 in. and a feed of 0.006 ipr. The Taylor equations obtained under these conditions were $vt^{0.1} = 250$ and $vt^{0.2} = 700$ for hss and carbide tools, respectively.

The 5.925 in. diameter is to be reduced to 5.725 in. diameter in one turning cut with a feed of 0.006 ipr on a production lathe. The length of the cut is $2\frac{1}{2}$ in. and the load-unload time is $\frac{1}{2}$ min. On the basis of the cost data listed in Table 6-8, calculate the following:

1. The cutting speed for the minimum cost for the three tools listed in Table 6-8.

2. The tool life that will result in the maximum production rate for the same three tools.

3. The minimum cost for this one turning operation for all three tools.

4. The cost when turning at the maximum production rate with hss tools and with carbide tools.

5. The cost when turning at a low speed (100 fpm) with hss tools.

TABLE 6-8. Cost of Labor and Tools

Cost Factors	$\frac{3}{8}$ in. sq. hss	Solid Insert	Throwaway
		Type of Tool	
		$\frac{3}{8}$ in. sq. Carbide	
Original cost of tool	$0.50	$5.25	$0.75
Tool regrinding time	2 min	15 min	0 min
Tool changing time	$\frac{1}{2}$ min	$\frac{1}{2}$ min	$\frac{1}{2}$ min
Number of cutting edges per grind	1	8	8
Number of regrinds per tool	20	10	0

Labor Rates	
Machine operators rate (per hr)	$2.25
Machine dept. burden rate	5.00
Tool grinders rate	2.50
Grinding dept. burden rate	6.00

For the following solution it is assumed that the production lathe used has an infinite number of speeds, and that the production tools have the same shape as the research tools.

The Solution. First calculate the constants K_1 and K_2

$$K_1 = \frac{2.25 + 5.00}{60} = \frac{7.25}{60} = \$0.121/\text{min}$$

$$K_2 = \text{initial} + \text{regrind cost}$$

For the hss tool

$$K_2 = \frac{0.50}{20} + 2 \times \frac{8.50}{60} = 0.025 + 0.283 = \$0.308/\text{cutting edge}$$

For the insert tool

$$K_2 = \frac{5.25}{10 \times 8} + \frac{15}{8} \times \frac{8.50}{60} = 0.066 + 0.266 = \$0.332/\text{cutting edge}$$

For the throwaway tool

$$K_2 = \frac{0.75}{8} + 0 = \$0.094/\text{cutting edge}$$

Next, calculate R from

$$R = \frac{K_1 t_{tc} + K_2}{K_1}$$

For the hss tool

$$R = \frac{0.121 \times \frac{1}{2} + 0.308}{0.121} = 3.04 \text{ min/edge}$$

For the insert tool

$$R = \frac{0.121 \times \frac{1}{2} + 0.332}{0.121} = 3.24 \text{ min/edge}$$

For the throwaway tool

$$R = \frac{0.121 \times \frac{1}{2} + 0.094}{0.121} = 1.27 \text{ min/edge}$$

1. Then the cutting speed for the minimum cost is calculated from

$$v_m = \frac{C}{\left[\left(\frac{1}{n} - 1\right)(R)\right]^n}$$

For the hss tool

$$v_m = \frac{250}{\left[\left(\frac{1}{0.1} - 1\right)(3.04)\right]^{0.1}} = \frac{250}{(9 \times 3.04)^{0.1}} = \frac{250}{27.36^{0.1}} = \frac{250}{1.392} = \underline{\underline{180 \text{ fpm}}}$$

For the insert tool

$$v_m = \cfrac{700}{\left[\left(\cfrac{1}{0.2} - 1\right)(3.24)\right]^{0.2}} = \frac{700}{(4 \times 3.24)^{0.2}} = \frac{700}{12.96^{0.2}} = \frac{700}{1.668} = \underline{\underline{420 \text{ fpm}}}$$

For the throwaway tool

$$v_m = \cfrac{700}{\left[\left(\cfrac{1}{0.2} - 1\right)(1.27)\right]^{0.2}} = \frac{700}{(4 \times 1.27)^{0.2}} = \frac{700}{5.08^{0.2}} = \frac{700}{1.385} = \underline{\underline{505 \text{ fpm}}}$$

2. The tool life for the maximum production rate is calculated from

$$t_p = \left(\frac{1}{n} - 1\right) t_{tc}$$

For the hss tool

$$t_p = \left(\frac{1}{0.1} - 1\right) \times \tfrac{1}{2} = 9 \times \tfrac{1}{2} = \underline{\underline{4\tfrac{1}{2} \text{ min}}}$$

For both the carbide tools

$$t_p = \left(\frac{1}{0.2} - 1\right) \times \tfrac{1}{2} = 4 \times \tfrac{1}{2} = \underline{\underline{2 \text{ min}}}$$

The equivalent cutting speeds for the maximum production rate are:

$$v_p = \frac{C}{t^n} = \frac{250}{4.5^{0.1}} = \frac{250}{1.163} = \underline{\underline{215 \text{ fpm}}}$$

$$v_p = \frac{C}{t^n} = \frac{700}{2^{0.2}} = \frac{700}{1.149} = \underline{\underline{610 \text{ fpm}}}$$

3. The minimum cost on the basis of the cutting speed in fpm is calculated from

$$(c_t)_m = c_l + c_c + c_{tc} + c_g$$

or

$$(c_t)_m = K_1 t_l + K_1 \frac{L\pi D}{12vf} + K_1 \frac{L\pi D v^{(1/n)-1}}{12fC^{1/n}} t_{tc} + K_2 \frac{L\pi D v^{(1/n)-1}}{12fC^{1/n}}$$

For the hss tool

$$(c_t)_m = 0.121 \times \tfrac{1}{2} + 0.121 \frac{2.5\pi \times 5.925}{12 \times 180 \times 0.006}$$

$$+ 0.121 \frac{2.5\pi \times 5.925 \times 180^9}{12 \times 0.006 \times 250^{10}} \times \tfrac{1}{2}$$

$$+ 0.308 \frac{2.5\pi \times 5.925 \times 180^9}{12 \times 0.006 \times 250^{10}}$$

$$= 0.06 + 0.435 + 0.121 \times \frac{646 \times 180^9}{250 \times 250^9} \times \tfrac{1}{2} + 0.308 \times \frac{646 \times 180^9}{250 \times 250^9}$$

$$= 0.06 + 0.436 + 0.008 + 0.039 = \underline{\underline{\$0.543}}$$

For the carbide solid insert tool

$$(c_t)_m = 0.06 + 0.121 \frac{2.5\pi \times 5.925}{12 \times 420 \times 0.006}$$

$$+ 0.121 \frac{2.5\pi \times 5.925 \times 420^4}{12 \times 0.006 \times 700 \times 700^4} \times \tfrac{1}{2}$$

$$+ 0.33 \frac{2.5\pi \times 5.925 \times 420^4}{12 \times 0.006 \times 700 \times 700^4}$$

$$= 0.06 + 0.186 + 0.06 \times 646 \times \frac{0.13}{700} + 0.33 \times 646 \times \frac{0.13}{700}$$

$$= 0.060 + 0.186 + 0.007 + 0.039$$

$$= \$0.292$$

For the carbide throwaway insert tool ($A = 646$)

$$(c_t)_m = 0.06 + 0.121 \times \frac{646}{505} + 0.06 \times \frac{646}{700} \frac{(505)^4}{(700)^4} + 0.094 \times \frac{646}{700} \frac{(505)^4}{(700)^4}$$

$$= 0.06 + 0.155 + 0.06 \times \frac{646}{700} \times 0.272 + 0.094 \times \frac{646}{700} \times 0.272$$

$$= 0.06 + 0.155 + 0.015 + 0.023$$

$$= \$0.253$$

The minimum cost on the basis of the cutting speed expressed in rpm is calculated as follows:

$$(c_t)_m = K_1 t_l + K_1 \frac{L}{fN} + K_1 t_{tc} \times \frac{L}{fNt} + K_2 \frac{L}{fNt}$$

For the hss tool

$$N = \frac{12v}{\pi D} = \frac{12 \times 180}{\pi \times 5.925} = 116 \text{ rpm} \qquad \text{and} \quad t = 27.36$$

$$(c_t)_m = 0.121 \times \tfrac{1}{2} + 0.121 \times \frac{2.5}{0.006 \times 116} + 0.121 \times \tfrac{1}{2}$$

$$\times \frac{2.5}{0.006 \times 116 \times 27.36} + 0.308 \frac{2.5}{0.006 \times 116 \times 27.36}$$

$$= 0.06 + 0.435 + 0.008 + 0.039 = \$0.543$$

For the carbide solid insert tool

$$N = \frac{12v}{\pi D} = \frac{12 \times 420}{\pi \times 5.925} = 271 \text{ rpm} \qquad \text{and} \quad t = 12.96$$

$$(c_t)_m = 0.121 \times \tfrac{1}{2} + 0.121 \times \frac{2.5}{0.006 \times 271} + 0.121$$

$$\times \tfrac{1}{2} \frac{2.5}{0.006 \times 271 \times 12.96} + 0.332 \frac{2.5}{0.006 \times 271 \times 12.96}$$

$$= 0.060 + 0.186 + 0.007 + 0.039 = \$0.292$$

For the carbide throwaway insert tool

$$N = \frac{12v}{\pi D} = \frac{12 \times 505}{\pi \times 5.925} = 326 \quad \text{and} \quad t = 5.08$$

$$(c_t)_m = 0.121 \times \tfrac{1}{2} + 0.121 \frac{2.5}{0.006 \times 326} + 0.121$$

$$\times \tfrac{1}{2} \frac{2.5}{0.006 \times 326 \times 5.08} + 0.094 \frac{2.5}{0.006 \times 326 \times 5.08}$$

$$= 0.060 + 0.155 + 0.015 + 0.023 = \$0.253$$

4. The cost when turning at the maximum production rate.

For hss tools

$$(c_t)_p = 0.121 \times \tfrac{1}{2} + 0.121 \frac{2.5\pi \times 5.925}{12 \times 215 \times 0.006} + 0.121 \frac{2.5\pi \times 5.925 \times 215^9}{12 \times 0.006 \times 250^{10}}$$

$$\times \tfrac{1}{2} + 0.308 \frac{2.5\pi \times 5.925 \times 215^9}{12 \times 0.006 \times 250^{10}}$$

$$= 0.06 + 0.363 + 0.06 \times \frac{646}{250}\left(\frac{215}{250}\right)^9 + 0.308 \frac{646}{250}\left(\frac{215}{250}\right)^9$$

$$= 0.06 + 0.363 + 0.040 + 0.198 = \$0.663$$

For the carbide solid insert and throwaway tools

$$(c_t)_p = 0.06 + 0.186 \times \frac{420}{610} + 0.06 \times \frac{646}{700} \times \left(\frac{610}{700}\right)^4 + 0.33 \times \frac{646}{700}\left(\frac{610}{700}\right)^4$$

$$= 0.06 + 0.128 + 0.06 \times \frac{646}{700} \times 0.576 + 0.33 \times \frac{646}{700} \times 0.576$$

$$= 0.060 + 0.128 + 0.032 + 0.175$$

$$= \$0.295$$

5. The cost when turning with an hss tool at 100 fpm.

The tool life from the Taylor equation is

$$t = \left(\frac{C}{v}\right)^{1/n} = \left(\frac{250}{100}\right)^{10} = 2.5^{10} = \frac{9,500}{60} = 158 \text{ hrs}$$

and the cost is

$$c_t = 0.06 + 0.435 \times \frac{180}{100} + 0.06\frac{646}{250}\left(\frac{100}{250}\right)^9 + 0.308\frac{646}{250}\left(\frac{100}{250}\right)^9$$

$$= 0.06 + 0.78 + 0.06\frac{646}{250} \times 0.00025 + 0.308 \times \frac{646}{250} \times 0.00025$$

$$= 0.06 + 0.78 + 0.0 + 0.0002$$

$$= \underline{\underline{\$0.84}}$$

From the above calculations we can see that the machining cost at the maximum production rate is not much higher than the cost when machining at the minimum cost speed, particularly when carbide tools are used. However, the costs are considerably higher when speeds lower than the minimum cost speed are used.

MACHINABILITY

Machining is primarily a severe plastic deformation process in which the material being cut is locally deformed to fracture. This deformation is accompanied by severe rubbing with high friction on both the tool face at the tool-chip interface and the tool flank at the tool-work contact surface. These three regions are shown in Figure 6-39.

Deforming the material during cutting as well as the friction caused by rubbing produce heat which makes the tool hot. As it becomes hot, its strength and wear-resistance decrease causing it to

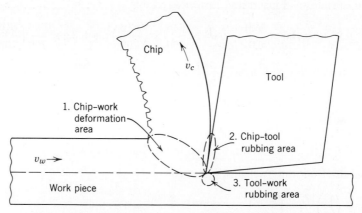

Figure 6-39. The three heat-producing zones in machining.

"fail," that is, its cutting edge to wear down. Most of the heat generated during machining is carried away with the chips, particularly at high speed, and a small amount is conducted to the work piece. The amount of heat transferred by conduction through the tool to the tool holder and surroundings is negligible. On a thermal basis, machining is essentially a steady-state process within a few seconds after cutting begins.

The term machinability, as used by engineers and technicians today, is a somewhat vague one that expresses the relative ease of machining a material. The basis for the evaluation or comparison may be any of the following: (1) tool life or cutting speed for a standard cutting condition; (2) cutting forces; (3) horsepower required; (4) surface finish; (5) chip disposal; and (6) dimensional stability. The concept of machinability used in this text is the first of the above-mentioned ones, namely, either the cutting speed for a given tool life or the tool life for a given cutting speed. This concept is the original one proposed by Herbert, Rosenhain, and Sturney in the 1920's. It is actually the most commonly used concept of machinability at the present time since all relative machinability ratings listed in all the handbooks are based on the cutting speed for a given tool life under some standard cutting conditions. Table 6-9 illustrates this kind of tabular data.

TABLE 6-9.   Machinability Ratings for Several Materials
(AISI B1112 Steel = 100%)

Material	Brinell Hardness	Machinability Rating (%)
Titanium	250	25
Tool Steel	200	30
18-8 Austenitic S.S.	155	30
Monel	200	40
AISI 4340	220	45
AISI 1080	220	45
AISI 1010	130	50
Aluminum bronze	150	60
AISI 1020	140	65
Berylium	–	65
Malleable iron	140	120
AISI B1113	190	135
Aluminum	–	300 to 1500
Magnesium	–	500 to 2000

In this context it is apparent that the machining efficiency of a material is dependent not only upon the physical properties of the material, but also on the tool material, tool shape, and cutting process. However, it is extremely desirable to have a *concept of machinability where it is a characteristic, or a secondary property dependent upon primary properties, of a material.* By this means it is possible to select or evaluate materials that are being considered during the design of component parts on the basis of economic fabrication as well as functional performance.

To achieve a machinability index that is a characteristic of the material, it is necessary to control the variables associated with the tool and cutting conditions. When a material's mechanical properties are evaluated by means of a tensile test, the testing temperature, pressure, environment, and specimen shape are all specified by testing standards. Similarly, when a material's machinability is being evaluated, everything concerned with the testing, exclusive of the material itself, should be fixed by specified standards. When this approach is taken, it is then possible to correlate a secondary property such as machinability with the primary physical properties, as is done in the next section.

To prevent the term machinability from becoming a vague, general word it is best to use it only when referring to *the characteristic of a material that indicates the cutting speed under standard conditions at which the material can be machined.* Thus machinability will have the units of length over time (ft/min). Whenever other machining parameters, such as cutting forces or surface finish, are being discussed, the term machinability should not be used to categorize the materials. Instead, the specific effect under study should itself be used. Thus, if the cutting force during the machining of one material is twice that of a second material, it should be so stated rather than confuse the subject by implying that the machinability of the second material is twice that of the first.

The physical properties of a material that affect its machinability fall into two classes, mechanical and thermal. The mechanical properties include the tensile strength, the strain-hardening exponent (or the Brinell hardness which is a measure of both the tensile strength and the strain-hardening exponent), and the final area ratio or per cent reduction of area. All these mechanical properties, as discussed in Chapters 1 and 2, can be correlated to and predicted from the microstructures of the material.

By referring to Figures 1-2, 6-39, and 6-40, the manner in which these physical properties influence a material's machinability may be

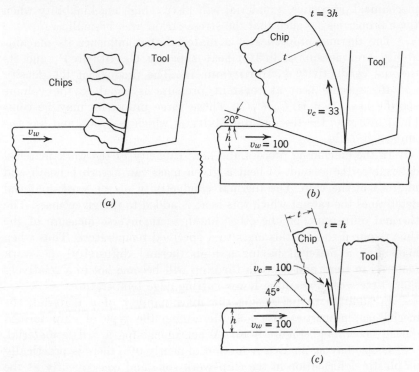

Figure 6-40. Types of chips formed in machining. (*a*) Discontinuous chips formed from brittle material. (*b*) and (*c*) Continuous chips formed with two materials of different ductility. (*b*) $\theta = 20°$. (*c*) $\theta = 45°$ (the ratio of t/h is called the chip-thickness ratio).

more easily understood. Heat is generated in the chip-work zone because of the tremendous amount of plastic deformation in that area, and in the tool-chip and tool-work zone because of friction. Since the life of the cutting tool depends upon its cutting-edge temperature, as discussed before, the amount of heat generated and the rate at which it is transferred to the work piece beneath the tool point is very important.

The area under the stress-strain curve, as illustrated in Figures 1-1 and 1-2, is an indication of the work (per unit volume) done on a material when it is plastically deformed to fracture, as in machining. This area may be determined if the tensile strength, the strain-harden-ing exponent, and the per cent reduction of area are known. Obviously, the larger this area is, the greater the amount of heat generated, with resulting higher tool-cutting edge temperatures. Thus, in terms of its mechanical properties, a material will have a high machinability when these properties are such that the stress-strain area is small.

The thermal properties of a material that influence its machinability are: density ρ, lb/ft^3; heat capacity C_p, Btu/lb°F; and its thermal conductivity k, Btu/ft/min/°F. The product of the density and the specific heat at constant pressure is equal to the volume specific heat, that is, $C_v = \rho C_p$. These three properties may be combined into one, the thermal diffusivity α, which is $k/\rho C_p$ and has the units of ft^2/min.

In the machining process, the heat capacity of the work material determines the amount of heat a given mass can absorb beneath and in front of the chip. The thermal conductivity of the work material determines the rate at which this heat is added to the given mass. The thermal diffusivity, on the other hand, is an inverse measure of the time required to heat this mass to a specified temperature. Thus when machining a material having a high thermal diffusivity, the work material in front and beneath the chip will become hot in a relatively short time with a resulting lower cutting edge temperature.

In addition to influencing the machinability of a material, the mechanical properties also help determine the type of chip formed during machining (Figure 6-40). When machining a brittle material, that is, one having an area reduction of nearly 0%, there is practically no plastic deformation in the chip-work zone and consequently as the tool progresses it causes the material in its path to fracture into small, irregularly shaped, undeformed chips as shown in Figure 6-40a. Chips of this type are desirable from a material handling, storing, and transporting point of view in that the chips have a relatively high bulk-density when compared to the stringy type of chips which are formed from ductile materials.

How thick and thin chips are formed when machining a ductile material is shown in Figure 6-40b and c. Both of these chips are referred to as the continuous type because they come off in long strings or coils. In b the shear angle ϕ is low, and consequently the thickness of the chip is greater than the thickness of the cut h. In this case ($\phi = 20°$) the chip-thickness ratio, h/t is 3. In other words, the length of the chip is one-third the length of the cut inasmuch as the volume of the material remains constant. The chip shown in c has a thickness equal to the thickness of the cut, or a cutting ratio of one. Unfortunately, the chip-thickness ratio, or the cutting ratio as it is sometimes called, cannot be determined from the mechanical properties at the present time, but must be determined by an actual machining test.

A Fundamental Machinability Equation

A comprehensive study of the influence of the physical properties of a material on its machinability was made by Henkin and Datsko.[5] This investigation yielded a relationship that equates the machinability of a material to the physical properties of thermal conductivity, Brinell hardness, and per cent reduction of area. The derivation of this fundamental machinability equation is presented below.

After considerable experimental and analytical study it was determined that seven independent variables, in addition to the tool-chip interface temperature, are required to completely define machinability. These eight variables are listed in Table 6-10. Many other parameters characterize the machining process, such as cutting forces, coefficient of friction, "shear" angle, chip ratio, and abrasion. However, all these additional parameters are really dependent upon the primary variables listed in Table 6-10, although the exact nature of this dependency is not known at the present. However, we will now briefly discuss these independent or primary variables.

TABLE 6-10.   Variables Used in Dimensional Analysis of Machinability

Variable	Dimensions	Description
H_B	$ML^{-1}t^{-2}$	Brinell hardness (kg/mm^2)
R_f	None	Area ratio at fracture
k	$MLt^{-3}T^{-1}$	Thermal conductivity (Btu/hr-ft-°F)
C_v or ρC_p	$ML^{-1}t^{-2}T^{-1}$	Volume specific heat (Btu/ft^3-°F)
h	L	Thickness (feed) of cut (in.)
w	L	Width (depth) of cut (in.)
v	Lt^{-1}	Cutting velocity (ft/min)
T	T	Tool-chip temperature (°F)

It was determined after several years of investigation of all the mechanical properties, including friction and wear-resistance, that the Brinell hardness and the area ratio at fracture (or per cent reduction of area) describe sufficiently well the plastic behavior of a material for the prediction of machinability. It is interesting to note that Herbert, in the 1920's, came to the conclusion that "The measure of machinability is the hardness of the chip."

Hardness implies resistance to penetration, or compressive deformation. The range of elastic deformation for materials, except for elastomers and the like, is quite small and therefore the hardness is primarily influenced by the plastic properties of the material: namely, the strength coefficient σ_o and the strain-hardening index m in the equation $\sigma = \sigma_o \epsilon^m$. Inasmuch as the average or effective strain a material is subjected to beneath the Brinell penetrator during a hardness test appears to be about the same as during a tensile test,* the Brinell hardness provides sufficient information of the plastic portion of a material's behavior. It is well known that the tensile strength is proportional to the Brinell hardness and that the proportionality constant is 500 for steel. For the analysis that follows, it must be recalled that the Brinell hardness has the units of stress, kg/mm^2, or energy per unit volume.

In order to determine the area under the stress-strain curve, which is a measure of the work per unit volume necessary to deform a material to fracture, the tensile strain at fracture ϵ_f must also be known. The strain at fracture may be determined from either the final area ratio or the per cent reduction of area by means of the following relationships that were developed in Chapter 1

$$\epsilon_f = \ln R_f = \ln \frac{100}{100 - A_r} \qquad (6\text{-}45)$$

As mentioned previously, the thermal properties that influence machinability are the volume specific heat ρC_p and the thermal conductivity k. This is valid provided the heat transfer through the tool as well as the heat convected to the surroundings are of second-order importance. Experimental data verify this condition for dry cutting, that is, machining without a cutting fluid.

The tool life also depends upon the cutting velocity v, the thickness of cut or feed h, and the width of cut w. As mentioned previously, parameters such as tool shape and tool material which actually in-

---

* By conducting a series of Meyer hardness tests in which the applied loads and diameter of ball are varied, a relationship such as

$$\frac{4L}{\pi d^2} = K \left(\frac{d}{D} \right)^{n-2}$$

is obtained where L is the load, d is the diameter of the indentation and D is diameter of the spherical indentor. The Meyer hardness is different from the Brinell hardness in that the area that is divided into the load is the projected area rather than the spherical contact area. The former is the proper value to use for determining stress. In the equation above it is apparent that the left side has the proper units of stress and that d/D has the units of strain. But the important fact is that it has been observed that when both tensile tests and the above-described hardness tests are conducted on the same material, $n\text{-}2$ is about equal to m, and K for many materials is equal to σ_o. Thus the hardness test may be considered as a compressive strain-hardening test.

fluence the tool life are considered to be fixed constants in this analysis so the resulting relationship is a reflection of the material's properties.

The cutting edge temperature T is a dependent variable, the magnitude of which is determined by the cutting velocity. As can be seen from the experimental data plotted in Figures 6-21 and 6-41 for a wide range of materials tested, the cutting edge temperature is $975 \pm 25°F$ for a cutting velocity that results in a 60 min tool life, designated as v_{60}. The velocity for a 60 min tool life is that which gives a tool cutting edge temperature of 975°F, and therefore it is not necessary to include time in the fundamental machinability relationship. Similarly, for a v_{20} the cutting edge temperature is found to be $1025 \pm 25°F$ in Figures 6-21 and 6-41.

The Pi-theorem of dimensional analysis states that the number of dimensionless groups needed to completely describe a physical phenomenon is equal to the difference between the total number of variables

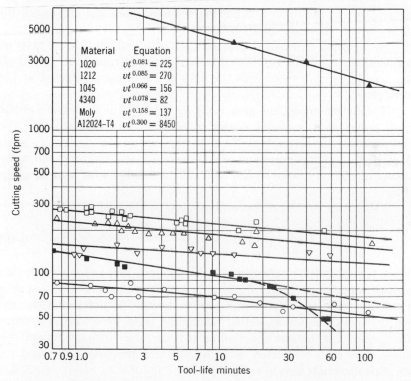

Material   Equation

Material	Equation
1020	$vt^{0.081} = 225$
1212	$vt^{0.085} = 270$
1045	$vt^{0.066} = 156$
4340	$vt^{0.078} = 82$
Moly	$vt^{0.158} = 137$
A12024-T4	$vt^{0.300} = 8450$

Figure 6-41. Relationship between cutting speed and tool-chip interface temperature for some metals.

and the number of primary variables. Four primary variables are used in this analysis: length L, time t, mass M, and temperature T. Since it was determined by experimental and analytical means that the eight variables listed in Table 6-10 are the total number needed to describe machinability, the number of dimensionless groups should be four.

Dimensionless analysis by itself does not indicate what the four dimensionless groups are. After the extensive study mentioned previously, it was established that the four required groups were: vh/α, w/h, $\rho C_p\, TJ/H_B$, and R_f. (α is the thermal diffusivity, $k/\rho C_p$; J is the mechanical equivalent of heat; R_f is the area ratio at fracture, A_o/A_f.)

The first group, vh/α, is the so-called thermal number whose importance was first recognized by Bisacre and Chao.[2] The thermal number governs the ratio of the heat conducted through the work to the heat transported by the moving chip. When machining with a large v and a small α, most of the heat goes out with the chips. But with a small v and large α, most of the heat goes into the work piece.

The second group, (w/h), represents the geometry of the cut and is discussed in detail in a following section where the exponents for these dimensionless groups are derived.

In the third dimensionless group, $\rho C_p\, J/H_B$ which has the units of temperature^{-1}, can be considered to represent a temperature rise if all the heat is carried away with the chip and none is conducted to the work piece.

The fourth group, the area ratio R_f or A_o/A_f, is a measure of the work done on a material during machining and consequently the machinability is inversely related to this group. In the limit, when $A_r = 100\%$ and $R_f = \infty$, or in other words, when a material can withstand an infinitely large strain, then the material should be unmachinable.

These four dimensionless groups may be equated as follows:

$$\left(\frac{v_x h}{\alpha}\right)\left(\frac{w}{h}\right)^b = K_p \left(\frac{\rho C_p T_x J}{H_B}\right)^c (R_f)^d \qquad (6\text{-}46)$$

where the subscript x refers to a particular tool life, and corresponding cutting edge temperature. K_p is a proportionality constant that is a function of the tool shape and tool material. To determine the exponents in this equation, actual machining tests were run on a range of experimental materials, including tool life and cutting temperature. These were then correlated with the physical properties obtained for the same materials that were machined.

In order to evaluate the machinability of materials it is necessary to select one set of standard conditions to serve as a basis, as is true of all physical tests. A convenient basis for establishing machinability, one that has been very frequently used in the past, is the cutting speed that results in a 60 min tool life, v_{60}. As mentioned previously, this corresponds to a cutting edge temperature of about 975°F, with the temperature increasing for a shorter tool life.

By carefully examining the deformation and shearing of the material in front of the tool and while observing the process of machining metallurgically polished and etched specimens through a microscope, it is apparent that most of the deformation occurs in the region where the temperature of the material is between room temperature and the cutting edge temperature. By correlating the experimental tool-life data with these microscopic studies, it was established that most of the deformation occurred at a temperature slightly above the average of the room temperature and the cutting edge temperature. On that basis, when machining with a v_{60}, the physical properties of the material used in the machinability equation to calculate the machinability must be those that are obtained at a testing temperature of approximately 600°F.

By plotting the 600°F physical properties versus the experimental machinability data, the numerical values of the exponents c and d were found to be 1 and —0.5, respectively.

The value of the exponent b can be determined by considering the effect of the size of cut on the velocity for a constant tool life. Woxen[14] introduced the concept of a "chip equivalent," q', defined as $(h + w)/hw$. He considered the cutting velocity as a function of q'. Interchanging the values of the width and the depth of cut, that is, changing a 0.100 in. depth with a 0.020 ipr feed to 0.020 in. depth with a 0.100 ipr feed, has no effect on the value of q'. However, experimental data conclusively shows that interchanging the width and depth has a major influence on the velocity for a constant tool life. Consequently, this concept is not valid.

To determine the effect of the size of the cut on the constant-life velocity, it is necessary to consider the two dimensionless groups vh/α and $(w/h)^b$. For a better understanding of the effect of the size of cut, these two groups can be combined into one, $v/\alpha(h^{1-b}w^b)$, where $(h^{1-b}w^b)$ may be considered as a "characteristic length" and designated as q. It should be noted that the exponent of q is unity. From experimental data as well as from physical considerations it is apparent that b is not a constant having one value, but instead it varies with the depth to width ratio of the size of the cut. The value of b can easily be determined from published experimental data for two extreme conditions of the w/h ratio.

It is known from machining experience that when the depth of cut is extremely large in comparison to the feed, the depth of cut has practically no effect on the constant-life velocity. This may be expressed mathematically as follows: as the ratio of w/h goes to infinity, the limit of b will be zero. Also, when $h = w$, the effect of each on the constant-life velocity obviously should be the same and therefore b will be $\frac{1}{2}$. These two limiting values are in agreement with published experimental data.

The value of b for w/h values between ∞ and 1 can be established by studying the published experimental values of the exponents for the feed and depth of cut. Many of the experimental studies summarize their results with an empirical equation of the form

$$v_x = C h^{-a} w^{-b} \qquad (6\text{-}47)$$

where a and b are about $\frac{2}{3}$ and $\frac{1}{3}$, respectively for average sized turning cuts. After analyzing many of the empirical equations, it was concluded that for a w/h ratio of about 6.7 the value of b is $\frac{1}{3}$ and thus the "characteristic length" q is $h^{2/3} w^{1/3}$. The relationships between b and the w/h ratio are summarized in Table 6-11. The feed exponent a is equal to $1-b$.

By substituting the numerical values of b, c, and d into Equation 6-46 and combining all of the constants into one, the equation becomes

$$\left(\frac{v_x}{\alpha}\right) q = A_1 \left(\frac{\rho C_p}{H_B}\right) R_f^{-0.5} \qquad (6\text{-}48)$$

where

$$A_1 = K_p J T_x$$

Solving explicitly for v_x and substituting k for its equivalent $\alpha \rho C_p$, Equation 6-48 may be written as

$$v_x = A_1 \frac{k}{q H_B R_f^{1/2}}$$

$$= \frac{A_1}{q} \left(\frac{k}{H_B R_f^{0.5}}\right) \qquad (6\text{-}49)$$

TABLE 6-11. Values of a, b, and q for Some w/h Ratios

w/h	h/w	b	a	q
∞	0	0	1	h
6.7	0.15	$\frac{1}{3}$	$\frac{2}{3}$	$h^{2/3} w^{1/3}$
1	1	$\frac{1}{2}$	$\frac{1}{2}$	$h^{1/2} w^{1/2}$

and for a given value of q it reduces to

$$v_x = A_2 \frac{k}{H_B R_f^{0.5}} \tag{6-50}$$

For the experimental conditions used in the study[5] mentioned above in which this relationship was derived, namely, $h = 0.0057$ in., $w = 0.050$ in., tool life = 60 min, the constant A_2 is 1150. Thus, for machining with hss tools with zero rake under the described conditions, the machinability is related to the physical properties according to the following equation:

$$v_{60} = 1150 \, k H_B^{-1} \, R_f^{-1/2} \tag{6-51}$$

Inasmuch as most handbooks list the per cent reduction of area rather than the more convenient ratio, Equation 6-50 can be rewritten as

$$v_{60} = 1150 k H_B^{-1} \left(1 - \frac{A_r}{100} \right)^{1/2} \tag{6-52}$$

or

$$v_{60} = \frac{13.55}{q} \frac{k}{H_B} \left(1 - \frac{A_r}{100} \right)^{1/2} \tag{6-53}$$

when the size of cut is not a depth of 0.050 in. and a feed of 0.0057 ipr.

This fundamental machinability equation has been found to be valid for materials as different as cast iron, steel, aluminum, zirconium, and titanium. It can also distinguish equally well between such nearly similar materials as 1020, 1045, 4340, and 1212 steels or the various stainless steels. Table 6-12 lists both the calculated (predicted) values of v_{60} and the experimentally obtained values for 25 different materials. The first seven materials as well as materials No. 22 through No. 24 were tested under conditions identical to those used in deriving the machinability equation. The remaining materials were actually tested under different cutting conditions; but were corrected by means of experimental conversion factors so that the values listed in the table are the equivalent v_{60} for the standard cutting conditions.

Of the materials listed, only the aluminum alloy (No. 6) and the molybdenum (No. 7) do not show a close correlation between the experimental and the calculated values. The reason that the aluminum alloy has an experimental v_{60} greater than the calculated value is that it has a phase transformation occurring in the temperature range of high speed machining (975 to 1050°F). This phase transformation utilizes some of the heat generated in the machining operation and

TABLE 6-12.   Comparison of Predicted and Experimental
Machinability Values

	Material	Cutting Speed for 60 Min Tool Life	
		Predicted*	Experimental†
1.	AISI 1020 steel	158	160
2.	AISI 1212 steel	190	190
3.	AISI 1045 steel	113	120
4.	AISI 4340 steel	61	60
5.	Al-1100-0	8650	8500
6.	Al-2024-T4	1960	2600
7.	Molybdenum	220	60
8.	Rene 41	20	17–20
9.	Ti-6 Al-4V	19	15–30
10.	Ti-155-A	21	15–30
11.	Udimet 500	26	25
12.	Inconel X	36	38
13.	301 Stainless steel	78	80
14.	303 Stainless steel	64	55–70
15.	310 Stainless steel	76	60–80
16.	347 Stainless steel	84	75–95
17.	410 Stainless steel	62	55–75
18.	430 Stainless steel	64	55–75
19.	446 Stainless steel	70	60–80
20.	Fe-Cr-Mo Alloy	66	55–75
21.	Zirconium	94	80–100
22.	Armco iron	220	225
23.	Grey cast iron	340	350
24.	Pearlitic cast iron	150	155
25.	Leaded red brass	745	500–1000

*Predicted from the general machinability equation

$$V_{60} = \frac{1150k}{H_B} (1 - A_r/100)^{1/2}$$

where k = thermal conductivity, H_B = Brinell hardness, and A_r = per cent reduction of area of tensile specimen.

†Materials 1 through 7, and 22 through 24 were tested under identical conditioning to those used in calculating the predicted values. The remaining materials were tested under different conditions and were corrected by means of emperical data to put them on the basis of the same cutting conditions as the previous data.

consequently the rise in temperature is less. The reason that the molybdenum can be machined at only one-fourth of its predicted velocity is apparent by examining the mechanism of chip formation of molybdenum as shown in Figure 6-42.

It is evident in this figure that molybdenum fails through the grain boundaries beneath the bottom of the cutting tool while the grains in front of the tool are being plastically deformed. The heat generated in the grains in front of the tool because of their deformation must flow down to the bulk of the work piece beneath the tool if the cutting edge temperature is to remain low. But the cracks through the grain boundaries serve as insulating surfaces and greatly retard the flow of heat into the work piece. Consequently, the cutting edge temperature and the chip temperature are much higher than they would be if the cracks were not present. In order to predict accurately the machinability of this material, the bulk thermal conductivity of the "cracked" metal would have to be used, and not the value of the sound metal as was done in obtaining the values listed in Table 6-12. Awareness of this type of chip formation brings to light a promising realization: if the molybdenum metal can be manufactured so that it

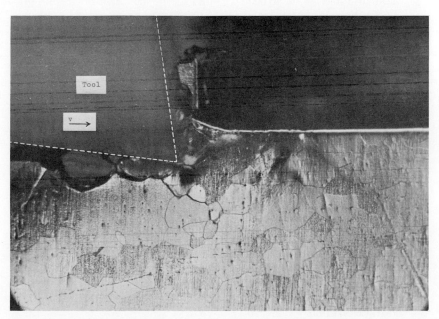

Figure 6-42. Photomicrograph of chip formation in molybdenum illustrating grain boundary failure beneath the tool.

does not fail through the grain boundaries (due to precipitated carbides in the grain boundaries) when deformed, its machinability can be increased by a factor of four.

The agreement between the predicted machinability and actual machinability of the remaining 23 materials is exceedingly good, considering the extreme range of materials covered—all the way from easy-to-machine 1100-0 aluminum having a v_{60} of 8500 fpm down to the extremely difficult to machine 6Al4Va titanium alloy having a v_{60} of only 19 fpm. On the basis of the above examination of the data listed in Table 6-12, these fundamental machinability equations can

TABLE 6-13. Physical Properties at 600°F for Some Metals
(Data compiled from many sources)

Material	Tensile Strength S_u psi	Area Reduction A_r %	Thermal Conductivity k Btu/hr-ft-°F	Brinell Hardness H_B kg/mm²
1. AISI 1020 steel	58,000	60	25.5	116
2. AISI 1212 steel	53,000	60	28.0	106
3. AISI 1045 steel	90,000	35	22.0	180
4. AISI 4340 steel	135,000	40	18.5	270
5. Al-1100-0	2,800	90	115.0	4.9
6. Al-2024-T4	15,700	65	80.0	27.5
7. Molybdenum	85,000	75	66.0	170
8. Rene 41	205,000	25	8.6	410
9. Ti-6 AL-4V	112,000	62	6.0	224
10. Ti-155-A	120,000	48	6.2	240
11. Udimet 500	175,000	15	8.5	350
12. Inconel X	155,000	34	11.9	310
13. 301 Stainless steel	70,000	40	12.4	140
14. 303 Stainless steel	72,000	53	11.9	144
15. 310 Stainless steel	50,000	55	9.9	100
16. 347 Stainless steel	62,000	32	11.1	124
17. 410 Stainless steel	73,000	74	15.6	146
18. 430 Stainless steel	64,000	75	14.4	128
19. 446 Stainless steel	83,000	40	13.2	166
20. Fe-Cr-Mo alloy	88,000	60	16.0	176
21. Zirconium	30,000	66	10.7	75
22. Armco iron	32,000	85	32.0	64
23. Gray cast iron	18,000	1–5	32.0	105
24. Pearlitic cast iron	25,000	1–5	26.0	192
25. Leaded red brass	29,000	15	41.0	58

be used with the following two qualifications: (1) the material should not have any transition temperatures below the cutting edge temperature (if it does, the machinability calculated will be lower than the actual machinability of the material) and (2) the predicted machinability values obtained are no more accurate than the physical properties used to compute them.

The predicted machinability values listed in Table 6-12 were calculated from the data listed in Table 6-13. These physical properties are those obtained by testing the material at 600°F, and not at room temperature. For some of the metals, particularly the higher melting temperature materials, the 600°F properties and the room temperature ones are almost identical.

Equations 6-48 and 6-53 are convenient for those researchers who are interested in determining how the machinability of a specific type of material may be improved or what properties of a material influence its machinability. However, these equations are not in as convenient a form as they might be for those engineers in industry who would like to have an equation that can be used in conjunction with simple tabulated data.

The Taylor equations of the type $v = Kt^{-n} f^{-a} d^{-b}$ (Equation 6-25) are very widely used since they are so convenient when the constant K and the exponents a, b, and n are known. The drawback of these later equations is that the constants must be determined experimentally for all the various materials and cutting conditions; and experimental tool-life testing is quite expensive. For these reasons the fundamental machinability Equation 6-53 derived previously is revised below in an attempt to obtain a machinability equation that can be used in conjunction with tabular data that can be prepared without the necessity of running actual tool-life tests.

By rearranging some of the terms in Equations 6-48 or 6-53, it is possible to put the fundamental machinability equation into the form[4]

$$v = \frac{AB}{q} \qquad (6\text{-}54)$$

where $A = K_p J T_x$ and is a tool-shape, tool-life constant,

$B = \dfrac{k}{H_B} \left(1 - \dfrac{A_r}{100}\right)^{1/2}$ and is a work material constant;

$q = (f + y)^a (d + y)^{1-a}$ and is a size of cut constant.

The first of these three constants, A, is a function of the tool shape, tool material, tool life desired, and cutting fluid used. Table 6-14 lists

TABLE 6-14.   Values for Tool Constant A for Hss Tool Shape: ASA Designation, 0, 0, 6, 6, 6, 0, 0

Tool Life	Cutting Temperature	Constant A
60 min	975°F	17.3
20 min	1025°F	18.6

the value of the constant A for two conditions when cutting with a hss tool. For a given tool material, the value of A is influenced primarily by the rake angle, the side-cutting edge angle, and the nose radius, as discussed in the preceding section under tool shape. Unfortunately, the constant A must still be obtained experimentally, and values for other tool shapes are not tabulated. However, if a cutting speed is calculated for a material with the standard tool shape listed in Table 6-14, then by means of the empirical relationships given in the preceding section under tool shape, the cutting speed for any other tool shape can be calculated.

Values for the material constant B are presented in Table 6-15 for a wide range of materials, listed in order of decreasing machinability. These values for the material constant were calculated from the physical properties listed in Table 6-13. The machinability of the structured steels decreases as the steel approaches eutectoid composition. It is interesting to note that very low-carbon steel, like armco iron, has about the same machinability as a free machining AISI 1212 steel. Also, AISI 4340 has about the same machinability as the stainless steels. Seven different stainless steels, including both ferritic and austenitic types, are included in Table 6-15 to illustrate that this fundamental machinability equation does differentiate between different compositions of the same class of material.

Although the size of cut constant q as originally expressed in Equation 6-46 and Table 6-11, namely $f^a d^{1-a}$, gives very good results for cuts having a feed of 0.0057 ipr or greater and a f/d ratio 0.1, the predicted results are in error when very small feeds or when large depths of cut are employed. A reason for this dicrepancy can be presented from a study of Figure 6-22 and 6-24. In these figures an annealed material is being machined by the so-called "orthogonal" or two-dimensional cutting in which the tool is wider than the work piece. When the first cut is taken on this specimen, the material at the top surface is annealed. But during cutting, the material in front and beneath the tool is plastically deformed and if during machining, the temperature of the metal at the new machined surface is below the

TABLE 6-15.   Values of Material Constant (B) For Some Metals
in the Annealed or Hot-Rolled Condition
(Properties at $600°F$ used to calculate B)

	Material	Material Constant (B)
1.	1100-0 Aluminum	7.420
2.	2024-T4 Aluminum	1.720
3.	Leaded red brass	0.652
4.	Gray cast iron ($105\ H_B$)	0.300
5.	Armco iron	0.194
6.	Molybdenum	0.194
7.	AISI 1212 steel	0.167
8.	AISI 1020 steel	0.139
9.	Pearlitic cast iron ($190\ H_B$)	0.133
10.	AISI 1045 steel	0.099
11.	Zirconium	0.083
12.	347 Stainless steel	0.074
13.	301 Stainless steel	0.069
14.	310 Stainless steel	0.066
15.	440 Stainless steel	0.062
16.	Fe-Cr-Mo alloy	0.058
17.	303 Stainless steel	0.057
18.	430 Stainless steel	0.056
19.	410 Stainless steel	0.054
20.	AISI 4340 steel	0.053
21.	Inconel X	0.031
22.	Udimet 500	0.022
23.	Ti-155A	0.019
24.	Rene 41	0.018
25.	Ti-6Al-4V	0.016

recrystallization temperature, the new surface of the metal is strain-hardened. Figure 6-43 is a sketch of an actual plot of microhardness distribution in a chip and work piece of annealed aluminum when machined with 0.012 in. thickness (feed) of cut in orthogonal cutting. The hardness readings are on the Tukon (Knoop) scale.

The annealed hardness varies between 32 and 40 H_k, so an average value of 37 is used. The isohardness line of 37 drawn in Figure 6-43 then separates the annealed material from the strain-hardened lines. The hardness increases toward the tool point to maximum values of about 88 H_K. This compares to a maximum value of 66 H_K in the neck

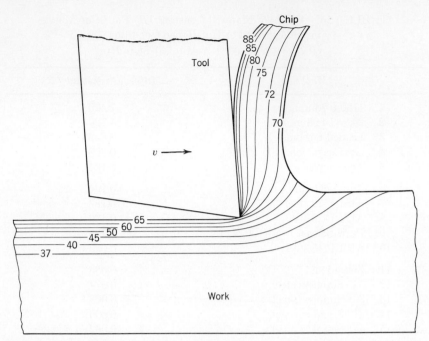

Figure 6-43. Sketch of isohardness in chip formation of annealed aluminum. Iso-hardness (Knoop) lines may be considered lines of constant strain.

of a fractured tensile specimen of annealed aluminum (See Figure 5-29). From this it is apparent that a machined surface of a metal may be severely strain hardened. Now what happens when a second cut is made on this material? Can it be assumed that the material is still annealed? Obviously not, even though only a thin surface layer is strain hardened. In reality, the thickness of the cut (feed) is not much greater than the depth of the coldworked layer. As the feed is decreased, the coldworked layer becomes a larger fraction of the total thickness of cut.

From the above discussion it appears that the strain-hardening characteristics (σ_o, m and ϵ_f) of a material must be included in the size of cut constant q to account for the presence of a strain-hardened layer during normal machining operations. Although analytically it is impossible to calculate the true value of the size of cut constant q on the basis of the material's properties, an experimental study[4] on AISI 1020 steel determined that better agreement between predicted and actual values was obtained when a constant was subtracted from the

TABLE 6-16.   Values for The Constant y for a Range of
Values of The Strain-Hardening Exponent m

m	y
0	0
0.05	0.0015
0.25	0.0025
0.50	0.004

TABLE 6-17. Values for the Size of Cut Constant q for
Typical Values of Feed and Depth

$$q = (f + y)^a (d + y)^{1-a} \qquad\qquad a = 0.6\left(\frac{f}{d}\right)^{-0.05}$$

d	f	$\left(\dfrac{f}{d}\right)$	a	q $y = 0.001$	$y = 0.004$
0.200	0.002	0.010	0.756	0.0084	0.0142
	0.005	0.025	0.723	0.0160	0.0212
	0.010	0.050	0.698	0.0265	0.0315
	0.020	0.100	0.674	0.0439	0.0483
	0.050	0.250	0.643	0.0834	0.0867
0.100	0.002	0.020	0.730	0.0078	0.0130
	0.005	0.050	0.698	0.0140	0.0189
	0.010	0.100	0.674	0.0228	0.0268
	0.020	0.200	0.651	0.0364	0.0399
	0.050	0.500	0.621	0.0665	0.0690
0.050	0.002	0.040	0.705	0.0070	0.0114
	0.005	0.100	0.674	0.0121	0.0162
	0.010	0.200	0.651	0.0188	0.0224
	0.020	0.400	0.627	0.0294	0.0324
	0.050	1.000	0.600	0.0511	0.0544
0.025	0.002	0.080	0.681	0.0060	0.0100
	0.005	0.200	0.651	0.0101	0.0135
	0.010	0.400	0.627	0.0151	0.0182
	0.020	0.800	0.607	0.0280	0.0254
	0.050	2.000	0.580	0.0385	0.0415

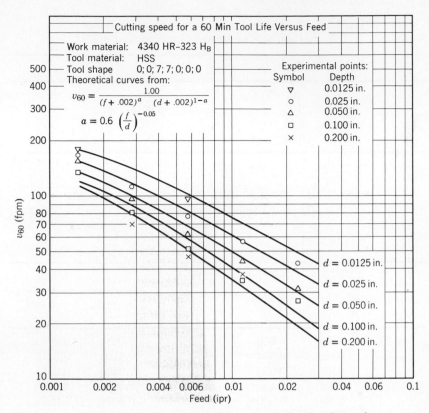

Figure 6-44. Comparison of experimental and calculated values of v_{60} versus feed. Solid lines are from calculated values and the points are experimental.

depth of cut. The modified empirical relationship for q on this basis is

$$q = f^a (d - x)^{1-a} \qquad (6\text{-}55)$$

where $\alpha = \frac{1}{2}(f/d)^{-0.03}$.

For 1020 steel, the value of x is 0.005 in.

However, it seems more reasonable to place the correction factor for strain-hardening on the feed rather than on the depth of cut. Recently, studies have yielded good results for a variety of metals when the size of cut constant has the form

$$q = (f + y)^a (d + y)^{1-a} \qquad (6\text{-}56)$$

The exponent a is influenced by the f/d ratio according to the relationship

$$a = 0.6 \left(\frac{f}{d}\right)^{-0.5} \tag{6-57}$$

The value of y varies from 0 for a material that does not strain harden to a maximum of 0.004 for a material that strain hardens the highest possible amount; that is, has both a large m and ϵ_f.

Table 6-16 lists values of the constant y for a range of values of strain-hardening exponent m. As an example, AISI 1020 HR steel has a strain-hardening exponent of 0.2 so it has a value of y equal to 0.001. Type 303 stainless steel has a strain-hardening exponent of 0.5 and therefore a y value of 0.004.

Table 6-17 lists values of the exponent a and size constant q for a range of feeds and depth of cut for two values of y; 0.001 and 0.004.

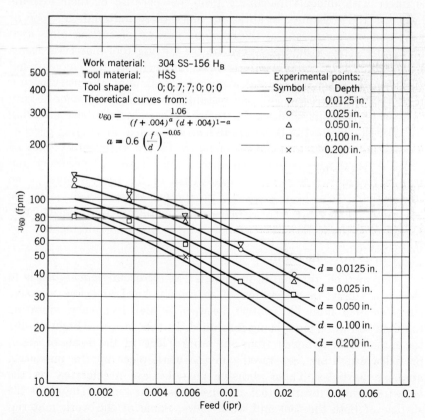

Figure 6-45. Comparison of experimental and calculated values of v_{60} versus feed. Solid lines are from calculated values and the points are experimental.

Figures 6-44 and 6-45 are plots of the cutting speed for a 60 min tool life, v_{60}, versus the feed where q was calculated by means of Equation 6-56. Although the two metals shown in these figures are metallurgically very different, their machinabilities are similar and quite low. The AISI 4340 is low because of its relatively high hardness; the 304 stainless because of its low thermal conductivity. The calculated values of v_{60} from Equation 6-54 are shown by the solid curves. The experimental data points are plotted for purposes of comparison. Although the data points do not fall perfectly on top of the calculated curves, the agreement is as good as most empirical plots of v_{60} versus feed obtained by completely experimental means.

MISCELLANEOUS MACHINING PROCESSES

Many materials developed in recent years have presented the engineer with difficult machining problems because of their extreme hardness and resistance to abrasion. Since these materials may be as hard and wear-resistant as the common variety of cutting tools used in metal cutting, (they may even be the cutting tool materials themselves) it is nearly impossible to machine them by the conventional methods. However, by concentrating a large amount of energy onto a relatively small area at any one instant, it is possible to remove very small chips without seriously fracturing or harming the base material.

For this method to be acceptable as a practical machining process, it must be repetitive and continuous so that a satisfactory rate of metal removal may be obtained with a high degree of accuracy and surface finish. In addition, the application of the process must be so simple that it can be used in the production shop as well as in the laboratory. There are several methods of applying this concentrated energy onto the work surface that fulfill the above requirements.

Ultrasonic Machining

One method, referred to in industry as *ultrasonic machining*, is to charge a slurry (a suspension of extremely hard and fine abrasive particles in a fluid like water) between a high-frequency vibrating tool and the work piece being machined. In this process (Figure 6-46) the material is removed from the work piece in the form of small particles which are "fractured" off the work piece by the impacting abrasive particles. These abrasive particles are accelerated by the high-frequency vibrating tool and dissipate their kinetic energy at the surface of both the tool and work piece. Some of the work material may be eroded because of cavitation—the formation of low pressure bubbles at the surface of the work piece caused by the rapidly re-

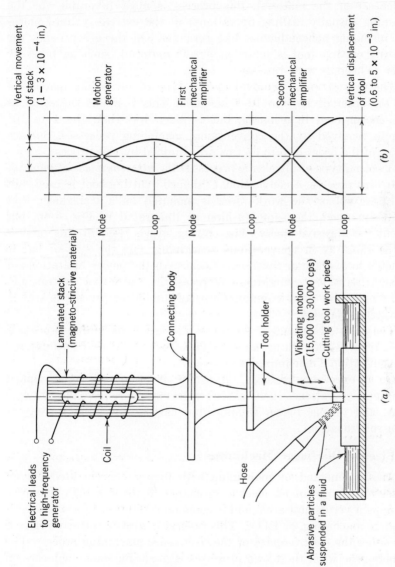

Figure 6-46. Schematic sketch of abrasive type of ultrasonic machining process. (*a*) Physical components. (*b*) Vertical displacements of various components.

ceding tool. To continue the cutting operation, the tool is fed down into the work piece as the material is abraded away.

Since the wear rate is directly proportional to the hardness (or brittleness) of the material, this process is most favorable for the machining (usually drilling operations) of the extremely hard materials, including nonconductors like ceramics. On the other hand, the vibrating cutting tool is made of a soft material, such as brass or copper, to keep its wear-rate low.

The rate of metal removal in this type of ultrasonic machining is of the order of 10^{-3} to 10^{-2} in.^{3}/min. This is about the same as those encountered in grinding, but is much less than the 1 to 10^2 in.^{3}/min removed by the conventional machining processes. Surface finishes of the order of 5 to 64 rms are obtained by this process.

A second type of ultrasonic process is the *ultrasonic-assist machining*. In this process, a conventional "shaped" cutting tool is used, but either the tool or the work piece is mounted on a transducer that vibrates in much the same fashion as illustrated in Fig. 6-46, but without the abrasive slurry. The cutting speeds used in this process are the same as in conventional machining, but the size of cut is restricted to average or finish cuts because of the power limitations of the high-frequency generators. Whereas the "abrasive" ultrasonic-machining is now used in manufacturing, this latter process is still in the experimental stage.

The main advantage of the ultrasonic-assist machining process is that it reduces the cutting force by 25% to 50% of that encountered with conventional machining.

On an experimental basis, ultrasonic vibrations are being applied to forming operations, such as wire drawing, to reduce the drawing forces; and during fusion welding and casting to refine the grains during solidification.

Electric Discharge Machining

Another method of machining with highly concentrated energy utilizes the energy of an electric discharge to focus a high temperature upon a very small area, and is commonly referred to as electrical-discharge machining, or EDM. This process is also frequently referred to as either the *electro-spark* or the *electro-arc* machining process. The distinction between these two processes is made by some engineers on the basis of whether the discharge (current flow) occurs as a spark when the electrode approaches the work piece or whether it occurs as an arc after the electrode has contacted the work piece at mutual asperities that become heated and vaporized because of the high current density. Since this is really a theoretical technicality (which came first, the contact or the flow), no distinction between these two is made in the following discussion.

The mechanism of metal removal in the electrical-discharge process is shown in the insert of Figure 6-47 and described below. This mechanism or theory was established after a very careful metallographic examination of the subsurface material of a variety of surfaces machined by the EDM process. It is most vividly displayed in the subsurface layers of carbon-tool steel which was previously heat treated to give primary, or untempered, martensite. In these layers, all the phase transformations and tempering stages encountered in conventional heat-treating processes are present. These include: new, reformed primary martensite at the immediate surface, high-temperature tempered martensite beneath this, followed by low-temperature tempered martensite, and finally, the unaffected original primary martensite. The depth of this heat-affected layer is normally about 0.010 to 0.020 in.

The sequence of operations responsible for the metal removal, as depicted in the schematic diagram of Figure 6-47, is as follows. The electrode, which may or may not be vibrating, in its slow downward travel contacts the work surface at a point corresponding to where projections on the surface of both the work and the tool coincide. This contact, which may not be physical but is a closeness of approach sufficient to cause electron flow, closes the electrical circuit. This causes, in the type of unit illustrated, a capacitor to discharge its stored energy. For most efficient metal removal, that is, a high rate of work material removal with a low rate of electrode loss, the electrode should be negative and the work piece positive during this part of the cycle.

As the electrode is raised, or the projections are boiled off, an arc of short duration is created. An approximate value of the duration of this arc may be obtained from the time constant of the circuit, which is the time required to charge a capacitor to 63% or to discharge it to 37% of its final charged value. The value of the time constant, RC, in seconds is equal to the product of the resistance in ohms and the capacitance in farads. Typical values of resistance and capacitance to obtain reasonably good surface finishes are 5 ohms and 200 microfarads. This gives a time constant of 1×10^{-3} sec.

The high temperature of the arc discharge (about 10,000°F or higher) causes the metal at both ends of the arc to melt and vaporize. Since about five-eighths of the arc energy is expended by the electrons striking the anode and three-eighths of the arc energy is expended by

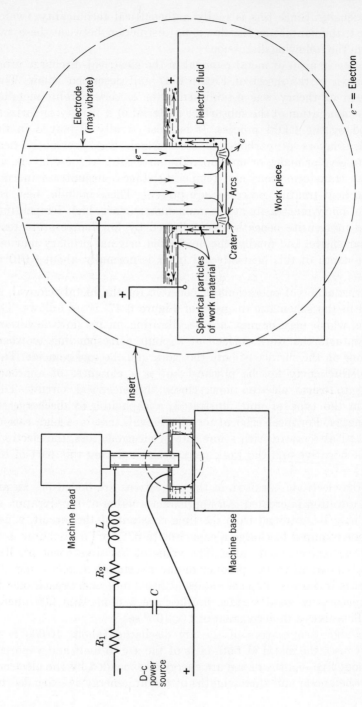

Figure 6-47. Schematic diagram of the electric discharge machining (EDM) process. R_2 and L are the resistance and inductance of the leads.

the ions striking the cathode, the electrode should be negative to reduce its errosion rate.

The arc is extinguished when the electrical circuit is broken, either by the discharge of the condensor or by some mechanical means. The dielectric cutting fluid then quenches and washes away the particles which became spherical while in the molten state. This sequence continues at a rapid rate—thousands of small arcs per second.

All EDM machines do not operate on the basis of a R-C circuit. Some machines employ a pulse circuit wherein either electron tubes or rotating machinery interrupt the flow of d-c electricity from the source to the tool. Generally the pulse type circuit operates at frequencies ten times that of an R-C circuit.

Because electrical discharges occur from the side of the electrode as well as from the end, the width of the hole produced is generally tapered and slightly wider than the electrode. The gap between the work and the tool is about 10^{-3} to 10^{-4} in. Surface finishes of 60 rms can be obtained by this process when small to modest-size pulses of energy are used. Under these conditions the metal removal rate is of the order of 10^{-3} in.^{3}/min. By increasing the energy of each pulse, the metal removal rate may be increased by a factor of 1000, but the resulting surface is very rough and pitted. Also, by resorting to a trepanning type of operation where a large O.D. hollow tool having a thin wall is used to remove a solid core from the work piece, a large overall metal-removal rate can be achieved.

There are several areas in the industrial field of machining in which the EDM process is the most economical. One of these areas is the drilling and tapping of sintered tungsten carbide parts, which because of their extreme hardness cannot be machined by the conventional methods. Another area is the machining of the cavities in forging dies where only one or two parts (dies) have to be made. In this case, the fabrication of the formed electrode by a casting process enables the EDM process to be more economical than the machining of the cavity on a "die sinking" type of milling machine. A third area is the machining of thin-wall parts that do not have the rigidity needed to withstand the cutting force of a conventional tool. On the other hand, the EDM process cannot be used in the machining of the hard nonconductive ceramic materials. For these materials, we resort to the ultrasonic machining process.

Electron Beam Machining

Another process utilizing highly concentrated energy is the *electron beam process*. It is used for both machining and welding. In this process a stream of electrons emitted from an electron gun is made to impinge upon the work piece which is in a vacuum (10^{-6} mm Hg) chamber. The electrons are accelerated by potentials of 100 to 200 kv with beam currents up to 20 ma. The electron beam is focused by electromagnetic lenses to diameters of 10^{-6} to 10^{-2} in. The impact of this electron beam upon the work piece causes the material it strikes to melt and vaporize.

The location of the electron beam with respect to the work piece can be accurately controlled by the use of optics that permit the work piece to be viewed coaxially with the beam at magnifications of 10X to 50X.

In general this process is applicable to micromachining operations, usually drilling, on hard materials where the conventional processes fail. Its main disadvantages are that the work must be performed in a vacuum, and deep holes have tapered sides.

The electron beam is used as a welding process in industry to a greater extent than it is used as a machining process.

Laser Machining

Lasers and *masers* provide energy sources similar to the electron beam in that the energy is confined to a small area. Masers, which were developed first, are ruby crystals (Al_2O_3) lightly alloyed (doped) with chromium and have the characteristics of amplifying rather than absorbing radiation of certain wave lengths. The word maser is derived from "microwave amplification by stimulated emission of radiation."

The laser, which is referred to as an optical maser, is replacing the maser as a technological tool. The word laser comes from "light amplification by stimulated emission of radiation." The alkaline earth fluorides, such as CaF_2, are replacing the ruby as the amplifier. Since the efficiency of the laser increases at very low temperatures, they are usually cooled by liquid nitrogen or helium. (Gas lasers are also being developed.)

The main disadvantage of the laser in terms of its being used as a tool in manufacturing processing is the low-power output. Consequently, it is only used for microdrilling or microwelding. It has one advantage over the electron beam in that it need not be operated in a vacuum.

Chemical and Electrochemical Machining

Two miscellaneous machining processes that do not use high intensity energy for material removal are the *chemical machining* (chem milling) and the *electrochemical machining* (ECM) processes. Chemical machining is the process where material is removed from a part by putting it in contact with a proper reagent so that the material is removed by means of a chemical reaction. This process is different from the cleaning processes only in that its objective is changing the shape of parts rather than removing "dirty" or unwanted materials.

The sequence of steps associated with chemical machining is: immersing in a bath to clean the part; drying; masking (by means of tape, paint, or plating) the areas that are not to be etched away; etching, usually by immersion; and cleaning.

Chemical machining is done on odd-shaped parts, usually large ones like spars or panels for aircraft frames, that can be machined by the conventional methods only with great difficulty or expense. The process is ideal for producing such parts as I-beams or angles having a decreasing cross section from one end to the other. This is accomplished by purchasing a standard structural beam, immersing it lengthwise into a deep bath of reagent and then raising the part out of the bath at a controlled rate. This is considerably more economical than machining a similar part on a conventional milling machine.

Very thin sections can be produced by this process, and very little distortion is induced in parts so machined. Also, hardened parts may be machined by this process as easily, if not more so, than soft pieces. One disadvantage is that the surface finish on coarse-grained parts is poor, particularly if much metal is etched away.

Flame cutting is a chemical machining process that is always classified under welding. The reason for this listing is that the same equipment used for flame cutting is also used more frequently for welding. Flame cutting is a process in which a locally preheated metal is moved through a fine jet of oxygen and is "machined" by oxidation according to the reaction $xM + yO \rightarrow M_xO_y$.

The electrochemical machining process is the equivalent of electroplating in reverse. For example, in silver plating an object the part is attached to the cathode of a d-c source and submerged in a proper electrolyte. A solid bar of silver is attached to the anode and also submerged. As the current flows, the silver bar slowly goes into solution in accordance with Faraday's law and a similar amount of silver is deposited on the negatively charged part. In the ECM process, the workpiece is made the anode. Probably the first practical applications of the ECM process were in the electropolishing and electroetching of metallographic specimens for microscopic examination.

In recent years (late 1940's) a special type of ECM process, called electrolytic grinding, was developed. In this process a metal-bonded diamond grinding wheel (diamond particles bonded together with metals such as brass or copper or nickel) is used. However, unlike conventional grinding, the diamond particles themselves do not "machine" or abrade away the work material. In this process the diamond particles serve as insulating spacers between the anodic workpiece and the periphery of cathodic matrix of the rotating disc and thus maintain a proper gap between the two electrodes to prevent arcing. Both diamond and tungsten carbide are nonconductors.

The diamond particles also serve to abrade from the surface of the workpiece any nonconducting inclusions or oxides that may be present. It is estimated that 90% of the workpiece removed is due to electrolytic action and 10% due to mechanical abrasion.

The electrolytic grinding process is used primarily as an alternate method to grind sintered carbide parts, usually cutting tools.

Surface finishes as fine as 4 rms are obtainable with tolerances of 10^{-4} in. A dull matte surface is produced in contrast to the bright ground surface and fine parallel grooves formed by conventional grinding. Mechanical and thermal stresses on the surface of the workpiece are low during this process. Consequently, no surface cracks are present on the finished part. Cutting tools sharpened by this process give the same tool life as tools ground by the conventional process.

AUTOMATIC AND NUMERICAL CONTROL

We will now discuss the role of automatic control in the manufacturing processes. If it is to be treated in depth, the subject of control should be viewed at from two different points of view. One approach is on the basis of automatic control theory, and the second is on the basis of descriptions of the various pieces of equipment (the hardware) associated with automatic control.

Automatic control theory is a subject area in itself. Many engineering schools offer one or more courses in feed-back and automatic control theory. There are several in-depth engineering and mathematical textbooks on the subject. It is both impossible and impractical to go into the theory of automatic control in a textbook such as this which treats the interrelationships between materials and processes. The intent of this textbook is to discuss briefly only the major or primary types of equipment associated with each of the processes, and a few of the more important types of attachments that are used on the primary equipment. Since automatic control devices of one sort or another are used as attachments on the manufacturing equipment of all of the processes, a general description of them is given here.

There are five types of automatic control devices, namely: mechanical, hydraulic, pneumatic, electrical, and numerical (tape). These are referred to as automatic control systems when their operating characteristics rather than their "hardware" are discussed. Although each one of these control systems is used in all five (heat treating, casting, welding, forming, and machining) of the manufacturing processes, they are discussed in this chapter on machining because it is in this area that they are most extensively used.

Mechanical Systems

The mechanical devices for automatic control of manufacturing processes are both the oldest and the most commonly used type. They are fast-acting and give positive (reliable) control with very little maintainance, which accounts for their widespread use—particularly in high production operations. Their one disadvantage is that when they are used on general purpose machines, such as cams on machine tools, the cost to make new cams and to reset the tooling is relatively high. Thus they are not economical for producing a small number of parts.

Mechanical devices are extensively used in the casting and welding processes in which a large number of pieces is made. The tooling associated with permanent-mold, die-, and shell-mold casting are examples of this type of control. The tooling and attachments used on sheet-metal forming equipment as well as bar forging and upsetting machines are examples of the extensive use of mechanical devices for automatic forming operations. Transfer-type machines, turret lathes, screw machines, and most production-type machine tools are examples of the use of mechanical devices for automatic control of machining operations.

Hydraulic Systems

Hydraulic devices are widely used for automatic control systems in all of the manufacturing processes, especially the forming and machining ones. Because of the noncompressibility of the fluid, hydraulic control devices are fast acting. This characteristic of fluids in combination with a high-pressure hydraulic system provides the large forces that are needed for the rapid acceleration, positioning, and deceleration of heavy loads. This is a very important requirement for the machines used in the manufacturing processes. Electro-magnetic devices such as motors and solenoids do not have the speed of response that the hydraulic devices do. In addition, hydraulic motors are usually smaller and and lighter than electric motors of equivalent horsepower ratings.

A hydraulic system consists of three basic components: pumps, valves, and actuators. The pumps provide the pressurized fluid that performs the required functions. There are three types of hydraulic pumps: gear pumps for low speed and pressure; vane pumps for variable-delivery of the quantity of fluid; piston pumps for high pressure and variable-delivery.

The direction and quantity of fluid flow in a hydraulic circuit is determined by the type and location of the valves. The principal valves and their functions are: relief valve, limits the maximum pressure in a line; pilot valve, controls the quantity and direction of fluid flow into an actuator; accumulator valve, stores reserve supply of fluid at a constant pressure; check valve, prevents flow in one direction; unloading valve, releases the pressure on the pump; reducing valve, lowers the pressure in a line to the required level; differential-pressure-regulating valve, maintains a constant-pressure drop between two locations.

The actuator is the device in a hydraulic circuit that actually performs the required function or motion. There are two classes of actuators, cylinders and motors. Cylinders impart straight line motion, and motors rotational motion.

Pneumatic Systems

The pneumatic control systems are very similar to the hydraulic systems just described. The primary difference between the two is that the pneumatic system employs a compressible fluid, usually air. Because of this compressibility, the pneumatic system is not as fast-acting or positive in action as the hydraulic system. A pneumatic system contains the same three basic components of a hydraulic system except that the power supply is usually called a compressor rather than a pump. Although a pump and a compressor perform the same function, that is, provide a pressurized fluid, the design of the two are slightly different because of the difference in the compressibilities of the two types of fluids. The valves and actuators for the pneumatic system are also very similar to those used in the hydraulic system.

Electro-mechanical and Electronic

Both electromechanical and electronic devices are extensively used for the automatic control of manufacturing processes. The ease of transmitting electrical power and the speed of transmitting and amplifying electrical signals makes this a very desirable control system. These electrical control devices fall into classes such as motors, generators, solenoids, limit switches, vacuum tubes, transistors and so forth. Since all engineering students become familiar with the general characteristics of all these electrical components in physics and electrical engineering courses, they are not described in this textbook.

Numerical or Tape Control

Machines and processes can also be automatically controlled by computers, tapes, cards, and related equipment. Although Numerical Control is used in such processes as inspection, assembly and forming operations, it gets its greatest recognition as an accessory to machine tools; particularly milling, drilling and turning machine tools. The first numerically controlled machine tools were milling machines designed and built for the U.S. Air Force to machine aircraft structures.

The term Numerical Control as used by the metal working industry, refers to the automatic control and operation of machine tools by information stored on tapes. The most commonly used tape today is a 1 in.-wide paper strip on which the information is stored by the proper spacing of punched holes in eight lines (channels) along the length of the tape. Binary numbers are used with a punched hole representing one and the absence of a hole representing zero. The holes are punched in the channels in predetermined standardized patterns to designate specific numerical codes. These coded numerical commands include all of the operations that the machine tool must perform to completely machine the programmed part.

Three steps, or functions, are necessary to transform a part-drawing into a finished part: 1) the blueprint is studied by a "part programmer" who prepares a program manuscript that includes the sequence of operations needed to machine the part, including tool designations, speeds, feeds and so forth; 2) the tape is prepared from the program on either a manual tape-writer or on a computerized one; 3) the tape is inserted in the tape-readout console of the appropriate machine tool which then automatically machines the part.

The most important function in Numerical Control, as is true in conventional machining if it is to be done efficiently, is the preparation of the program or process sheet. This task is done by a "programmer" in a Numerical Control system and by a "process engineer" in a conventional system. Which ever system is used, the manufacturing efficiency is no better than the processing—a poorly "processed" part cannot be made efficiently. However, since Numerical Control systems cost about three to five times as much as conventional machine tools, the need is greater for good processing in this newer system. In some cases the sole advantage of Numerical Control over conventional machining is the fact that the part is "processed" by a competent technician when the manufacturing is converted to Numerical Control whereas the part was just "made" by a machinist in the conventional system. The need for "processing" by a competent technician prior to machining is great even in the conventional system.

There are two principle types of numerically controlled machine tools; Point-To-Point (Positioning) and Continuous Path (Contouring). In the Point-To-Point type either the tool or the work piece goes from one programmed position to another in one or more straight lines, with no cutting occuring during this movement. In terms of cartesian coordinates the movement may be in the X direction, the Y direction, or in both directions at the same time. In the Continuous Path type of Numerical Control, the tool or work piece follows a predetermined line which may be straight or curved and the tool performs its intended task during this movement. This process is well adapted to three dimensional contouring such as that required in the machining of automobile body dies or aircraft-frame components that must be machined all over to achieve a minimum weight. Of the two types of Numerical Control systems, the Point-To-Point type is by far the more prevalent.

It is customary to specify Numerical Control Machine tools by the number of axes that have program-controlled motions. The simplest type is a two axis machine in which motions in two directions are controlled by the program. An example of a three axis machine tool is a drill press in which the table can be moved in two directions and the spindle can be moved vertically to control the depth of hole machined. The Electronic Industries Association lists 14 different axis designations, but no single machine tool is made with all of them. The most complex machine tools built today have five axes of motion. The additional axes, beyond the three principal perpendicular motions, are axes of rotation and inclination about each of the three principal directions.

The characteristics of Numerical Control makes this system the most economical in certain types of manufacturing situations. The following examples will serve to illustrate the favorable conditions for the application of Numerical Control.

1. The machining of complex contoured shapes. When these parts are machined by hydraulic, mechanical or electromechanical automatic systems a master pattern (made of wood, plaster or a soft metal) must be made first. This model is hand shaped and then placed on the machine tool where a tracer follows the surface of the model while a cutting tool duplicates the profile in the desired metal part.

With a Numerical Control system, the model need not be made if the surface of the contoured part can be represented by mathematical equations in terms of the X, Y, Z coordinates. This is an advantage especially when the parts to be made are large, complex, accurate and few in number.

2. The machining of parts that require a great number of individual "setups," each with its own set of tools, dies or fixtures. If the number of set-ups can be reduced and some of the tooling eliminated, the process will be economical. This advantage will result with any automated system. Another advantage of an automated system which eliminates or reduces the amount of tooling needed to make a part is that it also reduces the "lead time"—the time between when the part prints are finished and the finished parts are made.

3. When the machining time is small in comparison to the set-up and handling time, any fully automated system will be feasible since it is the nature of the automated system to either eliminate or greatly reduce the manual labor required.

REFERENCES

1. Boston, O. W., *Metal Processing*, 2nd Ed., John Wiley and Sons, New York, 1951.
2. Bisacre, G. H., and B. T. Chao, "The Effect of Speed and Feed on the Mechanics of Metal Cutting," *Proceedings Inst. Mech. Engr.*, **165**, 1951, pp. 1–13.
3. Coker, E. G., and K. C. Chakko, "Experiments on the Action of Cutting Tools," *Proceedings, Inst. Mech. Engr.*, 1922, p. 567.
4. Datsko, J., and A. Henkin, "Determining Machining Speeds from the Physical Properties of Metals," *Trans. SAE*, 1964, p. 486.
5. Henkin, A., and J. Datsko, "The Influence of Physical Properties on Machinability," *Trans. ASME*, **85**, Series B, No. 4.
6. Herbert, E. G., "Cutting Tools Research Committee, Report on Machinability," *Proceedings, Inst. Mech. Engr.*, 1928, pp. 175–825.
7. Hermann, G., edited by J. Weisbach, *Lehrbuch der Ingerieur und Maschinenmechanik*, 1896, p. 865.
8. Mallock, A., "The Action of Cutting Tools," *Proc. of the Royal Soc.*, **33**, 1881, pp. 127–139.
9. Nicolson, J. T., "Experiments With A Lathe Tool Dynamometer," *Proceedings, Inst. of Mech. Engr.*, 1904, p. 883.
10. Okochi, M., and M. Okoshi, "Researches on the Cutting Force," *Inst. of Physical and Chemical Res., Science Papers*, **5**, Tokyo, 1927, p. 261.
11. Rosenhain, W., and A. C. Sturney, "Flow and Rupture of Metals During Cutting," *Proceedings, Inst. Mech. Engr.*, 1925, p. 141.
12. Stanton, T. E., and J. H. Hyde, "An Experimental Study of the Forces Exerted on the Surface of a Cutting Tool," *Proceedings, Inst. Mech. Engr.*, 1925, p. 175.
13. Taylor, F. W., "On the Art of Cutting Metals," *Trans. ASME*, **28**, 1907, pp. 31–350.
14. Woxen, R., "A Theory and an Equation for the Life of Lathe Tools," *Ingeniors Vetenskaps Akademiens, Handlinger NR 119*, Stockholm, 1932.

15. Zvorikin, K. A., *Rabota i Usilie, Neobkhodimie dlaya Otdelenaya Metalliches-kikh Struyhek,* Moscow, 1893.

STUDY PROBLEMS

6-1   Calculate the cutting time to shape a $3\frac{1}{8}$ in. $\times$ 11 in. $\times$ 8 in. surface plate to 3 in. $\times$ 11 in. $\times$ 8 in. Assume it is done with one cut using a feed of 0.010 in./stroke and the average speed of the tool is 60 fpm. The shaper on which this work is to be done has the following speeds: 10, 15, 21, 30, 45, 65, 92, 130 spm.

6-2   Calculate the cutting time to mill the surface plate of Problem 6-1 by using a 40 tooth, 12 in. diameter face milling cutter with a feed of 0.004 ipt. Milling machine speeds are: 20, 26, 34, 44, 57, 75, 96, 124, 145, 214, 276, 355, 466 rpm. Cutting speed is 60 fpm.

6-3   Calculate the time to turn a 8 in. diameter shaft to 7.600 in. diameter for a length of 24 in. if a feed of 0.0057 ipr and a speed of 120 fpm is used.

6-4   How are the physical sizes of each of the basic machine tools specified?

6-5   It is required to press a steel rim onto cast iron flywheels that are 40 in. in outside diameter. From a design handbook it is found that the hole tolerance (class 6 fit) should be 0.0020 in., the shaft tolerance 0.0014 in. and the allowance 0.010 in. (allowance for press fit is negative). Specify the limits of the inside diameter of the steel band and the outside diameter of the cast iron wheel. What is the maximum and minimum interference that may be encountered?

6-6   If the flywheel in Problem 6-5 were 4 in. thick, could it be machined on a 36 in. swing engine lathe? From a manufacturing point of view (as opposed to the design point of view), are the tolerances good and reasonable?

6-7   List the tolerances and surface finishes that are obtainable on each of the basic machine tools.

6-8   a. T F   In general, longer tapers may be turned by offsetting the tailstock than by use of the taper attachment.

        b. T F   A shaft turned on a lathe with the tool below center will be tapered.

        c. T F   The feeds on most lathes, as is true of the speeds, are intentionally based on a geometric progression. $(a, ak, ak^2, ak^3, ak^4, \dots)$

        d. T F   For accurate thread cutting, the nonrotating half nuts on the carriage are engaged with the rotating lead screw rather than engaging the friction clutches between the keywayed feed rod and the carriage.

        e. T F   The helix angle on a drill corresponds to the rake angle on a single point tool.

6-9   A drill press equipped with a $\frac{1}{2}$ hp motor is being used to drill six $\frac{1}{2}$ in. diameter $\times$ 1 in. deep holes in an AISI 1020 cold-drawn steel part. A speed of 400 rpm and a feed of 0.005 ipr is being used. It is proposed to purchase a six-spindle drill head to drill all six holes simultaneously. Does the drill press have sufficient capacity?

6–10   1020 hot-rolled steel is being machined with a high-speed steel tool having 0° rake angles, 6° relief angles, 0° side cutting edge angle and no
nose radius. The size of cut (per cutting edge) is 0.250 in. deep and
0.020 in. thick (feed). Calculate the cutting force (F_c): (a) by means
of Table 6-4; (b) by means of unit horsepower—assume $hp_u = 1.0$;
(c) by means of the tensile strength equation.

6–11   A 2 in. diameter steel shaft is being ground on the outside diameter at a
cutting speed of 5000 fpm. The diameter of the shaft is reduced 0.002
in. each time the wheel passes over the work from one end to the other.
The work (shaft) is rotated at 200 rpm, and the wheel traverses the
length of the work at a rate of 50 in./min. The unit horsepower for this
grinding operation is 7.0. Determine the torque required to rotate the
shaft. (Neglect friction between work and centers.)

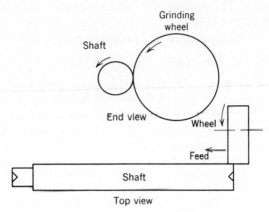

6–12   When drilling AISI 6150 steel, the equations for torque and thrust are:

$$\text{Torque } T = 1840\ f^{0.78}\ d^{1.8} \text{ (lb ft)}$$

$$\text{Thrust } L = 53{,}400\ f^{0.78}\ d^{1.0} \text{ (lb)}$$

where f is the feed in ipr., and d is the drill diameter in inches. (a.) Calculate the torque hp. for a $1\frac{1}{2}$ in. diameter drill rotating at 100 rpm and
a feed of 0.015 ipr. (b.) Calculate the thrust hp. (c.) Calculate the
unit hp.

6–13   If for the material in Problem 6-35, 33,000 ft lb/in.³ are required to
machine it, what torque would be required to rotate the work with a
0.010 ipr feed, 0.125 in. depth, and 100 fpm speed during a turning
operation?

6–14   If the speed (rpm) in Problem 6-13 were doubled, how much would the
torque increase?

6–15   Suppose no handbook at present has any empirical data concerning the
machining forces for beryllium and the company you have just gone to
work for is planning on ordering some standard machine tools to machine
beryllium, how would you estimate, as accurately and quickly as you
can, the unit horsepower requirements for beryllium. (No force dynamo-
meters are available.)

6–16   Estimate the unit horsepower needed to perform turning operations on a lathe for the newly developed material that has the following properties: Y.S. = 150,000 psi; T.S. = 200,000 psi; σ_f = 350,000 psi; A_r = 10%.

6–17   An engine lathe is being used to make a turning cut on gray cast iron. The depth of cut is 0.200 in. the feed is 0.015 ipr and the O.D. of the work at the cut is 10 in.
a. Determine the approximate torque required to rotate the work.
b. Estimate the net horsepower required at the cutter for a cutting speed of 330 fpm.

6–18   A cast steel flange 8 in. O.D. by 5 in. I.D. and 1 in. thick is to have six, $\frac{3}{4}$ in. diameter bolt holes drilled in it simultaneously. A multiple-spindle, fixed center drill head operates all drills at 450 rpm and at a feed rate of 5 in./min. The torque and thrust requirements per drill are given by the following equations:

Torque   (lb ft) $= 1840\ f^{0.78}\ d^{1.8}$

Thrust   (lb) $= 53,400\ f^{0.78}\ d^{1.0}$

where f = drill feed in inches per revolution
         d = drill diameter in inches.

Calculate
a. The maximum thrust acting on the flange when all drills are cutting.
b. The thrust horsepower.
c. The torque horsepower.
d. The total unit power (hp_u) required for overcoming both torque and thrust.

6–19   In process planning, the production of a hole is a problem because punching and drilling are quite competitive. For a 2 in. diameter hole in a 1 in. thick annealed 1040 steel plate:
a. How much force and energy is used in drilling?
b. How much force and energy is used in punching?

6–20   A cut is being made on a piece of material under the following conditions: $\frac{1}{8}$ in. depth, 0.20 ipr feed, 60 min tool life.
If, for this material the equation $v = 2.5\ t^{-0.1}\ f^{-0.7}\ d^{-0.5}$ is valid for the given conditions, what will be the cutting speed?

6–21   a. In machining the material of problem 5–9 with a high speed steel tool, would you expect continuous or discontinuous chips? Explain!
b. What would you estimate the unit horsepower of this material to be?
c. If for this material, experimental data shows that

$$v = 1.5\ t^{-0.1}\ f^{-0.7}\ d^{-0.5} \quad \text{and} \quad F_c = 200,000\ f^{0.9} d^{1.0},$$

could a machining cut with a $\frac{1}{8}$ in. depth, 0.010 ipr feed and a cutting speed that gives a 30 min tool life be used on a machine tool equipped with a 5 hp motor?

6–22   A 4 in. diameter bar is turned in one pass on a lathe to $3\frac{1}{2}$ in. diameter. The energy required at the tool is 30,000 ft lb/in.³. A tool life of 8 hr is desired. The appropriate equations for these conditions are:

$$v\, t^n = 200$$

$$v = 5\ t^{-0.1}\ f^{-0.8}\ d^{-0.6}$$

a. Find v, n, f, F_c, hp_c, for the desired cutting conditions.
b. Find the total hp and the overall efficiency if the no load hp is 2 and additional horsepower is transmitted with an efficiency of 85%.

6–23 If the speed (rpm) in Problem 6-13 were doubled, how much would the cutting time be changed? (Everything else is constant.)

6–24 Specify an "optimum" tool shape for rough turning the following materials with an HSS tool. Explain your choice briefly. (a.) Annealed medium carbon steel. (b.) Heat treated $(45R_c)$ medium carbon steel. (c.) Heat treated aluminum.

6–25 A process sheet specifies the following tool shape for rough turning AISI 5140 annealed shafts that are 2 in. diameter and 12 in. long: 5° BR, 0° SR, 6° ECA, 6° SCA, 6° ECEA, 0° SCEA, 0 in. R. By what per cent could the cutting time be reduced simply by changing the tool shape. Explain.

6–26 Refer to Figure 3-3. A similar pulley is made of AISI 1015 steel. The forged O.D. is $20\frac{1}{4}$ in. and it is to be rough turned on an engine lathe with a depth of cut of $\frac{1}{8}$ in. and a feed of 0.020 ipr with a proper HSS tool. If for these conditions the relationship $vt^{0.1} = 200$ is valid, what is the cutting time per piece if the cutting speed is such that the tool life is 2 hr?

6–27 A lathe operator is machining AISI 1018 hot-rolled steel axles and is reducing the diameter from 3.500 in. to 3.100 in. in one cut with a properly ground tool. He is using a feed of 0.006 ipr, a speed of 60 rpm, and the length of cut is 12 in. The loading–unloading time is 1 min, and the tool changing time is 1 min. Machinability studies show that for this tool-work combination, the following relationship is valid.

$$v = 2t^{-0.1}\ f^{-0.7}\ d^{-0.4}$$

After this turning operation, the shafts are ground to 3.090 in. diameter.

Assuming that a tool life of 30 min is satisfactory, by what per cent could you increase the daily productivity by specifying a change in *cutting conditions?* (420 *working* min in a day). (There is not one best answer, but several correct answers.)

6–28 A lathe is equipped with a 3 hp motor, and it may be assumed that the motor can be overloaded by an amount equal to the mechanical losses of the power-drive mechanisms. It is proposed to machine AISI 1045 cold drawn shafts by turning the diameter from 4 in. to 3.000 ± 0.010 in. for a length of 12 in.

Machinability tests on this material gave the following relationships:

$$F_C = 180,000\, f^{0.8} d^{1.0}$$

$$v = \frac{1.8}{t^{0.1} f^{0.8} d^{0.4}}$$

Assume that a minimum tool life of 1 hr is desirable; that a heavy cut is 0.750 in. deep with a feed of 0.040 ipr, and that a light cut is 0.050 in. deep with a feed of 0.003 ipr; the lathe has an infinite range of speeds and feeds.

Determine the minimum cutting time possible, in minutes per piece. (Again, there is not one answer but several correct answers.)

6-29   A machinist operating an engine lathe is turning AISI 1018 H.R. steel shafting with a HSS tool that has the approximate tool shape listed below:

5° BR, 5° SR, 6° ECA, 6° SCA, 6°ECEA, 0° SCEA, 0 in. radius

By what percent could you reduce the cutting time for this operation simply by changing the tool shape? Explain.

6-30   The operation in Problem 6-29 is being performed on three shifts, five days a week. During the next quarter the production schedule is going to be increased by 50% due to extremely good sales, so the foreman is planning on ordering another engine lathe to handle the additional parts. Each operator changes tools on this particular operation twice, at the beginning of the shift and again at lunch time, and the time to change the tool is about 2 min. How often should the tools be changed to get maximum production from this operation?

6-31   Some additional information on Problem 6-30 is as follows: The shaft is $3\frac{13}{16}$ in. diameter and is being reduced to $3\frac{9}{16}$ in. diameter in one cut with a feed of 0.006 ipr for a length of 18 in. at a speed of 60 rpm. In addition to the cutting time of this one particular operation, two other short operations requiring $1\frac{1}{2}$ min time and a loading-unloading time of 2 min complete the work on this one lathe. The shaft is ground afterward with 0.012 in. of grind stock provided on the diameter. (Diameter after grinding is 3.5500/3.5490.) Machinability tests on AISI 1018 HR steel with high speed tools (8, 14, 6, 6, 6, 15, $\frac{3}{16}$ in.) give the following empirical relationships:

$$v = 2.5 \ t^{-0.1} \ f^{-0.8} \ d^{-0.4}$$

Assume that the exponents are only slightly changed by tool shape while the constant "2.5" is greatly affected by tool shape.

a. For the above-mentioned tool, what feed and speed would you recommend for a 30 min tool life?

b. How many parts per shift would each operator get, assuming 400 "productive" min per shift?

c. How does this compare with the production presently being achieved?

6-32   Refer to Problem 6-26. Determine the cutting speed that would result in the maximum production if the tool changing time is 2 min.

6-33   Refer to Problem 6-26. Determine the cutting speed for minimum cost if the following conditions pertain to this operation.

Tool cost—$1.25	Lathe operator rate—$3.00/hr
Tool regrinds—20	Grinder rate— 2.50/hr
Tool grind time—3 min	Overhead— 5.50/hr
Tool change time—2 min	Load & unload time— 2 min

6–34   Refer to Problem 6-33. Calculate the cutting time if carbide tools were used.

6–35   AISI 9260 annealed steel shafts are to be machined on a turret lathe. One operation consists of turning a 3.500 in. to 3.250 diameter for a length of 8 in.

For a carbide tool, the relationship $v = t^{-0.2} \ d^{-0.5} \ f^{-0.7}$ is valid for this material under the appropriate cutting conditions.

If the carbide tool is of the throwaway type and a $\frac{1}{2}$ in. square tip used with a $-7°$ rake angle holder costs \$1.20; the operators rate is \$2.40/hr; with overhead at \$4.80/hr; load-unload time is 1 min and tool change time is $\frac{1}{2}$ min, then what cutting speed will result in the minimum cost if a feed of 0.010 ipr is used?

6–36   What is the minimum cost for the operation described in Problem 6-35?

6–37   If a high speed steel tool were to be used in Problem 6-35 instead of the carbide, what cutting speed would result in a 30 min tool life if the same feed and depth as above were used?

6–38   If a ceramic tool were to be used in Problem 6–35 instead of the carbide tool, what would be the *probable minimum* speed for which it would be superior to the carbide tool?

6–39   What surface finish and accuracy would you expect under conditions of Problem 6-35? What would you expect the "finest" tolerance and finish obtainable to be if the cutting conditions could be changed?

6–40   You are asked to specify the optimum cutting speed and tool life for a specific machining operation in which sintered carbide tools will be used. In looking through the handbooks, the only machinability data you can find for this particular material (hot-rolled 9140) is:

$$v = 1.8 \ t^{-0.1} \ f^{-0.8} \ d^{-0.4}$$

which pertains to machining with a HSS tool having the proper tool shape. Rewrite the above equation so that it will express the cutting speed-tool life relationship when cutting with a sintered carbide tool with $\frac{1}{4}$ in. depth of cut and 0.020 ipr feed.

6–41   In machining hot-rolled AISI 9140 (manganese) steel axles that are 6 in. O.D. $\times$ 5 ft long, a cut is made on each end simultaneously (the piece is chucked at its mid-length in a special lathe). The depth is $\frac{1}{4}$ in., the feed is 0.020 ipr and the length of cut is 10 in. For this work material and tool combination, the relationship

$$v = 1.8 \ t^{-0.1} \ f^{-0.8} \ d^{-0.4}$$

Other pertinent information is:

Machine operator's rate—	\$2.75/hr	Tool regrinding time—	2 min
Machine department burden—	6.25/hr	Tool changing time—	$\frac{1}{2}$ min
Tool grinder's rate—	2.75/hr	Load and unload	
Grinding department burden—	6.25/hr	(per piece)—	4 min
Original cost of tool—	0.90 ea.	Number of grinds/tool	10

a. Calculate tool life for minimum cost/piece.

   b. Calculate cutting speed for minimum cost/piece.
   c. Calculate minimum cost/piece.

6–42 For the material in Problem 6-16 the relationship

$$v = 2.5 \times t^{-0.2} f^{-0.8} d^{-0.6}$$

is valid for a sintered carbide tool and the following data applies to this particular plant:

Lathe operator's rate— $3.00/hr   Tool cost:
Grinder's rate—   3.20/hr   throwaway— $1.25
Overhead—   6.00/hr   solid insert—   6.00
Load and unload time— $\frac{1}{2}$ min   Tool life (cutting edges)
Tool change time: throwaway—6 edges,
   throwaway— $\frac{1}{3}$ min   no regrind
   solid insert—   1 min   solid insert—6 edges per
                                                regrind. 20 regrinds
                                                possible. 10 min to
                                                regrind.

   a. Calculate cutting speed for minimum cost using a throwaway insert.
   b. Would the solid insert or the throwaway insert result in a lower machining cost?

6–43 What is the cause and the result of residual stresses on a machined surface? Name two ways to eliminate the residual stresses?

6–44 What physical properties of a metal affect its machinability most? Explain each.

6–45 Sketch or state a hypothetical microstructure with excellent machineability and one with very poor machinability.

6–46 Rank the HCP materials listed in Appendix A in order of decreasing machinability (most machinable first).

6–47 Material x has the following machining characteristics with HSS tools of the shape 8, 14, 6, 6, 6, 15, and $\frac{1}{16}$.

$$vt^{0.1} f^{0.6} d^{0.4} = 2.0 \quad \text{and} \quad F_c = 165,000 f^{0.9} d$$

   a. A 6 in. O.D. $\times$ 4 in. I.D. $\times$ 15 in. long cylinder is to be bored to a $4\frac{1}{2}$ in. I.D. in one pass with a 0.010 ipr feed. For a 60 min tool life, what will be the cutting time?
   b. Determine the cutting speed for minimum cost when the depth of cut is 0.250 in. and the feed is 0.010 ipr for the following conditions: lathe operator rate = $2.75/hr; tool grinder rate = $3.00/hr; overhead = $5.00/hr; cost of tool = $2.00; no. of grinds = 10; grinding time = 5 min; tool changing time = 3 min.
   c. If a bar of this material is to be turned from a 4 in. O.D. to a 3.5 in. O.D. on a lathe having 5hp available at the cutting edge, what is a reasonable maximum rate of metal removal (in.^{3}/min.) that can be expected? A minimum tool life of 60 min is acceptable.

6–48 Two shops are machining a certain metal known as TYDIMB on lathes with carbide throwaway tools that cost $0.40 per cutting edge.

For this material and tool shape

$$vt^{0.2} f^{0.6} d^{0.4} = 1.6$$

$$F_c = 180{,}000 \, f^{0.8} \, d$$

Shop A is a production shop with a $3.00/hr labor rate and $6.00/hr overhead rate. Shop B is a machine shop associated with a company that has a lot of engineers and salesmen but sells only a small amount. Consequently the labor rate is $3.00/hr but the overhead is $18.00/hr. If the time to index a tool is $\frac{1}{2}$ min, how long should a tool be used in each shop?

6–49 We are designing a shaft and can use AISI 1045 annealed or cold-drawn (10%) steel. The cost, except for machining, is identical for both of these materials. Therefore, the one having the greater machinability should be used. Machinability handbooks do not have the data. Assume the thermal conductivity does not change appreciably with coldwork. Compare the v_{60}'s for the annealed and 10% cold-drawn bars for HSS tools of zero rake and zero radius with 0.005 ipr feed and 0.050 in. depth.

6–50 Calculate the cutting speed for a 60 minute tool life for the following materials and conditions: tool material—HSS; tool shape—0°,0°,6°, 6°, 6°, 0° 0 in.; feed—0.0057 ipr; depth of cut—0.50 in. (a) AISI 1020 HR steel. (b) 6 Al 4V Ti alloy. (c) AISI 4340 HR steel.

Appendix A

Physical Properties of Some Metals

Material	Lattice	Density ρ $\frac{gm}{cm^3}$	Specific Heat C_p $\frac{cal}{gm\,°C}$	Thermal Conductivity k $\frac{cal}{sec\,cm\,°C}$	Thermal Diffusivity α $\frac{cm^2}{sec}$	Melting Temperature, °F	Modulus of Elasticity, E psi	Yield Strength, S_y psi	Tensile Strength, S_u psi	Percent Elongation	Percent Reduction of Area, A_r	Heat of Fusion, ΔH_f $\frac{cal}{gm}$
Steel (Ferrite)	BCC	7.86	0.11	0.15	0.173	2780	30×10^6	30,000	40,000	45	75	58
Steel (1020)	–	7.86	0.11	0.15	0.173	2770	30×10^6	40,000	60,000	40	60	58
Steel (4340)	–	7.84	0.120	0.08	0.085	2750	30×10^6	135,000	153,000	10	35	58
Al (99.996)	FCC	2.70	0.22	0.53	0.89	1218	10×10^6	1,800	7,000	50	–	77
Al (2S-0)	FCC	2.71	0.23	0.53	0.88	1215	10×10^6	5,000	13,000	45	–	77
Zirconium	HCP	6.5	0.066	0.07	0.16	3200	12×10^6	16,000	36,000	30	–	60
Tantulum	BCC	16.6	0.036	0.13	0.22	5425	27×10^6	23,000	50,000	40	–	38
Columbium	BCC	8.57	0.065	0.13	0.23	4380	15×10^6	30,000	40,000	30	80	69
Beryllium	HCP	1.82	0.516	0.385	0.41	2340	40×10^6	26,500	33,000	1	–	260
Hafnium	HCP	13.09	0.0351	0.0533	0.116	3100	20×10^6	33,600	64,800	23	37	–
Molybdenum	BCC	10.2	0.061	0.35	0.56	4760	50×10^6	60,000	150,000	10	50	70
Copper	FCC	8.96	0.092	0.94	1.14	1981	16×10^6	8,000	32,000	55	78	42
70-30 Brass	FCC	8.5	0.09	0.25	0.33	1740	16×10^6	16,000	48,000	65	75	–
304 S.S.	FCC	7.9	0.12	0.039	0.054	2600	25×10^6	33,000	86,000	60	75	–
Titanium	HCP	4.54	0.126	0.0685	0.120	3300	16.8×10^6	63,000	79,000	25.2	50	97
Nickel	FCC	8.9	0.105	0.22	0.236	2651	30×10^6	8,500	46,000	30	70	74
Ni base alloy[1]	FCC	8.25	0.108	0.575	0.645	2300	31.7×10^6	154,000	206,000	14	–	–
Co base alloy[2]	FCC	9.13	0.092	0.27	0.322	2500	32.6×10^6	70,000	150,000	65	40	–

[1] 19 Cr, 11 Co, 10 Mo, 3 Ti, Bal Ni
[2] 10 Ni, 20 Cr, 15 W, Bal Co

Conversion Factors
1 cal = 3.968×10^{-3} Btu
1 cal/gm = 1.8 Btu/lb
1 cal/gm °C = 1 Btu/lb °F

Appendix B

Hardness Conversion Values

Conversion from diameter of indentation to Bhn is valid for all materials.
Conversion from Bhn to other hardness scales is valid only for steel.

Descriptive Hardness and Material	Brinell Hardness (10 mm Ball) Diameter of indentation (mm)	Bhn 500kg Load	Bhn 3000kg Load	Rockwell Hardness R_c	Rockwell Hardness R_b	Diamond Pyramid or Vickers Hardness	Knoop or Tukon	Scleroscope Hardness
File hard tool and abrasive resistant steel	2.20	130	780	68		942	905	100
	2.25	124	745	66		854	847	95
	2.30	119	712	64		789	807	90
	2.35	114	682	62		739	770	85
	2.40	109	653	60		695	719	81
	2.45	104	627	59		675	703	79
	2.50	100	601	58		655	672	77
Very high strength steels	2.55	96.3	578	57		636	644	75
	2.60	92.6	555	56		617	631	73
	2.65	89.0	534	54		580	593	71
	2.70	85.7	514	53		562	569	70
	2.75	82.6	495	52		545	558	68
	2.80	79.6	477	50		513	533	66
	2.85	76.8	461	49		498	519	65
	2.90	74.1	444	47		471	488	63
	2.95	71.5	429	46		458	479	61
	3.00	69.1	415	45		446	470	59

Appendix B (Continued)

Hardness Conversion Values

Conversion from diameter of indentation to Bhn is valid for all materials.
Conversion from Bhn to other hardness scales is valid only for steel.

Descriptive Hardness and Material	Brinell Hardness (10 mm Ball)			Rockwell Hardness		Diamond Pyramid or Vickers Hardness	Knoop or Tukon	Scleroscope Hardness
	Diameter of indentation (mm)	Bhn		R_c	R_b			
		500kg Load	3000kg Load					
High strength steels and titanium	3.05	66.8	401	43		424	438	58
	3.10	64.6	388	42		413	423	56
	3.15	62.5	375	40		393	412	54
	3.20	60.5	363	39		383	407	52
	3.25	58.6	352	38		373	391	51
	3.30	56.8	341	37		363	382	50
	3.35	55.1	331	36		353	375	48
	3.40	53.4	321	34		334	359	47
	3.45	51.8	311	33		325	353	46
	3.50	50.3	302	32		317	347	45
	3.55	48.9	293	31		309	337	43
	3.60	47.5	285	30		301	332	42
	3.65	46.1	277	29		293	327	41
	3.70	44.9	269	28		285	317	40
	3.75	43.6	262	27		278	303	39
	3.80	42.4	255	25		264	295	38
	3.85	41.3	248	24		257	290	37
	3.90	40.2	241	23	100	251	286	36
	3.95	39.1	235	22	99	246	282	35
	4.00	38.1	229	21	98	241	277	34

Appendix B (*Continued*)

Hardness Conversion Values

Conversion from diameter of indentation to Bhn is valid for all materials.
Conversion from Bhn to other hardness scales is valid only for steel.

Descriptive Hardness and Material	Diameter of indentation (mm)	Brinell Hardness (10 mm Ball) Bhn		Rockwell Hardness		Diamond Pyramid or Vickers Hardness	Knoop or Tukon	Scleroscope Hardness
		500kg Load	3000kg Load	R_c	R_b			
High strength and high toughness steels	4.05	37.1	223	20	97	236	270	32
	4.10	36.2	217	18	96	220	253	31
	4.15	35.3	212	17	95	209	250	30
	4.20	34.4	207	16	94	198	246	30
	4.25	33.6	201	15	93	188	240	29
	4.30	32.8	197	13	92	179	225	28
Pearlitic cast iron	4.35	32.0	192	12	91	171	219.5	27
	4.40	31.2	187	10	90	164	209.5	26
Hard brass	4.45	30.5	183		89	157	207.0	26
	4.50	29.8	179		88	151	203.0	25
Heat-treated aluminum	4.55	29.1	174		87	145	199.0	25
	4.60	28.4	170		86	140	195.6	24
	4.65	27.8	167		85	135	193.4	24
	4.70	27.1	163		84	130	190.4	24
	4.75	26.5	159		83	126	184.0	23
	4.80	25.9	156		82	122	180.0	23
	4.85	25.4	152		81	119	177.3	23
	4.90	24.8	149		80	115	174.0	22
	4.95	24.3	146		79	112	170.0	22
	5.00	23.8	143		78	108	167.0	21

Appendix B (*Continued*)

Hardness Conversion Values

Conversion from diameter of indentation to Bhn is valid for all materials.
Conversion from Bhn to other hardness scales is valid only for steel.

| Descriptive Hardness and Material | Brinell Hardness (10 mm Ball) | | | Rockwell Hardness | | Diamond Pyramid or Vickers Hardness | Knoop or Tukon | Sclero-scope Hardness |
| | Diameter of indentation (mm) | Bhn | | R_c | R_b | | | |
		500kg Load	3000kg Load					
Soft steels	5.05	23.3	140		77	106	163.0	21
	5.10	22.8	137		75	103	158.0	20
	5.15	22.3	134		74	100	153.0	20
	5.20	21.8	131		73	98	150.0	
Ferritic cast iron	5.25	21.4	128		71	95	148.0	
	5.30	20.9	126		70	93	147.0	
	5.35	20.5	123		69	91	143.5	
Aluminum and brass alloys	5.40	20.1	121		68	89		
	5.45	19.7	118		67	87		
	5.50	19.3	116		65	85		
	5.55	18.9	114		64	83		
	5.60	18.6	111		63	81		
	5.65	18.2	109		62	79		
	5.70	17.8	107		60	78		
	5.75	17.5	105		59	77		
	5.80	17.2	103		57			
	5.85	16.8	101		55			
	5.90	16.5	99.2		53			
	5.95	16.2	97.3		50			
	6.00	15.9	95.5		47			

Appendix C

Selected equilibrium phase diagrams. From *Metals Handbook*, 1948 edition.

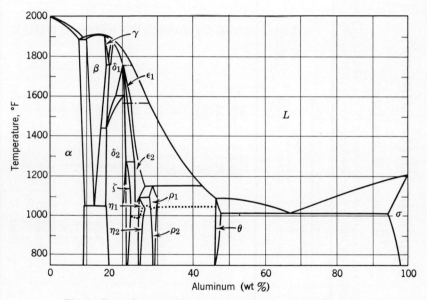

Figure C-1. Copper-aluminum equilibrium phase diagram.

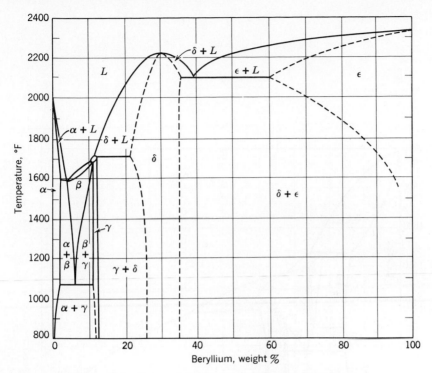

Figure C-2. Copper-beryllium equilibrium phase diagram.

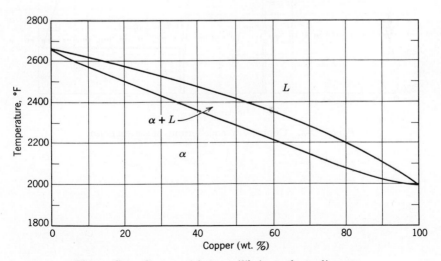

Figure C-3. Copper-nickel equilibrium phase diagram.

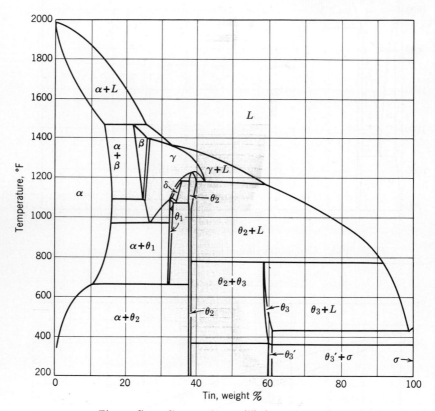

Figure C-4. Copper-tin equilibrium phase diagram.

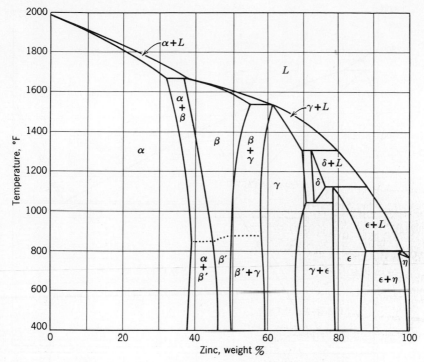

Figure C-5. Copper-zinc equilibrium phase diagram.

Figure C-6. Iron-cadmium equilibrium phase diagram. Iron and cadmium are mutually insoluble in the solid state.

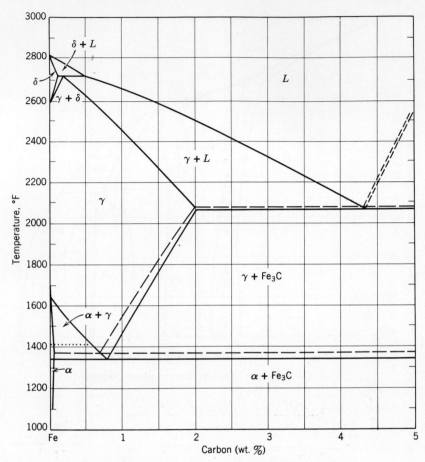

Figure C-7. Iron-carbon equilibrium phase diagram.

Figure C-8. Iron-lead equilibrium phase diagram. Iron and lead are mutually insoluble in both the liquid and solid states.

Figure C-9. Iron-silver equilibrium phase diagram. Iron and silver are virtually insoluble in both the liquid and solid states.

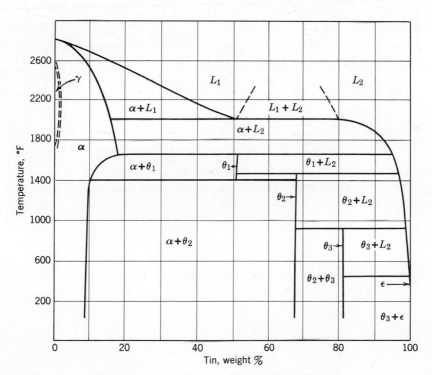

Figure C-10. Iron-tin equilibrium phase diagram.

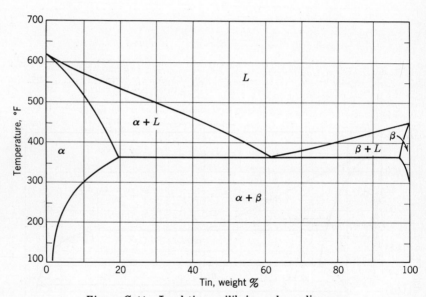

Figure C-11. Lead-tin equilibrium phase diagram.

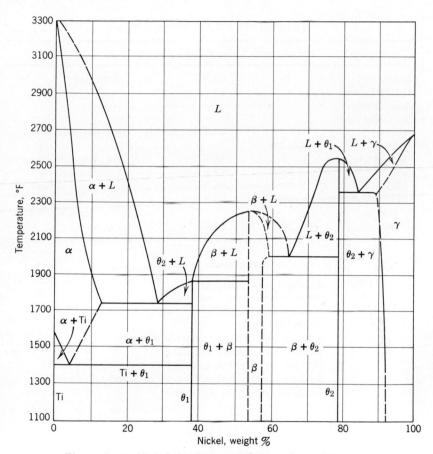

Figure C-12. Nickel-titanium equilibrium phase diagram.
Compounds: (θ_1) 38 wt.% Ni-Ti$_2$-Ni; (β) 57 wt.% Ni-TiNi; (θ_2) 78 wt.% Ni-TiNi$_3$.

Appendix D-1

Designations for Aluminum Alloys

Type	Old Number	New Number	Suffix	Meaning
Aluminum (99.00% min)	2s	1XXX	O	Annealed
Alloys (grouped by major alloy)				
Copper	11s, 14s, 17s, 24s	2XXX	H	Strain-hardened
Manganese	3s	3XXX	F	As fabricated
Silicon	32s	4XXX	W	Solution treated
Magnesium	52s	5XXX	T	Heat treat temper
Magnesium and silicon	61s	6XXX		(T2 to T10 for wrought materials)
Zinc	75s	7XXX		

Subdivisions of −T temper

−T2	Annealed (cost products only)
−T3	Solution heat treated and coldworked
−T4	Solution heat treated and naturally aged
−T5	Artificially aged
−T6	Solution heat treated and artificially aged
−T7	Solution heat treated and stabilized
−T8	Solution heat treated, coldworked, and artificially aged
−T9	Solution heat treated, artificially aged, and coldworked
−T10	Artificially aged and coldworked

Appendix D-2

Chemical Composition of Some Aluminum Alloys

Number	Principal Alloy Element	Alloy Elements				
		Cu	Mn	Si	Mg	Zn
1100	None	–	–	–	–	–
2011	Copper	5.5	–	–	–	–
2014	Copper	4.5	0.8	0.8	0.4	–
2017	Copper	4.0	0.5	–	0.5	–
2024	Copper	4.0	0.6	–	1.5	–
3003	Manganese	–	1.2	–	–	–
4032	Silicon	0.9	–	12.2	1.1	–
5052	Magnesium	–	–	–	2.5	–
6061	Magnesium	0.25	–	0.6	1.0	–
7075	Zinc	1.6	–	–	2.5	5.6

Appendix D-3

Typical Mechanical Properties of Wrought Aluminum Alloys

Alloy and Temper	Strength psi		Percent Elongation	Bhn-500kg
	Tensile	Yield		
1100-O	13,000	5,000	45	23
1100-H18	24,000	22,000	15	44
2011-T8	59,000	45,000	12	100
2014-O	27,000	14,000	18	45
2014-T6	70,000	60,000	13	135
2017-O	26,000	10,000	22	45
2017-T4	62,000	40,000	22	105
2024-O	27,000	11,000	22	47
2024-T3	70,000	50,000	18	120
3032-T6	55,000	46,000	9	120
6061-T6	45,000	40,000	17	95
7075-T6	82,000	72,000	11	150

Appendix E-1

AISI and SAE Designation of Structural Steels

The common steels are specified by a code consisting of four (4) numbers as illustrated below with the substitution of the letters X, Y, and Z for the numbers. A steel specification XYZZ has the following meaning:

X—indicates the type of alloy present
Y—indicates the per cent of principal alloys
ZZ—indicates the "points" of carbon (points of carbon are % × 100)

When X Is	Alloys Present Are
1[1]	None (plain carbon)
2	Nickel
3	Nickel-chromium
4	Molybdenum (+ nickel-chromium)
5	Chromium
6	Chromium-vanadium
8	Nickel-chromium-molybdenum
9	Silicon-manganese

Examples

2130 is a 1% nickel steel with 0.3% C
4340 is a 3% (molybdenum + Ni + Cr) steel with 0.4% C

[1] 11ZZ and 12ZZ indicate resulfurized free machining steel. 13ZZ indicates high manganese plain carbon steel.

Appendix E-2

Compositions of Some AISI Steels

AISI No.	C	Mn	P Max	S Max	Si	Ni	Cr	Mo
Plain Carbon								
C 1010	0.08–0.13	0.30–0.60	0.040	0.050	0.1 max	–	–	–
C 1018	0.15–0.20	0.60–0.90	0.040	0.050	0.10–0.30	–	–	–
C 1020	0.18–0.23	0.30–0.60	0.040	0.050	0.10–0.30	–	–	–
C 1040	0.37–0.44	0.60–0.90	0.040	0.050	0.10–0.30	–	–	–
C 1045	0.43–0.50	0.60–0.90	0.040	0.050	0.10–0.30	–	–	–
C 1080	0.75–0.88	0.60–0.90	0.040	0.050	0.10–0.30	–	–	–
Free Machining								
C 1113	0.10–0.16	1.00–1.30	0.040	0.24–0.33	–	–	–	–
C 1117	0.14–0.20	1.00–1.30	0.040	0.08–0.13	–	–	–	–
C 1141	0.37–0.45	1.35–1.65	0.040	0.08–0.13	–	–	–	–
B 1112	0.13 Max	0.70–1.00	0.07–0.12	0.16–0.23	–	–	–	–
C 1212	0.13 Max	0.70–1.00	0.07–0.12	0.16–0.23	–	–	–	–
High Manganese								
1320	0.18–0.23	1.60–1.90	0.040	0.040	0.20–0.35	–	–	–
1340	0.38–0.43	1.60–1.90	0.040	0.040	0.20–0.35	–	–	–

Appendix E-2 (*Continued*)

Compositions of Some AISI Steels

AISI No.	C	Mn	P Max	S Max	Si	Ni	Cr	Mo
Alloys								
2317	0.15-0.20	0.40-0.60	0.040	0.040	0.20-0.35	3.25-3.75	—	—
2340	0.38-0.43	0.70-0.90	0.040	0.040	0.20-0.35	3.25-3.75	—	—
3140	0.38-0.43	0.70-0.90	0.040	0.040	0.20-0.35	1.10-1.40	0.55-0.75	—
4037	0.35-0.40	0.70-0.90	0.040	0.040	0.20-0.35	—	—	0.20-0.30
4140	0.38-0.43	0.75-1.00	0.040	0.040	0.20-0.35	—	0.80-1.10	0.15-0.25
4150	0.48-0.53	0.75-1.00	0.040	0.040	0.20-0.35	—	0.80-1.10	0.15-0.25
4340	0.38-0.43	0.60-0.80	0.040	0.040	0.20-0.35	1.65-2.00	0.70-0.90	0.20-0.30
4640	0.38-0.43	0.60-0.80	0.040	0.040	0.20-0.35	1.65-2.00	—	0.20-0.30
4820	0.18-0.23	0.50-0.70	0.040	0.040	0.20-0.35	3.25-3.75	—	0.20-0.30
5140	0.38-0.43	0.70-0.90	0.040	0.040	0.20-0.35	—	0.70-0.90	—
6145	0.43-0.48	0.70-0.90	0.040	0.040	0.20-0.35	—	0.80-1.10	0.15 min V
8620	0.18-0.23	0.70-0.90	0.040	0.040	0.20-0.35	0.40-0.70	0.40-0.60	0.15-0.25
9260	0.55-0.65	0.75-1.00	0.040	0.040	1.80-2.20	—	0.25-0.40	—
9845	0.43-0.48	0.70-0.90	0.040	0.040	0.20-0.35	0.85-1.15	0.70-0.90	0.20-0.30

Code for Prefixes:

  B—Acid bessemer carbon steel

  C—Basic open hearth carbon steel

  D—Acid open hearth carbon steel

  E—Electric furnace steel

Appendix E-3

Standard Manufacturing Tolerances
(All Tolerances are Minus)

Cold-Finished Carbon Steel Bars and Shafting

Specified size in inches	Variations from Size in Inches		
	Carbon 0.28% Max	Carbon 0.29% to 0.55%	Carbon Over 0.55%
Cold-Drawn Rounds			
Up to 1 incl.	0.002	0.002	0.006
Over 1 to 2, incl.	0.003	0.004	0.008
Over 2 to 4, incl.	0.004	0.005	0.010
Over 4 to 6, incl.	0.005	0.006	0.012
Over 6 to $7\frac{3}{4}$, incl.	0.006	0.008	0.016
Over $7\frac{3}{4}$ to 9, incl.	0.007	0.010	0.018
Over 9	0.008	0.011	0.020
Cold-Drawn Hexagons			
Up to $\frac{5}{16}$, incl.	0.002	0.003	0.006
Over $\frac{5}{16}$ to 1, incl.	0.003	0.004	0.008
Over 1 to $2\frac{1}{2}$, incl.	0.004	0.005	0.010
Over $2\frac{1}{2}$ to 4, incl.	0.005	0.006	0.012
Cold-Drawn Squares			
Up to $\frac{5}{16}$, incl.	0.003	0.004	0.008
Over $\frac{5}{16}$ to 1, incl.	0.004	0.005	0.010
Over 1 to $2\frac{1}{2}$, incl.	0.005	0.006	0.012
Over $2\frac{1}{2}$ to 4, incl.	0.006	0.008	0.016

Cold-Finished Alloy Steels

Specified size in inches	Variations from Size in Inches		
	Carbon 0.28% Max	Carbon 0.29% to 0.55%	Carbon Over 0.55%
Cold-Drawn Rounds			
Up to 1 incl.	0.003	0.005	0.007
Over 1 to 2, incl.	0.004	0.006	0.009
Over to 4, incl.	0.005	0.007	0.011
Cold-Drawn Hexagons			
Up to $\frac{5}{16}$ incl.	0.003	0.005	0.007
Over $\frac{5}{16}$ to 1, incl.	0.005	0.007	0.011
Over 1 to $2\frac{1}{2}$, incl.	0.005	0.007	0.011
Over $2\frac{1}{2}$ to $3\frac{1}{8}$, incl.	0.006	0.008	0.013
Cold-Drawn Squares			
Up to $\frac{5}{16}$, incl.	0.004	0.006	0.009
Over $\frac{5}{16}$ to 1, incl.	0.005	0.007	0.011
Over 1 to $2\frac{1}{2}$, incl.	0.006	0.008	0.013
Over $2\frac{1}{2}$ to 4, incl.	0.007	0.010	0.017

Appendix E-3 (*Continued*)

Cold Drawn Flats

(Tolerances for flats apply to thickness as well as width)

Width in Inches			
To $\frac{3}{4}$ incl.	0.003	0.004	0.008
Over $\frac{3}{4}$ to $1\frac{1}{2}$, incl.	0.004	0.005	0.010
Over $1\frac{1}{2}$ to 3, incl.	0.005	0.006	0.012
Over 3 to 4, incl.	0.006	0.008	0.016
Over 4 to 6, incl.	0.008	0.010	0.020
Over 6	0.013		

Width in Inches			
Up to $\frac{3}{4}$ incl.	0.004	0.006	0.009
Over $\frac{3}{4}$ to $1\frac{1}{2}$, incl.	0.005	0.007	0.011
Over $1\frac{1}{2}$ to 3, incl.	0.006	0.008	0.013
Over 3 to 4, incl.	0.007	0.010	0.017
Over 4 to 6, incl.	0.009	0.012	0.021
Over 6	0.014		

Turned, Ground and Polished Rounds or Cold-Drawn, Ground and Polished Rounds

Diameters	Resulfurized	Non resulfurized
Less than $2\frac{1}{2}$ in.	0.002	0.002
$2\frac{1}{2}$ in. to 4 in. incl.	0.003	0.003
Over 4 in. to 6 in. incl.	0.004	0.005
Over 6	0.005	0.006

Diameters	Not Heat Treated	Heat Treated
Up to $2\frac{1}{2}$, excl.	0.002	0.003
$2\frac{1}{2}$ to 4, incl.	0.003	0.004
Over 4 to 6, incl.	0.004	0.005
Over 6	0.005	0.006

Appendix E-4

Machining Allowance for Hot-Rolled Steel

Hot-Rolled Carbon Steel Bars	
Nominal Diameter of Hot-Roller Bar in Inches	*Conventional Allowance for Turning on Diameter*
$1\frac{1}{2}$ to 3, incl.	$\frac{1}{8}$ in.
Over 3	$\frac{1}{4}$ in.

Hot-Rolled Alloy Steel Bars	
Specified Size in Inches	*Min. Stock Removal from Surface, Inches*
Up to $\frac{5}{8}$ incl.	0.016
Over $\frac{5}{8}$ to 1, incl.	0.023
Over 1 to $1\frac{1}{4}$, incl.	0.028
Over $1\frac{1}{4}$ to $1\frac{1}{2}$, incl.	0.032
Over $1\frac{1}{2}$ to $2\frac{1}{2}$, incl.	0.052
Over $2\frac{1}{2}$ to $4\frac{1}{2}$, incl.	0.090
Over $4\frac{1}{2}$ to $6\frac{1}{2}$, incl.	0.125

Appendix F

Selected isothermal transformation curves and end-quench harden-ability curves.

From *Atlas of Isothermal Transformation Diagrams*, United States Steel Corporation.

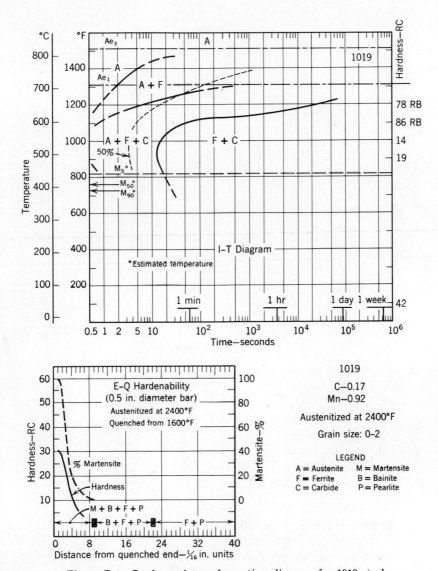

Figure F-1. Isothermal transformation diagram for 1019 steel.

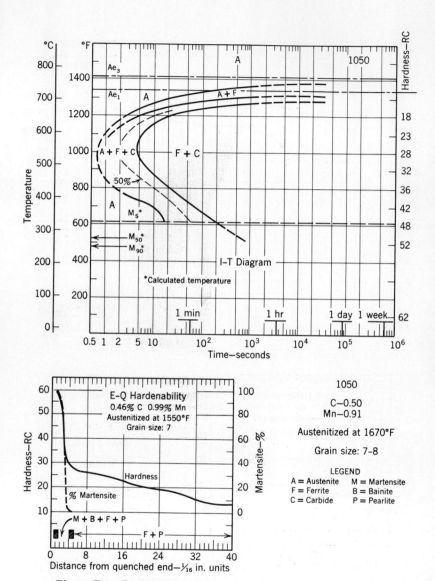

Figure F-2. Isothermal transformation diagram for 1050 steel.

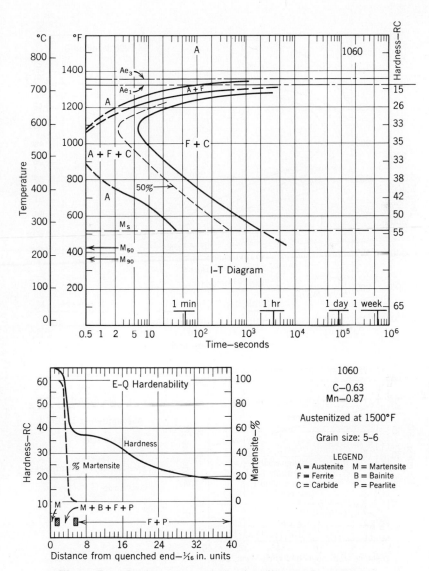

Figure F-3. Isothermal transformation diagram for 1060 steel.

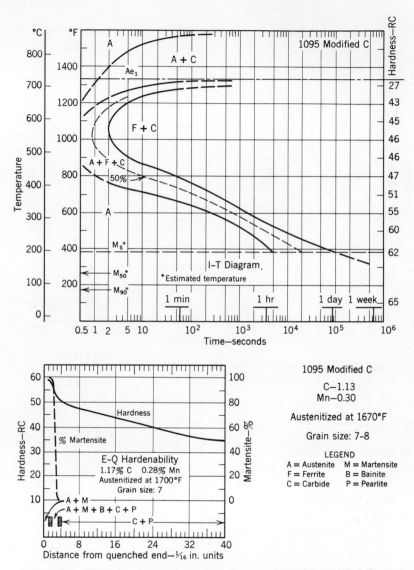

Figure F-4. Isothermal transformation diagram for 1095 modified C steel.

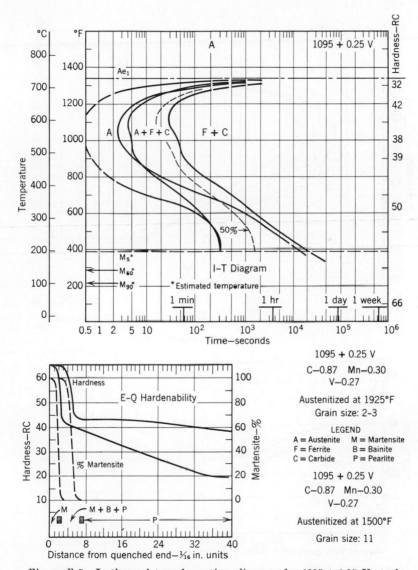

Figure F-5. Isothermal transformation diagram for 1095 + 0.25 V steel.

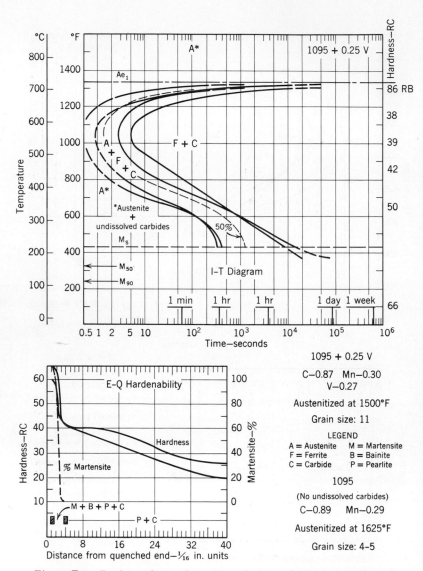

Figure F-6. Isothermal transformation diagram of 1095 + 0.25 V steel.

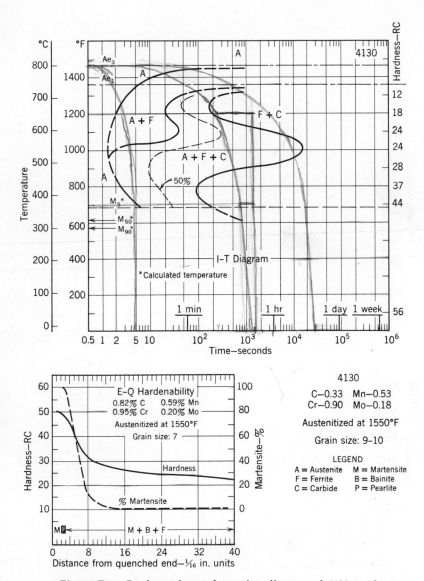

Figure F-7. Isothermal transformation diagram of 4130 steel.

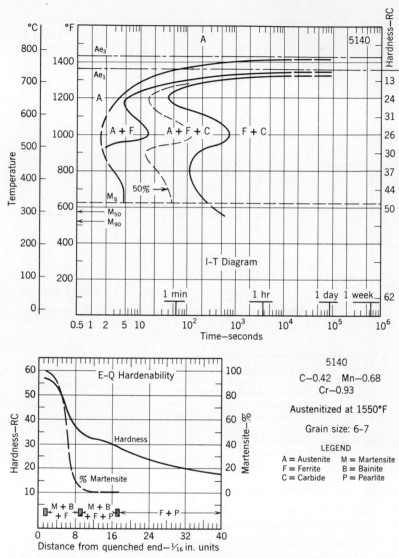

Figure F-8. Isothermal transformation diagram of 5140 steel.

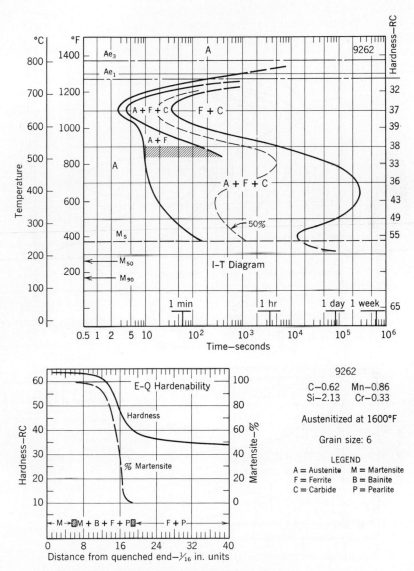

Figure F-9. Isothermal transformation diagram of 9262 steel.

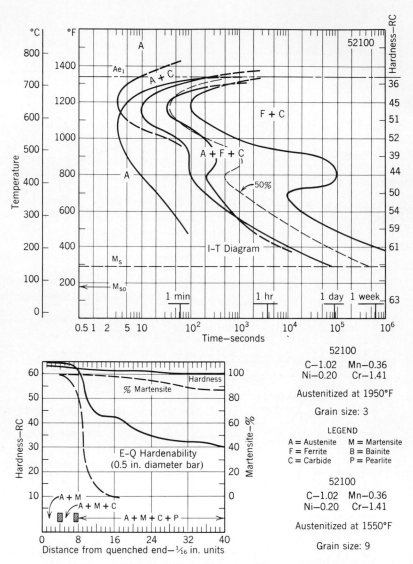

Figure F-10. Isothermal transformation diagram of 52100 steel.

Appendix G

End-Quench Hardenability Band Limits[1] for Some H Steels
From "Materials in Design Engineering," **56**, No. 5, October 1962

AISI Type	| "J" Distance, in.															
	1/8	1/4	3/8	1/2	5/8	3/4	7/8	1	1⅛	1¼	1⅜	1½	1⅝	1¾	1⅞	2
13XX																
1330 H²	56-47	53-40	50-31	45-26	42-23	39-21	37 max	35 max	34 max	33 max	32 max	31 max	31 max	31 max	30 max	30 max
1335 H³	57-49	55-44	52-34	48-29	44-26	41-24	39-22	37-21	35-20	34 max	33 max	32 max	31 max	31 max	30 max	30 max
1340 H³	60-52	58-49	56-40	54-33	51-29	48-27	44-25	41-24	39-23	38-23	37-22	36-22	35-21	35-21	34-20	34-20
25XX																
2515 H⁴	44-37	42-30	40-24	37-20	34 max	31 max	29 max	28 max	27 max	26 max	25 max	24 max	24 max	23 max	23 max	22 max
2517 H⁴	46-38	45-31	43-25	41-21	37 max	34 max	32 max	31 max	30 max	29 max	28 max	27 max	27 max	26 max	26 max	25 max
31XX																
3120 H³	47-39	42-30	35-23	30-20	28 max	27 max	26 max	25 max	24 max	23 max	23 max	22 max	22 max	21 max	21 max	21 max
3130 H²	55-47	52-42	49-34	45-30	41-28	38-25	35-24	34-22	33-21	32-20	32 max	31 max	31 max	31 max	30 max	30 max
3135 H³	57-50	55-47	53-41	50-35	48-33	44-30	39-28	37-26	36-25	35-23	34-22	34-20	34 max	34 max	33 max	33 max
3140 H³	60-52	59-49	57-45	56-41	54-36	52-33	50-31	48-30	46-29	44-28	43-28	42-27	41-27	40-26	40-26	39-25
33XX																
3310 H⁴	43-36	42-35	42-33	41-31	40-30	40-29	39-28	38-27	37-26	37-26	37-26	36-26	36-25	36-25	35-25	35-25
3316 H⁴	47-39	46-38	46-37	45-35	45-33	45-32	44-32	44-31	44-31	43-31	43-31	43-31	42-31	42-30	42-30	41-30
40XX																
4032 H²	54-45	46-29	34-23	29-21	26 max	25 max	24 max	23 max	23 max	22 max	22 max	21 max	21 max	20 max	—	—
4037 H³	57-49	51-35	38-26	32-22	29-20	27 max	26 max	25 max	25 max	25 max	25 max	24 max	24 max	24 max	23 max	23 max
4042 H³	60-52	55-40	45-29	36-26	33-24	31-23	30-23	29-22	28-22	28-21	28-20	27-20	27 max	27 max	26 max	26 max
4047 H³	62-55	58-42	52-32	43-28	38-27	35-26	33-25	32-25	31-24	30-24	30-23	30-23	30-22	29-22	29-21	29-21
4053 H³	65-59	62-53	59-38	55-32	47-30	42-29	38-28	36-28	34-27	33-27	33-27	32-26	32-26	32-26	31-25	31-25
4063 H³	60 min	65-56	64-39	61-35	57-33	51-32	46-31	43-31	41-30	40-30	39-29	38-29	38-28	37-28	37-27	36-27
4068 H³	60 min	59 min	64-45	62-36	58-34	52-33	47-32	44-32	42-31	41-31	40-30	39-30	38-29	38-29	38-28	37-28

521

Appendix G (*Continued*)

End-Quench Hardenability Band Limits[1] for Some H Steels
From "Materials in Design Engineering," **56**, No. 5. October 1962.

AISI Type	$\frac{1}{8}$	$\frac{1}{4}$	$\frac{3}{8}$	$\frac{1}{2}$	$\frac{5}{8}$	$\frac{3}{4}$	$\frac{7}{8}$	1	$1\frac{1}{8}$	$1\frac{1}{4}$	$1\frac{3}{8}$	$1\frac{1}{2}$	$1\frac{5}{8}$	$1\frac{3}{4}$	$1\frac{7}{8}$	2
41XX																
4118 H⁵	46-36	35-23	28 max	25 max	23 max	21 max	20 max	—	—	—	—	—	—	—	—	—
4130 H²	55-46	51-38	47-31	42-27	38-26	35-25	34-24	33-23	32-22	32-21	32-20	31 max	31 max	30 max	30 max	29 max
4135 H³	58-50	56-48	55-45	53-40	51-36	49-33	47-31	45-30	44-29	42-28	41-27	40-27	39-27	38-26	38-26	37-26
4137 H³	59-51	58-49	57-48	55-43	54-39	52-36	50-34	48-33	46-32	45-31	44-30	43-30	42-30	42-29	41-29	41-29
4140 H³	60-53	59-51	58-50	57-47	56-42	55-39	54-37	53-35	52-34	51-33	49-33	48-32	47-32	46-31	45-31	44-30
4142 H³	62-55	61-53	61-52	60-50	59-47	58-44	57-41	56-39	55-37	54-36	53-35	53-34	52-34	51-34	51-33	50-33
4145 H³	63-55	62-54	61-53	61-52	60-50	59-48	59-45	58-42	57-40	57-38	56-37	55-36	55-35	55-34	54-34	54-34
4147 H³	64-57	64-56	63-55	63-54	62-53	62-51	61-48	60-45	59-42	59-40	58-39	58-38	57-37	57-37	56-37	56-36
4150 H³	65-59	65-58	65-57	64-56	64-55	63-53	62-50	62-47	61-45	60-43	59-41	59-40	58-39	58-38	58-38	58-38
43XX																
4320 H⁵	47-38	43-32	38-27	34-23	31-21	29-20	27 max	26 max	25 max	25 max	24 max	24 max	24 max	24 max	24 max	24 max
4337 H⁵	59-52	59-52	58-51	58-51	57-50	57-49	57-47	57-46	56-44	56-42	55-41	55-40	55-39	54-39	54-39	53-39
4340 H⁵	60-53	60-53	60-53	60-52	60-52	59-51	58-49	58-48	58-47	57-46	57-45	57-44	57-43	56-42	56-41	56-40
E4340 H⁵	60-53	60-53	60-53	60-53	60-53	60-53	59-52	59-51	58-51	58-50	58-49	57-48	57-47	57-46	57-45	57-44
46XX																
4620 H⁵	45-35	39-24	31 max	27 max	25 max	23 max	22 max	21 max	21 max	20 max	—	—	—	—	—	—
4621 H⁵	47-38	44-30	37-25	32-22	28 max	26 max	25 max	24 max	24 max	23 max	23 max	22 max	22 max	22 max	21 max	21 max
4640 H³	60-52	58-50	56-44	53-37	49-32	44-29	41-27	39-27	38-26	37-26	36-26	35-25	35-25	34-25	34-24	33-24
47XX, 48XX																
4720 H⁵	47-39	39-27	32-21	28 max	26 max	24 max	23 max	22 max	21 max	21 max	21 max	20 max	—	—	—	—
4812 H⁴	43-34	41-26	37-21	33 max	29 max	27 max	25 max	24 max	24 max	23 max	23 max	22 max	22 max	21 max	21 max	21 max
4815 H⁴	44-37	42-30	39-24	35-21	31 max	29 max	28 max	27 max	26 max	25 max	24 max	24 max	24 max	23 max	23 max	23 max
4817 H⁴	46-38	44-32	41-27	37-23	33-21	31-20	29 max	28 max	27 max	26 max	25 max	25 max	25 max	25 max	24 max	24 max
4820 H⁴	48-40	46-38	43-31	40-27	37-25	35-23	33-22	31-21	29-20	28-20	28 max	27 max	27 max	26 max	26 max	25 max

"J" Distance, in.

Appendix G (*Continued*)

End-Quench Hardenability Band Limits[1] for Some H Steels

From "Materials in Design Engineering," **56**, No. 5. October 1962.

AISI Type	\(\tfrac{1}{8} \)	\(\tfrac{1}{4} \)	\(\tfrac{3}{8} \)	\(\tfrac{1}{2} \)	\(\tfrac{5}{8} \)	\(\tfrac{3}{4} \)	\(\tfrac{7}{8} \)	\(1 \)	\(1\tfrac{1}{8} \)	\(1\tfrac{1}{4} \)	\(1\tfrac{3}{8} \)	\(1\tfrac{1}{2} \)	\(1\tfrac{5}{8} \)	\(1\tfrac{3}{4} \)	\(1\tfrac{7}{8} \)	\(2 \)
50XX, 51XX																
5046 H³	62-55	56-32	46-27	35-25	33-24	32-23	31-22	30-21	29-20	28 max	27 max	26 max	25 max	24 max	23 max	23 max
5120 H⁵	46-34	36-23	30 max	27 max	24 max	22 max	21 max	—	—	—	—	—	—	—	—	—
5130 H²	55-46	51-39	47-32	42-28	38-25	36-22	34-20	33 max	32 max	31 max	30 max	29 max	27 max	26 max	25 max	24 max
5132 H²	56-47	52-40	48-32	42-27	38-24	36-22	34-20	33 max	32 max	31 max	30 max	29 max	28 max	27 max	26 max	25 max
5135 H³	57-49	55-43	52-35	47-30	43-27	40-24	38-22	37-21	36-20	35 max	34 max	33 max	32 max	32 max	31 max	30 max
5140 H⁵	59-52	54-38	54-38	46-30	43-28	43-28	40-27	38-25	37-24	36-23	35-21	34-20	34 max	33 max	33 max	32 max
5145 H⁵	62-55	60-51	58-42	56-35	53-32	50-30	47-29	44-28	42-26	41-25	39-24	38-23	37-22	37-21	36 max	35 max
5147 H⁵	64-56	62-54	61-52	60-45	59-37	58-34	57-32	56-31	55-30	54-29	53-27	52-26	51-25	50-24	49-22	48-21
5150 H⁵	65-58	63-56	61-49	59-38	56-34	53-32	50-31	47-30	45-29	43-28	42-27	41-26	40-25	39-24	39-23	38-22
5152 H⁵	65-58	64-57	63-55	62-51	60-45	59-39	58-37	57-35	56-34	55-32	53-31	51-30	50-29	48-27	47-26	45-25
5160 H⁵	60 min	65-59	64-56	63-47	61-39	59-36	56-35	52-34	48-33	47-32	46-31	45-30	44-29	43-28	43-28	42-27
61XX																
6120 H³	47-38	42-29	36-24	33-22	31-21	31-20	30 max	29 max	28 max	28 max	27 max	26 max	25 max	25 max	24 max	23 max
6145 H²	63-55	62-54	61-49	59-42	57-38	55-36	52-35	50-33	49-32	48-31	47-30	46-29	45-27	44-26	43-25	42-24
6150 H²	65-58	64-56	63-53	61-47	60-41	58-38	55-36	52-35	50-34	48-32	47-31	46-30	45-29	44-27	43-26	42-25
86XX																
8617 H⁵	44-33	38-24	31 max	27 max	25 max	23 max	22 max	21 max	21 max	20 max	—	—	—	—	—	—
8620 H⁵	47-37	41-27	34-21	30 max	28 max	26 max	25 max	24 max	23 max	23 max	23 max	23 max	23 max	22 max	22 max	22 max
8622 H⁵	49-39	44-30	37-24	32-20	30 max	28 max	26 max	25 max	25 max	24 max	24 max	24 max	24 max	24 max	24 max	24 max
8625 H²	51-41	46-32	40-27	35-23	32-21	30 max	28 max	27 max	27 max	26 max	26 max	26 max	26 max	25 max	25 max	25 max
8627 H²	52-43	48-35	43-29	38-26	34-24	32-22	30-21	29-20	28 max	28 max	28 max	27 max	27 max	27 max	27 max	27 max
8630 H²	55-46	52-39	47-32	41-28	37-26	34-24	33-22	31-21	30-21	30-20	29-20	29 max	29 max	29 max	29 max	29 max
8635 H⁵	57-49	55-45	53-39	50-33	46-30	43-28	40-26	37-25	36-24	35-23	34-23	33-23	33-23	33-22	32-22	32-22
8637 H³	58-51	57-48	55-42	53-36	49-32	46-30	43-28	40-26	39-25	37-25	36-24	36-24	35-24	35-24	35-23	35-23

"J" Distance, in.

Appendix G (*Continued*)

End-Quench Hardenability Band Limits[1] for Some H Steels

From "Materials in Design Engineering," **56**, No. 5. October 1962.

AISI Type	$\frac{1}{8}$	$\frac{1}{4}$	$\frac{3}{8}$	$\frac{1}{2}$	$\frac{5}{8}$	$\frac{3}{4}$	$\frac{7}{8}$	1	$1\frac{1}{8}$	$1\frac{1}{4}$	$1\frac{3}{8}$	$1\frac{1}{2}$	$1\frac{5}{8}$	$1\frac{3}{4}$	$1\frac{7}{8}$	2
8641 H3	60-53	59-51	58-46	55-39	52-34	49-31	45-29	42-28	41-26	39-26	38-25	38-25	37-24	37-24	37-24	37-24
8642 H3	62-54	61-52	60-48	58-42	55-37	52-33	49-31	46-29	44-28	42-28	41-27	40-27	40-26	39-26	39-26	39-26
8645 H3	63-56	63-54	61-50	60-45	58-39	55-35	52-33	49-31	47-30	45-29	43-28	42-28	42-27	41-27	41-27	41-27
8650 H3	65-58	64-57	63-54	62-50	60-44	59-39	58-36	56-34	55-33	53-32	52-31	50-31	49-30	47-30	46-29	45-29
8653 H3	65-59	65-58	64-57	64-56	63-53	62-47	62-44	61-42	61-40	60-39	59-38	59-37	59-36	59-35	58-35	58-34
8655 H3	59 min	58 min	56 min	54 min	65-49	64-43	63-40	62-38	61-37	60-35	59-34	58-34	57-33	56-33	55-32	53-32
8660 H3	60 min	60 min	59 min	57 min	53 min	47 min	44 min	65-42	64-40	64-39	63-38	62-37	62-36	61-36	60-35	60-35
87XX																
8720 H3	47-38	42-30	35-24	31-21	29 max	27 max	26 max	25 max	24 max	24 max	23 max	23 max	23 max	23 max	22 max	22 max
8740 H3	60-53	60-51	58-46	56-40	53-35	50-32	48-31	45-29	43-28	41-27	41-27	40-27	39-27	39-27	38-26	38-26
8742 H3	62-55	61-53	60-49	58-44	56-39	53-35	51-33	48-31	46-30	45-29	43-29	42-28	42-28	41-28	41-28	40-27
8750 H3	65-59	64-57	63-56	62-53	61-49	60-45	59-42	58-39	57-37	55-35	53-34	52-33	51-33	50-32	49-32	48-32
92XX																
9260 H2	60 min	64-53	62-41	58-36	52-35	47-34	43-33	40-32	38-31	37-31	36-30	36-30	35-29	35-29	35-28	34-28
9261 H2	60 min	65-59	64-52	63-42	60-37	54-36	45-35	42-34	39-33	38-32	37-31	37-31	36-30	36-30	35-29	35-29
9262 H2	60 min	60 min	65-56	64-48	62-39	59-37	55-36	48-35	45-34	43-33	41-33	39-32	38-31	37-31	36-30	36-30
93XX, 98XX																
9310 H4	43-35	42-34	42-31	41-29	40-27	38-26	36-26	35-26	35-26	35-25	34-25	34-25	34-25	34-25	33-24	33-24
9840 H3	60-53	60-53	60-53	60-52	59-51	58-48	58-45	57-43	56-41	55-39	55-38	55-36	54-36	54-35	53-34	53-34
9850 H3	65-59	65-59	65-56	65-58	65-58	65-58	64-57	64-56	63-54	62-50	62-50	61-49	61-48	61-47	60-47	60-47

[1]Rockwell C hardness value and distance from quenched end of standard end quench hardenability band. Range indicates maximum and minimum values. Steels heat treated as follows: [2]normalized at 1650 F, austenitized at 1600 F; [3]normalized at 1600 F, austenitized at 1550 F; [4]normalized at 1700 F, austenitized at 1550 F; [5]normalized at 1700 F, austenitized at 1700 F.

Appendix H

TABLE H-1.   Prices of Primary Materials (1965–66)

Common Materials	Cost $/lb	Density lb/in.³
Aluminum (ingot)	0.25	0.098
Copper (pig)	0.36	0.32
Iron (pig)	0.03	0.28
Iron (powder)	0.12	0.28
Lead (pig)	0.16	0.41
Magnesium (pig)	0.36	0.065
Nickel (pig)	0.80	0.32
Tin (pig)	1.25	0.26
Titanium (sponge)	1.35	0.16
Zinc (pig)	0.15	0.25
Polystyrene (powder)[1]	0.15	0.038
Bakelite (powder)[1]	0.22	0.05
Teflon (powder)[1]	3.50	0.077

Special Materials	Cost $/lb	Density lb/in.³
Antimony	0.44	0.24
Beryllium (97% lump)	62.00	0.066
Chromium (99.8%)	1.20	0.26
Cobalt (98%)	1.70	0.32
Germanium (refined)	125.00	0.19
Gold	420.00	0.70
Platinum	1,200.00	0.77
Silver	15.50	0.38
Thorium	20.00	0.42
Vanadium	3.65	0.21
Zirconium (sponge)	8.00	0.24

[1] General purpose, low strength powder.

TABLE H-2.   Prices of Mill Products (1965–66)

(In general mill prices are approximately two times the primary prices)

Material	Cost $/lb
1100-F aluminum sheet ($\frac{1}{16}$ ga.)	0.41[1]
6063-T5 aluminum bar (extr.)	0.39[1]
2011-T3 aluminum bar (1 in. dia.)	0.60[1]
AZ31B magnesium sheet ($\frac{1}{16}$ ga.)	0.80[3]
AZ31B magnesium bar	0.90[3]
Monel bar (HR)	1.00[3]
Copper bar	0.63[2]
70-Cu 30-Zn brass bar	0.57
18-4-1 hss tool steel	1.84
18-4-1-5 hss tool steel	2.50[3]
Low carbon steel	
HR sheet	0.053[4]
CR sheet	0.065[4]
HR strip	0.053[4]
HR structural shapes	0.057[4]
HR bars	0.059[4]
CF bars	0.080[4]
HR alloy steel bars	
(av. price)	0.070[3]
302 stainless bars	0.50[3]

[1] 30,000 lb lots   [2] 5,000 lb lots
[3] Fob mill   [4] 30,000 lb lots

TABLE H-3. Warehouse Prices (Detroit)

Material	Cost $/lb	Density lb/in.^{3}
1100-F aluminum ($\frac{1}{2}$ in. $\times$ 1 in. bar)	0.90[1]	0.098
2024-T4 aluminum ($\frac{1}{2}$ in. $\times$ 1 in. bar)	1.00[1]	0.10
70-30 brass ($\frac{1}{2}$ in. $\times$ 1 in. bar)	0.80[1]	0.30
302 stainless ($\frac{1}{2}$ in. $\times$ 1 in. bar)	1.00[1]	0.28
Plexiglass ($\frac{1}{4}$ in. sheet)	1.20[1]	0.043
Nylon (1 in. dia. extr.)	4.30[1]	0.042
Teflon (1 in. dia. extr.)	8.50[1]	0.077
Low carbon steel		
HR sheet (18 ga.)	0.097[2]	0.283
CR sheet (15 ga.)	0.106[2]	0.283
HR strip	0.117[2]	0.283
HR plate	0.100[2]	0.283
HR structural shapes	0.105[2]	0.283
HR bars (2 in. dia.)	0.100[2]	0.283
CF bars (2 in. dia.)	0.112[2]	0.283
Alloy steel bars		
HR 4615 (2 in. dia.)	0.164[2]	0.283
CR 4615 (2 in. dia.)	0.200[2]	0.283
HR 4140 (2 in. dia.)	0.158[2]	0.283
CD 4140 ann (2 in. dia.)	0.197[2]	0.283

[1] 500 lb lots
[2] 2000 lb lots

TABLE H-4. Approximate Prices of Castings[1]

Sand Castings		Die Castings	
Material	Cost $/lb	Material	Cost $/lb
Gray iron	0.10–0.25	Zinc base	0.30–0.50
Malleable iron	0.11–0.25	Aluminum	0.50–1.00
Steel	0.15–0.35	Brass	0.50–1.00
Aluminum	0.50–1.00	Plastic	0.50–0.75
Magnesium	0.60–1.25	Permanent mold iron	0.10–0.25
Brass	0.50–1.00		

[1] The lower cost figure will usually apply when the quantity is very large (in automotive or appliance field) and the shape is very simple. The higher cost figure will usually apply when the quantity is small and the shape of the casting is complex.

Appendix I

Practical Tolerances and Surface Finishes
Obtained by the Common Manufacturing Processes

Process	Surface Finish (rms)	Tolerance		Remarks
		Good	Best obtainable	
1. Flame cutting	250–2000	±0.060	±0.020	Distortion
2. Sawing	125–1000	±0.020	±0.005	
3. Shaping	63–1000	±0.010	±0.001	
4. Broaching	32–250	±0.005	±0.0005	
5. Milling	32–500	±0.005	±0.001	
6. Turning	32–500	±0.005	±0.001	
7. Drilling (dia.)	63–500	$(+0.010-000)L$	$(+0.002-000)S$	$(L \geqq 1$ in. dia.$)$
(loc.)		±0.015	±0.002 (with jig)	$(S \geqq \frac{1}{2}$ in. dia.$)$
8. Reaming (dia.)	16–125	±0.002	±0.0005	
9. Hobbing	32–250	±0.005	±0.001	
10. Grinding	8–125	±0.001	±0.0002	
11. Lapping	0–16	±0.0002	±0.000,050	50μ
12. Forming (brake)	Same as rolling	±0.060	±0.015	
(roll)	Same as rolling	±0.010	±0.005	
13. Stamping	Same as rolling	±0.010	±0.001	
14. Drawing	Same as rolling	±0.010	±0.002	

Appendix I (*Continued*)

Practical Tolerances and Surface Finishes
Obtained by the Common Manufacturing Processes

Process	Surface Finish (rms)	Tolerance		Remarks
		Good	Best obtainable	
15. Forging	125–1000	±0.060 (in./in.)	±0.030 (in./in.)	
16. Rolling (cold)	8–32	±0.010	±0.001	
17. Extrusion (hot)	63–250	±0.020	±0.005	
(cold)	8–63	±0.005	±0.001	
18. Sand casting	250–2000	$\pm\frac{1}{8}$ in./ft.	$\pm\frac{1}{32}$ in./ft.	
19. Permanent mold	40–125	±(0.030 + .002D)	±(0.010 + .002D)	
20. Die casting	40–100	±0.010	±0.002 in./in.	
21. Investment casting	60–125	–	±0.002 in./in.	Nonferrous
			±0.004 in./in.	Ferrous
22. Sintered metal	40–100	±0.005	±0.001	
23. Sintered ceramics	30–250	±0.030 in.	±0.020 in./in.	
24. Fusion welding	100–250	$\pm\frac{1}{8}$ in.	±0.010	
25. Spot welding	Same as parent metal	$\pm\frac{1}{16}$ in.	±0.010	
26. Heat treating	Same as parent metal	±0.030	±0.010	Grind stock

Index

531